OXFORD MEDICAL PUBLICATIONS

The Psychopharmacology and Treatment of Schizophrenia

BRITISH ASSOCIATION
FOR PSYCHOPHARMACOLOGY MONOGRAPHS

The Psychopharmacology and Treatment of Schizophrenia

BRITISH ASSOCIATION FOR
PSYCHOPHARMACOLOGY MONOGRAPH
No 8

Edited by

P.B. BRADLEY
Professor of Pharmacology, University of Birmingham

S.R. HIRSCH
Professor of Psychiatry,
Charing Cross and Westminster Medical School,
London

Oxford   New York   Tokyo
OXFORD UNIVERSITY PRESS
1986

Oxford University Press, Walton Street, Oxford OX2 6DP

Oxford New York Toronto
Delhi Bombay Calcutta Madras Karachi
Petaling Jaya Singapore Hong Kong Tokyo
Nairobi Dar es Salaam Cape Town
Melbourne Auckland

and associated companies in
Beirut Berlin Ibadan Nicosia

Oxford is a trade mark of Oxford University Press

Published in the United States
by Oxford University Press, New York

British Library Cataloguing in Publication Data
The Psychopharmacology and treatment of
schizophrenia——(British Association
for Psychopharmacology monograph;
no. 8)
1. Schizophrenia
I. Bradley, P.B.   II. Hirsch, Steven R.
III. Series
616.89'8206   RC514
ISBN 0-19-261260-3

Library of Congress Cataloging in Publication Data
Main entry under title:
The Psychopharmacology and treatment of schizophrenia.
(British Association for Psychopharmacology
monograph; no. 8) (Oxford medical publications)
Includes bibliographies and index.
1. Schizophrenia——Chemotherapy.   I. Bradley, P. B.
II. Hirsch, Steven R.   III. Series.   IV. Series:
Oxford medical publications. [DNLM: 1. Schizophrenia——
drug therapy.   W1 BR343D no. 8/WM 203 P9736]
RC514.P7188   1986   616.89'82061   85-30969
ISBN 0-19-261260-3

Set by Colset Private Limited, Singapore
Printed in Great Britain
at the University Printing House, Oxford
by David Stanford
Printer to the University

Dedicated to
John Wing and Joel Elkes
to whom we are indebted for
stimulating our interest in
psychopharmacology.

Preface

We were invited by the British Association of Psychopharmacology to produce this book with the aim of bringing together knowledge from basic and clinical disciplines on the pharmacology and treatment of schizophrenia. We have set out to provide an authoritative and critical review of the evidence as it relates to the current state of knowledge with respect to biochemistry, pharmacology, treatment, and research methodology in schizophrenia. We have tried to cover these areas comprehensively, and in so doing have omitted other areas which we do not feel are of major importance.

The first five chapters discuss the basis of our understanding of drug treatment and critically review various hypotheses which derive from our knowledge of drug action in schizophrenia. The middle section is concerned with an evaluation of the efficacy of treatment: the choice of a diagnostic system, the contribution of social factors to course and outcome, statistical and epidemiological concerns in the design of treatment trials, and rating scales available for assessing the effects of treatment along clinical and social parameters. The extension of the scope of this book to include what is known about social influences and outcomes, their interaction with treatment, and their importance in clinical trials is perhaps unique for a book on psychopharmacology.

The last three chapters attempt a thorough review of treatments of schizophrenia, biological and psychological, based on knowledge from systematic controlled studies; they review in depth what is known about the pathophysiology, clinical presentation, and treatment of unwanted effects of drugs on the various systems of the body.

The chapter on treatments is intended to review extensively the evidence concerning the clinical activity, efficacy, and use of medications by carefully considering the research findings. Conventional, fringe, and experimental treatments are all considered if there has been an attempt to consider systematically their effectiveness.

We hope the book will be used as an informative text and source of reference by clinicians, pharmacologists, and all of those interested in the psychopharmacology and treatment of schizophrenia.

Birmingham and *London*　　　　　　　　　　　　　　P. B. B.
October 1985　　　　　　　　　　　　　　　　　　　　S. R. H.

Contents

Contributors

PHILIP B. BRADLEY, *Professor of Pharmacology, The Medical School, University of Birmingham, Birmingham B15 2TJ, UK.*

IAN BROCKINGTON, *Professor of Psychiatry, Queen Elizabeth Hospital, Birmingham B15 2TH, UK.*

BRENDA COSTALL, *Reader in Neuropharmacology, Postgraduate School of Studies in Pharmacology, University of Bradford, Bradford BD7 1DP, UK.*

STEPHEN H. CURRY, *Professor and Director, Division of Clinical Pharmacokinetics, J. Hillis Miller Health Center (Box J-4), University of Florida, Gainesville, Florida 32610, USA.*

J. GUY EDWARDS, *Consultant Psychiatrist, Department of Psychiatry, Royal South Hants Hospital, Southampton SO9 4PE, UK.*

STEVEN R. HIRSCH, *Professor of Psychiatry, Charing Cross and Westminster Medical School, Fulham Palace Road, London W6 8RF, UK.*

SUSAN D. IVERSEN, *Merck Sharp & Dohme Research Laboratories, Neuroscience Research Centre, Terlings Park, Eastwick Road, Harlow, Essex CM20 2QR, UK.*

A. V. P. MACKAY, *Physician Superintendent, Argyll and Bute Hospital, Argyll PA31 8LD and MacKintosh Lecturer in Psychological Medicine, University of Glasgow, UK.*

K. D. MACRAE, *Reader in Medical Statistics, Department of Medicine, Charing Cross and Westminster Medical School, Fulham Palace Road, London W6 8RF, UK.*

R. MANCHANDA, *Assistant Professor of Psychiatry, University of Western Ontario and Director of Education, St. Thomas Psychiatric Hospital, St. Thomas N5P 3V9, Canada.*

C. D. MARSDEN, *Professor of Neurology, Institute of Psychiatry and King's Hospital Medical School, De Crespigny Park, London SE5 8AF, UK.*

R. H. S. MINDHAM, *Nuffield Professor of Psychiatry, University Department of Psychiatry, 15 Hyde Terrace, Leeds LS2 9LT, UK.*

ROBERT J. NAYLOR, *Reader in Pharmacology, Postgraduate School of Studies in Pharmacology, University of Bradford, Bradford BD7 1DP, UK.*

STEPHEN PLATT, *MRC Unit for Epidemiological Studies in Psychiatry, University Department of Psychiatry, Royal Edinburgh Hospital, Edinburgh EH10 5HF, UK.*

RICHARD RODNIGHT, *Professor of Neurochemistry, Institute of Psychiatry, De Crespigny Park, London SE5 8AF, UK.*

1

Peripheral biochemistry in schizophrenia

RICHARD RODNIGHT

INTRODUCTION

It is accepted that human behaviour is related, in ways we are only beginning to understand, to patterns of chemical events in the nervous system. It is therefore reasonable to suppose that behind the abnormal behaviour diagnosed by psychiatrists as 'schizophrenic' there must exist (however elusive) abnormal biochemistry. Unfortunately, in attempting to delineate these abnormalities investigators have been faced with intractable problems and uncertainties that have confounded the interpretation and comparison of results, so that after decades of intensive study the biochemistry of schizophrenia remains largely a mystery. However, even if we still lack any appreciable knowledge of the basic pathology of the disorder, there is now a greater awareness of the dimensions of the problem and of the reasons for past failures (see for example Baxter and Melnechuk 1980).

A major source of confusion relates to the nature of the patient populations considered by different researchers to justify the label 'schizophrenic'. Despite the progress achieved over the past decade in establishing internationally agreed criteria for diagnosing schizophrenia, patient groups defined as 'schizophrenic' by diverse centres are often too heterogeneous to be strictly comparable. The problem is widely recognized (Pope and Lipinski 1978). It is compounded when loosely defined 'schizophrenic' populations are compared with normal subjects living in the community without the inclusion of a population of 'non-schizophrenic' patients living in the same hospital environment. Another aspect of the problem of patient selection concerns the now widely held opinion that the aetiology of the schizophrenic syndrome is multifactorial and that individual loadings vary (Kety 1980; Leonhard 1980); if this is true it follows that even when patients are diagnosed on narrow criteria homogeneous biochemical parameters are not necessarily to be expected.

The confusion generated by different diagnostic practice and the putative multiple aetiologies of schizophrenia may be capable of resolution—for example, by employing dimensional techniques in which symptom spectra, instead of formal diagnosis, are examined in relation to biological variation (as exemplified by the Present State Examination pioneered by Wing *et al*. 1974), and by recognizing the possibility of biological heterogeneity even in narrowly defined groups (e.g. Buchsbaum and Haier 1978; Wyatt *et al*. 1981; Jeste *et al*. 1982). More intractable are the present limitations in the analytical tools available for studying the molecular bases of human behaviour. The complexity of human biochemical processes is daunting (Harris 1980); there are few clues as to which systems may be related to abnormal behaviour and even fewer probes available to study cerebral chemistry in the living subject. Many substances, among them body fluid constituents, exert powerful effects on the CNS in extremely low concentrations. Moreover there are few grounds for believing that a significant number of schizophrenic illnesses are related to one of the defined biochemical disorders associated with organic psychotic states (Davison and Bagley 1969; Lishman 1978). Occasional examples of metabolic disorder associated with psychosis with schizophrenic features appear sporadically in the literature (Freeman *et al*. 1975; Pepplin-khuizen *et al*. 1980; Besson 1980), but attempts to demonstrate these and other metabolic abnormalities in classic schizophrenia have so far been unsuccessful.

If we assume that schizophrenia, like diabetes, nephrosis, and a number of other diseases, is probably a multifactorial condition we need to consider how putative aetiological factors might give rise to the syndrome. A purely hypothetical scheme is suggested in Fig.1.1. This starts from the now generally accepted postulate that genetic factors are often involved in the aetiology of schizophrenia, but that, since the concordance rate for the condition in monozygotic twins is only about 50 per cent, non-genetic or environmental factors must also be important. The twin data are generally interpreted as implying a genetic vulnerability for the condition rather than the inheritance of genes that result directly in the development of the condition (Kety 1980). Figure 1.1. also assumes that schizophrenic behaviour is related to a disorder of central neurotransmission in which one or more neuronal systems are affected, resulting in an imbalance of transmitter function which constitutes the final common path generating the symptomatology. Now, the putative aetiological factors responsible for transmitter imbalance may be expressed or derived from a normal or abnormal environment. For example, the 'schizophrenic' genotype itself may be directly responsible through interactions in a normal environment for developmental defects in the molecular organization of the nervous system, eventually expressed as disordered neurotransmission. Clearly, because of the immense complexity of the nervous system, aetiologies of this kind in schizophrenia cannot be excluded, but in practice have yet to be demonstrated. Similarly, the idea that in a genetically vulnerable individual the sensory input (embracing all psychosocial experience in a normal environment) somehow results in a distortion of transmitter balance is conceivable, but virtually impossible to quantify or disprove.

With respect to the vulnerable individual in an abnormal environment, virus infections (Crow 1983), birth traumas (Schneider 1981; Parnas *et al*. 1981), and nutritional factors (Dickerson 1978) have all been discussed as possible aetiological agents, amongst others, involved in the genesis of schi-

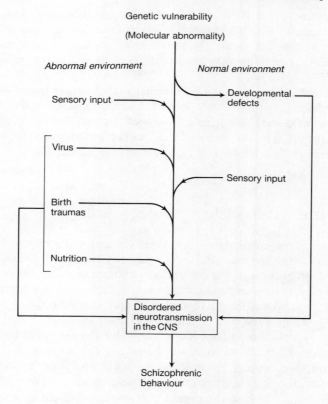

FIG. 1.1. A hypothetical scheme to suggest how putative aetiological factors might give rise to the schizophrenic syndrome.

zophrenic behaviour. Moreover, some of these putative aetiological agents may be posulated to lead to schizophrenic illness in genetically non-susceptible individuals.

Biochemical abnormality in schizophrenic patients could be related to any of the components of Figure 1.1. For instance, the demonstration of abnormal enzyme activity in the patient's cells may point to a molecular defect directly related to the genetic vulnerability. However, genetic markers are difficult to locate, as the extensive investigations into blood platelet monoamineoxidase in psychiatric illness shows (see below). Direct analysis of biopsy or autopsy brain tissue may uncover evidence for the putative disorder of cerebral neurotransmission; both the potential and the limitations of this approach have been discussed recently (Spokes 1979; Rodnight 1980). Between the molecular abnormality derived from the abnormal genotype and the biochemical 'lesion' in the CNS, there remains the possibility of pheno-typic variation in general bodily chemistry arising from interactions between the genetic component and the various environmental factors, typically leading to a distortion of metabolism and abnormal concentrations of some body fluid constituent. In psychotic illness, however, unusual body fluid compositions may be secondary products of stress and great caution is needed before concluding that abnormalities of this nature are indicative of aetiology.

The present chapter focuses on recent research into selected aspects of peripheral biochemistry in schizophrenia, leaving consideration of the putative disorder of central neurotransmission to Chapter 2. Recent reviews of the biochemistry of schizophrenia include works by Meltzer (1979), Lewis (1980), Crow (1980), Berger (1981), and Rodnight (1982, 1983).

TRANSMETHYLATING REACTIONS

The celebrated transmethylation hypothesis is now some 30 years old. In a seminal paper Osmond and Symthies (1952; see Gillin *et al*. 1978 and Baldessorini *et al*. 1979 for a recent reviews) drew attention to an observation of Harley-Mason concerning the similarity in structure of the hallucinogen, mescaline (trimethoxyphenylethylamine), and the catecholamine transmitters. They suggested that in schizophrenia an abnormal methylation of adrenaline to yield a putative endogenous hallucinogen might be an aetiological factor. At that time little was known of the biochemistry of transmethylation, the process by which the methyl group of methionine (as *S*-adenosylmethionine) is transferred a variety of acceptors. When, a few years later Julius Axelrod discovered that the catecholamines were indeed inactivated by *O*-methylation many felt that a breakthrough in schizophrenia research had been achieved, a conclusion reinforced by persistent reports (reviewed by Cohen *et al*. 1974) indicating that in many cases of chronic schizophrenia the characteristic acute symptomatology was exacerbated by the administration of large doses of *L*-methionine.

Subsequent attempts to demonstrate abnormal *O*-methylation of catecholamines in schizophrenia centred around the so-called 'pink spot' phenomenon which was controversially indentified as 3, 4-dimethoxyphenylethylamine and claimed by some groups to occur uniquely in urine from schizophrenics. The early work in this area is now generally discounted, but it has been established that some double methylation of dopamine to yield 3,4-dimethoxyphenylethylamine does occur in human subjects, and in one recent paper the urinary excretion of this substance was significantly increased in some acute drug-free schizophrenics (Friedhoff *et al*. 1977); in chronic subjects or patients receiving drugs, by contrast, the excretion was within normal limits. Since dimethoxyphenylethylamine differs from its trimethoxylated congener, mescaline, in possessing no pronounced actions on the CNS, and since the enzymic basis of the double *O*-methylation is obscure, the interpretation of these results, if replicated, in terms of the symptoms of schizophrenia is uncertain.

N-methylation

Whereas *O*-methylation of the catecholamines leads to inactivation, *N*-methylation of the amine groups of the indoleamines generally results in a change in pharmacological activity. For example, N',N'-dimethyltryptamine (DMT), the dimethylated derivative of tryptamine (a trace amine in brain) possesses short-acting hallucinogenic properties when administered parenterally to human subjects. Of the *N*-methyl indoles derived from serotonin, the principal endogenous indoleamine precursor, 5-hydroxy-N',N'-dimethyltryptamine or bufotenine is inactive, probably because it fails to penetrate the brain, and 5-methoxydimethyltryptamine, although reputedly a potent hallucinogen, is highly toxic to some species and has been little studied. Interest has therefore remained centred on DMT.

The potency of DMT is about four times that of mescaline. Subjects report sensations of 'inward withdrawal' rather than frank hallucinations (Mandell and Segal 1973; Gillin *et al.* 1976; Bickel *et al.* 1976), but as with other psychotomimetics it is debatable whether the model psychosis it induces bears any relation to the cardinal symptoms of schizophrenia. On the other hand it seems highly unlikely that any putative endogenous 'psychotoxin' responsible for the symptoms of schizophrenia would produce identical symptomatology when administered in a single dose to normal subjects.

In view of the psychotomimetic properties of DMT the discovery in mammalian tissues of an enzyme (indoleamine-*N*-methyltransferase, INMT) capable of synthesizing DMT *in vivo* and *in vitro* was of great interest (Saavectra *et al.* 1973). The reaction sequence is as follows:

(1) Tryptamine + *S*-adenosylmethionine
      <u>INMT</u>   > N'-methyltryptamine (NMT) + *S*-adenosylhomo-
                cysteine.

(2) NMT + *S*-adenosylmethionine
      <u>INMT</u>   > N',N'-dimethyltryptamine (DMT) + *S*-adenosyl-
                homocysteine.

The intermediate product NMT is pharmacologically inactive as a hallucinogen. The overall reaction is inhibited by one of its products, *S*-adenosylhomocysteine, and by endogenous inhibitors (see below). DMT is degraded ultimately by monoamine oxidase (MAO-B) to indoleactic acid and there is good evidence that its *in vivo* metabolism is very rapid (Kaplan *et al.* 1974).

INMT activity is widely distributed in animal tissue, with the highest concentration being found in the lung. The enzyme activity is very low in rodent brain, and it is doubtful whether it has been detected in human brain postmortem. However, traces of DMT have been detected in rodent brain (Stramentinoli and Baldessarini 1978).

There have been many attempts to detect DMT in the body fluids, but only recently have adequately specific methods been developed. Earlier work is reviewed by Rosengarten and Friedhoff (1976). Recent papers indicate that normal subjects excrete endogenous DMT in the range 0.1–0.5 μg/24 h (Carpenter *et al.* 1975; Oon *et al.* 1977; Raisanen and Karkkainen 1979). The application to mentally ill subjects of specific methods for determining DMT in urine has produced conflicting results. Carpenter *et al.* (1975), using a specific but relatively insensitive method, were unable to distinguish 26 acute schizophrenics (diagnosed on DSM-II criteria) from 10 normal subjects with respect to DMT excretion. By contrast a later study (Murray *et al.* 1979), in which a more sensitive method was used, reported an increased excretion of DMT, but not NMT, in recently-admitted drug-free patients who were considered by hospital psychiatrists to have a psychotic illness, and who included a group of 26 acute schizophrenics diagnosed on the stricter DSM-III criteria. About half of these patients, and a similar proportion of patients suffering from 'uncertain' psychotic illnesses (but excluding psychotic depression) excreted DMT in the range 1–4 μg/24 h. Excretion in patients with neurotic illnesses fell within the normal range. When DMT excretion was examined in relation to specific symptoms, without regard to hospital diagnosis, ratings on the Present State Examination (Wing *et al.* 1974) indicated that the increased excretion was clearly associated with psychotic rather than neurotic symptomatology. It was of interest that syndromes suggesting elation, perceptual abnormalities, and difficulty in thinking and communicating were most highly correlated with a raised excretion of DMT, since these have been described as being prominent in the model psychosis induced by DMT in normal subjects (Gillin *et al.* 1976). This suggested that either overproduction or inefficient degradation of DMT in acute psychosis might be responsible for generating these aspects of the symptomatology.

This hypothesis was apparently supported by further studies showing that abnormal excretion of DMT tended to decline to normal levels during the resolution of an acute psychosis (Murray *et al.* 1979). The decline did not appear to be related to therapy with neuroleptics because patients receiving neuroleptics occasionally excreted abnormal amounts. However, in a longitudinal study of DMT excretion in five patients with schizophrenic illnesses and four with cyclic manic depressive illnesses, no evidence was found for an association between the rate of DMT excretion and rapid changes in mood or psychotic symptomatology (Checkley *et al.* 1980). Thus although there was the usual tendency for DMT excretion to decline with treatment, short-term fluctuations in mental state did not correlate with urinary DMT.

The possibility that the extra-cerebral production of DMT was concerned in psychotic symtomatology was further considered by Checkley *et al.* (1979). These authors argued that if physical illnesses could be identified in which a high urinary excretion of DMT occurred in the absence of psychopathology, this would decrease the probability of a central role for DMT in symptom pathogenesis. Patients with severe liver disease were chosen since the liver contains INMT and is also a rich source of MAO; a combination of cellular damage and low MAO activity might result in higher levels of DMT circulating in the blood stream and therefore excreted in the urine. A proportion of such patients did indeed excrete DMT in the same range as often observed in psychotic illness, but in none of these patients was there any evidence of psychopathology (Checkley *et al.* 1979).

A further consideration, tending to discount an involvement of DMT in psychotic symptomatology concerns the magnitude of the excretion, which appears extremely low when compared with the doses (0.7 mg/kg body weight) required to induce a model psychosis in normal subjects. This discrepancy may be related to the fact that administered DMT is very rapidly metabolized or sequestered. Thus, Kaplan *et al.* (1974) found that less than 0.1 per cent of an injected dose of about 50 mg was recovered in the urine and the mean peak concentration (for 11 subjects) in the venous blood was only 100 ng/ml. These data led Kaplan *et al.* to conclude that: 'urinary levels of DMT would not appear to be a meaningful area for comparing psychotic and normal subjects, even if DMT were an endogenous psychotogen'. It was also felt that determinations of blood concentrations of DMT would be unlikely to produce evidence for an abnormal metabolism of DMT in the brain.

The latter conclusion appears justified and the question of a central abnormality in indoleamine *N*-methylation in schizophrenia must remain open. With respect to measurements of the urinary excretion of DMT, however, evidence from the relative levels of INMT in various tissues suggests that the major part is derived from the activity of the enzyme in the lung rather than in the CNS. If this is correct, it is reasonable to consider the possibility that an abnormal leakage of DMT from the lung into the arterial circulation might induce psychotic behaviour in vulnerable individuals. The available evidence tends to discount even this idea. Using a highly sensitive and specific GC-MS method for determining blood DMT, Walker *et al.* (1979) reported roughly comparable levels in simultaneous arterial and venous blood samples in nine schizophrenic patients whose clinical state was not described. The values ranged from < 10 pg/ml to 118 pg/ml; the highest value observed therefore was some 1000 times less than the peak levels found by Kaplan *et al.* (1974) in venous blood from normal subjects experiencing a model psychosis following intramuscular injection of DMT. Nevertheless, further research appears to be justified. In normal subjects arterial blood concentrations after giving DMT are likely to be lower than those in the venous blood due to the action of lung MAO. Further, in patients the output of DMT from the lung may occur in bursts which single arterial samples would not necessarily detect. There is a case, therefore, for studying DMT in serial arterial blood samples in acutely ill and actively hallucinating patients. However, it may be noted that there is no consistent evidence for a therapeutic effect of haemodialysis in schizophrenia (Carpenter *et al.* 1983).

Little is known about the regulation of DMT metabolism in man and animals. The availability of the methyl donor, *S*-adenosylmethionine, does not appear to be a factor (Stramentinoli and Baldessarini 1978). There have been a series of reports describing endogenous inhibitors of INMT activity.

One of these was identified as a copper–glutathionine complex (Marzullo and Friedhoff 1978). In a careful study Gomes and Shanley (1978; Gomes 1980) examined CSF for inhibitory activity towards a partially purified preparation of INMT from rabbit lung. Heat-stable inhibitory factors were indeed found in pooled CSF samples, but none of these had peptide-like properties, nor was any systematic comparison made between controls and patients. With respect to the catabolism of DMT, MAO-B, the enzyme responsible, has been extensively investigated in schizophrenia, as described below. It seems unlikely, however, that the non-specific decrease in platelet MAO often seen in schizophrenia is responsible for the intermittent increased excretion of DMT, since no correlation between the two parameters has been observed (R. Murray unpublished work). It may be relevant to note that inhibition of MAO in normal subjects by drugs led to an increased excretion of both NMT and DMT (Oon *et al*. 1977), whereas in patients only DMT is sometimes elevated. Further there is no consistent evidence that MAO inhibitors exacerbate schizophrenic symptomatology (see Checkley *et al*. 1979 for references), although a single case of a psychosis induced by phenelzine was reported recently (Sheehy and Maxmen 1978).

Other aspects of transmethylation

Recent studies have examined methionine metabolism in blood cells. Ismail *et al*. (1978) incubated [^{14}C-CH$_3$]-*S*-adenosylmethionine with leucocytes from 11 poorly characterized schizophrenics and seven normal controls, and observed a lower rate of oxidation of the methyl group to $^{14}CO_2$ in the patients, which was apparently unrelated to drug therapy. Significantly low values have been reported for two keys enzymes involved in the synthesis of *S*-adenosylmethionine, namely serine hydroxymethyltransferase (Carl *et al*. 1978) and methionine adenosine transferase (Carl *et al*. 1978; Kelsoe *et al*. 1983), in blood cells from schizophrenic patients. Both these studies require replication under more controlled conditions, but superficially they support the concept of Levi and Waxman (1975) of deficient rather than enhanced transmethylation in schizophrenia. Normal blood concentrations of *S*-adenosylmethionine were found in a group of 30 patients by Cohen *et al*. (1982).

Smythies (1980) drew attention to the potential importance of an aspect of transmethylation, as yet little studied in a clinical setting. This concerns the transfer of the methyl moiety to the carboxyl groups of proteins, a process implicated in several behavioural control mechanisms in prokaryotes and eukaryotes (Springer *et al*. 1979).

PLATELET MONOAMINE OXIDASE (MAO) ACTIVITY

The human blood platelet has proved popular in psychiatric research as an easily available source of biochemical mechanisms that process the monoamine transmitters: for example, a membrane-located uptake system for serotonin, cell surface receptors for noradrenaline, and the enzyme mono-amineoxidase (MAO). Several excellent reviews of platelet MAO in psychiatric research are available (Stahl 1977; Campbell 1981; Sandler *et al.* 1981; Fowler *et al.* 1982). Platelet MAO is the B type of the enzyme which preferentially hydrolyses non-hydroxylated substrates such as benzylamine, β-phenylethylamine, and tryptamine, in contrast to MAO-A which degrades the transmitter monoamines serotonin and noradrenaline. However, more than 50 per cent of the human brain enzyme is type B and the affinity of both types for dopamine is similar. Thus, although the relevance of the platelet enzyme to neuronal function is obscure, it may nevertheless be of importance in helping to degrade potentially neurotoxic amines in the blood stream such as β-phenylethylamine and the hallucinogenic methylated indoleamines.

There have been many reports over the last decade of abnormally low activities of platelet MAO in subgroups of patients with chronic schizophrenia and other psychiatric illnesses. In acute schizophrenics, however, the activity is usually within normal range. Despite differences in technique and the usual problems of equating diagnostic practice in different centres, a review of 26 investigations (Wyatt *et al.* 1979) concluded that the abnormally low activity frequently observed in a proportion of chronic patients is probably of biological significance. Several authors have claimed a significant association between low platelet MAO and paranoia (Potkin *et al.* 1978; Orsulak *et al.* 1978; Haier *et al.* 1979) and hallucinations (Bond *et al.* 1979; Meltzer *et al.* 1980 *a*). In typical studies of undifferentiated chronic schizophrenics the mean decrease ranges between -20 and -50 per cent but, since low activity is not a general phenomenon in schizophrenia, the average values obscure the fact that some patients have extremely low activities. Such low values may be repeatedly observed in the same patients suggesting a stable trait. Indeed there is evidence from twin studies pointing to a heritable factor in determining the observable level of MAO in platelets (Wyatt *et al.* 1973; Winter *et al.* 1978; Reveley *et al.* 1983). In the study of Wyatt *et al.* (1973) 13 pairs of monozygotic twins discordant for schizophrenia were examined: using tryptamine as substrate the mean activity of platelet MAO in the twins was abnormally low (-36 per cent, $p < 0.01$) and the activity between each pair of twins was significantly correlated ($r = 0.67; p < 0.01$). The correlation was all the more striking in view of the wide range of values observed (0.31–9.49 nmol of substrate/mg of protein). Almost identical results were obtained by Reveley *et al.* (1983) who examined a different cohort of monozygotic twins from the UK.

There are, however, many reasons for rejecting the hypothesis that platelet MAO activity is a genetic marker or that the low activity often reported in schizophrenia necessarily has aetiological significance. The activity is conditioned by endogenous and environmental factors including hormones and drug status (Murphy *et al.* 1977; Chojnacki *et al.* 1981; Del Vecchio *et al.* 1983). Several laboratories have consistently reported normal levels of the enzyme in schizophrenia: for example, Mann and Thomas (1979) were unable to distinguish chronic institutionalized schizophrenics from normals and other hospital patients with respect to MAO activity. One group (Groshong *et al.* 1979) was unable to detect subnormal activity in chronic schizophrenics of their own choice, but confirmed reported low activities in blood samples supplied by another centre. Low activity of the enzyme has been observed in normal populations and has in several reports been linked with individuals considered to be 'high risk subjects' for non-specific psychiatric disturbance (Coursey *et al.* 1979). This would make the phenomenon a non-specific vulnerability factor contributing to later psychopathology.

Low MAO activity has been reported in skeletal muscle biopsy samples taken from a variety of patients with functional psychoses (Meltzer and Arora 1980), although no correlation with platelet MAO was observed. By contrast platelet and leucocyte MAO activities have been found to correlate (Sullivan *et al.* 1978). This suggests the presence of factors in the plasma influencing the activity, but reports of such an inhibitor have not been confirmed (Wise *et al.* 1979).

While further work in this area appears justified, there seems little point in different laboratories continuing to accumulate data obtained from their local patients. Systematic kinetic studies and structural analysis of purified MAO isolated from patients consistently exhibiting low activity values are required.

IMMUNE SYSTEMS

In the pre-1970 studies on plasma proteins in schizophrenia (see Durell and Archer 1976 for review) there are observations suggesting abnormalities in immunoglobulins in the condition. At that time the enormous complexity of the body's immune systems, and the great range of individual differences in them, were only beginning to be understood; consequently there has been a tendency to discount these early studies. Recent interest in the subject stems from proposals that some patients with schizophrenia may have suffered a slow virus infection (Torrey and Peterson 1976; Crow 1978, 1983) as well as from the current interest in the role of autoimmune mechanisms in medicine and in the association of HLA (human leucocyte antigen) systems with certain diseases. It may be noted that none of these suggestions is necessarily mutually exclusive: viruses may damage the delicate equilibrium that regulates immune responses; and patients with some autoimmune diseases typically possess particular HLA types (Rose 1981). Moreover, it is now known that inborn errors in metabolic pathways not unique to lymphoid cells may lead to immunodeficiency syndromes and therefore to increased susceptibility to infection (Hirschhorn 1983).

The autoimmune hypothesis of schizophrenia predicts that some patients with the illness will exhibit circulating antibodies to specific substances in central neurones, much in the same way as patients with myasthenia gravis possess in their blood stream antibodies to the acetylcholine receptor of the neuromuscular junction. An intriguing hypothesis along these lines involving the dopamine receptor is due to Knight (1982). However, to investigate this and other autoimmune hypotheses in schizophrenia a test system is required, ideally one which demonstrates a relation between specific antibody titre and the symptoms of the illness. This has never been achieved. The first attempt is represented by Heath's early experiments (Heath and Krupp 1967) in which it was claimed that a γ-G-immunoglobulin fraction (IgG, and called 'taraxein') isolated from the blood of schizophrenic patients, when injected into the lateral ventricles of monkeys, gave rise to abnormal potentials in recordings from the septal area. Control IgG fractions uniformly failed to elicit this response. It was later reported that similar abnormal electrical activity could be observed in recordings from the septal area of patients. Further, by employing fluorescent antibody techniques, evidence was obtained for a specific binding of the IgG fraction to cell nuclei in post-mortem brain tissue from schizophrenic subjects. Heath's work stimulated a series of studies, most of which failed to support his findings, although a few (mainly of Russian origin) gave it qualified support; this literature was cogently reviewed by Durell and Archer (1976). However, the most direct attempt to replicate Heath's original studies appeared more recently (Bergen *et al.* 1980). IgG fractions were prepared from 'acutely-ill schizophrenics' and controls. Of 187 sera from 24 patients, 29 were found positive according to Heath's criteria. However, in a series of 50 sera from 30 control subjects, six were positive, and although the difference in incidence was highly significant, the finding of positive results with IgG fractions from psychiatrically normal individuals of comparable age detracts from the hypothesis.

In another study Pulkkinen (1977) attempted to correlate the gross concentration of three immunoglobulin fractions in serum (IgA, IgG, and IgM) with psychopathology in 76 patients loosely diagnosed as suffering from schizophrenia or schizophreniform psychosis. Only IgM showed a statistically significant correlation to psychopathology, particularly symptoms of withdrawal during first admission. Paranoid patients, on the other hand, exhibited the lowest concentrations of IgM. There was also a clear tendency for a high concentration of total immunoglobulins at time of admission to predict a short stay in hospital, but this may have been due to an age factor.

In the search for genetic markers for vulnerability to schizophrenia attention has focused recently on the HLA systems. These ubiquitous cell surface glycoproteins are the major determinants of transplant histocompatability (Svejgaard 1976). The HLA systems are polymorphic and exhibit an exceptionally wide spread of phenotypic variation; they are thus valuable genetic markers. Moreover, certain HLA types are associated specifically with a number of diseases, all of which have a familial basis and an uncertain aetiology; multiple sclerosis and juvenile onset diabetes are important examples. McGuffin (1980) proposed that HLA-disease associations may be accounted for in one of two ways: by a close proximity between the HLA loci on chromosome 6 and genes determining immune responses (the 'disease' genes) or because particular HLA types on the cell surface predispose to disease. Since the antigens are present on all cell surfaces, including the neuronal membrane, the latter hypothesis may be of relevance to psychiatric illness. For instance abnormal antigens bound to neuronal membranes may conceivably modify the sensitivity of receptors to their neurotransmitters. Recent Italian work lends some credence to this idea. Castellano *et al*. (1974) in a study of different strains of mice and their recombinants, showed that the effect of chlorpromazine adminstration on an avoidance behavioural response in this species is genetically determined and that the locus is linked to the HLA (H2) system. Another study reported that the clinical response to treatment with chlorpromazine in a group of 33 schizophrenic patients (WHO 1973, classification) was to some extent dependent upon the HLA profile of the subject (Smeraldi *et al*. 1976). Patients possessing the HLA-AI system responded more favourably to treatment than patients who were negative for this antigen. However, a recent study employing several neuroleptics (McGuffin 1979) failed to confirm this finding in a group of UK patients, although there was a relationship between HLA type and susceptibility to develop extrapyramidal side-effects. Moreover, the work of Smeraldi and Scorza-Smeraldi (1976) and Scorza-Smeraldi *et al*. (1977), which claimed that catecholamines and certain adrenergic receptor antagonists interfere with the specific binding of anti-HLA-AI antibodies to human lymphocytes, while provocative, also needs to be treated with caution, since the existence of true adrenergic receptors on these cells is uncertain.

With regard to the possible association of specific HLA subtypes and schizophrenic illnesses, a number of studies have appeared (reviewed by McGuffin 1979, 1980; McGuffin *et al*. 1983) but the position remains rather confused. Two approaches are possible: studies of populations and studies of families having one or more members affected by mental illness. The latter is perhaps potentially the most fruitful approach, but it is particularly demanding on resources. In the one available study (Turner 1979) a linkage between the HLA systems and psychotic symptoms (termed 'schizotaxia') was demonstrated, but subtypes were not determined. Population studies have not indicated any consistent specific associations with the syndrome of schizophrenia as a whole, but in the various subclassifications of schizophrenia more consistent results have emerged (McGuffin *et al*. 1981). Four studies (see McGuffin 1980) agree that the HLA-A9 type is increased in paranoid schizophrenia; the same conclusion may also apply to HLA-CW4 type. An association of HLA-AI with hebophrenic or nuclear schizophrenia has also been claimed (McGuffin 1979; Smeraldi *et al*. 1976). In another study awaiting replication Luchins *et al*. (1980*b*) showed an excess of HLA-A2 in patients without any evidence from CT scans of brain atrophy, while no such association was found in patients with some degree of cerebral atrophy. However, in a more recent study from the Maudsley group of 12 families containing two or more members diagnosed as schizophrenic, no linkage between the disorder and HLA types could be demonstrated (McGuffin *et al*. 1983).

Several centres have studied circulating levels of T-lymphocytes in schizophrenia, but with inconsistent results (Delisi *et al*. 1982; Coffey *et al*. 1983).

SERUM ENZYMES: CREATINE PHOSPHOKINASE AND DOPAMINE-β-HYDROXYLASE

The idea that the pathology of the schizophrenic psychoses may involve abnormal processes in peripheral structures as well as in the brain, appears to receive some support from studies on the concentration of tissue enzymes in the serum. Two enzymes that have been intensively investigated are creatine phosphokinase and dopamine-β-hydroxylase.

Creatine phosphokinase (CPK)

Abnormally high levels of serum CPK were initially reported by Schiavone and Kaldor (1965) in nine out of 24 schizophrenic subjects. The phenomenon has since been investigated by several groups, but in particular by Meltzer and co-workers (see Meltzer (1976) for review). The increased concentrations are only seen in a proportion of acutely psychotic subjects and usually last for five to ten days after the onset of psychotic symptoms. Very high values, as much as 50 times normal, are sometimes recorded, but typically the rise is 5–10 times normal and in a recent study even less (Schubert *et al.* 1982). Isoenzyme studies have shown that the abnormal enzyme levels are derived from skeletal muscle rather than cardiac muscle or the brain. The concentration of other enzymes from skeletal muscle, notably aldolase and pyruvate kinase, are also increased in patients with abnormal CPK levels indicating that the phenomenon reflects some general changes in the permeability or integrity of the muscle membrane.

The phenomenon is not confined to the schizophrenic psychoses. In a major study of newly admitted psychotic patients with psychosis, Meltzer (1976) observed abnormally high serum CPK levels in 47.1 per cent of the sample; this proportion was similar for patients with 'acute schizophrenia' (both paranoid and non-paranoid types), 'chronic schizophrenia' with exacerbation of symptoms and in bipolar affective illness. A similar overall incidence was reported by Taylor and Abichandani (1980) in a retrospective study of 322 admissions to a psychiatric hospital, but of these elevations of serum CPK, 56 per cent occurred in patients diagnosed as primary affective disorder (with psychotic features) and only 24 per cent in patients with schizophrenia. A similar over-representation of a diagnosis of mania in newly admitted patients with high serum CPK values was earlier noted by Gosling *et al.* (1972). Abnormally high levels of serum CPK have also been observed in acute brain disease, such as status epilepticus, vascular catastrophes, tumours and infective conditions. In these instances, however, leakage of the brain isoenzyme may at least partly account for the abnormal levels. The general problems in interpreting serum CPK levels have been discussed by Nevins *et al.* (1973).

There are several possible reasons for an excessive leakage of CPK from muscle into the serum which have to be assessed before the phenomenon can be considered to be of pathogenic significance. Drug therapy and altered corticosteroid secretion appear to have been excluded, but excessive physical exercise and intra-muscular injections have been clearly shown to result in moderate increases in serum CPK, although these are typically less than the levels observed in disturbed patients (Meltzer 1976; Goode *et al.* 1979). However in a group of 54 patients Soni (1976) found that CPK levels in the serum correlated with a measure of psychomotor activity, regardless of diagnosis. Nursing procedures involving limb restraint may make an even more significant contribution. For example, forcible restraint (and the ensuing struggle) applied to a group of normal volunteers resulted in increases in serum CPK that often exceeded 10-fold normal values and which persisted for 72 hours (Goode *et al.* 1977*a*). Thus in some acutely disturbed patients where this type of management is employed, abnormal CPK levels are readily explained.

There apparently remain instances of patients exhibiting high serum CPK who have not been restrained, who have not received intramuscular injections, and whose level of physical activity is not excessive, and in these cases the possibility of the phenomenon being related to a pathological process located in skeletal muscle cannot be excluded. This consideration has led to a search for abnormalities in muscle biopsies from psychiatric patients (Meltzer 1976). In the most recent paper from this group (Crayton and Meltzer 1979) abnormalities in the pattern of distribution of intramuscular nerve twigs were reported in 62 patients with schizophrenic or affective psychoses (classified according to DSM II criteria). These abnormalities consisted of increased collateral branching of the subterminal axons in the patient group compared with a much smaller group of eight normal controls; the incidence was significantly higher in patients with paranoid schizophrenic psychoses. There is no clear evidence to indicate whether this abnormal branching of subterminal axons is related to recent damage to the muscle fibres or to a primary neuropathic process. It is also uncertain whether the neuropathy is related to the appearance of high concentrations of CPK in the serum, since in the study of Crayton and Meltzer (1979) there was no correlation between the serum CPK level and the incidence of abnormal axonal branching. However, if the release of CPK into the serum is due to muscle damage and the neuropathic process reflects repair, a correlation between the two parameters would not be expected.

Several other abnormalities in the neuromuscular system of patients with various types of psychosis have been claimed (Goode *et al.* 1977*b*), but consideration of these is outside the scope of this chapter.

Dopamine-β-hydroxylase (DBH)

This enzyme catalyses the terminal step in the synthesis of noradrenaline and is therefore more directly related to CNS function than muscle CPK.

Evidence for a deficit in central noradrenergic pathways in schizophrenia was claimed by Wise *et al.* (1974) from studies of DBH levels in post-mortem brain samples, but these results have not been confirmed (Crow *et al.* 1979).

Serum DBH is believed to be derived from peripheral noradrenergic terminals, from which it is released stoichiometrically along with transmitter during synaptic transmission; changes in the rate of release of noradrenaline therefore may conceivably be reflected in the concentration of DBH in the serum, although the possibility of other regulatory factors being concerned has to be considered (see below and Stolk *et al.* 1980).

Initial attempts to demonstrate an abnormality in serum DBH in schizophrenia gave largely negative results, but recent studies using an improved assay in which maximum enzyme velocity is measured, appear to contradict the earlier findings. Fujita *et al.* (1978) compared serum DBH in 149 chronic schizophrenics (diagnosed on Schneider's criteria) and 153 normal non-hospitalized controls. The mean enzyme activity in the patients was significantly decreased (patients: 16.17 ± 12.6 μmol/min/l; controls: 42.53 ± 30.94 μmol/min/l; $\pm$ S. D., $p < 0.01$) and the difference was not related to age or treatment with drugs. However there was a large overlap in the values between the two groups. In another recent report Meltzer *et al.* (1980*b*) studied 78 'schizophrenics' and 90 normal subjects; there was no difference in the means for the two groups as a whole, but the mean for the patients with 'chronic paranoid schizophrenia' was significantly lower, a result partly confirmed by Castellani *et al.*, (1982). Book *et al.* (1978) in a study of three pedigrees in a Swedish geographical isolate, found a strong association between the presence of schizophrenic symptoms and low values for serum DBH. In view of the fact that DBH is a copper-dependent enzyme it may also be relevant to note that Tyrer *et al.* (1979) found abnormally low levels of copper in CSF samples from a small group of schizophrenic patients (see also Baron *et al.* 1982; Bowman and Lewis 1982).

Unfortunately these recent results cannot be taken as support for a deficiency of noradrenergic activity in schizophrenia as originally proposed by Wise *et al.* (1974). Recent work (reviewed by Weinshilboum 1979; Stolk *et al.* 1980) suggests that it is unlikely that serum DBH concentrations bear any relation to the level of noradrenergic activity in the individual. The range of observed serum DBH activity in both normal and patient populations is very wide, but the individual differences appear to reflect stable heritable traits rather than state-dependent variations. In fact fluctuations in the quantity of DBH released into the serum from noradrenergic terminals are probably insignificant compared with the total circulating DBH at any one time. Stolk *et al.* (1980) suggested that the 2000-fold range of serum DBH activity typically observed in man is related to individual differences in the rate of the extraneuronal disposal of the enzyme by metabolism, rather than a reflection of sympathetic nervous activity. On this basis the low mean activity for the enzyme observed by Fujita *et al.* (1978) and others can hardly be considered of primary aetiological significance, although it may indicate an inherited tendency to possess a high activity for a proteolytic pathway in the patients.

GLUTEN-SENSITIVITY

The suggestion that gluten-sensitivity may be an aetiological factor in some patients with schizophrenia is due to F. C. Dohan (see Dohan 1978, for a review of the evidence). Broadly speaking the hypothesis proposes that certain peptides derived from the breakdown of the gluten present in cereals possess properties that are neurotoxic in genetically susceptible individuals. Schizophrenia related to gluten-sensitivity is thus seen as analogous to coeliac disease, in which gluten-derived peptides are known to be cytotoxic for the intestinal mucosa. Indeed there is weak circumstantial evidence suggesting that some cases of schizophrenia and coeliac disease may be genetically related.

The main evidence for the gluten sensitivity hypothesis is pharmacological rather than biochemical: it is claimed that in selected patients the symptoms of schizophrenia are attenuated on a gluten-free diet and are precipitated on the re-introduction of cereals (Singh and Kay 1976; Dohan 1978). Experiments designed to establish such a causal connection between diet and symptomatology require to be conducted under double-blind conditions and have to be very carefully evaluated. The study of Singh and Kay (1976) goes some way towards satisfying these criteria. The patients ($n = 14$) were maintained on neuroleptics and fed a gluten-free diet for 14 weeks except for a period of four weeks during which their diet was supplemented with a gluten-containing drink; during the remainder of the test periods a placebo drink was substituted. Raters and patients were said to be blind to the nature of the drinks. Significant exacerbation of symptomatology as indicated by mean behavioural scores, was reported during the period of gluten administration. The suggestion that the exacerbation of symptoms during the 'gluten period' was related to a supposed effect of gluten in delaying the absorption of neuroleptics from the gut, now appears to be unlikely (Luchins *et al.* 1980*a*).

Further work in this area certainly seems justified, but the difficulties in establishing the putative toxicity of gluten as scientific fact are formidable (Hallert 1982; Singh and Kay 1983). In any case it seems accepted, even by the proponents of the hypothesis, that only a small proportion of schizophrenic patients are likely to fall in this category (Rice *et al.* 1978).

There have been claims for other nutritional factors as causative environmental agents in schizophrenia and some of these were discussed briefly by Dickerson (1978).

PROSTAGLANDINS (PGs)

The prostaglandins are a group of 20-carbon oxygenated fatty acids that contain a cyclopentane ring. They are classified according to the substitutions on the cyclopentane ring by the letters A–F and according to the number of carbon–carbon double bonds by a subscript. They are ubiquitously distributed in mammalian tissues and physiologically extremely potent. Their many actions include the modulation of inflammatory responses and the regulation of cyclic AMP synthesis. In the CNS there is evidence for an involvement of prostaglandins in synaptic transmission (Wolfe 1976).

In view of their widespread distribution and potency it is perhaps not surprising that prostaglandin metabolism has been considered as an aetiological factor in schizophrenia. Both prostaglandin excess (Feldberg 1976) and deficiency (Horrobin *et al.* 1978) have been proposed; according to the latter authors, both may be correct in view of the bell-shaped dose response curve observed for PGE_1 in some systems. The evidence for these hypotheses has been summarized by Rotrosen *et al.*, (1980). It is at best circumstantial. Feldberg (1976) drew attention to the catalepsy induced by injection of PGE_1 in animals and to the fact that raised concentrations of PGE_1 have been observed in endotoxin-induced cataleptic states; however, catalepsy in animals cannot be considered as a model for schizophrenia. The deficiency hypothesis relies mainly on analogy with disease states in which prostaglandin metabolism is disturbed, such as arthritis and acrodermatitis enteropathica. Excess prostaglandin synthesis is considered to be a factor in producing the inflammation of arthritis and schizophrenics are reported to have a lower than normal risk for rheumatoid arthritis (Baldwin 1979), as well as to be relatively resistant to pain. However, it should be noted that aspirin is not a psychotomimetic and yet it inhibits prostaglandin synthesis. Acrodermatitis enteropathica is perhaps more interesting for the hypothesis. This is a rare inherited condition, associated with schizophreniform symptoms, in which zinc transport is disturbed; zinc has therapeutic actions in the conditions and also stimulates prostaglandin synthesis.

Direct evidence for a disturbance of prostaglandin functions in schizophrenia has been difficult to establish. A major deficit in schizophrenia in prostaglandin synthesis induced by ADP in platelets was claimed by Abdullah and Hamadah (1975), but so far this work has not been replicated. More recently Rotrosen *et al.* (1980) and Kafka and Van Kammen (1983) studied the interaction of prostaglandins with cyclic AMP synthesis in platelets from schizophrenic subjects. The latter authors examined PGE_1 stimulation of cyclic AMP accumulation in relation to inhibition by noradrenaline through α_2-receptors. Stimulation was lower than normal in male patients ($n = 11$), but the difference was not evident in females. Rotrosen *et al.* studied PGE receptors in blood platelets linked to adenylate cyclase, using cells pulse-labelled with [^{3}H] adenine and measuring the production of [^{3}H] cyclic AMP. In a group of 39 carefully diagnosed schizophrenic patients, mean PGE-stimulated cyclic AMP accumulation was significantly decreased compared with matched control subjects; the difference was not related to drug treatment or length of illness. As in so many similar studies, however, there was the usual overlap between the patients and normals. There is no evidence at present to indicate whether the attenuated response to PGE in platelets from the patients is related to a decreased receptor sensitivity or to metabolic factors regulating the metabolism of cyclic AMP; furthermore, any relevance to CNS function is speculative.

By contrast Mathe *et al.* (1980) in a careful study reported a greatly increased content of immuno-reactive prostaglandin E in CSF from a group of schizophrenic patients; there was no difference in the CSF content of thrombaxane B_2. The authors postulated that the raised PGE concentration might affect the sensitivity of central receptors to transmitters.

CALCIUM IONS AND SCHIZOPHRENIA

There have been recurring reports over the years of abnormalities in calcium and magnesium metabolism in psychotic disorders, particularly in illnesses with pronounced periodicity. In these patients transient but significant increases in serum total calcium and inorganic phosphorus often coincide with regular exacerbations of psychotic symptoms or frank mania.

In the view of Carman and Wyatt (1979*a*) these transient increases in serum calcium may trigger exacerbation of psychotic behaviour, perhaps by provoking overcompensation of a homeostatic regulator of calcium levels in the CNS, and thus increase the general level of behavioural excitability (calcium ions are known to be membrane stabilizers). This is a very tenuous argument, but the general idea does receive some experimental support. The concentration of calcium in the CSF significantly increased concomitantly with remission in a group of acute schizophrenics (Jimerson *et al.* 1979) and low values for CSF calcium have several times been described in schizophrenia generally (see Carman and Wyatt 1979*b*). This suggested the possibility of therapeutic intervention. Having observed, in a double-blind study of 12 patients, that the compound dihydrotachysterol (which increases total calcium and phosphorous in the body fluids) tended to exacerbate psychotic symptoms, Carman and Wyatt (1979*a,b*) went on to study the effect of calcitonin, an agent that decreases serum calcium. In several patients calcitonin reduced the amplitude of the pre-psychotic rise in serum calcium and delayed or aborted the onset of the regular psychotic episode.

It may be noted that in a group of non-cycling schizophrenic patients Alexander and Bunney (1978) found no difference from controls in serum calcium or magnesium levels. However in six patients who developed catatonia a striking increase in serum calcium was observed at the onset of the exacerbation.

The calcium ion is such a ubiquitous and essential element in virtually all aspects of neuronal function that it is difficult to understand how a general disturbance in the regulation of its distribution and transport can lead to a relatively circumscribed behavioural disturbance without gross neurological signs. It is therefore possible that the changes in calcium seen in the periodic patients may be secondary to other biochemical events, and that the effect of calcitonin may be non-specific.

CONCLUSION

As the reader will have observed no attempt at an inclusive survey of the literature has been made in this review. The work selected to some extent reflects my own interests, but has also been chosen to illustrate the themes of the Introduction. Study of peripheral biochemistry is unlikely to delineate causative aetiological factors in psychotic illness; the body fluids are too remote from the CNS and any inherited molecular abnormality affecting peripheral as well as central processes is likely to present a clinical picture with physical symptoms, which are conspicuously absent in schizophrenia. Nevertheless, peripheral biochemistry is a relevant area of research; as well as contributing to our general knowledge of the biology of the schizophrenic subject, it may eventually provide clues as to the central molecular abnormalities that must underlie the condition. That is the justification for further research in this frustrating area.

ACKNOWLEDGEMENT

I am grateful to the Wellcome Trust and the Medical Research Council for support.

References

Abdullah, Y. H. and Hamadah, K. (1975). Effect of ADP of PGE₁ formation in blood platelets from patients with depression, mania and schizoprenia. *Br. J. Psychiat.* **127**, 591-5.

Alexander, P. E. and Bunney, W. E. Jr. (1978). Serum calcium and magnesium in schizophrenia: relationship to clinical phenomena and neuroleptic treatment. *Br. J. Psychiat.* **133**, 143-9.

Baldessarini, R. J., Stramentinoli, G., and Lipinski, F. (1979). Methylation hypothesis. *Arch gen. Psychiat.* **36**, 303-7.

Baldwin, J. A. (1979). Schizophrenia and physical disease *Psycholog. Med.* **9**, 611-8.

Baron, M., Perlman, R., Levitt, M., Meltzer, H., Given, R., and Asnis, L. (1982). Plasma copper and dopamine-β-hydroxylase in schizophrenia. *Biol. Psychiat.* **17**, 115-20.

Baxter, C. F. and Melnechuk, T. (Eds.) (1980). *Perspectives in schizophrenia research*. Raven Press, New York.

Bergen, J. R., Grinspoon, L., Pyle, H. M., Martinez, J. Jr. and Pennel, R. B. (1980). Immunologic studies in schizophrenic and control subjects. *Biol. Psychiat.* **15**, 369-79.

Berger, P. A. (1981). Biochemistry and the schizophrenias. Old concepts and new hypotheses. *J. nerv. ment. Dis.* **169**, 90-9.

Besson, J. A. O. (1980). A diagnostic pointer to adult metachromatic leucodystrophy. *Br. J. Psychiat.* **137**, 186-7.

Bickel, P., Dittrich, A., and Dchopf, J. (1976). Experimental study on altered states of consciousness induced by *N, N*-dimethyltryptamine (DMT). *Pharmakopsychiat. Neuropsychopharmakol.* **9**, 220-5.

Bond, P. A., Cundall, R. L., and Falloon, I. R. (1979). Monoamine oxidase (MAO) of platelet, plasma, lymphocytes and granulocytes in schizophrenia. *Br. J. Psychiat.* **134**, 360–5.

Book, J. A., Wetterberg, L., and Modrezewska, K. (1978). Schizophrenia in a North Swedish geographica isolate, 1900–1977. Epidemiology, genetics and biochemistry. *Clin. Genet.* **14**, 373–94.

Bowman, M. D. and Lewis, M. S. (1982). The copper hypothesis of schizophrenia. *Neurosci. Biobehav. Rev.* **6**, 321–8.

Buchsbaum, M. S. and Haier, P. J. (1978). Biological homogeneity, symptom heterogeneity and the diagnosis of schizophrenia. *Schiz. Bull.* **4**, 473–5.

Campbell, I. C. (1981). Blood platelets and psychiatry. *Br. J. Psychiat.* **138**, 78–80.

Carl. G. F., Crews, E. L., Carmichael, S. M., Benesh, F. C., and Symthies, J. R. (1978). Four enzymes of one-carbon metabolism in blood cells of schizophrenia. *Biol. Psychiat.* **13**, 773–6.

Carman, J. S. and Wyatt, R. J. (1979*a*). Calcium: pacesetting the periodic psychoses. *Am. J. Psychiat.* **136**, 1035–39.

——,—— (1979*b*). Use of calcitonin in psychotic agitations and mania. *Arch. gen. Psychiat.* **36**, 72–5.

Carpenter, W. T., Fink, E. G., Narasimhachari, N, and Himwich, H. E. (1975). A test of the transmethylation hypothesis in acute schizophrenic patients. *Am. J. Psychiat.* **132**, 1067–71.

—— Sadler, J. H., Light, P. D., Hanlon, T. E., Hurland, A. A., Penna, M. W., Reed, W. P., Wilkinson, E. H., and Bartko, J. J. (1983). The therapeutic efficacy of hemodialysis in schizophrenia. *New Engl. J. Med.,* **308**, 669–75.

Castellani, S., Ziegler, M. G., Van Kammen, D. P., Alexander, P. E., Sins, S. G., and Lake, C. R. (1982). Plasma norepinephrine and dopamine-β-hydroxylase activity in schizophrenia. *Arch. gen. Psychiat.* **39**, 1145–9.

Castellano, C., Eleftheriou, B. E., Barley, D. W., and Oliviero, A. (1974). Chlorpromazine and avoidance: a genetic analysis. *Psychopharmacologia* **34**, 309–16.

Checkley, S. A., Murray, R. M., Oon, M. C. H., Rodnight, R., and Birley, J. L. T. (1980). A longitudinal study of the excretion of N-N-dimethyltryptamine in patients with psychotic illness. *Br. J. Psychiat.* **137**, 236–9.

—— Oon, M. C. H., Rodnight, R., Murphy, M. P., Williams, R. S., and Birley, J. L. T. (1979). Urinary excretion of dimethyltryptamine in liver disease. *Am. J. Psychiat.* **136**, 439–41.

Chojnacki, M., Kralik, P., Allen, R. H., Ho, B. T., Schoolar, J. C., and Smith, R. C. (1981). Neuroleptic-induced decrease in platelet MAO activity of schizophrenic patients. *Am. J. Psychiat.* **138**, 838–40.

Coffey, C. E., Sullwan, J. L., and Rice, J. R. (1983) T-lymphocytes in schizophrenia. *Biol. Psychiat.* **18**, 113–19.

Cohen, B. M., Lipinski, J. F., Vuckovic, A., and Prosser, E. (1982). Blood S-adenosyl-L-methionine levels in psychiatric diorders. *Am. J. Psychiat.* **139**, 229–31.

Cohen, S. M., Nichols, A., Wyatt, R., and Pollin, W. (1974). The administration of methionine to chronic schizophrenic patients: a review of ten studies. *Biol. Psychiat.* **8**, 209–25.

Coursey, R. D., Buchsbaum, M. S., and Murphy, D. L. (1979). Platelet MAO activity and evoked potentials in the identification of subjects biologically at risk for psychiatric disorders. *Br. J. Psychiat.* **134**, 372–81.

Crayton, J. W. and Meltzer, H. Y. (1979). Degeneration and regeneration of motor neurons in psychiatric patients. *Biol. Psychiat.* **14**, 803–19.

Crow, T. J. (1978). Viral causes of psychiatric disease. *Postgrad. med. J.* **54**, 763–7.

—— (1980). Molecular pathology of schizophrenia: more than one disease process?

Br. med. J. i, 66–8.

—— (1983). Is schizophrenia an infectious disease? *Lancet* i, 173–5.

—— Baker, H. F., Cross, A. J., Joseph, M. H. Lofthouse, R., Longden, A., Owen, F., Riley, G. J., Glover, V., and Killpack, W. S. (1979). Monoamine mechanisms in chronic schizophrenia: post mortem neurochemical findings. *Br. J. Psychiat.* **134**, 249–56.

Davison, K. and Bagley, C. R. (1969). Schizophrenia like psychoses associated with organic disorders of the central nervous system: a review of the literature. In *Br. J. Psychiat.* Special Publications No. 4: *Current problems in neuropsychiatry* (ed. R.N. Herrington), pp. 113–84.

DeLisi, L. E., Goodman, S., Neckers, L. M., and Wyatt, R. S. (1982). An analysis of lymphocyte subpopulations in schizophrenic patients. *Biol. Psychiat.* **17**, 1003–9.

Del Vecchio, M., Maj, M., D'Ambrosio, A., and Kemali, D. (1983). Low platelet MAO activity in chronic schizophrenia: a long term effect of neuroleptic treatment. *Psychopharmacology* **79**, 177–9.

Dickerson, J. W. T. (1978). Nutrition and schizophrenia: implications and problems. In *The biological basis of schizophrenia* (ed. G. Hemmings, and W. A. Hemmings), pp. 197–208. MTP Press, Lancaster, UK.

Dohan, F. C. (1978). Schizophrenia: are some food-derived polypeptides pathogenic? Coeliac disease as a model. In *The biological basis of schizophrenia* (ed. G. Hemmings and W. A. Hemmings), pp. 167–77. MTP Press, Lancaster, UK.

Durell, J. and Archer, E. G. (1976). Plasma proteins in schizophrenia: a review. *Schiz. Bull.* **2**, 147–59.

Feldberg, W. (1976). Possible association of schizophrenia with a disturbance in prostaglandin metabolism. A physiological hypothesis. *Psychol. Med.* **6**, 359–69.

Fowler, C. J., Tipton, K. F., Mackay, A. V. P., and Youdim, M. B. H. (1982). Human platelet monoamine-oxidase—a useful enzyme in the study of psychiatric disorders? *Neuroscience* **7**, 1577–94.

Freeman, J. M., Finkelstein, J. D., and Mudd, S. H. (1975). Folate responsive homocystinuria and schizophrenia. *New Engl. J. Med.* **292**, 491–6.

Friedhoff, A. J., Park, S., Schweitzer, J. W., Burdock, E. I., and Armour, M. (1977). Excretion of 3,4-dimethoxyphenylethylamine (DMPEA) by acute schizophrenics and controls, *Biol. Psychiat.* **12**, 643–54.

Fujita, K., Ito, T., Maruta, K., Teradaira, R., Beppu, H., Nakagami, Y., Kato, Y., Nagatsu, T., and Kato, T. (1978). Serum dopamine-β-hydroxylase in schizophrenic patients, *J. Neurochem.* **30**, 1569–72.

Gillin, J. C., Kaplan, J., Stillman, R., and Wyatt, R. J. (1976). The psychodelic model of schizophrenia—the case of N,N-dimethyltryptamine. *Am. J. Psychiat.* **133**, 203–8.

—— Stoff, D. M., and Wyatt, R. J. (1978). Trans methylation hypothesis: a review of progress. In *Psychopharmacology: a generation of progress* (ed. M. A. Lipton, A. DiMascio, and K. F. Killam), pp. 1097–112. Raven Press, New York.

Gomes, U. C. R. (1980). Studies in the biochemistry of schizophrenia with special reference to the transmethylation hypothesis. PhD Thesis, University of Stellenbosch, Capetown, South Africa.

—— and Shanley, B. C. (1978). Endogenous inhibitor of indoleamine-N-methyltransferase in cerebrospinal fluid. *Life Sci.* **23**, 697–704.

—— Meltzer, H. Y. Moretti, R., Kupfer, D. J., and McCartland, R. J. (1979). Relationship between wrist-monitored motor activity and serum CPK activity in psychiatric patients. *Br. J. Psychiat.* **135**, 62–6.

——, —— Crayton, J., and Mazura, T. (1977b). Physiologic abnormalities of the neuromuscular system. *Schiz. Bull.* **3**, 121–38.

—— Weinberg, D. H., Mazura, J. A., Curtiss, G. Moretti, R. J., and Meltzer, H. Y.

(1977*a*). Effect of limit restraints on serum creatine phosphokinase activity in normal volunteers. *Biol. Psychiat.* **12**, 743–55.

Gosling, R., Kerry, R. J., Orme, J. E., and Owen, F. (1972). Creatine phosphokinase in newly admitted psychiatric patients. *Br. J. Psychiat.* **121**, 351–6.

Groshong, R., Baldessarini, R. J., Gibson, D. A., Lipinski, J. F., Axelrod, D., and Pope, A. (1979). Activities of type A and B MAO and catechol-*o*-methyltransferase in blood cells and skin fibroblasts of normal and chronic schizophrenic subjects. *Arch. gen. Psychiat.* **35**, 1198–205.

Haier, R. J., Murphy, D. L., and Buchsbaum, M. S. (1979). Paranoia and platelet MAO in normals and non-schizophrenic psychiatric group. *Am. J. Psychiat.* **136**, 309–10.

Hallert, C. (1982). Psychiatric illness, gluten and coeliac disease. *Biol. Psychiat.* **17**, 959–61.

Harris, H. (1980). *The principles of human biochemical genetics*, 3rd edn. Elsevier/North Holland, Amsterdam.

Heath, R. G. and Krupp, J. M. (1967). Schizophrenia as an autoimmunologic disorder. *Arch. gen. Psychiat.* **16**, 1–33.

Hirschhorn, R. (1983). Metabolic defects and immunodeficiency disorders. *New Engl. J. Med.* **308**, 714–16.

Horrobin, D. F., Ally, A. I., and Karmali, R. A. (1978). Prostaglandins and schizophrenia: further discussion of the evidence. *Psychol. Med.* **8**, 43–8.

Ismail, L., Sargent, T. III, Dobson, E. L., and Pollycore, M. (1978), Altered metabolism of the methionine methyl group in the leukocytes of patients with schizophrenia, *Biol. Psychiat.* **13**, 649–60.

Jeste, D. V., Kleinman, J. E., Potkin, S. G., Luchins, D. J., and Weinberger, D. R. (1982). *Ex uno multi*—subtyping the schizophrenic syndrome. *Biol. Psychiat.* **17**, 199–222.

Jimerson, D. C., Post, R. M., Carman, J. S. Van Kammen, D. P., Wood, J. H. Goodwin, F. K., and Bunney, W. E. Jr. (1979). CSF calcium: clinical correlates in affective illness and schizophrenia. *Biol. Psychiat.* **14**, 37–51.

Kafka, M. S. and Van Kammen, D. P. (1983). α-Adrenergic receptor function in schizophrenia. *Arch. gen. Psychiat.* **40**, 264–70.

Kaplan, J., Mandel, J. R., Stillman, R., Walker, R. W., Vandenheuvel, W. J. A. Gillin, J. C., and Wyatt, R. J. (1974). Blood and urine levels of *N,N*-dimethyltryptamine following administration of psychoactive doses to human subjects. *Psychopharmacologia* **38**, 239–45.

Kelsoe, J. R., Tolbert, L. C., Crews, E. L., and Smythies, J. R. (1983). Kinetic evidence for decreased methionine adenosyltransferase activity in erythrocytes from schizophrenics. *J. Neurosci. Res.* **8**, 99–103.

Kety, S. S. (1980). The syndrome of schizophrenia: unresolved questions and opportunities for research. *Br. J. Psychiat.* **136**, 421–36.

Knight, J. G. (1982). Dopamine-receptor-stimulating antibodies: a possible cause of schizophrenia. *Lancet.* **ii**, 1073–5.

Leonhard, K. (1980). Contradictory issues in the origin of schizophrenia. *Brit. J. Psychiat.* **136**, 437–44.

Levi, R. M. and Waxman, S. (1975). Schizophrenia, epilepsy, cancer, methionine and folate metabolism. *Lancet.* **ii**, 11.

Lewis, M. E. (1980). Biochemical aspects of schizophrenia. *Essays Neurochem. Neuropharm.* **4**, 1–67.

Lishman, W. A. (1978). Organic psychiatry. The psychological consequences of cerebral disorder. Blackwell Scientific Publications, Oxford.

Luchins, D., Freed, W. J., Potkin, S. Rosenblatt, J. E., Gillin, J. C., and Wyatt, R. J. (1980*a*). Wheat gluten and haloperidol. *Biol. Psychiat.* **15**, 819–20.

—— Torrey, E. F., Weinberger, D. R. Zalcman, S., Delsi, L., Johnson, A., Rogentine, N., and Wyatt, R. J. (1980*b*). HLA antigens in schizophrenia. Differences between patients with and without evidence of brain atrophies. *Br. J. Psychiat.* **136**, 243–8.

Mandell, A. J. and Segal, D. S. (1973). The psychobiology of dopamine and the methylated indoleamines with particular reference to psychiatry. In *Biological psychiatry* (ed. J. Mendels), pp. 101–12. J.Wiley, New York.

Mann, J. and Thomas, K. M. (1979). Platelet monoamine oxidase activity in schizophrenia. Relationship to disease, treatment, institutionalization and outcome. *Br. J. Psychiat.* **134**, 366–71.

Marzullo, G. and Friedhoff, A. J. (1978). An inhibitor of opiate receptor binding from human erythrocytes identified as a glutathione–copper complex. *Life Sci.* **21**, 1559–68.

Mathe, A. A., Sedvall, G., Wiesel, F. A., and Nyback, H. (1980). Increased content of immunoreactive prostaglandin E in cerebrospinal fluid of patients with schizophrenia. *Lancet* **i**, 16–18.

McGuffin, P. (1979), Is schizophrenia an HLA-associated disease. *Psychol. Med.* **9**, 721–8.

—— (1980). What have transplant antigens got to do with psychosis? *Br. J. Psychiat.* **136**, 510–12.

—— Farmer, A. E., and Yonace, A. H. (1981). HLA antigens and sub types of schizophrenia. *Psychiat. Res.* **5**, 115–22.

—— Festenstein, H., and Murray, R. (1983). A family study of HLA antigens and other genetic markers in schizophrenia. *Psychol. Med.* **13**, 31–43.

Meltzer, H. Y. (1976). Neuromuscular dysfunction in schizophrenia. *Schiz. Bull.* **2**, 106–35.

—— (1979). Biochemical studies in schizophrenia. In *Disorders of the schizophrenic syndrome* (ed. L. Bellak), pp. 45–135. Basic Books, New York.

—— and Arora, R. C. (1980). Skeletal muscle MAO activity in the major psychoses. Relationship with platelet and MAO activities. *Arch. gen. Psychiat.* **37**, 333–9.

——, —— Babar, R., Jackman, H., Nasr, S., Pscheidt, G., Smith, M., and Strahilevitz, M. (1980*a*). Platelet monoamine oxidase activity and schizophrenia. *Arch. gen. Psychiat.* **37**, 357.

—— Nasr, S. J., and Tong, C. (1980*b*). Serum dopamine-β-hydroxylase activity in schizophrenia. *Biol. Psychiat.* **15**, 781–8.

Murphy, D. L., Belmaker, R., Carpenter, W. T., and Wyatt, R. J. (1977). Monoamine oxidase in chronic schizophrenia: studies of hormonal and other factors affecting enzyme activity. *Br. J. Psychiat.* **130**, 151–8.

Murray, R. M., Oon, M. C. H., Rodnight, R., Birley, J. L. T., and Smith, A. (1979). Increased excretion of dimethyltryptamine and certain features of psychosis. *Arch. gen. Psychiat.* **36**, 644–49.

Nevins, M. A., Saran, M., Bright, M., and Lyons, L. J. (1973). Pitfalls in creatine phosphokinase activity. *J. Am. med. Assoc.* **224**, 1382–7.

Oon, M. C. H., Murray, R. M., Rodnight, R., Murphy, M. P., and Birley, J. L. T (1977). Factors affecting the urinary excretion of endogenously formed dimethyltryptamine in normal human subjects. *Psychopharmacology* **54**, 171–5.

Orsulak, P. J., Schildkraut, J. J., Schatzberg, A. F., and Herzog, J. M. (1978). Differences in platelet monoamine oxidase activity in subgroups of schizophrenic and depressive disorders, *Biol. Psychiat.* **13**, 637–47.

Osmond, H. and Smythies, J. R. (1952). Schizophrenia: a new approach. *J. ment. Sci.* **98**, 309–15.

Parnas, J., Mednick, S. A. and Moffitt, T. E. (1981). Perinatal complication and adult schizophrenia. *Trends in Neurosciences* October, 262–4.

Pepplinkhuizen, L., Bruinvels, J., Blom, W., and Moleman, P. (1980). Schizophrenia-like psychosis by a metabolic disorder. *Lancet* i, 454–6.

Pope, H. G., Jr. and Lipinski, J. F. (1978). Diagnosis in schizophrenia and manic depressive illness. A reassessment of the specificity of 'schizophrenic' symptoms in the light of current research. *Arch. gen. Psychiat.* **35**, 811–28.

Potkin, S. G., Cannon, H. E., Murphy, D. L., and Wyatt, R. J. (1978). Are paranoid schizophrenics different from other schizophrenics? *New Engl. J. Med.* **298** 61–6.

Pulkkinen, E. (1977). Immunoglobulins, psychopathology and prognosis in schizophrenia. *Acta psychiat. scand.* **56**, 173–82.

Raisanen, M. and Karkkainen, J. (1979). Mass fragmentographic quantification of urinary *N,N*-dimethyltryptamine and bufotenine. *J. Chromatog.* **162**, 579–84.

Reveley, M. A., Reveley, A. M., Clifford, C. A., and Murray, R. M. (1983). The genetics of platelet MAO activity in discordant schizophrenic and normal twins. *Br. J. Psychiat* **142**, 560–5.

Rice, J. R., Ham, C. H., and Gore, W. E. (1978). Another look at gluten in schizophrenia. *Amer. J. Psychiat.* **135**, 1417–18.

Rodnight, R. (1980). Biochemical perspectives in psychiatric research. In *Priorities in psychiatric research* (ed. M. G. Lader), pp. 1–16. John Wiley, Chichester, UK.

—— (1982). Biochemistry and pathology of schizophrenia. In *Handbook of psychiatry* Vol. 3. Psychoses of uncertain aetiology (ed. J. K. Wing), pp. 69–73. Cambridge University Press, Cambridge, UK.

—— (1983). Schizophrenia: some current neurochemical approaches. *J. Neurochem.* **41**, 12–21.

Rose, N. R. (1981). Autoimmune disease, *Scientific Am.* **244**, 70–81.

Rosengarten, H. and Friedhoff, A. (1976). A review of recent studies of the biosynthesis and excretion of hallucinogens formed by methylation of neurotransmitters or related substances. *Schiz. Bull.* **2**, 90–105.

Rotrosen, J., Miller, A. D., Maudio, D., Traficante, L. J., and Gershon, S. (1980). Prostaglandins, platelets and schizophrenia, *Arch. gen. Psychiat.* **37**, 1047–54.

Sandler, M., Reveley, M. A., and Glover, V. (1981). Human platelet monoamine-oxidase in health and disease: a review. *J. clin. Path.* **34**, 292–302.

Schiavone, D. J. and Kaldor, J. (1965). Creatine phosphokinase levels and cerebral disease. *Med. J. Australia* **52**, 709–92.

Schneider, G. E. (1981). Early lesions and abnormal neuronal connections. *Trends in Neurosciences* July, 187–9.

Schubert, D. S. P., Brocco, K., Miller, F. T., and Patterson, M. (1982). Serum creatine phosphokinase levels in patients meeting the St Louis research diagnostic criteria for schizophrenia. *Am. J. Psychiat.* **139**, 491–3.

Scorza-Smeraldi, R., Smeraldi, E., Fabio, G., Bellodi, L., Sacchetti, E. and Rugarli, C. (1977). Interference between anti-HLA antibodies and adrenergic receptor binding drugs. *Tissue Antigens* **9**, 163–6.

Sheehy, L. M. and Maxmen, J. S. (1978). Phenelzine-induced psychosis. *Am. J. Psychiat.* **135**, 1422–3.

Singh, M. M. and Kay, S. R. (1976). Wheat gluten as a pathogenic factor in schizophrenia. *Science* **191**, 401–2.

——, —— (1983). Study of gluten effect in schizophrenia. *Arch. gen. Psychiat.* **40**, 345.

Smeraldi, E., Bellodi, L., Sacchetti, E., and Cazzullo. C. L. (1976). The HLA system and the clinical response to treatment with chlorpromazine. *Br. J. Psychiat.* **129**, 486–9.

—— and Scorza-Smeraldi, R. (1976). Interference between anti-HLA antibodies and chlorpromazine. *Nature, Lond.* **260**, 532–4.

Smythies, J. R. (1980). Brain protein carboxymethylases and schizophrenia. *Psychoneuroendocrinology* **5**, 177–8.

Soni, S. D. (1976). Serum creatine phosphokinase in acute psychosis. *Br. J. Psychiat.* **128**, 181–3.

Spokes, E. G. S. (1979). An analysis of factors influencing measurements of dopamine, noradrenaline, glutamate decarboxylase and choline acetylase in human post mortem brain tissue. *Brain* **102**, 333–46.

Springer, M. S., Goy, M. F., and Adler, J. (1979). Protein methylation in behavioural control mechanisms and in signal transduction. *Nature, Lond.* **280**, 279–84.

Stahl, M. S. (1977). The human platelet. A diagnostic and research tool for the study of biogenic amines in psychiatric and neurologic disorders. *Arch. gen. Psychiat.* **34**, 509–16.

Stolk, J. M., Hurst, J. H. Friedman, M. J., Harris, P. Q., Van Riper, D. A., and Nisula, B. C. (1980). Serum dopamine-β-hydroxylase: indicator of what? In *Enzymes and neurotransmitters in mental disease* (ed. E. Cesdin, T. L. Sourkes, and M. H. B. Youdim), pp. 171–92. J. Wiley, New York.

Stramentinoli, G. and Baldessarini, R. J. (1978). Lack of enhancement of DMT formation in rat brain and rabbit lung *in vivo* by methionine or S-adenosylmethionine. *J. Neurochem.* **31**, 1015–20.

Sullivan, J. L., Cavenar, J. D. Stanfield, C. N., and Hammett, E. B. (1978). Reduced MAO activity in platelets and lymphocytes of chronic schizophrenics. *Am. J. Psychiat.* **135**, 597–8.

Svejgaard, A. (1976). *The HLA System: an introductory survey.* Monographs in Human Genetics No 7. S. Karger, Basel.

Taylor, J. R. and Abichandani, L. (1980). Creatine phosphokinase elevations and psychiatric symptomatology. *Biol. Psychiat.* **15**, 865–70.

Torrey, E. F. and Petterson, M. R. (1976). The viral hypothesis of schizophrenia. *Schiz. Bull.* **2**, 136–6.

Turner, W. J. (1979). Genetic markers for schizotoxia. *Biol. Psychiat.* **14**, 177–206.

Tyrer. S. P., Delves, H. T., and Weller, M. P. I. (1979). CSF copper in schizophrenia. *Am. J. Psychiat.* **136**, 937–9.

Walker, R. W., Mandel, L. R., Kleinman, J. E., Gillin, J. C., Wyatt, R. J., and Vandenheuvel, W. J. A. (1979). Improved selective ion monitoring mass-spectrometric assay for the determination of *N,N*-dimethyltryptamine in human blood utilizing capillary column gas chromatography. *J. Chromatog.* **162**, 539–46.

Weinshilboum, R. M. (1979), Serum dopamine-β-hydroxylase. *Pharmacol. Rev.* **30**, 133–66.

Wing, J. K., Copper, J. E., and Sartorius, N. (1974). *The measurement and classification of psychiatric symptoms.* Cambridge University Press, London.

Winter, H., Herschel, M., Propping, P., Friedl, W., and Vogel, F. (1978). A twin study of three enzymes (DBH, COMT, MAO) of catecholamine metabolism. *Psychopharmacology* **57**, 63–9.

Wise, C. D., Baden, M. M., and Stein, L. (1974). Post mortem measurements of enzymes in human brain: evidence of a central noradrenergic deficit in schizophrenia. *J. Psychiat. Res.* **11**, 185–98.

—— Potkin, S., Bridge, P., and Wyatt, R. J. (1979). Endogenous inhibitor of platelet MAO activity in chronic schizophrenia—failure to replicate. *Am. J. Psychiat.* **136**, 1336–7.

Wolfe, L. S. (1976). Prostaglandins and synaptic transmission. In *Basic neurochemistry* (2nd edn.) (ed. G. J. Siegel, R. A. Albers, R. Katzman, and B. W. Agranoff), pp. 263–75. Little Brown, Boston.

Wyatt, R. J., Murphy, D. L., Belamker, R., Cohen, S., Donnelly, C. H., and Pollin, W. (1973). Reduced monoamine oxidase activity in platelets: a possible genetic marker for vulnerability to schizophrenia. *Science* **179**, 916–18.

—— Potkin, S. G., and Murphy, D. L. (1979). Platelet monoamine oxidase activity in schizophrenia: a review of the data. *Am. J. Psychiat.* **136**, 377–85.

——, —— Kleinman, J. E., Weinberger, D. R., Luchins, D. L., and Jeste, D. V. (1981). The schizophrenic syndrome. Examples of biological tools for sub-classification. *J. nerv. ment. Dis.* **169**, 100–12.

2

Pharmacology of antipsychotic drugs

P. B. BRADLEY

INTRODUCTION

The antipsychotic drugs, or major tranquillizers, are chemically very diverse but possess the common property of alleviating the symptoms of both functional and organic psychoses. They are effective not only in the acute phase of psychotic disorders but also as maintenance therapy, to reduce the risk of relapse. Most, if not all, antipsychotic drugs are sedative if given in sufficiently large doses. However, some are only very weakly sedative and, in the dose levels needed for the control of the symptoms of psychotic states, marked reduction of consciousness is rarely observed with any of the antipsychotic drugs. This property, in fact, distinguishes the antipsychotic drugs from other types of central depressants, e.g. barbiturates.

Although extracts of the climbing shrub, *Rauwolfia serpentina*, had been in use in India for centuries for the treatment of insanity and high blood pressure, the discovery of the antipsychotic drugs is usually attributed to the French psychiatrists, Jean Delay and Pierre Deniker, who also coined the term 'neuroleptic' which was subsequently adopted by the World Health Organisation (WHO Tech. Rep. No. 371). Other names which have been used for these drugs are: 'psycholeptic', 'ataractic', and 'antischizophrenic'. There are perhaps subtle distinctions between the precise meanings of these different terms. However, the only distinction which needs to be considered here is between the terms 'antipsychotic' and 'neuroleptic', which unfortunately are often used interchangeably. An antipsychotic action implies an action against a specific clinical syndrome, i.e. psychosis, whereas the term neuroleptic has a much wider connotation and includes many types of action on the nervous system. Neuroleptic is, therefore, the most appropriate term to use in discussing the pharmacology of these drugs.

The drug which Delay and Deniker used was chlorpromazine, a phenothiazine, and the 'prototype' for many other antipsychotic drugs. The discovery was empirical, rather than being based on a knowledge of the mechanism of action of the drug and of the pathophysiology of psychosis, but the effects were dramatic and led to what has been termed a 'pharmacological revolution' in psychiatry. The stimulus provided by this discovery in the early-1950s led to a search for antipsychotic activity in other, more chemically diverse compounds, as well as other drugs chemically related to chlorpromazine. Thus, the thioxanthines, which are structurally related to the phenothiazines, and the butyrophenones and diphenylbutyl-piperidines, which are not, were discovered during the next decade. No significant new discoveries were made for almost another 20 years, but recently another new group of drugs with antipsychotic properties has appeared, the substituted benzamides. There are also some miscellaneous agents for which at times antipsychotic properties have been claimed. These include the β-blocker, propranolol, certain opioid peptides, and even the psychotomimetic drug, *D*-lysergic acid diethylamide (LSD 25).

Initially, there was a great deal of controversy concerning the specificity of antipsychotic drugs, as it was thought that the drugs did not really alleviate the symptoms of psychotic illness, but merely sedated or 'tranquillized' otherwise recalcitrant patients. However, a number of studies comparing the effects of antipsychotic drugs with those of general sedatives (e.g. barbiturates) has shown that there is a specific antipsychotic action which is not possessed by general sedatives (Klein and Davis 1969).

THE CLASSIFICATION OF ANTIPSYCHOTIC DRUGS

Probably the best method of classification for antipsychotic drugs at the present time is in terms of their chemical structure. In the following pages the pharmacological properties of each of the main groups will therefore be discussed. The groups are:

1. Rauwolfia alkaloids and related substances
2. Phenothiazines
3. Thioxanthenes
4. Butyrophenones and diphenylbutylpiperidines
5. Dibenzazepines
6. Substituted benzamides
7. Miscellaneous.

Rauwolfia alkaloids and related substances

Reserpine

The shrub *Rauwolfia* is indigenous to India, Africa, and South America and is an abundant source of alkaloids. It seems certain that extracts of *Rauwolfia* roots were known in folk medicine for many centuries as effective in mania and for the treatment of snake bites. However, in spite of reports in the Indian literature (Sen and Bose 1931), the drug was largely ignored in Western medicine until the principal psychopharmacologically active constituent, reserpine, was isolated in 1952.

Reserpine (Fig. 2.1) is an indole. Its most important pharmacological action is to deplete tissue levels of amines which, in the central nervous system, are mainly noradrenaline (NA), 5-hydroxytryptamine (5-HT), and dopamine (DA). However, the drug also has peripheral actions and causes

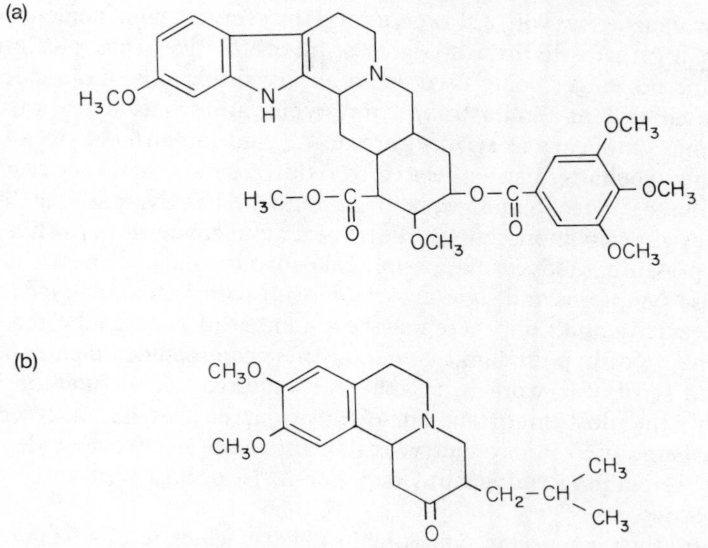

(a)

(b)

FIG. 2.1.   The chemical structures of (a) reserpine and (b) tetrabenazine.

the release of 5-HT and histamine from platelets, and catecholamines from the heart. Other peripheral sites, e.g. the adrenal medulla and the gut, are less affected by reserpine.

Reserpine is highly lipid soluble and therefore rapidly permeates cell membranes where it binds with the granular membranes of amine-containing nerve terminals (Wagner 1975). This prevents the uptake of the amines into the intracellular storage vesicles and has the ultimate effect of causing a failure of transmission, since it is the bound transmitter in the granular vesicles which is released synaptically. This action of reserpine is thought to be due to inhibition of the ATPase-dependent uptake mechanism in the vesicle membranes. Thus, any amine which diffuses out will not be pumped back in again and may be degraded by monoamine oxidase (MAO) in the cytoplasm.

Doses of reserpine which are just sufficient to cause failure of transmission produce a reversible impairment of the storage vesicles and, in this case, function can be restored by the administration of an exogenous amine or its precursor. Larger doses of reserpine cause irreversible damage to the storage vesicles and the effects are much less easily reversed. Chronic administration of reserpine has been found to cause increased activity of the enzymes, tyrosine hydroxylase, and tryptophan hydroxylase, leading therefore to a compensatory increase in amine synthesis. A stimulatory action on choline acetyltransferase, thus increasing the levels of acetylcholine (ACh) in brain, has also been reported, together with effects on amino acids and prostaglandins, though the significance of these latter effects is not clear.

Clinically, the effects of reserpine appear to be similar to those of chlorpromazine but with a slower onset. However, the high incidence of side-effects, together with the availability of more effective drugs, has resulted in reserpine no longer being used as an antipsychotic. The main side-effects associated with the administration of reserpine are: sedation, extrapyramidal symptoms, lowering of seizure thresholds, and impairment of autonomic function. The latter can be related to reduced sympathetic activity, due to depletion of catecholamines, and consequent parasympathetic 'release'. Thus, excess salivation, nausea, diarrhoea, nasal congestion, flushing, fall in blood pressure, bradycardia, peripheral oedema, and acute peptic ulcer, i.e. all those symptoms and signs associated with parasympathetic overactivity, may occur. In addition, there may be a number of hormonal effects due to disturbance of hypothalamic function; these can include amenorrhoea and reduced fertility in women, together with altered sexual function in men. Possibly the most important side-effect which has resulted in reserpine no longer being used in psychiatry, is the tendency for iatrogenic depression, closely resembling endogenous depression, to occur, even with relatively small doses.

Due to the reduction in sympathetic activity, which results from depletion of amines both centrally and peripherally, reserpine still has a place in the treatment of hypertension. Reserpine has also been a very useful drug in experimental pharmacology, particularly in elucidating mechanisms of monoamine storage and release, the mode of action of sympathomimetic drugs and the fundamental processes involved in the activity of the autonomic nervous system. The drug has also been used to provide an animal model for the testing of drugs with potential antidepressant properties.

Two substances, closely related to reserpine, deserpidine and rescinnamine, have also been used as antipsychotic drugs. Their properties are very similar to those of reserpine and they, too, are now only of historical interest.

For a review of reserpine and related drugs, see Bein (1980).

Tetrabenazine

This substance is a benzoquinolizine derivative (Fig. 2.1b) and therefore is not chemically related to reserpine. It is considered here because its pharmacological actions are similar to those of reserpine. Thus, tetrabenazine causes depletion of amines by disrupting storage mechanisms; however, its effect is mainly on the central nervous system (CNS) and it has little or no peripheral action. It is less hypotensive than reserpine and the effects are of shorter duration and with a more rapid onset. However, the side-effects of tetrabenazine, including depression and extrapyramidal symptoms, are just as prevalent. Therefore, tetrabenazine, too, is only of historical interest. The drug has an application in the treatment of movement disorders due to Huntington's chorea, senile chorea, and related neurological conditions.

Phenothiazines

The first of the substituted phenothiazines to be successfully used in psy-

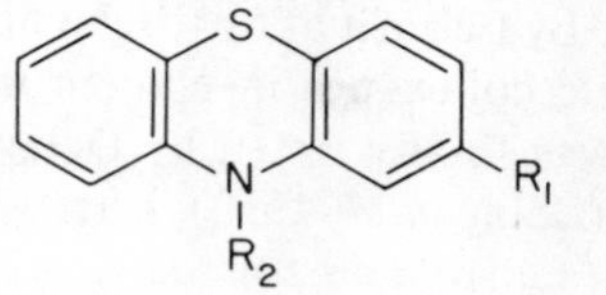

R_1	R_2	
H	$CH_2.CH_2.N(C_2H_5)_2$	Diethazine
H	$CH_2.CH_2.CH_2.N(CH_3)_2$	Promazine
H	$CH_2.CH(CH_3).N(CH_3)_2$	Promethazine
Cl	$CH_2.CH_2.CH_2.N(CH_3)_2$	Chlorpromazine

FIG. 2.2.   The chemical structures of some substituted phenothiazines.

chiatry was chlorpromazine and is therefore widely regarded as the 'proto-type' antipsychotic. The first phenothiazine derivatives were synthesized in 1883, although interest then was in making the dye methylene blue. Phenothiazine itself was used for a time as an antiseptic and anthelminthic but was abandoned because of toxic effects. However, following the discovery of antihistamine activity by Bovet in 1937, various phenothiazine derivatives were synthesized in the Rhone–Poulenc laboratories in Paris for their antihistamine properties. These were aminophenothiazines with substitutions on the nitrogen atom of the pyridine ring (R_2, Fig. 2.2). Two of these derivatives are promethazine and diethazine which are analogues of chlorpromazine. Promethazine quickly became known as an excellent antihistaminic and has been widely used ever since. It is however, sedative, a property which is often regarded as a 'side-effect'. Promethazine was tested in schizophrenic patients but was found to be no more effective than other sedatives (e.g. barbiturates). It was also found to potentiate the actions of barbiturates and was introduced into surgery by Laborit in 1949 as part of his 'lytic cocktail' which was designed to reduce postoperative shock. As well as reducing the amount of general anaesthetic required, the lytic cocktail was found to induce a state of somnolence or calm sleep, from which the patient could easily be roused. Another phenothiazine derivative synthesized by the chemist Charpentier was chlorophenothiazine, with a chlorine atom in the position R_2 of the phenothiazine molecule (Fig. 2.2.) and this compound was subsequently renamed chlorpromazine. Chlorpromazine had less antihistamine activity but was both sympatholytic and parasympatholytic, i.e. it reduced autonomic activity. The drug was found to abolish pre-operative anxiety as well as reducing surgical stress and postoperative shock. Patients who had been given chlorpromazine were alert, but were strikingly indifferent to their environment, a state described by Laborit as 'artificial hibernation'. Laborit tried to interest his psychiatric colleagues in chlorpromazine but without much success until the drug was finally tested by Delay and Deniker, who reported their results in 1952 (Delay *et al*. 1952), after which it became very widely used as an antipsychotic drug and for many other purposes. In the treatment of schizophrenia the phenothiazines have, from the early days of their introduction, held a unique position. It soon became clear that these drugs had a completely different action to that of sedatives and that the fundamental symptoms of schizophrenia, many of which are uniquely characteristic of the disorder, responded selectively.

General properties and structure–activity relationships

Chlorpromazine, as the prototype phenothiazine, possesses in addition to its antipsychotic action, numerous other properties. Many of these are, to a greater or lesser extent, also possessed by other phenothiazine neuroleptics (see below). The most important of these actions are: cardiovascular effects, e.g. disturbances of vasomotor control, interference with temperature control mechanisms, and an anti-emetic action. In experimental animals, there is a reduction in motor activity, a tendency to induce a catatonia-like state, and the blocking of conditioned avoidance responses. However, another action, common to most phenothiazines (and in fact, most antipsychotic drugs), is the ability to induce extra-pyramidal symptoms, closely resembling those associated with Parkinson's disease. This ability to induce iatrogenic parkinsonism is of course undesirable and is therefore regarded as a side-effect of antipsychotic drugs.

The phenothiazines have a wide range of pharmacological actions. Their antihistamine actions have already been referred to. In addition they have weak antagonist actions to 5-hydroxytryptamine (serotonin, 5-HT) and to acetylcholine. These actions may be responsible for some of the side-effects produced by the drugs and will be referred to in more detail. The most marked peripheral action of the phenothiazines is a blockade of adrenergic receptors, especially α-receptors. This action causes loss of vasomotor tone and is thought to be responsible, at least in part, for the postural hypotension which is sometimes associated with the use of therapeutic doses of drugs such as chlorpromazine.

Chemically, the phenothiazines are tricyclic molecules (Fig. 2.2) with substitutions on the carbon atom at position 2 (R_1) and, on the nitrogen atom at position 10 (R_2). The substitution on one of the benzene rings (i.e. R_1) is essential for neuroleptic activity and is always in the same position (i.e. carbon atom 2). Thus, the structure of promazine and chlorpromazine are very similar, differing only in the presence of a chlorine atom at R_1 (Fig. 2.2), the side-chain attached at R_2 being the same in both drugs. Chlorpromazine, which possesses the chlorine at R_1, is a potent neuroleptic drug with only moderate sedative activity, while promazine is not a useful antipsychotic but is strongly sedative. Thus, the presence of the halogen at R_1 imparts neuroleptic activity. Other non-neuroleptic phenothiazines (i.e. no substitution at R_1) are promethazine, which is a powerful antihistamine and has already been referred to, and diethazine (see Fig. 2.2), which is a weak antihistamine but has marked anticholinergic properties which are atropine-like, i.e. anti-muscarinic, and the drug has been used successfully in the treatment of Parkinson's disease. Apart from chlorine, other substituents at R_1 include trifluoromethyl ($- CF_3$, viz. trifluopromazine and trifluoperazine, Fig. 2.3), which increases the neuroleptic potency, and methyl-mercapto ($- SCH_3$, viz. thioridazine, Fig. 2.3), which is approximately equipotent with chlor-promazine as a neuroleptic.

The phenothiazine neuroleptics can be divided into three classes according to the type of substitution on the nitrogen atom (R_2) at position 10. This side-chain can be aliphatic or contain piperidine or piperazine moities. Many

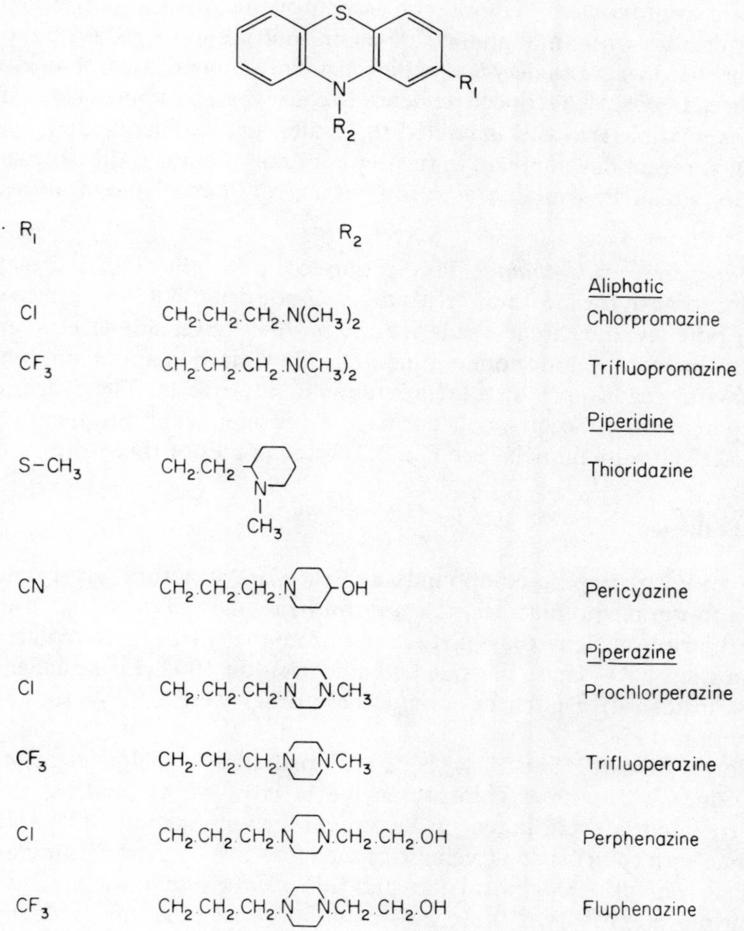

R_1	R_2	
		Aliphatic
Cl	$CH_2.CH_2.CH_2.N(CH_3)_2$	Chlorpromazine
CF_3	$CH_2.CH_2.CH_2.N(CH_3)_2$	Trifluopromazine
		Piperidine
$S-CH_3$	$CH_2.CH_2$ — (piperidine, N–CH_3)	Thioridazine
CN	$CH_2.CH_2.CH_2.N$ (piperidine) —OH	Pericyazine
		Piperazine
Cl	$CH_2.CH_2.CH_2.N$ (piperazine) $N.CH_3$	Prochlorperazine
CF_3	$CH_2.CH_2.CH_2.N$ (piperazine) $N.CH_3$	Trifluoperazine
Cl	$CH_2.CH_2.CH_2.N$ (piperazine) $N.CH_2.CH_2.OH$	Perphenazine
CF_3	$CH_2.CH_2.CH_2.N$ (piperazine) $N.CH_2.CH_2.OH$	Fluphenazine

FIG. 2.3. The chemical structures of some phenothiazine neuroleptics.

thousands of compounds have been synthesized with varying side-chain structures in attempts to make more potent antipsychotic drugs and to eliminate side-effects. Only a few, particularly those in use clinically, will be considered here.

1. *Aliphatic side-chain.*   These are all aminoalkyl compounds in which the basic nitrogen atom in the side-chain is tertiary and is separated from the nitrogen atom in the central ring by a three-carbon chain (e.g. chlorpromazine and trifluopromazine, Fig. 2.3). Phenothiazines with shorter side-chains, (e.g. promethazine, Fig. 2.2) have potent antihistamine and sedative properties but are not neuroleptics.

2. *Piperidine side-chain.*   Although a number of neuroleptic drugs with piperidine side-chains has been developed, only a few are now used as antipsychotics, the principal ones being thioridazine and pericyazine (Fig. 2.3). They are approximately equipotent as neuroleptics to the corresponding phenothiazines with an aliphatic side-chain, but are more sedative and are therefore used where anxiety and agitation are prominent. Also, thioridazine is reported to possess a reduced tendency to cause extrapyramidal side-effects and it is possible that this is related to greater anticholinergic activity (see below). A recent development in this series of compounds is the drug, pipothiazine, which is available as a long-acting or 'depot' preparation (see Chapter 4).

3. *Piperazine side-chain.*   This group of phenothiazine neuroleptics contains some of the most powerful antipsychotic drugs but, apart from their greater potency, they are less sedative and produce fewer side-effects related to disturbances of autonomic function. They have marked anti-emetic actions and readily produce extrapyramidal side-effects. These drugs are more potent than the other phenothiazine neuroleptics in producing catatonia-like states in animals. See Fig. 2.3 for examples of this group.

Thioxanthenes

These are also tricyclic compounds and they are structurally very closely related to the phenothiazines, the thioxanthene nucleus differing from the phenothiazine nucleus only in that the aromatic nitrogen is replaced by carbon (Fig. 2.4). Thus, the side-chain at position 10 (R_2) is attached to a carbon instead of a nitrogen atom. These drugs were first synthesized in Denmark in 1958.

Chlorprothixene (Fig. 2.4) is the thioxanthene analogue of chlorpromazine. It resembles chlorpromazine in most of its pharmacological properties but is more potent in its anticholinergic, atropine-like activity. Thus, as with thioridazine (see above) the incidence of extrapyramidal side effects is less with chlorprothixine, and this may be due to the greater antimuscarinic potency. On the other hand, there is a greater tendency for anticholinergic side-effects, e.g. cardiovascular symptoms, to occur with chlorprothixine. The drug is a potent anti-emetic and is claimed to be less

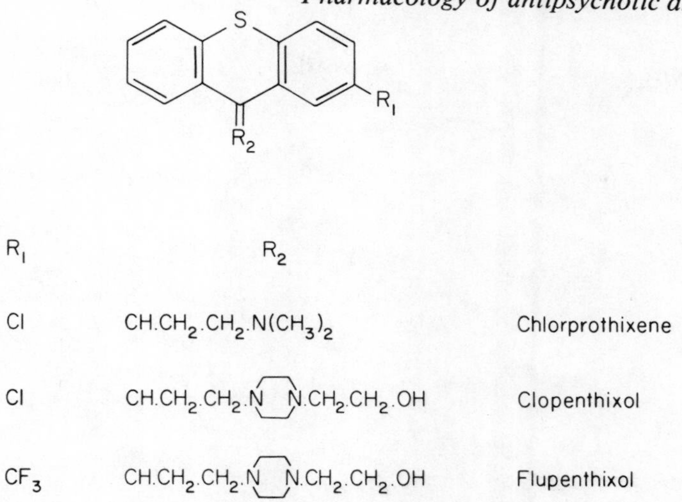

R_1	R_2	
Cl	$CH.CH_2.CH_2.N(CH_3)_2$	Chlorprothixene
Cl	$CH.CH_2.CH_2.N\frown N.CH_2.CH_2.OH$	Clopenthixol
CF_3	$CH.CH_2.CH_2.N\frown N.CH_2.CH_2.OH$	Flupenthixol

FIG. 2.4. The chemical structures of thioxanthenes used clinically.

sedative than chlorpromazine. It is the least potent of the thioxanthene neuroleptics but possesses some antidepressant activity.

The other members of this group, e.g. clopenthixol and flupenthixol (Fig. 2.4) have piperazine side-chains at R_2. Thus, clopenthixol is the thioxanthene analogue of perphenazine, and flupenthixol is the analogue of fluphenazine. These drugs are very similar in their properties to the corresponding phenothiazines. However, the carbon atom at position 10 in the tricyclic ring results in the formation of a double bond with the first carbon atom of the side-chain. The resulting asymmetry means that two stereoisometric forms exist and, in the case of flupenthixol, the isomers have been separated and tested for both pharmacological and clinical activity. The α- or *cis*-isomer has been found to be active and the β- or *trans*-isomer, inactive (see below). Both clopenthixol and flupenthixol are used as depot forms for maintenance therapy, e.g. as the decanoate, which can be administered at intervals of two to four weeks. The pharmacological properties of these formulations appear to be the same as the other forms of these drugs.

For further details of the structure–activity relationships of the tricyclic neuroleptic drugs, i.e. the phenothiazine and the thioxanthenes, see Schmutz and Picard (1980).

Butyrophenones and diphenylbutylpiperidines

These drugs do not possess a tricyclic structure and they are chemically related to the analgesic, pethidine. They were discovered in the Janssen laboratories in Belgium in 1957 when a series of propiophenones, derived from norpethidine, was being screened for potential analgesic activity. Some compounds with potent analgesic activity were found, others showed mixed

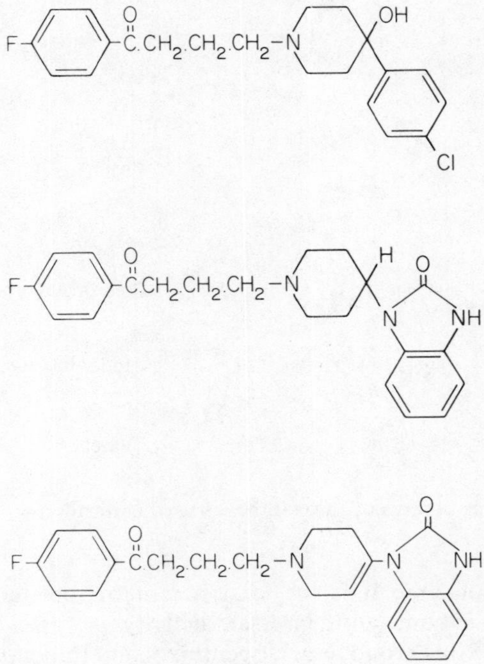

FIG. 2.5. The chemical structures of clinically-important butyrophenones.

analgesic–neuroleptic activity, and yet another group were devoid of morphine-like actions but were found to closely resemble chlorpromazine in their pharmacological profile. The first of these drugs to be used clinically as an antipsychotic was haloperidol (Fig. 2.5), and it is still very widely used. Others are benperidol and droperidol (Fig. 2.5). The pharmacological properties of these three compounds appear to be similar. They have strong antipsychotic actions but lack some of the other properties of the phenothiazines. Thus, they have little or no antihistaminic, anticholinergic, or antiadrenergic activity, and they therefore lack sedative properties and have a reduced tendency to cause autonomic disturbances compared to the phenothiazines. The lack of sedative properties is notable although it may not be so marked with droperidol, and haloperidol has been known to cause insomnia. All the butyrophenones have a very marked propensity to cause extrapyramidal symptoms and this has been attributed to a greater affinity for the extrapyramidal system, but it is more likely to be associated with the low anticholinergic potency.

Benperidol is more potent than haloperidol but otherwise does not have any advantage over the latter. Benperidol has also been used to suppress antisocial sexual behaviour. Droperidol is relatively short-acting and is the drug of choice, in combination with the potent analgesic fentanyl, to induce neuroleptanalgesia. Droperidol is also sometimes used for premedication when it

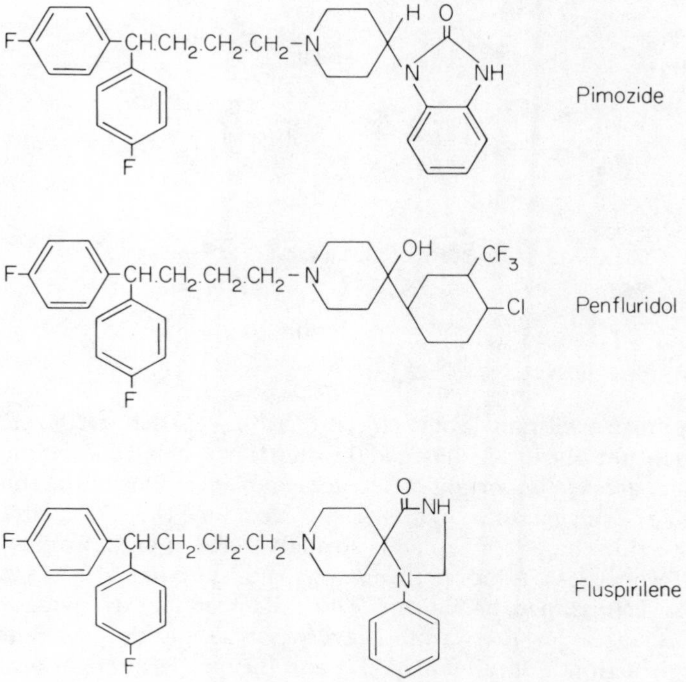

FIG. 2.6. The chemical structures of some clinically-important diphenylbutyro-piperidines.

produces a quiet relaxed state. The most potent representative of this group of drugs is spiperone or spiroperidol. This substance is not used clinically but has proved to be a useful tool in experimental studies, especially in receptor binding assays where the radiolabelled form is used as a ligand.

The diphenylbutyropiperidines are very similar in chemical structure to the butyrophenones (Fig. 2.6). They were made five years after the synthesis of haloperidol by modification of the keto function of the butyrophenone side-chain. Pimozide, which is probably the best known of this group of anti-psychotic drugs and was also the first to be used, is a derivative of the buty-rophenone, benperidol. It is not sedative even when given in large doses and has a reduced tendency to produce extrapyramidal symptoms compared to most other antipsychotic drugs. However, the full range of extrapyramidal side-effects can still be observed, particularly with high doses. The reduction in extrapyramidal side-effects with pimozide may be related to the anticho-linergic property of the drug. Epileptiform convulsions have been known to occur following the withdrawal of pimozide.

Two other representative drugs of this group are penfluridol and flus-pirilene (Fig. 2.6). These are longer-acting than pimozide, and penfluridol, which is active when given orally, can be administered at weekly intervals.

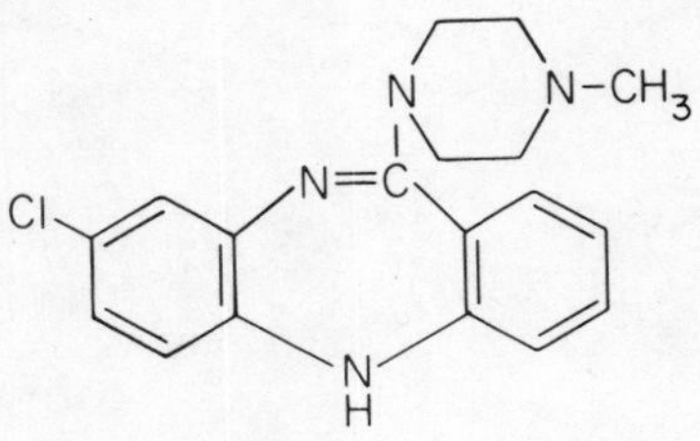

FIG. 2.7.   The chemical structure of clozapine.

Dibenzazepine derivatives

These are drugs with a tricyclic structure, although the centre ring differs from that of the phenothiazines and thioxanthenes, being a seven-membered ring. There are also important differences in the positions of the substituent groups. The principal drug in this class is clozapine (Fig. 2.7), which has a piperazine side-chain. Clozapine is strongly sedative and also has muscle-relaxant properties. It does not cause any cataleptic-like effects in animals and it has been claimed that clozapine does not produce extrapyramidal side-effects in man. So far, this seems to have been true. The drug has potent anticholinergic actions (Bürki *et al.* 1977) and this property might account, at least in part, for the absence of extrapyramidal side-effects. Clozapine also interacts with other neurotransmitter systems, e.g. 5-HT and other receptors in the CNS, e.g. histamine receptors.

Because of the absence of Parkinson-like side-effects associated with its use, clozapine has been referred to as an 'atypical' neuroleptic. Unfortunately, due to the high incidence of agranulocytosis in patients being treated with clozapine, the drug is no longer available. It is of theoretical interest as the first of the so-called 'atypical' neuroleptics, and it is also of use as an experimental drug. Furthermore, it is highly likely that new dibenzazepine neuroleptics will emerge in the future.

Substituted benzamides

This is a relatively new class of antipsychotic drugs which are chemically related to the anti-emetic, metoclopramide (Fig. 2.8). The parent substance is procainamide which was synthesized in 1942 for use as an orally-effective anti-arrhythmic agent. Further developments led to metoclopramide (5-chloro-2-methoxy procainamide) which, apart from being anti-emetic also has effects on gastric motility. It was noted that metoclopramide had a pharmacological profile which, in some aspects, resembled that of neuroleptic drugs, particularly in antagonizing effects produced by apomorphine. When tested clinically, metoclopramide was found to be an effective, though not very potent, antipsychotic drug (Stanley *et al.* 1980). A related drug, sulpiride (Fig. 2.8) which was synthesized in the same laboratory, was at first used

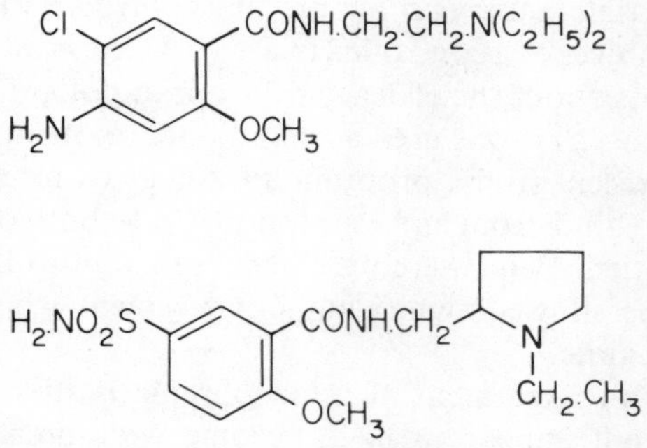

FIG. 2.8. The chemical structures of the substituted benzamides, metoclopramide and sulpiride.

clinically in gastroenterology, but was soon found to be a useful antipsychotic agent. Apart from its successful use in the treatment of schizophrenia, sulpiride has been reported to be effective in treating chronic 'defect state' syndromes (Borenstein *et al.* 1969). Since, when tested in animals, sulpiride showed only part of the spectrum of activity common to most neuroleptic drugs, it was classed as 'atypical'. Thus, this drug did not induce catalepsy in animals and was ineffective in antagonizing the effects of apomorphine and amphetamine. For this reason it was suggested that sulpiride might lack extrapyramidal side-effects. However, this is not the case and Parkinson-like effects are regularly seen although the incidence of these side-effects may be less than with other antipsychotic drugs. Sulpiride is non-sedative and has been reported to have antidepressant effects. A related substance, sultopride is a more potent antipsychotic than sulpiride but is sedative.

Because they are relatively new and are 'atypical' with respect to the older types of neuroleptic drugs, the substituted benzamides have been studied in considerable detail. Their pharmacological properties will be considered again below.

Miscellaneous compounds

Many substances have been used at different times for the treatment of schizophrenia and varying degrees of success have been claimed. However, only those which are important or are of particular pharmacological interest will be discussed here.

Beta-adrenoceptor antagonists

Interest in the possibility that β-blockers might have a role in the treatment of schizophrenia was aroused by the discovery that, in the treatment of acute porphyria with large doses of propranolol, psychotic symptoms were also reduced (Atsmon and Blum 1970). Other studies followed and it has been reported that, as well as propranolol, pindolol, oxprenolol, and acebutolol may also reduce symptoms of schizophrenia. However, many of the reports are anecdotal or are of open trials lacking proper placebo controls. Only propranolol itself has been the subject of a controlled trial (Yorkston *et al*. 1977), but even here there are doubts about the efficacy of propranolol as an antipsychotic drug in its own right, as it was used as an adjunct to therapy with chlorpromazine. In a more recent study, propranolol was given to patients receiving depot flupenthixol (Lindström and Persson 1980). In both of these studies it was found that patients who were previously resistant to therapy with neuroleptic drugs alone showed significant improvement when propranolol was added to the regime.

The role of β-blockers in the treatment of schizophrenia is still controversial and their use does not appear to have become widespread. One problem is that, in most studies, large doses have been used, much larger than are required for complete peripheral β-receptor blockade. Thus, mechanisms of action other than β-blockade are possible, for example non-specific membrane stabilization or interactions with 5-HT systems, etc. It is possible to explain the effects of β-blockers, when they are used as an adjunct to therapy with traditional neuroleptics, in terms of pharmacokinetic phenomena.

Psychotomimetics

Perhaps the most remarkable use of a drug in the treatment of schizophrenia is that of *D*-lysergic acid diethylamide (LSD 25), a psychotomimetic drug which produces, in normal human subjects (Bradley *et al*. 1953), many symptoms resembling those of schizophrenia, especially hallucinations, mood changes, and distortions of perception and other sensory modalities. So closely do the symptoms produced by small doses of LSD 25 in normal subjects resemble those of naturally-occurring psychosis, that the state induced by the drug has been described as a 'model psychosis'. It was found that schizophrenics reacted differently to the administration of LSD 25 than did normal controls (Sandison 1963) and were also more resistant to the drug. This may have justified the use of relatively large doses. However, the main effects of LSD 25, which appeared from the many reports of its use in schizophrenia in the 1950s and 1960s, suggest that it was an adjunct to psychotherapy rather than having a direct action of its own on schizophrenia symptomatology. As LSD 25 is no longer available, and would not be prescribed if it were, this drug is now only of historical and pharmacological interest, the latter because of its interaction with 5-HT receptors.

Opiate antagonists

The discovery in brain of endogenous opiates or 'endorphins' led to the formulation of many different hypotheses concerning their functional role. Thus, it was considered that an excess of endorphins, or of abnormal endorphins, might result in mental disturbances, and, conversely, that some mental disease states might be related to a deficiency of endorphins. In line with the first hypothesis, the opiate antagonist, naloxone, has been administered to chronic schizophrenic patients (Gunne *et al*. 1977; Emrich *et al.* 1977) with reportedly favourable results. Not all symptoms were equally affected, however, although naloxone was consistently found to reduce acoustic hallucinations. Other groups have not been able to confirm these findings and the use of opiate antagonists in the treatment of schizophrenia has not become widespread.

γ-Type endorphins

Another hypothesis which proposes an involvement of endorphins in psychosis has arisen from studies of the effects of γ-type endorphins (des-tyrosine-γ-endorphin, β-endorphin and des-enkephalin-γ-endorphin) in animals, where it was found that these substances possessed a similar profile of activity to that of the classical neuroleptics, such as haloperidol, in terms of antagonism of the effects of apomorphine, amphetamine etc. To explain these observations it was proposed that the γ-type endorphins modulate the activity of dopamine systems in the brain, possibly by an action at presynaptic receptors (Van Ree and de Wied 1982). Furthermore, the effects of γ-type endorphins have been tested in schizophrenic patients with relief of the symptoms in some cases (about 25 per cent). However, extensive trials with γ-type endorphins have not been carried out and it is not clear how effective these substances are as antipsychotic drugs.

Summary

It is clear from the foregoing that, apart from the classical neuroleptic drugs, both 'typical' and 'atypical', a number of agents with widely varying pharmacological properties can influence the psychotic state. A tentative explanation as to how some of these effects may be brought about will be given at the end of this chapter.

THE BIOLOGICAL ACTIONS OF ANTIPSYCHOTIC DRUGS

In the previous section reference was made to the diverse chemical structures of the antipsychotic drugs and it is also apparent that these drugs possess many and varied pharmacological properties. In this section, the biological actions of neuroleptic drugs as a group will be discussed in more detail in relation to their pharmacological properties and an attempt made to relate the latter to their clinical antipsychotic actions.

There is a vast literature reporting the results of biochemical, neurophysiological, and behavioural studies of the actions of neuroleptic drugs. This is partly due to the intense research interest which the discovery of these drugs provoked, since, at the time that they were discovered, their action on the central nervous system was completely novel and, secondly, because they have such a wide range of actions. In fact, it is highly improbable that any biological system exists on which the action of chlorpromazine has not been tested and, furthermore, not found to have some effect (hence the name *Largactil*). Since the biochemical aspects of the actions of antipsychotic drugs are discussed in Chapter 1, and their behavioural effects in Chapter 3, this section will concentrate mainly on neurophysiological effects, together with those pharmacological properties which relate most closely to the clinical effects. Inevitably, most of the data comes from studies on experimental animals and the majority of these have utilized the 'prototype' neuroleptic, chlorpromazine.

In general, animals which have been given neuroleptic drugs show reduced motor activity; they also show diminished responses to external stimuli and have little interest in their environment. However, there is no reduction in motor power or co-ordination, nor is there a tendency for excessive somnolence, unless very large doses are administered. Cats, treated with neuroleptic drugs, show increased sociability and reduced hostility and, in those species which are normally aggressive or defensive, neuroleptic drugs have a 'taming' effect. This property is made use of in veterinary practice. The electroencephalogram or electrocorticogram, where this has been recorded in experimental animals (see below) shows the appropriate changes which correlate with the behavioural state. Thus, the effects of neuroleptic drugs in animals resemble fairly closely those seen in man and the use of animal models for analysing the mode of action of these drugs is considered to be valid.

Peripherally, chlorpromazine, as the prototype neuroleptic, has a wide range of pharmacological actions, mostly as an antagonist of different neurotransmitter systems. The antihistamine properties of the phenothiazines have already been referred to, together with the fact that chlorpromazine is relatively weak in this respect, being 40 to 100 times less potent than promethazine, depending upon the test used. It is also a weak antagonist of the action of 5-hydroxytryptamine and acetylcholine. The most marked peripheral action of chlorpromazine is as an antagonist at α-adrenergic receptors. This action causes a loss of vasomotor tone and is probably responsible, at least in part, for the postural hypotension which is sometimes associated with the use of therapeutic doses of the drug. However, although chlorpromazine appears to have little or no ganglion blocking activity, the hypotensive effect is probably complex and involves central actions as well as peripheral ones, e.g. depression of the vasomotor control centre in the hypothalamus and medullary region of the brainstem. Chlorpromazine is a potent local anaesthetic but does not appear to have been used for this purpose. (For further details of the peripheral pharmacology of the phenothiazines, and of other neuroleptics, see Courvoisier *et al.* 1953, and for reviews see Bradley 1963; Domino *et al.* 1968.)

Centrally too, the neuroleptics, and especially phenothiazines such as chlorpromazine, produce many different effects and it is quite obvious that they must act at more than one site in the brain. In addition to their antihistaminic, antiserotonergic, anticholinergic, and anti-adrenergic actions which the phenothiazines demonstrate peripherally, in the central nervous system they are also antagonists of dopamine, as are all other neuroleptic drugs. This latter action can explain many, but not all, of the central effects. For example, the anti-emetic action of many neuroleptic drugs can be related to an antidopamine action on the chemoreceptor trigger zone of the vomiting centre in the medullary region of the brainstem. The chemoreceptor centre can be stimulated by the dopamine agonist apomorphine, which causes emesis, and this action of apomorphine is antagonized by chlorpromazine. Similarly, an antidopamine action can explain some of the endocrine effects of the neuroleptics. Thus, dopamine receptors in the tuberoinfundibular tract normally inhibit the release of prolactin, and an antagonist action at these receptors can account for the increased release of prolactin which is associated with the use of neuroleptic drugs in man. Other endocrine effects which can be related to a depressant action on the hypothalamus include the inhibition of growth hormone and a reduced release of gonadotropin. While large doses of chlorpromazine have been found to inhibit the release of ACTH in response to stress, moderate doses appear to stimulate its release. These effects have been correlated with an action of chlorpromazine in increasing the ability of living organisms to resist stress.

An increase in appetite is often associated with the administration of neuroleptic drugs to psychotic patients and this effect is thought to be due to a depression of the satiety centre in the hypothalamus. Effects on temperature regulation are also thought to be due to an action on the hypothalamus, although the precise mechanism is not known. The disturbance of temperature regulation can result in either hypo- or hyperthermia, depending upon the ambient temperature. Thus, in the 'lytic cocktail', used by Laborit, the actions of promethazine and chlorpromazine were to produce a state of artificial hibernation due to a lowering of body temperature. However, in climates where the ambient temperature is high, patients taking phenothiazine medication may suffer hyperthermic episodes.

There is no clear correlation between any of the central effects of the phenothiazine neuroleptics and their antihistamine potency, as measured peripherally. Also, since this property is minimal in some of the most potent antipsychotic drugs, it seems unlikely that an antihistamine action contributes significantly to the therapeutic effects. It is possible that this property may be responsible for the sedative actions of some of these drugs, especially as the most potent antihistamine phenothiazines are markedly sedative and are used for their sedative action (e.g. promethazine). Similarly, there is no clear relationship between the antiserotonin actions and central effects of antipsychotic drugs, although drugs which affect 5-HT systems in brain do have effects on mental function (e.g. tricyclic antidepressants, psychotomimetics). Again, there could be a link with sedation although an antiserotonin action in the CNS would be expected to cause increased wakefulness. The anticholinergic action of the phenothiazines is atropine-like, i.e. it is antimuscarinic, and the use of certain non-neuroleptic phenothiazines (e.g. diethazine) in the treatment of Parkinson's disease has already been referred to. It is considered likely that the reduced incidence of extrapyramidal side-effects of the Parkinson-type, associated with the use of drugs such as thioridazine, and their virtual absence with clozapine, may be explained by the greater anticholinergic potency of these two drugs. Thus, the anticholinergic activity as measured by *in vitro* receptor binding, is for thioridazine 10 times, and for clozapine 20 times that of chlorpromazine, whereas for the butyrophenones, e.g. haloperidol, it is one-tenth or less.

By far the most potent actions of neuroleptic drugs (not just the phenothiazines) in the brain are the interactions with catecholamines, and especially with dopamine. Thus, the 'dopamine hypothesis of schizophrenia' which attributes the antipsychotic action of the neuroleptic drugs to an antagonism of the actions of dopamine, as well as attributing the production of extrapyramidal side-effects to a similar action, is the hypothesis currently in vogue, although not universally accepted. Since this hypothesis is discussed in detail in Chapter 5, it will not be treated here. A blockade of dopamine receptors in the brain can also account for some of the other actions and side-effects of neuroleptic drugs, viz. anti-emetic effects, tardive dyskinesias, etc. It is necessary, therefore, to consider some of these actions in more detail.

Interactions between neuroleptic drugs and catecholaminergic neurones

One of the first indications that effects on catecholamines in the brain might be important for the actions of neuroleptic drugs came from the observation that reserpine caused depletion of monoamine stores in brain (Brodie and Shore 1957). However, although reserpine has similar clinical effects to other neuroleptic drugs, the latter, e.g. phenothiazines and butyrophenones, differ from reserpine in not causing depletion. Carlsson and Lindqvist (1963) studied the effects of various neuroleptic drugs on the metabolism of catecholamines by measuring the levels of the methylated metabolites of dopamine and noradrenaline in brain. They found that small doses of chlorpromazine and haloperidol, but not of the non-neuroleptic promethazine, caused accumulation of these metabolites. Thus, only chlorpromazine and haloperidol elevated the level of 3-methoxytyramine, the metabolite of dopamine, and in this haloperidol was more effective than chlorpromazine. Promethazine was without effect on the levels of 3-methoxytyramine. On the other hand, all three drugs produced increased levels of normetanephrine, the metabolite of noradrenaline, although in this, promethazine was less potent than chlorpromazine or haloperidol. It was found that the clinical potencies of the drugs correlated better with their influence on the levels of 3-methoxytyramine (i.e. with dopamine metabolism), than on the levels of normetanephrine (noradrenaline metabolism). These findings are best explained on the basis of increased metabolism and synthesis of the transmitter, i.e. increased turnover. It was proposed by Carlsson that the increase in turnover of the transmitter was caused by feedback activation of catecholaminergic neurones as a result of the blockade of the postsynaptic receptors by the neuroleptic drugs. This hypothesis, which is supported by additional evidence, is now generally accepted. Thus, it has been extended to include other classes of neuroleptic drugs and it has also been shown that chronic therapy with neuroleptics is associated with increased levels of catecholamine metabolites in schizophrenic patients (Sedvall *et al*. 1974). Opposite effects on turnover, i.e. depression of synthesis and metabolism, by agonist drugs, together with electrophysiological data (Bunney *et al*. 1973) are consistent with the Carlsson hypothesis. However, it is now thought that the feedback is through activation of presynaptic receptors, i.e. 'autoreceptors', rather than through a neuronal feedback circuit (Carlsson 1978; Bartholini and Lloyd 1980).

Site of action of neuroleptic drugs in the brain

The wide variety of biological effects which results from the central actions of neuroleptic drugs clearly indicates that there must be more than one site of action in the brain. In fact, it is thought that there are four principal ana-tomical sites involved in the actions of these drugs. These are: (1) the brainstem, where sedation and effects on sensory input are mediated; (2) the hypothalamus—anti-emetic actions, effects on body temperature, appetite, and endocrine effects; (3) the basal ganglia, where the extrapyramidal side-effects are likely to be mediated; (4) the limbic system—effects on emotion and mood. In addition, it is probable that neuroleptic drugs have some actions on the cerebral cortex, since they can influence seizure activity, and most probably on the spinal cord as well, as they can affect spinal reflexes, although some of these actions could be mediated via descending influences from the brainstem.

The brainstem

Studies on the effects of neuroleptic drugs in experimental animals with per-manently implanted recording electrodes, so that changes in the electrocor-ticogram could be observed concomitantly with behavioural changes, showed that chlorpromazine caused a marked reduction in responsiveness to sensory stimuli without inducing any appreciable degree of sedation (Bradley and Hance 1957). These effects were ascribed to inhibition of the activation of the brainstem reticular activating system by afferent impulses from colla-terals of the sensory pathways, rather than to a direct depression of reticular neurones. Support for this hypothesis came from the finding that chlor-promazine had little effect on the threshold of arousal produced by direct electrical stimulation of the brainstem reticular formation, but caused marked elevation of thresholds for sensory-induced arousal (Fig. 2.9) (Bradley and Key 1958). A depression of arousal in the limbic cortex by chlor-promazine was also demonstrated (Killam and Killam 1956). It was also shown that the reduced responsiveness to sensory stimulation produced by chlorpromazine closely resembled the process of habituation, in which responses to non-significant stimuli are progressively reduced and eventually lost. Thus, chlorpromazine appeared to potentiate this process, while psy-chotomimetic drugs, such as LSD 25, had opposite effects (Key and Bradley 1960). The reduction of sensory influences on brainstem mechanisms by the neuroleptic drugs led to the suggestion that these drugs produced a state of

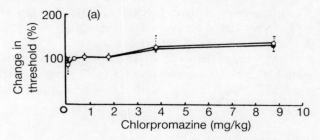

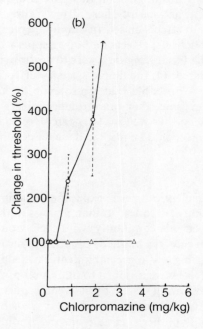

FIG. 2.9.   The effects of chlorpromazine, given in incremental doses, on: (a) the threshold for arousal produced by direct electrical stimulation of the brainstem (○ EEG arousal; •,behavioural arousal) and (b) the threshold for arousal produced by sensory (auditory) stimulation. Also shown in (b) is the threshold for click responses recorded from the auditory cortex (○ EEG and behavioural arousal; △, click response). In both graphs the percentage change in threshold has been plotted against the dose of the drug. (From Bradley and Key 1958.)

'pharmacological deafferentiation' of the brainstem (Bradley 1965).

In experiments in which the activity of single neurones in the brainstem was recorded, it was found that systemic administration of chlorpromazine reduced the responses of neurones to peripheral stimuli to which they had previously shown convergence (Fig. 2.10) (Bradley 1957). The administration

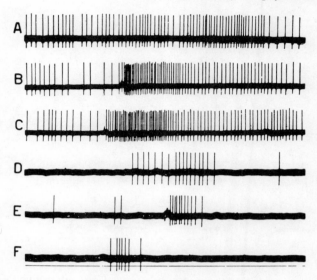

FIG. 2.10.   Effects of chlorpromazine on spontaneous and evoked activity of a single neurone in the mesencephalic reticular formation. (A) control spontaneous discharge; (B) control response to tapping right anterior leg; (C) control response to trigeminal stimulation; (D) spontaneous activity after 2.0 mg/kg chlorpromazine (i.v.); (E) response to tapping right anterior leg; (F) response to trigeminal stimulation. (E) and (F) after chlorpromazine. (From Bradley 1957.)

of chlorpromazine locally to single neurones in the brainstem, either by microtap (Avanzino *et al.* 1966), or by microiontophoresis (Bradley *et al.* 1966), resulted in antagonism of excitatory responses produced by microiontophoretically-applied noradrenaline (Fig. 2.11). Excitation produced by acetylcholine or 5-hydroxytryptamine was not antagonized, nor were inhibitory responses to these substances, although chlorpromazine sometimes mimicked the inhibition of neuronal activity produced by noradrenaline. Many of the neurones on which chlorpromazine blocked noradrenaline-induced excitation were identified physiologically as having ascending axons and were therefore thought to be part of the ascending catecholamine system arising in the brainstem (Anden *et al.* 1966).

The neurones of the locus coeruleus contain large amounts of catecholamines, and pathways have been traced from this nucleus into the limbic cortex, the hippocampus, neocortex, and other brainstem nuclei. However, the responses of the neurones in the locus coeruleus appear to be somewhat complex. For example, their spontaneous activity is depressed by intravenous injections of small amounts of *d*-amphetamine (Graham and Aghajanian 1971), whereas amphetamine excites neurones in the brainstem reticular formation (Bradley 1968). Similarly, noradrenaline, applied by microiontophoresis, has been found to inhibit neurones in the locus coeruleus (Svensson *et al.* 1975). The effect of amphetamine in the locus coeruleus has been

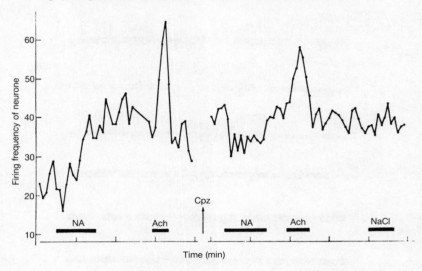

FIG. 2.11.   Antagonism of the excitatory effects of *l*-noradrenaline (NA), but not those of acetylcholine (Ach) by chlorpromazine (Cpz), on the firing rate of a single spontaneously active medullary neurone. All drugs were applied micro-iontophoretically with a current of 50 nA. NaCl represents a current control, also 50 nA. The firing frequency of the neurone (f) has been plotted against time. (From Bradley *et al*. 1966.)

interpreted as inhibition due to neuronal feedback after presynaptic release of catecholamines from the terminals, and the inhibitory effects of nor-adrenaline, as due to self-inhibition of the neurones. However, chlor-promazine was found to block the depression of neuronal firing produced by amphetamine in the locus coeruleus (Graham and Aghajanian 1971). These actions of chlorpromazine, antagonizing the effects of noradrenaline on neuronal activity, as well as those of the indirectly-acting sympathomimetic amine, amphetamine, are consistent with its potent α-adrenergic receptor blocking action peripherally.

The anti-emetic effects of the neuroleptics have already been discussed. This action, which is attributed to an antidopamine action in the chemo-receptor trigger zone of the area postrema of the medulla oblongata, is shown by reserpine, chlorpromazine, and by other phenothiazine neuroleptics, by various butyrophenones such as haloperidol, droperidol, and spiroperidol, by pimozide and by the substituted benzamides, e.g. sulpiride. Of the non-neuroleptic phenothiazines, promazine has only a weak anti-emetic action and promethazine none at all.

The hypothalamus

Reference has already been made to many effects of the neuroleptics which are mediated by an action on the hypothalamus, e.g. effects on appetite, temperature regulation, etc. All known antipsychotic drugs, including 'atypical' agents such as sulpiride, cause increased secretion of prolactin and decreased release of growth hormone. The hypothalamus exerts humoural control over adenohypophysial function and can stimulate or inhibit the release of hormones by the pituitary. Hypophysial portal blood has been found to contain significant quantities of dopamine, which is known to inhibit the secretion of prolactin, while dopamine receptors have been detected in the pituitary. Thus, it is thought that an antagonist action by neuroleptic drugs at dopamine receptors in the hypothalamus, and probably in the pituitary also, is responsible for the increased levels of prolactin and decreased growth hormone associated with treatment with these drugs.

The effects of neuroleptic drugs on cardiovascular function are complex and are almost certainly due to actions at both peripheral and central sites. Thus, antagonism of peripheral adrenergic receptors will lead to loss of vaso-motor tone and result in a tendency for the blood pressure to fall. Centrally, the drugs cause depression of vasomotor control mechanisms in the hypo-thalamus and bulbospinal regions of the brain, and this action also con-tributes to the hypotension. Thus, the postural hypotension which can occur when antipsychotic drugs are administered in large doses, is due to an antagonism of α-adrenergic receptors, probably at all three sites.

The basal ganglia

Of the many side-effects produced by antipsychotic drugs, their ability to induce iatrogenic Parkinsonism is perhaps the most notable, and was observed soon after the introduction of chlorpromazine. All the anti-psychotic drugs which are currently available have been found to cause extra-pyramidal side-effects to some extent. These effects are most marked in the case of the butyrophenones and are less prevalent with drugs which possess strong anticholinergic actions, e.g. thioridazine. However, there are also certain drugs without a high anticholinergic potency which also lack a pro-pensity to induce extrapyramidal effects to any marked extent, e.g. pimozide and sulpiride. It is difficult to account for this in terms of pharmacological properties, although in the case of sulpiride, its low potency may be relevant. The one exception to this rule appears to be clozapine, but the lack of reports of extrapyramidal side-effects with clozapine may have been due to the com-paratively short time the drug was in use. A second possibility is that the sedation produced by clozapine might mask the appearance of Parkinson-like side-effects, but this is thought to be unlikely. If, as is anticipated, new dibenzazepine neuroleptics are developed in the future, their potential for producing extrapyramidal side-effects will be examined most carefully.

Idiopathic Parkinson's disease has long been known to be a disorder of the basal ganglia and the successful treatment of this condition with L-dopa, which results from the finding that there were lower levels of dopamine in the basal ganglia of patients with Parkinson's disease (Hornykiewicz 1972) led to the generally accepted hypothesis that the symptoms of the disease could be due to a defect in dopaminergic transmission. Thus, the almost universal ability of neuroleptic drugs to induce symptoms of Parkinson's disease could be attributed to an interference with dopaminergic transmission.

The main dopamine-containing pathways in the brain, apart from the tuberoinfundibular system in the hypothalamus, which has already been discussed, are: (a) an ascending pathway from dopamine-containing cell bodies in the substantia nigra, projecting to the corpus striatum (caudate nucleus and globus pallidus), the so-called nigro-striatal pathway, and (b) a meso-limbic pathway, with cell bodies in the ventral mesencephalic tegmentum, projecting to the nucleus accumbens, the olfactory tubercle, the limbic cortex, and amygdala (Fig. 2.12). Degeneration of the nigro-striatal system is associated with the symptoms of Parkinson's disease and is generally thought to be the site of action at which the neuroleptic drugs produce their extra-pyramidal side-effects which so closely resemble the symptoms of Parkinsonism.

A biochemical model for drug action at dopamine receptors in the CNS was provided by the dopamine-stimulated adenylate cyclase system (Kebabian and Greengard 1971), in which it was shown that dopamine activated the cyclase which transforms ATP to cyclic AMP. In homogenates of brain regions which are rich in dopamine, e.g. caudate nucleus, it was found that neuroleptic drugs blocked the synthesis of cyclic AMP which was stimulated by dopamine. Thus, the drugs inhibited dopamine-stimulated adenylate cyclase activity, the inhibition was dose-dependent, and the drug-induced effect was competitive with dopamine (Miller *et al.* 1974). Related drugs which lack antipsychotic properties, e.g. promazine and promethazine, did

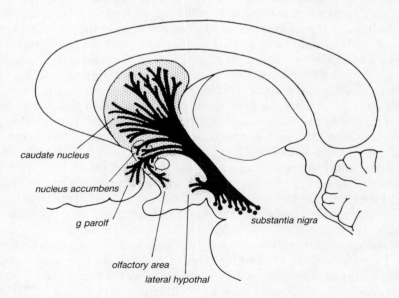

FIG. 2.12.   Diagrammatic sagittal section of the human brain showing the principal dopamine-containing neurones and their projections. In this diagram the substantia nigra (s. nigra) also includes cells in the ventral mesencephalic tegmentum. Also, the caudate nucleus includes the putamen.

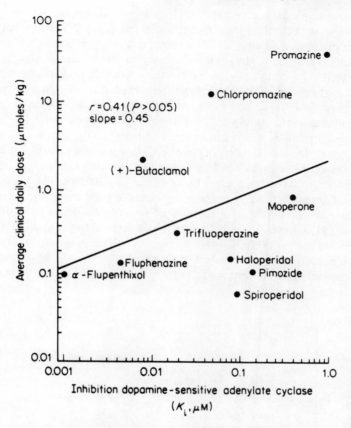

FIG. 2.13.   Lack of correlation between the ability of a number of neuroleptic drugs to inhibit dopamine-sensitive adenylate cyclase activity and their clinical potencies. (From Creese *et al.* 1978.)

not produce this effect. However, when a wider range of neuroleptic drugs was tested on this system, no clear correlation between the clinical potencies of the drugs and their ability to inhibit dopamine-stimulated adenylate cyclase activity was found (Fig. 2.13) (Iversen *et al.* 1976). Nevertheless, in similar studies which made use of the fact that some thioxanthene neuroleptics exist in stereoisomeric forms, e.g. flupenthixol, the isomers were found to differ substantially in their potencies as dopamine antagonists and these differences correlated well with their clinical effectiveness. Thus, while both stereoisomers of flupenthixol are present in the preparation which is used clinically, the α(*cis*)-isomer is 1000 times more potent than the β(*trans*)-isomer in blocking adenylate cyclase activity (Miller *et al.* 1974) and a clinical trial with the two isomers (Johnstone *et al.* 1978) demonstrated that the antipsychotic activity was restricted to the α-isomer. Therefore, while there appears to be a correlation between the clinical antipsychotic potency of certain neuroleptic drugs and their ability to inhibit dopamine-stimulated adenylate cyclase activity, many discrepancies exist (Fig. 2.13). For example, the butyrophenones, haloperidol and spiroperidol, together with pimozide, are far more potent clinically than is chlorpromazine but are weaker in terms of their ability to inhibit dopamine-sensitive adenylate cyclase activity *in vitro*. Inconsistencies of this type have been explained in terms of the differences between *in vivo* and *in vitro* observations and also by the possibility that pharmacokinetic factors may influence clinical efficacy.

A better correlation has been established between the actions of neuroleptic drugs at dopamine receptors in the CNS and their clinical potencies, through the use of receptor binding techniques utilizing radioactive ligands. Such techniques have been used to examine the affinities of a range of neuroleptic drugs for the dopamine receptor and a good correlation has been found between the ability of a number of neuroleptic drugs to inhibit the binding of [³H]haloperidol to homogenates of striatal tissue and the clinical potency of these drugs (Fig. 2.14) (Creese *et al.* 1976). A similarly good correlation has also been established between the inhibition of binding of [³H]haloperidol in brain homogenates by neuroleptic drugs and their ability

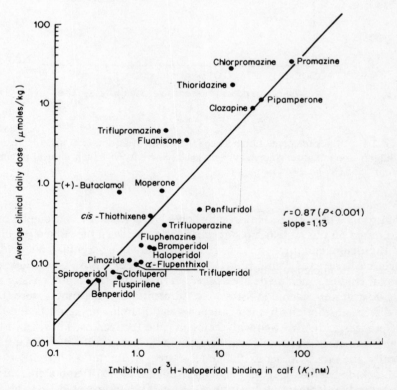

FIG. 2.14.   Correlation between the affinities of neuroleptic drugs for the [³H]haloperidol binding site and their clinical potencies. (From Creese *et al.* 1978.)

to block behavioural responses in animals produced by activation of dopamine receptors, e.g. amphetamine-induced stereotypy in rats and apomorphine-induced emesis in dogs (Creese *et al.* 1978).

It has always been assumed that the antipsychotic actions of the neuroleptic drugs were inextricably linked to their ability to produce extrapyramidal side-effects, possibily by an action at a common site. This assumption is now being questioned since antipsychotic drugs now exist with an apparently reduced potential to produce extrapyramidal side-effects and, furthermore, the presence of Parkinson's disease does not appear either to protect or to predispose patients to schizophrenia. Thus, it is possible that these two main actions of neuroleptic drugs, i.e. the antipsychotic action and the ability to induce symptoms of Parkinson's disease, may be mediated by actions at different sites in the brain. Since the main function of the nigrostriatal dopaminergic pathway is the control of motor performance, and the degeneration of this pathway is responsible for the symptoms of iodopathic Parkinsonism, this site in the brain is usually assumed to be the region where the neuroleptic drugs produce their extrapyramidal side-effects, by blockade of dopamine receptors. It has been suggested, on the other hand, that the antipsychotic effects of the neuroleptic drugs may be mediated at another site, the mesolimbic system.

The mesolimbic system

Anatomically, this system consists of dopamine-containing cell bodies in the interpeduncular nucleus which project in a tract lying close to the nigrostriatal tract, to the mesolimbic forebrain, i.e. the nucleus accumbens and olfactory tubercles (Fig. 2.12). The possibility that neuroleptic drugs might produce their therapeutic antipsychotic effects by an action on the mesolimbic dopamine system has been investigated by examining the effects of neuroleptic drugs on the turnover of dopamine in the striatum and nucleus accumbens (Crow *et al.* 1977). Three neuroleptic drugs were chosen which differed widely in their ability to produce extrapyramidal side-effects and the turnover of dopamine was assessed by measuring the increase in the dopamine metabolite, homovanillic acid. In the striatum the three drugs, fluphenazine, chlorpromazine, and thioridazine, had markedly different effects on turnover but there was, nevertheless, a good correlation between this action and their potencies in producing extrapyramidal side-effects (Fig. 2.15). In the nucleus accumbens, on the other hand, the three drugs had equal effects on turnover, reflecting equal clinical potencies (Fig. 2.15). Similar results have been obtained in a comparison of the effects of clozapine, which produces little or no extrapyramidal side-effects, with those of haloperidol, which has very marked side-effects, on the turnover of dopamine in these same two structures, using doses which were equipotent with regard to clinical antipsychotic activity (Andén and Stock 1973). There is also electrophysiological data which supports the concept that the antipsychotic effect of the neuroleptic drugs may be mediated by an action on the mesolimbic system. Thus, intravenous injections of small amounts of amphetamine were

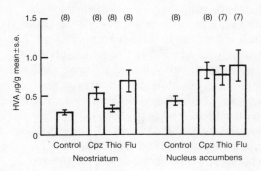

FIG. 2.15.   The effects of three phenothiazines, given in doses equivalent to their clinical potencies, on the turnover of dopamine, measured by the concentration of homovanillic acid (HVA) in two different regions of the rat brain, the striatum and nucleus accumbens. The doses used were: chlorpromazine (Cpz) 5 mg/kg, thioridazine (Thio) 5 mg/kg, and fluphenazine (Flu) 0.25 mg/kg. (From Crow *et al.* 1977.)

found to reduce the firing rate of neurones in both the striatum and meso-limbic region (Bunney and Aghajanian 1973). Chlorpromazine abolished this effect in both regions but thioridazine and clozapine were effective in anta-gonizing the effects of amphetamine only in the mesolimbic region, i.e. not in the striatum. This finding is consistent with the fact that both thioridazine and clozapine are antipsychotic but are weak in producing extrapyramidal side-effects.

The hypothesis that neuroleptic drugs, such as chlorpromazine and halo-peridol, produce their antipsychotic effects by an antidopamine action on the mesolimbic system and their extrapyramidal side-effects by virtue of an action in the striatum, is attractive but the evidence for it is still largely circumstantial. According to this hypothesis, drugs which are antipsychotic but relatively weak in producing extrapyramidal side-effects, e.g. thio-ridazine and clozapine, should act selectively on the dopaminergic mesolimbic system and have little effect on the striatum, but there is no direct evidence to suggest that this is the case. On the other hand, the inability of both thioridazine and clozapine to produce extrapyramidal side-effects is readily explained by their high anticholinergic potencies, as already dis-cussed. However, this may not be the whole story and the discovery that there are subtypes of dopamine receptors, which may mediate different responses, and for which different types of neuroleptic drugs show a differential affinity, may be relevant.

Multiple receptors for dopamine

There are many precedents for the existence of different sub-types of receptors for neurotransmitters. Thus, acetylcholine interacts with nicotinic and muscarinic receptors, catecholamines with α- and β-adrenergic receptors, histamine with H_1 and H_2 receptors, and so on. In the case of dopamine, the classification of receptor subtypes is controversial and confusing. Not only have up to eight different subtypes been proposed, but the same designations, i.e. D_1 or D_2, or DA_1 and DA_2, have been used to define receptor subtypes on the basis of *different* criteria. Thus, on the basis of behavioural data, DAe (excitatory) and DAi (inhibitory) receptors have been postulated (Cools and van Rossum 1976), and also DA_1 for hyperactivity and DA_2 for the induction of dyskinesias (Costall and Naylor 1975). Another classification has been based on the peripheral actions of dopamine: thus, a DA_1 receptor subserves vasodilation in the canine renal vascular bed, and has also been shown to be present at other sites on smooth muscle, both vascular and non-vascular (e.g. gastrointestinal tract), while the DA_2 receptor is located on post-ganglionic sympathetic nerve terminals at which dopamine agonists cause a reduction in the release of noradrenaline. It seems unlikely that these peripheral dopamine receptors can have any significance for the actions of antipsychotic drugs.

One of the biological actions of dopamine already referred to, is its ability to increase the synthesis of cyclic AMP by stimulating the enzyme adenylate cyclase. This enzyme, which is specific for dopamine, has a wide distribution in nervous tissue throughout the animal kingdom, from snails to man. However, although neuroleptic drugs are inhibitors of the dopamine-induced stimulation of adenylate cyclase in the striatum, and non-neuroleptics are not (see above), there is lacking a complete correlation with clinical potency, particularly in the case of the butyrophenones. Also, some of the actions of dopamine, especially the inhibition of prolactin release, do not appear to be associated with the formation of cyclic AMP. Thus, it has been proposed (Kebabian and Calne 1979) that the dopamine receptors which are associated with the formation of cyclic AMP should be designated D_1 receptors and those whose actions are *not* related to the second messenger, D_2. The prototype for the D_1 receptor is the bovine parathyroid gland, where activation of dopamine receptors causes release of parathyroid hormone. D_2 receptors have been identified in the intermediate lobe of the anterior pituitary of the rat, which is innervated by dopaminergic neurones with cell bodies in the arcuate nucleus and axons passing through the pituitary stalk to terminate in the vicinity of the melanotrophs. Here, stimulation of dopamine receptors is associated with inhibition of the release of prolactin and α-MSH in many species. However, it has been necessary to change the criteria for dopamine D_2 receptors, as another action of dopamine in the pituitary is to inhibit the β-adrenergic stimulation of the synthesis of cyclic AMP, i.e. to depress synthesis of cyclic AMP. Thus, while the D_1 receptor of Kebabian and Calne is exclusively associated with dopamine-stimulated adenylate cyclase activity, the D_2 receptor is correlated with either no effect on cyclic AMP or a decreased synthesis.

The classification of dopamine receptor subtypes on the basis of biochemical or behavioural data alone is unsatisfactory and leads to confusion. The classification of receptor subtypes for other neurotransmitters, e.g. acetylcholine, noradrenaline, and histamine, has been based on sound

TABLE 2.1.   *Pharmacological characteristics of D_1 and D_2 dopamine receptors*

	D_1 receptor	D_2 receptor
Adenylate cyclase activity	Stimulated	Unaffected or inhibited
Dopamine	Agonist (μM potency)	Agonist (nM potency)
Apomorphine	Partial agonist or antagonist	Agonist (nM potency)
Bromocriptine	Antagonist (μM potency)	Agonist (nM potency)
Thioxanthenes	Antagonists	= Antagonists
Phenothiazines	Antagonists	< Antagonists
Butyrophenones	Weak antagonists	≪ Potent antagonists
Sulpriide	No effect	Antagonist

After Kebabian and Calne (1979) and others.

pharmacological principles, i.e. the actions of selective agonists and anta-gonists mediating different physiological or pharmacological effects. There is however some pharmacological data which lends credibility to the D_1, D_2 classification outlined above (Table 2.1). For example, dopamine itself exhibits a differential potency at the two receptor sites, being effective in micromolar concentrations at D_1 receptors and in nanomolar concentrations at D_2 sites. Apomorphine, which is classically a dopamine agonist, has dif-ferent effects at the two receptor sites. At many sites apomorphine closely mimics the action of dopamine and has a similar potency; these are actions of dopamine which are mainly mediated by D_2 receptors. However, where the actions of dopamine are linked to activation of adenylate cyclase (D_1 receptors), apomorphine can act either as an antagonist or as a partial agonist, depending upon the concentration used. Similar effects are shown by some ergot derivatives with dopaminergic activity, e.g. bromocriptine (Table 2.1). It is the D_2 receptors which are believed to be defective in Par-kinson's disease (Offermeier and van Rooyen 1983) and it is at these receptors that bromocriptine, which is effective in the treatment of Parkinson's disease, displays the greatest agonist activity.

Probably more interesting are the effects of dopamine antagonists at the receptor subtypes. Thus, 'classical' neuroleptics, such as the phenothiazines and thioxanthenes, are effective antagonists at both D_1 and D_2 receptors, while the butyrophenones have only weak activity at D_1 receptors, and the benzamides, metaclopramide, sulpiride, and tiapride, are active at D_2 sites but almost inactive at D_1 receptors. Thus, it has been concluded that the clinical effects of the neuroleptic drugs are most probably mediated by a blockade of dopamine receptors which are *not* associated with stimulation of adenylate cyclase, i.e. D_2 receptors (Creese *et al.* 1976; Seeman *et al.* 1976). In fact, at the present time, it is not possible to ascribe any definite function to the dopamine receptors linked to adenylate cyclase (i.e. D_1 receptors).

The analysis of dopamine receptor subtypes has been facilitated by exten-sive *in vitro* studies of the binding of neuroleptic drugs to sites in the brain which show some of the characteristics of dopamine receptors. Various ligands have been used in these studies; thus, [^{3}H]haloperidol and [^{3}H]spiperone bind to receptor sites which can be distinguished from the sites associated with the enzyme adenylate cyclase. It is therefore believed that [^{3}H]haloperidol and [^{3}H]spiperone show a selective affinity for D_2 dopamine receptors and, in fact, selectively label these receptors. On the other hand, there are no selective ligands for D_1 receptors, but, by using a high concentration of a selective D_2 antagonist, such as sulpiride or spiroperidol, to mask the D_2 sites, it is possible to examine binding at D_1 sites, using a ligand such as [^{3}H]flupenthixol which normally has an equal affinity at both sites (Hyttel 1981, 1982). Using other neuroleptic drugs to displace these ligands, it has been shown that, whereas the thioxanthenes have an equal affinity for both D_1 and D_2 binding sites, the butyrophenones, diphenylbutylpiperidines and the substituted benzamides are almost completely selective for the D_2 site, and the phenothiazines occupy an intermediate position, having a greater affinity for D_2 than for D_1 binding sites (Hyttel *et al.* 1983). Also, the affinities of neuroleptics for the D_2 binding site ([^{3}H]haloperidol binding) correlates well with their clinical potencies (Fig. 2.14) (Creese *et al.* 1976). Both D_1 and D_2 receptors occur in the striatum and in the nucleus accumbens (Leysen and Laduron 1977), and so far no differentiation has been found between the binding of neuroleptic drugs to D_1 and D_2 dopamine receptors in the striatum as compared to the mesolimbic system (Leysen 1981). Furthermore, in spite of the findings of Kebabian and Greengard (1971), relating the antipsychotic actions of neuroleptic drugs to their ability to inhibit dopamine-stimulated adenylate cyclase, it seems very likely that actions at D_2 receptors are responsible for both the antipsychotic and extrapyramidal side-effects of the neuroleptics. In fact it seems likely that various effects of dopamine, in different areas and in a variety of animal species, are mediated by D_2 receptors (Leysen 1984). This idea is supported by the finding that the number of D_2 receptors is increased in the brains of schizophrenics (as shown by increased binding of [^{3}H]haloperidol or [^{3}H]spiroperidol) (Lee *et al.* 1978; Owen *et al.* 1978), whereas no changes have been found with D_1 receptor binding (Owen *et al.* 1981).

The 'atypical' neuroleptic, sulpiride, is unique as it does not influence dopamine-stimulated adenylate cyclase and appears to interact only with dopamine D_2 receptors. Sulpiride is also unique in that it only binds to D_2 receptors in the presence of sodium ions, a property not shown by other neuroleptic drugs. However, the functional significance of this is not known.

Receptor binding studies with neuroleptic drugs, utilizing ligands for neurotransmitter receptors other than dopamine, serve to emphasize the wide range of pharmacological interactions of this group of drugs (Table 2.2) (Leyson 1981, 1984).

In addition to D_1 and D_2 dopamine receptors, binding sites designated as D_3 and D_4 have been identified. However, no relationship between these binding sites and any known pharmacological, physiological, or biochemical action of dopamine has been demonstrated and it is, therefore, not justified to suggest that these binding sites represent functional receptors.

TABLE 2.2.   *Bindings affinities of neuroleptic drugs at receptors for different neurotransmitters*

	Dopamine[1]	Serotonin[2]	Histamine[3]	Noradrenaline[4]	Acetylcholine[5]
Chlorpromazine	50	20	7	2	162
Thioridazine	15	36	40	3	77
Chlorprothixene	11	3.5	6	1	39
Haloperidol	1	48	4 390	8	4 370
Pimozide	1	33	>10 000	41	1 022
Clozapine	156	16	4	7	31
Sulpiride	31	>10 000	>10 000	>1 000	>10 000

After Leysen 1981.

Affinity expressed as equilibrium inhibition constant, K_i in nM, for ligands indicated.

[1] Binding of [³H]haloperidol in striatum of rat (Leysen et al. 1977).
[2] Binding of [³H]spiperone in frontal cortex of rat (Leysen et al. 1978).
[3] Binding of [³H]pyrilamine, H_1 receptors, in guinea pig cerebellum (Chang et al. 1978).
[4] Binding of [³H]WB4101, α_1 receptors, in forebrain of rat (Greenberg et al. 1976).
[5] Binding of [³H]dexetimide, muscarinic receptors, in striatum of rat (Laduron et al. 1979)

Presynaptic dopamine receptors

During the past decade it has become increasingly apparent that complex regulatory processes are involved in synaptic transmission. Feedback regulation of dopamine turnover has already been referred to. In addition, it has been found that dopamine agonists inhibit, and its antagonists facilitate, the release of [³H]dopamine from slices of caudate nucleus from the rat pretreated with tritiated dopamine (Farnabo and Hamberger 1971). This phenomenom can be explained by the existence of presynaptic receptors on the nerve terminals which regulate the release of transmitter. The presence of presynaptic receptors can also explain the depression of the firing of mesencephalic neurones by dopamine agonists and the reversal of this effect by antagonists, e.g. neuroleptics (Bunney *et al.* 1973). Presynaptic receptors which are acted upon by the transmitter which the neurone releases, are usually designated as 'autoreceptors' (Starke and Langer 1979) and the action of the released transmitter is to *inhibit* further release, thus providing a negative feedback mechanism. Apart from dopamine, autoreceptors are known to exist for transmitter systems utilizing acetylcholine, noradrenaline, GABA, and 5-HT; they are found both peripherally and centrally.

The presence of presynaptic receptors controlling the release of dopamine can help to explain the dual action of apomorphine on locomotor activity. In small doses apomorphine inhibits locomotor activity and it is thought that this is due to a presynaptic agonist action, reducing the release of dopamine, while larger doses cause increased locomotor activity, presumably by stimulating postsynaptic dopamine receptors (Di Chiara *et al.* 1976).

It is suggested that the autoreceptor on dopaminergic nerve terminals not only controls the release of transmitter but also influences the activity of the enzyme tyrosine hydroxylase, thus affecting transmitter synthesis as well (Arbilla *et al.* 1982). Thus, the net effect of activation of dopamine autoreceptors will be to *reduce* dopaminergic synaptic transmission. The dopamine autoreceptors appear to be of the D_2 subtype (Kebabian and Saavedra 1976). Autoreceptors are very sensitive to the actions of agonist drugs and can be activated by very small concentrations of agonists.

The concept of presynaptic autoreceptors has been reinforced by the discovery of drugs with selective actions at these sites, e.g. clonidine and α-methylnoradrenaline (Langer *et al.* 1980), and an analogue of dopamine, 3-(3-hydroxyphenyl)-*N*-*n*-propylpiperidine (3-PPP) has been found to mimic the effects of small doses of apomorphine (Nilsson and Carlsson 1982) in animals. This substance appeared to have no actions which could be attributed to stimulation of postsynaptic dopamine receptors, only those associated with presynaptic actions, e.g. inhibition of turnover of dopamine. Whether or not dopamine agonists with selectivity for autoreceptors will have any antipsychotic actions remains to be seen, but if they do, then this could represent an important new approach. In fact, it has been suggested that the 'atypical' neuroleptic sulpiride acts at presynaptic receptors, both from the results of *in vitro* receptor binding studies (Jenner and Marsden 1981) and electrophysiological experiments (Mereu 1983).

Presynaptic receptors for other neurotransmitters

In addition to autoreceptors which are activated by the transmitter which the neurone releases, there is evidence that presynaptic receptors for endogenous substances *other* than the neurone's own transmitter, may be present on presynaptic nerve terminals and can have a regulatory or 'modulatory' role. These presynaptic receptors can be activated by transmitter substances released from adjacent terminals, or by locally-produced or blood-borne substances (Langer 1981). There is good evidence that the release of dopamine from nerve terminals in both the striatum and the nucleus accumbens can be affected by cholinergic and serotoninergic influences, as well as by both excitatory and inhibitory amino acids, e.g. glutamate and GABA, and also by many peptides, including opioid peptides. Thus, acetylcholine and cholinergic agonists have been shown to enhance the release of dopamine from preparations of CNS tissue, and both muscarinic and nicotinic presynaptic receptors have been found on dopamine terminals (Westfall 1974; de Belleroche and Gardiner 1982). On the other hand, 5-HT has been shown to decrease the turnover of dopamine in the striatum (Awazi and Guldberg 1978) and to reduce dopamine release (Ennis *et al.* 1981). Gultamate stimulates dopamine release (Besson *et al.* 1979) and GABA inhibits it (Lloyd *et al.* 1979). Cholecystokinin, TRH, neurotensin, and Substance P have all been shown to modulate the release of dopamine, though whether the action is mediated by presynaptic receptors in all cases is not clear. In the case of opioid peptides, an analogue of met-enkephalin, D-Ala^2-*met*-enkephalinamide, has been found to increase dopamine release in the rat striatum and cat caudate nucleus, and it has been suggested that this effect is mediated by an action on opiate receptors located on dopaminergic nerve terminals, or through interneurones in contact with dopaminergic nerve endings (Chesselet *et al.* 1982).

Much of the evidence for the existence of presynaptic receptors has come from studies using *in vitro* preparations, e.g. synaptosomes or tissue slices, and while some effects have been confirmed *in vivo*, no physiological role for the various modulatory influences on dopaminergic transmission in the brain has been established. Obviously, these are complex mechanisms and further elucidation and study is needed. At the present time, presynaptic modulatory influences on dopaminergic transmission in the brain do not appear to have any direct relevance for the actions of neuroleptic drugs, except that certain drugs, e.g. sulpiride, appear to have effects on dopamine antoreceptors. However, it is possible that presynaptic mechanisms may be important and might possibly provide an explanation for the effectiveness of non-neuroleptic therapy in the treatment of schizophrenia (see Summary and conclusions).

Long-term effects of neuroleptic drugs

One of the problems with attempting to relate the clinical effects of neu-roleptic drugs to their pharmacological actions is that the latter are usually assessed from the results of acute experiments in animals, whereas the drugs are used clinically over long periods of time and very often the therapeutic action does not appear immediately. Thus, the full therapeutic response to an antipsychotic drug may require several weeks in which to appear and con-versely, it may last for a considerable time after the cessation of therapy. Fur-thermore, there are some effects, e.g. tardive dyskinesias, which may take even longer to appear (see Chapter 12). There are reasons for believing that the primary pharmacological actions of the neuroleptics, observed mainly in acute experiments, induce a series of secondary effects, the precise nature of which is not yet fully understood.

The development of long-term adaptive changes in synaptic function is a phenomenon of increasing importance in CNS pharmacology. The devel-opment of supersensitivity of receptors as a result of denervation is well known in peripheral tissues, and similar changes have been observed in the CNS after lesions or after chronic administration of drugs. In the latter case, it is probably the presence of an antagonist drug in the vicinity of the post-synaptic receptor for long periods of time, that causes an adaptive change in the receptor mechanism to take place, whereby it can respond to the reduced amount of transmitter present in the synaptic cleft. Thus, the receptor will become supersensitive to *normal* levels of the transmitter. In the case of dopamine receptors, supersensitivity of the postsynaptic receptors, following unilateral lesions of the nigro-striatal pathway in animals, is thought to be responsible for the turning behaviour which develops subsequently and which can be induced by administration of dopamine agonists, e.g. apo-morphine and amphetamine (Ungerstedt 1971). Long-term administration of neuroleptic drugs to animals results in the development of enhanced beha-vioural responses, e.g. the stereotyped behaviour induced by apomorphine (Asper *et al*. 1973). Increased sensitivity of dopamine-stimulated adenylate cyclase and increased binding of dopamine receptor ligands (i.e. [³H]spiperone) in the striatum have also been reported (Clow *et al*. 1979; Clow *et al*. 1980). In other studies, denervation supersensitivity developed in the striatum after lesions induced with the neurotoxic agent 6-hydro-xydopamine, which is selective for catecholamine-containing nerve terminals, as indicated by the increased binding of [³H]haloperidol (Creese *et al*. 1977). Since these two ligands are thought to be relatively specific for the D_2 receptor, it is generally assumed that it is the D_2 receptor which develops supersensitivity, although the increased sensitivity of dopamine-stimulated adenylate cyclase activity suggests that the D_1 receptor may also become supersensitive.

Changes in the sensitivity of postsynaptic dopamine receptors are thought to be responsible for the development of tardive dyskinesias (Chapter 12) as a result of long-term therapy with antipsychotic drugs (Klawans 1973). In man, the extrapyramidal side-effects which may appear early, tend to diminish in the course of therapy, suggesting that tolerance at the D_2 receptor may be developing, while increased prolactin levels are maintained (Meltzer and Fang 1976). *Post-mortem* studies of the brains of schizophrenic patients, using receptor binding techniques, have demonstrated increased binding at D_2 receptors, with no change at D_1 receptors (Owen *et al*. 1978; Lee and Seeman 1980). This data is interpreted as indicating that there is an increase in the number of D_2 receptors in the brains of schizophrenics following long-term treatment with antipsychotic drugs. However, some changes in D_2 receptors have also been found in patients who received no medication. Therefore, such data must be treated with caution.

There is evidence from animal experiments that changes in the sensitivity of dopamine autoreceptors can occur following long-term treatment with neuroleptic drugs (Arbilla *et al*. 1982). The development of supersensitivity of presynaptic dopamine receptors might possibly enhance autoinhibition of dopaminergic transmission. Such an effect should be favourable in the treatment of schizophrenia in the sense that dopaminergic transmission would be reduced. However, if the changes in the sensitivity of the presynaptic auto-receptors occurred simultaneously with the corresponding changes in the sensitivity of postsynaptic receptors, the two effects would tend to cancel out unless they followed different time courses. Furthermore, if supersensitivity of presynaptic dopamine receptors contributed to the therapeutic action of neuroleptic drugs, then supersensitivity of *post*synaptic receptors could account for the development of chronic side-effects, e.g. tardive dyskinesias.

While most studies of the consequences of long-term administration of neuroleptic drugs have concentrated on changes in dopamine receptors, it is possible that changes in other neurotransmitter systems might also be important. These systems might influence dopaminergic transmission either directly, i.e. via presynaptic receptors on dopamine nerve terminals, or indirectly, e.g. through interneurones. Supersensitivity of 5-HT (Dawbarn *et al*. 1981) and GABA (Gale 1980) receptors after chronic administration of neuroleptic drugs has been demonstrated. Thus, a role for adaptive changes in transmitter systems other than dopamine cannot be ignored.

Summary and conclusions

The antipsychotic drugs are the example, *par excellence*, of the analysis of the pharmacology of the drugs increasing our knowledge of the physiological and biochemical mechanisms with which they interact and helping in the understanding of the disease which the drugs are used to treat. Hence, we have the 'Dopamine theory of schizophrenia' which is discussed in detail elsewhere (Chapter 5). Unfortunately, it is true that the drugs appear to relieve only the symptoms of the schizophrenia and not to influence the underlying cause.

The antipsychotic drugs are diverse, both chemically and in their pharmacological properties. There has been a tendency to look for common factors in their pharmacological actions, but it is possible that the variations between the different drugs might prove to be more interesting and more informative in the long run. Thus, antihistamine potency seems to account reasonably well for the sedative properties of some neuroleptics and antagonism at α-adrenergic receptors, for the hypotensive effects. The high anticholinergic potency of drugs such as thioridazine and clozapine certainly accounts well for the reduced incidence of extrapyramidal side-effects encountered with these drugs. Much has been made of the fact that the 'atypical' neuroleptic, sulpiride, is a selective antagonist at the dopamine D_2 receptor. Sulpiride was categorized as 'atypical' because its profile of activity in behavioural tests in animals did not correspond to that of the 'typical' neuroleptics. In particular, sulpiride failed to induce catalepsy in mice and was found to be ineffective in blocking stereotyped behaviour induced by apomorphine and amphetamine in rats. On the basis of this profile of activity, it was predicted that the drug might be less likely to induce extrapyramidal side-effects and possibly cause less tardive dyskinesia. However, these predictions have not been fulfilled and the incidence of extrapyramidal symptoms such as parkinsonism, akathisia, and dystonic reactions is not significantly different to that with other neuroleptics. At the present time there is no evidence that a selective action at D_2 receptors has any significance for the antipsychotic actions of neuroleptic drugs. In fact, this could be a 'red herring' since no clear physiological function has yet been demonstrated for the D_1 receptor, and it seems likely that the D_2 receptor is responsible for mediating both the antipsychotic action and the production of extrapyramidal side-effects. Sulpiride does not pass the blood–brain barrier readily and one possibility is that a metabolite of the drug is responsible for the therapeutic effect. However, this seems unlikely since, when sulpiride is injected directly into the brain in animals, it produces typical dopamine antagonist effects (Moore 1982). Sulpiride also differs from other neuroleptics in two other respects. First, the affinity of [³H]sulpiride for dopamine receptors appears to be critically dependent upon the presence of sodium ions, which is not true for the binding of other neuroleptic drugs, and, second, sulpiride appears to bind only to dopamine receptors and not to interact with 5-HT, histamine, noradrenaline, acetylcholine, or GABA receptors (Jenner and Marsden 1981) (see Table 2.2). It is perhaps somewhat disappointing that a drug which binds selectively to one subtype of dopamine receptor, and does not interact with other neurotransmitter systems, fails to show any unique clinical properties. The one antipsychotic drug which does appear to be unique clinically is clozapine for which there were no reports of extrapyramidal side-effects when it was in use (Jenner and Marsden 1983). However, because of its bone marrow toxicity the drug was never widely used and one cannot help but speculate that if it had been more widely used, reports of extrapyramidal side-effects might have eventually appeared. If, as seems likely, a new generation of dibenzazepine neuroleptics does appear, then this question may be answered. Nevertheless, clozapine does not possess a unique spectrum of pharmacological properties as does sulpiride, and the absence of extrapyramidal side-effects with clozapine may be accounted for by the high anticholinergic potency, higher in fact than for any other neuroleptic drug.

While differential effects on D_1 and D_2 subtypes of dopamine receptors (according to the criteria of Kebabian and Calne (1979)) have not helped in the analysis of the mechanism of action of neuroleptic drugs, studies which can differentiate between actions at presynaptic, as opposed to postsynaptic sites may provide important information, especially if drugs which are selective agonists at presynaptic autoreceptors are shown to be active in man. While a therapeutic action has been predicted for such drugs (Nilssen and Carlsson 1982), they might conceivably exacerbate the symptoms of schizophrenia, or produce more marked side-effects.

It would be interesting too, if neuroleptic drugs which had selective actions on the mesolimbic system, as opposed to the nigro-striatal system, could be developed, as this might help in the separation of antipsychotic actions from extrapyramidal side-effects. So far, there is only circumstantial evidence to support the concept that the antipsychotic action is mediated in the mesolimbic system (Crow *et al.* 1977), and although claims for such an action are being made, particularly in manufacturers' literature, the definitive evidence is not yet available.

It is interesting to speculate on the possible consequence of the presence of presynaptic receptors for neurotransmitters, other than dopamine, on dopaminergic nerve terminals. For example, could the regulation of dopaminergic transmission by other neurotransmitters account for the claimed effectiveness of non-neuroleptic drug treatments in schizophrenia, e.g. β-blockers, such as propranolol, and endorphins? While the overactivity of dopamine systems could account at least for some of the symptoms of schizophrenia, there is no evidence from human studies to support this hypothesis (Crow 1980; Crow *et al.* 1983). While the dopamine hypothesis can explain much of the symptomatology of schizophrenia, the aetiology of the disease could be quite different. For example, it has been proposed that schizophrenia might be due to a virus (Crow 1983) or that it is an autoimmune disease (Knight 1982). Apart from such considerations, it is probably naïve to think of a defect of a single neurotransmitter system as being responsible for such a complex state, which itself may not represent a unitary disease state. From our current knowledge of brain function, it is clear that it does not work in a unitary manner and the various functional states must represent the outcome of complex interactions between various neurotransmitter systems, and some of these interactions will be taking place at presynaptic sites.

It is also clear that the neuroleptic drugs have actions at a number of different sites in the brain. Some of these actions, e.g. the anti-emetic effect, have a clearly localized site of action. With others, especially the therapeutic action in schizophrenia, it is less easy to be precise. In schizophrenia there is inappropriate responding to the environment, both external and internal. Thus, schizophrenics are extremely aware of external stimuli but have difficulty in sorting out their meaning. The region of the brain in which neural integrative mechanisms are involved in the filtering of sensory information and in many facets of behavioural activity, including emotion, perception, and motivation, is the brainstem reticular formation. A disturbance of these filtering and integrative mechanisms could easily account for inappropriate responses. Conversely, a 'pharmacological deafferentation' by neuroleptic drugs (Bradley 1965) can equally well account for the therapeutic actions of these drugs.

References

Andén, N-E., Dahlström, A., Fuxe, K., Olsen, L., and Ungerstedt, U. (1966). Ascending noradrenaline neurons from the pons and the medulla oblongata *Experientia* **22**, 44–45.

—— and Stock, G. (1973). Effect of clozapine on the turnover of dopamine in the corpus striatum and in the limbic system. *J. Pharm. Pharmacol.* **25**, 346–8.

Arbilla, S., Nowak, J. Z., and Langer, S. Z. (1982). Presynaptic autoregulation of dopamine release. In *Presynaptic receptors, mechanisms and functions* (ed. J. de Belleroche), pp. 30–45. Ellis Horwood, Chicester.

Asper, H., Baggiolini, M., Bürki, H. R., Lauener, H., Ruch, W., and Stille, G. (1973). Tolerance phenomena with neuroleptics: catalepsy, apomorphine stereotypies and striatal dopamine metabolism in the rat after single and repeated administration of loxapine and haloperidol. *Eur. J. Pharmacol.* **22**, 287–94.

Atsmon, A. I. and Blum, M. (1970). Treatment of acute porphyria variegata with propranolol. *Lancet* **i**, 196–7.

Avanzino, G. L., Bradley, P. B., Comis, S. D., and Wolstencroft, J. H. (1966). A comparison of the actions of ergothioneine and chlorpromazine applied to single neurones by two different methods. *Int. J. Neuropharmacol.* **5**, 331–3.

Awazi, N. and Guldberg, H. C. (1978). On the interaction of 5-hydroxytryptophan and 5-hydroxytryptamine with dopamine metabolism in the rat striatum. *Naunyn-Schmiedeb. Arch. Pharmac.* **303**, 63–72.

Bartholini, G. and Lloyd, K. G. (1980). Biochemical effects of neuroleptic drugs. In *Psychotropic drugs, Part 1, Antipsychotic and antidepressants* (ed. F. Hoffmeister and G. Stille), pp. 193–212. Springer-Verlag, Berlin.

Bein, H. J. (1980). Centrally acting rauwolfia alkaloids. In *Psychotropic drugs, Part 1, Antipsychotics and antidepressants* (ed. F. Hoffmeister and G. Stille), pp. 43–58. Springer-Verlag, Berlin.

Besson, M. J., Kemel., M. J., Glowinski, J., and Giorguieff, M. F. (1979). Presynaptic control of dopamine release from striatal dopaminergic terminals by various striatal transmitters. In *Presynaptic receptors, Advances in biosciences,* Vol. 18 (ed. S. Z. Langer, K. Starke, and M. L. Dubocovich), pp. 159–63. Pergamon Press, Oxford.

Borenstein, P., Champion, C., Cujo, P., Gekiere, F., Olivenstein, C., and Kramarz, P. (1969). Un psychotrope original: Le Sulpiride. *Sem. Hôp. Paris.* **45**, 1301–14.

Bradley, P. B. (1957). Microelectrode approach to the neuropharmacology of the reticular formation. In *Psychotropic drugs* (ed. Garattini and V. Ghetti), pp. 207–16. Elsevier, Amsterdam.

—— (1963). Phenothiazine derivatives. In *Physiological pharmacology* (ed. W. S. Root and F. G. Hofmann), pp. 417–77. Academic Press, New York.

—— (1965). Neurophysical mechanisms of pharmacological deafferentation. In *Désafférentation expérimentale et clinique, 2nd. Bel-Air Symposium*, pp. 37–46. Georg et Cie, Geneva.

—— (1968). Synaptic transmission in the central nervous system and its relevance for

drug action. *Int. Rev. Neurobiol.* **11**, 1–56.
—— Elkes, C., and Elkes, J. (1953). On some effects of lysergic acid diethylamide (LSD 25) in normal volunteers, *J. Physiol.* **121**, 50P.
—— and Hance, A. J. (1957). The effect of chlorpromazine and methopromazine on the electrical activity of the brain in the cat. *EEG Clin. Neurophysiol.* **9**, 191–215.
—— and Key, B. J. (1958). The effects of drugs on arousal responses produced by electrical stimulation of the reticular formation of the brain *EEG Clin. Neurophysiol.* **10**, 97–110.
—— Wolstencroff, J. H., and Avanzino, G. L. (1966). Neuronal basis for the central action of chlorpromazine *Nature, Lond.* **212**, 1425–7.
Brodie, B. B. and Shore, P. A. (1957). On a role for serotonin and norepinephrine as chemical mediators in the central autonomic nervous system. In *Hormones, brain function and behaviour* (ed. H. Hoagland), pp. 161–79. Academic Press, New York.
Bunney, B. S. and Aghajanian, G. K. (1973). Electrophysiological effects of amphetamine on dopaminergic neurons. In *Frontiers in catecholamine research* (ed. S. H. Snyder and E. Usdin), pp. 957–62. Pergamon Press, Oxford.
—— Walters, J. R., Roth, R. H., and Aghajanian, G. K. (1973). Dopaminergic neurons: effect of antipsychotic drugs and amphetamine on single cell activity. *J. Pharm. exp. Ther.* **185**, 560–71.
Bürki, H. R., Sayers, A. C., Ruch, W., and Asper, H. (1977). Effects of clozapine and other dibenzo-epines on central dopaminergic and cholinergic systems. Structure–activity relationships. *Arzneim. Forsch.* **27**, 1561–5.
Carlsson, A. (1978). Mechanism of action of neuroleptic drugs. In *Psychopharmacology: a generation of progress.* (ed. M. A. Lipton, A. DiMascio, and K. F. Killam), pp. 1057–70. Raven Press, New York.
—— and Lindqvist, J. (1963). Effect of chlorpromazine and haloperidol of formation of 3-methoxytryamine and normetanephrine in mouse brain. *Acta pharmacol. toxicol.* **20**, 140–4.
Chang, R. S. L., Tran, V. T., and Snyder, S. H. (1978). Histamine H_1 receptors in brain labelled with ^{3}H-mepyramine. *Eur. J. Pharmacol.* **48**, 463–4.
Chesselet, M. F., Lubetski, C., Cheramy, A. Reishine, T. D., and Glowinski, J. (1982). Modulation of striatal dopamine release by opiates. In *Presynaptic receptors, mechanisms and functions* (ed. J. de Belleroche), pp. 152–64. Ellis Horwood, Chicester.
Clow, A., Jenner, P., and Marsden, C. D. (1979). Changes in dopamine-mediated behaviour during one year's neuroleptic administration. *Eur. J. Pharmacol.* **57**, 365–75.
—— Theodorou, A. Jenner, P., and Marsden, C. D. (1980). Changes in rat striatal dopamine turnover and receptor activity during one year's neuroleptic administration. *Eur. J. Pharmacol.* **63**, 135–44.
Cools, A. R. and van Rossum, J. M. (1976). Excitation-mediating and inhibition-mediating dopamine receptors. A new concept towards a better understanding of electrophysiological, biochemical, pharmacological, functional and clinical data. *Psychopharm.* **45**, 243–54.
Costall, B. and Naylor, R. J. (1975). Neuroleptic antagonism of dyskinetic phenomena. *Eur. J. Pharmacol.* **33**, 301–12.
Courvoisier, S., Fournel, J., Ducrot, R., Kolsky, M., and Koetschet, P. (1953). Propriétés pharmacodynamiques du chlorhydrate de chloro-3-(diméthyl-amino-3'prolyl)-10 phénothiazine (4.560 R.P.). (1) Étude expérimentale d'un nouveau corps utilisé dans l-anesthésie potentialisée et dans l'hibernation artificielle. *Arch. intern. Pharmacodynamie* **92**, 305.
Creese, I., Burt, D. R., and Snyder, S. H. (1976). Dopamine receptor binding predicts

clinical and pharmacological potencies of antischizophrenic drugs. *Science* **192**, 481–3.

——, ——, —— (1977). Dopamine receptor binding enhancement accompanies lesion-induced behavioural supersensitivity *Science* **197**, 596–8.

——, ——, —— (1978). Biochemical actions of neuroleptic drugs: focus on the dopamine receptor. In *Handbook of psychopharmacology*, Vol. 10, *Neuroleptics and schizophrenia* (ed. L. L. Iversen, S. D. Iversen, and S. H. Snyder), pp. 37–89. Plenum, New York.

Crow, T. J. (1980). Molecular pathology of schizophrenia: more than one disease process? *Br. Med. J.* **28**, 66–8.

—— (1983). Is schizophrenia an infectious disease? *Lancet* i, 173–5.

—— Deakin, J. F. W., and Longden, A. (1977). The nucleus accumbens—a possible site of antipsychotic action of neuroleptic drugs. *Psychol. Med.* **7**, 213–21.

—— Owens, D. G. C., Johnstone, E. C., Cross, A. J., and Owen, F. (1983). Does tardive dyskinesia exist? In: *New directions in tardive dyskinesia research, Modern problems in pharmacopsychiatry*, Vol. 21 (ed. J. Bannet and R. H. Belmaker), pp. 206–19. Karger, Basel.

Dawbarn, D., Long, S. K., and Pycock, C. J. (1981). Increased central 5-hydro-xytryptamine receptor mechanisms in rats after chronic neuroleptic treatment. *Br. J. Pharmacol.* **73**, 149–56.

de Belleroche, J. S. and Gardiner, I. M. (1982). Cholinergic action in the nucleus accumbens: modulation of dopamine and acetylcholine release. *Br. J. Pharmacol.* **75**, 359–65.

Delay, J., Deniker, P., and Harl, J. M. (1952). Utilisation en thérapeutique psychia-trique d'une phénothiazine d'action centrale élective (4560 R.P.). *Ann. med. Psychol.* **2**, 112–17.

DiChiara, G., Porceddu, M. L., Vargiu, L., Argiolas, A., and Gessa, G. L. (1976). Evidence for dopamine receptors mediating sedation in the mouse brain. *Nature, Lond.* **264**, 564–7.

Domino, E. F., Hudson, R. D., and Zografi, G. (1968). Substituted phenothiazines: pharmacology and chemical structure. In *Drugs affecting the central nervous system* (ed. A. Burger), pp. 327–97. Dekker, New York.

Emrich, H. M., Cording, C., Piree, S., Kölling, A., Zerssen, D. V., and Herz, A. (1977). Indication of an antipsychotic action of the opiate antagonist naloxone. *Pharmakopsychiat. Neuropsychopharmakol.* **10**, 265–70.

Ennis, C., Kemp, J. D., and Cox, B. (1981). Characterisation of inhibitory 5-hydroxytryptamine receptors that modulate dopamine release in the striatum. *J. Neurochem*, **36**, 1515–20.

Farnabo, L. O. and Hamberger, B. (1971). Drug-induced changes in the release of ^{3}H-monoamines from field stimulated rat brain slices. *Acta physiol. scand.* **371**, 35–44.

Gale, K. (1980). Chronic blockade of dopamine receptors by antischizophrenic drugs enhances GABA binding in substantia nigra. *Nature, Lond.* **283**, 569–70.

Graham, A. and Aghajanian, G. K. (1971). Effects of amphetamine on single cell activity in catecholamine nucleus, the locus coeruleus. *Nature, Lond.* **234**, 100–2.

Greenberg, D. A., U'Prichard, D. C., and Snyder, S. H. (1976). α-Noradrenergic receptor binding in mammalian brain. *Life Sci.* **19**, 69–76.

Gunne, L. M., Lindström, L., and Terenius, L. (1977). Naloxone-induced reversal of schizophrenic hallucinations. *J. Neurol. Transm.* **40**, 13–19.

Hornykiewicz, O. (1972). Neurochemistry of Parkinsonism. In *Handbook of neu-rochemistry*, Vol. 7 (ed. A. Lajtha), pp. 465–501. Plenum, New York.

Hyttel, J. (1981). Similarities between the binding of ^{3}H-piflutixol and ^{3}H-flupentixol to rat striatal dopamine receptors *in vitro*. *Life Sci.* **28**, 563–9.

—— (1982). Preferential labelling of adenylate cyclase coupled dopamine receptors with thioxanthene neuroleptics. *Adv. Biosci.* **37**, 147–52.

—— Christensen, A. V., and Arnt, J. (1983). Neuropletic classification: implications for Tardive dyskinesia. In *New directors in tardive dyskinesia research, Modern problems in pharmacopsychiatry*, Vol. 21 (ed. J. Bannet and R. H. Belmaker), pp. 49–64. Karger, Basel.

Iversen, L. L., Rogawski, M. A. and Miller, R. J. (1976). Comparison of the effects of neuroleptic drugs on pre- and postsynaptic dopaminergic mechanisms in the rat striatum. *Mol. Pharmacol.* **12**, 251–3.

Jenner, P. and Marsden, C. D. (1981). Substituted benzamide drugs as selective neuroleptic agents. *Neuropharmacol.* **20**, 1285–93.

——, —— (1983). Neuroleptics. In *Psychopharmacology, Part 1, Preclinical psychopharmacology* (ed. D. G. Graham-Smith and P. J. Cowen), pp. 180–247. Excerpta Medica, Amsterdam.

Johnstone, E. C., Crow, T. J., Frith, C. D., Carney, M. W. P., and Price, J. S. (1978). Mechanism of the antipsychotic effect in the treatment of acute schizophrenia. *Lancet* i, 848–57.

Kebabian, J. W. and Calne, D. B. (1979). Multiple receptors for dopamine. *Nature, Lond.*, **277**, 93–6.

—— and Greengard, P. (1971). Dopamine-sensitive adenyl cyclase: Possible role in synaptic transmission. *Science* **174**, 1346–9.

—— and Saavedra, J. M. (1976). Dopamine-sensitive adenylate cyclase occurs in a region of the substantia nigra containing dopaminergic dendrites. *Science* **193**, 683–5.

Key, B. J. and Bradley, P. B. (1960). The effects of drugs on conditioning and habituation to arousal stimuli in animals. *Psychopharmacology* **1**, 450–62.

Killam, E. K. and Killam, K. F. (1956). A comparison of the effects of reserpine and chlorpromazine to those of barbiturates on central afferent systems in the cat. *J. Pharm. exp. Ther.* **116**, 35.

Klawans, H. L. (1973). *Pharmacology of extrapyramidal movements disorders.* Karger, Basel.

Klein, D. F. and Davis, J. M. (1969). *Diagnosis and drug treatment of psychiatric disorders.* Williams and Wilkins, Baltimore.

Knight, J. G. (1982). Dopamine-receptor-stimulating autoantibodies: A possible cause of schizophrenia. *Lancet* ii, 1073–6.

Laduron, P. M., Verwimp, M., and Leysen, J. E. (1979). Stereospecific *in vitro* binding of ³H-dexetimide to brain muscarinic receptors *J. Neurochem.* **32**, 421–7.

Langer, S. Z. (1981). Pharmacological implications of presynaptic control of neurotransmitter secretion. In *Chemical neurotransmission–75 years* (ed. L. Stjärne, P. Hedqvist, H. Lagercrantz, and A. Wennmalm), pp. 301–12. Academic Press, New York.

—— Arbilla, S., and Kamal, L. (1980). Autoregulation of noradrenaline and dopamine release through presynaptic receptors. In *Neurotransmitters and their receptors* (ed. U. Z. Littauer, Y. Dudai, I. Silman, V. I. Teichberg, and Z. Vogel), pp. 7–21. John Wiley, New York.

Lee, T. and Seeman, P. (1980). Elevation of brain neuroleptic/dopamine receptors in schizophrenia. *Am. J. Psychiat* **137**, 191–7.

——, —— Tourtelotte, W. W., Farley, I. J., and Hornkiewicz, O. (1978). Binding of ³H-neuroleptics and ³H-apomorphine in schizophrenic brains. *Nature, Lond.* **274**, 897–900.

Leysen, J. E. (1981). Review on neuroleptic receptors: specificity and multiplicity of *in vitro* binding related to pharmacological activity. In *Clinical pharmacology in psychiatry: neuroleptic and antidepressant research* (ed. E. Usdin, S. G. Dahl, L. F. Gram, and O. Lingjaerde), pp. 35–62. Macmillan, London.

—— (1984). Receptors for neuroleptic drugs. In *Advances in human psychopharmacology* (ed. G.D. Burrows and J. Werry) Vol. 3, pp. 315–56. Jai Press, Greenwich, Connecticut, USA.

—— and Laduron, P. M. (1977). Differential distribution of opiate and neuroleptic receptors and dopamine-sensitive adenylate cyclase in rat brain. *Life Sci.* **20**, 281–8.

—— Tollenaere, J. P., Koch, M. H. J., and Laduron, P. M. (1977). Differentiation of opiate and neuroleptic receptor binding in rat brain. *Eur. J. Pharmacol.* **43**, 253–67.

—— Niemegeers, C. J. E., Tollenaere, J. P., and Laduron, P. M. (1978). Serotonergic component of neuroleptic receptors. *Nature, Lond.* **272**, 168–71.

Lindström, L. H. and Persson, E. (1980). Propranolol in chronic schizophrenia: a controlled study in neuroleptic-treated patients. *Br. J. Psychiat.* **137**, 126–30.

Lloyd, K. G., Worms, P., Scatton, B., Zivkovic, B., and Bartholini, G. (1979). The influence of GABA on dopamine neuron activity. In *Presynaptic receptors, Advances in biosciences*, Vol. 18 (ed. S. Z. Langer, K. Starke, and M. L. Dubocovich), pp. 207–12. Pergamon Press, Oxford.

Meltzer, H. Y. and Fang, V. S. (1976). Serum prolactin levels in schizophrenia: effect of antipsychotic drugs. A preliminary report. In *Hormones, behaviour and psychopathology* (ed. E. J. Sachar). Raven Press, New York.

Mereu, G. P. (1983). Activation of dopaminergic neurons by sulpiride. In *Receptors and supramolecular entities, Advances in biosciences*, Vol. 44 (ed. G. Biggio, E. Costa, G. L. Gessa, and P. F. Spano), pp. 147–53. Pergamon Press, Oxford.

Miller, R. J., Horn, A. S., and Iversen, L. L. (1974). The action of neuroleptic drugs on dopamine-stimulated adenosine cyclic 3', 5'-monophosphate production in rat neostriatum and limbic forebrain. *Mol. Pharmacol.* **10**, 759–66.

Moore, N. A. (1982). The modification of dopamine-induced behaviour by antipsychotic drugs. PhD Thesis, University of Birmingham.

Nilssen, J. L. G. and Carlsson, A. (1982). Dopamine-receptor agonist with apparent selectivity for autoreceptors: A new principle for antipsychotic action? *Trends Pharmacol. Sci.* **3**, 322–5.

Offermeier, J. and van Rooyen, J. M. (1983). Dopamine inhibitory and excitatory systems in tardive dyskinesias. In *New directions in tardive dyskinesia research, Modern problems in pharmacopsychiatry*, Vol. 21 (ed. J. Bannet and R. H. Belmaker), pp. 124–42, Karger, Basel.

Owen, F., Cross, A. J., Crow, T. J., Longden, A., Poulter, M., and Riley, G. L. (1978). Increased dopamine receptor sensitivity in schizophrenia. *Lancet* ii, 223.

——, ——, ——, Lofthouse, R., and Poulter, M. (1981). Neurotransmitter receptors in brain in schizophrenia. *Acta psychiat. scand.* **291** 20–6.

Sandison, R. A. (1963). In *Hallucinogenic drugs and their psychotherapeutic use* (ed. R. Crockett, R. A. Sandison, and A. Walk), p. 33. H. K. Lewis, London.

Schmutz, J. and Picard, C. W. (1980). Tricyclic neuroleptics structure–activity relationships. In *Psychotropic agents. Part I. Antipsychotics and antidepressants* (ed. F. Hoffmeister and G. Stille), pp. 3–26. Springer-Verlag, Berlin.

Sedvall, G., Fyro, B., Nyback, H., Wiesel, F. A., and Wode-Helgodt, B. (1974). Mass fragmentometric determination of homovanillic acid in lumbar cerebrospinal fluid of schizophrenic patients during treatment with antipsychotic drugs. *J. psychiat. Res.* **11**, 75–80.

Seeman, P., Lee, T., Chau-Wong, M., and Wong, K. (1976). Antipsychotic drug doses and neuroleptic/dopamine receptors. *Nature, Lond.* **261**, 717–19.

Sen, G. and Bose, K. C. (1931). Rauwolfia serpentina, a new Indian drug for insanity and high blood pressure. *Indian med. World* **2**, 194–201.

Stanley, M., Lautin, A., Rotrosen, J., Gershon, S., and Kleinberg, D. (1980).

Metoclopramide: antipsychotic efficacy of a drug lacking in potency in receptor models. *Psychopharmacology* **71**, 219–25.

Starke, K. E. and Langer, S. Z. (1979). A note on terminology for presynaptic receptors. In *Presynaptic receptors, Advances in biosciences*, Vol. 18 (ed. S. Z. Langer, K. Starke, and M. L. Dubocovich), pp. 1–3. Pergamon Press, Oxford.

Svensson, T. H., Bunney, B. S., and Aghajanian, G. K. (1975). Inhibition of both noradrenergic and serotonergic neurons in brain by the α-adrenergic agonist, clonidine. *Brain Res.* **92**, 291–306.

Ungerstedt, U. (1971). Striatal dopamine release after amphetamine or nerve degeneration revealed by rotational behaviour. *Acta physiol. scand.* **82**, 49–68.

Van Ree, J. M. and de Wied, D. (1982). Neuroleptic-like profile of γ-type endorphins as related to schizophrenia. *Trends Pharmacol. Sci.* **3**, 358–61.

Wagner, L. A. (1975). Minireview. Subcellular storage of biogenic amines. *Life Sci.* **17**, 1755–62.

Westfall, T. C. (1974). The effect of cholinergic agents on the release of ^{3}H-dopamine from rat striatal slices by nicotine, potassium and electrical stimulation. *Fedn. Proc.* **33**, 524.

Yorkston, N. J., Gruzelier, J. H., Saki, S. A., Hollander, D., Pitcher, D. R., and Sergeant, H. G. (1977). Propranolol as an adjunct to the treatment of schizophrenia. *Lancet* **ii**, 575–8.

3

Animal models of schizophrenia

SUSAN D. IVERSEN

The possibility of developing animal models of human psychiatric disorders continues to attract attention. The widespread use of pharmacological agents in the treatment of mental illness has generated the need for appropriate animal models with which to test the efficacy of newly developed drugs. But at the theoretical level there is also a growing concern to define the neuro-biological basis of such illness and to advance understanding of the aetiology of psychiatric disorders.

In this chapter attention is focused on schizophrenia, although the scientific approaches illustrated apply equally well to studies of depression, anxiety (see Iversen 1979a), mania (Robbins and Sahakian 1980), psychiatric disorders of childhood, or those associated with minimal brain dysfunction (Cohen and Young 1977). Furthermore, pharmacological models of schizophrenia receive the most detailed treatment. Much less progress has been made in devising animal models where manipulation of the environment induces psychotic behaviour in animals, although such studies could begin to indicate the importance of environmental events in the aetiology of schizophrenia in man. Clearly, in man complex environmental and sociological factors operate and in this domain study of animals cannot enter in any relevant way. Thus, the approach has limitations, and it is for these reasons that some clinicians remain sceptical. Some hold a fundamental opposing view, believing that the core of psychopathology is disordered symbolic processing, the essence of which is not reflected in observed behaviour. If such a position is held, analysis of abnormal behaviour in animals or man, whether drug or environmentally induced, is irrelevant to an understanding of mental illness. In animals this argument is said to be even stronger because their capacity for symbolic processing is itself very limited. It is reasonable to question both these premises (McKinney 1974) and there are many who believe that observation of behaviour represents the only reliable way to define psychiatric disorders.

CRITERIA FOR AN ANIMAL MODEL OF SCHIZOPHRENIA

McKinney and Bunney (1969) put forward a set of four criteria for evaluating animal models of mental illness. No doubt more exhaustive lists could be produced but this one is useful at the present state of the art. The clinical condition and the animal's behaviour should show:

1. Similarity of the inducing conditions;
2. Similarity of behavioural states produced;
3. Common underlying neurobiological mechanisms;
4. Reversal by clinically effective treatment techniques.

It is of paramount importance to know what one is attempting to model before undertaking experimental work in animals. Yet it is immediately apparent that it is difficult, if not possible, to answer these questions about most of the common human psychiatric conditions. This point is particularly pertinent in the present chapter, as recently there has been a recurrence of interest in nosological approaches to schizophrenia. It seems worthwhile to refer to these discussions on the classification of schizophrenic illnesses and the diagnostic features of these illnesses, before turning to the animal models.

NOSOLOGICAL APPROACHES TO SCHIZOPHRENIA

Kraepelin (1913) introduced the term 'dementia praecox' to describe a psychotic illness with poor prognosis. The course of the illness tended to be chronic and although it could be marked by intermittent attacks and patterns of remission, *restitutio ad integrum* (in the words of Bleuler) did not occur. It was Bleuler (1911) who coined the term 'schizophrenia' because he found Kraepelin's terminology awkward and considered that it described the disease but not the diseased. Both he and Kraepelin defined the fundamental symptoms of schizophrenia which they considered to be of diagnostic importance. These were impoverished affect, disturbances of personal contact and rapport, ambivalence, lack of motivation, depersonalization, and stereotyped behaviour which resulted in a 'specific type of alteration of thinking, feeling and relation to the external world which appears nowhere else in this particular fashion'. These are often termed the negative symptoms of schizophrenia. Bleuler and Kraepelin also described additional accessory symptoms including delusions and hallucinations. Fifty years later, Schneider (1959) focused on these positive symptoms and advocated the use of a checklist defining their absence or presence for diagnosing schizophrenia. This was widely adopted because unlike some of the negative symptoms, the positive ones were easier to define, to identify, and to rate. The enthusiasm with which Schneider's proposals were greeted led to a loss of interest in nosological approaches to schizophrenia for two decades, and it is only in the last few years that clinicians have turned again to this important question of fundamental diagnostic criteria.

Soon after Schneider's ideas were published biological research in psychiatry, and especially that related to schizophrenia, saw a rapid increase and his ideas on diagnostic criteria, as we shall see, had a major influence on the development of animal models of schizophrenia (Kety 1980; Crow 1980; Mackay 1980). A number of clinicians have recently pointed out that

Kraepelin and Bleuler would clearly have disagreed with Schneider's proposals. Both viewed hallucinations and delusions as accessory symptoms. Bleuler considered them 'partial phenomena of the most varied diseases. Their presence is often helpful in making the diagnosis but not in diagnosing the presence of schizophrenia'. Mackay (1980) stated that it has never been demonstrated that the positive symptoms of Schneider either more accurately describe or delineate the original disease. It was considered relevant to raise these nosological issues before turning to a description of the experimental work on models and particularly animal models of schizophrenia, because as we do so we must ask which of the symptoms are being modelled in each case. We must also refer back to the criteria of McKinney and Bunney to see how far these are met.

PHARMACOLOGICAL MODELS OF SCHIZOPHRENIA

The dopamine overactivity hypothesis of schizophrenia

Many excellent overviews of this topic have appeared and it is not necessary to describe scientific results which have converged to support the working hypothesis that in schizophrenia dopamine overactivity exists (Iversen 1978). Neuroleptic drugs, such as the phenothiazine, chlorpromazine, were introduced in the 1940s and rapidly came into widespread use for controlling the florid symptoms of schizophrenia. It was demonstrated with *in vitro* biochemical methods that such drugs interact with catecholamine (dopamine and noradrenaline) receptors in the peripheral and central nervous system to block chemical transmission at the synapse.

At the dopamine postsynpatic site in brain, receptor blockade resulted in inhibition of dopamine-stimulated adenylate cyclase. An important group of antischizophrenic drugs were subsequently developed, the butyrophenones (including haloperidol, spiroperidol, and pimozide) which blocked dopamine (DA) rather than noradrenaline (NA) receptors, confirming the view that DA dysfunction (rather than NA) is associated with schizophrenia. The butyrophenones, however, had a relatively weak inhibitory effect on the adenylate cyclase response. This observation led to the discovery that brain contained two DA receptor types; the D_1 receptor linked to adenylate cyclase and a D_2 receptor, not linked to cyclase to which radio-labelled butyrophenones bind. Since both the phenothiazines and the butyrophenones are potent antischizophrenic agents, it has come to be generally accepted that the D_2 receptor is the more important target for this pharmacological effect.

Recently, more selective D_2 antagonists, the substituted benzamides such as sulpiride (Jenner and Marsden 1979) and remoxipride (Ogren *et al.* 1984) have been discovered. These compounds are also reported to have a greater effect on D_2 mechanisms in the limbic areas than in the striatum, which could account for the claim that they do not produce tardive dyskinesia. With the discovery of a highly specific D_1 receptor antagonist, SCH 23390 (Christensen *et al.* 1984), it will be possible to evaluate directly the importance of the adenylate cyclase-linked DA_1 receptor in the antipsychotic action of neuroleptics.

A second powerful line of evidence correlating dopamine receptors with antipsychotic action became available when receptor binding assays were developed for quantifying the interaction of neuroleptics with dopamine receptors. A highly significant correlation exists between occupancy of the DA receptor and clinical efficacy of the drug. (Creese *et al.* 1976) and a striking relationship is shown in Fig. 3.1 using displacement of radioactive ligand haloperidol as a measure of the interaction of the neuroleptic with the dopamine receptor (Seeman *et al.* 19076).

A number of other findings have strengthened the proposed relationship between dopamine overactivity and schizophrenia. Drugs which increase brain dopaminergic activity would be expected to exacerbate schizophrenic symptoms. Janowsky *et al.* (1973) found that intravenous methylphenidate accentuated psychotic symptoms during the florid state of schizophrenia.

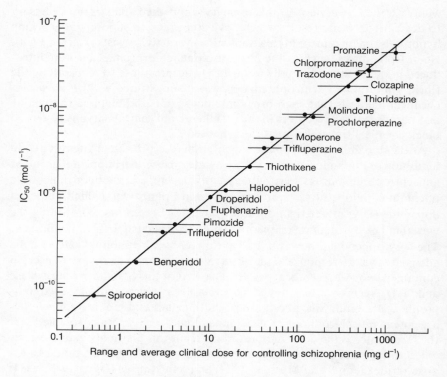

FIG. 3.1.   Comparison of the clinical potencies of neuroleptic drugs, measured as average daily dose in treating schizophrenia, with potencies of the same drugs in displacing [^{3}H]-haloperidol from DA receptor binding sites *in vitro* (concentration of drug required to displace 50 per cent of specific haloperidol binding). (Reprinted by permission from *Nature, Lond.* **261**, 717. Copyright © 1976, Macmillan Journals Ltd.)

Similarly, Angrist *et al.* (1973) found significant worsening of symptoms in schizophrenics treated with L-dopa.

It is generally accepted that manipulations of the central nervous system which result in enhanced dopaminergic activity might, on the one hand, result in behavioural symptoms comparable to those seen clinically in schizophrenia and, on the other, provide useful models for evaluating the relative efficacy of drugs developed to reduce dopamine activity by receptor blockade or some other biochemical action on the DA neurone.

Enhanced dopaminergic function may be achieved by drugs interfering with the synthesis, degradation, re-uptake, and release of dopamine or by mimicking the effect of dopamine directly at the receptor level with agonist drugs. The behavioural effects of indirect-acting sympathomimetic drugs, such as *d*-amphetamine which releases dopamine (Kuczenski 1983), or the dopamine receptor agonists, such as apomorphine, have been extensively studied. Models in animals and man have emerged from chronic and acute dosage with such drugs (Ridley 1985).

Psychosis in man following chronic high doses of amphetamine

Amphetamine abuse has occurred whenever the drug has not been carefully regulated. In the 1960s when the hippie movement flourished (Angrist and Sudilovsky 1978), it was reported in several countries that humans taking consistently large doses of amphetamine or related stimulants were presenting to psychiatric clinics, and were misdiagnosed as suffering from paranoid schizophrenia. Neuroleptic drugs were successful in treating this psychotic behaviour, reinforcing the view that amphetamine psychosis and schizophrenia had some common neurobiological element.

The phenomenon itself was described under experimental conditions (Angrist and Gershon 1970) in volunteer addicts who were given hourly oral doses of amphetamine as the racemic sulphate over about 24 hours. The cardiovascular responses were monitored carefully and the behavioural responses noted. A summary of the results of one of these patients who received 325 mg amphetamine over 28.75 hours is shown in Fig. 3.2. Clinical notes reported in the figure legend reveal thought disorder, delusions, paranoia, and auditory hallucinations in this patient. The conclusion of Angrist and Gershon that in some individuals amphetamine psychosis mirrors very closely paranoid schizophrenia is much in line with the views in Connell's (1958) monograph. In these earlier studies the individuals became addicted to stimulants which had been prescribed initially for medical reasons; for example amphetamine for the treatment of narcolepsy (Prinzmetal and Bloomberg 1935; Youngs and Scoville 1938), or benzedrine inhalers (Monroe and Drell 1947; Herman and Nagler 1954) for the treatment of nasal congestion.

Connell stated:

Psychosis associated with amphetamine usage is much more frequent than would be expected from reports in the literature. . . . The clinical picture is primarily a

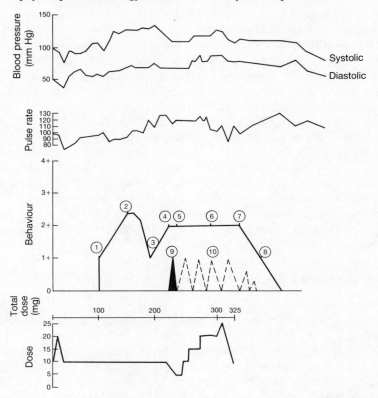

FIG. 3.2.   Clinical notes made at times 1–10 as indicated on behaviour graph above. 1. 'The other patients went to bed and the atmosphere changed. I was the centre of attention. I didn't want to talk because I was afraid I'd say something and the nurses would make a report and you'd cut me off. I felt the nurse behind me and felt like I had to hide or something.' 2. During the night one patient awoke, came into the day-room and spoke of 'brainwashing'. 'It seemed she thought I was doing it to her, making her sicker with my mind. Then I thought there was another person involved — putting thoughts into both our minds or using my mind to cure her.' Asked if he believed in telepathy, he answered; 'When I'm stoned I do because it feels so real.' 3. He then began to feel more relaxed but still worried about the nurses' observations and thought others could notice his body odour. 4. He thought discussions between other patients and the investigator concerned him and was afraid to get up from a table for fear that they could tell he was high and would watch him. 5. After lunch he was told to lie down by an aide. He didn't want to but did so 'to avoid an argument'. Lying down he 'felt sure' that the investigator had 'sneakily' cut his medication by substituting placebo tablets and that the amphetamine was being excreted in his perspiration causing a strong body odour that he actually smelled. 6. At this time he heard the voices of other patients in the ward discussing him in the third person, i.e. 'He's stupid. Why's he doing it? He's not doing anything. He's just staying up.' 7. He was afraid to leave the ward for a taped interview because 'other people look at you and seem to know'. He also smelled faeces and thought he had been incontinent but checked and found none. 8. Taking his temperature in the bathroom he noticed some-one in a lab across the street and felt that he had been 'planted' there to watch him.

paranoid psychosis with ideas of reference, delusions of persecution, auditory and visual hallucinations in a setting of clear consciousness . . . The mental picture may be indistinguishable from acute or chronic paranoid schizophrenia.

The preponderance of delusions and hallucinations are often dramatic in amphetamine psychosis. However, unlike schizophrenia, visual and tactile hallucinations appear to be more common than auditory ones. In many unrelated toxic drug states and in fever, visual hallucinations are common and this has led some clinicians to view amphetamine psychosis merely as a toxic response to the drug.

Tactile hallucinations are also seen which lead to intense investigation of an area of skin and then to the feeling that there are insects under the skin causing irritation. This feature of the syndrome is seen particularly dramatically when cocaine, another indirect sympathomimetic amine, is abused (Siegel 1978).

For this and other reasons, Slater (1959) and Bell (1965) put forward the view that amphetamine psychosis and schizophrenia can be distinguished on clinical grounds. Both stressed three important features characteristic of the drug condition which distinguish it from schizophrenia: (1) lack of thought disorder; (2) frequency of visual hallucinations; and (3) brisk affective responses. Angrist and Gershon (1970) certainly described in their subjects the most convincing parallel of the two conditions, as they obtained evidence of auditory hallucinations and formal thought disorder in some of their volunteers. It is possible that the more aggressive induction of amphetamine intoxication they employed with hourly treatment accounts for the severity and broad range of symptoms they observed. The earlier studies described the syndrome in patients with varied histories in terms of drug, dose, and dosage regime.

Animal studies of amphetamine psychosis after chronic exposure to drug

Ellinwood pioneered the study of chronic amphetamine treatment in rats, cats, dogs, and monkeys (Ellinwood and Escalante 1972). The comparative aspect of this work has been important because it is now clear that the natural fabric of behaviour varies across species and that these biological constraints are important in determining the characteristics of the abnormal behaviour in a given species.

Repeated escalating doses of amphetamine produce motor repetition or stereotypy which becomes more and more obvious. Ellinwood was not satisfied merely to quantify stereotypy but carefully analysed the progressive deterioration of organized behaviour as the motor stereotypy emerged. In

9. Four hours after amphetamine was cut he still felt that other patients on the ward were watching him; this subsided after three additional hours. 10. He also noticed that the odour he attributed to the amphetamine in his perspiration intensified whenever he was in close proximity to the nursing staff, i.e. when pulses and blood pressures were taken. (Reprinted with permission from *Biological Psychiatry* **2**, 95.)

studies of cats and dogs and of monkeys, two aspects of the disorganized behaviour were conspicuous in amphetamine psychosis—the disruption of postural adjustment and behavioural set (Ellinwood *et al.* 1972). In the cat study, methamphetamine was given over an 11-day period and 16 elements of behaviour were recorded and classified under the following headings:

1. Physical location (place and orientation);
2. Relation with the environment (attitude);
3. Level of activity (activity scale);
4. Positions and movements (body changes);
5. Looking activity;
6. Sniffing involvement;
7. Grooming activity;
8. Autonomic responses;
9. Miscellaneous (including infrequent and often complex behaviours).

In the early phases stereotyped responses were observed and it was noted how a particular response, with repetition, evolved into only a remnant of the original behaviour; grooming evolved to simply raising a leg, and sniffing finally evolved to mere deviation of the head. Ellinwood was equally impressed by what he described as drug-induced changes of posture and attitude, which persisted even after the more specific movement patterns of stereotypy had broken down. 'Dyssynchrony' is the term he introduced to describe 'one body part or body segment moving without proper relation to other parts to make a flowing vector of behaviour'. It was suggested that the initiative to change attitude, that is, one's relationship with the environment, or to modify postural-movement sets, is a prerequisite for normal behavioural organization. The intrinsic postural–attitudinal sets are the substrates of attention and organize and direct the normal sequences of behaviour.

A number of defects, including abnormal righting reflexes, poor postural adjustment, and catatonia, are cited which are observed in schizophrenia and are thought to reflect disruption of postural sets. Kraepelin (1913) himself called attention to a number of ocular signs in schizophrenia including pupillary abnormalities, staring nystagmus, abnormal blinking, and blepharospasm. Recently, Stevens (1978) made a careful study of these ocular signs in drug-free patients and considered they provide clues about the pathology of schizophrenia. She pointed out that in schizophrenics abnormal electrical activity has been recorded from the nucleus accumbens and other limbic structures innervated by the dopamine neurones of the ventral tegmental area lying medial to the substantia nigra. The nucleus accumbens, being a more medially placed structure than the striatum, projects to more medial aspects of the diencephalon and mesencephalon, including the paramedian pontine reticular formation and the optic tectum. These connections of the limbic dopamine neurones with the visual midbrain may account for the abnormal eye movements in schizophrenia.

Ellinwood and Escalante (1972) extended their cat studies and performed similar experiments on amphetamine intoxication in monkeys using escalating daily treatment for many months. Motor stereotypies could be seen readily but, in the later stages, it seemed that there was no longer any relationship between the motor acts and the objects to which the behaviour was generated; a deterioration of 'object relatedness'. In understanding stereotypy it is important to know if the animal is actually perceiving the object or objects being explored. Observation suggests that, at least in the early stage of drug intoxication, this is the case. Ellinwood and Escalante (1972) describe one of their monkeys:

Over a period of months, another female rhesus (Tanya) developed a repertoire of hand–eye examination patterns. The major component in these behaviours was picking or probing minute objects . . . The stereotypies included a picking and examination of sawdust in the cage and parts of the cage itself, picking and examining as part of grooming, and repeated examination of the feet. Several component behaviours composed these patterns. Picking or clasping a given object, followed by repeated examination of the hand, was an often displayed sequence. Tanya's examination of her hand consisted in repeatedly rubbing the thumb against the first three fingers and opening and closing the hand under close visual regard. This behavioural component was frequently manifested in a repetitious grooming response, in which the monkey would clasp her nose and then examine her hand for the results of that clasp. Early in the drug cycle, the repetitious examining patterns were carried out slowly and deliberately, with considerable visual attention. Later, it was noted that Tanya would frequently pick and clasp an object while visual attention was easily distracted or even directed elsewhere. Still later, the picking behaviour appeared autonomous and unrelated to the original purpose. At the same time, hand movements took on an athetoid quality. As the animal scrabbled on the floor of the cage, she frequently would pay no attention to this hand movement, which had evolved out of earlier examination of the contents of the cage floor.

In interpreting such observations, Ellinwood and Kilbey (1975) suggested that in its early stages, stereotypy represents more than a simple repetitious motor pattern; that indeed, it represents some level of perception but that deterioration in the perception and utilization of objects then occurs 'which may be analogous to the deterioration of thought processes observed in humans'.

A few experimenters have treated animals with very large doses of amphetamine over a short time period and have produced a rapid onset of behavioural changes. Ellison devised a passive pump mechanism to deliver amphetamine continuously to rats. A small silicone-walled pellet containing a high concentration of amphetamine base is prepared and implanted subcutaneously. For about 10 days amphetamine is released continuously but at a declining rate (Huberman *et al.* 1977). The effects of the drug were evaluated in rats living in a stable social environment (Ellison *et al.* 1978). Forty rats were thoroughly habituated to the large and interesting living chambers with sleeping burrows attached. Half were implanted with amphetamine pellets and the behaviour of the colony was monitored continuously. Over the first two days or so, the expected increases in locomotor activity and the emergence of species-specific stereotyped responding were observed in amphetamine-treated rats, with a concomitant decrease in social contact. After this the drugged rats withdrew for about 24 hours to the burrows and then emerged on Day 4 to show a high level of social interaction with the control animals, but this social behaviour was abnormal. The amphetamine-treated rats tended to goad the controls and to initiate antagonistic encounters which ended to their disadvantage; exaggerated fight-or-flight responses, fear-like startle responses, and vocalization were commonly observed in the drugged animals, which resulted in their being chased by the normal rats. Ellison pointed out that humans given small, frequent doses of amphetamines are initially aroused but become irritable and depressed, often withdrawing in isolation to their rooms. When they re-emerge paranoid delusions are often observed (Griffiths *et al*. 1972).

The slow-release amphetamine pellet has now been modified for use in monkeys. We have studied the behavioural effects of continuous amphetamine administration in three species of non-human primate, rhesus monkey, cynomologous monkey, and baboon, and studies have also been performed on the vervet monkey (Lyon and Nielsen 1979; Ellison *et al*. 1981).

In our study, with striking similarity in all species, profound behavioural changes occurred over a 10-day period after the implanation of the osmotic pump primed with *d*-amphetamine base (characteristic responses from a rhesus monkey are summarized in Fig. 3.3).

Enhanced arousal is initially noted which is characterized by increased *crossings* in the cage and rapid side-to-side head movements, *checking behaviour*. This phase merges rapidly into *stereotypy*, the repetition of fragmented abnormal motor acts which in monkeys tend to be individual-specific rather than the highly predictable species-specific patterns seen in rodents, other mammals, and lower vertebrates, (Randrup and Munkvad 1970, 1974). This is followed by a quiet phase before the emergence of abnormal and interesting behavioural patterns, The most prominent responses at this late stage were fixed *staring* at an abitrary point outside the cage or fixed staring at a part of the body, for no apparent reason. Similar responses have been reported in the Japanese macaque (Machiyama *et al*. 1970) and Cercopithecus (Kjellberg and Randrup 1972). These patterns of inappropriate staring were frequently interrupted by the behavioural elements classed as *sudden orient startle*. In the visual mode the monkey suddenly orientates to a place and then apparently flees, leaping across the cage, from an imaginary stimulus.

Behaviour was recorded throughout the 24 hours and, since these responses were observed in the middle of the night when all was quiet, we are encouraged to believe that the behaviour reflects hallucinations. In the tactile mode the same thing appears to happen; the monkey suddenly focuses attention to an area of skin and shows vigorous *grooming*. Complete grooming sequences are observed culminating in the animal bringing the non-existent groomed material to its mouth and chewing as if to consume an offending insect or bug. The behaviour may also be directed to the wall of the cage. The behaviour described as bug-catching is seen in all species, but most dramatically in the cynomologous monkeys and vervet monkeys (Ellison *et al*. 1981; Nielsen *et al*. 1983) and involves well-organized catching responses

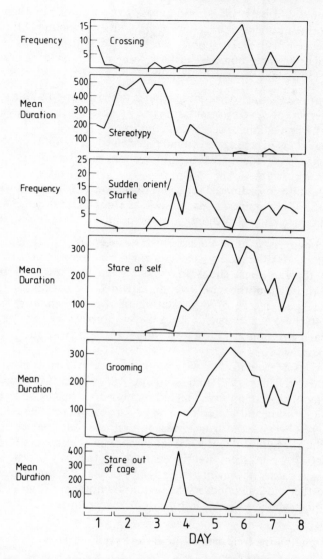

FIG. 3.3. Frequency and duration of six behavioural responses recorded over 24 hours per day for 8 days after implantation of amphetamine pellet. Behaviour was filmed and recorded for 1 minute every 30 minutes throughout the day and night. The scores from 4 rhesus monkeys were averaged to produce this figure.

into the air. The most important thing about these behaviours is that they are observed in the behavioural repertoire of the normal monkey but, under the influence of amphetamine, they occur in the absence of any detectable external stimulus. The high correlation of occurrence for startle/flee and self-stare/groom is suggestive of an introversion of attention and the latter behaviours have been likened to the delusions of parasitosis experienced by amphetamine, but particularly cocaine addicts (Gould and Gragg 1976).

While it is tempting to equate these behaviours with hallucinations in man, in the absence of subjective report, caution is demanded. Lyon and Nielsen (1979) suggested three objective criteria to be met in order to say with any degree of confidence that the probability of perceptual hallucination is high:

1. Clear orientating to a stimulus that is not visible or audible to a human observer, preferably orientating to a point in space within the confines of the immediate observation situation;
2. Clear signs of strong emotional reaction to this stimulus point (typical reactions include stiffening, piloerection, pupillary dilation, flight, or threat postures);
3. A definite co-ordinated sequence of responses orientated with respect to the given point in space (such as threatening action, scratching, biting, striking, or fleeing from the point of initial orientation).

The behaviours cannot be ascribed to sleep deprivation induced by amphetamine. Hallucinatory episodes did not develop in control monkeys placed in the same test situation, whose sleep was regularly but briefly disrupted throughout the night over an extended test period. The vividness, persistence, and degree of organization of the hallucinatory behaviours observed in these experiments and in vervet monkeys by Lyon and Nielsen (1979) when continuous drug exposure exists, is without precedent in previous studies.

Chronic, escalating dosage with amphetamine was used in rats and cats (Ellinwood and Kilbey 1977) and monkeys (Ridley *et al*. 1982) and some late-stage behaviours were observed including 'wet-dog' shakes, limb flick behaviour, hand staring and snatching. The slow-release experimental techniques are of interest because the drug is present for an extended period and thus the chronic pharmacological feature of schizophrenia or amphetamine psychosis is modelled. It would seem that the determining factor is not the level of the drug present, rather its *chronicity*. This may be why it is much more difficult to induce the late hallucinatory behaviours with acute drug dosage, even repeated high, daily doses, as in Ellinwood's experiments.

Acute amphetamine treatments—high-dose regimes

Acute treatment with amphetamine also provides models which fulfil the criteria of McKinney and, since they are much simpler to work with, they are used widely for evaluating antischizophrenic drugs.

In many species, the effects of acute treatment with high doses of amphetamine have been described. Motor behaviour becomes compulsive and stereotyped. It is interesting that motor stereotypy was presented by Bleuler as a fundamental symptom in schizophrenia. Rylander (1969) first drew attention to drug-induced motor stereotypy in addicts abusing the stimulant drug, phenmetrazine (*Preludin*) and he introduced the Swedish term 'punding' to describe a syndrome in which patients analyse objects of interest in a repetitive manner. Complex mechanical items such as clocks or cars are taken apart and reassembled; women sort their handbags or clean their apartment repetitively. The form of the stereotypy is idiosyncratic to the individual. Overt motor stereotypy is also observed, including pacing and grimacing.

Randrup and his colleagues provided a comprehensive study and description of amphetamine-induced stereotyped behaviour in many species and generated interest in the relationship between animal models of stereotypy and dopamine theories of schizophrenia (Munkvad *et al.* 1968). Rats, when treated with 5 mg/kg *d*-amphetamine remain in the same place with the head directed to the floor of the cage and persistent dorsal/ventral neck movements, sniffing, licking, and gnawing are observed for several hours. Some behaviours including self-grooming and social interaction are eliminated from the behavioural repertoire (Randrup and Munkvad 1971). Stereotyped behaviour takes different forms in different species. Cats move their head continuously from side to side as if looking about and dogs run continually in circles or back and forth along a fixed route. In primates, overt motor stereotypy may also be seen. Marmosets show a characteristic lateral head movement termed checking (Scraggs and Ridley 1978) and similar behaviour has been described in vervet monkeys (Lyon and Nielsen 1979). Interestingly, locomotor stereotypes have rarely been reported in primates.

If animals are first trained to make a particular response, this will be selectively enhanced under the drug. Rats, for example, stereotype lever-pressing once they have been trained on the operant task, although they rarely take the earned reinforcements (Randrup and Munkvad 1971). If the response element stimulated is compatible with the conditioned behaviour, amphetamine may actually enhance the output of conditioned behaviour. If, on the other hand, the preferentially stimulated response is incompatible with the conditioned behaviour, disruption of performance is seen. Lyon and Randrup (1972) reported an experiment in rats trained either to press and release a lever or to hold a lever down to obtain reward. Under stereotypic doses of amphetamine, performance on the former task was enhanced, while in the second condition holding down the lever was severely disrupted by the tendency to press and release. Such results suggest that the tendency to perform motor acts is stimulated by amphetamine. Lyon and Robbins (1975) presented a comprehensive theory of amphetamine action which suggests that as the dose of drug is raised response output is stimulated. However, those responses requiring a relatively long time for completion, e.g. a grooming sequence or social interaction, become progressively truncated and finally eliminated as behaviour comes to be dominated by brief motor acts repeated at a very high frequency.

As we shall see later, activation of the nigro-striatal DA system results in stereotyped behaviour. The striatum is a major forebrain output to the motor apparatus but also receives massive input from neocortex, particularly from areas like the frontal cortex involved in higher aspects of stimulus integration or cognition (Iversen 1984*a*). Thus, any model of stereotyped behaviour must account for the fact that in monkeys, and particularly in man, while stereo-typy has the essential feature of motor repetition, complex acts and thoughts may also be affected (Ridley and Baker 1982, 1983). A distinction was made between those processes which initiate and organize a motor response and those processes involved in the choice between possible behaviours (Ridley and Baker 1982, 1983). These authors distinguished and characterized the effect of amphetamine on both mechanisms by the use of a variety of dis-crimination tasks. For example, marmosets were trained within one session to discriminate reliably a pair of visual objects and then immediately to reverse that pattern of discriminative behaviour (e.g. stop responding to pre-viously rewarded toy ballerina and start responding to toy Indian, previously unrewarded but now, in the reversal phase, rewarded). When treated with 0.3 or 0.6 mg/kg amphetamine, difficulty was experienced in learning the reversal discrimination, although the initial discrimination of the session was unimpaired (Ridley *et al.* 1981). Failure could not be ascribed to the general perceptual disability since only reversal discrimination and not initial dis-crimination was impaired. Equally, motor repetition to the left or right response plaque did not account for the finding since the tendency to respond to the previously-rewarded object requires responses to left and right as the objects are randomly moved on each trial. Ridley and Baker (1983) suggested that amphetamine can act on the nervous system to maintain a neural programme which represents stimulus–reward associations, even when neural activity that determines stimulus choice and motor activity is changing. Since under the influence of amphetamine these neural programmes are maintained in the face of the contrary evidence from the environment, 'it is our belief that they may be equivalent to those which con-tribute to the maintenance of delusional beliefs in psychosis'. These effects were blocked by haloperidol reinforcing the view that neuroleptics do indeed suppress the cognitive disorders of schizophrenia and do not merely block striatal motor function.

Acute amphetamine treatment—low-dose regimes

Finally, we will consider the behavioural effects of low doses of amphetamine given acutely. In all species there is an increase in behavioural arousal.

In rodents, stimulation of locomotor arousal is seen clearly after low doses of amphetamine (0.5–1.5 mg/kg in the rat). There continues to be dispute as to whether or not exploration of interesting stimuli in the environment is also increased. File and Wardill (1975) using a hole board apparatus reported a decrease in exploration of the holes whereas Makajuola *et al.* (1977), also using a hole board, but with a slightly different test and rating conditions, claimed that amphetamine increases both hole exploration and stereotyped motor behaviour. The design of the test apparatus is crucial and if the stimuli are placed in a localized part of the apparatus, such as an alcove, it is clearly shown that amphetamine reduces exploration. This was the case in the study of Robbins and Iversen (1973) who explained the apparent reduction in exploration in terms of response incompatibility. The persistent locomotor behaviour induced by the drug occurred in the main body of the apparatus and this prevented the rat from approaching the interesting visual stimuli in the alcoves.

Acute or chronic amphetamine treatment failed to stimulate patterns of locomotor behaviour in the rhesus monkey (Fig.3.3). This is in agreement with the findings of Scraggs and Ridley (1978) in the marmoset, where *d*- and *l*-amphetamine increased lateral head movements (checking) and decreased grooming, social behaviour, and eating, but had no obvious effect on the amount of whole-body movement.

Fischman and Schuster (1977) studied, in the rhesus monkey, the effects of *d*-amphetamine on operantly conditioned behaviour. A DRL schedule was used which demands controlled low rates of operant responding. This species is extremely sensitive to the stimulant effects of amphetamine and, initially, doses of 0.0625 mg/kg increased lever pressing, disrupting operant behaviour in a manner suggesting that motor programmes were running out of control. However, tolerance to the disruptive motoric effects of amphetamine developed rapidly.

In man, amphetamine-like drugs have been used to improve performance, commonly in examination candidates, athletes, and military men in action. The characteristic effects of a minimal effective (2.5–15 mg) dose of amphetamine consist of feelings of relaxed alertness, energetic vitality, and confident assertiveness. Appetite and fatigue disappear; the person is not inclined to eat and cannot sleep. As the drug wears off some individuals experience tension and irritability. Larger doses (20–50 mg) often produce dysphoric anxiety and relaxed alertness is replaced by a 'driven' feeling. These increases in responsiveness have been likened to the heightened arousal and the disorders of attention seen in schizophrenia in which patients claim they are unable to deal with the barrage of sensory information hitting them.

NEUROPHARMACOLOGICAL BASIS OF AMPHETAMINE EFFECTS

Drugs which enhance the availability of dopamine at the receptor induce behavioural symptoms considered equivalent to features of schizophrenic behaviour. The identification of the brain dopamine pathways specifically mediating these behavioural responses would offer a neurological approach to the modelling of schizophrenia. A considerable amount of experimental work has been directed to this question. If such pathways were identified, it would be premature to assume that their dysfunction results in schizophrenia, but in view of the clinical efficacy of dopamine receptor-blocking drugs in schizophrenic illness it is reasonable to suppose that activity in these pathways is a corollary of schizophrenia. Accordingly, animal models involving damage, stimulation, or chronic dysfunction of the dopamine pathways could provide neurological symptoms, which themselves are not seen in schizophrenia and yet could provide a further means of evaluating novel drugs capable of modifying dopaminergic function.

Amphetamine releases dopamine and noradrenaline in brain and blocks the active re-uptake process in the nerve terminals by which the catecholamines released at the synapse are inactivated. Many experimenters have used biochemial tools to evaluate the role of NA and DA in the behavioural effects of amphetamine. Few, if any, of these tools have the biochemical selectivity demanded for such experiments. α-Methyltyrosine prevents the synthesis of NA and DA and convincingly blocks all the behavioural effects of amphetamine, but is also tends to suppress spontaneous behaviour. This is also true of dopamine-β-hydroxylase inhibitors which block the synthesis of NA and DA. These, and related studies, were admirably reviewed in Moore (1978).

Taylor and Snyder (1971) approached the problem in a different way. *In vitro* biochemical studies demonstrated that the *d*- and *l*-isomers of amphetamine have different potencies on a number of biochemical measures. *d*-Amphetamine was 10 times more potent than the *l*-isomer in blocking catecholamine uptake into crude synaptosomes prepared from cerebral cortex, a tissue rich in NA rather than DA. By contrast, on striatal (predominantly DA innervation) synaptosomes, the isomers were roughly equipotent (Coyle and Snyder 1969). Similar results were obtained by Taylor and Snyder (1971) studying the effects of amphetamine isomers on uptake of intraventricularly administered, radioactively labelled NA or DA. It was suggested that the greater stereoselectivity of the response of noradrenergic than of dopaminergic neurones to amphetamine, afforded a way of evaluating if the behavioural effects induced by amphetamine were mediated by NA or DA neuronal systems.

In other words, behaviours mediated by NA should be affected more by *d*-than *l*-amphetamine, whereas the isomers should be equipotent on behaviours mediated by DA. In behavioural studies, Taylor and Snyder (1971) found a 10:1 potency ratio of the isomers on locomotor behaviour and a 2:1 ratio of stereotypy. The heuristic value of this suggestion was appealing and generated much interest and work. Angrist *et al.* (1971) found both isomers equipotent in inducing amphetamine psychosis in man and interpreted this as support for the dopaminergic hypothesis of amphetamine psychosis.

In the ensuing decade the clear initial findings have been progressively eroded. A number of experimenters have failed to replicate the equal or 2:1 ratio of the *d*- and *l*-isomers on dopamine systems. Harris and Baldessarini (1973) found a 4:1 ratio on dopamine uptake into striatal synaptosomes and a 2:1 ratio in cortex. Holmes and Ruttledge (1976), using amphetamine-induced release of dopamine as a measure, reported ratios of 5:1 and 2:1 in striatum and cortex respectively.

Thus, it is now generally accepted that selective involvement of the NA rather than DA system cannot be concluded on the basis of greater stimulation by the *d*- than the *l*-isomer of the behaviour under study. In the words of Bunney *et al.* (1975) 'What appeared at first as a simple clear cut pharmacological tool for determining the specific catecholamine system responsible for mediating certain behaviours has become exceedingly complex'.

Lesion studies have played a more important part in defining the relative roles of DA and NA in the behavioural effects of amphetamine. In pioneering studies of this kind, Randrup and his colleagues demonstrated in a number of different ways that striatal dopamine mediated the stereotyped behaviour induced by amphetamine.

With selective lesion studies it has now been demonstrated that brain DA is necessary for both the locomotor and stereotyped response to amphetamine. Creese and Iversen (1975) injected the catecholeamine toxin 6-hydroxydopamine (6-OHDA) bilaterally into the substantia nigra of the rat to deplete both the nigro-striatal and the mesolimbic DA-containing pathways and found blockade of both the locomotor and stereotyped response to acute doses of amphetamine. Subsequently, Kelly *et al.* (1975) refined the lesion technique by injecting 6-OHDA locally into the DA-terminal regions of the caudate/putamen or nucleus accumbens, to achieve selective lesions to either the nigro-striatal or the limbic DA pathways. Testing low and high doses of *d*-amphetamine and the DA agonist apomorphine, they demonstrated that limbic DA loss abolished locomotor arousal induced by 1.5 mg/kg *d*-amphetamine and enhanced apomorphine-induced locomotion. In contrast, striatal DA loss prevented the emergence of stereotyped behaviour in response to higher doses of amphetamine. This double dissociation of the stimulant effects of amphetamine and apomorphine to different sectors of the forebrain DA trajectory has now been verified in a number of laboratories.

Since experimental psychosis following chronic amphetamine exposure models florid schizophrenia most closely, it would be interesting to study the effect of selective dopamine lesions on the emergence and pattern of abnormal behaviour after such drug regimes. Equally appropriate are non-invasive imageing techniques for quantifying activity in brain during drug-induced behavioural states. The 2-deoxyglucose method can be used to measure activity in the nigro-striatal and mesolimbic dopamine pathways of rats exposed to acute high doses of amphetamine or to chronic amphetamine released from a slow diffusion device; the former drug regime induces stereotyped motor behaviour and the latter late-stage 'hallucinatory' behaviours. It was found that both the striatal and limbic dopamine areas were activated after acute drug treatment but only the mesolimbic system in the late stage of amphetamine intoxication (Eison *et al.* 1981; Orzi *et al.* 1983). These findings support the lesion results implicating the nigro-striatal system in stereotyped motor behaviour and the limbic system in the florid affective features of amphetamine psychosis and, it is suggested, of schizophrenia.

THE USE OF ANIMAL MODELS FOR EVALUATING ANTISCHIZOPHRENIC DRUGS

All effective antipsychotic drugs, with varying selectivity, block either or both D_1 and D_2 receptors and, since D_1 and D_2 receptors exist in both striatal and limbic areas, models involving activation or damage to either sector of the forebrain DA system may be used. An animal model does not have to fulfil all the criteria of McKinney and Bunney to be useful for drug screening purposes. In fact the most widely used models for detecting dopamine receptor blocking drugs involve behaviours remote from the schizophrenia syndrome but nevertheless dependent on forebrain dopamine pathways. In rats, amphetamine and apomorphine-induced locomotor behaviour (models of the limbic dopamine pathway) and stereotyped behaviour (models of the striatal dopamine pathway) are used extensively for evaluating neuroleptics. Locomotor activity can be measured automatically with photocell devices and stereotypy rated with ordinal scales, although it is important to remember that such scales do not imply any lawful relationship between the behaviours rated, nor should the ratings be interpreted in quantitative terms.

Dopamine or dopamine agonists can be injected directly into the dopamine-rich terminal areas of striatum to induce locomotor or stereotyped behaviour (Pijnenburg *et al.* 1975; Costall and Naylor 1976). In mice, systemic apomorphine induces a robust climbing behaviour (Costall *et al.* 1982) which is simple to measure and has been very useful for evaluating neuroleptics. There are striking correlations between neuroleptic antagonism of these behaviours and the clinical efficacy of the drugs.

Models even further from the clinical state involve experimental manipulation of the dopamine pathways. Notable amongst them is the screening test developed by Ungerstedt (1971) which capitalized on the symmetric nature of the basal ganglia motor circuits. In rodents, a unilateral 6-OHDA lesion to the nigro-striatal dopamine neurones results in motor asymmetry, which can be enhanced with dopaminergic stimulant drugs to induce rotational behaviour. The frequency and the direction of the rotation is determined by the degree of activation of the intact or denervated dopamine system. Drugs which reduce dopamine function block rotational behaviour.

DA neurone autoreceptors provide an alternative and powerful means of reducing functional activity in the nigro-striatal DA pathway (Bannon and Roth 1983). Low doses of apomorphine and other DA agonists activate these receptors to lower activity in DA neurones and reduce the output of spontaneous motor behaviour, whereas higher doses activate the post-synaptic receptor to enhance motor behaviour. Systemic administration of DA agonists to mice induces a dose-related reduction in locomotor behaviour blocked by DA receptor antagonists (Martin and Bendesky 1984).

MODELS FOR ATYPICAL OR MORE SELECTIVE NEUROLEPTICS

It is accepted that there are at least two DA receptor types, that the different dopamine pathways are involved in different motor functions, and that neuroleptic drugs have neuropharmacological actions in addition to dopamine receptor blockade. It now becomes important to identify and use a range of models which will differentiate compounds in terms of these additional properties.

For example, the phenothiazine and butyrophenone drugs effectively antagonize amphetamine- or apomorphine-induced rotation in the nigro-striatal model. However, it was reported that thioridazine and clozapine, two effective antipsychotic agents which block dopamine receptors, were unable to antagonize rotational behaviour (Kelly and Miller 1975). It was demonstrated that these compounds have anticholinergic, in addition to antidopaminergic activity.

In striatum, dopamine and acetylcholine exist in functional balance, such that dopamine over- or under-activity is reflected in a reciprocal change in cholinergic function. Since, in striatum, thioridazine and clozapine simultaneously block both dopamine receptors and the induced cholinergic imbalance (Seeger *et al.* 1982), the output of the striatum is essentially unchanged and thus motor output (rotation) remains unchanged. In the case of these drugs, a secondary pharmacological property masks the primary effect when the rotational model is used for their evaluation. Other models of the nigro-striatal system, including neuroleptic-induced catalepsy or impairment of shock avoidance behaviour are also relatively insensitive to these atypical neuroleptics. At the neurophysiological level it has been demonstrated that, whereas classical neuroleptics increase the firing of both the substantia nigra A9 DA neurones and the ventral tegmental A10 DA neurones, clozapine, thioridazine, and sulpiride increase the firing only in the limbic DA neurones (White and Wang 1983).

If the dopamine blockade achieved by the atypical neuroleptics in striatum is functionally neutralized by their anticholinergic activity, then their proven antipsychotic activity must depend on dopamine receptor blockade outside the striatal system, i.e. in limbic or cortical areas. Thus, it would be predicted that in models of non-striatal DA function, these neuroleptics would be active. Indeed this is the case. In models of limbic DA function, including locomotor activity induced with systemic (Iversen and Koob 1977) or intracerebral drug infusions (Pijnenburg *et al.* 1975; Costall and Naylor 1976) all classes of neuroleptic drug, including thioridazine and clozapine (Costall and Naylor 1975) and other so-called atypical neuroleptics, are active.

Chronic treatment with neuroleptic drugs results in unwanted motor side-effects (dyskinesias of late onset, so-called tardive dyskinesia), and there is reason to believe that this is due to their effect in striatum. The atypical neuroleptics with their minimal functional disruption of striatum do not result in tardive dyskinesia as frequently as the phenothiazines and butyrophenones. If the supposition is upheld that the unwanted side-effects of neuroleptics are related to the striatal site of action, then neuroleptics with more selective action on limbic and cortical dopamine targets should be interesting antipsychotic agents with a low risk for parkinsonian symptoms and tardive dyskinesia. This is claimed for the limbic selective D2 antagonists, sulpiride, and remoxipride.

A corollary of this is that, when new neuroleptics are studied, animal models of the dopamine receptors in striatum (rotation, catalepsy, avoidance behaviour) are the most relevant for predicting the risk of unwanted side-effects. Indeed, it is generally accepted that the ability of neuroleptics to induce catalepsy in rodents correlates well with this risk factor. The phenothiazines and butyrophenones have profound effects on striatal as well as non-striatal DA systems and have induced marked catalepsy in animals. Clozapine, thioridazine, and the substituted benzamides have their major effect on the limbic system and do not induce severe catalepsy in rodents.

Much has been said of the ability of neuroleptic drugs to block dopamine-mediated behaviours. But ultimately we have to ask if these drugs normalize schizophreniform behaviour in the patient or the animal model or merely dampen all behavioural output and thus apparently achieve improvement of the symptomatology. Clinical opinion appears divided and many doubt that neuroleptics control the fundamental symptoms of schizophrenia and restructure disorganized behaviour. It has become generally accepted that the florid symptoms, including hallucinations and delusions as assessed by standard rating scales, are controlled by neuroleptic treatment and intensified by amphetamine (Angrist *et al.* 1980*a*). Less attention has been paid to the fine structure of the 'controlled' behaviour. Further quantitative studies of the effect of neuroleptics on the thought disorders of schizophrenia and on the animal models of this condition are badly needed.

In one of the few studies of this kind Ridley *et al.* (1979) reported that in marmosets, although a number of behavioural elements enhanced by the drug amphetamine were reduced with haloperidol, some aspects of the behavioural disruption were not improved. Social interaction, which was dramatically reduced after chronic amphetamine treatment was, for example, not reinstated by haloperidol. However, the lack of social behaviour in amphetamine-treated animals has been likened to the emotional deterioration seen in schizophrenia and classed as a defect or negative symptoms rather than a feature of the florid disease state. What is becoming clear is that in man the negative or defect features of schizophrenia are not improved by neuroleptics or exacerbated by amphetamine (Angrist *et al.* 1980*b*).

THE ROLE OF NA AND 5HT IN MODELS OF SCHIZOPHRENIA

NA pathways of the forebrain appear not to be involved directly in amphetamine models of schizophrenia. Lesions to the forebrain NA pathways did not result in attenuation of the motoric effects of amphetamine (Creese and Iversen 1975). On the contrary, it has generally been found that responses to amphetamine are enhanced when brain NA function is reduced with biochemical treatments or lesions, suggesting a reciprocal relationship between NA and DA innervations in forebrain (Antelman and Caggiula 1977).

Bearing in mind that amphetamine releases NA as well as DA, and that the phenothiazines, which are highly effective antipsychotics, block NA as well as DA receptors, one cannot feel entirely confident in ruling out a component of NA dysfunction in schizophrenia.

5HT is also found in high concentration in dopamine terminal areas of brain. The median raphe is the origin of the striatal innervation. 5HT lesions, 5HT agonists and antagonists modify the behavioural response to acute doses of amphetamine and apomorphine. Amphetamine stereotypy is decreased when 5HT synthesis is increased and enhanced when 5HT synthesis is inhibited or 5HT receptors blocked with drugs or lesions to 5HT pathways (Breese *et al.* 1974; Costall and Naylor 1974). These results suggest a normal inhibitory role of 5HT in forebrain. On the other hand, selective increase in brain 5HT itself achieved with 5HT-releasing drugs such as *p*-chloroamphetamine or fenfluramine (Jacobs 1976) or by treatment with the 5HT percursor, tryptophan (+ MAO inhibitor) (Green and Grahame-Smith 1974), produces a characteristic motor syndrome including increased locomotion, hindlimb abduction, head weaving, forepaw treading, tremor, 'wet dog' shakes, and straub tail.

This pattern of results suggests that 5HT may have an excitatory effect and it remains to be clarified if the same or different neural substrates mediate these opposing effects of 5HT release. Gerson and Baldessarini (1980) concluded 'recent evidence suggests that different components of such motor behaviour have dissimilar neurophysiologic bases. We propose that inhibitory effects of 5HT on spontaneous activity may be mediated by ascending projections of 5HT to forebrain, whereas excitatory influences on other motor behaviours may be activated by descending or spinal tracts'.

Simultaneous release of or increase in brain of DA and 5HT results in yet another behavioural syndrome characterized by backward walking and circling. High doses of amphetamine (15–25 mg/kg) or fenfluramine and *p*-chloroamphetamine (25 mg/kg) induce this behaviour. Curzon *et al.* (1980) discussed this syndrome in relation to schizophrenia pointing out that in man both amphetamine and fenfluramine (Griffiths *et al.* 1975) in very high doses cause psychotic behaviour including hallucinations. A wide range of hallucinogens including psilocybin, LSD, mescaline, and the mixed morphine agonist/antagonist drugs like cyclazocine, pentazocine, and levallorphan all produce backward walking in animals suggesting a relationship between this element of abnormal behaviour and hallucinations. Hallucinations figure prominently in amphetamine psychosis and in schizophrenia, which it resembles; thus it is speculated that 'not only catecholamine neurones but also 5HT neurones are involved in the development of amphetamine psychosis and that backward walking may be an animal model of human amphetamine psychosis and perhaps also for paranoid schizophrenia' (Curzon *et al.* 1980). Before the advent of the DA hypothesis, serious attention was given to the possibility that abnormal 5HT activity was involved in schizophrenia. Recent findings suggest that it is timely to reconsider this possibility. Sedval (1980) obtained evidence of raised 5HT turnover in familial schizophrenia and Enna (1980) reported lowered LSD binding sites in autopsy brain material from schizophrenics. Finally, Leysen *et al.*

(1978) discovered that certain neuroleptics act as antagonists at 5HT receptors as well as at DA receptors. This is particularly dramatic in frontal cortex and they commented: 'The present observations do not detract from the dopamine theory of schizophrenia, but they do imply that a broadening of this theory to cover serotonergic processes may increase our understanding of the complexity of disorders'.

BEHAVIOURAL MODELS OF SCHIZOPHRENIA

In recent years studies of schizophrenia have focused closely on pharmacological models. To date, it is the positive or Type I symptoms of the illness which have been effectively modelled in animals and we have not yet come to grips with the fundamental negative symptoms of Kraepelin's disease state.

Thus, it is a matter of importance to consider other approaches to the study of schizophrenia. While it seems likely that chemical imbalance is a neurobiological correlate of psychosis, the precipitating factor in schizophrenia is clearly not a drug. To pursue the aetiology of schizophrenia we must look to genetic and environmental factors which presumably predispose to chemical imbalance.

Studies on the role of dopamine systems of brain in relation to behavioural control lead to a model which proposes that the mesolimbic and nigro-striatal DA systems operate in parallel to mediate motivation and arousal and initiate sequencing of appropriate motor behaviour (Iversen 1984a). A third dopamine pathway has been described, the mesocortical system which innervates frontal cortex and other areas of juxta-allocortex. Our knowledge of this pathway is based largely on studies of the frontal cortex innervated by mesencephalic DA neurones, an area of cortex, which has topographical efferent projections to both dorsal and ventral striatum, the areas receiving nigro-striatal and mesolimbic dopamine innervation. The role of the cortical DA loop may be to inhibit the dorsal and ventral striata since it has been found that lesions of the frontal cortex in rat enhance behavioural responses mediated by the striatum such as amphetamine-induced stereotypy and locomotor activity (Carter and Pycock 1980).

In man the frontal lobes are concerned with complex cognitive behaviour and, via efferent projections to striatum, have their access to motor behaviour (Iversen 1984a). It is probably at this frontal site (Brozoski *et al.* 1979) that DA could be said to be involved in intellectual functions and thus influence the interaction between thought and action. It is tempting to speculate that imbalance in these three co-ordinated DA systems could account for the range of florid positive symptoms in schizophrenia and amphetamine psychosis.

ANATOMICAL MODELS OF SCHIZOPHRENIA

But how could the DA system become overactive? One possibility is that the dopamine neurones become spontaneously overactive. Stevens and Livermore (1978) emphasized that the DA neurones do not operate in isolation but are modulated by a number of chemically coded inputs to the substantia nigra (SN) or ventral tegmental area (VTA). Pathways containing NA, ACh, GABA, Substance P, and a number of other neuropeptides innervate the SN and VTA and influence the activity of DA neurones. Chronic dysfunction of such modulatory pathways could be expected to influence dopaminergic activity and thereby the function of the forebrain structures innervated by these neurones. It is suggested that the dorsal and ventral striata function to gate or filter information from neo- and limbic cortex and interference with dopamine-mediated modulation of these striatal gates should 'lead to characteristic species-specific disturbance of perception and behaviour' (Stevens and Livermore 1978).

This model was developed on the basis of experiments on freely moving cats given repeated injections of the GABA blocking drug, bicuculline, into the ventral tegmental origins of the mesolimbic/cortical DA pathways to reduce inhibitory control. Marked behavioural changes were observed including intense arousal, hypervigilance, orientating, slinking, crouching, searching, sniffing, and side-to-side looking behaviour. Similar experiments were performed using the kindling method described by Goddard *et al.* (1969) to induce changes in cerebral excitability by repeated focal stimulation of the brain with an electrical current that is initially too low to elicit any detectable behavioural change. Activation of the dopamine neurones of the VTA in this way resulted in a behaviour similar to that seen after bicuculline injection and in both cases abnormal electrical spike activity was recorded in the nucleus accumbens. Similar electrical abnormality has been demonstrated in chronic schizophrenics and Stevens and Livermore (1978) raised the possibility that experimental kindling of the inhibitory pathways impinging on dopamine neurones in schizophrenia might provide a viable means of down regulating dopamine overactivity.

It has been demonstrated in rats that dopaminergic neurones are readily sensitized by certain chronic sensory inputs. In a number of different experimental paradigms it has been shown that the behavioural responses to amphetamine are enhanced if the rat is exposed to unavoidable, albeit mild stress. For example, tail pinch has been studied as a non-specific arousing stimulus in the rat which activates dopaminergic neurones (Antelman *et al.* 1980). After experiencing tail pinch for 12 daily test sessions, rats showed enhanced locomotor and stereotypy in response to amphetamine. Similarly, low doses of amphetamine sensitize to further doses of the drug and a single dose of amphetamine (Antelman and Chiodo 1983) enhances the species-specific behaviour induced by subsequent tail pinch. Antelman proposed that stress 'is an important factor in any model of schizophrenia and that interchangeability of stress and amphetamine can account for a number of observations in the literature'. Acute psychosis can be precipitated by stress (Gardos and Cole 1978) and stress can reinstate amphetamine psychosis in abstinent individuals during remission (Utena 1974). Likewise, schizophrenics appear to be especially sensitive to the psychotogenic effects of amphetamine (Janowsky and Davis 1974) and individuals with a vulnerability to stress would show an enhanced response to amphetamine, which could account for the extreme variation in amphetamine dosage required to induce psychotic reactions in individuals with no record of schizophrenia. The midbrain-cortical DA pathway could be involved in the pathological response to stress. In experimental animals stress activates the frontal dopamine system (Thierry *et al.* 1976) and this biochemical response, like that to neuroleptic drugs (Scatton 1977), does not show the rapid tolerance observed in subcortical dopamine systems under the same experimental conditions (Thierry *et al.* 1978).

The unique responsiveness of the cortical DA system is ascribed to the lack of DA autoreceptor control of this subpopulation of the ventral tegmental DA neurones (Bannon and Roth 1983). Since these neurones maintain their response to neuroleptics during chronic treatment, it has been suggested that they play a crucial part in the therapeutic effect of these drugs.

Chronic stress in susceptible individuals could result in dysfunction in this cortical control system and a consequent release of subcortical sites from cortical control. The biochemical correlate of this circuitry imbalance may not be revealed as dramatic changes of transmitter level in DA neurones and yet blockade of the basal ganglia output with neuroleptic drugs would be clinically efficacious. According to this hypothesis the failure to observe heightened dopamine activity in the brains of patients dying with schizophrenia would not be unexpected.

Biochemical changes should be sought in other parts of the complex circuitry interacting with the mesencephalic DA system (Iversen 1984*b*). A recent finding of raised DA in the left amygdala is particularly interesting (Reynolds 1983) and illustrates the importance of investigating interhemispheric dysfunction in widespread forebrain circuits rather than focusing only on the DA neurones of the basal ganglia.

The direct evidence for cortical pathology in florid schizophrenia is equally limited, although comparisons have been made between the psychological defects in schizophrenia and those seen in frontal lobe pathology. Already there is evidence from EEG studies of abnormal asymmetric electrical activity in psychosis (Tucker 1983; Gruzelier 1983). The search for an anatomical basis of schizophrenia has not been exhaustive and, with the introduction of new brain imaging techniques, a revival of interest will be seen.

Dynamic interactions in CNS mechanisms are difficult to study and to date have been impossible to investigate in the living brain. With new imaging techniques it will become possible to detect regional changes and fluctuations in the activity of brain circuits in living man and evaluate the neuropathological correlates of scizophrenia *in situ*.

Such methods will also allow us to evaluate the closely related hypothesis which suggests that neuronal degeneration processes occur in schizophrenia. Circuitry dysfunctions of the kind referred to could occur as a consequence of degeneration in related anatomical systems. Indeed, there is evidence that acute damage to one forebrain monoamine system results in increased activity in another pathway innervating the same target area (Emson and Koob 1978).

Reibaud *et al.* (1984) showed that the responsiveness of the dopamine receptors (D_1) of the nucleus accumbens is controlled both by the dopaminergic input from the ventral tegmental area and the non-dopaminergic input from the frontal cortex. After frontal cortex lesions dopamine receptor binding in NAS increased by 14 per cent but, after a combined lesion to the dopamine neurones innervating NAS and the frontal cortex, binding increased by 52 per cent. The implication of these findings is that a progressive functional pathology of the monoamine system and the frontal cortex could account for the dopamine overactivity in schizophrenia.

Could a progressive degeneration also account for the symptoms of the defect state schizophrenia? Crow (1980) suggested that the florid symptoms of schizophrenia represent one disease state related to dopamine overactivity and the defect state reflects a distinct disease, characterized by degeneration of the brain and not specifically related to dopamine dysfunction. Since in a proportion of patients positive symptoms give way to negative ones, it is tempting to speculate that at least in some schizophrenics a progressive change in some essential brain system occurs which controls the output of the striatum.

Degeneration or chronic dysfunction of the non-striatal dopamine pathway could account for the clinical observations. Minimal damage or temporary blockade of dopamine neurones leads to supersensitivity of the postsynaptic dopamine receptors. With experimental lesions to the dopamine cell bodies, such a process can be demonstrated dramatically. A partial lesion to the nigro-striatal DA pathway in rats results in supersensitivity of the DA receptors, the increase correlating with the level of depletion (Creese *et al.* 1977). The remaining DA neurones show enhanced levels of neurophysiological (Schultz and Ungerstedt 1978) and biochemical activity (Agid *et al.* 1973). The net outcome of these two compensatory factors is supra-normal levels of stimulation at the postsynaptic site. Under such experimental conditions amphetamine responses are enhanced rather than attenuated (Brook and Iversen 1975).

Could such a mechanism account for florid psychosis involving imbalance in perception (hallucinations), cognition (thought disorder), and emotion (paranoia)? After progressive and chronic dysfunction these mechanisms may no longer be able to compensate and a lack of behavioural output or negative symptoms is seen. It is at this stage that pathological changes associated with ventricular enlargement have been consistently observed (Crow 1980) and, in schizophrenic patients with verified brain atrophy, van Kammen *et al.* (1983) found reduced DA metabolites and dopamine-β-hydroxylase activity in spinal fluid. Long-term changes in limbic and cortical areas with the concurrent imbalance in related chemical systems of brain could be expected to result in profound and varied disorders of behaviour and cognition rather than the frank motor deficiencies seen after nigro-striatal dopamine damage in Parkinson's disease. It is exactly this slow degeneration of DA neurones which occurs in the nigro-striatal system of parkinsonian patients, and although the final outcome in this disease fits the proposed model, the early overactivity phase has no obvious clinical concomitant. The limitation of animal experimentation is that we try to achieve with a single manipulation in time, a model of a disease progressing over many years. This proved to be the case when attempting to model Parkinson's disease with acute non-specific lesions to the basal ganglia in the monkey, and I have no doubt that we face the same problem in attempting to model schizophrenia in animals.

ACKNOWLEDGEMENT

The author received support from the Wellcome Trust for experimental work on amphetamine psychosis. The help of Burt Angrist is gratefully acknowledged both in discussion at the time the manuscript was prepared and in reviewing the text.

References

Agid, Y., Javoy, F., and Glowinski, J. (1973). Hyperactivity of remaining dopaminergic neurones after partial destruction of the nigro-striatal dopaminergic system in the rat. *Nature, New Biol.* **245**, 150-1.

Angrist, B. M. and Gershon, S. (1970). The phenomenology of experimentally induced amphetamine psychosis—preliminary observations. *Biol. Psychiat.* **2**, 95-107.

—— Rotrosen, J., and Gershon, S. (1980*a*). Response to apomorphine, amphetamine and neuroleptics in schizophrenic subjects . *Psychopharmacology* **67**, 31-8.

——, ——, —— (1980*b*) Differential effects of amphetamine and neuroleptics on negative vs. positive symptoms in schizophrenia. *Psychopharmacology* **72**, 17-19.

—— Sathananthan, G., and Gershon, S. (1973). Behavioural effects of L-Dopa in schizophrenic patients. *Psychopharmacologia* **31**, 1-12.

—— and Sudilovsky, A. (1978). Central nervous system stimulants: historical aspects and clinical effects. In *Handbook of psychopharmacology* (ed. S. D. Iversen and S. H. Snyder), Vol. 2, p. 99-165. Plenum Press, New York.

Antelman, S. M. and Caggiula, A. R. (1977). Norepinephrine–dopamine interactions and behaviour. *Science* **195**, 646-53.

—— and Chiodo, L. A. (1983). Amphetamine, as a stressor. In *Stimulants: Neurochemical, behavioural and clinical prospectives* (ed. I. Creese), pp. 269-99. Raven Press, New York.

—— Eichler, H. T., Black, C. A., and Kocen, D. (1980). Interchangeability of stress and amphetamine in sensitization. *Science* **207**, 329-31.

Bannon, M. J. and Roth, R. H. (1983). Pharmacology of mesocortical dopamine neurons. *Pharm. Rev.* **35**, 53-68.

Bell, D. S. (1965). Comparison of amphetamine psychosis and schizophrenia. *Br. J. Psychiat.* **111**, 701-7.

Bleuler, E. (1911). *Dementia praecox.* (Translated in 1950 by H. Zinkin.) International University Press, New York.

Breese, G. R., Cooper, B. R., and Mueller, R. A. (1974). Evidence for involvement of 5-hydroxytryptamine in the actions of amphetamine. *Br. J. Pharmacol.* **52**, 307-14.

Brook, M. C. and Iversen, S. D. (1975), Changed eating and locomotor behaviour in rat after 6-hydroxydopamine lesions to the substantia nigra. *Neuropharmacology* **14**, 95–105.

Brozoski, T. J., Brown, R. M., Rosvold, H. E., and Goldman, P. S. (1979). Cognitive deficit caused by regional depletion of dopamine in prefrontal cortex of rhesus monkey. *Science* **205**, 929–32.

Bunney, B. S., Walters, J. R., Kuhar, M. J., Roth, R. H., and Aghajanian, G. K. (1975). D- and L-amphetamine stereo-isomers: Comparative potencies in affecting the firing of central dopaminergic and noradrenergic neurons. *Psychopharmacol. Commun.* **1**, 177–90.

Carter, C. J. and Pycock, C. J. (1980). Behavioural and biochemical effects of dopamine and noradrenaline depletion within the medial prefrontal cortex of the rat. *Brain Res.* **192**, 163–76.

Christensen, A. V., Hyttel, A. J., Larsen, J. J., and Sevendson, O. (1984). Pharmacological effects of a specific dopamine D1 antagonist SCH 23390 in comparison with neuroleptics. *Life Sci.* **34**, 1529–40.

Cohen D. J. and Young J. G. (1977). Neurochemistry and child psychiatry. *J. Am. Acad. Child Psychiat.* **16**, 353–411.

Connell, P. H. (1958). *Amphetamine psychosis*. Maudsley Monograph No. 5, Oxford University Press, Oxford.

Costall, B., Eniojukan, J. F., and Naylor, R. J. (1982). Spontaneous climbing behaviour of mice, its measurement and dopaminergic involvement. *Eur. J. Pharmacol.* **85**, 125–32.

—— and Naylor, R. J. (1974). Stereotyped circling behaviour induced by dopaminergic agonists after lesions of the midbrain raphe nuclei. *Eur. J. Pharmacol.* **29**, 206–22.

——, —— (1975). Detection of neuroleptic properties of clozapine, sulpiride and thioridazine. *Psychopharmacologia* **43**, 69–74.

——, —— (1976). Antagonism of the hyperactivity induced by dopamine applied intracerebrally to the nucleus accumbens septi by typical neuroleptics and by clozapine, sulpiride and thioridazine. *Eur. J. Pharmacol.* **35**, 161–8.

Coyle, J. T. and Snyder, S. H. (1969). Catecholamine uptake by synaptosomes in homogenates of rat brain: stereospecificity in different area. *J. Pharmacol. exp. Ther.* **170**, 221–31.

Creese, I. N. R., Burt, D. R., and Snyder, S. H. (1976). Dopamine receptor binding predicts clinical and pharmacological potencies of antischizophrenic drugs. *Science* **192**, 481–3.

——, ——, —— (1977). Dopamine receptor binding enchancement accompanying lesion-induced behavioural supersensitivity. *Science* **197**, 596–8.

—— and Iversen, S. D. (1975). The pharmacological and anatomical substrates of the amphetamine response in the rat. *Brain Res.* **83**, 419–36.

Crow, T. J. (1980). Molecular pathology of schizophrenia: more than one disease process? *Bri. med. J.* **280**, 66–8.

Curzon, G., Fernando, J. C. R., and Lees, A. J. (1980). Behaviour provoked by simultaneous release of dopamine and serotonin: possible relevance to psychotic behaviour. In *Enzymes and neurotransmitters in mental disease* (ed. E., Usdin, T. L., Sourkes, and M. B. H., Youdim), pp. 411–30. Wiley, Chichester.

Eison, M. S., Eison, A. S., and Ellison, G. (1981). The distribution of *d*-amphetamine and local glucose utilization in rat brain during continuous amphetamine administration. *Exp. Brain Res.* **43**, 281–8.

Ellinwood, E. H. and Escalante, D. O. (1972). Chronic methamphetamine intoxication in three species of experimental animals. In *Current concepts of amphetamine abuse* (ed. E. H. Ellinwood and S. Cohen), p. 959. US Government Printing Office, Washington DC.

—— and Kilbey, M. M. (1975). Amphetamine stereotypy: The influence of environmental factors and prepotent behavioural patterns on its topography and development. *Biol. Psychiat.* **10**, 3–16.

——, —— (1977). Chronic stimulant intoxication models of psychosis. In *Animal models in psychiatry and neurology* (ed. I. Hanin and E. Usdin), pp. 61–74. Pergamon Press, Oxford.

—— Sudilovsky, A., and Nelson, L. (1972). Behavioural analysis of chronic amphetamine intoxication. *Biol. Psychiat.* **4**, 215–30.

Ellison, G., Eison, M. S., and Huberman, H. S. (1978). Stages of constant amphetamine intoxication: Delayed appearance of paranoid-like behaviours in rat colonies. *Psychopharmacology* **56**, 293–9.

—— Nielsen, E. B., and Lyon, M. (1981). Animal model of psychosis: Hallucinatory behaviours in monkeys during the late stage of continuous amphetamine intoxication. *J. Psychiat. Res.* **16**, 13–22.

Emson, P. C. and Koob, G. F. (1978). The origin and distribution of dopamine-containing afferents to the rat cortex. *Brain Res.* **142**, 249–67.

Enna, S. J. (1980). Drug and disease induced alterations in brain serotonin receptors. In *Serotonin: current aspects of neurochemistry and function* (ed. B. Haber), pp. 347–58. Plenum, New York.

File, S. E. and Wardill, A. C. (1975). Validity of head-dipping as a measure of exploration in a modified hole board. *Psychopharmacologia* **44**, 53–9.

Fischman, M. W. and Schuster, C. R. (1977). Long-term behavioural changes in the rhesus monkey after multiple daily injections of *d*-methylamphetamine. *J. Pharmacol. exp. Ther.* **201**, 593.

Gardos, G. and Cole, J. O. (1978). Maintenance antipsychotic therapy: From whom and how long? In *Psychopharmacology: a generation of progress* (ed. M. A. Lipton, A. Di Mascio, and K. F. Killman), pp. 1169–78. Raven Press, New York.

Gerson, S. C. and Baldessarini, R. J. (1980). Motor effects of serotonin in the central nervous system. *Life Sci.* **27**, 1435–51.

Goddard, G. V., McIntyre, D. C., and Leech, C. K. (1969). A permanent change in brain function resulting from daily electrical stimulation. *Exp. Neurol.* **25**, 296–330.

Gould, W. M. and Gragg, T. M. (1976). Delusions of parasitosis: an approach to the problem. *Arch. Dermatol.* **112**, 1745–8.

Green, A. R. and Grahame-Smith, D. G. (1974). The role of brain dopamine in the hyperactivity syndrome produced by increased 5-hydroxytryptamine synthesis in rats. *Neuropharm.* **13**, 949–59.

Griffiths, J. D., Cavanaugh, J., Held, J., and Oates, J. (1972). Dextroamphetamine: evaluation of psychomimetic properties in man. *Arch. gen. Psychiat.* **26**, 97–100.

—— Nutt, J. G., and Jasinski, D. R. (1975). A comparison of fenfluramine and amphetamine in man. *Clin. Pharmacol. Ther.* **18**, 563–70.

Gruzelier, J. (1983). Left-and-right-sided dysfunction in psychosis: implications for electroencephalographic measurement. *Adv. Biol. Psychiat.* **13**, 192–5.

Harris, J. E. and Baldesssarini, R. J. (1973). Uptake of [³H]-catecholamine by homogenates of the rat corpus striatum and cerebral cortex: effects of amphetamine analogues. *Neuropharmacology* **12**, 669–79.

Herman, M. and Nagler, S. H. (1954). Psychosis due to amphetamine. *J. nerv. ment. Dis.* **120**, 268–72.

Holmes, J. C. and Ruttledge, C. D. (1976). Effects of the *d*- and *l*-isomers of amphetamine on uptake, release and catabolism of norepinephrine, dopamine and

5-hydroxtryptamine in several regions of rat brain. *Biochem. Pharmacol.* **25**, 447–51.

Huberman, H. S., Eison, M. S., Bryan, K. S., and Ellison, G. (1977). A slow-release silicone pellet for chronic amphetamine administration. *Eur. J. Pharmacol.* **45**, 237–42.

Iversen, L. L. (1978). Biochemical and pharmacological studies: the dopamine hypothesis. In *Schizophrenia* (ed. J. K. Wing), p. 89. Academic Press, London.

Iversen, S. D. (1979*a*). Animal models of relevance to biological psychiatry. In: *Handbook of biological psychiatry* (ed. H. M. Lader, O. J. Rafaelsen and E. J. Sachar), Vol. I, pp. 303–35.

—— (1979*b*). Neural substrates mediating amphetamine responses. In *Cocaine and other stimulants* (ed. E. H. Ellinwood and M. M. Kilbey), *Adv. in behavioural biology* Vol. 21, p. 31. Plenum Press, New York.

—— (1984*a*). Behavioural aspects of the cortico–subcortical interaction with special reference to frontostriatal relations. In *Cortical integration*: Basic, archicortical and corticol association levels of neural integration (ed. F. Reinoso-Suarez and C. Ajmone-Marsah), IBRO Monograph Series, Vol. 11, pp. 237–54. Raven Press, New York.

—— (1984*b*). Recent advance in the anatomy and chemistry of the limbic system. In *Psychopharmacology of the limbic system* (ed. M. R. Trimble and E. Zarifian), Br. Ass. Psychopharm. Monograph 5, pp. 1–16. Oxford University Press, Oxford.

—— and Koob, G. F. (1977). Behavioural implications of dopaminergic neurons in the mesolimbic system. In *Advances in biochemical psychopharmacology* (ed. E. Costa and G. L. Gessa), Vol. 16, pp. 209–14. Raven Press, New York.

Jacobs, B. L. (1976). An animal behaviour model for studying central serotonergic synapses. *Life Sci.* **19**, 777–86.

Jenner, P. and Marsden, C. D. (1979). The substituted benzamides—a novel class of dopamine antagonists. *Life Sci.* **25**, 479–86.

Janowsky, D. S. and Davis, J. B. (1974). Dopamine psychomotor stimulants and schizophrenia: Effects of methylphenidate and the stereoisomers of amphetamine in schizophrenics. In *Neuropsychopharmacology of amines and their regulatory enzymes* (ed. E. Usdin), pp. 317–23. Raven Press, New York.

—— El-Yousef, M. K., Davis, J. M., and Sekerke, H. S. (1973). Provocation of schizophrenic symptoms by intravenous administration of methylphenidate. *Arch. gen. Psychiat.* **28**, 185–91.

Johnston, E. C., Crow, T. J., Frith, C. D., Carney, M. N. P., and Price, J. S. (1978). Mechanism of the antipsychotic effect in the treatment of acute schizophrenia. *Lancet* **i**, 848–51.

Kelly, P. H., and Miller R. J. (1975). The interaction of neuroleptics and muscarinic agents with central dopaminergic systems. *Br. J. Pharmacol.* **54**, 115–21.

—— Seviour, P. W., and Iversen, S. D. (1975). Amphetamine and apomorphine responses in the rat following 6-OHDA lesions of the nucleus accumbens septi and corpus striatum. *Brain Res.* **94**, 507–22.

Kety, S. S. (1980). The syndrome of schizophrenia: unresolved questions and opportunities for research. *Br. J. Psychiat.* **136**, 421–36.

Kjellberg, B. and Randrup. A. (1972), Stereotypy with selective stimulation of certain items of behaviour observed in amphetamine-treated monkeys (Cercopithecus). *Pharmakopsychiatrie* **5**, 1–12.

Kraepelin, W. (1913). Dementia praecox and paraphrenia. Translated by R. M. Barclay from 8th German edition of the *Textbook of psychiatry*, Vol. III, Part 2. *On endogenous dementias*. E. and S. Livingstone, Edinburgh.

Kuczenski, R. (1983). Biochemical actions of amphetamine and other stimulants. In

Stimulants: neurochemical behavioural and clinical perspectives (ed. I. Creese), pp. 31–61. Raven Press, New York.

Leysen, J. E., Niemegeers, C. J. E., Tollanaere, J. P., and Ladinton, P. M. (1978). Serotonergic component of neuroleptic receptors. *Nature, Lond.* **272**, 168–71.

Lyon, M. and Nielsen, E. B. (1979). Psychosis and drug-induced stereotypies. In *Psychopathology in animals: Research and clinical implications* (ed. J. D. Keehn), pp. 103–42. Academic Press. New York.

—— and Randrup, A. (1972). The dose–response effect of amphetamine upon avoidance behaviour in the rat, seen as a function of increasing stereotypy. *Psychopharmacologia* **23**, 334–47.

—— and Robbins, T. W. (1975). The action of central nervous system stimulant drugs: A general theory concerning amphetamine effects. In *Current developments in psychopharmacology* (ed. W. Essman and J. Valzelli), Vol. 2, pp. 80–163. Spectrum Press, New York.

Machiyama, Y., Utena, H., and Kikuchi, M. (1970). Behavioural disorders in Japanese monkeys produced by long-term administration of methamphetamine. *Proc. Jap. Acad.* **46**, 738.

Mackay, A. V. P. (1980). Positive and negative schizophrenic symptoms and the role of dopamine. *Br. J. Psychiat.* **137**, 379–86.

MacLennan, A. J. and Maier, S. F. (1983). Coping and the stress-induced potentiation of stimulant stereotypy in the rat. *Science* **219**, 1091–3.

Makajuola, R. O. A., Hill, G., Dow, R. C., Cambell, G., and Ashcroft, G. W. (1977). The effects of psychotropic drugs on exploratory and stereotyped behaviour of rats studied in a hole board. *Psychopharmacology* **55**, 67–74.

Martin, G. E. and Bendesky, R. J. (1984). Mouse locomotor activity: An *in vivo* test for dopamine autoreceptor activation. *J. Pharmacol. exp. Ther.* **229**, 706–11.

McKinney, W. T., (1974). Animal models in psychiatry. *Pers. in Biol. and Med.* **17**, 529–41.

—— and Bunney, W. F. (1969). Animal models of depression. I. Review of evidence: implications for research. *Arch. gen. Psychiat.* **21**, 240–8.

Monroe, R. R. and Drell, H. Z. (1947). Oral use of stimulants obtained from inhalers. *J. Am. med. Ass.* **135**, 909–15.

Moore, K. E. (1978). Amphetamines: biochemical and behavioural actions in animals. In *Handbook of psychopharmacology* (ed. L. L. Iversen, S. D. Iversen, and S. H. Snyder), Vol. 11, pp. 41–98. Plenum Press, New York.

Munkvad, I., Pakkenberg, H., and Randrup, A. (1968). Aminergic systems in basal ganglia associated with stereotyped hyperactive behaviour and catalepsy. *Brain Behav. Evol.* **1**, 89–100.

Nielsen, E. B., Lyon, M., and Ellison, G. (1983). Apparent hallucinations in monkeys during around-the-clock amphetamine for seven to fourteen days. *J. Neur. ment. Dis.* **171**, 222–223.

Ogren, S. O., Hall, H., Kohler, C., Magnusson, O., Lindbom, L. O., Angeby, K., and Florvall, L. (1984). Remoxipride, a new potential antipsychotic compound with selective antidopaminergic actions in the rat brain. *Eur. J. Pharmacol.* **102**, 459–74.

Orzi, F., Dow-Edwards, Jehle, J., Kennedy, C., and Sokoloff, L. (1983). Comparative effects of acute and chronic administration of amphetamine on local cerebral glucose utilization in the conscious rat. *J. cereb. Blood Flow Metab.* **3**, 154–60.

Pijnenburg, A. J. J., Honig, W. M. M., and van Rossum, J. M. (1975). Effects of antagonists upon locomotor stimulation induced by injection of dopamine and noradrenaline into the nucleus accumbens of nialamide-pretreated rats. *Psychopharmacologia* **41**, 175–80.

—— and van Rossum, J. M. (1973). Stimulation of locomotor activity following injection of dopamine into the nucleus accumbens. *J. Pharm.* **25**, 1003–5.

Prinzmetal, M. and Bloomberg., W. (1935). Use of benzedrine for the treatment of narcolepsy. *J. Am. med. Ass.* **105**, 2051–4.

Randrup, A. and Munkvad, I. (1970). Biochemical, anatomical and psychological investigations of stereotyped behaviour induced by amphetamines. In *Amphetamines and related compounds* (ed. E. Costa and S. Garattini), pp. 695–713. Raven Press, New York.

——, —— (1971). Behavioural toxicity of amphetamines studies in animal experiments. In *The correlation of adverse effects in man, with observations in animals* (ed. S. B. de Baker) Excerpta Medica International Congress Series. No. 220, pp. 6–17. Excerpta Medica, Amsterdam.

——, —— (1974). Pharmacology and physiology of stereotyped behaviour. *J. Psychiat. Res.* **11**, 1–10.

Reibaud, M., Blanc, G., Studler, J. M., Glowinksi, J., and Tassin, J. P. (1984). Non-DA prefronto-cortical efferents modulate D_1 receptors in the nucleus accumbens. *Brain Res.* **305**, 43–50.

Reynolds, G. P. (1983). Increased concentrations and lateral asymmetry of amygdala dopamine in schizophrenia. *Nature, Lond.* **305**, 527–9.

Ridley, R. M. (1985). *Psychostimulants in psychopharmacology*, Vol. 2, Part I. *Preclinical psychopharmacology* (ed. D. G. Grahame-Smith, H. Hippins, and G. Winokur). pp. 152–79. Excerpta Medica, Amsterdam.

—— and Baker, H. F. (1982). Stereotypy in monkeys and humans. *Psychol. Med.* **12**, 61–72.

——, ——, (1983). Is there a relationship between social isolation, cognitive flexibility, and behavioural stereotypy? An analysis of the effects of amphetamine in the marmoset. In *Ethology: Primate models of neuropsychiatric disorders* (ed. K. A. Miczek), pp. 101–35. Alan R. Liss, Inc. New York.

——, —— Owen, F., Cross, A. J., and Crow, T. J. (1982). Behavioural and biochemical effects of chronic amphetamine treatment in the vervet monkey. *Psychopharmacology* **78**, 245-51.

——, —— and Scraggs, P. R. (1979). The time course of the behavioural effects of amphetamine and their reversal by haloperidol in a primate species. *Biol. Psychiat.* **14**, 753–65.

—— Haystead, T. A., and Baker, H. F. (1981). An involvement of dopamine in higher order choice mechanisms in the monkey. *Psychopharmacologia, Berlin* **72**, 173–7.

Robbins, T. W. and Iversen, S. D. (1973). A dissociation of the effects of *d*-amphetamine on locomotor activity and exploration in rats. *Psychopharmacology* **28**, 155–64.

Robbins, T. R. and Sahakian, B. J. (1980). Animal models of Mania. In *Mania—an evolving concept* (ed. R. Belmaker and H. van Praag), pp. 143–216. Spectrum, New York.

Rylander, K. (1969). Clinical and medico-criminological aspects of addictions to central stimulating drugs. In *Abuse of central stimulants* (ed. F. Sjoqvist and M. Tottle), pp. 251–73. Raven Press, New York.

Scatton, B. (1977). Differential regional development of tolerance to increase in dopamine turnover upon repeated neuroleptic administration. *Eur. J. Pharmacol.* **46**, 363–9.

Schneider, K. (1959). *Clinical psychopathology* (Translated by M. W. Hamilton). Grune and Stratton, New York.

Schultz, W. and Ungerstedt, U. (1978). Short-term increase and long-term reversion of striatal cell activity after degeneration of the nigro-striatal dopamine system. *Exp. Brain Res.* **33**, 159–71.

Scraggs, P. R. and Ridley, R. M. (1978). Behavioural effects of amphetamine in small primate: relative potencies of the *d*- and *l*-isomers. *Psychopharmacology* **59**, 243–5.

Sedvall, D. G. (1980). Serotonin metabolite concentrations in cerebrospinal fluid from schizophrenic patients: relationship to family history. In *Serotonin: current aspects of neurochemistry and functions* (ed. B. Haber), pp. 719–25. Plenum, New York.

Seeger, T. F., Thal, L., and Gardner, E. L. (1982). Behavioural and biochemical aspects of neuroleptic-induced dopaminergic supersensitivity: studies with chronic clozapine and haloperidol. *Psychopharmacology* **76**, 182–7.

Seeman, P., Lee, T., Chau-Wong, M., and Wong, K. (1976). Antipsychotic drug doses and neuroleptic/dopamine receptors. *Nature, Lond.* **261**, 717.

Siegel, R. K. (1978). Cocaine hallucinations. *Am. J. Psychiat.* **135**, 309–14.

Slater, E. (1959). Book review of *Amphetamine psychosis*, by P. H. Connell. *Br. med. J.* **1959**, 488.

Snyder, S. H., Richelson, E., Weingartner, H., and Faillace, L. A. (1970). Psychotrophic methoxyamphetamine: structure and activity in man. In *Amphetamine and related compounds* (ed. E. Costa and S. Garattini), pp. 905–28. Raven Press, New York.

Stevens, J. R. (1978). Disturbances of ocular movements and blinking in schizophrenia. *J. Neurol. Neurosurg. Psychiat.* **41**, 1024–30.

—— and Livermore, A. (1978). Kindling of the mesolimbic dopamine system: animal models of psychosis. *Neurology* **28**, 36–46.

Stoof, J. C. and Kebabian, J. W. (1981). Opposing roles for D-1 and D-2 dopamine receptors in efflux of cyclic AMP from rat striatum. *Nature, Lond.* **294**, 366–8.

Taylor, K. M. and Snyder, S. H. (1971). Differential effects of *d*- and *l*-amphetamine on behaviour and on catecholamine disposition in dopamine and norepinephrine containing neurones of the rat brain. *Brain Res.* **28**, 295–309.

Thierry, A. M., Tassin, J. P., Blanc, G., and Glowsinki, J. (1976). Selective activation of the mesocortical DA system by stress. *Nature, Lond.* **263**, 242–4.

——, ——, ——, —— (1978). Studies on mesocortical dopamine systems. In *Advances in biochem. psychopharmacol.* (ed. P. J. Roberts, G. N. Woodruff, and L. L. Iversen), Vol. 19, pp. 205–16. Raven Press, New York.

Tucker, D. M. (1983). Asymmetries of activation and arousal in psychopathology. *Adv. Biol. Psychiat.* **13**, 19–25.

Ungerstedt, U. (1971). Post synaptic supersensitivity after 6-hydroxydopamine induced generation of the nigro striatal dopamine system. *Acta physiol. scand. Suppl.* **367**, 69–93.

Utena, H. (1974). On relapse-liability schizophrenia, amphetamine psychosis and animal model. In *Biological mechanism of schizophrenia and schizophrenia-like psychosis* (ed. H. Mitsuda and T. Fukuda), p. 285. Igaku Shoin, Tokyo.

van Kammen, D. P. Mann, L. S., Sternberg, D. E., Scheinin, U., Niwan, P. T., Marder, S. R., Kammen, W. B. van, Rieder, R. O., and Linnoila, M. (1983). Dopamine-β-hydroxylase activity and homovanillic acid in spinal fluids of schizophrenics with brain atrophy. *Science* **220**, 974–7.

White, F. J. and Wang, R. Y. (1983). Differential effects of classical and atypical antipsychotic drugs on A9 and A10 dopamine neurons. *Science* **221**, 1054–7.

Youngs, D. and Scoville, W. B. (1938). Paranoid psychosis in narcolepsy and the possible danger of benzedrine treatment. *Med. Clin. N. Am.* **22**, 637–46.

4

Applied clinical pharmacology of schizophrenia

STEPHEN H. CURRY

The drugs that are used in the treatment of schizophrenia were mostly discovered without the assistance of specialist clinical pharmacologists. They emerged from industrial screening programmes, and most of our knowledge of their effects in humans has been gained from astute observation during their therapeutic use by pharmacologically orientated clinicians. As evidence of this, the prototype drug, chlorpromazine, was a by-product of clinical studies of the antihistamines, and of other agents designed to potentiate anaesthesia (Delay *et al*. 1952). Haloperidol was discovered in a basic science unit in a pharmaceutical company in 1958. The thioxanthenes represent no more than a change in emphasis from the phenothiazine ring as the chemical nucleus to a second, very closely related, chemical structure in the hope of increasing the chances of successful new discoveries (Byck 1975).

As the subject of clinical pharmacology developed, a series of reviews describing the human pharmacology of the major tranquillizers appeared (Domino 1962; Hamilton 1965; Ban 1966; Hollister 1968). These early reviews were mostly concerned with: (1) classification of the drugs used in the treatment of schizophrenia, largely on the basis of their chemical formulae; (2) descriptions of the basic actions of the compounds in humans; and (3) applications to particular psychiatric conditions. These reviews were also concerned with whether or not any specificity in tranquillizer action really existed.

It seems that most psychiatrists would now agree that there is, in fact, a specific effect of the major tranquillizers useful in the treatment of schizophrenia. Indeed, just 10 years after chlorpromazine was introduced, the view was expressed that few psychiatrists would like to practise psychiatry without it, or without one of the other related compounds (Hamilton 1965). By about the same time, the studies of the National Institute of Mental Health–Psychopharmacology Research Branch (NIMH-PSC 1964), and of other groups, had established the efficacy of the phenothiazines in schizophrenia beyond doubt, and the action clearly has specificity (Davis 1965; May 1968). Nowadays there is a sharp distinction between the antischizophrenic drugs (now often called 'neuroleptics'), the antidepressants, and the minor tranquillizers of the diazepam type, although that statement is not intended to imply that there are no patients able to benefit from combinations of examples of two or even all three of these groups of drugs.

More recently, and in contrast with much of the foregoing, clinical phar-macologists have examined more systematically the reasons for variations between patients in their responses to the major tranquillizers, and have also searched for better, increasingly objective, measures of drug effect. The present review is largely, but not exclusively concerned with these two areas. The need for work in these areas was pointed out nearly 20 years ago. 'The astonishingly wide range of dosage of phenothiazines is a very peculiar problem . . . For this reason, it is very difficult to consider an individual patient and have some notion of what is a reasonable dose for him' (Hamilton 1965). It was about this time that Brodie was expressing the view vigorously that pharmacokinetic differences among psychiatric patients might account for some or all of the variations implicit in these comments (Brodie 1967).

Historically speaking, it is probably true to say that, following the lead given by Brodie and until 1980, clinical pharmacological investigation of the neuroleptics was the preserve of a small group of investigators, notably including this author, M. H. Lader, L. E. Hollister, J. M. Davis and groups in Oxford and Cambridge, UK. The first 15 years of this work have been reviewed by this author (Curry 1976*a, b,* 1980*a,* 1981*a, b,* 1984*a–d*). Since 1980, there has been an escalation of analytical work, and of studies in phar-macokinetics in particular, brought on by the introduction of new tech-niques, and the purpose of this review is partly to relate these two phases of the work one to the other.

PHARMACOKINETIC DIFFERENCES AS A BASIS FOR VARIATIONS IN RESPONSE

It is appropriate to summarize the ways in which pharmacokinetic factors might influence drug response. First, the drug must be absorbed from its site of administration. Variations in *rates* of absorption will affect how quickly drug responses will occur (onset times). They will also affect how long they last, as slow onset of effect often (but not always) goes hand-in-hand with a long-lasting effect. Variations in the *extent* of absorption will affect the overall exposure of the body to the drug. Related to this, first-pass effects (metabolism of oral doses in the intestine or liver during absorption) will reduce the availability of unmetabolized drug to the body, although it must be remembered that if a first-pass effect leads to increased production of an active metabolite, the effect will be enhanced. Variations in blood–brain transfer, in binding, and in rates of metabolism and excretion will also affect the availability of drug molecules to sites of action at particular times (Curry 1980*a*).

These phenomena have been studied to various extents with the neuroleptic drugs. Of some 30 readily available examples, only a minority have been evaluated pharmacokinetically to any great extent. This minority includes chlorpromazine, thioridazine, butaperazine, fluphenazine, flupenthixol, and haloperidol. A number of other compounds has been evaluated to a small extent. However, a pattern is emerging and the key points seem to be as set out in the following paragraphs. These points have largely been determined with chlorpromazine (Curry 1980*b*).

Absorption and first-pass effects

It is generally supposed that there are variations in rates of absorption of oral doses but much more important is the major first-pass problem. It is known to affect chlorpromazine and fluphenazine to a considerable degree. It also affects haloperidol to some extent. First-pass effects are classically studied in humans by comparison of concentrations of the drug in venous plasma following intravenous and oral doses given in exactly comparable conditions. More detailed studies in animals are possible by means of intraperitoneal injections and also injections directly into the portal circulation. In addition, various *in vitro* techniques are available. In the case of chlorpromazine, calculation of areas under the curves following doses by various routes shows similarity for intravenous, intraperitoneal (dogs and rats), and intramascular doses, with the oral dose leading to an area anywhere between 0.1 and 1.0 times that after the intravenous dose. This indicates conversion of orally administered chlorpromazine to metabolites at some point before the molecules reach the general circulation. The significance of the intraperitoneal dose is that it bypasses the gastrointestinal tract but not the portal circulation, so the major site of conversion appears to be associated with the gastrointestinal tract itself (Curry *et al.* 1970*a*). Following this up, *in vitro* studies have shown that there is a microsomal P-450 system in the intestinal mucosa, and that chlorpromazine can be converted to oxides in isolated intestinal loops (Curry *et al.* 1971; Curry and Mould 1975).

Variations between and within individuals in the degree of the first-pass effect are undoubtedly a major reason for the wide variations in plasma levels of chlorpromazine first reported in the earliest studies (Curry and Marshall 1968; Curry *et al.* 1970). In regard to other drugs, very little has been done with intravenous doses. However, comparison of intramuscular and oral doses of fluphenazine has revealed a considerable first-pass problem, possibly with as little as one per cent of the oral dose reaching the general circulation as unmetabolized drug (Curry *et al.* 1979*a*). Also, fluphenazine is one of the drugs given clinically by intramuscular injection and there are clearly variations in rates of absorption from the injection site.

In evaluating the first-pass problem it should be noted that the metabolic reactions involved are relatively simple, being oxidations of the ring sulphur of the phenothiazines to sulphoxides, of side-chain tertiary amine groups to *N*-oxides, and possibly conjugation of side-chain aliphatic hydroxyl groups with glucuronic acid in such compounds as fluphenazine and flupenthixol. One or more of these reactions can occur alone or in combination in a wide range of compounds, and so it seems likely that first-pass metabolism is a problem to some extent with most if not all of the major tranquillizers.

Surprisingly, after nearly 20 years of research into the pharmacokinetics of neuroleptics, it is still fair to say that there has been very little *systematic* investigation of absorption. We do know the scale of the first-pass effect for the major examples, mentioned earlier for chlorpromazine and fluphenazine, and approximately 30 per cent for haloperidol. However, we know nothing objectively about precise rates of absorption. Only in the last few years have attempts been made even to study trifluperazine kinetics at any level. Thus clinical judgement remains the best indicator of relative rates of absorption among the drugs and between individuals. Against this it is undoubtedly true to say that intramuscular injections and oral doses exert their effects more slowly than do intravenous doses, but few investigators would claim that there is certainty of knowledge as to whether oral or intramuscular doses reach their maximum effects most rapidly. The significance of this was highlighted recently in relation to emergency psychiatry (Curry 1984*c, d*; Donlon *et al.* 1979; Menuck and Voineskos 1981).

Metabolites

There are vast numbers of metabolites of most of the neuroleptics (Williams and Parke 1964; Curry 1980*b*). The only important exception to this appears to be haloperidol, which is converted to a relatively small number of products. Chlorpromazine is known to undergo sulphoxidation and *N*-oxidation (already mentioned in relation to first-pass effects), plus demethylation and hydroxylation, then conjugation of the hydroxylated products with glucuronic acid. Deamination probably also occurs, and it is further believed that other, as yet unidentified routes may be important. The reactions occur in combination, yielding vast numbers of products. Even the old idea of a possible 168 metabolites must now be considered an underestimate, and so careful consideration must be given as to whether or not the metabolites occur in important quantities in plasma and/or brain.

Chlorpromazine sulphoxide reaches substantial concentrations in human plasma, its concentrations occasionally exceeding those of chlorpromazine. There is disagreement about other metabolites. In the earlier studies, only the demethylated derivatives were examined and they were found in quantities less than 10 per cent of those of the unchanged drug. More recently, a similar observation was made concerning 7-hydroxylated analogues. Other authors have found larger quantities of demonomethylchlorpromazine and 7-hydroxychlorpromazine in human plasma. There are at least three possible reasons for this disagreement. First, patients groups vary, and positive metabolite reports are confined generally, but not always to groups of patients treated for long periods of time. Detection of metabolites after single doses is not common. Second, there could be analytical errors. Demonomethylchlorpromazine has generally been detected in extracts in which its presence could have been as a decomposition product of chlorpromazine *N*-oxide. Third, substantial quantities of 7-hydroxychlorpromazine and other hydroxylated metabolites are found in erythrocytes and this contrasts with the non-hydroxylated products. Haemolysis during blood collection can lead to invalid measurements in plasma.

The consensus view is that chlorpromazine sulphoxide often approaches concentrations similar to those of the parent drug, while 7-hydroxychlorpromazine sometimes reaches these levels. The concentrations of the demethylated analogues are only rarely above 10 per cent of those of the unmetabolized drug. The only other metabolite usually occurring in more than trace quantities is the glucuronide (or possibly a mixture of glucuronides) of 7-hydroxychlorpromazine. There is one report of possibly important quantities of a compound with the properties of 7, 8 dihydroxychlorpromazine.

As to the metabolites in brain, the sulphoxidized and demethylated compounds cross the blood–brain barrier in animals. The compounds in the 7-hydroxychlorpromazine group also cross to some extent. Presumably the glucuronides do not, as total radioactivity after administration of [^{35}S]-chlorpromazine is cleared from brain more rapidly than is the unchanged drug, while it is cleared from plasma more slowly than is the unchanged drug. Total radioactivity increasingly comprises relatively polar metabolites at time intervals increasingly distant from the time of dosage.

There are undoubtedly wide interpatient variations in the rate and degree of conversion to particular metabolites. The pharmacological action of the metabolites will be considered later.

Tissue residues

There is a general belief that neuroleptic drugs persist in the body for long periods following cessation of dosage. The conventional doctrine is that: 'the ultimate sojourn of the phenothiazine drugs in the body is exceedingly long, (Byck 1975). This idea developed between 1950 and 1970 as the outcome of the excellent urinary excretion studies of Forrest and her co-workers, in which it was shown that drug-derived material was detectable in urine as long as two years after treatment with phenothiazines stopped (Forrest and Green 1972). Tissue studies in animals after single doses have confirmed a high degree of reversible localization in lung, muscle (cardiac, smooth, and voluntary) fat, kidney, etc., in the sense that the concentrations of chlorpromazine in the tissues (measured in mass. mass^{-1} units such as μg.g^{-1}) exceed by several-fold those in plasma measured in the same units. Bearing in mind the degree of protein binding of unmetabolized chlorpromazine (> 90 per cent), this represents concentrations exceeding by as much as several-fold those in plasma water (Curry 1980*b*).

It seems that the whole body amount (tissue and plasma concentrations) declines slowly after stopping dosing, and it has been estimated that the terminal phase half-life of chlorpromazine in plasma, which represents whole body decline when tissue localization is reversible, is in the region of 60 days. In addition, there may be a small degree of non-reversible tissue localization (possibly by covalent binding), which would have serious toxicological implications.

Measurement of the half-life values of neuroleptic drugs has, in fact, proved very difficult. For example, the earliest reports put the half-life of chlorpromazine at approximately six hours, which is the half-life of fall in plasma levels from maximum concentration postdosage to trough just before dosage. The 60-day figure mentioned in the previous paragraph seems to contradict this. It seems that the six-hour phase is a distributional half-life, representing principally loss from plasma to tissues, as a six-hour half-life would lead to 99 per cent clearance from the body in 42 hours. On withdrawing the drug, the very slow loss from tissues dominates. The 60-day half-life means easy detection for one to two years after cessation of treatment. Similar investigations of the half-life values of the other drugs have produced a range of figures. However, it is very difficult to evaluate the significance of a drug half-life to schizophrenia. This will be discussed later, but it should be recognized at this point that patients do not necessarily relapse when the concentrations in plasma fall below a certain threshold, and that the probability of relapse is highly dependent on the stage and severity of the illness.

Recent research has seen an escalation in the volume of available information on the pharmacokinetics of chlorpromazine (Loo *et al.* 1980), perazine (Schley *et al.* 1981), fluphenazine (Dysken *et al.* 1981), promazine (Harris *et al.* 1983), and thiothixene (Yesavage *et al.* 1982*a*), but there is still insufficient data available.

A 'tissue' that has been of considerable interest is cerebrospinal fluid (CSF). Studies of CSF have been confined to chlorpromazine, thioridazine, and haloperidol, and have mostly been conducted in Scandinavia. Alfredsson and Sedvall (1981) and Wode-Heldgodt and Alfredsson (1981) showed that chlorpromazine equilibrates between plasma water and CSF. Alfredsson *et al.* (1982) detected penetration of CSF by 7-hydroxychlorpromazine. Nyberg *et al.* (1981) showed that comparable principles are applicable to thioridazine. Romon *et al.* (1981) studied serum and CSF levels of haloperidol by means of radioimmunoassay and radioreceptor assay.

Enzyme induction

Chlorpromazine is a potent enzyme inducer, in that the activity of the P-450 microsomal oxidase system of the liver, which is responsible for metabolizing chlorpromazine and other drugs, is increased as the result of prolonged exposure to the drug. This is shown in humans as a fall in plasma concentrations of the unchanged drug per unit of dose from day 8 to day 36 of treatment and in decreased antipyrine half times (which can be used to some extent to monitor the activity of the system) (Loga *et al.* 1975). By the same token, metabolite concentrations will tend to increase during this time. It can be presumed that chlorpromazine induces activity in the P-450 system of intestinal mucosa, and this might increase the first-pass effect. There are undoubtedly interpatient variations in the rate and degree of enzyme induction (Harmon *et al*. 1980).

Protein binding

Protein binding remains an enigmatic problem. As already mentioned, chlorpromazine and the other neuroleptic drugs are reversibly bound to plasma protein such that the unchanged drugs are 90 per cent or more bound at therapeutic concentrations. The metabolites have lower per cent bound figures, down to effectively zero for the glucuronides. It must be remembered that (1) binding is reversible and dynamic, and that the kinetic constants involved are such that re-equilibration takes place in milliseconds if a factor disturbing binding appears; (2) in spite of this comment, it is still valid to think of the nonbound molecules at any moment as the only ones available at that time for tissue penetration and hence for pharmacological action; (3) binding is certainly to albumin, but possibly also to α_1-acid-glycoprotein and other proteins as well; (4) displacement of one drug by another is possible, but on the whole this is not known to be an important phenomenon with neuroleptics; and (5) although binding is saturable, differences in per cent free have not been observed within individuals when total concentration varies, or indeed when any other circumstances change (Alfredsson and Sedvall 1981; Axelsson *et al*. 1982; Brinkschulte *et al*. 1982; Nyberg and Mastensson 1982; Schley 1983).

There are important variations *between* patients in protein binding (Curry 1970). However, it must be appreciated that, within the normal range of protein concentrations encountered in healthy individuals, there is little scope for more than a two-fold range in per cent nonbound. Nevertheless, organic disease problems change the concentrations of the binding proteins, and chlorpromazine binding has been shown to vary from 91 up to 99 per cent in a mixed group of hospitalized patients. This would lead to a 10-fold range of nonbound concentration at the same total concentration in plasma.

Biopharmaceutical problems

Pharmaceutical formulation is a major factor controlling concentrations of many drugs in biological fluids. In general, solutions, be they injected or swallowed, render 100 per cent of the dose available at the site of administration. Tablets, capsules, and injection solutions are generally designed to present drugs rapidly and efficiently at their site of administration, *except* when there is a deliberate attempt to prolong the absorption phase by means of timed-release capsules or depot injections. Generally speaking, the neuroleptics do not suffer from biopharmaceutical problems, but there are timed-release capsules available and these are of dubious value. Depot injections are considered in a separate section of this review.

General aspects of pharmacokinetics

It has become standard practice in pharmacokinetics to relate the measures of pharmacokinetic variables to a wide range of physiological and pathological variables, such as age, sex, weight, renal disease, hepatic disease, metabolic disease (e.g. thyrotoxicosis), cardiovascular disease, dietary habits, and exercise. Very little investigation of this type has taken place with neuroleptics. In particular, age has been virtually neglected. In one study, the response to, but not the pharmacokinetics of, chlorpromazine was shown to be modified in liver disease. The response was enhanced in disease. Recent additions to the literature in this area include isolated studies of 'drug holidays' (Hershey *et al.* 1981), alcoholism (Axelsson *et al.* 1982), and cimetidine interactions (Howes *et al.* 1983), smoking (Pantuck *et al.* 1982), and one paper on age (Yesevage *et al.* 1982*b*).

NONPHARMACOKINETIC FACTORS IN CLINICAL PSYCHOPHARMACOLOGY

The subject of pharmacokinetics is generally considered to involve the assessment of drug concentrations in biological fluids. There is no reason why pharmacokinetics should not be extended to the kinetics of drug effect, but for the time being it is convenient to consider this as a nonpharmacokinetic area.

Dose–response, therapeutic index and toxicity

The difficulty of applying the dose–response concept to populations treated with neuroleptic drugs is a classic problem of huge dimensions (Domino 1962). A proportion of patients will show a response even to placebo. Another proportion will not respond to the drugs at all. In between there is a wide range of doses for a given effect. Possibly this could be tidied up with improved selection of patients but this is not as easy as it sounds. In one reasonably successful study, a group in Oklahoma organized a behavioural dose–response study with chlorpromazine. Doses were randomly assigned to patients. A dose of 150 mg/day^{-1} was found to be more effective than placebo. Doses of 300 and 600 mg/day^{-1} gave better clinical responses, but there was little difference between these two higher doses in clinical effect. However, side-effects were more prevalent at the highest dose (Clark *et al.* 1970).

The neuroleptic drugs do, in a sense, have a high therapeutic index in that the dose for severe toxicity is considerably above that for clinical response in any individual patient, although a dose causing toxicity in one patient may be inadequate for clinical success in another. However, it must be realized that this 'margin of safety' is a somewhat tenuous concept, as some side-effects occur at doses within the clinically needed range (e.g. drowsiness and postural hypotension in the early stages of treatment with chlorpromazine;

short-term extrapyramidal reactions with the piperazine and other low-dose phenothiazines). Furthermore, some of the long-term severe toxicity reactions are not related to acute dose. Instead, they occur as the result of prolonged exposure to the drugs. Hence, the common belief that patients should receive the lowest dose for the shortest time needed to achieve the desired clinical result.

Another major problem of the dose–response relation is the fact that patients overdosed with neuroleptic drugs may be difficult to distinguish from untreated schizophrenics. Neuroleptics in overdose can cause problems with perception, thought processes, and movement, such that the patient may be dulled, confused and passive, rigid or presenting with an unusual gait. Along the same lines, it has even been suggested that too much chlorpromazine could be 'psychotoxic' and one of the interesting by-products of the kinetic studies discussed earlier has been evidence that patients are rated poorly more frequently when they have relatively high concentrations of chlorpromazine sulphoxide (Chaffin 1964; Mackay *et al.* 1974). This area deserves further research, although it seems probable that the psychotoxicity is not a real induction of a psychotic reaction, and that the chlorpromazine sulphoxide data arose from a relatively inactive metabolite being produced in higher amounts by first-pass metabolism in patients responding poorly for reasons of their disease state, but treated with relatively high chlorpromazine doses as a psychiatrist reaction to the problem of a refractory illness. Chlorpromazine sulphoxide has been shown in clinical trials to have approximately one-seventh the activity of the parent drug (Davidson *et al.* 1957).

In a sense, the plasma level can be considered as the dose, so that the relationship between plasma levels and effect becomes a dose–response study. However, in this review this topic is the subject of a separate section.

Time-course of treatment

One of the basic problems in understanding quantitative psychopharmacology is the failure of many investigators to appreciate the fact that response of schizophrenics to treatment of any kind occurs over a period of time. With the drugs there may be a measurable response after the first dose, but it will not represent an important change in psychiatric status. There may be some improvement after three to four days, but generally speaking three weeks are needed to establish an effect with six weeks to six months needed for the full stable response to be obtained. However, rapid changes in global ratings have been claimed after starting treatment with parenterally-administered drugs, which may reflect the higher plasma levels per unit of doses obtained by such methods (Shopsin *et al.* 1969). On withdrawal of treatment, there may be no more than a 40 per cent lesser incidence of relapses in the six months following withdrawal of active medication compared with a placebo group selected and handled similarly (Prien and Klett 1972; Hirsch *et al.* 1973).

It seems that schizophrenia is a vicious circle of self-perpetuating pathology. The drugs do little more than interrupt this vicious circle, although hopefully they can put it into reverse. They at least assist in the creation of a situation in which the patient can resist the undesired elements in his thinking and set himself, with the assistance of psychotherapy, on a course of improvement. As Dally said, speaking of tranquillizers '. . . they are able to arrest the progress of psychotic disorders which, if allowed to continue, would lead to further impairment of the patient's contact with reality. They interrupt a vicious circle and allow the patient's CNS to function in a normal matter' (Dally 1967). The implications for this in relation to dose–response relationships and studies of the relation of kinetics and effect, are that every patient starts from a different baseline with a different degree of pathology and with a different potential for improvement. Only when patients are selected for study with an attempt to standardize this factor will improved relationships be shown. And all this presumes qualitative homogeneity of the illness which clearly does not occur.

Tolerance

There are a number of mechanisms of tolerance relevant to the action of neuroleptics. First, the enzyme induction phenomenon, which was discussed earlier as leading to a reduction in concentrations of the unchanged drug per unit of dose is an exemplification of pharmacokinetic tolerance. Second, there is some form of pharmacodynamic or receptor tolerance. An initial dose of chlorpromazine can cause sedation and postural hypotension in a way that later, higher doses do not. Furthermore, the initial dose may lead to plasma concentrations that are greatly exceeded during later treatment with higher doses. So tolerance develops to the sedative and hypotensive effects. Indeed, without this, it is quite likely that it would be impossible to administer the scale of dosage needed to reverse the symptoms of schizophrenia (Loga *et al.* 1975).

   This demonstrates one way in which individual patients vary in their sensitivity to neuroleptic drugs. It would be naive of us to think that there is not a similar range of receptor responsivity at whatever site is important to the neuroleptic response.

Kinetics of changes in effects of chlorpromazine

One particular research group has published data on the changes in effects of chlorpromazine as a function of time (Smolen *et al.* 1975*a–c*; Smolen *et al.* personal communication, Williams *et al.* personal communication). Starting with the established observation of the relation between drug kinetics and pupil size (usually constriction, resulting from blockade of α-adrenoceptors), Smolen and his colleagues studied eye changes (including intraocular pressure by tonometry), resting heart rate, and body temperature, in animals and humans, as a function of dose and time following the dose. Effects have been detected at doses well below those necessary for the chemical detection of chlorpromazine in biological fluids and the importance of this lies in the intended use of the effects of the drug in the study of biopharmaceutical problems. Some of the more interesting observations have been: (1) delay in effects, even after giving the drug by intravenous injection; (2) qualitative differences in eye effects between different species; and (3) a suggestion of a qualitative difference in effects when the drug is given intravenously or orally; although this probably resulted from the vastly different concentrations involved, it equally could relate to the fact that chlorpromazine sulphoxide is formed much more readily from the oral dose. Further progress in this area will be awaited with great interest.

RELATION BETWEEN TREATMENT OUTCOME AND PHARMACOKINETIC MEASUREMENTS

Studies of the relation between outcome of treatment and plasma levels of neuroleptics have given conflicting and sometimes confusing results. For example, in one of the more recently published studies, morbidity scores were positively correlated with plasma chlorpromazine levels after two weeks treatment of acute schizophrenics, but not after four weeks treatment of the same patients, and then only in females (Wode-Helgodt *et al.* 1978). Two earlier studies failed to reveal a positive correlation between plasma chlorpromazine and effect (Sakalis *et al.* 1972; Mackay *et al.* 1974), although two further research groups demonstrated a therapeutic range of over 30–35 ng ml^{-1}, but under 300–350 ng ml^{-1} as optimal (Curry *et al.* 1970*b*; Rivera-Calimlin *et al.* 1973; Curry 1976*c*). With thioridazine, one paper recorded a curvilinear relation between effect and level, and two others showed no relation (Bergling *et al.* 1975; Gottschalk *et al.* 1975). With butaperazine, a tenuous relation was shown (Simpson *et al.* 1973; Smith *et al.* 1977). This has been reinforced more recently, leading to the suggestion that a 'therapeutic window' of optimal butaperazine plasma levels exists. Other work with butaperazine related the red-cell concentration to plasma concentration ratio, to effect, using the hypothesis that red-cell localization could be a model for brain localization. The problem here is that very few people see butaperazine as an important drug (Casper *et al.* 1980).

With penfluridol, the one report in this context is of failure to show a concentration–effect relationship (Chouinard *et al.* 1977). Other recent reports of concentration–effect relationships with neuroleptics have been concerned with chlorpromazine (Cohen *et al.* 1980; May *et al.* 1981; Van Putten *et al.* 1980, 1981; Sedvall 1981), thioridazine (Crammer 1981; Papadopoulos *et al.* 1980; Vaisanen *et al.* 1981), fluphenazine (Sakalis and Traficante 1981), and haloperidol (Morselli and Zarifian 1980). Recent studies have done little to advance our knowledge in this area, even failing to build up a vast literature of controversy, as has occurred with tricyclic antidepressants. It seems that the old idea still prevails, that in a very crude verse, too little is not enough, and too much is too much. With chlorpromazine, below 30 ng ml^{-1} is often too little. Above 350 ng ml^{-1} is usually too much. A more sophisticated delineation of the therapeutic range remains to be made.

All of the studies mentioned in the previous two paragraphs were of between-patient correlations. Arguably, such studies miss the point, but they are of course essential if a clinical monitoring programme is under test. The distinction must be made between correlation studies with populations, based on the hypothesis that all patients treated with the same drug concentration will show the same response, and longitudinal studies in individuals. Longitudinal studies are the more realistic, as it is clearly an oversimplification to think that all patients would show the same response to any particular plasma level.

The pattern of longitudinal change in patients treated for approximately six weeks with chlorpromazine has been studied in detail (Sakalis *et al.* 1972). In the first eight days, improvement is seen against a rising overall plasma chlorpromazine level. Thereafter, improvement continues against a falling level. The overall fall results from enzyme induction, and it was suggested that this could indicate that clinical improvement is more dependent on the concentrations of active metabolites than on those of the parent drug. However, the metabolites with known activity are not detectable in important amounts until much later stages of treatment. Furthermore, studies of population correlations, which included metabolite measurements, were no more successful than population studies in which only the parent drug was measured.

The link between long-term toxicity and pharmacokinetics has fascinating implications. Problems such as tardive diskinesia do not disappear abruptly on reducing the plasma level of drugs such as chlorpromazine. Indeed, they do not necessarily disappear at all. However, there is a consensus view that they can be reduced as a future problem by minimizing the long-term drug exposure of new patients. Thus, the incidence and severity of toxicity can be considered as a function of the multiple of cumulative dose and overall mean plasma concentration. This can be reduced by prescribing the least amount needed for successful therapy, and monitoring patients with the objective of reducing plasma levels continuously until relapse occurs or the need for no more drug is shown. In at least one American state (Texas) this is now standard practice. Bolvig-Hannsen *et al.* (1981), Widerlov *et al.* (1982), and Jeste *et al.* (1982) all made special references to toxicity in their work.

ACTIVITY OF METABOLITES OF NEUROLEPTIC DRUGS

This is a crucial and controversial area. Almost all of the work has been done with chlorpromazine, for which model metabolites have been synthesized on a large scale, but the chlorpromazine results have implications for other compounds (Curry 1980*b*; Davidson *et al.* 1957; Kleinman *et al.* 1980).

Much of the early urinary excretion work with chlorpromazine and its metabolites was done in the hope of finding particular metabolic routes associated with particular responses. Generally speaking, this work has drawn a very important blank and there is no evidence for different metabolic routes in different kinds of patients or patients responding in different ways. There are, of course, differences in rates of metabolism down common routes. It is worth noting in particular that metabolic conversion down a particular route could not be essential for neuroleptic action, as there is no metabolic route common to all neuroleptics.

There is now a reasonable consensus that pharmacological studies can be confined to the parent drug plus the first two demethylated metabolites, chlorpromazine sulphoxide and 7-hydroxychlorpromazine (and possibly 7,8-dihydroxychlorpromazine). Generally speaking, these compounds show activity related to their lipid solubilities. Lipid solubility is progressively reduced on metabolism so that the general rule is activity in the metabolites but less than in the parent drug. However, 7,8-dihydroxychlorpromazine is relatively potent in affecting ATPase *in vitro*, and 7-hydroxychlorpromazine is a little more potent than chlorpromazine in certain systems. In addition, since these compounds tend to be present in plasma at lower concentrations than those of the parent drug and, since their lesser lipid solubility causes lesser brain penetration, it seems that the metabolites probably make a contribution but do not dominate the response. Nevertheless, it must be remembered that the metabolites show less protein binding, and so the concentration nonbound for a given total concentration is greater. As discussed earlier, the nonbound fraction is the active one. Also, these comments concerned the desired effects of the drug. There is good evidence that 7-hydroxychlorpromazine is especially toxic and oxidation of the amine group may also be important in adverse reactions.

An interesting aspect when considering metabolites is the application of radioreceptor assays in the measurement of total neuroleptic activity (Creese and Snyder 1977). The principle is based on the fact that neuroleptic drugs appear to bind to the content of certain fractions of brain homogenates in proportion to their clinical potency. The basis for this is tenuous, as definition of a standard active dose of a neuroleptics is really impossible. Even more tenuous is the evidence that metabolites bind similarly in proportion to clinical potency, as chlorpromazine sulphoxide and 7-hydroxychlorpromazine apart, no phenothiazine metabolite has ever been given a 'clinical potency'. The argument in favour of the radioreceptor assay goes on that the neuroleptics displace a model radioactive neuroleptic from its binding sites in relation to clinical potency. So the degree of, for example, ^{3}H-spiroperidol binding, indicates the total neuropleptic content, weighted for potency of the various drugs and their metabolites if present. The approach is impressive as shown by a recent report of a positive relation between mini-PSE score and radioreceptor assay score (Tune *et al.* 1980), except for the flaw in the basic argument.

Apart from the points indicated in the previous paragraph, the existence but relatively low incidence of application, of the radioreceptor assay method raises questions concerning its widespread acceptance. Nearly ten years have passed since its development, and its simplicity should have led to an outburst of activity. This has not occurred. Verbal comments heard by this reviewer have been concerned with lack of reproducibility, and a 30 per cent coefficient of variation. Perhaps its only real deficiency is its use of radioactivity. Whatever its problem, this method has not had the impact expected (Curry 1985).

ENDOCRINE AND OTHER BIOCHEMICAL RELATIONSHIPS

A series of reports on relationships between concentrations of chlorpromazine and biochemical indices of endocrine or physiological function has been published, mostly by a group working in Oxford (Boullin *et al.* 1975*a, b*; Kolakowska *et al.* 1975, 1976; Wiles *et al.* 1976; Meltzer *et al.* 1981). The search is on for an index of pharmacological effect which will show changes as a function of time following doses. The earlier work used platelet aggregation induced by 5-hydroxytryptamine, which is inhibited by chlorpromazine, as an *in vitro* indicator of the chlorpromazine effect, and found that the response was greatly increased in blood from chlorpromazine-treated patients. After stopping chlorpromazine the response did not return to normal until three weeks had elapsed, while chlorpromazine levels dropped below the limit of assay within one week. Chlorpromazine sulphoxide and demonomethylchlorpromazine were detected in conventional amounts by these workers, and these metabolites were present in the same samples as those in which the parent drug was found. Platelet responses are in fact very complex as chlorpromazine and/or its metabolites added to blood *in vitro*, rather than by dosage *in vivo* followed by analysis *in vitro*, actually inhibits the aggregation response.

The Oxford group has more recently focused its attention on prolactin. The importance of prolactin is: (1) plasma prolactin rises in human subjects given chlorpromazine; (2) circulating levels of prolactin are raised in psychiatric patients receiving neuroleptics; and (3) prolactin release relates to function of dopaminergic nerves in the hypothalamus, and other dopaminergic nerves may be important in psychoses (Martin 1973; Frantz *et al.* 1972). Dopaminergic nerves in the basal ganglia are certainly important in extrapyramidal effects of chlorpromazine as chlorpromazine blocks dopamine receptors. The questions arising are: (1) is the prolactin response related to dose or concentration of chlorpromazine; and (2) is the prolactin response related to clinical effects of the drug?

The Oxford group at first showed no relation between chlorpromazine dose and prolactin levels, but did show a significant correlation ($r = 0.67$) between concentrations in plasma and prolactin levels in a group of newly diagnosed schizophrenics. In addition, they showed that low plasma prolactin correlated with low incidence of extrapyramidal symptoms. Also, mean plasma chlorpromazine was higher in patients showing these symptoms. There was little useful correlation data for clinical effects or autonomic nervous system side-effects.

In a second paper the same group repeated their extrapyramidal system/plasma chlorpromazine/prolactin observations, but this time in a group of patients from among whom six of the seven who showed no clinical improvement actually had plasma chlorpromazine levels equal to or higher than those who improved. In their third paper, the same investigators reported on 18 chronic schizophrenics receiving a miscellany of other drugs and with the diffuse pathology of chronic disease. The relationships seen in the acute dose study now disappeared. The drug concentrations in the acutely-treated and chronically-treated patients were similar and all-in-all prolactin is not emerging as obviously useful in monitoring the clinical pharmacology of neuroleptic action. However, interesting observations have been made more recently with long-acting neuroleptics (see next section).

PHARMACOKINETICS OF LONG-ACTING NEUROLEPTICS

Certain neuroleptics are specifically designed to exert effects for times longer than those expected with conventional oral preparations. There are approximately eight neuroleptic drugs in this group, available either as prescribable drugs or research compounds. Despite the fact that these compounds are basically pharmacokinetic variants of other drugs, objective pharmacokinetic evidence for differences between the long-acting and short-acting compounds has rarely been obtained. Indeed, all neuroleptics exert effects for a long time (Leff and Wing 1973; Hirsch *et al.* 1973). The important distinction is between compounds administered daily (or more frequently) on the one hand, and those administered weekly (or less frequently) on the other. The latter are classified as long-acting (Johnson 1977).

Measurement of the plasma levels of the long-acting drugs has proved extremely difficult. These drugs are given in low doses, spread over long intervals, and this has led to very low concentrations, with consequent high demands for technical power in methods involved. However, various pieces of information are now available, and we can begin to build up a picture.

Fluphenazine

The oldest of the long-acting neuroleptics is fluphenazine enanthate, although this compound has been largely replaced by fluphenazine decanoate. These two drugs were first marketed more than 10 years ago, and over the years a number of largely unsuccessful attempts have been made to assess their pharmacokinetic properties. Amongst these attempts, there is a fluorimetric study which recorded concentrations in the body higher than those possible from the dose given distributed through the total body water. There is also a study of total radioactivity, never published in full. In recent years progress has been made with radioimmunoassay and with studies of fractionated radioactivity (Curry *et al.* 1979*a*). This report has been wrongly reviewed as involving the study of unfractionated radioactivity (Jann *et al.* 1985). Both have yielded unexpected observations. The enanthate behaves much as expected from animal data and from basic principles. The fluphenazine concentration rises to a maximum 2–3 days after the dose, and falls with a half-life of approximately 3–5 days. This results in a 75 per cent drop in plasma fluphenazine from the peak to the trough in a once-a-week regime, and a quadrupling of the predosage level to the peak after each dose. This is a substantial degree of fluctuation. In contrast the decanoate shows two phases of fluphenazine concentration. There is an initial short-lasting peak in the first 8–12 hours, reaching levels far above those arising from the enanthate, then a plateau for 2–3 weeks, with relatively small changes, and a half-life of 6–10 days. This plateau is at a level below the peak, but above the trough resulting from enanthate. The clinical significance of this will be considered later (Altamura *et al.* 1985; Curry *et al.* 1979*a*; Wiles and Gelder 1980).

Perphenazine

The enanthate ester of perphenazine shows a smooth rise and fall of the parent drug. Perphenazine concentrations rise from approximately 1 nmol l^{-1} before the dose to 6–12 nmol l^{-1} at the peak, which is around 3–4 days. The half-life is then several days, with exact details dependent on individual characteristics (Eggert-Hansen *et al.* 1976).

Flupenthixol

Flupenthixol decanoate has been assessed by various techniques, including measurement of unfractionated radioactivity and radioimmunoassay. The unfractionated radioactivity measurements are of little value although it has been suggested that because the excretion patterns of known metabolites indicate faster elimination than that of flupenthixol itself, the majority of serum radioactivity represents flupenthixol (Jorgensen 1978b). This is probably fallacious, as the analogous studies with fluphenazine showed that only a small proportion of the total radioactivity represented the parent drug. Also, a later study actually proved metabolites to be present (Stauning *et al.* 1979). The same applied in animals given flupenthixol, and there was some similar evidence in one poorly documented study with flupenthixol decanoate. In spite of all this, the unfractionated radioactivity data from flupenthixol decanoate does seem to rule out the occurrence of an early peak as seen with fluphenazine decanoate. This may have considerable clinical importance (Aaes-Jorgensen *et al.* 1977; Johnstone *et al.* 1980, Jorgensen 1978*a*, *b*; Lundbeck Ltd. 1974; Stauning *et al.* 1979).

Penfluridol

This compound is of especial interest because of its oral administration. Three reports of pharmacokinetic data can be quoted. First, on a once weekly regimen, the peak was at 24–72 hours after the dose. The drug was detectable at seven days. In another study, detailed assessment in the thirteenth week of once-weekly treatment showed a background concentration of 10–15 ng ml^{-1}, a peak at 12 hours of approximately 55 ng ml^{-1}, and a biphasic fall, rapid at first, slower later, to approximately 11 ng ml^{-1} by 168 hours after the dose, which was 120 mg. In the third study with a gradually increasing dose over 13 weeks, approximately similar data were obtained, but at a lower over-all level (Chouinard *et al.* 1977; Cooper *et al.* 1977; Gallant *et al.* 1974; Migdalof *et al.* 1979).

The fascinating implication of this, is that during long-term treatment, the time course of rise and fall of penfluridol concentrations and the percentage rise and fall, is remarkably similar to that of chlorpromazine in similar circumstances. And chlorpromazine is the typical 'short-acting' neuroleptic! Of course, 'short' and 'long' are relative terms. Chlorpromazine definitely exerts its effects for long periods, and this probably relates to the long-term retention in the body. Clinical relapse does not occur when plasma chlor-promazine falls acutely. Indeed, the highest incidence of relapse is in the *second month* after cessation of treatment, when final residues of the drug are slowly disappearing from the body (Leff and Wing 1973; Hirsch *et al.* 1973). Perhaps, with the appropriate psychological follow-up, and with suitable promotion, chlorpromazine could be marketed as a once-weekly, long-acting drug. I am sure that infrequent intramuscular chlorpromazine could be proved long-acting, especially if formulated in an oily injection. This might lead to lesser overall dosage of this compound, which would be excellent if accompanied by sufficient clinical effect. A similar argument could be applicable to haloperidol. However, it must still be recognized that the difference between therapeutic doses and doses causing side-effects may be a limiting factor. For a drug to be acceptable for weekly dosing, it must be possible to administer a sufficient quantity in the weekly dose.

Haloperidol has in fact emerged in recent years as a potentially long-acting drug in decanoate form. Compared with the phenothiazines, haloperidol has always appeared to be a simpler drug to study, having less active metabolite problems, less of a first-pass effect, and reasonably predictable phar-macokinetics, such as in the relation between dose and concentrations. There is now an opportunity to study long-acting haloperidol in comparison with long-acting fluphenazine, regardless of the fact that haloperidol seems more popular in emergency psychiatry than in long-term maintenance (Evans 1981; Itoh *et al.* 1980; Magliozzi *et al.* 1981; Rubin *et al.* 1980; Menuck and Voineskos 1981; Donlon *et al.* 1979).

Other examples

Genuine pharmacokinetic information is short on the other long-acting examples. Technical data on fluspirilene is restricted to total radioactivity measurements (Smith, Kline, and French Ltd). The time-course of pipothia-zine has been studied pharmacologically (Julou *et al.* 1973).

Implications for clinical effect

Objective study of the duration of neuroleptic effect is obviously very difficult. Weekly, two-weekly, or monthly dosage regimens for particular drugs have become standard practice, largely on the basis of manufacturers' recommendations, animal work, or intuitive reasoning with empirical observation of patients as a major influence, and incidence of unwanted effects playing a part. It would certainly be useful if the time-course of neuroleptic effect could be elucidated, but it must be remembered that clinical deterioration will not necessarily set in when the drug has ceased to be detectable in the body.

There are, however, implications for side-effects of a transient nature, such as drowsiness, and some extrapyramidal problems arising from presence of too much drug and reversible by reduction of plasma levels. This has been clearly shown with fluphenazine enanthate and decanoate (Altamura *et al*. 1985; Curry *et al*. 1979*b*). Thus, the enanthate caused a higher overall incidence of side-effects, with maximum occurrence at 2–3 days. The decanoate caused side-effects on the day of injection, and there were also changes in plasma prolactin which showed a similar time-course. Similar studies have not been carried out with other drugs.

The data also raises important questions concerning mechanisms of release from intramuscular injection sites. It is thought that the speed of loss from the injection site controls the duration of action. However, fluphenazine decanoate seems to leave the injection site in two phases. The initial loss is rapid, and leads to the early peak. The later loss is slow and leads to the long plateau. In contrast, the loss of the enanthates of fluphenazine and perphenazine from their sites of injection is steady and monophasic. Perhaps decanoates bind differently to muscle tissue, or perhaps fluphenazine decanoate is unique, as there is no evidence as yet of anything unusual with flupenthixol decanoate (Dreyfuss *et al*. 1971*a, b*; 1976; Altamura *et al*. 1979).

Thus we still have much to learn about the pharmacokinetics and clinical influence of the long-acting neuroleptics. Problems are still basic, relating to assay methods, release from injection sites, and duration of effect among other factors. This lack of information must be considered remarkable in view of the reason for existence of, and the series of claims made for, these compounds.

Drug interactions

Neuroleptic drugs are commonly administered in combination with either one or more other neuroleptics or with drugs of different groups. There have been no reports of interactions between neuroleptic drugs although there has been a certain amount of speculation. Similarly, there are few studies reported to date concerning interactions between neuroleptics and drugs from the other major groups of psychotropic agents. One recent report concerned the effect of neuroleptics on tricyclic antidepressant levels and effects (Vandel *et al.* 1979).

Loga *et al.* (1981) studied the interaction of chlorpromazine and nortriptyline. Seven male in-patients suffering from acute schizophrenia were treated with chlorpromazine elixir 100 mg 8-hourly for nine weeks. Nortriptyline, 50 mg every 8 hours, was added during weeks four, five, and six. Plasma chlorpromazine levels rose when nortriptyline was added, and the antipyrine half-life was prolonged. Blood pressure, which had dropped on institution of the chlorpromazine, dropped further when nortriptyline was added to the regimen. Pulse rate rose, with a further rise on adding nortriptyline. Pupil size, salivation, and handwriting length were diminished (probably maximally) by the chlorpromazine, and no further change was initiated by the nortriptyline. Clinically speaking, the addition of nortriptyline dramatically reversed the therapeutic action of the chlorpromazine, presumably by a pharmacodynamic effect. It was concluded that this combination is potentially deleterious and must be used with care.

The interaction of greatest interest is that between neuroleptics and the centrally-acting anticholinergic drugs used in the treatment of drug-induced extrapyramidal side-effects. The importance of this interaction relates to the not uncommon practice of administering orphenadrine and other such compounds prophylactically to prevent any adverse reactions that might occur. Orphenadrine is a classic enzyme-inducing compound and it has been shown to reduce plasma chlorpromazine concentrations in patients treated longterm, and this results in reductions in peripheral effects such as changes in pupil size, gland activity, and cardiovascular changes which relate quite closely to plasma chlorpromazine levels. It does not cause a noticeable change in psychiatric rating during a two- to three-week period, as the plasma level change is within a relatively small range over which clinical changes would not be expected. As regards handwriting length, which is an exemplification of extrapyramidal system problems, and which is sensitive to chlorpromazine and orphenadrine, the orphenadrine reverses the micrographia caused by chlorpromazine.

The question arose as to whether this was merely the result of reduced plasma chlorpromazine and this was determined by use of phenobarbitone as the enzyme inducer. This compound has no anticholinergic effects, but it does reduce plasma chlorpromazine. It does not reverse micrographia. Thus, the effect of orphenadrine is a genuine anticholinergic effect, of value in treatment of schizophrenics showing side-effects of neuroleptics, although its prophylactic use is probably illogical (Loga *et al.* 1975).

CLINICAL MONITORING

Monitoring of plasma chlorpromazine concentrations in patients is useful up to a point. It is not recommended as a routine procedure, as clinical judgement is obviously better for determining the status of a patient. However, it is useful in the determination of reasons for poor response in refractory patients, as a low level ($<$ 35 ng ml^{-1}) indicates a massive first-pass effect or inconsistent tablet taking, an intermediate level ($>$ 35 but $<$ 350 ng ml^{-1}) indicates adequate drug treatment, and, in a refractory patient, the presence of other important factors and high levels ($>$ 350 ng ml^{-1}) indicate overdosing. However, these are only guidelines and there are two important riders. First, the time of sampling is important, and it is best to obtain an estimate of the mean concentration over 24 hours. Second, low levels can indicate successful tablet taking with a high first-pass effect, and this is best detected by urinary excretion studies. Labelling of a person who is an efficient tablet taker with a high first-pass effect as a patient with poor compliance could be disastrous psychologically. Patients with high levels should be tried at lower levels. Patients with low levels can be given higher doses (but at the risk of long-term toxicity caused by metabolites) or intramuscular preparations which by pass the first-pass problems (Cooper 1978; Curry 1985).

CONCLUSION

This review represents an attempt to evaluate the extent to which contemporary clinical pharmacological approaches can be used to determine reasons for differences among the neuroleptic drugs and among the patients treated with them. At present, explanations are partial, in a field strewn with false pathways leading to illusory success. Continued research with ever improving methods is needed, but there is no doubt that, as the result of past efforts, the neuroleptics are vastly better understood than was the case 15 years ago when Brodie encouraged the scientific community to look at their kinetics in greater depth.

APPENDIX: ASSAY TECHNIQUES

Chemical analysis of drugs is not strictly a technique of clinical pharmacology, but the importance of the results obtained by means of chemical analysis to the clinical pharmacology of neuroleptic drugs is so obvious, that a brief summary of relevant points is given here. The application of gas chromatography to chlorpromazine assay in 1968 started the pharmacokinetic work going (Curry 1968). Approximately the same technique was then applied to thioridazine and butaperazine with considerable success, and to fluphenazine, pipothiazine, and trifluoperazine with limited success (Gillespie and Sipes 1981; Javaid *et al.* 1981, 1982; Cooper and Lapierre 1981). However, there were always problems, notably with reproducibility and with the need to assay the parent drug and the metabolites separately. The advent of liquid chromatography, particularly with electrochemical detection, has overcome most if not all of the problems. A strategy for all neuroleptics was presented in 1982 (Curry *et al.* 1982) and specific assays using liquid chromatography are now available for fluphenazine (Davis and Fenimore 1983; Goldstein and Van Vunakis 1981; Heyes *et al.* 1980), thioridazine (Kilts *et al.* 1982; Skinner *et al.* 1980), trimeprazine (McKay *et al.* 1982*a*), promethazine (Melethil *et al.* 1983; Taylor and Houston 1983), chlorpromazine (Murakami *et al.* 1982; Stevenson and Reid 1981), and levomepromazine (Murakami *et al.* 1982).

Along the way there have been more specialized approaches, such as the use of gas chromatography and mass spectrometry combined (Dahl *et al.* 1982; McKay *et al.* 1982*b*; Midha *et al.* 1982; Whelpton *et al.* 1982), radioimmunoassay (Midha *et al.* 1980, 1981), and radioreceptor assay (Kurland *et al.* 1980; Tune and Coyle 1981; Tune *et al.* 1981). Availability of methods is no longer a limiting factor in this research, but all available methods still require careful application.

References

Aaes-Jorgensen, T., Fredricson Overo, K., Bogeso, K. P., and Jorgensen, A. (1977). Pharmacokinetic studies on clopenthixol decanoate; a comparison with clopenthixol in dogs and rats. *Acta pharmacol toxicol.* **41**, 103–20.

Alfredsson, G., Lindberg, M., and Sedvall, G. (1982). The presence of 7-hydroxy-chlorpromazine in CSF of chlorpromazine treated patients. *Psychopharmacology* **77**, 376–8.

—— and Sedvall, G. (1981). Protein binding of chlorpromazine in cerebrospinal fluid and serum. *Int. Pharmacol. Psychiat.* **73**, 55–62.

Altamura, A. C., Whelpton, R., and Curry, S. H. (1979). Animal model for investigation of fluphenazine kinetics after administration of long-acting esters. *Biopharmaceut. Drug Dis.* **1**, 65–72.

——, Curry, S.H., Montgomery, S., and Wiles, D.H. (1985). Early unwanted effects of fluphenazine esters related to plasma fluphenazine concentrations in schizophrenic patients. *Psychopharmacology* **87** 30–3.

Axelsson, R., Martensson, E., and Alling. C. (1982). Serum concentration and protein binding of thioridazine and its metabolites in patients with chronic alcoholism. *Eur. J. clin. Pharmacol.* **23**, 359–63.

Ban, T. A. (1966). Clinical pharmacology of the phenothiazines. *Appl. Therapeut.* **8**, 423–7.

Bergling, R., Mjorndal, T., Oreland, L., Rapp, W., and Wold, S. (1975). Plasma levels and clinical effects of thioridazine and thiothixine. *J. clin. Pharmacol.* **15**, 178–86.

Bolvig-Hannsen, L., Larsen, F. F., and Vestergard, P. (1981). Plasma levels of perphenazine (Trilafon) related to development of side effects. *Psychopharmacology* **74**, 306–9.

Boullin, D. J., Grahame-Smith, D. G., Grimes, R. P. J., and Woods, H. F. (1975*a*). Inhibition of human blood platelet aggregation by chlorpromazine and its metabolites. *Br. J. Pharmacol.* **53**, 121–6.

—— Woods, H.F., Grimes, R.P.J., Grahame-Smith, D.G., Wiles, D., Gelder, M.G., and Kolakowska, T. (1975*b*). Increased platelet aggregation responses to 5-hydroxytryptamine in patients taking chlorpromazine. *Br. J. clin. Pharmacol.* **2**, 29–35.

Brinkschulte, M., Gaertner, H. J., Schied, H. W., and Breyer-Pfaff, V. (1982). Plasma protein binding of perazine and amitriptyline in psychiatric patients. *Eur. J. clin. Pharmacol.* **22**, 367–73.

Brodie, B. B. (1976). Physicochemical and biochemical aspects of pharmacology. *J. Amer. med. Ass.* **202**, 600–9.

Byck, R. (1975). Drugs and the treatment of psychiatric diorders, *The pharmacological basis of therapeutics*, (5th edn) (ed. L. S. Goodman and A. Gilman). Macmillan, New York.

Casper, R., Garver, D. L., Dekirmenjian, H., Chang, S., and Davis, J. M. (1980). Phenothiazine levels in plasma and red blood cells. *Arch. gen. Psychiat.* 37, 301-5.

Chaffin, D. S. (1964). Phenothiazine induce acute psychotic reaction: the 'psychotoxicity' of a drug. *Am. J. Psychiat.* 121, 26-32.

Chouinard, G., Annable, L., and Cooper, S. (1977). Antiparkinson drug administration and plasma levels of penfluridol, a new long-acting neuroleptic. *Commun. Psychopharmacol.* 1, 325-31.

Clark, M. L., Ramsey, H. R., Ragland, R. E., Rahhal, D. K., Serafetinides, E. A. and Costiloe, J. P. (1970). Chlorpromazine in chronic schizophrenia: behavioural dose-response relationships. *Psychopharmacologia, Berlin* 18, 260-70.

Cohen, B. M., Lipinski, J. F., Pope, H. G., Harris, P. O., and Altesman, R. I. (1980). Neuroleptic blood levels and therapeutic effect. *Psychopharmacology* 70, 191-3.

Cooper, S. F., Dugal, R., Albert, J. M. and Bertrand, M. (1977). Penfluridol steady-state kinetics in psychiatric patients. *Clin. Pharmacol. Ther.* 18, 352-9.

—— and Lapierre, T. D. (1981). Gas liquid chromatographic determination of pipotiazine in plasma of psychiatric patients. *J. Chromatog.* 223, 95-102.

Cooper, T. B. (1978). Plasma level monitoring of antipsychotic drugs. *Clin. Pharmacokinet.* 3, 14-38.

Crammer, J. L. (1981). Antipsychotic agents: Thioridazine; pharmacokinetics, plasma levels, and clinical response. In *Psychotropic drugs: plasma concentration and clinical response* (ed. G. D. Burrows and T. R. Norman), pp. 303-18. Marcel Dekker, New York.

Creese, I. and Snyder, S. H. (1977). A simple and sensitive radioreceptor assay for antischizophrenic drugs in blood. *Nature, Lond.* 270, 180-2.

Curry, S. H. (1968). Determination of nanogram quantities of chlorpromazine and some of its metabolites in plasma using gas-liquid chromatography with an electron capture detector. *Anal. Chem.* 40, 1251-5.

—— (1970). Plasma protein binding of chlorpromazine. *J. Pharmacol.* 22, 193-7.

—— (1976a). Metabolism and kinetics of chlorpromazine in relation to effect. In *Antipsychotic drugs: pharmacokinetics and pharmacodynamics* (ed. G. Sedvall, B. Uvnas, and Y. Zolterman), pp. 343-52. Pergamon, Oxford.

—— (1976b). Plasma level studies in psychotropic drug evaluation. *Br. J. Clin. Pharmacol.* 3, 20-8.

—— (1976c). Gas chromatographic methods for the study of chlorpromazine and some of its metabolites in plasma. *Psychopharmacol. Commun.* 2, 1-15.

—— (1980a). Methodological pitfalls; the influence of experimental design on results. In *Drug concentrations in neuropsychiatry* (ed. R. Porters, J. Rivers, and J. Whelan), pp. 35-49. Excerpta Medica, Amsterdam.

—— (1980b). *Drug disposition and pharmacokinetics*, (3rd edn). Blackwell, Oxford.

—— (1981a). Antipsychotic drugs: I. chlorpromazine—pharmacokinetics, plasma levels and clinical response. In *Plasma levels of psychotropic drugs and clinical response* (ed. G. D. Burrows and T. Norman). Marcel Dekker, New York.

—— (1981b). Binding of psychotropic drugs to plasma protein and its influence on drug distribution. In *Clinical pharmacology in psychiatry* (ed. E. Usdin), pp. 213-23. Elsevier, New York.

—— (1984a). Assessment of psychotropic drugs following acute doses: I. Pharmacodynamics and pharmacokinetics. In *Guidelines for the use of psychotropic drugs* (ed. H. Stancer), pp. 381-8. Spectrum, New York.

—— (1984b). Assessment of psychotropic drugs following acute doses: II. Clinical significance of neuroleptic plasma levels. In *Guidelines for the use of psychotropic drugs* (ed. H. Stancer), pp. 239–44. Spectrum, New York.

—— (1984*c*). Recent developments in pharmacokinetics relevant to the practice of psychiatry. In Advances in neuropsychopharmacology (ed. G. D. Burrows and T. Norman), pp. 1–5. Libbey, London.

—— (1984*d*). Phenothiazines: Metabolism and pharmacokinetics. In *Drugs in psychiatry* (ed. G. D. Burrows and T. Norman), Vol. 3, pp. 79–97. Elsevier, Amsterdam.

—— (1985). Commentary: the strategy and value of neuroleptic drug monitoring. *J. clin. Psychopharm.* **5** 263–71.

—— Altamura, A. C., and Montgomery, S. (1979*b*). Unwanted effects of fluphenazine enanthate and decanoate. *Lancet* **i**, 331–3.

—— Brown, E. A., Hu, O. Y-P, and Perrin, J. H. (1982). LC assay of phenothiazine, thiothixene, and butyrophene neuroleptics and antihistamines in biological fluids with conventional and radial compression columns and UV and electro-chemical detection. *J. Chromatog.* **231**, 361–76.

—— Davis, J. M., Janowsky, D. S., and Marshall, J. H. L. (1970*b*). Factors affecting chlorpromazine plasma levels in psychiatric patients. *Arch. gen. Psychiat.* **22**, 207–15.

—— Derr, J. E., and Maling, H. M. (1970*a*). The physiological disposition of chlorpromazine in the rat and dog. *Proc. Soc. exp. Biol. Med.* **134**, 314–18.

—— D'Mello, A., and Mould, G. P. (1971). Destruction of chlorpromazine during absorption in the rat *in vivo* and *in vitro*. *Br. J. Pharmacol.* **42**, 403–11.

—— and Marshall, J. H. L. (1968). Plasma levels of chlorpromazine and some of its relatively non-polar metabolites in psychiatric patients. *Life Sci.* **7**, 9–17.

—— and Mould, G. P. (1975). A microsomal oxidase system in rat intestinal mucosa. *Br. J. Pharmacol.* **54**, 229P–30P.

—— Whelpton, R., de Schepper, P. J., Vranckx, S., and Schiff, A. A. (1979*a*). Kinetics of fluphenazine after fluphenazine dihydrochloride, enanthate and decanoate administration to man. *Br. J. clin. Pharmacol.* **7**, 325–31.

Dahl, S. G., Johnsen, H., and Lee, C. R. (1982). Gas chromatographic mass spectrometric identification of *O*-demethylated and monohydroxylated metabolites of levomepromazine in blood from psychiatric patients by selected ion recording with high resolution. *Biomed. Mass Spectrom.* **9**, 534–8.

Dally, P. (1967). *Chemotherapy of psychiatric disorders.* Logos Press, London.

Davidson, J. D., Terry, L. L., and Sjoerdsma, A. (1957). Action and metabolism of chlorpromazine sulfoxide in man. *J. Pharmacol. exp. Ther.* **121**, 8–12.

Davis, C. M. and Fenimore, D. C. (1983), Determination of fluphenazine in plasma by high-performance thin-layer chromatography. *J. Chromatog.* **272**, 157–65.

Davis, J. M. (1965). The efficacy of the tranquillizing and antidepressant drugs. *Arch. gen. Psychiat.* **13**, 552–72.

Delay, J., Deniker, P. and Harl, J. M. (1952). Utilisation en therapeutique psychiatrique d'une phenothiazine d'action central elective (4560 RP). *Ann. Med. Psychol.* **110**, 112–17.

Domino, E. F. (1962). Human pharmacology of tranquillizing drugs. *Am. clin. Pharmacol. Ther.* **3**, 599–664.

Donlon, P. T., Hopkin, J., and Tupin, J. P. (1979). Overview: efficacy and safety of the rapid neuroleptization method with injectable haloperidol. *Am. J. Psychiat.* **136**, 273–8.

Dreyfuss, J., Ross, J. J., and Schreiber, E. C. (1971*a*). Excretion and biotransformation of the enanthate ester of fluphenazine 14-C by the dog. *J. Pharm. Sci.* **60**, 829–33.

——, ——, —— (1971*b*). Biological disposition and metabolic fate of fluphenazine-14-C in the dog and rhesus monkey. *J. Pharm. Sci.* **60**, 821–5.

——, —— Shaw, J. M., Miller, I., and Schreiber, E. C. (1976). Release and elimination of 14-C-fluphenazine enanthate and decanoate esters administered in sesame oil to dogs. *J. Pharm. Sci.* **65**, 502–7.

Dysken, M. W., Javaid, J. I., Chang, S. S., Schaffer, C., Shaid, A., and Davis, J. M. (1981). Fluphenazine pharmacokinetics and therapeutic response. *Psychopharmacology* **73**, 205–10.

Eggert-Hansen, C., Rosted, Christensen, T., Elley, J., Bolvig, Hansen, L., Kragh-Sorensen, P., Narsen, N. E., Naestoft, J., and Hvidberg, E. F. (1976). Clinical pharmacokinetic studies of perphenazine. *Br. J. clin. Pharmacol.* **3**, 915–23.

Evans, L. (1981). Butyropherones: plasma levels and therapeutic effect. In *Psychotropic drugs: plasma concentrations and clinical response* (ed. G. D. Burrows and T. R. Norman), pp. 319–29. Marcel Dekker, New York.

Forrest, I. S., Green, D. E. (1972). Phenothiazines: metabolism and analytical detection. *J. forensic Sci.* **17**, 592–617.

Frantz, A. G., Kleinberg, D. L., and Noel, G. L. (1972). Studies on prolactin in man. *Rec. Prog. Horm. Res.* **28**, 527–73.

Gallant, D. M., Mielke, D. G., Spirtes, M. A., Swanson, W. C., and Bost, R. (1974). Penfluridol: an efficacious long-acting oral antipsychotic compound. *Am. J. Psychiat.* **131**, 699–702.

Gillespie, T. J. and Sipes, I. G. (1981). Sensitive gas chromatographic determination of trifluoperazine in human plasma. *J. Chromatog.* **223**, 95–102.

Goldstein, S. A. and Van Vunakis, H. (1981). Determination of fluphenazine, related phenothiazine drugs and metabolites by combined high-performance liquid chromatography and radio-immunoassay. *J. Pharmacol. exp. Ther.* **217**, 36–43.

Gottschalk, L. A., Biener, R., Noble, E. P., Birch, H., Wilbert, D. E., and Heiser, J. F. (1975). Thioridazine plasma levels and clinical response. *Comprehens. Psychiat.* **16**, 323–7.

Hamilton, M. (1965). Ten years of chlorpromazine. *Comprehens. Psychiat.* **6**, 291–97.

Harmon, A. W., Frewin, D. B., and Priestly, B. G. (1980). Comparative enzyme-inducing effects of chlorpromazine and fluphenazine therapies in psychotic patients. *Psychopharmacology* **69**, 35–7.

Harris, J. P., Phillipson, O. T., Watkins, G. M., and Whelpton, R. (1983). Effects of chlorpromazine and promazine on the visual after effects of tilt and movement. *Psychopharmacology* **79**, 49–57.

Hershey, L. A., Gift, T., Atkins, R. W., and Rivera-Calimlin, L. (1981). Effects of a drug holiday on plasma chlorpromazine levels in chronic schizophrenic patients. *Psychopharmacology* **73**, 355–8.

Heyes, W. F., Salmon, J. R., and Marlow, W. (1980). High performance liquid chromatographic separation of the *N*- and *S*-oxides of fluphenazine decanoate. *J. Chromatog.* **194**, 416–20.

Hirsch, S. R. Gaind, R., Ronde, P. D., Stevens, B. C., and Wing, J. K. (1973). Outpatient maintenance of chronic schizophrenic patients with long-acting fluphenazine: double-blind placebo trial. *Br. med. J.* **1**, 633–7.

Hollister, L. E. (1968). Human pharmacology of antipsychotic and antidepressant drugs. *Ann. Rev. Pharmacol.* **8**, 491–516.

Howes, C. A., Pullar, T., Sourindhrin, I., Mistra, P. C., Capel, H., Lawson, D. H., and Tilstone, W. J. (1983). Reduced steady-state plasma concentrations of chlorpromazine and indomethacin in patients receiving cimetidine. *Eur. J. clin. Pharmacol.* **24**, 99–102.

Itoh, H., Yagi, G., Ohtsuka, N., Iwamura, K., and Ichikawa, K. (1980). Serum level of haloperidol and its clinical significance. *Prog. Neuro-Psychopharm.* **4**, 117–183.

Jann, M.W., Ereshefsky, L., and Saklad, S.R. (1985). Clinical pharmacokinetics of the depot antipsychotics. *Clinical Pharmacokinetics* **10** 315–33.

Javaid, J. I., Dekirmenjian, H., and Davis, J. M. (1982). GLC analysis of trifluoperazine in human plasma. *J. Pharm. Sci.* **71**, 63–6.

—— —— Liskevych, V., Lin, R-I., and Davis, J. M. (1981). Fluphenazine determination in human plasma by a sensitive gas chromatographic method using nitrogen detector. *J. chromatog. Sci.* **19**, 439–43.

Jeste, D. V., Linnoila, M., Wagner, R. L., and Wyatt, R. J. (1982). Serum neuroleptic concentrations and tardive dyskinesia. *Psychopharmacology* **76**, 377–80.

Johnson, D. A. W. (1977). Practical considerations in the use of depot neuroleptics for the treatment of schizophrenia. *Br. J. hosp. Med.* **17**, 546–59.

Johnstone, E. C., Bourne, R. C., Cotes, P. M., Crow, T. J., Ferrier, I. N., Owen, F., and Robinson, J. D. (1980). Blood levels of flupenthixol in patients with acute and chronic schizophrenia. In *Drug concentrations in neuropsychiatry* (ed. R. Porter, J. Rivers, and J. Whelan). Excerpta Medica, Amsterdam.

Jorgensen, A. (1978a). A sensitive and specific radioimmunoassay for *cis (z)*-flupenthixol in human serum. *Life Sci.* **23**, 1533–42.

—— (1978b). Pharmacokinetic studies on flupenthixol decanoate: a depot neuroleptic of the thiaxanthine group. *Drug Metab. Rev.* **8**, 235–49.

Julou, L., Bourat, G., Ducrot, R., Fournel, J., and Garret, C. (1973). Pharmacological study of pipotiazine (19, 366 RP) and its undercylenic (19, 551 RP) and palmitic (19, 552 RP) esters. *Acta psychiat. scand.* **241**, 9–30.

Kilts, C. D., Patrick, K. S., Breese, G. R., and Mailman, R. B. (1982). Simultaneous determination of thioridazine and its *S*-oxidized and demethylated metabolites using high performance liquid chromatography on radially compressed silica. *J. Chromatog.* **231**, 377–91.

Kleinman, J.E., Bigelow, L.B., Rogol, A., Weinberger, D.R., Nasrallah, H.A., Wyatt, R.J., and Gillin, J.C. (1980). A clinical trial of 7-hydrooxychlorpormazine in chronic schizophrenia. In *Phenothiazines and structurally related drugs* (ed. E. Usdin *et al.*). Elsevier, New York.

Kolakowska, T., Wiles, D. H., McNeilly, A. S., and Gelder, M. G. (1975), Correlation between plasma levels of prolactin and chlorpromazine in psychiatric patients. *Psychol. Med.* **5**, 214–5.

—— —— Gelder, M. G., and McNeilly, A. S. (1976b). Clinical significance of plasma chlorpromazine levels: II. Plasma levels of the drug, some of its metabolites and prolactin in patients receiving long-term phenothiazine treatment. *Psychopharmacology* **49**, 101–7.

Kurland, A. A., Nagaraju, A. and Hanlon, T. E. (1980). The dopamine radioreceptor assay—a clinical application. *J. clin. Pharmacol.* **20**, 191–3.

Leff, J. P. and Wing, J. K. (1973). Trial of maintenance therapy in schizophrenia. *Br. med. J.* **3**, 599–604.

Loga, S., Curry, S. H., and Lader, M. H. (1975). Interactions of orphenadrine and phenobarbitone with chlorpromazine: Plasma concentrations and effects in man. *Br. J. clin. Pharmacol.* **2**, 197–208.

—— —— —— (1981). Interaction of chlorpromazine and nortriptyline in patients with schizophrenia. *Clin. Pharmacokinet.* **6**, 454–62.

Loo, J. C. K., Midha, K. K., and McGilveray, I.J. (1980). Pharmacokinetics of chlorpromazine in normal volunteers. *Commun. Psychopharmacol.* **4**, 121–9.

Lundbeck Limited (Luton UK) (1974). Depixol Depot Injection. Technical Information.

Mackay, A. V. P., Healey, A. F., and Baker, J. (1974). The relationship of plasma chlorpromazine to its 7-hydroxy and sulphoxide metabolites in a large population of chronic schizophrenics. *Br. J. clin. Pharmacol.* **1**, 425–30.

Magliozzi, J. R., Hollister, L. E., Arnold, K. V., and Earle, G. M. (1981). Relationship of serum haloperidol levels to clinical response in schizophrenic patients. *Am. J. Psychiat.* **138**, 365–7.

Martin, J. B. (1973). Neural regulation of growth hormone secretion. *New Engl. J. Med.* **288**, 1384–93.

May, P. R. A. (1968). *Treatment of schizophrenia: a comparative study of five treatment methods.* Science House, New York.

——, Van Putten, T., Jenden, D. J., Yale, D., and Dixon, W. J. (1981). Chlorpromazine levels and the outcome of treatment in schizophrenic patients. *Arch. gen. Psychiat.* **38**, 202–7.

McKay, G., Cooper, J. K., Midha, K. K., Hall, K., and Hawes, E. M. (1982*a*). Simple and sensitive high-performance liquid chromatographic procedure with electrochemical detection for the determination of plasma concentrations of trimeprazine following single oral doses. *J. Chromatog.* **233**, 417–22.

—— Hall, K., Cooper, J. K., Hawes, E. M., and Midha, K. K. (1982*b*). Gas-chromatographic–mass spectrometric procedure for the quantitation of chlorpromazine in plasma and its comparison with a new high-performance liquid chromatographic assay with electrochemical detection. *J. Chromatog.* **232**, 275–82.

Melethil, S., Dutta, A., Chungi, V., and Dittert, L. (1983). Liquid chromatographic assay for promethazine in plasma using electrochemical detection. *Analyt. Lett.* **16 (B9)** 701–9.

Meltzer, H. Y., Busch, D. A., and Fang, V. S. (1981). Effect of neuroleptics on serum prolactin levels in relation to clinical response and neuroleptic blood levels. In *Clinical pharmacology in psychiatry* (ed. E. Usdin), pp. 51–168. Elsevier, New York.

Menuck, M., and Voineskos, G. (1981). Rapid parenteral treatment of acute psychosis, *Comprehens. Psychiat.* **22**, 351–61.

Midha, K. K., Cooper, J. K., and Hubbard, J. W. (1980). Radioimmunoassay for fluphenazine in plasma. *Commun. Psychopharmacol.* **4**, 107–14.

—— —— McGilveray, I. J., Butterfield, A. G., and Hubbard, J. W. (1981). High-performance liquid chromatographic assay for nanogram determination of chlorpromazine and its comparison with radioimmunoassay. *J. Pharm. Sci.* **70**, 1043–6.

—— Roscoe, R. M. H., Hall, K., Hawes, E. M., Cooper, J. K., McKay, G., and Shetty, H. V. (1982). A gas chromatographic mass spectrometric assay for plasma trifluoperazine concentrations following single doses. *Biomed. Mass Spectrom.* **9**, 186–90.

Migdalof, B. H., Grinder, J. M., Heykants, J. J. P., and Janssen, P. A. T. (1979). Penfluridol: a neuroleptic drug designed for long duration of action. *Drug Metab. Rev.* **9**, 281–99.

Morselli, P. L. and Zarifian, E. (1980). Clinical significance of monitoring plasma levels of psychotropic drugs. In *Drug concentrations in neuropsychiatry* (ed. R. Portes, J. Rivers, and J. Whelan), pp. 115–139. Excerpta Medica, Amsterdam.

Murakami, Kazuo, Murakami, Koji, Veno, T., Hajikata, J., Shirasawa, K., and Muto, T. (1982). Simultaneous determination of chlorpromazine and levomepromazine in human plasma and urine by high-performance liquid chromatography using electrochemical detection. *J. Chromatog.* **227**, 103–12.

NIMH-PSC Collaborative Study Group (1964). Phenothiazine treatment in acute schizophrenia. *Arch. gen. Psychiat.* **10**, 246–61.

Nyberg, G. L., Axelsson, R., and Martensson, E. (1981). Cerebrospinal fluid concentrations of thioridazine and its main metabolites in psychiatric patients. *Eur. J. clin. Pharmacol.* **19**, 139–48.

—— and Martensson, E. (1982). Binding of thioridazine and thioridazine metabolites to serum protein. *Naunyn-Schmiedeberg's Arch. Pharmacol.* **319**, 189–96.

Pantuck, E. J., Pantuck, C. B., Anderson, K. E., Conney, A. H., and Kappas, A. (1982). Cigarette smoking and chlorpromazine disposition and actions. *Clin. Pharmacol. Ther.* **31**, 533–8.

Papadopoulos, A. S., Chand, T. G., Crammer, J. L., and Lader, S. (1980). A pilot study of plasma thioridazine and metabolites in chronically treated patients. *Br. J. Psychiat.* **126**, 591–6.

Prien, R. F. and Klett, C. J. (1972). An appraisal of the long-term use of tranquillizing medication with hospitalized schizophrenics: a review of the literature. *Schiz. Bull.* **5**, 64–73.

Rivera-Calimlin, L., Casteneda, L., and Lasagna, L. (1973). Effect of mode of management on plasma chlorpromazine in psychiatric patients. *Clin. Pharmacol. Ther.* **14**, 978–86.

Romon, R., Averbuch, I., Rozick, P., Fijman-Danilovich, L., Kara, T., Dasberg, H., Ebstein, R. P., and Belmaker, R. H. (1981). Serum and CSF levels of haloperidol by radioimmunoassay and radioreceptor assay during high-dose therapy of resistant schizophrenic patients. *Psychopharmacology* **73**, 197–9.

Rubin, T. T., Forsman, A., Heykants, J., Ohman, R., Towes, B., and Michiels, M. (1980). Serum haloperidol determinations in psychiatric patients. *Arch. gen. Psychiat.* **37**, 1069–74.

Sakalis, G., Curry, S. H., Mould, G. P., and Lader, M. H. (1972). Physiologic and clinical effects of chlorpromazine and their relation to plasma level. *Clin. Pharmacol. Ther.* **13**, 931–46.

—— and Traficante, L. (1981). Antipsychotic agents: Fluphenazine. In *Psychotropic drugs: plasma concentration clinical response* (ed. G. D. Burrows and T. R. Norman), pp. 287–301. Marcel Dekker, New York.

Schley, V. J. (1983). Über die Bindung verschiedener Perazio-Metaboliten und Phenothiazine-Derivate an saures a_1-Glykoprotein. *Arzneim.-Forsch.* **33**, 185–87.

—— Riedel, E., and Muller-Oerlinghausen, B. (1981). Metabolism and excretion of the neuroleptic drug perazine in healthy volunteers. *Int. Pharmacol. Psychiat.* **16**, 201–5.

Sedvall, G. (1981). Correlations between clinical biochemical and pharmacokinetic data in chlorpromazine-treated patients. In *Clinical pharmacology in psychiatry* (ed. E. Usdin), pp. 243–9. Elsevier, New York.

Shopsin, B. Hekimian, L. J. Gershon, S., and Floyd, A. (1969). A controlled evaluation of haloperidol, chlorpromazine and sodium amobarbital: Intramuscular short-term use in acute psychotic patients. *Curr. ther. Res.* **11**, 561–73.

Simpson, G. M., Lament, R., Cooper, T. B., Lee, J. H., and Bruce, R. B. (1973). The relationship between blood levels of different forms of butaperazine and clinical response. *J. clin. Pharmacol.* **13**, 288–97.

Skinner, T., Gochnauer, R., and Linnoila, M. (1980). Liquid chromatographic method to measure thioridazine and its active metabolites in plasma. *Acta pharmacol. toxicol.* **48**, 416–20.

Smith, R. C., Dekirmenjian, J., Davis, J. M., Crayton, J. and Evans, J. (1977). Plasma butaperazine levels in long-term chronic nonresponding schizophrenics. *Commun. Psychopharmacol.* **1**, 319–24.

Smith, Kline & French Laboratories Limited (Welwyn Garden City, UK). Redeptin: Technical Information (undated).

Smolen, V. F., Murdock, H. B., Stoltman, W. P., Clevenger, J. W., Combs, L. W., and Williams, E. J. (1975a). Pharmacological response data for comparative bioavailability studies of chlorpromazine oral dosage forms in humans: I. pupilometry. *J. clin. Pharmacol.* **15**, 734–51.

—— —— and Williams, E. J. (1975*b*). Bioavailability analysis of chlorpromazine in humans from pupilometric data. *J. Pharmacol. exp. Ther.* **195**, 404–15.

—— Williams, E. J., and Kuehn, P. B. (1975*c*). Bioavailability and pharmacokinetic analysis of chlorpromazine in humans and animals using pharmacological data. *Canad. J. pharm. Sci.* **10**, 95–106.

Stauning, J. A., Kirk, L., and Jorgensen. A. (1979). Comparison of serum levels after intramuscular injections of 2% and 10% *Cis(z)*-Flupentixol decanoate in viscoleo to patients. *Psychopharmacology* **65**, 69–72.

Stevenson, D. and Reid, E. (1981). Determination of chlorpromazine and its sulphoxide and 7-hydroxy metabolites by ion-pair high pressure liquid chromatography. *Analyt. Lett.* **14 (B20)**, 1785–1805.

Taylor, G. and Houston, J. B. (1983). Determinants of systemic availability of promethazine in rabbits. *J. Pharm. Pharmacol.* **35**, 284–8.

Tune, L. and Coyle, J. T. (1981). Acute extrapyramidal side-effects: serum level of neuroleptics and anitcholinergics. *Psychopharmacology* **75**, 9–15.

—— Creese, I., DePaul, J. R., Slavney, P. R, Coyle, J. T., and Snyder, S. H. (1980) Clinical state and serum neuroleptic levels measured by radioreceptor assay in schizophrenia. *Am. J. Psychiat.* **137**, 187–90.

——, ——, ——, —— and Snyder, S. H. (1981). Neuroleptic serum levels measured by radioreceptor assay and clinical response in schizophrenic patients. *J. nerv. ment. Dis.* **169**, 60–3.

Vaisanen, K., Viukari, M., Rimon, R., and Raisanen, P. (1981). Haloperidol, thioridazine and placebo in mentally subnormal patients—serum levels and clinical effects. *Acta psychiat. scand.* **63**, 262–5.

Vandel, B., Vandel, S., Allers, G., Bechtel, P., and Volmat, R. (1979). Interaction between antitriptyline and phenothiazine in man: Effect on plasma concentration of antitriptyline and its metabolite nortriptyline and the correlation with clinical response. *Psychopharmacology* **65**, 187–90.

Van Putten, T., May, P. R. A., and Jenden, D. J. (1981). Does a plasma level of chlorpromazine help? *Psychol. Med.* **11**, 729–34.

——, ——, —— Cho, A. K., and Yale, C. (1980). Plasma and saliva levels of chlorpromazine and subjective response. *Am. J. Psychiat.* **137**, 1241–2.

Whelpton, R., Curry, S. H., and Watkins, G. M. (1982). Analysis of plasma trifluoperazine by gas chromatography and selected ion monitoring. *J. Chromatog.* **228**, 321–6.

Widerlov, E., Haggstrom, J-E., Kilts, C. D., Andersson, V., Breese, G. R., and Mailman, R. B. (1982). Serum concentrations of thioridazine, its major metabolites and serum neuroleptic-like activities in schizophrenics with and without tardive dyskinesia. *Acta psychiat. scand.* **66**, 294–305.

Wiles, D. H. and Gelder, M. G. (1979). Plasma fluphenazine levels by radioimmunoassay in schizophrenic patients treated with depot injections of fluphenazine decanoate. *Br. J. clin. Pharmacol.*

—— Kolakowska, T., McNeilly, A. S., Mandelbrote, B. M., and Gelder, M. G. (1976). Clinical significance of plasma chlorpromazine levels: I, Plasma levels of the drug, some of its metabolites, and prolactin during acute treatment. *Psychol. Med.* **6**, 407–15.

Williams, R. T. and Parke, D. V. (1964). The metabolic fate of drugs. *Ann. Rev. Pharmacol.* **4**, 85–114.

Wode-Helgodt, B. and Alfredsson, G. (1981). Concentration of chlorpromazine and two of its active metabolites in plasma and cerebrospinal fluid of psychotic patients treated with fixed drug doses. *Psychopharmacology* **73**, 55–62.

—— Borg, S., Fyro, B. and Sedvall, G. (1978). Clinical effects and drug concentrations in plasma and cerebrospinal fluid in psychotic patients treated with fixed doses of chlorpromazine. *Acta psychiat. scand.* **58**, 149–73.

Yesevage, J. A., Becker, J., Werner, R. D., Mills, M. J., Holman, C. A., and Cohn, R. (1982*a*). Serum level monitoring of thiothixene in schizophrenia: acute single dose levels at fixed doses. *Am. J. Psychiat.* **139**, 174–8.

—— Holman, C. A., and Cohn, R. (1982*a*). Rapid parenteral treatment of acute psychosis. *Comprehens. Psychiat.* **22**, 351–61.

5

Neurotransmitter hypothesis of schizophrenia

BRENDA COSTALL AND ROBERT J. NAYLOR

Bleuler's original treatise on 'schizophrenia' was entitled 'Dementia praecox or the group of schizophrenias' (Bleuler 1911) and thus, from its conception, schizophrenia has been considered as more than one illness. Subsequently, 70 years of clinical experience of schizophrenia has suggested that schizophrenics may be differentiated into subgroups, for example, catatonic, hebephrenic, simple, and paranoid, dependent on obvious differences in behavioural presentation. An understanding of schizophrenia has ranged from a belief that it is a social invention designed to remove from society those who prove to be an embarrassment (Szasz 1978) to a consideration that it reflects an exceedingly complex disease aetiology involving both genetic and environmental factors (Kety *et al.* 1978; Gottesman 1978; Crow 1980; De Feudis and Charras 1982).

Whilst the clinical boundaries of schizophrenia are sometimes ill-defined, and the conveniently applied clinical labels cannot necessarily be taken to denote the existence of specific disease types, it is clear that schizophrenia may reflect in a number of presentations, and the first requirement of the present chapter is to identify those key symptoms which characterize schizophrenia. These primarily include, in various combinations, thought disorders, hallucinations, delusions, and frequently, affective and volitional disturbances. In addition, there may be deleterious emotional, intellectual, memory, perceptual and personality changes (Liberman 1982). Second, it is implicit in the title of this chapter, 'Neurotransmitter hypothesis of schizophrenia', that schizophrenia is a functional disorder, and the remission of psychotic episodes would support this hypothesis.

Yet this is too simplistic an interpretation. Whilst historically it was considered that schizophrenia and manic-depressive psychosis could be distinguished from the organic psychoses, Crow (1982) effectively argued that there is a group of schizophrenics who demonstrate psychological changes which may be associated with essentially irreversible structural changes in the brain. The fundamental finding is that there is a group of chronic schizophrenic patients who have an abnormal ventricular size, with the increased ventricular area relating to the intellectual impairment and the presence of 'negative' symptoms, for example, loss of drive and flattening of affect (see Crow 1982 for references). Crow suggested that there may be two broad symptom groups which represent relatively independent dimensions of psychopathology and may reflect different underlying disease processes. The type I syndrome (of positive symptoms) is more characteristically seen in acute psychotic episodes and the type II syndrome (of negative symptoms) is more frequent in chronic illnesses. However, this is not an invariable rule since positive symptoms may still be present after many years in an institution and negative symptoms are seen in some patients with acute schizophrenia. Patients may have symptoms of both types, either at the same time or sequentially, although for many patients repeated episodes of psychoses may finally lead to the emergence of type II symptoms.

It is against this background of an exceedingly complex disease aetiology that an attempt is made to critically analyse the evidence for a neurotransmitter dysfunction in schizophrenia. A broader perspective of the definitions, aetiologies, and treatments of schizophrenia can be found in recent reviews (Ban and Lehmann 1977; Stevens 1978; Horrobin 1979; Berger 1981, Wyatt *et al.* 1979, 1981; Meltzer *et al.* 1981; Crow 1982; Haracz 1982; Liberman 1982; Snyder 1982).

THE DOPAMINE HYPOTHESIS OF SCHIZOPHRENIA

The most frutiful and most widely accepted neurotransmitter hypothesis of schizophrenia relates to an involvement of cerebral dopamine. The basis of the hypothesis is very simple—an influence which tends to enhance cerebral dopaminergic activity will exacerbate schizophrenia whilst an influence to reduce dopaminergic activity will ameliorate the symptoms of schizophrenia. However, the evidence reviewed in this chapter indicates that an uncritical acceptance of the hypothesis may disadvantage a future and improved understanding of the involvement of dopamine in schizophrenia. The dopamine hypothesis is based on a wealth of neuropharmacological data and inferences, and on restricted clinical findings.

Neurophamacological data indicative of a dopamine involvement in schizophrenia: dopamine agonist studies

The ability of amphetamine to induce a psychosis in man has been known for many years, the symptomatology being likened to that of a 'paranoid psychosis' (Young and Scoville 1938). Connell (1958) distinguished the amphetamine psychosis from toxic organic psychosis but considered it indistinguishable from schizophrenia. However, Ellinwood (1972) thought that the amphetamine psychosis may be distinguished from schizophrenia by the high incidence of visual hallucinations and by the retention of reasonably appropriate affect (see also Bell 1965; Griffith *et al.* 1972). Whilst the range of schizophrenic psychopathology is too extensive to be initiated in its entirety by any one drug, the use of amphetamine probably provides a reasonable model of paranoid schizophrenia (Angrist and Gershon 1972).

An understanding of the central sites and mechanisms via which amphetamine may induce its 'psychotic' effects has been derived almost exclusively from animal experimentation. Numerous behavioural studies in the rodent have shown that amphetamine can induce hyperactivity and stereotyped motor behaviour which are blocked by prior disruption of catecholamine biosynthesis using α-methylparatyrosine (Weissman *et al.* 1966). From biochemical experiments, an extensive literature attests to the ability of amphetamine to cause a release of catecholamines from nerve terminals and to inhibit reuptake processes (Moore *et al.* 1977; Horn 1979; Glowinski *et al.* 1979). Therefore, it has been concluded that the behavioural effects elicited by amphetamine in the rodent are catecholamine-dependent. Attempts to elucidate the relative roles of noradrenaline and dopamine in the mediation of the amphetamine effects have used selective noradrenaline synthesis inhibition and selective antagonism by dopamine and noradrenaline antagonists. It has been concluded that dopamine plays the crucial role in the development of amphetamine-induced stereotyped behaviour and hyperactivity, although a noradrenergic influence on the latter response cannot be dismissed (Kokkinidis and Anisman 1981). An additional and interesting study using *d*- and *l*-amphetamine indicated *d*-amphetamine to be 10 times more potent than *l*-amphetamine to induce motor hyperactivity in rats and to inhibit noradrenaline uptake, whilst the isomers were equipotent to inhibit (striatal) dopamine uptake and to induce stereotyped behaviour (Coyle and Snyder 1969). Whatever the correctness of these observations (Ferris *et al.* 1972; Horn 1979), both the *d*- and the *l*-isomer of amphetamine have been used to induce psychosis in man (Janowsky and Davis 1974), and to assess the relative roles of noradrenaline and dopamine.

The administration of *d*-amphetamine to man causes increased drive, hyperactivity, and stereotyped behaviour as behavioural antecedents to the psychotic phase (Ellinwood 1972). An extrapolation of the animal findings to man has led to the conclusion that amphetamine evokes its effects in man by enhancing catecholaminergic activity. It is therefore surprising that Griffith (1972) (as reported by Angrist and Gershon 1972) reported α-methylparatyrosine treatment, in doses of 2–3 g per day, sufficient to partially antagonize the peripheral actions of amphetamine, to actually enhance the psychotogenic effects of amphetamine by a factor of two. Clearly, more detailed studies to ensure correct dosage of α-methylparatyrosine would be highly relevant. In any event, the ability of dopamine antagonists to antagonize amphetamine psychosis (see below), would argue for an important dopamine involvement and, whilst not negating a possible role for noradrenaline, it is unlikely that amphetamine induces psychosis via two mechanisms, a dopamine-mediated schizophrenia component and a paranoid psychosis mediated via noradrenaline (Snyder 1974).

It is a rather obvious, but frequently neglected point, that the above behavioural and biochemical changes caused by amphetamine in normal laboratory animals are the result of an acute challenge. If these actions of amphetamine were immediately relevant to its ability to cause psychosis in man, then the administration of single doses of amphetamine to the 'normal' human would be expected to cause psychosis. However, whilst acute amphetamine treatment can increase arousal and drive in normal subjects, which attests to a clear central action, equally obvious is the absence of stereotyped behaviour and psychosis. Assuming that the action of amphetamine in the human brain is broadly comparable to that occurring in laboratory animals, the conclusion is that a simple modest increase in catecholamine function is inadequate to induce psychosis.

Yet it is apparent that continued treatment of human subjects with amphetamine, at doses in the order of hundreds of milligrams of *d*-amphetamine, can finally result in stereotyped behaviour patterns and a psychotic behaviour generally considered to most closely reflect paranoid schizophrenia. Such doses are probably comparable to those required to induce stereotyped responding in the rodent expressed on a mg per kg basis. Further, the acute single administration of modest doses of *d*-amphetamine can precipitate or intensify psychotic symptoms in schizophrenic patients (van Kammen *et al*. 1982). It becomes clear that if the psychosis induced by *d*-amphetamine does involve an enhancement of dopamine function, then such actions are best observed after a period of persistent dopamine receptor stimulation. However, it is a critical observation that an acute amphetamine treatment can intensify schizophrenic psychosis indicating the immediacy of dopamine involvement with schizophrenia. This may reflect an action of dopamine on dopamine receptors of modified sensitivity and/or an action of dopamine on dopamine receptors where the functional activity of other controlling neurotransmitter systems has been modified by prior persistent dopamine overactivity.

The above findings offer support for a 'simple' dopamine hypothesis of schizophrenia—that an enhanced dopamine activity can induce psychosis. However, perhaps the most intriguing finding in an examination of data on dopamine agonist administration to schizophrenic patients is that not all subjects respond with an enhanced psychosis to *d*-amphetamine challenge. Van Kammen *et al*. (1982) reviewed the literature which showed that, of 285 patients examined in 12 studies, only 25 per cent showed exacerbated symptoms to *d*-amphetamine challenge, 46 per cent were reported to show no change, and 29 per cent were actually reported to show an improvement. The authors suggested that such data may be indicative of two types of schizophrenia, a dopamine-sensitive and a dopamine-insensitive group, classified as type I and type II respectively according to the hypothesis of Crow (1982). Results obtained by Van Kammen *et al*. (1982) also indicate not merely a worsening of psychotic behaviour following the administration of amphetamine to schizophrenic subjects but also an acute improvement in 29 per cent. However, the authors also found that when patients were rechallenged with amphetamine identical effects were only recorded when patients were in a similar clinical state, thus indicating a 'state-dependent' rather than a 'yes or no' response to amphetamine. In demonstrating this variability in response to *d*-amphetamine the authors questioned the simplicity of the 'dopamine supersensitivity' model of schizophrenia as well as the model proposed by Crow.

In retrospect, it would have been more accurate for the authors to divide their 'dopamine-sensitive' responders into positive (i.e. psychosis exacerbation) and negative (i.e. psychosis amelioration) groups with a third group showing genuine insensitivity, i.e. no clinical change. In terms of 'sensitivity' and 'insensitivity' to amphetamine the authors' groupings sit uncomfortably on the classification of Crow. Dopamine agonists may induce a worsening of psychosis in type I patients, but rarely induce psychotic symptoms in patients showing a negative symptomatology (type II) (see Cesarec *et al*. 1974; Gerlach and Luhdorf 1975; Inanaga *et al*. 1975; Brambilla *et al*. 1979). Hence, an amelioration in schizophrenia caused by dopamine agonists may to some extent involve an improvement in the negative symptoms (Cesarec *et al*. 1974; Gerlach and Luhdorf 1975; Buchanan *et al*. 1975; Ogura *et al*. 1976; Angrist *et al*. 1982). Whilst this is undoubtedly an over-simplification (van Kammen and Bunney 1979), the observations that dopamine agonists can cause worsening or improvement in psychotic behaviour allowed the formulation of hypotheses of 'at least two different types of schizophrenia' (Segal and Janowsky 1978) or 'two different disease processes' (Brambilla *et al*. 1979).

In any event, there is ever-increasing evidence that to use the 'dopamine hypothesis' of schizophrenia to indicate the universal presence of an enhanced dopamine activity in schizoprenia may be seriously misleading. That amphetamine may reduce psychotic symptoms is of fundamental importance for a revision of the dopamine hypothesis, but in which direction? It remains the most important observation that psychotic states have been induced in normal man by high doses of, and/or chronic treatment with, amphetamine and other agents known to increase cerebral dopaminergic function, for example, methylphenidate (McCormick and McNeil 1963) and levodopa (Jenkins and Groh 1970; Goodwin *et al*. 1970), and that lower doses of these agents have precipitated or intensified psychotic symptoms in schizophrenia (van Kammen *et al*. 1977; Angrist *et al*. 1975, 1980; Janowsky *et al*. 1973*a*, 1977*b*; Janowsky and Davis 1976; Yaryura-Tobias *et al*. 1970). However, all such agents have an ability to enhance dopamine and noradrenaline function, and it has proved difficult to identify with precision the relative roles played by the two catecholamines. The most relevant experiment would be to specifically inhibit the synthesis of noradrenaline by inhibiting dopamine-β-hydroxylase. In practice, it is difficult to achieve a complete enzyme inhibition and the agents which do exert a reasonable effect, for example fusaric acid, are potentially toxic. Nevertheless, the administration of fusaric acid was found to exacerbate psychotic symptoms in certain patients (Sack and Goodwin 1974) and it has been hypothesized that a biological deficit in schizophrenia involves a block in the dopamine-β-hydroxylase step to result in increased formation of dopamine, but in noradrenaline neurones (Hartmann 1976). That temporary dopamine-β-hydroxylase inhibition combined with levodopa administration might produce mental changes in normal subjects was assessed by Hartmann and Keller-Teschke (1977) who found a significant deviation in 'total psychopathology' using the BPRS rating scale. Whilst such findings are preliminary, they support an involvement of dopamine rather than noradrenaline in psychosis. Nevertheless, it remains possible that a reduced noradrenaline function might contribute to the development of psychosis and, indeed, Kokkinidis and Anisman (1981) argued this point on the basis of animal experimentation. However, Rebec and Bashore (1982) indicated the difficulties in too ready a translation of animal findings to the clinic. Furthermore, whilst Hornykiewicz (1982) most ably reviewed the case for a noradrenaline involvement in the pathology of schizophrenia (essentially on the basis of clinical biochemical findings—see below), the author clearly considered the animal data to be of a tenuous nature. From animal experimentation the case for a noradrenergic involvement in psychosis is not proven, and it is well established that α_1- and α_2-adrenoceptor agonists cannot evoke the behavioural spectrum of activities evoked by dopamine and that the α_1- and α_2-adrenoceptor antagonists have no significant ability to antagonize the dopamine-induced behaviours in widely used animal models of psychosis.

Having established a prima facie case for an enhanced dopaminergic activity contributing to schizophrenia, how can this be reconciled to a reduction in schizophrenia symptoms in some patients by dopamine agonists? The most reasonable explanation can be derived from animal experimentation where a recent and very rapidly developing literature attests to a very potent action of many dopamine agonists to reduce motor responding in rodents (Sumners *et al.* 1981; Costall *et al.* 1980, 1981; Strömbom 1976; Costentin *et al.* 1977; Bradbury *et al.* 1982). The critical factor is that apomorphine and numerous other dopamine agonists can secure motor inhibition at doses too low to stimulate postsynaptic dopamine receptors. The inhibitory action involves an effect within the mesolimbic and striatal brain regions (Bradbury *et al.* 1982; Van Ree and Wolterink 1981), most probably on presynaptic receptors to decrease the synthesis and/or release of dopamine (Carlsson 1975). In addition, dopamine agonist action on autoreceptors located on the dendrites/cell body of the dopamine neurone affords a further important site of action (Bunney 1979; Bradbury *et al.* 1983).

The action of apomorphine to reduce the core symptoms of schizophrenia (Smith *et al.* 1977; Tamminga *et al.* 1978b; Corsini *et al.* 1977, 1981) was hypothesized to involve a similar action on dopamine autoreceptors (a corresponding action of apomorphine to reduce movement disorders believed to be associated with a raised dopamine activity has also been shown; see Corsini *et al.* (1981) for references), and this concept may be extended to the abilities of amphetamine, methylphenidate, L-dopa (and other agents) to reduce the symptoms of schizophrenia. Thus, these agonists will act to increase the synaptic activity of dopamine which, in the terminal areas, will allow for a post- and presynaptic action and, in the cell body region, for an activation of the dopamine cell body to reduce dopamine cell firing. For example, *d*-amphetamine infused into the pars compacta of the substantia nigra inhibits neuronal activity (Groves *et al.* 1975, 1976), *in vivo* experiments measuring dopamine release have confirmed that amphetamine facilitates the local release of dopamine in this region (Cheramy *et al.* 1981), and dopamine injected directly into the area of the substantia nigra is potent to reduce locomotor responding (Bradbury *et al.* 1983). It would be of immediate interest to extend these studies to the more medially located dopamine cell groups innervating the limbic and cortical areas, for an action here of the dopamine agonists to reduce ascending dopamine activities would seem entirely logical. In contrast, it is more difficult to envisage that dopamine released in the nerve terminal regions would normally have a major action to decrease neuronally released dopamine without a postsynaptic consequence. In support of this hypothesis, recent studies have shown that, whilst apomorphine and other 'directly acting' dopamine agonists may decrease locomotor activity from nerve terminal regions of the rodent brain (see above), dopamine caused essentially postsynaptic motor facilitation, motor depressant actions proving inconsistent and non-dose-related (Bradbury *et al.* unpublished data). Therefore, the ability of peripherally administered 'indirectly-acting' dopamine agonists to decrease dopamine function is best understood as a midbrain action involving the release of endogenous dopamine on to autoreceptor mechanisms.

Yet these considerations ignore two points central to the dopamine hypothesis. First, with agents such as amphetamine and methylphenidate it is difficult to achieve motor depression in normal animals and, second, no explanation is provided for the observation that some schizophrenic patients show an exacerbation, and others an amelioration, of psychotic symptoms. An explanation, of necessity somewhat speculative, must relate to the changes in neuronal circumstances following continued drug treatment (see below).

Neuropharmacological data indicative of dopamine involvement in schizophrenia: dopamine antagonist studies

It is now over 30 years since the phenothiazines were introduced into psychiatry to transform a clinical situation from one of custodial restraint to the beginnings of a therapy. The subsequent pharmacological investigations of the early 'antischizophrenic' phenothiazine drugs in experimental animals established a plethora of pharmacological antagonisms not only of enzymatic mechanisms and protein synthesis but also at specific neurotransmitter receptor sites, cholinergic, serotonergic, noradrenergic and, finally, dopaminergic. From this array of data the first indication that one particular effect may be related to the antischizophrenic action came when Carlsson and Lindqvist (1963) noted that an increase in dopamine metabolites caused by the neuroleptic agents was in proportion to their clinical potencies. This action of the neuroleptics was considered to be secondary to a blockade of postsynaptic dopamine receptors. Subsequently, antischizophrenic agents developed from other chemical series, the butyrophenones, thioxanthenes, dibenzazepines, diphenylbutylpiperidines, and, particularly, the substituted benzamide derivatives, have shown the essential requirement for securing an antipsychotic effect to be an ability to antagonize at dopamine receptors. Agents such as reserpine and tetrabenazine which deplete neuronal stores of dopamine are also antipsychotic agents.

An incisive inhibition of dopamine function in laboratory animals can be demonstrated within minutes of administration by effects such as catalepsy induction, antagonism of conditioned avoidance responding, antagonism of drug-induced stereotyped behaviour patterns, and inhibition of locomotor activity responses. Many of these behavioural effects are the result of inhibitory actions on mesolimbic and striatal dopamine function, with the potency of the neuroleptics closely paralleling their clinical antipsychotic activity (Costall and Naylor 1980). Of the sites of neuroleptic action, that in the striatum is generally considered to determine ability to induce extrapyramidal side-effects in man, for example, pseudoparkinsonism, dystonias, and dyskinesias, whilst an action on the limbic and cortical dopamine systems is considered to more reasonably reflect antipsychotic action. Many studies have shown the neuroleptic agents to modify dopamine turnover in the striatal, limbic, and cortical systems (see Costall and Naylor 1980 for references). In addition, the potencies of neuroleptic drugs to displace a labelled neuroleptic agent such as [^{3}H]spiperone from striatal membranes correlates with clinical potency (Creese *et al.* 1976; Seeman *et al.* 1976). Comparable studies performed using limbic and cortical tissue would be of considerable interest.

There would seem little doubt that neuroleptic agents specifically antagonize dopamine function and exert unique antischizophrenic activity and, indeed, such evidence forms the second major support for the dopamine hypothesis of schizophrenia. Yet how relevant are the above observations to an understanding of the aetiology and treatment of schizophrenia?

The immediate requirement for the 'treatment' of an acutely disturbed schizophrenic patient is a rapid control of the agitation and motor disturbance to prevent self-induced harm and permit a more manageable nursing and medical care. Neuroleptic agents, frequently administered in high dosage, are routinely employed to secure patient cooperation. The grossly disturbed behaviour and excessive psychomotor activity may partly reflect an enhanced dopaminergic activity and justify neuroleptic intervention. Yet is is curious that the potent and very specific dopamine receptor-blocking drug pimozide is consistently indicated to be of limited use in the treatment of the acute schizophrenic presentation (Chouinard and Annable 1982). Does this indicate that the less specific neuroleptics, having an ability to inhibit noradrenergic function at the higher doses used, are exerting a more general 'tranquillizing' and akinetic action? Whatever the complexities of the catecholamine receptor antagonism, the 'tranquillizing' action and the ability to produce signs of extrapyramidal disturbance are an acute neuroleptic action and undoubtedly involve important dopamine receptor antagonism. Yet the immediacy of such actions are *not* accompanied by antagonism of the psychoses and, indeed, are temporally distanced from the antipsychotic action to ameliorate the hallucinations, delusions, and thought disorders by some two or more weeks. Hence it is immediately apparent that a simple antagonism of dopamine function either by dopamine receptor blockade or dopamine depletion is insufficient to ameliorate the core symptoms of schizophrenia. Furthermore, whilst one group of investigators reported that α-methylparatyrosine treatment can reduce the dosage of neuroleptic agent required for the treatment of schizophrenia (Carlsson *et al*. 1972, 1973; Wälinder *et al*. 1976), two other groups reported that α-methylparatyrosine, given alone, is ineffective in the treatment of acute or chronic schizophrenia (Gershon *et al*. 1967; Charalampous and Brown 1967). In a more recent double-blind trial, where α-methylparatyrosine was administered to chronic schizophrenic patients who were maintained on suboptimal doses of neuroleptic agent, no clinical improvement was observed, notwithstanding evidence of dopamine synthesis inhibition as indicated by the development of extrapyramidal side-effects (Nasrallah *et al*. 1977).

Yet do such discrepancies justify a serious questioning of the 'dopamine hypothesis'? It is reasonable to reflect that the immediate neuronal consequence of a raised dopamine activity in the brain will be an immediate compensatory adjustment of the other (unspecified) neuronal mechanisms which normally interact to maintain the status quo. The effects of an exaggerated dopamine function will only be evident when the compensatory capacities of these other neuronal mechanisms have been exceeded. The changes caused in these systems may be of a persistent nature and a sudden inhibition of dopamine function may require the re-establishment of receptor mechanisms over a period of many days or longer. This could reasonably and readily account for the delayed appearance of the antipsychotic action of the neuroleptic agents. It must be emphasized that neuroleptic agents are the only drugs that can satisfactorily reduce the psychotic disorder of schizophrenia and their only known common property is to reduce dopamine function (Niemegeers and Leysen 1982).

There remain two further points. First, neuroleptic treatment does not 'cure' schizophrenia and the basic causation of the disease process is not influenced by dopamine antagonists or any other drug. Whilst this does not detract from the 'dopamine hypothesis', a second point offers a more serious challenge to the theory. This is the point that some schizophrenics show only a partial response or no response to neuroleptic treatment (see Buckley 1982). Whilst this may be due in some cases to inadequate dosing, and idiosyncratic drug absorption and metabolism patterns, these effects cannot satisfactorily explain all failures. There would appear to be two possibilities, either that the treatment failures have a psychosis which was never associated in any way with dopamine dysfunction, or that dopamine may have been a contributory aetiological factor earlier in the disease process which subsequently incurred alteration in other neuronal mechanisms and perhaps irreversible brain changes.

If one accepts that a positive (psychosis amelioration) or negative (no effect) response of schizophrenic patients to neuroleptic therapy reflects the presence of 'dopamine-sensitive' and 'dopamine-insensitive' responders, do such patients divide on the basis of a response to both dopamine agonists and antagonists? Angrist *et al.* (1980) reported that lack of psychotogenic effect to *d*-amphetamine predicted lack of improvement following neuroleptic treatment. However, van Kammen *et al.* (1982) indicated that, whilst a *d*-amphetamine response may predict the subsequent antipsychotic response to pimozide treatment, this response was not in the direction suggested by the 'dopamine hypothesis'. Thus, patients who showed an *anti*psychotic effect to *d*-amphetamine also showed an antipsychotic response to pimozide. This paradoxical positive relationship could be attributed to a complex action via the dopamine systems and was taken to broadly support a dopamine involvement, but with differences in pre- and postsynaptic dopamine actions (see van Kammen *et al.* 1982 for full discussion). At least as important was the observation that the patients' response to dopamine agonist challenge may change over time to reflect a 'state dependent' rather than a 'trait-dependent' phenomenon, and that the responsiveness to neuroleptic agents may similarly vary during treatment (Van der Velde 1976; Docherty *et al.* 1978).

It is generally accepted that the 'positive' symptoms of schizophrenia respond most favourably to neuroleptic treatment whilst there may be little amelioration in the negative symptoms. Whether that group of patients failing to respond to neuroleptic therapy can pose a serious question for the validity of the 'dopamine hypothesis' is debatable, for it could easily be argued that these patients are suffering irreversible changes in brain function subsequent to initial dopamine dysfunction. The 'dopamine hypothesis' is thus afforded general support from a consideration of the use of neuroleptic agents, but with tentative indications of a complex interaction between drug and disease process.

Clinical biochemical data indicative of a dopamine involvement with schizophrenia

The possibility that central catecholaminergic processes may show disturbed function in schizophrenia was investigated by measurement of neurochemical changes occurring in brain tissue and body fluids. The assessment of changes in catecholamine function by measurement of precursors, neurotransmitters and their metabolites, and of enzyme activities in body fluids, urine, blood, and cerebrospinal fluid, has an important advantage that measurements can be taken during the onset, progression, and treatment of disease. The major disadvantage is that changes occurring in such gross body systems may have little relevance to a biochemical change occurring in a discrete brain region. The use of brain tissue has the advantage of tissue relevance, but the disadvantage that the use of autopsy material is attempting to detect meaningful neurochemical changes which were instituted decades earlier.

Measurement of changes in cerebrospinal fluid (CSF)

Central dopaminergic activity in schizophrenia was assessed by measuring the levels of the dopamine metabolites homovanillic acid (HVA) and 3,4-dihydroxyphenylacetic acid (DOPAC) in the CSF. Relevant studies were reviewed by Meltzer (1979) and Haracz (1982) and only the major findings are summarized here. It has proved impossible to determine the source of the metabolites which, however, are most reasonably derived from those structures bordering the ventricles, for example, the striatum (Sourkes 1973). Van Praag and Korf (1976) indicated that increased motor activity may be related to the increase in HVA levels in schizophrenia but it is uncertain that a minor change in a discrete limbic or cortical structure can seriously influence the levels of HVA or DOPAC in the CSF. Whilst a number of studies have reported interesting differences between subgroups of schizophrenic patients, the significance of these observations is very difficult to determine (Meltzer 1979). Perhaps the most relevant finding is that dopamine metabolite levels vary considerably within any schizophrenic population, but one finally must conclude that such measures only afford a useful means of studying 'cerebral' dopamine metabolism.

Modified enzyme activities in platelets and erythrocytes

A reduction in the activity of the dopamine degrading enzymes, monoamine oxidase (MAO) and catechol-*O*-methyltransferase (COMT), in schizophrenia could be relevant to the 'dopamine hypothesis'. Wyatt *et al.* (1980*a*) reviewed the literature reporting on changes in monoamine oxidase and concluded that approximately two-thirds of chronic schizophrenic patients have lowered platelet MAO activity, although acute schizophrenics have apparently 'normal' platelet MAO activity. The significance of these changes is most uncertain, particularly since brain MAO activity is not reduced in schizophrenia (Meltzer *et al.* 1980; Reveley *et al.* 1981). Similarly, whilst some differences in COMT activity in erythrocytes from schizophrenic patients were reported, no difference in post-mortem cerebral COMT activity between schizophrenics and 'controls' could be determined (Haracz 1982).

Urinary metabolites

An assessment of cerebral dopamine metabolism from measurement of urine constituents has the insuperable difficulty of contamination by peripheral catecholamine metabolism (Goodwin and Post 1975). Nevertheless, there are a number of reports of abnormally high concentrations of phenylethylamine in the urine of schizophrenic patients (Wyatt *et al.* 1980*b*) although the significance of this remains to be determined (Haracz 1982).

It is apparent that the above investigational approaches are so indirect and inconclusive that they neither support nor discourage the dopamine hypothesis. Direct biochemical analysis of brain tissue is ostensibly the more logical approach.

Biochemical analysis of schizophrenic brain tissue post-mortem

If cerebral dopamine function of schizophrenic patients is enhanced, then the final critical evidence to support or dismiss the dopamine hypothesis could be obtained from an analysis of schizophrenic brain tissue. These important findings are discussed in relation to levels of dopamine, homovanillic acid (HVA), and 3,4-dihydroxyphenylacetic acid (DOPAC), and changes in the dopamine receptors.

In the original study reporting on preliminary findings, Bird *et al.* (1977) concluded that there were major biochemical abnormalities in post-mortem brain from patients with schizophrenia or schizophrenia-like psychoses. Four brain regions were examined, nucleus accumbens, putamen, amygdala, and hippocampus, and of the two regions containing detectable concentrations of dopamine, nucleus accumbens and putamen, dopamine concentrations in the nucleus accumbens were shown to be elevated approximately 50 per cent above control values, whilst dopamine levels in the putamen were normal. The authors emphasized that it was unknown whether the neurochemical abnormality was related to the disease state or to the consequence of long-term neuroleptic treatment. Furthermore, the authors stressed that the results must be interpreted with caution since an increased dopamine concentration does not necessarily imply an increased activity of dopaminergic nerve terminals. Such caution was appropriate since Crow *et al.* (1978*a*, 1980) reported that dopamine and HVA levels in the nucleus accumbens were the same in tissue from chronic schizophrenics and control patients. In the caudate nucleus, however, dopamine levels were increased and HVA levels decreased. In another study, Crow *et al.* (1979) found a significant increase in dopamine levels in both the caudate and putamen but HVA and DOPAC levels were not modified.

Bacopoulos *et al.* (1979) determined HVA levels in the brains of 25 schizophrenics who had received neuroleptic treatment and found significant increases in HVA levels in the cingulate gyrus, orbital frontal cortex, and temporal lobe, but HVA levels in the nucleus accumbens and putamen were normal.

Winblad *et al.* (1979) measured dopamine and HVA concentrations in the brains of 12 schizophrenics who had received neuroleptic medication, and six patients had additionally been lobotomized at least 25 years before death. Dopamine concentrations in the caudate, putamen, cingulate gyrus, and frontal lobe were the same in schizophrenic and control brains. In addition, HVA levels which were measured in the caudate nucleus and putamen did not significantly differ between the two groups.

A further group (Kleinman *et al.* 1980; Wyatt *et al.* 1981) assessed dopamine, HVA and DOPAC concentrations in post-mortem brain obtained from patients diagnosed as having chronic undifferentiated schizophrenia, chronic paranoid schizophrenia, and a third group of unspecified 'psychiatric disorders'. No significant differences for dopamine, homovanillic acid, and DOPAC were found in the nucleus accumbens of any of the patient groups relative to controls.

Farley *et al*. (1980), using brain samples from four chronic paranoid schizophrenics, failed to find any differences in dopamine and HVA concentrations between the schizophrenic and control samples from the caudate nucleus, putamen, nucleus accumbens, and medial and lateral olfactory areas. However, dopamine but not HVA was found to be significantly elevated in the tissue sample taken from the ventral septum of the schizophrenic brains. An earlier paper from this group (Farley *et al*. 1978) indicated above normal noradrenaline levels in the ventral septum, the bed nucleus of the stria terminalis, the nucleus accumbens, and the mammillary bodies of brains taken from chronic paranoid schizophrenic patients.

Toru *et al*. (1982), analysing dopamine and HVA concentrations in the nucleus accumbens, caudate, and putamen of six schizophrenic and control brains, found no significant change in dopamine concentrations in these areas of the schizophrenic brains, although HVA levels were significantly higher in the basal ganglia. Mackay and colleagues (1982), however, in an analysis of the dopamine content in post-mortem samples of caudate nucleus and nucleus accumbens from psychotic patients, found that dopamine concentrations were significantly elevated (by 37 per cent) in the caudate nucleus of early-onset schizophrenics and in the nucleus accumbens of schizophrenic and early-onset schizophrenics by 20 and 43 per cent respectively.

Reynolds (1983) also recorded a significant increase of 68 per cent in dopamine concentration in the amygdala of schizophrenic brains, the increase showing an intriguing laterality to the left hemisphere. Dopamine levels in the caudate nucleus were similar to those found in control brains.

Together, these studies offer little support for dopamine function, as measured by changes in dopamine/metabolite concentrations, being enhanced in mesolimbic areas of schizophrenic brain. When changes do occur, they are generally small or inconsistent with the exception of the data reported by Reynolds (1983). Such findings offer little support to the 'dopamine hypothesis', but it would be premature to suggest that such data detracts from the hypothesis. Thus, virtually all the autopsy material was obtained from schizophrenic patients who had received neuroleptic medication for many years, and this alone may alter cerebral dopamine metabolism in unspecified ways (see Mackay *et al*. 1982). Second, almost all the material was obtained from chronic schizophrenics. Yet as the disease progresses it is well established that the prognosis is less favourable and the effectiveness of the neuroleptic agents on the negative symptoms becomes questionable. Of what relevance are such changes occurring in chronic schizophrenic brains to the earlier schizophrenic symptomatology occurring years or literally decades earlier? Until non-invasive biochemical techniques can be developed to investigate changes occurring in the functioning brain during disease development and treatment these questions will remain unanswered.

A second major series of investigations to analyse the biochemistry of post-mortem schizophrenic brain used receptor labelling assays to determine the nature and number of dopamine receptors in the schizophrenic brain. The ability of labelled dopamine and neuroleptics to bind with high affinity to brain tissue in a saturable and stereospecific manner was used to define 'dopamine receptors' (Burt *et al*. 1976; Seeman *et al*. 1976). It is believed that these binding sites reflect the locus of antipsychotic action of the neuroleptic drugs. The possibility that there may exist different types of binding sites is beyond the scope of this review and is the subject of lively discussion (see Seeman 1982; Creese and Sibley 1982).

In one of the first studies, Owen *et al*. (1978) found that [³H]spiperone binding in the caudate, putamen, and nucleus accumbens of brain autopsy material obtained from schizophrenic patients was higher than control values. The increased binding was attributed to an increase in receptor numbers rather than an increase in affinity for the receptor. Indeed the receptor affinity was shown to decrease, although, on the basis of animal experiments, this was attributed to the presence of residual neuroleptics in the brain samples. Lee *et al*. (1978), Lee and Seeman (1980*a, b*), and Reisine *et al*. (1980*a, b*) also recorded an elevated binding of [³H]haloperidol and/or [³H]spiperone in the caudate and putamen of schizophrenics. Similarly, Mackay *et al*. (1980*a, b*) recorded an increase in [³H]spiperone binding but with decreased receptor affinity in the caudate and nucleus accumbens of schizophrenic brains. The authors considered that the decreased receptor affinity observed in schizophrenics was due to the presence of residual neuroleptic drug treatment and emphasized that the receptor alterations were not seen in a subgroup of schizophrenics who were free of neuroleptic medication for at least one month before death. In partial contrast to the results obtained from the above four groups of workers, Reynolds *et al*. (1980, 1981) found that the binding (receptor numbers) of [³H]spiperone to putamen did not differ in tissue taken from schizophrenics and control non-psychiatric patients but that, in agreement with the above studies, the receptor affinities were lower in the neuroleptic-treated schizophrenics as compared to the control or 'drug-free' patients. Mackay *et al*. (1978) in an earlier study also reported a non-significant elevation of [³H]spiperone binding in the nucleus accumbens of schizophrenic patients.

What is the significance of such observations to the dopamine hypothesis of schizophrenia? The determined application by many authors in these pioneer studies has led to inconclusive findings. A major and insuperable ethical and practical difficulty is that the autopsy material was obtained from patients who, in the majority of cases, had properly received neuroleptic treatment. Even when neuroleptic treatment had been discontinued the persistence of neuroleptic drug within the body is remarkable. It must be a continuing cause for concern that, where studies did report a change in the binding of [³H]spiperone or [³H]haloperidol, prior neuroleptic treatment may have contributed to such changes (Seeman 1981; Iversen and Mackay 1981). This is particularly important when there is conflicting evidence as to the presence of neuroleptic receptor abnormalities in drug-free schizophrenics (Mackay *et al*. 1980*b*; Lee and Seeman 1980*a, b*; Cross *et al*. 1981; Reisine *et al*. 1980*a, b*). It also remains a curious observation that [³H]agonist binding, [³H]apomorphine, [³H]ADTN, did not differ in the brain tissue of schizophrenic and control groups of patients (Cross *et al.* 1979*a*), and this is surely worthy of more detailed investigation. In addition, it is a disappointment that not all workers included mesolimbic tissue in their brain region analyses, for it is difficult to consider the basal ganglia as the sole site of antipsychotic action of the neuroleptic drugs, and extrapolations to effects occurring in other more relevant brain areas are entirely speculative. Also, it is completely unknown whether the increased number of neuroleptic binding sites represents an increase in both pre- and postsynaptic receptors or a decrease in one and marked increase in the other, and whether these additional receptors have any functional relevance. Finally, to emphasize the limitations of having no choice in the selection of the patient population (as indicated in the above dopamine and HVA analyses) for obtaining the postmortem material, is it reasonable to predict from the biochemical data obtained from chronic schizophrenic brains (where patients are considered to be markedly less responsive to neuroleptic drugs) as to events occurring years and decades earlier in the acute presentations? In this immensely difficult area of investigation, it is premature to suggest that such data can be forwarded to support or criticize the 'dopamine hypothesis'.

General conclusion

The 'dopamine hypothesis' of schizophrenia dictates that an enhanced dopaminergic activity will facilitate psychotic disorder. Evidence from human autopsy material obtained from the brains of schizophrenic patients offers no consistent evidence of an increased dopamine turnover and the relevance of increased numbers of neuroleptic receptors in the brains of such patients remains to be established. However, such studies have used chronic schizophrenic brains and the significance of the findings to events occurring earlier in the disease process is unknown. The major evidence to support the 'dopamine hypothesis' is neuropharmacological—dopamine agonists exacerbating and neuroleptic drugs ameliorating the psychotic symptoms. However, it is a critical finding that some schizophrenic patients fail to show exacerbation to dopamine agonists and some are not helped by neuroleptic therapy, thus indicating a subpopulation of schizophrenics where a dopamine dysfunction is not critical. However, even in such patients it is possible that an initial dopamine dysfunction may have contributed to the disorder.

It is very important to note that the neuropharmacological evidence is essentially based on the effects of acute drug administration to animals, yet such agents are administered chronically to man. Creese and Sibley (1981) and Kokkinidis and Anisman (1981) reviewed the now extensive literature on how the chronic administration of dopamine agonists and antagonists to animals can cause changes at variance with acute effects. Rupniak *et al.* (1983) reviewed their data suggesting that continued neuroleptic administration causes the development of tolerance and subsequently the emergence of dopamine receptor supersensitivity. Costall *et al.* (1982) also showed that the persistent infusion of dopamine into the nucleus accumbens of rat brain for only a few days can cause drastic alterations in the behavioural responsiveness of the animals to dopamine agonist–antagonist challenge which are detectable for many months, a period of time equivalent to many years of disruption in the human. A consideration of such changes may allow a much better understanding of the limitations of neuroleptic therapy, the aetiology of the disease process of schizophrenia, and a future development of the 'dopamine hypothesis'.

HYPOTHESES OF SCHIZOPHRENIA WHICH CONSIDER NEUROTRANSMITTER OR CENTRALLY-LOCATED SUBSTANCES OTHER THAN DOPAMINE

Noradrenaline

Whilst antipsychotic drugs frequently antagonize at both dopamine and noradrenaline receptors, the antischizophrenic actions do not correlate with blockade of α-adrenoceptors (Peroutka *et al.* 1977). It is therefore unlikely that an enhanced noradrenergic function is essentially involved in schizophrenia. Nevertheless, some reports indicate higher than normal levels of noradrenaline in limbic forebrain regions of schizophrenic brains (Farley *et al.* 1978; Kleinman *et al.* 1979; Carlsson 1979). Yet the total patient population reported on is very small, and controversy exists as to whether the schizophrenia produced the changes in noradrenaline, whether the raised noradrenaline contributed to the schizophrenia, or whether the changes were simply the result of neuroleptic treatment. Kety (1979) proposed that the negative symptoms of schizophrenia may result from a reduced noradrenergic activity but, in this most speculative of areas, no meaningful conclusion can be drawn.

Serotonin

The possibility that serotonergic systems may dysfunction in schizophrenia was critically reviewed by Weil-Malherbe (1978), who also assessed the evidence for the 'methylation theory'. We summarize that no consistent abnormality in serotonin synthesis or metabolism has been established in schizophrenia (see Joseph *et al.* 1979). However, with the development of select agonist and antagonist drugs to influence different subclassifications of the serotonin receptor (see Iversen 1985), it is now being revealed that serotonin may perform important neuromodulatory functions which are particularly relevant to dopamine and the suppression of events when cerebral dopamine function is elevated (Costall *et al.* unpublished).

γ-Aminobutyric acid (GABA)

Perry *et al.* (1979) measured the concentration of GABA in the nucleus accumbens and thalamus of brains taken from patients who died whilst suffering from schizophrenia or Huntington's chorea. Mean GABA content was significantly decreased in both brain areas in both disease states and the authors concluded that 'GABA deficiency may be a biochemical characteristic of some forms of schizophrenia'. However, there is general agreement that the activity of glutamate decarboxylase is normal in post-mortem brains of schizophrenics (Crow *et al.* 1978*b*; Perry *et al.* 1978) and in a subsequent study Cross *et al.* (1979*b*) found normal concentrations of GABA in both the thalamus and nucleus accumbens in brains of schizophrenics. Also, whilst baclofen was claimed to have a therapeutic action in schizophrenia (Frederiksen 1975), subsequent reports suggested baclofen to be ineffective or even detrimental (Simpson *et al.* 1976; Beckman *et al.* 1977). In addition, the very potent GABA agonist muscimol and the GABA-inhibitor γ-acetylenic-GABA are ineffective to alleviate schizophrenic symptoms (Tamminga *et al.* 1978*a*; Palfreyman 1981). These results would suggest that schizophrenia is unlikely to result from a GABA deficiency.

Acetylcholine

There are a number of pharmacological and neurochemical indications to suggest that there may be changes in cholinergic activity in the schizophrenic brain and/or that a cholinergic system might be activated to moderate the schizophrenic illness. The first indications came from a pharmacological approach, indicating that the cholinomimetics arecoline and oxotremorine produced periods of 'lucidity' in patients with catatonic and withdrawn schizophrenia (Pfeiffer and Jenny 1957; Collard *et al.* 1965). The very short-lived actions of such agents predictably caused only transient remissions but longer remissions were recorded following the combination of neuroleptics with physostigmine (Rosenthal and Bigelow 1973). Physostigmine was also shown to reverse the exacerbation of schizophrenic symptoms caused by methylphenidate (Janowsky *et al.* 1973*b*). Whilst such evidence would support the hypothesis that an increase in central cholinergic activity might improve the schizophrenic symptoms, it should be noted that intravenous physostigmine and the potent cholinesterase inhibitor diisopropylfluorophosphonate did not improve schizophrenic symptoms (Rowntree *et al.* 1950; Modestin *et al.* 1973). More recently the administration of choline chloride was reported to have no significant effect in schizophrenia (Davis *et al.* 1980). It would be expected that anticholinergic drugs might perhaps exacerbate schizophrenic symptoms, but such studies have been confounded by the very potent deliriant effects of agents such as ditran (Itil *et al.* 1969). Similarly, whilst antiparkinson drugs have been considered to reduce the efficacy of antipsychotic drug therapy, this is a variable response (see Costall *et al.* 1979 for references). Also, neuroleptic drugs having potent anticholinergic effects, for example clozapine and thioridazine, are effective antipsychotic agents. It is obvious that the use of drugs capable of modifying cerebral cholinergic processes has produced conflicting data in support of a cholinergic involvement in schizophrenia. Equally as evident is the difficulty in use of such agents which can so powerfully affect the peripheral autonomic nervous system with the attendent discomfort. The use of agents with a selectivity of action for the central cholinergic mechanisms would help to clarify the existing discrepancies, but such agents remain to be developed.

The neurochemical data from schizophrenic brains has proved equally difficult to interpret. Early comparative studies of total cholinesterase or acetylcholinesterase activity in schizophrenic and control brains indicated either normal or enhanced activities in the schizophrenic brains (Birkhauser 1941; Pope *et al.* 1949; Takahashi and Ogushi 1953). Domino *et al.* (1973) measured cholinesterase activity in 15 brain regions; specific acetylcholinesterase was significantly depressed in the septal area and head of the caudate, total cholinesterase was depressed in the septal area, whilst pseudocholinesterase was markedly enhanced in numerous brain regions of the schizophrenic brains. The authors also recorded that choline acetyltransferase activity was normal in the caudate, hippocampus, and in many other brain areas, but was elevated in the amygdala. In contrast, McGeer and McGeer (1977) recorded an increased choline acetyltransferase activity in the caudate, putamen, nucleus accumbens, and hippocampus of schizophrenic brains. (The latter study is particularly instructive in emphasizing the immense interpretational complexities inherent in the use of autopsy material. Thus, post-mortem delays ranged from 1½ to 20 hours; death was caused by suicide, bronchopneumonia, coronary occlusion, heart disease, cardiac arrest, pulmonary emphysema, aspiration of food, and multiple myeloma; drug usage by patients in the last month of life included phenothiazines, haloperidol, benztropine, phenytoin, aspirin, meperidine, acetaminophen, penicillin, gentamicin, cephalexin, aminophylline, multivitamins, prednisone, digoxin, and furosemide. It is all too apparent that, notwithstanding the authors' careful scientific approach, their best endeavours might be defeated by the 'variability' in quality of the autopsy material—was one studying genuine brain changes caused by schizophrenia, or schizophrenic changes modified by brain deterioration, schizophrenic changes modified by other pathologies or drug treatments? Clearly these problems are common to all such investigations, although not generally so clearly reported.) In any event, further studies are clearly required to clarify the neurochemical changes occurring in cholinergic processes in schizophrenic brains to allow serious comment as to the role played by cholinergic processes in schizophrenia.

Neuropeptides

The possibility that peptides within the central nervous system may have potential neurotransmitter or neuromodulatory roles to regulate brain function and behaviour is presently one of the most exciting areas in neuroscience. Numerous peptides are being discovered or synthesized and many may finally be shown to have important physiological, pharmacological and perhaps therapeutic value. The majority of peptides have received very little investigation as to their involvement in schizophrenia and this remains a difficult area to assess. Major limiting factors are the measurement and differentiation of one particular peptide among others of similar structure, the absence of suitable antagonists, and limited clinical studies. For example, neurotensin has been subject to intensive investigation in animals and has been shown to modify behaviour in a similar manner to neuroleptics in a number of tests (Nemeroff *et al*. 1982). Further, Widerlöv *et al*. (1982) reported that a subgroup of schizophrenic patients showing marked psychomotor retardation/catatonia had lower immunoreactive neurotensin levels than control patients. However, Manberg *et al*. (1982) found normal levels of neurotensin in the limbic structures of schizophrenic brains but emphasized that such findings are of little value to an understanding of peptide *turnover*. The reader is referred to the first conference on neurotensin indicating the breadth of interest in this peptide and its possible role in central disease processes (see above references).

Within the neuropeptide area, one of quite extraordinary growth, only one group of peptides, the 'opioid peptides' (endorphins), have been used in sufficient studies to allow a reasonable discussion of an involvement in schizophrenia. The role of the endorphins in schizophrenia has been reviewed in depth by Van Ree and De Wied (1981) and only the key points are considered here.

The pentapeptide enkephalins are the best understood of the opioid peptides. They are widely distributed in neural pathways throughout the brain (Elde *et al*. 1976) with a considerable degree of overlap with the monoamine-containing neuronal systems. They are present in high concentrations around the midbrain dopamine cell bodies and their dopamine terminal areas. Hypotheses on the nature of an involvement of endorphins in schizophrenia have considered that schizophrenia may result from an endorphin excess, a deficiency or changes in β-endorphin fragments.

Endorphin excess hypothesis

An increase in 'endorphin-like material' in the cerebrospinal fluid of schizophrenic patients was first reported by Terenius and colleagues in 1976, and the same group subsequently confirmed their findings (Lindström *et al*. 1978; Rimon *et al*. 1980). However, such data is only of significant value if the endorphin-like material is precisely identified. Another report indicates levels of CSF 'β-endorphin-like immunoreactive substance' to be markedly increased in acute schizophrenia but reduced in chronic schizophrenia (Domschke *et al*. 1979), but this was not confirmed (Emrich *et al*. 1979). Studies on post-mortem schizophrenic brains failed to reveal any significant change from 'normal' of levels of 'β-endorphin-like immunoreactivity' in various brain areas (Lightman *et al*. 1979). Hence, there is no convincing evidence for an alteration in brain β-endorphin levels in schizophrenia, and a definitive series of experiments must await the development of a highly specific assay procedure. Further, if an excess of β-endorphin were to result in schizophrenia, it is surprising that acute administration of potent opiate agonists does not result in psychosis (Smith and Beecher 1961) (although psychotomimetic effects are observed with opiates having partial agonist/antagonist action).

A different approach has been to use a narcotic antagonist in an attempt to block the presumed excessive β-endorphin activity. The first trial by Gunne *et al.* (1977) reported that naloxone greatly reduced hallucinations, but this trial was non-placebo controlled and could not be repeated by Gunne *et al.* (1979). Many other independent groups using doses of naloxone known to antagonize opioid actions in man similarly confirmed that naloxone has no demonstrable antipsychotic effect (Janowsky *et al.* 1977*a*; Davis *et al.* 1977; Kurland *et al.* 1977; Volavka *et al.* 1977). It is emphasized that these studies were double-blind cross-over studies. Yet it remains possible that the doses of naloxone used in these studies, whilst adequate to antagonize morphine, were inadequate to antagonize the effects of endogenous opioid peptides, for in two double-blind placebo-controlled cross-over studies Emrich *et al.* (1977) and Watson *et al.* (1978) reported that higher doses of naloxone (some 5–10-fold greater than used in the above studies) did significantly reduce hallucinations, particularly auditory hallucinations. Yet Watson *et al.* (1979) indicated:

'studies of alterations of schizophrenia with naloxone are intrinsically flawed. Target symptoms such as auditory hallucinations are subjective, short-lived and uniquely susceptible to suggestion or psychological "set" factors. To further complicate matters, the short duration of action of naloxone requires the selection of subjects who are simultaneously good reporters and experience persistent (or frequent) hallucinations. In our experience it was necessary to screen more than 1000 psychiatric patients to locate those acceptable for this study.'

The authors concluded that 'in carefully selected, relatively rare subjects, higher doses of naloxone seem to decrease the reported frequency and intensity of auditory hallucinations'. Whilst this may involve an antagonism of endogenous opioid activity, it should be considered that naloxone also has a GABA receptor antagonist action (Dingledine *et al.* 1978). It should be noted that two preliminary studies have shown another long-acting opiate antagonist, naltrexone, to lack antipsychotic action (Simpson *et al.* 1977; Micke and Gallant 1977). Such evidence offers no support for an endorphin excess in the majority of schizophrenia patients.

Endorphin deficiency hypothesis

That psychoses may be related to an endorphin deficiency was suggested on the basis of the finding that β-endorphin induced postural rigidity when injected into the brainstem, and this was likened to neuroleptic catalepsy (Jacquet and Marks 1976). This inference was quite misleading (see Segal *et al.* 1977) although it was postulated that β-endorphin may be an endogenous antipsychotic compound. In a trial involving four schizophrenic patients, Kline *et al.* (1977) reported that one to three days following the intravenous injection of β-endorphin there occurred a long-term progressive reduction in psychotic symptoms. In double-blind trials the immediate effects of β-endorphin appeared to be a slightly worsening (behavioural withdrawal and increased psychotic experience) whereas a small magnitude of improvement (as measured using BPRS scores) was apparent after longer treatment, although the improvement was not clinically obvious (Berger *et al.* 1980; *see also* Gerner *et al.* 1980; Pickar *et al.* 1981; Pethö *et al.* 1981). However, Berger (1981) argued against a too ready dismissal of the possible long-term improvements suggesting that single-dose studies are a dubious indicator of therapeutic potential. Further trials using repeated doses would at least be informative. Nevertheless, on the available data there is no clear evidence to indicate that schizophrenia is related to endorphin deficiency.

Hypotheses for an involvement of endorphin fragments

In a challenging hypothesis De Wied (1979) considered that schizophrenia is an 'inborn error in the degradation of β-endorphin'. In animal neuropharmacological studies it was noted that, whilst β-endorphin and α-endorphin (γ-endorphin fragment) could delay the extinction of pole-jumping avoidance behaviour (a non-opiate action) (De Wied *et al.* 1978*a*), γ-endorphin and des-tyr-γ-endorphin (DTγE) (endorphin fragment) facilitate the extinction of pole-jumping avoidance behaviour (De Wied *et al.* 1978*b*). The latter response is characteristic of neuroleptic action and the behavioural effects of DTγE were examined in other neuroleptic test procedures (De Wied *et al.* 1978*b*; Van Ree *et al.* 1980*a*). It was reasoned that DTγE or a closely related peptide may possess endogenous neuroleptic action and that an absence of such factors was an aetiological factor in psychopathology (De Wied *et al.* 1978*c*).

In an open study DTγE was administered daily for 8–10 days to six schizophrenic patients and all were reported to show improvement, albeit short-lived in three patients (Verhoeven *et al.* 1978). A double-blind crossover study subsequently confirmed an antipsychotic action in some patients, for example, hebephrenic patients, whilst others with residual schizophrenia and schizoaffective psychosis did not respond (Verhoeven *et al.* 1979). A factor alleged to be involved in determining patient response was a negative relationship between the response and the duration of the last psychotic episode. Other open and double-blind trials have suggested an antipsychotic effect in acute but not in chronic schizophrenics (Emrich *et al.* 1980; Machanda and Hirsch 1981; Tamminga *et al.* 1981); it may also be noted that DTγE did not affect neuroleptic-induced tardive dyskinesia or parkinsonism in chronic schizophrenics (Casey *et al.* 1981). In a double-blind placebo-controlled trial in 13 schizophrenic patients a similar spectrum of antipsychotic action was claimed for (des-enkephalin)-γ- endorphin (Van Ree *et al.* 1980*b*). Many important issues are raised by the results of these experiments which must be confirmed in a much larger population of schizophrenic patients before one may elaborate on subtypes of schizophrenia showing differential responses. Until this is accomplished, this must remain an area of intriguing challenge (see Van Ree and De Wied 1981 for detailed discussion).

Prostaglandins

The mammalian central nervous system contains the enzymatic mechanisms necessary for the synthesis of prostaglandins which are hypothesized to have a neuromodulatory role. There are two hypotheses relating schizophrenia to a prostaglandin dysfunction. Matthe *et al.* (1980) suggested that schizophrenia is associated with an excess of prostaglandin-like compounds in the brain. This was based on their findings of a high prostaglandin-like immunoreactivity in the cerebrospinal fluid. However, the specificity of the radioimmunoassay was not validated using mass fragmentography and, in a later study using a highly sensitive and specific assay for prostaglandins, Linnoila *et al.* (1983), measuring PGE_2, $PGF_{2\alpha}$, and $6\text{-}keto\text{-}PGE_{1\alpha}$, could not confirm the presence of raised prostaglandins in the cerebrospinal fluid of chronic schizophrenic patients.

The second hypothesis considers a PGE_1 deficiency in schizophrenia (Horrobin *et al.* 1980) and is based on the circumstantial evidence (1) that schizophrenics are resistant to conditions such as rheumatoid arthritis in which increased prostaglandin synthesis may play a role; (2) most effective antischizophrenic drugs enhance the secretion of prolactin which increases the production of PGE_1; (3) platelets from schizophrenics seem to form much less PGE_1 than those from normal individuals; (4) platelets from schizophrenics fail to form normal amounts of cAMP when exposed to PGE_1 (Horrobin *et al.* 1980). The authors developed the concept that schizophrenia-like states will occur when the PGE_1: dopamine ratio is too low and advocated attempts to increase PGE_1 formation. Clearly it is difficult to test this hypothesis. First, the measurement of prostaglandins is not easy and attempts to determine such levels, particularly if these are reduced from normal in discrete areas of the schizophrenia brain, may pose many problems. Second, assuming a deficiency disease, then attempts will be required to increase prostaglandin synthesis by administration of precursor. Whether this will incur the disadvantages of a peripherally raised prostaglandin activity is uncertain, but the use of dihomogammalinolenic acid in schizophrenia would at least be instructive. Finally, a detailed assessment of the actions of prostaglandins to modify discrete dopamine systems in the rodent brain is being attempted (Costall *et al.* unpublished) which may help to clarify the precise interaction between prostaglandins and dopamine.

CONCLUSIONS

To 'prove' a neurotransmitter hypothesis of schizophrenia would require a demonstration of dysfunction in neurotransmitter synthesis, release or receptor function, or associated neurotransmitter/neuromodulatory changes in the brains of schizophrenic patients, followed as the disease progresses, and in the different types of disease states. Notwithstanding an immense application, an examination of chronic schizophrenic brains has failed to reveal any consistent neurotransmitter abnormality. In particular, the clinical evidence for a disturbed dopamine function in schizophrenia remains speculative. Whilst striatal and limbic neuroleptic receptors may increase in the brains of chronic schizophrenics, like all biochemical parameters measured in autopsy material, such effects must be carefully distinguised from the changes caused by previous drug therapy or associated disease processes.

Nevertheless, the dopamine hypothesis of schizophrenia, which rests almost exclusively on neuropharmacological evidence, has proven immensely useful for an explanation of the actions of antischizophrenic drugs. In addition, it has provided a cornerstone to our understanding of the ability of agents such as amphetamine to induce or exacerbate psychoses. It may also be finally shown to be a useful concept in explaining the paradoxical actions of dopamine agonist treatment where, for example, drug action on dopamine autoreceptors in some patients may reduce schizophrenic behaviour. Its continued usefulness will be found in studies attempting to understand the functioning of discrete dopamine and interrelated systems within the brain and in the detection of agents with a selectivity of action for the cortical and limbic systems. Further, the development of initial studies showing that chronic treatment with dopamine antagonists and agonists may induce changes not observed on acute drug challenge may afford a better understanding of the aetiology and treatment of schizophrenia.

Yet it is an important observation that an ill-defined proportion of schizophrenics do not respond to neuroleptic treatment, suggesting an involvement of neurotransmitter(s) in addition to dopamine. Whilst these remain essentially obscure, of the various neurotransmitter and neuromodulator substances currently investigated, hyotheses relating to an involvement of neuropeptides, prostaglandins, and serotonin provide the most provocative working hypotheses for future vigorous clinical and pharmacological investigation.

References

Angrist, B. and Gershon, S. (1972). Some recent studies on amphetamine psychosis—unresolved issues. In *Current concepts on amphetamine abuse* (ed. E. H. Ellinwood, S. Cohen., and M. Rockville), pp. 193–204. National Institute of Mental Health.
—— Peselow, E., Rubinstein, M., Corwin, J., and Rotrosen, J. (1982). Partial improvement in negative schizophrenic symptoms after amphetamine. *Psychopharmacology* **78**, 128–30.
—— Rotrosen, J., and Gershon, S. (1980). Responses to apomorphine, amphetamine, and neuroleptics in schizophrenic subjects. *Psychopharmacology* **67**, 31–8.

—— Thompson, H., and Shopsin, B. (1975). Clinical studies with dopamine receptor stimulants. *Psychopharmacologia* **44**, 273–80.

Bacopoulos, N., Bird, E. D., and Roth, R. (1979). Dopamine metabolites in brain regions of schizophrenics. In *Catecholamines, basic and clinical frontiers*, Vol. 2 (ed. E., Usdin, I. J. Kopin, and J. D. Barchas), pp. 1884–6. Pergamon Press, New York.

Ban, T. A. and Lehmann, H. E. (1977). Myths, theories and treatment of schizophrenia. *Dis. nerv. Syst.* **38**, 665–71.

Beckman, H., Frische, M., Ruther, E., and Zimmer, R. (1977). Baclofen (para-chlorphenyl-GABA) in schizophrenia. *Pharmakopsychiat.* **10**, 26-31.

Bell, D. S. (1965). Comparison of amphetamine psychosis and schizophrenia. *Br. J. Psychiat.* **111**, 701–7.

Berger, P. A. (1981). Biochemistry and the schizophrenias old concepts and new hypotheses. *J. nerv. ment. Dis.* **169**, 90–9.

—— Watson, S. J., Akil, H., Elliott, G. R., Rubin, R. T., Pfefferbaum, A., Davis, K. L., Barchas, J. D. and Li, C. H. (1980). β-endorphin and schizophrenia. *Arch. gen. Psychiat.* **37**, 635–40.

Bird, E. D., Barnes, J., Iversen, L. L., Spokes, E. G., Mackay, A. V. P., and Shepherd, M. (1977). Increased brain dopamine and reduced glutamic acid decarboxylase and choline acetyltransferase activity in schizophrenics and related psychoses. *Lancet* **ii**, 1157–9.

Birkhauser, H. (1941). Cholinesterase und mon-aminoxydase in zentralen Nervensystem. *Schweiz Med. Wochenschr.* **71**, 750–2.

Bleuler, E. (1911). *Dementia praecox or the group of schizophrenias.* (English edition 1950). International University Press, New York.

Bradbury, A. J., Costall, B., Lim, S. K., and Naylor, R. J. (1982). Differentiation of dopamine agonist action to facilitate or inhibit motor behaviour. In *Advances in the biosciences*, Vol. 37. *Advances in dopamine research.* (ed. M. Kohsaka, Y. Shohmori, Y. Tsukada, G. N. Woodruff and), pp. 413–24. Pergamon Press, Oxford.

——, —— and Naylor, R. J. (1983). Reduction in motor responding of the mouse by dopamine agonist action in the midbrain. *Neuropharmacology* **22**, 1171–6.

Brambilla, F., Scarone, S., Ponzano, M., Maffei, C., Nobile, P., Rovere, C., and Guastalla, A. (1979). Catecholaminergic drugs in chronic schizophrenia. *Neuropsychobiology* **5**, 185–200.

Buchannan, F. H., Parton, R. V., Warren, J. W., and Baker, E. P. (1975). Double-blind trial of L-dopa in chronic schizophrenia. *Aust. and NZ J. Psychiat.* **9**, 269–71.

Buckley, P. (1982). Identifying schizophrenic patients who should not receive medication. *Schiz. Bull.* **8**, 429–32.

Bunney, B. S. (1979). The electrophysiological pharmacology of midbrain dopamine systems. In *The neurobiology of dopamine* (ed. A. S. Horn, J. Korf, and B. H. C. Westerink), pp. 417–52. Academic Press, New York.

Burt, D. R., Creese, I., and Snyder, S. H.(1976). Properties of [³H]haloperidol and [³H]dopamine binding associated with dopamine receptors in calf brain membranes. *Mol. Pharmacol.* **12**, 800–12.

Carlsson, A. (1975). Receptor-mediated control of dopamine metabolism. In *Pre- and post-synaptic receptors* (ed. E. Usdin and W. E. Bunney), pp. 49–65. Marcel Dekker, New York.

—— (1979). The impact of catecholamine research on medical science and practice. In *Catecholamines: basic and clinical frontiers*, Vol. 1 (ed. E. Usdin, I. Kopin, and J. Barchas), pp. 4–19. Pergamon Press, New York.

—— and Lindqvist, M (1963). Effect of chlorpromazine and haloperidol on formation of 3-methoxy-tyramine and normetanephrine in mouse brain. *Acta pharmacol. toxicol.* **20**, 140-4.

—— Persson, T., Roose, B.-E., and Walinder, J. (1972). Potentiation of phenothiazines by alpha-methyl-tyrosine in treatment of chronic schizophrenic. *J. Neural. Trans.* **33**, 83-90.

—— Roose, B.-E., Waldiner, J., and Skott, A. (1973). Further studies on the mechanism of anti-psychotic action: potentiation by alpha-methyl-tyrosine of thioridazine effects in chronic schizophrenics. *J. Neural. Trans.* **34**, 125-32.

Casey, D. E., Korsgaard, S., Gerlach, J., Jorgensen, A., and Simelsgaard, H. (1981). Effect of Des-Tyrosine-γ-endorphin in tardive dyskinesia. *Arch. gen. Psychiat.* **38**, 158-60.

Cesarec, Z., Eberhard, G, and Nordgren, L. (1974). A controlled study of the antipyschotic and sedative effects of neuroleptic drugs and amphetamine in chronic schizophrenia. *Acta psychiat. scand.* **249**, 65-77.

Charalampous, K. D., and Brown, S. (1967). A clinical trial of α-methyl-para-tyrosine in mentally ill patients. *Psychopharmacologia* **11**, 422-5.

Cheramy, A., Leviel, V., and Glowinski, J. (1981). Dendritic release of dopamine in the substantia nigra. *Nature, Lond.* **289**, 537-42.

Chouinard, G. and Annable, L. (1982). Pimozide in the treatment of newly admitted schizophrenic patients. *Psychopharmacology* **76**, 13-19.

Collard, J., Lecoq, R., and Demaret, A. (1965). Un essai de therapeutique pathogenique de la schizophrenie par un acetylcholinique: L'oxotremorine. *Acta neurol. belg.* **65**, 122-7.

Connell, H. P. (1958). *Amphetamine psychosis*. Maudsley Monograph No. 5. Chapman and Hall, London.

Corsini, G. U., Del Zompo, M., Manconi, S., Cianchetti, C., Mangoni, A., and Gessa, G. L. (1977). In *Advances in biochemical psychopharmacology*, Vol. 16 (ed. E. Costa, and G. L. Gessa), pp. 645-8. Raven Press, New York.

—— Piccardi, M. P., Bochetta, A., Bernardi, F., and Del Zompo, M. (1981). Behavioural effects of apomorphine in man: dopamine receptor implications. In *Apomorphine and other dopaminomimetics*, Vol. 2 (ed. G. U. Corsini and G. L. Gessa), pp. 13-24. Raven Press, New York.

Costall, B., Domeney, A. M., Naylor, R. J.(1982). Behavioural and biochemical consequences of persistent overstimulation of mesolimbic dopamine systems in the rat. *Neuropharmacology* **21**, 327-35.

—— Fortune, D. H., Hui, S.-C. G., Naylor, R. J. (1980). Neuroleptic antagonism of the motor inhibitory effects of apomorphine within the nucleus accumbens: drug interaction at presynaptic receptors? *Eur. J. Pharmacol.* **63**, 347-58.

—— Hui, S-C. G. and Naylor, R. J. (1979). Hyperactivity induced by injection of dopamine into the nucleus accumbens: actions and interactions of neuroleptic, cholinomimetic and cholinolytic agents. *Neuropharmacology* **18**, 661-5.

—— Lim, S. K., and Naylor, R. J. (1981). Characterisation of the mechanisms by which purported dopamine agonists reduce spontaneous locomotor activity of mice. *Eur. J. Pharmacol.* **73**, 175-88.

—— and Naylor, R. J. (1980). Assessment of the test procedures used to analyse neuroleptic action. *Rev. pure appl. Pharm. Sci.* **1**, 3-83.

Costentin, J., Marcais, H., Protais, P., and Schwartz, J.-C. (1977). Tolerance to hypokinesia elicited by dopamine agonists in mice: hyposensitisation of autoreceptors? *Life Sci.* **20**, 883-6.

Coyle, J. T. and Snyder, S. H. (1969). Catecholamine uptake by synaptosomes in homogenates of rat brain: stereospecificity in different areas. *J. Pharmacol. exp. Ther.* **170**, 221-31.

Creese, I., Burt, D. R., and Snyder, S. H. (1976). Dopamine receptor binding predicts clinical and pharmacological potencies of antischizophrenic drugs. *Science.* **192**, 481–3.

—— and Sibley, D. R. (1981). Receptor adaptations to centrally acting drugs. *Ann. Rev. Pharmacol. Toxicol.* **21**, 357–91.

——, —— (1982). Comments on the commentary by Dr Seeman. *Biochem. Pharmacol.* **31**, 2568–9.

Cross, A. J., Crow, T. J., and Owen, F. (1979a). The use of ADTN (2-amino-6,7-di-hydroxy-1,2,3,4-tetrahydronaphthalene) as a ligand for brain dopamine receptors. *Br. J. Pharmacol.* **66**, 87.

——, ——, —— (1979b). Gamma-aminobutyric acid in the brain in schizophrenia. *Lancet* i, 560–1.

——, ——, —— (1981). ^{3}H.flupenthixol binding in *post-mortem* brains of schizophrenics: evidence for a selective increase in dopamine D_2 receptors. *Psychopharmacology* **74**, 122–4.

Crow, T. J. (1980). The search for an environmental agent in schizophrenia. *Trends Neurosci.* **3**(7), XIII–XIV.

—— (1982). The biology of schizophrenia. *Experientia* **38**, 1275–82.

—— Baker, H. F., Cross, H. J., Jospeh, M. H., Lofthouse, R., Longden, A., Owen, F., Riley, G. J., Glover, V., and Killpack, W. S. (1979). Monoamine mechanisms in chronic schizophrenia: post-mortem neurochemical findings. *Br. J. Psychiat.* **134**, 249–56.

—— Cross, A. J., Johnstone, E. C., Longden, A., Owen, F., and Ridley, R. M. (1980). Time course of the antipsychotic effect in schizophrenia and some changes in *post mortem* brain and their relation to neuroleptic medication. *Adv. biochem. Psychopharmacol.* **24**, 495–503.

—— Johnstone, E. C., Longden, A. J., and Owen, F. (1978a). Dopaminergic mechanisms in schizophrenia: The antipsychotic effect and the disease process. *Life Sci.* **23**, 563–8.

—— Owen, F., Cross, A. J., Lofthouse, R., and Longden, A. (1978b). Brain biochemistry in schizophrenia. *Lancet* i, 36–7.

Davis, G. C., Bunney, W. E., Deraites, E. G., Kleinman, J. E. and Wyatt, R. J. (1977). Intravenous naloxone administration in schizophrenia and affective illness. *Science* **197**, 74–7.

Davis, K. L., Hollister, L. E. and Berger, P. A. (1980). Choline chloride in schizophrenia. *Am. J. Psychiat.* **136**, 1581–3.

De Feudis, F. V. and Charras, C. (1982). A theory of schizophrenia: role of environment. *Gen. Pharmacol.* **13**, 95–8.

De Wied, D. (1979). Schizophrenia as an inborn error in the degradation of β-endorphin—a hypothesis. *Trends Neurosci.* **2**, 79–82.

—— Bohus, B., Van Ree, J. M., and Urban, I. (1978a). Behavioural and electrophysiological effects of peptides related to lipotropin (β-LPH). *J. Pharmacol. exp. Ther.* **204**, 570–80.

——, ——, —— Kovacs, G. L., Greven, H. M. (1978b). Neuroleptic-like activity of (Des-Tyr^1)-γ-endorphin in rats. *Lancet* i, 1046.

—— Kovács, G. L., Bohus, B., Van Ree, J. M., and Greven, H. M. (1978c). Neuroleptic activity of the neuropeptide β-LPH$_{62-77}$((des-Tyr^1)-γ-endorphin: DTγE). *Eur. J. Pharmacol.* **49**, 427–36.

Dingledine, R., Iversen, L. L., and Breuker, E. (1978). Naloxone as a GABA antagonist: evidence from iontrophoretic receptor binding and convulsant studies. *Eur. J. Pharmacol.* **47**, 19–27.

Docherty, J. P., van Kammen, D. P., and Siris, S. G. (1978). Stages of onset of schizophrenia psychosis. *Am. J. Psychiat.* **135**, 420–6.

Domino, E. F., Krause, R. R., and Bowers, J. (1973). Various enzymes involved with putative neurotransmitters. *Arch. gen. Psychiat.* **29**, 195–201.

Domschke, W., Dickschas, A., and Mitznegg, P. (1979). CSF. β-endorphin in schizophrenia. *Lancet* **i**, 1024.

Elde, R., Hökfelt, T., Johansson, O., and Terenius, L. (1976). Immunohistochemical studies using antibodies to leucine–enkephalin. Initial observations on the nervous system of the rat. *Neuroscience* **1**, 349–51.

Ellinwood, E. H., Jr. (1972). Amphetamine psychosis: Individuals settings and sequences. In *Current concepts on amphetamine abuse* (ed. E. H. Ellinwood, S. Cohen, and M. Rockville), pp. 143–57. National Institute of Mental Health.

Emrich, H. M., Cording, C., Pirée, S., Möller, H.-J., van Zerssen, C., and Herz, A. (1977). Actions of naloxone in different types of psychoses. In *Endorphins and mental health research* (ed. E. Usdin, W. W. Bunney, N. S. Kline), pp. 452–60. Macmillan, London.

—— Höllt, V., Kissling, W., Fischler, M., Laspe, H., Heinmann, H., van Zerssen, D., and Herz, A. (1979). β-Endorphin like immunoreactivity in cerebrospinal fluid and plasma of patients with schizophrenia and neuropsychiatric disorders. *Pharmakopsychiatrie* **12**, 269–76.

—— Zaudig, M., Kissling, W., Dirlich, G., Von Zerssen, D., and Herz, A. (1980). Des-Tyrosyl-γ-endorphin in schizophrenia: a double blind trial in 13 patients. *Pharmakopsychiatrie* **13**, 290–8.

Farley, I. J., Price, K. S., McCullough, E., Deck, J. H. N., Hordynski, W., and Hornykiewicz, O. (1978). Norepinephrine in chronic paranoid schizophrenia: above-normal levels in limbic forebrain. *Science* **200**, 456–8.

—— Sharnak, K. S., and Hornykiewicz, O. (1980). Brain monoamine changes in chronic paranoid schizophrenia and their possible relation to increased dopamine receptor sensitivity. *Adv. biochem. Psychopharmacol.* **21**, 427–33.

Ferris, R. M., Tang, F. L., and Maxwell, R. A. (1972). A comparison of the capacities of isomers of amphetamine, deoxypipradel, and methylphenidate to inhibit the uptake of tritiated catecholamines in rat cerebral cortex slices, synaptosomal preparations of rat cerebral cortex, hypothalamus and striatum and into adrenergic nerves of rabbit aorta. *J. Pharmacol. exp. Ther.* **181**, 407–16.

Fredericksen, P. K. (1975). Baclofen in the treatment of schizophrenia. *Lancet* **i**, 702–3.

Gerlach, J. and Luhdorf, D. (1975). The effect of L-dopa on young patients with simple schizophrenia treated wtih neuroleptic drugs. *Psychopharmacologia* **44**, 105–10.

Gerner, R. H., Catlin, D. H., Gorelick, D. A., Hui, K. K. and Li, C. H. (1980). β-endorphin: intravenous infusion causes behavioural change in psychiatric patients. *Arch. gen. Psychiat.* **37**, 642–7.

Gershon, S., Hekimian, L. J., Floyd, A., Jr., and Hollister, L. E. (1967). Alpha-methyl-*p*-tyrosine (AMT) in schizophrenia. *Psychopharmacologia* **11**, 189–94.

Glowinski, J., Cheramy, A., and Giorguieff, M. F. (1979). *In-vivo* and *in-vitro* release of dopamine. In *The neurobiology of dopamine* (ed. A. S. Horn, J. Korf, and B. H. C. Westerink), pp. 199–216. Academic Press, London.

Goodwin, F. K., Murphy, D. L., and Brodie, H. K. H. (1970). L-dopa, catecholamines and behaviour: a clinical and biochemical study in depressed patients. *Biol. Psychiat.* **2**, 341–66.

—— and Post, R. M. (1975). Studies of amine metabolites in affective illness and in schizophrenia: a comparative analysis. In *Biology of the major psychoses: a comparative analysis* (ed. D. X. Freedman), pp. 299–332. Raven Press, New York.

Gottesman, I. I. (1978). In *The nature of schizophrenia* (ed. L. C. Wynne, R. L. Cromwell, and S. Matthysse), pp. 59–69. Wiley, New York.

Griffith, J. D., Fann, W. E., and Oates, J. A. (1972). The amphetamine psychosis:

experimental manifestations. In *Current concepts on amphetamine abuse* (ed. E. H. Ellinwood, S. Cohen, and M. Rockville), pp. 185–91. National Institute of Mental Health.

Groves, P. M., Wilson, C. J., Young, S. J., and Rebec, G. V. (1975). Self-inhibition by dopaminergic neurones. *Science* 190, 522–9.

—— Young, S. J., and Wilson, C. J. (1976). Self-inhibition by dopaminergic neurons: disruption by (±) alpha-methyl-paratyrosine pretreatment on anterior diencephalic lesions. *Neuropharmacology* 15, 755–62.

Gunne, L. M., Lindström, L., and Terenius, L. (1977). Naloxone-induced reversal of schizophrenic hallucinations. *J. Neural. Trans.* 40, 13–19.

——, —— and Widerlov, E. (1979). Possible role of endorphins in schizophrenia and other psychiatric disorders. In *Endorphins and mental health research* (ed. E. Usdin, W. W. Bunney, and N. S. Kline), pp. 547–60. Macmillan, London.

Haracz, J. L. (1982). The dopamine hypothesis: an overview of studies with schizophrenic patients. *Schiz. Bull.* 8, 438–69.

Hartmann, E. (1976). Schizophrenia: a theory. *Psychopharmacology* 49, 1–16.

—— and Keller-Teschke, M. (1977). Biology of schizophrenia: mental effects of dopamine-β-hydroxylase inhibition in normal man. *Lancet* i, 37–8.

Horn, A. S. (1979). Characteristics of dopamine uptake. In *The neurobiology of dopamine* (ed. A. S. Horn, J. Korf, and B. H. C. Westerink), pp. 217–35. Academic Press, London.

Hornykiewicz, O. (1982). Brain catecholamines in schizophrenia–a good case for noradrenaline. *Nature, Lond.* 299, 484–6.

Horrobin, D. F. (1979). Schizophrenia: reconciliation of the dopamine, prostaglandin, and opioid concepts and the role of the pineal. *Lancet* i, 529–31.

—— Manku, M. S., Oka, M., and Cunnane, S. C. (1980). The role of a prostaglandin E_1 deficiency in schizophrenia: interaction with dopamine and opiates. In *The biochemistry of schizophrenia and addiction* (ed. G. Hemmings), pp. 3–17. MTP Press Ltd, Lancaster.

Inanaga, K., Nakazawa, Y., Inoue, K., Tachibana, H., Ochima, M., Katori, T., Tanaka, M., and Ogasa, N. (1975). Double-blind controlled study of L-dopa therapy in schizophrenia. *Fol. Psychiat. Neurol. Jap.* 29, 123–43.

Itil, T. M., Keskiner, A., and Holden, O. M. C. (1969). The use of LSD and ditran in the treatment of therapy resistant schizophrenics (symptom provocation approach). *Dis. nerv. Syst.* 30, 90–103.

Iversen, L. L. (1985). Superpotent serotonin blockers. *Nature, Lond.* 316, 107–8.

—— and Mackay, A. V. P. (1981). Brain dopamine receptor densities in schizophrenics. *Lancet* 11, 149.

Jacquet, Y. F. and Marks. N. (1976). The C-fragment of β-lipotropin: an endogenous neuroleptic or antipsychotogen? *Science* 194, 632–5.

Janowsky, D. S. and Davis, J. M. (1974). Dopamine, psychomotor stimulants, and schizophrenia: effects of methylphenidate and the stereoisomers of amphetamines in schizophrenia. In *Neuropsychopharmacology of monoamines and their regulatory enzymes* (ed. E. Usdin), pp. 317–23. Raven Press, New York.

——, —— (1976). Methylphenidate, dextroamphetamine and levamphetamine: effects of schizophrenic symptoms. *Arch. gen. Psychiat.* 33, 304–8.

—— El-Yousef, M. K., and Davis. J. M. (1973a). Provocation of schizophrenic symptoms by intravenous administration of methylphenidate. *Arch. gen. Psychiat.* 28, 185–91.

——, ——, —— and Sekerke, H. J. (1973b). Antagonistic effects of physostigmine and methylphenidate in man. *Am. J. Psychiat.* 130, 1370–6.

—— Segal, D. S., Bloom, F., Abrams, A., and Guilleman, R. (1977a). Lack of effect of naloxone in chronic schizophrenia. *Am. J. Psychiat.* **134**, 926–7.

—— Storms, L., and Judd, L. L. (1977*b*). Methylphenidate hydrochloride effects of psychological tests in acute schizophrenic and nonpsychotic patients. *Arch. gen. Psychiat.* **34**, 189–94.

Jenkins, R. B. and Groh, R. H. (1970). Mental symptoms in parkinsonian patients treated with L-dopa. *Lancet* **ii**, 177–9.

Joseph, M. H., Baker, H. F., Crow, T. J., Riley, G. J., and Risby, D. (1979). Brain tryptophan metabolism in schizophrenia: a post-mortem study of metabolism on the serotonin and kynurenine pathways in schizophrenic and control subjects. *Psychopharmacology* **62**, 279–85.

Kety, S. S. (1979). Roles of neurotransmitters and polypeptides in schizophrenia. In *World issues in the problems of schizophrenic psychoses* (ed. T. Fukuda, and H. Mitsuda), pp. 128–9. Igaku-Shoin, Tokyo.

—— Rosenthal, D., Wender, P. H., Schulsinger, F., and Jacobsen, B. (1978). In *The nature of schizophrenia* (ed. L. C. Wynne, R. L. Cromwell, and S. Matthysse), pp. 25–37. Wiley, New York.

Kleinman, J., Bridge, P., and Karoum, R. (1979). Catecholamines and metabolites in the brains of psychotics and normals: post-mortem studies. In *Catecholamines: Basic and clinical frontiers* (ed. E. Usdin, I. Kopin, and T. Barchas), pp. 413–19. Pergamon Press, New York.

——, ——, —— Speciale, S. Jr, Staub, R., Zalcman, S., Gillin, J. C., and Wyatt, R. J. (1980). Chronic schizophrenia: post-mortem studies. In *Perspectives in schizophrenia research* (ed. C. Baxter and T. Melnechuk), pp. 227–36. Raven Press, New York.

Kline, N. S., Li, C. H., Lehmann, H. E., Lajtha, A., Laski, E., and Cooper, T. (1977). β-endorphin-induced changes in schizophrenic and depressed patients. *Arch. gen. psychiat.* **34**, 1111–13.

Kokkinidis, L. and Anisman, H. (1981). Amphetamine psychosis and schizophrenia: a dual model. *Neurosci. Biobehav. Rev.* **5**, 449–61.

Kurland, A. A., McCabe, O., Hanlon, T. E., and Sullivan, D. (1977). The treatment of perceptual disturbances in schizophrenia with naloxone hydrochloride. *Am. J. Psychiat.* **134**, 1408–10.

Lee, T. and Seeman, P. (1980*a*). Abnormal neuroleptic/dopamine receptors in schizophrenia. *Adv. biochem. Psychopharmacol.* **21**, 435–42.

—(1980*b*). Elevation of brain neuroleptic/dopamine receptors in schizophrenia. *Am. J. Psychiat* **137**, 191–7.

——, —— Tourtellote, W. W., Farley, I. J., and Hornykiewicz, O. (1978). Binding of [³H]neuroleptics and [³H]apomorphine in schizophrenic brains. *Nature, Lond.* **274**, 897–900.

Liberman, R. P. (1982). What is schizophrenia? *Schiz. Bull.,* **8**, 433–7.

Lightman, S. L., Spokes, E. G., Sagnella, G. A., Gordon, D., and Bird, E. D. (1979). Distribution of β-endorphin in normal and schizophrenic human brains. *Eur. J. clin. Invest.* **9**, 377–9.

Lindström, L. H., Widerlöv, E., Gunne, L.-M., Wahlström, A., and Terenius, L. (1978). Endorphins in human cerebrospinal fluid: clinical correlations to some psychotic states. *Acta psychiat. scand.* **57**, 153–64.

Linnoila, M., Whorton, A. R., Rubinow, D. R., Cowdry, R. W., Ninan, P. T., and Waters, R. N. (1983). CSF prostaglandin levels in depressed and schizophrenic patients. *Arch. gen. Psychiat* **40**, 405–6.

Machanda, R., and Hirsch, S. R. (1981). (Des-Tyr¹)-γ-endorphin in the treatment of schizophrenia. *Psychol. Med.* **11**, 401–4.

Mackay, A. V. P., Bird, E. D., Iversen, L. L., Spokes, E. G., Creese, I., and Snyder, S. H. (1980*a*). Dopaminergic abnormalities in post-mortem schizophrenic brain.

Adv. biochem. Psychopharmacol. **24**, 325–33.

——, —— Spokes, E. G., Rossor, M., Iversen, L. L., Creese, I., and Snyder, S. H. (1980*b*). Dopamine receptors and schizophrenia: drug effect or illness? *Lancet* **ii**, 915–16.

—— Doble, A., Bird, E. D., Spokes, E. G., Quik, M., and Iversen, L. L. (1978). [³H]Spiperone binding in normal and schizophrenic *post mortem* human brain. *Life Sci.* **23**, 527–32.

—— Iversen, L. L., Rosser, M., Spokes, E., Bird, E., Arregui, A., Creese, I., and Snyder, S. H. (1982). Increased brain dopamine and dopamine receptors in schizophrenia. *Arch. gen. Psychiat.* **39**, 991–7.

Manberg, P. J., Nemeroff, C. B., Iversen, L. L., Rosser, M. N., Kizer, J. S., and Prange, A. J. Jr. (1982). Human brain distribution of neurotensin in normals, schizophrenics and Huntington Choreics. *Ann. NY Acad. Sci.* **400**, 354–67.

Mathe, A. A., Sedvall, G., Wiesel, F. A., Nybäck, H. (1980). Increased content of immunocreative prostaglandin E in cerebrospinal fluid of patients with schizophrenia. *Lancet* **i**, 16–18.

McCormick, T. K. and McNeil, T. W. (1963), Acute psychosis and Ritalin abuse. *Tex. State J. Med.* **59**, 99–100.

McGeer, P. L. and McGeer, E. G. (1977). Possible changes in striatal and limbic cholinergic systems in schizophrenia. *Arch. gen. Psychiat.* **34**, 1319–23.

Meltzer, H. Y. (1979). Biology of schizophrenia subtypes: a review and proposal for method of study. *Schiz. Bull.* **5**, 460–79.

—— Busch, D., and Fang, V. S. (1981). Hormones, dopamine receptors and schizophrenia. *Psychoneuroendocrinology* **6**, 17–36.

—— Jackson, H., Arora, R. C. (1980). Brain and skeletal muscle monoamine oxidase activity in schizophrenia. *Schiz. Bull.* **6**, 208–12.

Micke, D. H. and Gallant, D. M. (1977). An oral opiate antagonist in chronic schizophrenia. *Am. J. Psychiat.* **134**, 1430–1.

Modestin, J., Schwartz, R. B., and Hunger, J. (1973). Zur Frage Beeinflussung schizophrener Symptome durch Physostigmin. *Pharmakopsychiat. Neuropsychopharmakol.* **6**, 300–4.

Moore, K. E., Chiueh, C. C., and Zeldes, G. (1977). Release of neurotransmitters from the brain *in vivo* by amphetamine, methylphenidate and cocaine. In *Cocaine and other stimulants* (ed. E. H. Ellinwood, and M. M. Kilbey), pp. 143–60. Plenum Press, New York.

Nasrallah, M. A., Donnelly, E. F., Bigelow, L. B., Rivera-Calimlin, L., Rogol, A., Potkin, S, Rauscher, F. P., Wyatt, R. J., and Gillin, C. (1977). Inhibition of dopamine synthesis in schizophrenia. *Arch. gen. Psychiat.* **34**, 649–55.

Nemeroff, C. B., Hernandez, D. E., Luttinger, D., Kalivas, P. W., and Prange, A. J. Jr. (1982). Interactions of neurotensin with brain dopamine systems. *Ann. NY Acad. Sci.* **400**, 330–44.

Niemegeers, C. J. E. and Leysen, J. E. (1982). The pharmacological and biochemical basis of neuroleptic treatment in schizophrenia. *Pharmaceutisch Weekblad, Scientific Edition* **4**, 71–8.

Ogura, C., Kishimoto, A., and Nakao, T. (1976). Clinical effect of L-dopa on schizophrenia. *Curr. ther. Res.* **20**, 308–18.

Owen, F., Cross, A. J., Crow, T. J., Longden, A., Poulter, M., and Riley, G. T. (1978). Increased dopamine receptor sensitivity in schizophrenia. *Lancet* **ii**, 223–6.

Palfreyman, M. (1981). Recent studies on the pharmacology of GABA: therapeutic perspective. *Trends Pharmacol. Sci.* **2**, VI–IX.

Peroutka, S. J., U'Prichard, D. C., Greenberg, D. A., and Snyder, S. H. (1977). Neuroleptic drug interactions with norepinephrine alpha-receptor binding sites in rat brain. *Neuropharmacology* **16**, 549–56.

Perry, E. K., Blessed, G., Perry, R. H., and Tomlinson, B. E. (1978). Brain bio-chemistry in schizophrenia. *Lancet* **i**, 35–6.

Perry, T. L., Kisk, S. J., Buchanan, J., and Hansen, S. (1979). Gamma amino butyric acid: the deficiency in brain of schizophrenic patients. *Lancet* **i**, 237–9.

Pethö, B., Gräf, L., Larczag, I., Bitter, I., Tolna, J., Baraczka, K., and Li, C. H. (1981). β-endorphin and schizophrenia. *Lancet* **i**, 212–13.

Pfeiffer, C. C. and Jenny, E. H. (1957). The inhibition of the conditioned response and the counteraction of schizophrenia by muscarinic stimulation of the brain. *Ann. NY Acad. Sci.* **66**, 753–64.

Pickar, D., Davis, G. C., Schultz, S. Ch., Extein, I., Wagner, R., Naber, D., Gold, Ph. W., Van Kammen, D. P., Goodwin, F. K., Wyatt, R. J., Li, C. H., and Bunney, W. E. Jr. (1981). Behavioural and biological effects of acute β-endorphin injection in schizophrenic and depressed patients. *Am. J. Psychiat.* **138**, 160–6.

Pope, A., Meath, J. A. Jr and Caveness, W. F. (1949). Histochemical distribution of cholinesterase and acid phosphatase in the prefrontal cortex of psychotic and non-psychotic patients. *Trans. Am. neurol Ass.* **74**, 147–53.

Rebec, G. V. Bashore, T. R. (1982). Comments on 'amphetamine models of paranoid schizophrenia': a precautionary note. *Psychol. Bull.* **62**, 403–9.

Reisine, T. D., Pedigo, N. W., Regan, P., Ling, N., and Yamamura, H. I. (1980*a*). Abnormal brain opiate mechanisms in schizophrenia. In *Endogenous and exogenous opiate agonists and antagonists* (ed. E. L. Way), pp. 117–20. Pergamon Press, New York.

—— Rosser, M., Spokes, E., Iversen, L. L., and Yamamura, H. I. (1980*b*). Opiate and neuroleptic receptor alterations in human schizophrenic brain tissue. *Adv. biochem. Psychopharmacol.* **21**, 443–50.

Reveley, M. A., Glover, V., Sandler, M. and Spokes, E. G. (1981). Brain monoamine oxidase activity in schizophrenics and control. *Arch. gen. Psychiat.* **38**, 663–5.

Reynolds, G. P. (1983). Increased concentrations and lateral asymmetry of amygdala dopamine in schizophrenia. *Nature, Lond.* **305**, 527–9.

—— Reyolds, L. M., Riederer, P., Jellinger, K., and Gabriel, E. (1980). Dopamine receptors and schizophrenia: drug effect or illness? *Lancet* **ii**, 1251.

—— Riederer, P., Jellinger, K., and Gabriel, E. (1981). Dopamine receptors and schizophrenia: the neuroleptic drug problem. *Neuropharmacology* **20**, 1319–20.

Rimon, R., Terenius, L., and Kampman, R. (1980). Cerebrospinal fluid endorphins in schizophrenia. *Acta psychiat. scand.* **61**, 395–403.

Rosenthal, R., and Bigelow, L. G. (1973). The effects of physostigmine in phenothia-zine resistant chronic schizophrenic patients: preliminary observations. *Comprehens. Psychiat.* **14**, 489–95.

Rowntree, D. W., Nevin, S., and Wilson, A. (1950). The effects of diisopropylfluoro-phosphonate in schizophrenic and manic depressive psychosis. *J. Neurol. Neurosurg. Psychiat.* **13**, 47–59.

Rupniak, N. M. J., Jenner, P., and Marsden, C. D. (1983). The effect of chronic neuroleptic administration on cerebral dopamine receptor function. *Life Sci.* **32**, 2289–311.

Sack, R. L. and Goodwin, F. K. (1974). Inhibition of dopamine-β-hydroxylase in manic patients. A clinical trial and fusaric acid. *Arch. gen. Psychiat.* **31**, 649–54.

Seeman, P. (1981). Dopamine receptors in post-mortem schizophrenic brains. *Lancet* **i**, 1103.

—— (1982). Nomenclature of central and peripheral dopaminergic sites and receptors. *Biochem. Pharmacol.* **31**, 2563–8.

—— Lee, T., Chau-Wong, M., and Wong, K. (1976). Antipsychotic drug doses and neuroleptic/dopamine receptors. *Nature, Lond.* **261**, 717–19.

Segal, D. S., Browne, R. G., Bloom, F., Ling, N., and Guillemin, R. (1977). β-endorphin: endogenous opiate or neuroleptic. *Science* **198**, 411–13.

—— and Janowsky, D. S. (1978). Psychostimulant-induced behavioural effects: possible models of schizophrenia. In *Psychopharmacology: a generation of progress* (ed. M. A. Lipton, A. Di Mascio, and K. F. Killam), pp. 1113–23. Raven Press, New York.

Simpson, G. M., Branchly, M. H., and Lee, J. H. (1977). A trial of naltrexone in chronic schizophrenia. *Curr. ther. Res.* **22**, 909–13.

——, —— and Shrivastava, R. K. (1976). Baclofen in schizophrenia. *Lancet* i, 966–7.

Smith, G. M. and Beecher, H. K. (1961). Subjective effects of heroin and morphine in normal subjects. *J. Pharmacol. exp. Ther.* **136**, 47–52.

Smith, R. C., Tamminga, C. and Davis, J. M. (1977). Effect of apomorphine on schizophrenic symptoms. *J. Neural. Trans.* **40**, 171–6.

Snyder, S. H. (1974). *Madness and the brain*. McGraw Hill, New York.

—— (1982). Schizophrenia. *Lancet*, **ii**, 970–3.

Sourkes, T. L. (1973). On the origin of homovanillic acid (HVA) in the cerebrospinal fluid. *J. Neural. Trans.* **34**, 153–7.

Stevens, J. R. (1978). Research in schizophrenia: regulation of dopamine in the meso-limbic system. *Imp. Sci. Soc.* **28**, 39–56.

Strömbom, U. (1976), Catecholamine receptor agonists. Effects on motor activity and rate of tyrosine hydroxylation in mouse brain. *Naunyn-Schmiedeberg's Arch. Pharmacol.* **292**, 167–76.

Sumners, C., de Vries, T. B., and Horn, A. S. (1981). Behavioural and neurochemical studies on apomorphine-induced hypomotility in mice. *Neuropharmacology* **20**, 1203–8.

Szasz, T. (1978). Schizophrenia—a category error. *Trends Neurosci.* **1**, 26–8.

Takahashi, Y., and Ogushi, T. (1953). On biochemical studies of schizophrenia. Report 1. An enzymological study on brain tissue and serum of schizophrenic patients: choline esterase. *Fol. Psychiat. Neurol. Jap.* **6**, 244–61.

Tamminga, C. A., Crayton, J. W., and Chase, T. N. (1978a). Muscimol: GABA agonist therapy in schizophrenia. *Am. J. Psychiat.* **135**, 746–47.

—— Schaffer, M. H., Smith, R. C., and Davis, J. M. (1978b). Schizophrenic symptoms improve with apomorphine. *Science* **200**, 567–8.

—— Tighe, P. J., Chase, T. N., De Fraites, E. G., and Schaffer, M. H. (1981). Des-Tyrosine-γ-endorphin administration in chronic schizophrenics. *Arch. gen. Psychiat.* **38**, 167–8.

Terenius, L., Wahlström, A., Lindström, L., and Widerlöv, E. (1976). Increased CSF levels of endorphins in chronic psychosis. *Neurosci. Lett.* **3**, 157–62.

Toru, M., Nishikawa, T., Mataga, N., and Takashima, M. (1982). Dopamine metabolism increases in *post mortem* schizophrenic basal ganglia. *J. Neural. Trans.* **54**, 181–91.

Van der Velde, C. D. (1976). Variability in schizophrenia. *Arch. gen. Psychiat.* **33**, 489–96.

Van Kammen, D. P. and Bunney, W. E. (1979). Heterogeneity in response to amphetamine in schizophrenia: effects of placebo, chronic pimozide and pimozide withdrawal. In *Catecholamines: basic and clinical frontiers* (ed. E. Usdin, I. J. Kopin, and J. D. Barchas), pp. 44–48. Pergamon Press, New York.

——, —— Docherty, J. P., Jimmerson, D. C., Post,R. M., Siris, M., Ebert, M., and Gillin, J. C. (1977). Amphetamine induced catecholamine activation in schizophrenia and depression. Behavioural and physiological effects. In *Advances in biochemical psychopharmacology* Vol. 16 (ed. E. Costa., G. L. Gessa), pp. 655–9. Raven Press, New York.

—— Docherty, J. P., Marder, S. R., Schulz, S. C., Dalton, L., and Bunney, W. E.

(1982). Antipsychotic effects of pimozide in schizophrenia. *Arch gen. Psychiat.* **39**, 261–6.

Van Praag, H. M. and Korf, J. (1976). Importance of dopamine metabolism for clinical effects and side-effects of neuroleptics. *Am. J. Psychiat.* **133**, 1171–7.

Van Ree, J. M., Bohus, B., and De Wied, D. (1980*a*). Similarity between behavioural effects of Des-Tyrosine-γ-endorphin and haloperidol and of α-endorphin and amphetamine. In *Endogenous and exogenous opiate agonists and antagonists* (ed. E. Leong Way), pp. 459–62. Pergamon Press, New York.

—— and De Wied, D. (1981). Endorphins in schizophrenia. *Neuropharmacology* **20**, 1271–7.

——, —— Verhoeven, W. M. A., and Van Praag, H. M. (1980*b*). Antipsychotic effect of γ-type endorphins in schizophrenia. *Lancet* **ii**, 1363–5.

—— and Wolterink, G. (1981). Injection of low doses of apomorphine into the nucleus accumbens of rats reduces locomotor activity. *Eur. J. Pharmacol.* **72**, 107–11.

Verhoeven, W. M. A., Van Praag, H. M., Botter, P. A., Sunier, A., Van Ree, J. M., and De Wied, D. (1978), (Des-Tyr¹)-γ-endorphin in schizophrenia. *Lancet* **i**, 1046–7.

——, —— Van Ree, J. M., and De Wied, D. (1979). Improvement of schizophrenic patients by treatment with (Des-Tyr¹)-γ-endorphin (DTγE). *Arch. gen. Psychiat.* **36**, 294–8.

Volavka, J., Mallya, A., Baig, S., and Perez-Cruet, J. (1977). Naloxone in chronic schizophrenia. *Science* **196**, 1227–8.

Wällinder, J., Skott, A., Carlsson, A., and Roos, B.-E (1976). Potentiation by metyrosine of thioridazine in chronic schizophrenics. *Arch. gen. Psychiat.* **33**, 501–5.

Watson, S. J., Akil, H., Berger, A. P., and Barchas, J. D. (1979). Some observations on the opiate peptides and schizophrenia. *Arch. gen. Psychiat.* **36**, 35–41.

—— Berger, P. A., Akil, H., Mills, M. J., and Barchas, J. D. (1978). Effects of naloxone in schizophrenia: reduction in hallucinations in a subpopulation of subjects. *Science* **201**, 73–6.

Weil-Malherbe, H. (1978). Serotonin and schizophrenia. In *Serotonin in health and disease*, Vol. III (ed. W. B. Essman), pp. 231–91. Spectrum Publications New York.

Weissman, A., Koe, B., and Tenen, S. (1966), Amphetamine effects following inhibition of tyrosine hydroxylase. *J. Pharmacol. exp. Ther.* **151**, 339–52.

Widerlöv, E., Lindström, L. H., Besev, G., Manberg, P. J., Nemeroff, C. B., Breese, G. R., Kizer, J. S., and Prange, A. J. (1982). Subnormal CSF levels of neurotensin in a subgroup of schizophrenics and normalization after neuroleptic treatment. In *Ann. NY Acad. Sci.* **400**, 418–19.

Winblad, B., Bucht, G., Gottfries, C. G., and Roos, B. E. (1979), Monoamines and monoamine metabolites in brains from demented schizophrenics. *Acta psychiat. scand.* **60**, 17–28.

Wyatt, R. J., Bigelow, L. B., and Gillan, J. C. (1979). Catecholamine related substances and schizophrenia: a review. In *Catecholamines: basic and clinical frontiers,* Vol. 2 (ed. E. Usdin, I. J. Kopin, and J. D. Barchas), pp. 1820–5. Pergamon Press, New York.

Wyatt, R. J., Moja, E. A., Karoum, F., Stoff, D. M., Potkin, S. G., and Kleinman, J. E. (1980*b*). Phenylethylamine, dopamine and norepinephrine in schizophrenia. In *Apomorphine and other dopaminomimetics,* Vol. 2 (ed. G. U. Corsini, and G. L. Gessa), pp. 39–44. Raven Press, New York.

—— Potkin, S. G., Bridge, T. P., Phelps, B. H. and Wise, C. D. (1980*a*). Monoamine oxidase in schizophrenia: an overview. *Schiz Bull.* **6**, 199–207.

——, —— Kleinman, J. E., Weinberger, D. R., Luchins, D. J., and Jeste, D. V. (1981). The schizophrenia syndrome: examples of biological tools for subclassification. *J. nerv. ment. Dis.* **169**, 110–12.

Yaryura-Tobias, J. A., Diamond, B., and Merlis, S. (1970). The action of L-dopa on schizophrenic patients (a preliminary report). *Curr. ther. Res.* **12**, 528–31.

Young, D. and Scoville, B. W. (1938). Paranoid psychosis in narcolepsy and the possible danger of benzedrine treatment. *Med. Clin. N. Am.* **22**, 637–45.

6

Diagnosis of schizophrenia and schizoaffective psychoses

IAN BROCKINGTON

INTRODUCTION

The nature of schizophrenia

'Schizophrenia' is one of the most important concepts in psychiatry, but there is little agreement on what the term means. It is often spoken of as a clinical syndrome or disease entity. A 'syndrome' is a group of symptoms which occur together in a characteristic pattern creating a spark of recognition in the eyes of the experienced observer, but schizophrenia is not a concurring cluster of symptoms but a loose collection of overlapping disease pictures covering almost the whole range of severe psychiatric disturbance, involving delusions, hallucinations, passivity experiences, thought disorder, motility disturbances, loss of volition, and affective changes (e.g. flattening, suspicion, perplexity) in a variety of combinations. It is doubtful whether there are any characteristic symptoms, and it has never been proved that any definition of schizophrenia selects a population of patients sharply separated from other psychotic patients. A 'disease entity' implies that a single thread runs through the course of an illness, determining its main features; for example the invasion of the body by the tubercle bacillus is the essential feature which determines the diverse manifestations of tuberculosis, and lack of endogenous insulin is the central feature of diabetes. It seems doubtful whether there is a single morbid process at the heart of the phenomenon of schizophrenia. There seem to be not one but several vectors of disturbance in the patient's mental life, including paranoid thinking, auditory hallucinosis, and social incompetence, and it is not at present clear how these can be related to a single essential abnormality. Kraepelin's original idea, that a group of different clinical pictures followed a common path to a state resembling dementia, no longer commands general acceptance; it has been abandoned by those who conceive schizophrenia in terms of characteristic symptoms without reference to the course, including Schneider (1959) who wrote,

Whoever like us emphasizes the condition will, if the psychosis shows any schizophrenic symptoms of first rank importance, hold firmly to such a diagnosis, although the psychosis clears up completely.

In the absence of a distinct pathognomonic cluster of symptoms *and* an agreed essential feature, the conceptualization of schizophrenia as a syndrome or disease entity is misleading.

Schizophrenia is neither a syndrome nor disease entity. It is simply a classificatory notion, a provisional category linking together 'only for the purpose of preliminary enquiry' (Kraepelin 1919) a number of patients who have something in common in their symptoms and course. The fact that it does not stand out as a syndrome, and that there is no agreement whether it is to be defined in terms of its natural history or its symptoms, makes the task of finding a definition acceptable to all particularly difficult; up till now this modest objective has proved too much for the psychiatric community. At present, we have a Babel of discordant definitions. This does not mean that we should abandon the term. Without it, nineteenth-century nosology was even more of a shambles. It means that we should refine the concepts we have, working towards the goal of classifying patients into homogeneous groups having useful and verifiable associations with aetiological factors, treatment response, outcome, etc. This will involve improving our methods of clinical observation, and choosing between rival formulations of the schizophrenic concept. This chapter reviews progress made towards this goal.

Schizoaffective and cycloid psychoses

From the earliest times, psychiatrists have been dissatisfied with Kraepelin's division of the functional psychoses into two entities—dementia praecox and manic depressive insanity—while acknowledging his achievement in focusing attention on the temporal pattern of an illness and using it as the main classificatory principle. In Germany itself Wernicke and Kleist developed the idea of the motility and degeneration psychoses, which later became the 'cycloid psychoses' of Leonhard and Perris (Perris 1974). The cycloid psychoses are comparable to schizophrenia and manic depression in having the requirements of a putative disease entity—their own heredity, characteristic symptoms, and course. The characteristic symptoms are confusion or perplexity, and in some cases there is a clinical 'polymorphism', i.e. a jumble of different psychotic symptoms in the absence of a persistent manic, depressive, or paranoid syndrome. The course is marked by an acute onset, variability in the clinical picture during the episode, and full recovery. The concept of cycloid psychoses as a nosological entity is used in Germany and Scandinavia, but has never gained acceptance in France, Britain, or America, nor in the World Health Organization's International Classification of Diseases.

In America, disaffection with the two-entities principle has generated a literature on 'schizoaffective psychoses' which started with a thoughtful article by Jacob Kasanin (1933). Under the name of 'acute schizoaffective psychoses' he called attention to

a group of . . . fairly young individuals, quite well integrated socially, who suddenly blow up in a dramatic psychosis and present a clinical picture in whom the differential diagnosis is extremely difficult.

He emphasized the good premorbid adjustment, the difficult environmental situation which served as a precipitant, the emotional turmoil, and the sudden development of a psychosis which resolved equally suddenly. He mentioned nine cases, but gave details of only five of them. His work was neglected for many years, but in 1963, at a time when 'schizophrenia' in America was coterminous with 'psychosis', Vaillant reviewed the literature on benign schizophrenia-like psychoses and drew up a list of features predictive of a favourable outcome including, for example, the absence of schizoid traits and a concern with dying. As the over-inclusive idea of schizophrenia was replaced, in the 1970s, by a narrowly defined psychosis with characteristic symptoms in the absence of major mood disorder, there was less need for the concept of 'good prognosis schizophrenia' but there emerged a large group of patients with *both* characteristic symptoms *and* a fully developed manic or depressive syndrome. These were called 'schizo-affective psychoses', borrowing Kasanin's term which he introduced to denote a very different group of disease pictures probably closer to acute paranoid disturbances. At the present time, schizoaffective psychoses (as defined by the Research Diagnostic Criteria of Spitzer *et al.*, 1978) are receiving a good deal of attention in an attempt to decide whether they belong to manic depressive disease, to schizophrenia, to both, or to a third disease entity. The purpose of this article is not to answer those questions, but to review the definitions of schizoaffective psychosis which have been proposed.

HOW A DIAGNOSIS IS MADE

Observations of symptoms and behaviour

Although this chapter is mainly concerned with definitions of diagnostic categories, these definitions have to be applied to a corpus of information about a patient's behaviour and symptoms. It is obvious from the nature of the subject matter—psychological experiences described by persons whose judgement may be awry, and transient behavioural disturbances—that it is difficult to build up a full and accurate representation of the psychotic episode. Ideally the patient would be under continuous observation by people who knew him well and have an extensive experience of mental illness, and he would on several occasions be questioned about his experiences by a trained interviewer. This ideal is, however, unattainable, and the best that can be done is to construct as complete a picture as possible by tapping a number of different sources of information.

The most systematic and reliable source of information about symptomatology is the structured interview (Spitzer *et al.* 1970; Wing *et al.* 1974). The patient is questioned about his symptoms by a person trained in the skills of interviewing and familiar with a glossary of defined phenomena. Such interviews are indispensable but they are not sufficient in themselves. When interview ratings are compared with ratings made from more comprehensive data (Carpenter *et al.* 1976; Downing *et al.* 1980) it is apparent that a great deal is missed. It is not surprising that behavioural disturbances are missed because the interviewer observes the patient for only one hour under special circumstances. It is surprising, however, that the interviewer also obtains an incomplete account of symptoms. The concordance between symptom ratings made by interviewers seeing the patient a few days apart is quite low, for example 0.41 (intraclass correlation coefficient) in one study of the present state examination (Cooper *et al.* 1972). It seems wise, therefore, to interview the patient on more than one occasion. Long structured interviews are tiring for both the patient and interviewer, and therefore it seems sensible to conduct rather briefer interviews on two or three occasions. The first interview should be as early as possible after admission in order to establish the main complaints and preoccupations, and to observe the disturbances which precipitated admission. The later interview(s) should complete the cross-examination and routine probes.

Unfortunately, some research studies base a diagnosis on a single structured interview, although no experienced psychiatrist would rely on such a limited source to make his clinical decisions. One would expect that when relatively small samples of patients are involved, a clinical research worker would make the best possible use of every source of information including an interview with a relative, who has observed the development of the psychosis and can thus compare the sick person with his former self. Allowance would have to be made for the relative's lack of formal knowledge of psychiatry, and perhaps limited powers of description. After admission the nursing staff take over the relative's role in relating closely to and observing the patient. Their frame of reference differs from that of the relative in that they have an extensive experience of mental illness (though their concepts may differ from the psychiatrist's) but they do not know their patient prior to admission and before the onset of illness. Bunney and Hamburg (1963) argued cogently that nursing staff are the only trained personnel who can observe the patient throughout the day and night in an extensive range of activities and interpersonal exchanges. It has been held against nurse *rating* that it is often hard to achieve adequate reliability. However, it is not necessary for nurses to make ratings. All that is necessary is for them to make observations. Other sources of information are more controversial. The use of film or videotape seems to offer an obvious advantage over unrecorded interviews, as the most difficult judgements (e.g. of affect) can be made by the most senior investigator or by several raters, and measurements can be made of speech and movement; in practice these methods have not been used very often because of the time involved in analysing recorded material. Although there is some evidence that videotape ratings are more sensitive in their recognition of change in state (Katz and Itil 1974) they have not been shown to improve diagnosis. Self-rating by patients has an intrinsic appeal because it is a source of information which is relatively free from observer bias, but again it is not clear that it can make a special contribution to diagnosis.

The basic information about a psychosis consists of what the patient said and did. At some stage this has to be transformed into numerical form, so that powerful statistical tools can be brought into use. In the writer's opinion the time to make this transformation is at the end, when all sources of information have been recruited, including several interviews, psychological reports, relatives' accounts, nursing observations, etc. At this stage the whole dossier, consisting of some thousands of words of verbatim statements by the patient and narrative description of his behaviour, is reviewed by experienced raters. Since it is necessary to weigh the value of each item of information and to resolve conflicting accounts, the rating task is highly judgmental and bound to be unreliable. For this reason it is mandatory that at least two raters are involved. This is expensive and time-consuming, but the challenge of eliminating error from clinical psychiatric method justifies the effort. Establishing the psychopathology of a psychotic episode requires a prolonged effort of observation, recording, and analysis.

Defining criteria

Once the clinical features of the psychosis have been established, the second stage in making a diagnosis is the application of a set of rules based on some classificatory system. Since it was realized that psychiatric diagnosis had a low inter-rater reliability (Kreitman 1961), efforts have been made to develop fool-proof criteria which will impose identical diagnostic procedures on all who use them. These include Feighner's criteria (Feighner *et al.* 1972), Catego (Wing *et al.* 1974), the Research Diagnostic (RDC) (Spitzer *et al.* 1975), and the 3rd Edition of the *American Psychiatric Association Diagnostic and Statistical Manual* (1980) (DSMIII). Although these efforts were necessary and have been justified by improved diagnostic uniformity, the differences between definitions in different research centres or in different parts of the world remain great. Table 6. 1 shows the number of patients with the diagnosis of schizophrenia, using a number of different

TABLE 6.1.   *Number of patients diagnosed schizophrenic in three series of patients*

Definition			
Catego S + , P + , O + , S?, P?, or O?	56	—	79
Catego S + , P + , or O +	44	41	67
Astrachan's New Haven Schizophrenia Index	48	45	—
Carpenter's flexible system, 5 symptoms present	48	—	45
Spitzer's Research Diagnostic Criteria, (incl. probable)	44	—	12
Schneider's first rank symptoms	38	29	43
Langfeldt's poor prognosis schizophrenia	37	22	42
Carpenter's flexible system, 6 symptoms present	24	29	21
DSMIII schizophrenia	19*	—	—
Feighner's criteria	18*	10	—
Number of psychotic patients	134*	119	108

* Only 125 patients were included in the analysis when the Feighner and DSMIII criteria were applied.

systems in three series of patients. In the Netherne series of 134 consecutive psychotic admission, originally interviewed by the US/UK Diagnostic Project in 1966–68, the number of patients meeting various definitions of schizophrenia range from 18 to 56; in the same series the project team made the diagnosis in 57 patients and the hospital consultants made the diagnosis in 70. In a series of 119 consecutive psychotic first admissions gathered from Camberwell in 1973–74, the number diagnosed ranged from 10 to 45, and in a series of 108 schizoaffective patients collected from the Maudsley, Bethlem Royal, and St Francis hospitals in 1972–75 the extremes were 12 to 79. When several definitions of schizoaffective psychosis were applied to the Camberwell first admission series (Brockington and Leff 1979), the numbers ranged from 1 to 17.

Although the enumeration of patients diagnosed by different systems gives a graphic impression of quite large differences between definitions, a coefficient of concordance such as Cohen's kappa (Cohen 1968) better describes the relation between them. Kappa is calculated from the equation.

$$\kappa = P_{.} - P_c / 1 - P_c$$

where $P_{.}$ is the percentage agreement between two definitions, and P_c is the agreement due to chance. When this descriptive statistic was applied to six widely used definitions of schizophrenia and the project diagnosis in the Netherne series, the average of the pair-wise kappa coefficients was 0.59. In the Camberwell first admission series the average kappa of a list of five definitions was 0.54. In the schizoaffective series, the average kappa for five definitions and the Maudsley hospital diagnosis was only 0.19. A kappa coefficient of 0.54, which is representative of the agreement between definitions of schizophrenia, is illustrated by Fig. 6.1, showing the overlap between

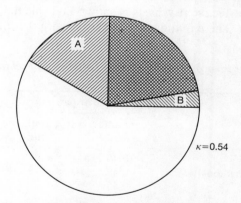

FIG. 6.1.   Concordance between Schneider's and Astrachan's definitions of schizophrenia showing the agreement between them in the Camberwell series of 119 psychotic first admissions. The cross-hatched segment shows the patients who satisfied both definitions, the unshaded area shows those who satisfied neither, and shaded areas A and B show those who satisfied Astrachan's and Schneider's definitions, respectively.

TABLE 6.2.   *Inter-rater reliabilities of some definitions of schizophrenia*

Definition	Source of patients	
	Camberwell study	Netherne study
Schneider's first rank symptoms	0.90	—
Carpenter's flexible system	0.66	—
Langfeldt's	0.65	—
Feighner's	0.48	0.50
Astrachan's	0.37	—
Research Diagnostic Criteria	—	0.45
DSMIII	—	0.49

Schneider's first rank symptoms and the Yale definition of Astrachan *et al.* (1972); the two criteria agreed on the presence of schizophrenia in 95 out of 119 patients (80 per cent), some of this being chance agreement. This level of agreement would have been higher had the denominator comprised all admissions rather than 119 psychotic admissions, because almost all the non-psychotic patients would have been agreed non-schizophrenic. Conversely it would have been lower had a borderline or schizoaffective sample been used. The level of agreement between definitions of schizoaffective psychosis is lower than between definitions of schizophrenia, with an average kappa of only 0.19 in the Camberwell first admission series.

Some of the error in making a diagnosis is due to the difficulty of applying a set of precise but complex rules to an agreed data base. This is expressed by the inter-rater reliability of the definitions. Some figures for the inter-rater reliability of definitions of schizophrenia are given in Table 6.2. They range from 0.37 (Cohen's kappa) to 0.90. A comparable set of figures for definitions of schizoaffective psychosis is shown in Table 6.3, and they range from 0.27 to 0.60. These findings are consistent with the commonsense view

TABLE 6.3.   *Inter-rater reliabilities of some definitions of schizoaffective disorders*

Definition	Source of patients		
	Camberwell study	Netherne study	Schizoaffective study
Kendell schizomania	0.40		
Kendell schizodepression	0.49		
Kasanin	0.35		
Stephens' good prognosis schizophrenia	0.50		
Welner's	0.53		
RDC schizoaffective mania	0.39		0.33
RDC schizoaffective depression	0.60	0.30	
DSMIII mood incongruent psychotic depression		0.27	

that the more complex the definition, the more difficult it is to apply. Schneider's rules are very simple, requiring the presence of only one out of 11 symptoms, and their inter-rater reliability was 0.90. A diagnosis of schizophrenia in terms of DSMIII however, requires about nine decisions in order to exclude depression, eight more to exclude mania, nine to establish the presence of schizophrenia and a further difficult judgement about the duration of illness. The inter-rater reliability of DSMIII, when applied to the Netherne series was only 0.49. It was disturbing to discover that the application of the *same* definition (RDC schizophrenia) to the *same* collection of data (the Netherne series) by two sets of raters (Kendell and Leff on the one hand, and Helzer and Brockington on the other) produced quite different results—one pair diagnosing 33 definite and eight probables, and the other 23 definites and five probables ($\kappa = 0.68$ for definite and 0.70 for definite + probable). The Netherne data base consisted of detailed history and mental state schedules, taking about 15 minutes to review. If the data had been more voluminous, it is probable that the error in applying definitions would have been greater.

It is clear that merely to create or adopt a set of definitions does not solve the problems of diagnosis. For the scientist concerned with chemistry, neurophysiology, or pathology, who does not wish to tangle with nosological issues, one can only advise the use of several different systems to improve the chance of comparing results with other laboratories. In view of the unreliability of applying these systems, the proper practice should be to employ at least two raters, who work independently at first, and then defend their ratings to each other and reach an agreed verdict. Alternatively (and this is perhaps the better counsel), the phenomena should be established using two or more raters and a computer program should be used to apply the definitions.

Choosing between definitions

Where definitions differ so much in the patients they select, one must try to decide which is the best for a particular purpose, and to base this on objective criteria. There is no use appealing to authority, since the leading authorities (Kraepelin, Bleuler, Schneider) disagree; that would in any case make schizophrenia a social rather than scientific concept. It is not easy to find suitable criteria for choosing between definitions. Using concordance itself as a criterion is unsatisfactory both in theory and practice; unsatisfactory in theory because it depends partly on social influences, and in practice because we find that some definitions concerned with phenomena have a high concordance (e.g. RDC and Langfeldt's, $\kappa = 0.74$) and some concerned with chronicity have an even higher concordance (e.g. Feighner's and DSMIII $\kappa = 0.84$), but the two sets have a poor concordance with each other. Thus the concordance data suggest two different concepts of schizophrenia. If one were looking for a statistical test based on the clinical phenomena themselves, it might be interesting to examine the homogeneity of groups of patients diagnosed as schizophrenic by different systems. Classification aims to create homogeneous classes of patients similar to each other and differing sharply from patients excluded from the class. If a satisfactory method of cluster analysis could be discovered, this test would be equivalent to finding out which defined group corresponded most exactly to a natural cluster.

The other ways of choosing between definitions depend on employing validating criteria, based on the facts which have been laboriously pieced together, in spite of semantic chaos, in the last 75 years. One of them is its heritability, firmly founded on twin and adoption studies. Shields and Gottesman (1972) compared some definitions in respect of the concordance rates in monozygotic twins. Unfortunately, manic depressive illness is even more heritable and this criterion would favour definitions which failed to distinguish schizophrenia from mania. A more stringent test is the concordance of diagnosis in a pair of monozygotic twins, both of whom had a psychosis; since the same genes are involved, the same diagnosis should be made.

Another established finding is the therapeutic effect of neuroleptic drugs; therefore it would be pertinent to compare the treatment response of variously defined groups of schizophrenics in a randomized, double-blind controlled trial, arguing that the 'best' definitions will show a marked effect. Again there is the obvious snag that schizophrenia is not the only psychosis which responds to neuroleptics, and, indeed, many chronic schizophrenics fail to respond to neuroleptics. A promising new criterion recently came to light through the work of Johnstone *et al.* (1976), confirmed by Weinberger *et al.* (1980) and Golden *et al.* (1980), who found lateral ventricular enlargement and other evidence of neurological damage in chronic schizophrenics. It would be possible to compare the merits of different definitions in predicting this finding.

Ideally, one would wish to apply all these criteria, together with the outcome criterion (to be considered next), to the same population of patients who had been subjected to a diagnostic analysis searching for a definition which selected a homogeneous group of patients having all the known characteristics of schizophrenia. If it could be shown that this group also met the criteria laid down by Kendell for a distinct disease entity, i.e. bimodality of discriminant scores or a non-linear relationship between symptomatology and a criterion measure (Kendell and Brockington 1980), we would have a definition of schizophrenia which would command universal respect.

The outcome criterion

At the time of writing the only measures which show large differences between schizophrenics and affective psychotics are those concerned with outcome. The patients whom Kraepelin recognized as liable to follow a deteriorating course in the nineteenth century are still distinguished (as a group) by the loss, or the lack, of social success and of the capacity for independent living. Modern therapy has not obscured this tendency. For example, in the Netherne series, 25 of the 28 patients with definite social breakdown were given a final diagnosis of schizophrenia. Unfortunately, there are a number of reasons for feeling less than happy about this criterion too. The outcome criterion is concerned with assessments of sociability, employability, independence, and clinical recovery. Of these, the first three may be profoundly affected by the attitude of society to schizophrenic patients. Ratings of *social involvement* are essentially concerned with the quality of relationships which are among the most difficult of all judgements to make in the field of psychiatry. The assessment of the *work record* is complicated by the different ways in which failure can be shown—frequent unnecessary changes, prolonged unemployment, a slide to less skilled jobs, or a failure to perform at a level consistent with intelligence or training.

If one uses separate measures for each of these criteria, one is left with several skewed ratings, each of which is rather insensitive. In men it is usually possible to obtain an overall view of employment during a span of five years, but it is less easy to obtain a comparable measure in women many of whom show their competence in the home and in the quality of their care of their children. *Independence* can be crudely assessed by the precise measure of duration of stay in hospital (which is liable to clerical errors only). Capacity for independent living, however, is only one of several influences which affect the duration of stay in hospital; others include the presence of uncontrolled psychotic symptoms and hospital admission policies which vary from country to country and from time to time. The degree of *clinical recovery* depends on the assessment of symptomatology in the intervals between episodes, but, unfortunately, even in the best follow-up studies, most of the detailed information is concerned with the episodes rather than the intervals. The outcome criterion aims at the recognition and assessment of schizophrenic defect, i.e.

. . . a peculiar destruction of the internal connections of the psychic personality with the most marked damage to the emotional life and volition.

(Kraepelin 1919).

However, it may be difficult to distinguish this enfeeblement from depression, or a phobic loss of confidence and narrowing of the personal horizons which may complicate mental breakdown, or from 'institutionalization'.

In our own follow-up studies of the Netherne and schizoaffective series (Brockington *et al.* 1978*a*, 1980*a*, *b*) we developed two scores which summarize the outcome of each patient. The first score deals with general outcome, amalgamating the measures described in the paragraph above. It was derived by multiple linear regression from 233 patients using five variables, and their standardized weights were as follows:

Employment record	+ 0.66
Social involvement	+ 0.65
Degree of clinical recovery	+ 0.53
Percentage of time in hospital	+ 0.45
Number of admissions per year	− 0.11

The second score deals with the balance of schizophrenic and affective symptoms during the follow-up period; it was derived by discriminant function analysis using a total of 87 typical schizophrenic and affective patients as criterion groups, and seven variables. The standardized weights were as follows:

Auditory hallucinosis	– 0.57
Delusion formation	– 0.52
Defect state	– 0.49
Passivity experiences	– 0.28
Persecution	– 0.18
Biological depressive symptoms	+ 0.45
Manic symptoms	+ 0.54

These are pragmatic measures which gloss over theoretical difficulties; they have proved to be sensitive enough to demonstrate differences between small groups of patients, for example in the general outcome of DSMIII schizophrenics (19 patients) and schizophreniform patients (7 patients), and in the psychopathological outcome of mood-congruent (11 patients) and mood-incongruent (14 patients) psychotic depressions. They will be used in some of the comparisons between definitions of schizophrenia and schizoaffective states which will now be reported.

COMPARISON BETWEEN DEFINITIONS OF SCHIZOPHRENIA

Schneider's first rank symptoms

Kurt Schneider published his 'first rank symptoms' in a few paragraphs of his book *Clinical psychopathology*. In M. W. Hamilton's translation (1959) we read,

We have emphasized these symptoms of first rank importance above and illustrated them with examples. Following the order in which we have reviewed them, they are: audible thoughts, voices heard arguing, voices heard commenting on one's actions; the experience of influences playing on the body (somatic passivity experiences), thought withdrawal and other interferences with thoughts; diffusion of thought, delusional perception and all feelings, impulses (drives) and volitional acts that are experienced by the patient as the work or influence of others.

Schneider did not advocate these symptoms as a sufficient basis for diagnosing schizophrenia because he recognized that they could also occur in

psychotic states that arise from a known physical illness: alcoholic psychoses, for example, epileptic twilight states, the psychoses of anaemia, and other such symptomatic psychoses, as well as a number of diverse morbid cerebral processes.

In a few paragraphs, Schneider gives a slightly more detailed account for the symptoms, describing, for example, experiences of physical interference that include hallucinations of intercourse in the context of erotomania. By 'thought withdrawal' Schneider does not mean the universally common symptom of thought blocking, but the delusion that other people are taking the thoughts away. 'Thought insertion' is diagnosed when 'thoughts are ascribed to other people who intrude their thoughts upon the patient'. 'Thought broadcasting' or 'diffusion' is present when thoughts 'are no longer private but are shared by others, the whole town or the whole world', and this 'does not signify message-bearing voices, nor the delusional perceptions of paranoid patients who note certain gestures or remarks and believe that those who make them know what is going on in their minds'. Delusional perception is recognized 'when some abnormal significance, usually with self-reference, is attached to a genuine perception without any comprehensible rational or emotional justification'. Disturbances of impulse will involve 'the direct experience of some alien control . . . the usual explanation advanced is that of alien suggestion, possession, hypnotic influences, or the use of some technical apparatus'. Koehler (1979) recently discussed some of the ambiguities in the interpretation of Schneider's first rank symptoms.

Schneider's symptoms have had an influence on British psychiatrists that is hard to understand in view of the lack of any explanation of the reasons for his assertions. Perhaps this influence is due to the intrinsic interest in and bizarre quality of the experiences he regards as diagnostic. The rules for distinguishing his symptoms are easy to learn and have high inter-rater reliability (Table 6.2). The first rank symptoms, or slight modifications of them, are incorporated in the Catego system (S +), Taylor and Abrams' criteria (1975), the Research Diagnostic Criteria, and DSMIII, and those symptoms which concern passivity experiences correspond to one of Langfeldt's five criteria for poor prognosis schizophrenia. It is not surprising therefore that the concordance between Schneider's and these other definitions is high. In the Netherne study the kappa coefficient between Schneider's schizophrenia and Catego S + was 0.87, RDC schizophrenia 0.72, and Langfeldt's poor prognosis group 0.76. The concordance with Feighner's criteria in the Camberwell study, however, was poor (0.21) (Brockington *et al.* 1978*a*).

There have been a number of studies of the predictive validity of Schneider's symptoms. Carpenter *et al.* (1973*a*) followed up a series of 165 patients studied in Maryland, USA, as part of the International Pilot Study of Schizophrenia. They found Schneider's symptoms in 51 per cent of 103 schizophrenics (diagnosed by DSMII). An outcome measure based on the severity of symptoms, time spent in hospital, work record, and social relationships, showed that those with first rank symptoms had a slightly better outcome than other schizophrenics. Later (Hawk *et al.* 1975), they reported a five-year follow-up study, interviewing 63 per cent of this sample, and found no difference between the outcome of 33 Schneider-positive and 28 Schneider-negative patients. The value of this finding is reduced by its failure to demonstrate outcome differences between any of the subgroups that were examined, including a comparison between 15 acute or schizoaffective and 46 other schizophrenics. Since others have found large and statistically significant differences between similar groups of acute and chronic schizophrenics in a total sample less than half the size (e.g. Helzer *et al.* 1981), it is possible that the outcome measures used by Hawk *et al.* were relatively insensitive. Silverstein and Harrow (1978) collected a sample of 126 patients in Chicago, of whom 72 had 'schizophrenia' but only 19 had first rank symptoms; at follow-up 2.7 years later they found no significant differences in re-admission rate nor in social, work, or role functioning between those who had the symptoms and those who did not. Bland and Orn (1980) compared various criteria in a case note study of patients admitted in 1963 and followed up in 1977; 40 out of 50 had first rank symptoms, but no differences in outcome were found.

In our own studies (Brockington *et al.* 1978a) we have looked at the outcome of Schneider Schizophrenics in the Netherne and schizoaffective series. Schneider's symptoms were partly successful in predicting the symptomatology of subsequent admissions. When general outcome is considered, however, Schneider's definition is one of the few definitions of schizophrenia which is *not* capable of selecting patients with a poor outcome. The outcome index of Schneider schizophrenia is close to the mean for psychotic patients. The reason for this failure is probably that the definition does not exclude patients with major mood disorders. There is no doubt that the first rank symptoms occur in psychoses with an excellent outcome, including mania (Abrams and Taylor 1976) and puerperal psychosis (Kadrmas *et al.* 1980). The addition of a clause concerned with the exclusion of severe depression and mania would improve the predictive powers of the Schneider criteria, which would then become similar to the RDC. They would have some use as a means of distinguishing schizophrenics with 'positive symptoms' from those without (e.g. the catatonics, hebephrenics, and residual schizophrenics), but they would still omit some patients with chronic auditory hallucinosis or systematized delusions. In summary, Schneider's first rank symptoms offer a narrow definition of schizophrenia, emphasizing the florid symptoms which are often found in psychoses with a good prognosis.

Langfeldt's criteria

Whereas Schneider's first rank symptoms are derived from general clinical experience, Langfeldt's criteria for poor prognosis schizophrenia were the product of a particular follow-up study carried out in Norway, examining the prognostic value of symptomatology empirically (Langfeldt 1937). His guidelines were described in a paper published in the Proceedings of the Royal College of Medicine (Langfeldt 1960), from which I abstracted the following definition.

The patient must have one of five groups of symptoms:

1. A special type of emotional blunting followed by lack of initiative and altered frequently peculiar behaviour ('more difficult to describe than to apprehend but the experienced psychiatrist regularly feels intui-

tively that he is confronted with a morbid personality of the genuine schizophrenic type').

2. Catatonia with 'history and signs in the periods of restlessness and stupor—negativism, catalepsy, vegetative symptoms—frequently so characteristic that no doubt can exist'.

3. Paranoid symptoms with depersonalization and derealization (meaning *Ichstörungen* with no insight, experiencing the disturbances as originating outside himself—he must *experience* the outside influences and changes).

4. Paranoid symptoms with primary delusions.

5. Chronic hallucinations not due to organic disease.

In a personal communication (1975) Langfeldt said that 'points 1, 2, and 3 correspond very well to my own clues to the typical ('progressive') schizophrenias running a chronic course. As to point 4, it concerns schizophrenias characterized by delusions to which it is not possible to detect any psychogenic or other origin, (and) . . . resistant against any type of directive psychotherapy'. His qualifications of point 5 were lengthy and were concerned with chronic hallucinations 'certainly occurring in patients suffering from reactive psychosis' so that in themselves they were insufficient to diagnose schizophrenia and required the presence of other essential symptoms. Since we were unclear about the diagnosis of 'reactive psychosis', we used the definition as it stood; it is important to note that our interpretation of Langfeldt's rules may differ from his own interpretation, and from that of Strauss and Carpenter (1974) who also attempted to replicate his findings.

In spite of the very general terms in which this definition is expressed, it has turned out to be easy to use and quite reliable ($\kappa = 0.65$). It is clearly a broader concept than Schneider's since it includes hebephrenia and catatonia, but the number qualifying (36 in the Netherne series, 41 in the schizoaffective, and 22 in the Camberwell first admissions) is about the same because somatic passivity experiences do not qualify under criterion 3 above and auditory hallucinations have to be chronic. The success of this definition in predicting outcome is shown in Table 6.4. The balance of symptomatology was schizophrenic in all three series. Langfeldt was more successful in predicting general outcome than Schneider, selecting a group with outcome significantly worse than the mean for psychotic patients in the Netherne and schizomanic, but not the schizoaffective depressed series. Strauss and Carpenter (1974) also found a poorer outcome in the group of patients they diagnosed as Langfeldt schizophrenics, with a mean score of 11.5 compared with 12.9 for non-schizophrenics, but this was not a significant difference. Only 29 patients qualified, compared with 52 Schneider-positive and 85 DSMII schizophrenics. We conclude that we have had difficulty in translating Langfeldt's views into Anglo-American ways of conceptualizing psychopathology, but we have found that patients we think correspond with his guidelines have a rather poorer prognosis than other psychotic patients.

TABLE 6.4.   *Outcome of patients with Langfeldt's poor prognosis schizophrenia*

	Langfeldt schizophrenia			Whole series		
	N	General outcome score	Psycho-pathology score	N	General outcome score	Psycho-pathology score
Netherne series	36	2.02†	− 0.05‡	125	1.67	+ 0.89
Schizoaffectives (manic)	8	1.85*	− 0.70	32 ⎫	1.58	− 0.83
Schizoaffectives (depressed)	33	1.65	− 1.35*	76 ⎭		

* Differs from the remainder of the patients in the series (p = <0.05).
† Differs from the remainder of the patients in the series (p = <0.01).
‡ Differs from the remainder of the patients in the series (p = <0.0001).

Catego

'Catego' is a computer program incorporating diagnostic rules designed to process data from the Present State Examination (Wing *et al.* 1974). It can be used by those employing the 9th edition of this well constructed interview. The first step in the program is to convert the 140 ratings into 38 'syndrome scores', and those using earlier editions of the Present State Examination, or working from other interviews or direct from case records (charts) can enter the program by converting their data into syndrome scores. The second step of the program involved searching for certain syndromes considered important in the hierarchy. At the top of the hierarchy is class S + which depends on the presence of the 'nuclear syndrome', i.e. the presence of *either* one of the following symptoms:

Thought intrusion
Thought broadcast
Thought commentary
Thought withdrawal
Voices discussing the patient in the third person or commenting on his thoughts or actions
Delusions of control
Delusions of alien penetration
Primary delusions

or the combination of other auditory hallucinations (not affectively based) and other delusions. A patient with these symptoms is always S + whatever other symptoms may be present. Other symptoms high up in the hierarchy are catatonic symptoms, incoherent speech, depression, depressive delusions and hallucinations, manic symptoms, and obsessional symptoms. The effect is to base classification mainly on the presence of certain characteristic symptoms rather than the overall balance.

There are two other classes which would fall into a broad concept of schizophrenia. P + designates delusional or paranoid psychoses, and contains patients with delusions and hallucinations other than depressive, grandiose, or those listed under class S +. O + refers to patients with catatonic symptoms or 'residual syndrome' (non-social speech and behaviour suggesting hallucinations). In our three series of patients there were many more S + than P + or O +, namely 119 S +, 15 P + and 6 O +. Catego also designates a group of patients falling into classes S?, P?, and O? who have some but not convincing evidence of the main classes. In the Netherne and schizoaffective series there were 23 of these patients. The concordance of Catego S + is very high with Schneider schizophrenia ($\kappa = 0.87$). When all the classes are taken together (including P? etc), its concordance in the Netherne series was quite high with Langfeldt's criteria ($\kappa = 0.63$) but very low with Feighner's criteria ($\kappa = 0.24$).

It was found in the Netherne follow-up study that Catego S + did not predict social outcome, but when all the classes (including P? etc.) were included in a very broad concept of schizophrenia, they did predict social outcome, apparently because P? and O? selected a few cases with particularly poor prognosis. It seems therefore useful to consider the merits of this broad concept, and the results of our outcome studies are shown in Table 6.5. The number of patients is high because so many of those in the schizoaffective (depressed) series qualified for S +. Table 6.5 shows that Catego in this broad form was successful in selecting patients with predominantly schizophrenic symptoms in the schizoaffective series, but not in the Netherne; in the Netherne series the mean psychopathology score was positive (indicating an excess of affective symptoms) although significantly less so than in psychotic patients in general. Catego was successful in selecting a relatively poor outcome group in two series—the Netherne patients and the schizomanics.

TABLE 6.5.   *Outcome of patients falling into Catego classes* S +, P +, O +, S?, P?, or O?

	Catego schizophrenia			Whole series		
	N	General outcome score	Psycho-pathology score	N	General outcome score	Psycho-pathology score
Netherne series	52	1.88*	+ 0.29†	125	1.67	+ 0.89
Schizoaffective series (manic)	15	1.71*	− 0.69	32 ⎫	1.58	− 0.83
Schizoaffectives (depressed)	60	1.61	− 1.07	76 ⎭		

* Differs from the remainder of the patients in the series ($p = <0.05$).
† Differs from the remainder of the patients in the series ($p = <0.0001$).
N.B. If the schizoaffective manics and depressed patients are taken together, the psychopathology score for Catego schizophrenics was significantly different from the remainder ($p = 0.01$).

If outcome prediction is accepted as an appropriate test, we can conclude that Catego is best used in its broadest form (including P? etc. within schizophrenia) and that it is slightly less successful than Langfeldt's criteria. The strengths of Catego are several—it is based on a disciplined approach to the psychiatric interview and (once this data base has been accepted) it is completely reliable. It allows diagnoses to be made in exactly the same way throughout the world, and it offers a whole diagnostic system, not just for schizophrenia but for other psychoses and neurotic states as well. In the author's experience, the particular value of Catego is that it gives a very broad but standardized concept of schizophrenia within which other ideas (e.g. cycloid psychosis, Feighner's definition) can be examined.

The New Haven schizophrenia index

This definition, originating in the Department of Clinical Psychiatry at Yale University (Astrachan *et al.* 1972), is the only one which seems to embody the Bleulerian concept of schizophrenia which was widely used in the USA before the US/UK diagnostic project published their findings. To qualify, a patient must score four points from the following list of items:

1. (a) Delusions (other than depressive); (b) auditory hallucinations (c) visual hallucinations; (d) other hallucinations.
2. (a) Bizarre thinking; (b) autism or grossly unrealistic private thoughts; (c) looseness of association; illogical thinking; overinclusion; (d) blocking; (e) concreteness; (f) derealization; (g) depersonalization.
3. Inappropriate affect.
4. Confusion.
5. Paranoid ideation (self-referential thinking, suspiciousness).
6. Catatonia (a) excitement; (b) stupor; (c) waxy flexibility; (d) negativism; (e) mutism; (f) echolalia; (g) stereotyped motor activity.

Items 1(a)–(d) and 2(a)–(c) count two points and the rest one point. A patient must have at least one symptom from item 1 or 2(a)–(c) and cannot score more than one for catatonia, and two for hallucinations.

Some of the items, including visual hallucinations, derealization and depersonalization, confusion, and self-referential thinking, would not be considered characteristic of schizophrenia by many European and American psychiatrists. Major mood disorder is not excluded. A particular feature is the emphasis on thought disorder. Unfortunately some of these concepts of thought disorder are not understood elsewhere. Trained in Britain, we were ill-qualified to apply them when we attempted to use the definition in the Netherne series. It is probable that we missed a number of patients who would have been selected by the Yale psychiatrists as schizophrenic on grounds of autism or bizarre thinking. The patients we did select had a general outcome score of 1.83 and a symptomatology score of +0.33, and were thus similar to Catego.

Feighner's criteria

The Department of Psychiatry at Washington University in St. Louis was the first to introduce a complete set of research criteria for general use (Feighner *et al*. 1972); these are sometimes called 'the Renard criteria' (named after the Renard Hospital in St. Louis). Their definition of schizophrenia is quite different from those discussed so far because it excludes those with an acute illness and those with major mood disorder. The definition is as follows, A through C being required:

A. *Both* (1) A chronic illness with at least 6 months of symptoms prior to the index evaluation without return to the premorbid level of psychosocial adjustment, *and* (2) absence of a period of depressive or manic symptoms sufficient to qualify for affective disorder or probable affective disorder (which are defined elsewhere).

B. *Either* (1) Delusions or hallucinations without sufficient perplexity or disorientation associated with them, *or* (2) verbal production that makes communication difficult because of lack of logical or understandable organization. (In the presence of muteness the diagnostic decision must be deferred).

C. *At least 3 of* (1) Single state, (2) poor premorbid social adjustment or work history, (3) family history of schizophrenia; (4) absence of alcoholism or drug abuse within one year of the onset of the psychosis; and (5) onset of the illness prior to the age of 40. If only 2 are present, the diagnosis is 'probable schizophrenia'.

In spite of the fact that almost any psychotic phenomena are sufficient to meet criterion B, the effect of this definition is to select a much smaller group of patients than the others so far considered. In the Netherne series only 18 qualified, and in the Camberwell series only 10. On this basis the incidence of schizophrenia would be only $3/10^5$ population per year, about one-third the usual quoted figure. Schizophrenia would have about the same incidence as mania or cycloid illness. The concordance between this definition and others is low, with the exception of the DSMIII definition (see below). Probably because of the complexity of the definition, its inter-rater reliability was only 0.48 in the Camberwell series and 0.50 in the Netherne.

The definition includes evidence of chronicity before the index evaluation, so it is not surprising that it selects a group with poor prognosis. Using the patients from the 'Iowa 500', Morrison *et al*. (1973) found that only 8 per cent of schizophrenics defined in this way recovered. and 20 per cent were continuously hospitalized. Johnstone *et al*. (1979) found that 15/20 had a poor outcome compared with 6/16 schizophrenics who did not meet Feighner criteria. We have studied this criterion only in the Netherne series where we found that the mean general outcome score was 2.49, and the psychopathology score – 0.53, indicating a prognosis much worse than Catego schizophrenics, and a marked excess of schizophrenic symptoms during the follow-up period. Further, we were able to show that this small group of

TABLE 6.6.   *Comparison between Catego schizophrenics who met Feighner criteria and those who did not (Netherne series)*

Variable	Feighner-positive	Feighner-negative	p
Number of patients	14*	38	
Passivity scale	22.2	8.7	0.07
Delusion scale	41.4	24.5	0.03
Defect scale	22.7	9.6	0.04
Psychopathology score	– 0.47	+ 0.57	0.01
Time in hospital	53.9%	17.0%	0.0001
General outcome score	2.48	1.65	0.004
Final diagnosis of schizophrenia	14	23	0.003

* Four Feighner schizophrenics did not meet Catego criteria.

patients contained most of the poor outcome schizophrenics selected by Catego. Table 6.6 compares 14 Catego schizophrenics who met Feighner's criteria with 38 who did not. Not only are there several large and statistically significant differences, but the Feighner-negative patients had a marked excess of affective symptoms in subsequent admissions. Thus, it is possible that the Feighner criteria select a group of patients qualitatively different from others patients with Catego schizophrenia.

Carpenter's flexible system

An interesting method of diagnosing schizophrenia was introduced by Carpenter *et al.* (1973*b*) following their analysis of 1121 patients from the International Pilot Study of Schizophrenia. Using symptoms ascertained by a modified Present State Examination and diagnoses made by the Field Centres in nine countries, they selected 69 statistically significant discriminators and entered them into a step-wise discriminant function analysis; the criterion groups were 405 schizophrenic patients and 155 with other diagnoses. The 12 symptoms that emerged as most discriminating were:

Restricted affect
Poor insight
Thoughts aloud
Waking early
Poor rapport
Depressed facies
Elation
Widespread delusions
Incoherent speech
Unreliable information
Bizarre delusions
Nihilistic delusions

Three of these symptoms count in favour of schizophrenia when absent (early waking, elation, and depressed facies). The list includes some items (poor rapport, widespread delusions, bizarre delusions, and unreliable information) which we found difficult to apply. One notices, with surprise, that Cotard's delusion counts towards schizophrenia, while auditory hallucinosis (which many regard as one of the principal schizophrenic phenomena) has been omitted, but one must admire the methods by which the list of symptoms was obtained especially the high ratio of patients to discriminating symptoms (at least 20:1). The flexible system has the virtue of selecting patients without affective symptoms, but it does so more readily in relation to depression than mania; manic patients tend to qualify because they score three points immediately for poor insight, and lack of early waking and depressed facies. One of the merits of the system is that it allows schizophrenia to be diagnosed at different levels of confidence, e.g. at five symptoms present, or at six symptoms present. The system proves to be reasonably reliable (e.g. $\kappa = 0.66$ in the Camberwell series (six symptoms present); this is partly due to the overall score being built up from 12 individual ratings, so that it is possible for two raters to agree that five symptoms are present, even though they disagree about each one of those symptoms. Carpenter *et al.* (1980) recently retracted their flexible system as a sufficient method of diagnosing schizophrenia, stating that it must be used in conjuction with general clinical judgement. In the results shown in Table 6.7, however, we were using the 12-point rules without reference to any other data.

At the threshold of five symptoms present, the number of patients qualifying is about the same as meet Langfeldt's and Schneider's definitions; it is clear that a higher proportion of manic than depressed schizoaffectives

TABLE 6.7. *Outcome of schizophrenic patients diagnosed by Carpenter's Flexible System*

		Carpenter schizophrenia			Whole series		
		N	General outcome score	Psycho-pathology score	*N*	General outcome score	Psycho-pathology score
Netherne series	5	43	2.02†	+ 0.16‡	125	1.67	+ 0.89
	6	22	2.03*	− 0.26‡			
Schizoaffectives	5	15	1.54	− 0.82*	32		
(manic)	6	8	1.82	− 0.78		1.58	− 0.83
Schizoaffectives	5	28	1.52	− 1.02	76		
(depressed)	6	13	1.38	− 0.66			

* Differs from the remainder of the patients in the series (p = <0.05).
† Differs from the remainder of the patients in the series (p = <0.01).
‡ Differs from the remainder of the patients in the series (p = <0.0001).
The figures 5 & 6 in the first column refer to the number of symptoms present.

qualify. At the six-symptom threshold it emerges as a strict definition; almost as strict as Feighner's. The flexible system's prediction of outcome in the Netherne series is much worse than Feighner's and similar to Langfeldt's. Outcome is no worse in patients with six rather than five symptoms, but they have more schizophrenic symptoms in subsequent admissions. In the schizomanic series a score of five predicts symptomatology, but not general outcome, and the addition of the sixth symptom improves the prediction of general outcome making the system as effective as Langfeldt's. In the schizoaffective (depressed) group, the system fails to select a poor outcome group. The few patients who qualify have a better outcome than schizodepressive patients in general, and paradoxically those with six Carpenter symptoms do better than those with five.

Taylor and Abrams's criteria

In 1975, a team of workers in Chicago published criteria requiring the simultaneous presence of delusions or hallucinations, thought disorder, and blunting for the diagnosis of schizophrenia (Taylor *et al.* 1975). Bearing in mind that the last two are more strictly defined in Britain than in USA, we found that Taylor and Abram's criteria excluded almost all our patients and, thus, have not studied its outcome prediction. Taylor and Abrams have now modified their criteria to allow the diagnosis to be made when only one of these is present. The criteria now require

1. At least one of (a) formal thought disorder (drivelling, tangentiality, neologisms, paraphasias, non sequiturs, private words, stock words); (b) first rank symptoms; (c) emotional blunting (a constricted, inappropriate unrelated affect of decreased intensity, with indifference/unconcern for loved ones, lack of emotional responsivity, and a loss of social graces.)
2. Clear consciousness.
3. No diagnosable affective disorder (for which they have rules).
4. No diagnosable coarse brain disease, no past hallucinogenic or psychostimulant drug abuse, and no medical condition known to cause schizophrenic symptoms.

This new definition was used by Young, Tanner, and Meltzer (unpublished) and was found to select about the same number of patients as Schneider's and Carpenter's system at six symptoms present (58, 52, and 55 respectively), much less than Astrachan's (129) and more than the Research Diagnostic Criteria (38) from a series of 196 psychotic patients studied by the Laboratory of Biological Psychiatry at Illinois State Psychiatric Institute. The analysis indicated that the definitions shared a core concept of schizophrenia and that this was identified more accurately by Taylor and Abrams' criteria than any of the others. Although the definition is concise and relatively easy to use, this finding needs to be replicated in other series.

The research diagnostic criteria

The Research Diagnostic Criteria (RDC) of Spitzer *et al*. (1975) are comparable to Feighner's set of research criteria in providing detailed rules for the whole range of psychiatric diagnoses. Their definition of schizophrenia, however, is very different, replacing six months by two weeks' duration, and narrowing the range of symptoms. The patient must fulfil three conditions—duration of two weeks, absence of depression and mania, and the presence of at least one (for probable) or two (for definite) of the following symptoms:

1. Thought broadcasting, insertion, or withdrawal.
2. Delusions of control, other bizarre delusions, or multiple delusions.
3. Delusions other than persecutory or jealousy lasting at least one week.
4. Delusions of any type if accompanied by hallucinations of any type lasting at least one week.
5. Auditory hallucinations in which a voice keeps up a running commentary on the subject's behaviours or thoughts as they occur, or two or more voices converse with each other.
6. Non-affective verbal hallucinations spoken to the subject.
7. Hallucinations of any type throughout the day for several days or intermittently for at least one month.
8. Definite instances of formal thought disorder.
9. Obvious catatonic motor behaviour.

There are 24 separate decisions required to make the diagnosis including seven to exclude mania and eight to exclude depression. It is not surprising, therefore, that inter-rater reliability is low. We found an inter-rater reliability of $\kappa = 0.45$ when two raters were compared with each other, improving to $\kappa = 0.68$ when their agreed verdict was compared with that of another pair of raters; it is interesting that this last figure is similar to the inter-rater reliability of Langfeldt's criteria which seem relatively vague but require only five decisions. In practice, the definition is easy to apply. The rater feels the satisfaction of making a careful diagnostic assessment and, unlike Catego, it can be applied to any material without employing a computer program.

The outcome characteristics of RDC schizophrenia could only be tested in the Netherne series, because there were too few schizoaffectives meeting this definition. The results shown in Table 6.8 show that these patients have a rather worse outcome than Langfeldt schizophrenics but a better outcome than Feighner schizophrenics. In an earlier comparison (Brockington *et al*. 1978a) using the RDC schizophrenics diagnosed by Kendell and Leff, there appeared to be only a slight difference in outcome prediction by RDC and Catego; a further analysis, however, using the patients selected by Helzer and Brockington and more sensitive outcome measures has shown a significant difference in the symptomatic outcome of the two groups, with Catego schizophrenics having an excess of affective symptoms during the follow-up period, while RDC schizophrenics had an excess of schizophrenic symptoms.

TABLE 6.8.   *Outcome of schizophrenic patients diagnosed by Spitzer's RDC*

	RDC schizophrenia			Whole series		
	N	General outcome score	Psycho-pathology score	N	General outcome score	Psycho-pathology score
Netherne series	28[6]	2.11†	− 0.25‡	125	1.67	+ 0.89
Schizoaffectives (manic)	7	1.85	− 0.61	32 ⎫	1.58	− 0.83
Schizoaffectives (depressed)	4	1.97	− 1.86	76 ⎭		
RDC negative Catego schizophrenics	28	1.73	+ 0.68*			

* Differs from RDC schizophrenia (p = <0.05).
† Differs from the remainder of the Netherne patients (p = <0.01).
‡ Differs from the remainder of the Netherne patients (p = <0.0001).
These are the 28 patients selected by Helzer and Brockington; Kendell and Leff
selected a larger number.

The diagnostic and statistical manual, 3rd ed.

The latest manual of the American Psychiatric Association (1980) is an
extensive revision of the Research Diagnostic Criteria. It returns to
Feighner's concept of schizophrenia as a chronic psychosis, and introduces
categories of schizophreniform disorder, paranoid disorder, brief reactive
psychosis, mood-incongruent mania, and mood-incongruent depression to
classify the acute psychoses. The psychopathological requirements for schizophrenia are very similar to the RDC and again there must be no manic or
depressive syndrome, but in addition the patient must have (or have had) a
continuous illness lasting at least six months, and a deterioration from a
previous level of functioning in work, social relations, or self-care. Patients
whose illness began after the age of 44, or was due to organic brain disease or
mental retardation are excluded. The schizophreniform disorders have the
same symptomatology as schizophrenia, but their duration is between two
weeks and six months.

These rules prove to be very strict. In the Netherne series, only 19 patients
met the criteria for schizophrenia, seven schizophreniform, two paranoid,
one brief reactive, one mood-incongruent mania, and 14 mood-incongruent
depression. Inter-rater reliability was low ($\kappa = 0.49$) for schizophrenia and
zero for schizophreniform disorder. Concordance with Feighner's schizophrenia was high ($\kappa = 0.84$), with RDC fairly high ($\kappa = 0.71$), and with other
definitions low ($\kappa = 0.26$ to 0.48). The outcome characteristics of these
patients have been studied only in the Netherne series (Table 6.9). DSMIII
schizophrenia has an outcome corresponding to Kraepelin's notion of poor
prognosis with continuing evidence of schizophrenic symptoms. The schizophreniform disorders, which differ only in their shorter duration, have a

TABLE 6.9. *Outcome of patients with DSMIII schizophrenia and schizophreniform states*

	DSMIII schizophrenics			Whole series		
	N	General outcome score	Psycho-pathology score	N	General outcome score	Psycho-pathology score
DSMIII schizophrenia	19	2.53†	− 0.51			
DSMIII schizophreniform	7	1.46	+ 0.17	125	1.67	+ 0.89
DSMIII negative RDC schizophrenia	10	1.45*	+ 0.21			

* Differs significantly from DSMIII schizophrenia (p = <0.001).
† Differs significantly from remainder of Netherne series (p = <0.001).

prognosis which is better than the mean for psychotic patients. When we reflect that DSMIII and Feighner's schizophrenia, which have the same outcome, share the requirement for chronicity and the absence of affective symptoms, but have completely different psychopathology clauses (one strict and the other broad), while DSMIII schizophrenia and schizophreniform disorder, which have totally different outcomes, share exactly the same symptoms, it is clear that chronicity and not symptomatology is the main predictor of outcome. Paradoxically, chronicity predicts not only general outcome, but also the balance of schizophrenic and affective symptoms.

Table 6.9 also shows that RDC schizophrenics who did not fulfil DSMIII criteria had a relatively good outcome. All this suggests that, nested within the broadly defined group of schizophrenia with its great diversity of outcomes, is a smaller group marked by their chronicity and perhaps by a mild form of neurological damage (Johnstone *et al.* 1976) who correspond to Kraepelin's dementia praecox.

COMPARISON BETWEEN DEFINITIONS OF SCHIZOAFFECTIVE AND CYCLOID PSYCHOSIS

Kasanin acute schizoaffective psychosis

Kasanin (1933) gave no definition of the psychosis he described, and we have been unsuccessful in writing an operational definition with adequate inter-rater reliability. In the Camberwell study Brockington and Leff (1979) used a definition which proved to have the lowest inter-rater reliability of all ($\kappa = 0.35$), and when this was revised for a diagnostic study of the Netherne series by Brockington and Helzer, the reliability was even lower ($\kappa = 0.09$). The elements of the Kasanin psychosis are (1) a 'very sudden onset in a setting of marked emotional turmoil', and (2) their occurrence in young people in sound psychological health. Presumably puerperal and postoperative psychoses are excluded. In the three series of psychotic patients we have studied with a total of 361 patients, there were 27 who met one of our

TABLE 6.10.   *Outcome of patients with Kasanin's 'acute schizoaffective psychosis'*

	Kasanin's psychosis			Whole series		
	N	General outcome score	Psycho-pathology score	N	General outcome score	Psycho-pathology score
Netherne series	9	1.18	+ 1.26	125	1.67	+ 0.89
Schizoaffective series	14	1.13†	− 0.30*	108	1.58	− 0.83

* Differs significantly from the remainder of the schizoaffective series (p = <0.05).
† Differs significantly from the remainder of the schizoaffective series (p = <0.01).

definitions (7 per cent). The concordance with other definitions of schizo-affective states was low, for example $\kappa = 0.16$ with Kendell's definition (Brockington *et al.* 1978*b*). It was rather higher with good prognosis schizophrenia ($\kappa = 0.50$) and cycloid psychosis (0.41 in the Camberwell series and 0.37 in the Netherne series). The outcome of these patients has been studied in two series. The general outcome was in each case much better than the mean for psychotic patients (Table 6.10) and the psychopathology shown in the follow-up period was significantly more affective than the other patients in both series, although the scores themselves were very different in the Netherne and schizoaffective patients. The success of this concept in predicting recovery was particularly evident in the schizoaffective depressed group in which it was hard to find any symptoms or definitions capable of predicting outcome, yet the Kasanin concept selected seven patients with an excellent outcome and a mean general outcome score of 0.99 (cf. 1.58 for all schizoaffectives, $p = 0.003$). Kasanin's 'acute schizoaffective psychosis' is not representative of the schizoaffective group as a whole, but applies to a small group of hyper-acute illnesses which may be of interest in their own right, because of their excellent prognosis.

Good prognosis schizophrenia

The concept of 'good prognosis schizophrenia' was abroad in the USA in the 1960s at a time when almost all psychotic patients were diagnosed schizophrenic. In a scholarly review, Vaillant (1964) identified a number of historical and clinical features which enabled those with favourable outcomes to be recognized. Subsequently, these criteria were revised by Stephens (1966, 1970) as a result of a 15–16 year follow-up of 472 patients admitted to the Phipps clinic in Baltimore. The guidelines drawn up by Vaillant or Stephens have been used in a number of replicating studies. Fowler *et al.* (1972) studied the first-degree relatives of 25 poor-prognosis and 28 good-prognosis schizophrenics and found 13 cases of schizophrenia and three affective disorder in the former, and five cases of schizophrenia and 14 of affective disorder in the latter—clear evidence that these patients were suffering fron affective disorders. Taylor and Abrams (1975) found that 54 out of 64 good-prognosis schizophrenics had a marked improvement compared with only four out of 24 poor-prognosis schizophrenics. We applied a modification of the Stephens definition to the schizoaffective series, and found that it selected a group with a better general outcome than the rest of the patients (mean score 1.25, $N = 35$, cf. 1.58 for the whole group, $p = 0.0004$) and fewer schizophrenic symptoms during the follow-up period (psychopathology score -0.53, cf. -0.83 for the whole group, $p = 0.03$). As with Kasanin's, Stephens' criteria were particularly useful in selecting patients with good prognosis from the schizoaffective (depressed) group.

Welner's criteria

The two definitions of schizoaffective disorders so far considered have drawn largely from the patient's history. By contrast Welner's definition (Welner *et al.* 1974), a development of Feighner's research criteria, is largely concerned with symptomatology. As evidence of affective disorder the patient must have six of the following symptoms:

Dysphoric mood
Euphoria
Irritability
Poor appetite or weight loss
Sleep difficulty
Loss of energy
Agitation or retardation
Loss of interest or libido
Self-reproach or guilt
Difficulty in concentrating, slowed-up or mixed-up thoughts
Suicidal thoughts
Hyperactivity
Push of speech
Flight of ideas
Grandiosity
Decreased need for sleep
Distractibility

As evidence of schizophrenia, the patient must have two of the following:

Any type of delusion
Any type of hallucination
Formal thought disorder (including tangential speech, neologisms, loose associations, blocking, word salad, echolalia, clang associations, but not circumstantial speech or flight of ideas associated with push of speech)
Inability to communicate in a logical manner (autistic or dereistic thinking)
Bizarre or strikingly inappropriate behaviour.

There must be no history of alcoholism, drug abuse, or organic brain disease, and there must be one of the following:

Acute onset
Severe precipitating factor
Episodic course
Pronounced perplexity, confusion or bewilderment

Welner and his colleagues (Croughan *et al.* 1974) found that 4 per cent of all admissions met this complex definition. They later followed up 128 patients diagnosed from the charts, interviewing 77 per cent of those still living (Welner *et al.* 1977); they found that 71 per cent ran a chronic course, and the remainder either ran an episodic course or remained well with medication. They did not compare the outcome with schizophrenic and affective patients. Most of their patients had depressed rather than manic symptoms at index admission. We obtained very different results when we applied their definition to our patients. We found it to be a rather strict definition met by only five patients in the Camberwell series (2 per cent of those under the age of 65 years), only 12/32 schizoaffective manics and 25/76 in the schizo-affective (depressed) series. Its inter-rater reliability was 0.53, and its concordance with other definitions low ($\kappa = 0.16$ to 0.32). The patients selected continued to show an excess of schizophrenic symptoms during the follow-up period (psychopathology score -0.75) but their general outcome (mean 1.32) was much better than that of other schizoaffective patients. ($p = 0.004$) and considerably better than the mean for Netherne psychotics.

The research diagnostic criteria

In terms of the Research Diagnostic Criteris (RDC)(Spitzer *et al.* 1975, 1978), a patient with a prominent manic or depressive syndrome cannot be diagnosed as suffering from schizophrenia. If certain schizophrenic symptoms are present, a diagnosis of schizoaffective disorder is made. For a diagnosis of schizoaffective disorder (depressed type) the patient must have an illness lasting at least a week, evidence of depressed mood, and four (for probable) or five (for definite) of the following symptoms:

Poor appetite or weight loss, or increased appetite or weight
Sleep difficulty or sleeping too much
Loss of energy, fatiguability or tiredness
Psychomotor retardation or agitation
Loss of interest or pleasure
Feelings of self-reproach or excessive inappropriate guilt
Complaints or evidence of diminished ability to think or concentrate
Recurrent thoughts of death or suicide or any suicidal behaviour.

These symptoms must overlap temporally with at least one of the following:

Delusions of being controlled or influenced, or of thought broadcasting, insertion or withdrawal;

Non-affective hallucinations of any type throughout the day for several days or intermittently throughout a one-week period;

Auditory hallucinations in which a voice keeps up a running commentary on the subject's thoughts or behaviours as they occur or two or more voices converse with each other;

Preoccupation with a delusion or hallucination to the relative exclusion of other symptoms or concerns (other than typical depressive delusions);

Definite instances of marked formal thought disorder accompanied by blunted affect, delusions or hallucinations or grossly disorganized behaviour.

Alternatively delusions or hallucinations (without depressive content) must be present for at least a month in the absence of the depressive syndrome.

The criteria for schizoaffective disorder (manic type) are similar. They require an illness lasting a week, elevated, expansive, or irritable mood, and the overlap of manic and depressive symptoms. For mania the patient must have three of the following symptoms (or four if the mood is only irritable):

More active than usual;
More talkative than usual;
Flight of ideas or subjective experience that thoughts are racing;
Inflated self-esteem;
Decreased need for sleep;
Distractibility;
Excessive involvement in risk-taking activities.

In addition, there must be at least one schizophrenic symptom, and here the list is similar to that for depressed patients, except that excessive pre-occupation with a delusion or hallucination is not included.

Some evaluative studies have been published. Rosenthal *et al.* (1980) applied them to a series of 71 manic depressive patients and found that 25 qualified. Pope *et al.* (1980) found that 52 out of 219 patients consecutively admitted to a hospital in Massachusetts met RDC criteria for schizoaffective mania, and that these patients resembled mania rather than schizophrenia in family history, treatment response, and outcome. We applied these criteria to all three series of patients we studied. In the Camberwell series eight patients (4 per cent of consecutive first admissions under the age of 65 years) qualified (seven depressed and one manic). In the Netherne series, 15 qualified (11 per cent of consecutive psychotic admissions, 6 per cent of all admissions), and included 11 depressed and four manic. In the schizoaffective series, 15 out of 32 manic patients and 59 out of 76 depressed qualified. The inter-rater reliability measured in the Netherne and Camberwell series was 0.39 and zero (using Cohen's kappa) for schizoaffective mania and 0.60 and 0.30 for schizoaffective depression. These are among the lowest inter-rater reliabilities we have obtained and they show how difficult it is to apply such complex criteria reliably. One notes, with astonishment, a more than 10-fold difference between the proportions of patients diagnosed schizoaffective (manic) by Pope in New England and by us in London. Can these differences be explained solely by admission policies in British and American mental hospitals? Taking the manic and depressed subgroups together, the concordance with other schizoaffective definitions was at the low level of $\kappa = 0.20$–0.3. We studied the outcome of these patients in the Netherne and schizoaffective series and the results are shown in Table 6.11. We found that RDC schizoaffective patients, whether manic or depressed, continued to show an excess of schizophrenic symptoms during their subsequent admissions, and in this they differed strikingly from ordinary depressed and manic patients. In terms of general outcome, the manic and depressed subgroups differed from each other. The schizoaffective manic patients had an outcome which was slightly worse than mania, and better than psychotic patients as a whole. The schizoaffective depressed patients fared significantly worse than depressed patients and worse than the remainder of the psychotic patients; their general outcome was similar to that of Catego schizophrenics.

DSMIII concepts of mood-congruent and mood-incongruent affective psychoses

The third edition of the Diagnostic and Statistical Manual has abolished the defined categories of schizoaffective disorder. All patients with at least four of the depressive symptoms or at least three of the manic symptoms listed in the previous section are considered to suffer from affective disorders. If the patient has delusions, hallucinations, or bizarre behaviour, he is diagnosed as a psychotic affective disorder, which may be mood-congruent or mood-incongruent. The distinction between these two subclasses is made on the content of the delusions and hallucinations. Mood-congruent mania is marked by 'themes of inflated worth, power, knowledge, identity or special relationship to a deity or famous person' and mood-congruent depression by 'personal inadequacy, guilt, disease, death, nihilism or deserved punishment'. In mood-incongruent affective disorders the themes are persecution, thought insertion, being controlled etc. Depressive stupor is considered mood-congruent but catatonic phenomena mood-incongruent. DSMIII mood-incongruent affective psychoses are nearly, but not quite, the same as RDC schizoaffective disorders. We found that concordance between the manic categories to be $\kappa = 0.75$, and the depressive $\kappa = 0.68$ and $\kappa = 0.78$ in two different series. The value of the DSMIII classification is that it distinguishes between simple affective disorder and mood-congruent affective psychosis. We found no difference in general outcome between these two, but we did find marked differences in the psychopathology of subsequent admissions, for example mood-congruent psychotic depression had more mania, depression, persecution, delusion formation, auditory hallucinations, and schizoaffective episodes than simple depression (Brockington *et al.* 1982).

Cycloid psychosis

In Perris' operational definition (1974), cycloid psychoses are 'syndromes characterized by affective symptoms' (mood swings) and two or more of the following:

1. Various degress of confusion (from slight perplexity to gross disorientation) with agitation or retardation.
2. Paranoia-like symptoms (delusions of reference or influence or persecution etc.) and/or hallucinations not syntonic with levels of mood
3. Motility disturbances (hypo- or hyperkinesia)
4. Occasional episodes or states of ecstasy
5. Pananxiety

The symptoms are further explained in the monograph. When Perris made diagnoses of cycloid psychoses in our three series of patients, the most important clues appeared to be the acute onset, the presence of confusion, and the pleomorphic character of the disease picture, with an admixture of symptoms from different syndromes and a tendency to change completely from one part of the episode to another. The number of patients diagnosed was considerable—10 in the Netherne series, 20 in the schizoaffective, and 13 in the Camberwell series, i.e. about 10 per cent of psychotic admissions. This agrees with Cutting's finding that 8 per cent of admissions with functional psychosis to the Maudsley professorial unit met Perris' criteria (Cutting *et al.* 1978). Thus, cycloid psychosis is more common than mania and about as frequent as Feighner's schizophrenia. Our studies of concordance showed that cycloid psychosis did not correspond to any Anglo-American concept of psychosis, and certainly not to schizoaffective psychosis, though there was some

TABLE 6.11. *Outcome of patients with RDC schizoaffective disorder and cycloid psychosis*

	RDC schizoaffective disorder			Whole series		
	N	General outcome score	Psycho- pathology score	N	General outcome score	Psycho- pathology score
Schizoaffective depressed (Netherne series)	11	− 1.87*	− 0.22†	125	1.67	+ 0.89
Schizoaffective manic (Netherne and schizoaffective series together)	19	1.38	− 0.56†	230	1.63	+ 0.10
Cycloid psychosis (Netherne and schizoaffective series together)	30	1.23‡	− 0.92	see above		

* Differs from outcome of 55 patients with major depression (mean 1.37) (*p* = <0.05).
† Differ from outcome of the respective comparison groups with major depression and mania (*p* = <0.001).
‡ Significantly better than non-cycloid psychotic patients (*p* = <0.01).

overlap with schizoaffective mania and Kasanin's psychosis. Many of the patients had thought disorder, auditory hallucinosis, and passivity phenomena, and were classified by Catego as S + ; they were recruited from those conventionally diagnosed as schizophrenic.

Our studies of outcome in these patients, however, showed their prognosis to be far better than for schizophrenia in every respect, and indeed much better than for psychotic patients in general(Table 6.11). Cycloid psychoses, using Vaillant's metaphor, has the head of schizophrenia but the body and tail of affective disorders. Their relation to the latter, particularly to manic depression, is controversial, but they should certainly be distinguished from chronic schizophrenia.

CONCLUSIONS

In the study of schizophrenia, the determination of the clinical state requires the same attention to detail and the elimination of error as is required for the measurement of biological variables. The clinical method consists of two stages—establishing the phenomena of the episode and applying diagnostic criteria. The first stage requires the use of multiple information sources, including standardized interviews and nursing observations; more than one trained rater should be involved in deciding what symptoms and signs are present. The second stage involves operational definitions, that can be applied either by computer or by rating (at least two raters being required).

Some assessment of the relative merits of the available definitions has been made, though only in terms of outcome. Definitions differ enormously in the number and type of patients they select and, in order to obtain results which have some chance of general comparability, it is necessary to use several different definitions in any study of schizophrenia. It is suggested that these definitions should include one which selects a broad range of patients with schizophrenic phenomena (e.g. Catego), one which excludes major mood disorders (e.g. the Research Diagnostic Criteria), and one which selects only chronic schizophrenics (e.g. DSMIII).

A comprehensive approach would also include one or more definitions of schizoaffective disorders, although there is no consensus as to what a schizoaffective psychosis is, and this concept is not to be compared with schizophrenia in its clarity and usefulness. Fortunately the RDC and DSMIII each provide definitions of schizoaffective or mood-incongruent affective disorders. Cycloid psychosis is perhaps a more promising concept since it has its own pathognomonic clinical picture and appears prognostically homogenous. Thus the use of the three complete systems—Catego, the Research Diagnostic Criteria and the Diagnostic and Statistical Manual, 3rd edition—together with Perris' definition of cycloid psychosis can be recommended as a comprehensive diagnostic approach at the present time.

References

Abrams, R. and Taylor, M. A. (1976). Mania and schizoaffective disorder, Manic type: a comparison. *Am. J. Psychiat.* **133**, 1445–7.
American Psychiatric Association (1980). *Diagnostic and statistical manual of mental disorders*, 3rd edn. American Psychiatric Association, Washington, DC.
Astrachan, B. M., Harrow, M., Adler, D., Brauer, L., Schwartz, A., Schwartz, C., and Tucker, G. (1972). A checklist for the diagnosis of schizophrenia. *Br. J. Psychiat.* **121**, 529–39.
Bland, R. C., and Orn, H. (1980). Schizophrenia: Schneider's first rank symptoms and outcome. *Br. J. Psychiat.* **137**, 63–8.
—— Kendell, R. E., and Leff, J. P. (1978a). Definitions of schizophrenia: concordance and prediction of outcome. *Psycholog. Med.* **8**, 387–98.
——, —— Kellett, J. M., Curry, S. H., and Wainwright, S. (1978b). Trials of lithium, chlorpromazine and amitriptyline in schizoaffective psychosis. *Br. J. Psychiat.* **133**, 162–8.
Brockington, I. F., and Leff, J. P. (1979). Schizoaffective psychosis: definitions and incidence. *Psycholog. Med.* **9**, 91–9.
—— Wainwright, S., and Kendell, R. E. (1980a). Manic patients with schizophrenic or paranoid symptoms. *Psycholog. Med.* **10**, 73–83.
——, —— and Wainwright, S. (1980b). Depressed patients with schizophrenic or paranoid symptoms. *Psycholog. Med.* **10**, 665–75.
——, Helzer, J.E., Hollier, V.F., and Francis, A.F. (1982). Definitions of depression: concordance and prediction of outcome. *Am. J. Psychiat.* **139**, 1022–7.
Carpenter, W. T., Strauss, J. S., and Muleh, S. (1973a). Are there pathognomonic symptoms in schizophrenia? *Arch. gen. Psychiat.* **28**, 347–52.
——, —— and Bartko, J. J. (1973b). Flexible system for the diagnosis of schizophrenia: report from the WHO Pilot Study of Schizophrenia. *Science* **182**, 1275–8.
——, ——, —— (1980). Diagnostic systems and prognostic validity. *Arch. gen. Psychiat.* **37**, 228–9.
—— Sachs, M. H., Strauss, J. S., Bartko, J. J., and Raynor, J. (1976). Evaluating signs and symptoms: a comparison of structured interview and clinical approaches. *Br. J. Psychiat.* **128**, 397–403.
Cohen, J. (1968). Weighted kappa: nominal scale agreement with provision for scaled disagreement or partial credit. *Psychol. Bull.* **70**, 213–20.
Cooper, J. E., Kendell, R. E., Gurland, B. J., Sharpe, L., Copeland, J. R. M., and Simon, R. (1972). *Psychiatric diagnosis in New York and London.* Institute of Psychiatry Maudsley Monographs, No. 20, Oxford University Press, Oxford.
Croughan, J. L., Weiner, A., and Robins, E. (1974). The group of schizoaffective and related psychoses—critique, record, follow-up and family studies. II. Record studies. *Arch. gen. Psychiat.* **31**, 632–7.
Cutting, J. C., Clare, A. W., and Mann, A. H. (1978). Cycloid psychosis: an investigation of the diagnostic concept. *Psycholog. Med.* **8**, 637–48.
Downing, A. R., Francis, A., and Brockington, I. F. (1980). A comparison of information sources in the study of psychotic illness. *Br. J. Psychiat.* **137**, 38–44.
Feighner, J. P., Robins, E., Guze, S. B., Woodruffe, R. A., Winokur, G., and Munoz, R. (1972). Diagnostic criteria for use in psychiatric research. *Arch. gen. Psychiat.* **26**, 57–63.
Fowler, R. C., McCabe, M. E., Cadoret, R. J. *et al.* (1972). The validity of good prognosis schizophrenia. *Arch. gen. Psychiat.* **26**, 182–5.
Golden, C. J., Moses, J. A., Zelazowski, R., Graber, B., Zatz, L. M., Horvath,

T. B., and Berger, R. A. (1980). Cerebral ventricular size and neurophysiological impairment in young chronic schizophrenics. *Arch. gen. Psychiat.* **37**, 619–23.

Hawk, A. B., Carpenter, W. T., and Strauss, J. S. (1975). Diagnostic criteria and five-year outcome in schizophrenia. *Arch. gen. Psychiat.* **32**, 343–7.

Helzer, J. E., Brockington, I. F., and Kendell, R. E. (1981). The predictive validity of DSMIII and Feighner definitions of schizophrenia: a comparison with Research Diagnostic Criteria and Catego. *Arch. gen. Psychiat.* **38**, 791–7.

Johnstone, E. C., Crow, T. J., Frith C. D., Husband, J., and Kreel, L. (1976). Cerebral ventricular size and cognitive impairment in chronic schizophrenia. *Lancet* **ii**, 924–6.

—— Frith, C. P., Gold, A., and Stevens, M. (1979). The outcome of severe acute schizophrenic illness after one year. *Br. J. Psychiat.* **134**, 28–33.

Kadrmas, A., Winokur, G., and Crowe, R. (1980). Postpartum mania. *Br. J. Psychiat.* **135**, 551–4.

Kasanin, J. (1933). The acute schizoaffective psychoses. *Am. J. Psychiat.* **90**, 97–126.

Katz, M. M. and Itil, T. M. (1974). Video methodology for research in psychopathology and psychopharmacology. *Arch. gen. Psychiat.* **31**, 204–10.

Kendell, R. E. and Brockington, I. F. (1980). The identification of disease entitles and the relationship between schizophrenia and the affective psychoses. *Br. J. Psychiat.* **137**, 324–31.

Koehler, K. (1979). First rank symptoms of Schneider: questions concerning clinical boundaries. *Br. J. Psychiat.* **134**, 236–48.

Kraepelin, E. (1919). *Dementia praecox.* [Translated by R. M. Barclay in 1921.] Churchill Livingstone, Edinburgh.

Kreitman, N. (1961). The reliability of psychiatric diagnosis. *J. ment. Sci.* **107**, 876–86.

Langfeldt, G. (1937). *The prognosis in schizophrenia and the factors influencing the course of the disease.* E. Munksgaard, Copenhagen.

—— (1960). Diagnosis and prognosis in schizophrenia. *Proc. R. Soc. Med.* **53**, 1047–52.

Morrison, J., Winokur, G., Crewe, R., and Clancy, J. (1973). The Iowa 500. First follow-up. *Arch. gen. Psychiat.* **29**, 678–82.

Perris, C. (1974). A study of cycloid psychoses. *Acta. psychiat. scand. Suppl.* **253**.

Pope, H. G., Lipinski, J. F., Cohen, B. M. and Axelrod, D. T. (1980). Schizoaffective disorder: an invalid diagnosis? A comparison of schizoaffective disorder, schizophrenia and affective disorder. *Am. J. Psychiat.* **137**, 921–7.

Rosenthal, N. E., Rosenthal, L. N., Stallone, F., Dunner, D. L., and Fieve, R. R. (1980). Toward the validation of RDC schizoaffective disorder. *Arch. gen. Psychiat.* **37**, 804–11.

Schneider, K. (1959). *Clinical psychopathology.* (translated by M. W. Hamilton), pp. 133–4. Grune and Stratton, New York.

Shields, J. and Gottesman, I. I. (1972). Cross-national diagnosis of schizophrenia in twins. *Arch. gen. Psychiat.* **27**, 725–30.

Silverstein, M. L. and Harrow, M. (1978). First-rank symptoms in the postacute schizophrenic: a follow-up study. *Am. J. Psychiat.* **135**, 1481–6.

Spitzer, R. L., Endicott, J., Fleiss, J. L., and Cohen, J. (1970). The psychiatric status schedule. A technique for evaluating psychopathology and impairment in role functioning. *Arch. gen. Psychiat.* **23**, 41–55.

——, —— and Robins, E. (1975 and 1978). *Research diagnostic criteria*, Instrument No. 58. New York State Psychiatric Institute, New York.

Stephens, J. H. (1970). Long-term and prognosis in schizophrenia. *Sem. Psychiat.* **2**, 464–85.

—— Astrup, C., and Mangrum, J. G. (1966). Prognostic factors in recovered and deteriorated schizophrenics. *Am. J. Psychiat.* **122**, 1116–21.

Strauss, J. S. and Carpenter, W. T. (1974). Characteristic symptoms and outcome in schizophrenia. *Arch. gen. Psychiat.* **30**, 429–34.

Taylor, M. A. and Abrams, R. (1975). Manic depressive illness and good prognosis schizophrenia. *Am. J. Psychiat.* **132**, 741–2.

——, —— and Gaztanaga, P. (1975). Manic depressive illness and schizophrenia—a partial validation of research diagnostic criteria utilizing neuropsychiatric testing. *Comp. Psychiat.* **16**, 91–6.

Vaillant, G. E. (1964). An historial review of the remitting schizophrenias. *J. nerv. ment. Dis.* **138**, 48–56.

Weinberger, D. R., Bigelow, L. B., Kleinman, J. E., Klein, S. T., Rosenblatt, J. E., and Wyatt, R. J. (1980). Cerebral ventricular enlargement in chronic schizophrenia. *Arch. gen. Psychiat.* **37**, 11–13.

Welner, A., Croughan, J., Fishman, R., and Robins, E. (1977). The group of schizoaffective and related psychoses: a follow-up study. *Comprehens. Psychiat.* **18**, 413–22.

——, —— and Robins, E. (1974). The group of schizoaffective and related psychoses–critique, record, follow-up and family studies. 1. A persistent enigma. *Arch. gen. Psychiat.* **31**, 628–31.

Wing, J. K., Cooper, J. E., and Sartorius, N. (1974). *The measurement and classification of psychiatric symptoms.* Cambridge University Press, Cambridge.

7

Influence of social experience and environment on the course of schizophrenia

S. R. HIRSCH

Anyone carrying out clinical trials in schizophrenia or evaluating results with a view to treating patients needs to be aware of the ways that the social environment can influence the course and prognosis of schizophrenia. Our experience in attempting to evaluate claims that renal dialysis can be used to treat chronic refractory patients illustrates the pitfalls. The first patient treated in this way showed no response, but the second, who had failed to respond to high doses of neuroleptics, rehabilitation, or ECT, brightened up and became remarkably more active after two weeks of dialysis. After several months he deteriorated. The fact then emerged that he had been infatuated by the nurse who administered the dialysis and he deteriorated when she was transferred to another service. A considerable body of evidence has grown up confirming the sensitivity of schizophrenics to social influences and demonstrating their vulnerability both to environments devoid of adequate stimulation, and to environments having an excess of it. An awareness of how the social environment influences the course and outcome of schizophrenia is therefore very relevant to clinical studies so that their influence can be anticipated and accounted for in clinical trials. As mentioned in Chapter 11 the correlation between relapse and social environment is of the same order as between relapse and continuing to take medication, and the two factors are independent of each other (Vaughn and Leff 1976).

This chapter considers social influences at different stages in the development of schizophrenia and their interaction with drug treatment.

EARLY FORMATIVE INFLUENCES

The influence of social factors can be better understood if a distinction is made between *formative* influences which affect the individual early in life at a time remote from the development of symptoms, and *provocative* influences which just precede a florid episode of schizophrenia, precipitating the illness at that point in time (Brown *et al.* 1973). Genetic influences, like social ones, are formative in this sense and cause a vulnerability to develop the illness later in life. In such a model, genetic influences may create a special vulnerability to exogenous physical or social factors arising from outside the patient. Thus, biological as well as social events early in life may predispose to schizophrenia independently, or only if a predisposing factor, such as genetic influence, is also present. For example, perinatal injury has been cited (Pollin and Stabenau 1968) as a possible environmental experience which can be critical in the presence of a predisposing vulnerability.

A careful critical review of the methodology of all research purporting to demonstrate that parental rearing can specifically predispose to schizophrenia failed to find convincing, well-supported evidence. Studies were either methodologically unsound or the evidence of an abnormality in the parents or in the families' interaction could equally be explained as resulting from genetic effects or the effect the abnormal child had on the family (Hirsch and Leff 1975). Indirect evidence that verbal communication is a decisive early influence (Singer *et al.* 1978; Wynne *et al.* 1977) has not been well substantiated or corroborated by rigorous studies elsewhere. Despite the dearth of evidence that social experience of any kind *predisposes* to schizophrenia, there are a number of prospective studies of children with a high genetic risk for schizophrenia which may shed new light by overcoming previous methodological difficulties (Wynne *et al.* 1978).

PREMORBID FACTORS AND THEIR INFLUENCE ON SUBSEQUENT COURSE

We refer here to factors which are neither predisposing nor provocative. Premorbid factors include those aspects of the patient's developmental and premorbid experience which affect his ability to cope with the consequences of the illness once it has occurred. They are handicaps acquired before the illness which hinder recovery and rehabilitation. Poverty, or failure to acquire education, culture, or working skills, when linked with an unsupportive family, or failure to develop a social role in the community prior to the illness, are examples of premorbid factors which influence recovery from any chronic disabling illness. They are not specific to schizophrenia but are mentioned here for logical completeness.

PROVOKING FACTORS WHICH LEAD TO ACUTE ILLNESS OR RELAPSE, AND THEIR RELEVANCE TO THE PATIENT'S RESPONSE TO TREATMENT

Any number of stressful experiences may precipitate an acute episode of schizophrenia. Two general forms of precipitants have been identified, 'Life Events' and 'High Expressed Emotions'. Brown and Birley (1968) found that Life Events occurred during the three-week period before onset in 60 per cent of 50 admissions for schizophrenia to the Maudsley Hospital. By comparison only 20 per cent of a group of 175 factory workers matched for age, sex, and social class had such experiences prior to interview. Leff and colleagues (1973) noted that the majority of Brown and Birley's patients who had had a Life Event were on maintenance neuroleptics. To confirm the importance of Life Events in schizophrenia, the incidence of Life Events occurring during

TABLE 7.1.   *Number of patients with Life Events five weeks before interviews*

		On placebo Number (per cent)		On drug Number (per cent)	
$n = 82$	Well patients — start of trial	10	(24)	12	(34)
$n = 68$	Well patients — end of 9 months	6	(38)	14	(27)
$n = 48$	Relapsed patients — when relapsed	12	(31)	8	(89)

Adapted from Leff *et al.* 1973.

three months prior to interview was examined in a sample of chronic schizophrenic out-patients maintained in the community and a sample of recovered acute schizophrenics about to be discharged from hospital. Both groups were thought to require long-term maintenance treatment. Using Brown and Birley's scale, all patients were assessed for the frequency of Life Events at the end of nine months observation or following an intercurrent relapse ($n = 116$). The 82 chronic patients were also examined when entering their trials. Table 7.1 shows the results. The timing of Life Events was calculated back from the date of admission or interview. Between 24 and 28 per cent of patients who were well at the time of interview had had a Life Event in the previous five-week period. Of the nine patients who relapsed on maintenance treatment eight, or 89 per cent had had a Life Event in the preceding five-week period, but patients who relapsed on placebo did not have an excess of Life Events (31 per cent). The underlying, if not explicit, assumption in this work is that, if schizophrenia is precipitated by Life Events, it should be more frequent just prior to a relapse than at random times in the patient's life. Brown and Birley's results were consistent with this but Leff and his colleagues (1973) suggested that the relationship is more complicated. One possible interpretation is that vulnerable schizophrenics, such as those requiring long-term treatment, can relapse with little or no definitive provocation if they are not on medication. If they are on medication a relapse without a Life Event is unlikely. Thus, it would appear that medication protects the patient by raising the threshold of susceptibility to stress in everyday life when it is 'Event' free.

These results were supported by Jacobs and Myers (1976) who found an increased incidence of Life Events in the year prior to onset, but further conformation is required. The same questionnaire for Life Events was used in Brown's and Leff's studies. Life Events include a birth, death, or serious illness in the family, having a visitor come to stay, witnessing a serious accident, being laid off from work, moving house, etc. Certain positive events, such as the birth of a baby, or a promotion at work are included. Complementary to the role of Life Events is the effect of close exposure to family members but this has been identified as a separate factor in its own right and is discussed below.

In passing it is worth noting that Life Events are equally important in the aetiology of depressive illness but their effect accumulates over a much longer time than the evidence suggests for schizophrenia (Brown *et al.* 1973; Leff and Vaughan 1980).

THE INFLUENCE OF KEY PERSONS AND HIGH EXPRESSED EMOTION

Brown and his colleagues found that the risk of re-admission following discharge from hospital for schizophrenia could be related to the type of living group to which the patient returned (Brown *et al.* 1962). Subsequently, a follow-up study of 339 patients found that the risk of re-admission was higher in patients living with a spouse or parent than those living alone (Brown *et al.* 1966). A prospective study of 101 schizophrenic admissions who lived with relatives was therefore carried out to examine the relapse rate of patients returning to live with a relative (Brown *et al.* 1972). An interview with the relative just after admission provided ratings of the emotional attitude of the closest relative which was called 'Expressed Emotion' (EE) and proved highly predictive of subsequent relapse. Ratings were made from tape recordings of the interview. Criticism and hostility were rated on the tone as well as content of speech. Emotional over-involvement was rated when the informant expressed unusual concern or anxiety about the patient in the interview, or reported over-protected or over-involved behaviour outside it. Examples are constant anxiety about the patient's diet or the time he comes home, or marked over-protectiveness, such as not letting the patient go out by himself (Leff 1978). In a subsequent analysis Vaughn and Leff noted that high EE relatives react with anger and frustration to the patient's negative symptoms and failures, while low EE relatives are more tolerant, respect the patient's desire for social distance, and avoid intrusive behaviour (Vaughn and Leff 1981).

In the largest study (Brown *et al.* 1972) 58 per cent of patients whose relatives were rated as high EE relapsed within nine months of discharge compared to 16 per cent returning to live with low EE relatives ($p < 0.001$). This finding was independently confirmed by Vaughn and Leff (1976) in a sample of 37 patients using the same method and has subsequently been replicated in a similar study in California (Falloon and Lieberman 1984). Evidence was produced by both studies to show that relapse was not correlated with the patients' symptoms, degree of behavioural disturbance, or work impairment. Statistical analysis showed that controlling for differences between patients in the severity of their symptoms and behavioural disturbances did not decrease the difference between high and low EE patients or reduce the power of the EE factor to predict relapse. A follow-up of 36 of the 37 patients showed a highly significant difference in the relapse rates between patients living with high and low EE relatives even two years after discharge (Leff and Vaughn 1981). The results shown in Fig. 7.2, also demonstrate a prophylactic effect of maintenance medication with no relapse after two years on drugs compared to 50 per cent relapse without drugs.

IMPORTANCE OF AMOUNT OF FREQUENT CONTACT

A further indication of the importance of the social experiences when accounting for the relapse of schizophrenics is the observation in both studies that patients who spent more than 35 hours per week in the same room with a high EE relative had much higher relapse rates. However, a problem with this observation is that the patients one would expect to be more severely disturbed are those unable to find work or attend a day centre. This may be the reason why they are in greater contact with their relatives.

To try and examine the possible contribution of behavioural disturbance to high EE in the relatives, Vaughn and Leff made a correlation matrix and stepwise regression of a number of factors possibly linked to relapse. They showed that the relatives' rating for EE was as closely correlated to relapse ($r = 0.45$) as lack of maintenance medication ($r = 0.39$), yet independent of it, and was just as strong after the contribution of the patient's behaviour disturbance was partialled out ($r = 0.52$) (Vaughn and Leff 1976). In a prospective controlled trial, Leff and colleagues have now demonstrated a causal relationship between Expressed Emotion and relapse, and between high contact with high relatives and relapse. This is discussed below.

MODIFICATION OF THE EFFECT OF EXPRESSED EMOTION BY MEDICATION

Vaughn and Leff (1976) combined their results with those of Brown *et al.* (1972) to produce the results shown in Fig. 7.1. This shows that medication modulated the influences of high EE and contact, but made no difference to the relapse rate of patients living with a low EE relative during the first nine months after discharge. However, a two-year follow-up revealed an increased cumulative relapse rate (50 per cent) for patients living in low EE homes who were *not* on medication, but not for patients in low EE homes who took maintenance medication (no relapses), though the numbers were

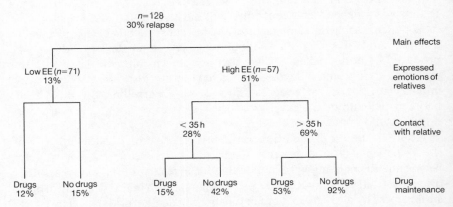

FIG. 7.1.   Relapse rates (percentage) over nine months following discharge for schizophrenia. (After Vaughn and Leff 1976.)

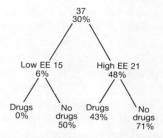

FIG. 7.2.   Two-year cumulative relapse rate in 37 schizophrenic patients. (After Leff and Vaughn 1981.) LEE ≡ low Expressed Emotion. HEE ≡ high Expressed Emotion.

small (see Fig. 7.2)(Leff and Vaughn 1981). The difference between patients in the high EE homes narrowed, with gradually more patients in high EE homes who remained on drugs relapsing. One interpretation is that the ability of drugs to prevent relapse in the face of high EE environment diminishes after nine months. Similar results have been reported by Falloon and Lieberman (1984).

THE INTERACTION OF LIFE EVENTS AND RELATIVES' EXPRESSED EMOTION

In a further analysis of their data Leff and Vaughn (1980) looked at the proportion of patients with a Life Event prior to admission who lived with relatives rated high or low in Expressed Emotion. The rate of Life Events in the preceding three weeks was significantly higher (56 per cent) in patients who came from a low EE home than a high EE home (5 per cent). Of 37 patients, only seven did not have either a high EE relative or a Life Event in the three weeks preceding the onset of their acute episode of schizophrenia. Thus, the provoking influence of arousing or stressful social stimuli in the form of a high EE relative or Life Event could account for the onset of acute schizophrenia in 81 per cent of their sample. In another recent report, Leff and Vaughn (1980) state that six of seven high EE patients (86 per cent) who relapsed on medication had had a life event, compared to 27 per cent in the non-relapsed group. The facts that medication reduces susceptibility to relapse in patients living with a high EE relative in the short run, and over a longer period in low EE homes too, and that Life Events were found in almost all patients who relapsed on maintenance medication (see above), but are not excessively frequent in patients not on medication, point to the likelihood that medication acts by reducing the patient's susceptibility to a stressful environment.

In general terms the Life Events and the Expressed Emotion research indicate two ways of identifying different sources of emotional stress. Unfortunately, we cannot completely equate the arousing effects of social factors identified in this way with the concept of physiological arousal as identified by psychophysiologists. Though something is known about psychophysiological indicators of arousal, stress is a well defined and more complicated emotion which can be better defended as useful, in this context, for its conceptual and heuristic value, than for its scientific precision. Tarrier and Leff (Tarrier *et al.* 1979) demonstrated that in a novel situation, such as being tested at home or in a laboratory, low EE relatives entering the room cause a decrease in arousal as indicated by the number of spontaneous fluctuations in the galvanized skin response. When the high EE relatives enter the room, the patient's high level of spontaneous fluctuations does not alter, but patients with low EE relatives show a decrease in fluctuations (arousal) when their relatives enter the room. Moreover, the base-line rate of fluctuations is higher in patients with high EE relatives than the low EE group. More recent work by Sturgeon and colleagues (1984) confirms that this is the most important difference between high and low EE patients (Sturgeon *et al.* 1984). The prediction that social intervention, if successful in reducing EE and relapse rates, would be associated with corresponding changes in skin conductance response frequencies was not confirmed; fluctuation in skin conductance were independently related to relapse.

CONFIRMATION OF THE CAUSAL ROLE OF HIGH EE AND HIGH CONTACT

The fact that a very high relapse rate was observed in patients with more than 35 hours per week contact with high EE relatives left unanswered the questions of whether patients relapsed as a result of contact with high EE relatives, or because the patients who are most in contact with relatives are those most likely to relapse. These are the ones who do not leave home to work or attend day centres, etc. Leff *et al.* (1982) clarified this issue by showing, in a controlled trial, that they could significantly lower the relapse rate in such patients either by reducing the key relatives' Expressed Emotions or hours of contact.

Twenty-four recently discharged schizophrenics having more than 35 hours per week contact with a relative, spouse, or parent, rated high in Expressed Emotion, were randomly allocated to continue with standard out-patient follow-up or to have the experimental family intervention programme. The expected nine-month relapse rate for these patients on the basis of previous studies was about 50 per cent (Fig. 7.1). Experimental families were educated about the illness, the nature of schizophrenia as a cause of lack of drive, difficulty getting out of bed, social distancing and coldness, etc. Groups were run fortnightly, mixing high and low EE relatives to discuss family difficulties and ways to cope, and about six sessions were held with patients and their relatives at home to explore dynamics or introduce a behavioural approach. The relapse rate after nine months for the control groups was as predicted, 50 per cent, but only 9 per cent in the experimental ($p = 0.04$) and the effect was still present at two years, by which time 77 per cent of controls who remained on medication and 14 per cent of schizophrenics who had social intervention had relapsed ($p = 0.02$). (Leff *et al*. 1985).

Falloon and colleagues (1982) provided further confirmation that family treatment can reduce the severity of acute exacerbations, and the number of admissions to hospital of patients receiving maintenance medication. They used an education plus behaviourally-oriented problem-solving approach, meeting with the whole family at home ($n = 18$), and the control group ($n = 18$) had a monthly follow-up at a clinic. Only one family-treated patient (6 per cent) relapsed over nine months compared to eight (44 per cent) of patients treated individually.

These recent studies confirm the importance of key relatives in the aetiology of relapse. They indicate that medication alone can prevent relapse in patients living with low EE relatives (Fig. 7.2), but that higher rates of relapse will occur among patients who live with high EE relatives unless contact on Expressed Emotion is reduced by psychosocial treatment of the family.

These studies leave no doubt that social milieu can be as powerful a factor as neuroleptic medication in influencing the course of treatment and must be controlled in any clinical trial.

THE EFFECT OF THE SOCIAL MILIEU IN HOSPITAL AND THE PROCESS OF REHABILITATION

Any review of the importance of social factors on the course of schizophrenia would be incomplete if it did not review the effect of hospitalization itself. Studies of the effects of new treatments are often faulted by their failure to overlook the effect a clinical trial can have in altering the social milieu which itself may be more important than medication in producing a change in behaviour. It is too easy to forget that chronic patients in long-stay wards face little prospect of leaving hospital, have sparse or no interaction with the public, and rarely, if ever, see visitors. They may have no productive occupation, no opportunity for satisfaction from work or hobbies, no house or garden to work on, little or no intellectual activity, no close friends, no loving relationships, and no sexual relationships. They rarely receive compliments from others, have little opportunity for achievement, and only rarely play sports or experience entertainment. Holidays do not exist. They live in institutions which must be more authoritarian than not. As Goffman pointed out (1961), efficiency in running the institution takes precedence over the patient's needs. Individualism is suppressed, initiative discouraged, and individual identity inevitably submerged.

Social poverty, understimulation

Wing and Brown (1961) showed that the longer the patient remains in hospital the less likely he will want to leave. More recently, Mann and Sproule (1972) showed that within a year of entering hospital most long-stay patients lose their initiative and don't want to leave. The end result is the withdrawn, inert, apathetic patient for which Kraepelin conceived the term *Dementia Praecox* who has little spontaneous speech or activity. This is an effect which can be seen in chronic inmates of any 'total institutions' as Goffman called them, such as subnormality hospitals, long-term prisons, and the back wards of the worst mental hospitals. The difference is that schizophrenia and brain-damaged individuals are much more rapidly susceptible to these effects than medically normal ones. The researcher can appreciate that the *intervention involved in a clinical trial which requires medical staff to take a close interest in the patients' condition and progress, carry out rating scales, and offer the hope and promise of a 'new treatment'* can have a powerful socially stimulating effect of the patient's behaviour independent of any pharmacological effect.

Experimental evidence to support this contention comes from Wing and Brown's study (1961, 1970) of long-stay female schizophrenics in three hospitals which differed in the amount of freedom and social stimulation they provided for patients. Patients in each hospital were equated for previous clinical history, length of hospitalizations, and current symptoms. Various measures which can be regarded as indices of social deprivations were measured such as being locked in the ward, having no access to kitchen facilities, lack of personal possessions such as a comb, scissors, toothbrush, and the time patients spend doing nothing. The ranking of the three hospitals was the same on all measures. There was a strong association between negative symptoms of schizophrenia including blunting of affect, poverty of speech, catatonic postures, mutism and social withdrawal, and the ranking on social deprivation.

The hospitals were followed up over 8 years. The worst hospital had improved on the social indices at the five-year follow-up subsequent to a change in the hospital's administration. There was a corresponding improvement in the clinical indices particularly related to a reduction in the amount of time patients spent doing nothing. Later, following the resignation of the medical superintendent, the hospital deteriorated and the patients' clinical state deteriorated accordingly, on the same variables measured before.

The study of McClelland and colleagues (1974) illustrates how the non-specific effects of treatment can effect the outcome of clinical trials. Attempting to investigate the effect of withdrawing anticholinergics on 99 chronically hospitalized schizophrenics, on maintenance neuroleptics, they carried out a double-blind study substituting placebo for anticholinergic in half the patients. Only a slight deterioration in the parkinsonian symptoms of those withdrawn from anticholinergics occurred, but there was a general trend for more patients to improve than deteriorate in *both* treatment groups, including frank psychotic behaviour, laughing and talking to oneself, posturing, and mannerism. Clearly, the extra attention patients received by being in the trial was the most powerful factor. Had a placebo control not been included, the improvement might have been ascribed to the change in medication.

OVERSTIMULATION DURING HOSPITAL TREATMENT AND REHABILITATION

While this study is quoted to show the importance of social poverty and lack of stimulation as a determinant of negative symptoms in schizophrenia, it must be noted that chronic schizophrenics are also sensitive to over-stimulation. Events within hospital which are analogous to Life Events can cause a recrudescence of positive symptoms, florid hallucinations, and delusions which were dormant for many years. Wing and colleagues (1964) showed that too vigorous an attempt at rehabilitation caused long-term patients, who, without preparation, were put directly into an Industrial Rehabilitation Unit, to develop florid symptoms. Similar patients given slow, gradual preparation did not show these effects. This is the theoretical basis for the rehabilitation concept of a gradual increase in time spent working and the difficulty of tasks assigned to patients with chronic difficulties. Preferably, this should take place in a safe familiar environment, with a gradual move to the more demanding atmosphere of an Industrial Therapy Unit. Negative symptoms such as mannerisms, talking to oneself, and restlessness, have been shown to very gradually improve as output improves in an Occupational Therapy Unit, but there may be little generalization of the improvement of the same kind of behaviour on the ward (Wing and Freudenberg 1961). A controlled trial has demonstrated that patients matched for severity did better in an Industrial Rehabilitation Unit than the matched group not offered the IRU but only moderately handicapped patients returned to open employment (Wing and Freudenberg 1961).

CONCLUSION—SOCIAL EFFECTS IN SCHIZOPHRENIA

This review summarizes the wide body of evidence which indicates that schizophrenics are highly susceptible to social influences. There is no evidence that social influences have a formative effect producing a susceptibility to develop schizophrenia, but there is strong evidence that in a vulnerable patient the timing and onset of acute psychotic episodes with hallucinations and delusions can usually be accounted for by the quality of the patient's social environment at home or the experience of disturbing Life Events. Medication reduces the susceptibility to both classes of stimuli, but has a less important role in their absence. Deprivation of social stimulation, on the other hand, exacerbates the negative features of schizophrenia—social withdrawal, poverty of speech, flatness of affect, and loss of drive—effects which are not modified by medication in the chronic state. Any attempt to evaluate new treatments must take account of these facts. Failure to employ double-blind control procedures or appreciate the social value of new treatment regimes, even when pharmacologically inactive, is probably the biggest source of misleading conclusions about the efficacy of new treatments. Their importance will be considered further in the Chapter 8.

References

Brown, G. W. and Birley, J. T. (1968). Crises and life changes and the onset of schizophrenia. *J. H. Soc. Behav.* **9**, 203.

——, —— and Wing, J. K. (1972). Influence of family life on the course of schizophrenia disorders: a replication. *Br. J. Psychiat.* **121**, 241–58.

—— Bone, M., Dalison, B., and Wing, J. K. (1966). *Schizophrenia and social care: a comparative follow-up of 339 schizophrenic patients.* Maudsley Monograph, No. 17. Oxford University Press, Oxford.

—— Harris, T. O., and Peto, J. (1973). Life Events and psychiatric disorders. Part 2—Nature of the causal link. *Psychol. Med.* **3**, 159–76.

—— Monck, E., Carstairs, G. M., and Wing, J. K. (1962). The influence of family life on the course of schizophrenic illness. *Br. J. Psychiat.* (Previously *Soc. Med.)* **16**, 55.

Falloon, I., Boyd, J., McGill, C., Rayani, J. Moss, H., and Gilderman, A. (1982). Family management in the prevention of exacerbation of schizophrenia: a controlled study. *New Engl. J. Med.* **306**, 1437–40.

—— and Lieberman, R. P. (1984). Interaction between drug and psychosocial therapy in schizophrenia. *Schiz. Bull.* **9**, 453–4.

—— Boyde, J. L., McGill, C. V., Williamson, M., Razani, S., Moss, H., Gilderman, A., and Simpson, G. (1965). Family management in the prevention of clinical morbidity in schizophrenia: clinical outcome of a 2-year longitudinal study. *Arch. gen. Psychiat.* **42**, 887–96.

Goffman, E. (1961). *Asylums: essays on the social situation of mental patients and other inmates.* Anchor Books, Doubleday, New York.

Hirsch, S. and Leff, J. (1975). *Abnormalities in the parents of schizophrenics: A review of the literature and an investigation of communication defects and deviances.* Maudsley Monograph, No. 22. Oxford University Press, Oxford

Jacobs, S. and Myers, J. (1976). Recent life events and acute schizophrenic psychosis: a controlled study. *J. nerv. ment. Dis.* **162**, 75–87.

Leff, J. (1978). Social and psychological causes of the acute attack. In *Schizophrenia: towards a new synthesis* (ed. J. K. Wing). Academic Press, London.

—— Hirsch, S. R., Rhode, P., Gaind, R., and Stevens, B. C. (1973). Life events and maintenance. therapy in schizophrenic relapse. *Br. J. Psychiat.* **123**, 659–60.

—— Kuipers, L., Berkowitz, R., Ebestein-Vries, R., and Sturgeon, D. (1982). A controlled trial of social interventions in families of schizophrenic patients. *Br. J. Psychiat.* **141**, 1437–40.

—— Kuipers, L., Berkowitz, R., and Sturgeon, D. (1985). A controlled trial of social intervention in the families of schizophrenic patients: two-year follow-up. *Br. J. Psychiat.* **146**, 594–600.

—— and Vaughn, C. (1980). The interaction of life events and relatives expressed emotion in schizophrenia and depressive neurosis. *Br. J. Psychiat.* **136**, 146–53.

——, —— (1981). The role of maintenance therapy and relatives expressed emotion in relapse of schizophrenia. A two-year follow-up. *Br. J. Psychiat.* **139**, 102–4.

Mann, S. and Sproule, J., (1972). Reasons for a six-month stay. In *Evaluating a community psychiatric service* (ed. J. Wing and D. Harley). Oxford University Press, Oxford.

McClelland, H., Blessed, B., Bhate, S, Ali, N., and Clark, P. (1974). The abrupt withdrawal of anti-Parkinsonian drugs in schizophrenic patients. *Br. J. Psychiat.* **124**, 151–9.

Pollin, W. and Stabenau, J. (1968). Biological, psychological and historical differences in a series of monozygotic twins discordant for schizophrenia. In *The trans-*

mission of schizophrenia (ed. D. Rosenthal and S. Kety). Oxford University Press, Oxford.

Singer, M., Wynne, L., and Toohey, M. L. (1978). Communication disorders and the families of schizophrenics. In *The nature of schizophrenia* (ed. L. Wynne, R. Cromwell, and S. Matthysse). John Wiley, New York.

Sturgeon, D. R., Turpin, G., Kuipers, L. Berkowitz, R., Leff, J. (1984). Psychophysiological responses of schizophrenic patients to High and Low Expressed Emotion relatives: a follow-up study. *Br. J. Psychiat.* **145**, 62–9.

Tarrier, N., Vaughn, C., Lader, M. H., and Leff, J. (1979). Bodily reaction to people and events in schizophrenia. *Arch. gen. Psychiat.* **36**, 311–16.

Vaughn, C. and Leff, J. (1976). The influence of family and social factors on the course of psychiatric illness. *Br. J. Psychiat.* **129**, 125–37.

——, —— (1981). Patterns of emotional response in relatives of schizophrenic patients. *Schiz. Bull.* **7**, 43–4.

Wing, J. K., Bennett, D. H., and Denham, J. (1964). *The industrial rehabilitation of long-stay schizophrenic patients.* Medical Research Council Memo No. 42. HMSO, London.

—— and Brown, G. W. (1961). Social treatment of chronic schizophrenia: a comparative survey in three mental hospitals. *J. ment. Sci.* **107**, 847.

——, —— (1970). *Institutionalism and schizophrenia: a comparative study of three mental hospitals 1966–1968.* Cambridge University Press, Cambridge.

Wynne, L., Cromwell, R., and Matthysse, S. (1978). *The nature of schizophrenia.* John Wiley, New York.

—— and Freudenberg, R. K. (1961). The response of severely ill chronic schizophrenic patients to social stimulation. *Am. J. Psychiat.* **118**, 311.

—— Singer, M. T., Bartko, J. J., and Toohey, M. L. (1977). Schizophrenics and their families: research on parental communication. In *Developments in psychiatric research* (ed. J. M. Tanner). Hodder and Stoughton, London.

8

Essential elements in the design of clinical trials

S. R. HIRSCH AND K. D. MACRAE

INTRODUCTION

The problems involved in assessing the effects of treatment are still under-rated by clinicians, who tend to be convinced by their own personal obser-vation and experience that a treatment is effective, and who therefore often doubt the efforts of researchers who wish to test their observations in controlled trials. Clinicians are partly justified in their faith in clinical obser-vation because it is the most sensitive way of detecting the possible benefits of treatment. Unfortunately, this sensitivity to the benefit of possible treatment effects carries with it is high probability of over-estimating a treatment's value. It is now generally accepted that clinical observations should rather be used as the source of inspiration for hypotheses which should then be formally tested in controlled trials. An opposite danger is to rely too heavily on the results of research without sufficient regard to the context in which it is conducted; distorted over-generalizations can arise from research results as well as in their absence. The problem which most beleaguers our attempts to achieve accurate results and draw valid conclusions is bias—'anything which tends to turn a man to a particular course . . . an inclination, leaning, pro-pensity, or prejudice' (*OED*). Much of what we call methodology is an effort to eliminate bias. This chapter deals with the problem of bias in a number of fundamental ways. The section of statistics discusses ways of overcoming sources of bias which arise within a controlled trial, and gives particular emphasis to those aspects of research design which deal with the problem of random error and when to terminate a clinical trial.

The special problem of confidently demonstrating that two treatments do not differ is a common source of false conclusions about the effectiveness of new treatments which is often overlooked by clinical researchers. For example, the efficacy of new antidepressants is generally tested by comparing them to established older ones and showing they do not significantly differ, but failure to show a significant difference between two treatments does not imply that there is no difference or that one treatment is as good as the other. A placebo control group would show if the new treatment is pharmaco-logically active, but placebo controls are rarely employed. In fact the use of placebos is virtually prohibited in some countries, such as West Germany, if there is an available drug which has some therapeutic benefit. Unfortunately this practice fails to take account of the fact that most patients, especially psychiatric ones, improve simply with the passing of time; therefore any improvement which occurs within both the experimental and the comparison reference treatment may be spontaneous or due to non-specific effects. Woggan *et al.* (1978) reported that in her multicentred trial of antidepressants, the most powerful factor accounting for change was the tendency for patients to be rated as less severe over time regardless of treatment. She called this a 'time dependent bias'. Silverman (1980) studied the properties of rating scales and observed that there is a tendency for the most abnormal or extremely rated items to be scored less severely on a subsequent occasion—a phenomenon which he attributes to a change in the rater's response set when retesting. The discussion of statistics which follows deals with this problem neatly. 'Power' rather than 'statistical significance' provides a means to estimate the likelihood that the failure to show a difference between two treatments may merely be due to chance (Type II error), and the 'confidence interval' can be used to indicate how wide a range of differences between two treatments could be predicted to occur by chance alone, given a specified *n* and confidence level. When one believes there is no difference between treatments, the correct test is one of power, just as *significance* is the relevant test when one believes there is a difference. Failure to assess power can lead to the incorrect conclusion that two drugs are similar when they may not be, and this is the most common statistical fallacy in the current clinical trial literature.

A different form of bias, which cannot be dealt with statistically, arises from the misinterpretation of results which, though valid in themselves, are wrongly applied to dissimilar groups of patients. This bias can lead to misjudgements about the effectiveness or ineffectiveness of a treatment, and will be dealt with in the section on the effects of case selection on the apparent effects of treatment (see p. 222) where it is argued that selection criteria can be the most critical variable which determines the outcome of a clinical trial. This section shows how the difference in results from one study to the next, with the same treatment, can be due to the choice of patients put into the study. This can have as large an effect on the outcome as the effect of the treatment under test. Chapter 7 provides a useful background for this section because it reviews the influence of social factors on clinical state and prognosis, and therefore highlights the need to take social factors into account when interpreting results of research. Chapter 9 reviews the main rating scales for schizophrenia available to assess symptomatic change in response to treatment, outlining their descriptive characteristics, evidence on their reliability, validity, and applicability, and highlighting weak and strong points. Chapter 10 reviews in a similar manner scales available to assess social behaviour and functioning.

STATISTICAL ANALYSIS AND INTERPRETATION OF CLINICAL TRIALS

The fundamental requirement in evaluating the success achieved by any treatment in medicine is that the fallacy of affirming the consequent be avoided. This fallacy has bedevilled therapeutic medicine throughout its history, and only in this century, with the development of the randomized controlled clinical trial, has a real attempt been made to avoid this fallacy. Perhaps it is first worth examining the logical structure of this fallacy. The deductively valid form of this sort of argument is known as the *modus tollens* in logic (Hempel 1966). For example:

> If treatment X is effective in treating patient Y's illness, then patient Y will recover. Patient Y does not recover. Therefore treatment X was not effective in patient Y.

In the above the efficacy of the treatment in a particular patient is being tested, and the conclusion that the treatment is ineffective for that patient is logically valid. However consider the argument:

> If treatment X is effective in treating patient Y's illness then patient Y will recover. Patient Y recovers. Therefore treatment X was effective in treating patient Y's illness.

The above argument is not deductively valid. It is of course possible that the conclusion is true but the truth of the conclusion has not been logically established by the chain of reasoning.

The reality of the problem of establishing treatment efficacy can be illustrated by two examples. First, even a disease with a very poor prognosis, such as cancer of the female breast, can show a very variable course when untreated. In Bloom's (1968) series of untreated cases some were still alive over 25 years later. Second, the power of the fallacy of affirming the consequent can be seen in the examples of discarded operations given by Barnes (1977).

Surgery for ptosis, a displacement of the internal organs (e.g. kidneys), was widely practised in the early part of this century in order to relieve such problems as neurosis, fetid breath, back pain, or constipation. Some patients required two or more operations to relieve their symptoms but the reported success rate of the treatment was high.

The resolution of this problem came, as has been mentioned, through the use of randomized controlled trials. Controlled, in the context of a clinical trial, means that evaluation of a treatment is through comparison with another—the other treatment may be an alternative of proven efficacy, a placebo, or even a no-treatment policy of wait-and-see. To make the treatment comparison valid in assessing the alternative treatment policies it is necessary that no systematic bias has been introduced to the trial. Bias can come in two forms, either by having differences between the groups of patients being compared—allocation or group membership bias, or by not measuring the outcomes of the treatments in exactly the same way for each treatment—assessment or measurement bias. As well as systematic bias, random or sampling bias can be a problem. By chance alone two treatments may give different results despite every precaution that has been taken to prevent allocation and assessment bias. A successful clinical trial requires that all three sorts of bias be suitably dealt with and we shall now therefore consider each of the biases in turn.

Elimination of bias

Allocation bias

It would be very misleading to compare two treatments if the patients who had received the treatments differed on some characteristic that could affect the success of treatment. If the patients receiving one of the treatments were older, iller, poorer, or better looked after in other ways, then it would be extremely unsafe to conclude that any differences in success seen were solely a result of a difference between the treatments. Also many factors that determine whether treatments succeed or fail in a particular patient are unknown or difficult to quantify.

To overcome the problem of allocation bias, patients should be sorted into the alternative treatment groups randomly. First, it should be decided whether the patient is suitable for the trial, regardless of which of the treatments he or she will eventually receive. Exclusions, because the patient is too ill, pregnant, has concurrent disease, etc. should be made before the randomization is carried out if at all possible. Removing the patient from the trial after randomization to a treatment is known as a withdrawal, and there is always a danger that bias can be introduced by the use of different withdrawal policies for different treatments. Of course, making the treatment allocation 'blind' by coding the treatments so that the identity of each treatment is concealed from doctor and patient can prevent deliberate or unconscious bias being introduced through withdrawals or, as we shall see later, in the assessment of success.

Random allocation to treatments, supplemented by a careful control of patient withdrawals, will prevent systematic bias producing groups of patients that differ, thereby making a fair comparison of the treatments impossible. This absence of systematic bias will apply to all possible confounding factors not just those which are known and measurable. Random bias can still occur and by chance produce differences between the groups. It is just this possibility that is being tested when a statistical test of significance is used, but more of that later.

Assessment bias

Unfairness could also be introduced to the treatment comparison if there were some systematic bias in the assessments of success or failure of treatment. The use of objective measurements wherever possible can help in this respect, if they are relevant to the disease being studied. For example, weight, lung-function studies, laboratory measurements, and even paper-and-pencil psychosomatic tests may be relatively free from possible assessment bias arising from a clinician's opinion of relative treatment efficacy. A standard device where the patients have to be assessed clinically is to use the double-blind procedure where neither the assessing doctor nor the patient knows which of the alternative treatments the patient has received. In some studies, especially when several clinicians, perhaps in several centres, are involved, an overall independent clinical audit of the data may be advisable in order to ensure uniformity of assessment criteria.

Of course, depending on the illness and assessments involved in a particular trial, other methods of preventing assessment bias may be possible. For example, assessments may be carried out by individuals not involved with the trial treatments, such as biochemists, psychologists, physiologists, or independent clinicians. Or, two clinicians may both separately assess the patient's state.

A subtle sort of assessment bias can occur if withdrawals and defaulters are not dealt with suitably. If, for example, one of the treatments is unpleasant or even toxic, this may give a much higher withdrawal rate for that treatment than for the other. If the patients who fail to complete the course of treatment are ignored in the analysis of results, this may overstate the success of the more unpleasant or toxic treatment. Indeed, it is the success of treatment policies, not just treatments, that ought to be compared in clinical trials. A treatment's success rate is an academic question whilst a treatment policy's success is a medical question.

Random bias—Type I and Type II errors

Having eliminated as far as possible allocation or group-membership bias and assessment or measurement bias by rigorous attention to the design of the trial and its patient assessment procedures, we now have to deal with the problem of random bias, the bias that is specifically considered by the statistical analysis of the resulting data. The principal aim of the statistical analysis is to assess how likely the treatment difference (if any) seen in the data resulting from the trial would be if, in truth, no real difference between the treatments existed. This is of course the question of determining the statistical significance of any difference. A statistically significant difference is one that is unlikely to occur if the treatment difference was really nil. 'Unlikely' is usually, by convention, a probability of less than 5 per cent.

It should be remembered that, even if the true treatment difference is zero, differences large enough to be judged statistically significant will occur as a matter of chance due to random bias with the probability chosen as the significance level (i.e. 5 per cent). A misleading result arising in this way is known as the Type I error.

However, although significance testing is the primary aim of the statistical analysis, two other matters ought to be considered in examining the trial data. A second sort of error, the Type II error, should be considered, an error in which again, through the effects of random bias, it is falsely concluded that no difference exists between the treatments, although in fact the treatments do differ. Perhaps even more important than testing for Type I and Type II errors is the question of estimation. The outcome of the clinical trial allows an inductive inference to be made about the likely range or interval within which the true treatment difference can be estimated to lie.

To summarize, the type I error occurs when, through random bias, it is decided that a treatment difference exists when in fact there is no such difference. The statistical analysis ensures that this is sufficiently unlikely, a probability of at most 5 per cent being used as the criterion of statistical significance. A Type II error has been made when it is decided that the treatments do not differ, when in fact they do. It is very desirable that a clinical trial should not make this error either. The probability that a Type II error has not been made in a trial is known as the *power* of the trial. To make a Type II error unlikely it is necessary to have a sufficiently large trial. Indeed, only by having enough data can the trial simultaneously have low probabilities of both types of error.

Estimating the required sample size

To calculate how large the trial needs to be, it is necessary to consider how sensitive it is required to be. The 'trial sensitivity' is defined as the magnitude of the difference between the treatments the trial is designed to detect. It is intuitively obvious that a very small trial may be capable of detecting only very large differences between the treatments, whereas a very large trial can show if a small difference exists. How the treatment difference is measured depends, of course, on the sort of data produced by the assessments made in the trial. With simple qualitative (binary) data, a percentage success (e.g. response to treatment, survival at a certain time, or cure) is obtained for each treatment. The treatment difference is the difference between the two percentages of success. If, for example, it is known that one treatment can cure

TABLE 8.1. *Number of patients per treatment group required to detect a given treatment improvement, for significance level 5 per cent and power 95 per cent, for a binary qualitative measurement. (After Paulson and Wallis 1947)*

Percentage success of first treatment (per cent)	Number of patients required to detect a given percentage improvement (difference) over first treatment						
	5%	10%	15%	20%	25%	35%	50%
5	702	220	115	74	52	31	17
10	1127	323	160	98	68	38	20
25	2069	543	251	145	95	49	24
50	2591	641	280	153	95	44	—
75	1808	410	160	74	—	—	—
90	702	—	—	—	—	—	—

TABLE 8.2.   *Numbers of patients per treatment group required to detect a given treatment difference (T) for quantitative data; T is the difference between the two treatment means expressed in numbers of standard deviations; the table is for significance level = 5 per cent and power = 95 per cent (based on Kastenbaum et al. 1970)*

T	n	T	n	T	n
0.16	1000	0.66	60	1.11	22
0.23	500	0.82	40	1.32	16
0.36	200	0.95	30	1.71	10
0.52	100	1.02	26	2.10	7

50 per cent of cases we might wish to see if a new treatment can improve this to 60 per cent—a difference (or sensitivity) of 10 per cent. When a quantitative measurement is possible (e.g. systolic blood pressure, heart rate, or leukocyte count) it is a difference between two means, the mean levels achieved by each of the treatments, that is being considered. The size of a difference between two means is expressed statistically in terms of the variability of the quantity being considered. This is done by converting the difference to standard deviation (S.D.) units. For instance, if the mean for one treatment is 100 units, with a standard deviation of 10 units, and it is wished to see if the other treatment can increase the mean to 120 units, we are looking for a difference of 20 units—or 20/10 = 2 S.D. Tables 8.1 and 8.2 show the numbers of patients required per treatment group to detect various differences with qualitative and quantitative data respectively. Both tables are for a significance level of 5 per cent and a power of 95 per cent (i.e. Type I and Type II error rates both equal to 5 per cent).

From Table 8.1 we can see that a clinical trial in which it is wished to see if a response rate of 50 per cent with the first treatment can be improved to 60 per cent (an improvement of 10 per cent), 641 patients per treatment group would be required—nearly 1300 in all.

The superiority of quantitative data especially when the standard deviation of the measurement is small will become readily apparent from Table 8.2. The hypothetical trial in which a 2 S.D. difference is being sought (i.e. $T = 2$) would require just about seven patients per group. Even a difference of just half a S.D. ($T = 0.5$) needs only 100 cases per group.

A common misunderstanding with tables for determining sample size is that one needs to know the likely difference in advance. This is not so. The trial sensitivity is the difference it is wished to detect, or perhaps more often, the difference it is possible to detect given the numbers of patients that are likely to be available for inclusion into the trial. How small or large a difference the trial ought to find is a value judgement of course. At the very least, the use of tables for determining sample size makes the matter of sensitivity and trial size a matter for explicit consideration before a trial is embarked on. If the numbers of cases available for trial purposes is small, a trial that would have been futile can be reconsidered without the wasted effort of being wise after the event.

Estimation—confidence intervals

The final matter to consider under the heading of random bias is, as was mentioned earlier, estimation. The hypothesis test, the decision as to whether we conclude there is or is not a treatment difference, results in just a bald statement that there is, or there is not, a difference. Indeed, the significance level, the probability that the data would have occurred if the difference were indeed zero, may be the only, and a very indirect, expression of the size of the difference. A low probability, 1 per cent, 0.1 per cent, or even less, is taken as being the final measure of authenticity. However, even this naive view runs into problems when the difference is not significant. What do we conclude in a situation such as the following, for example? The clinical trial comprised 20 patients with each of two treatments. With one of the treatments 10 patients were successes (i.e. 50 per cent response rate) and with the other treatment 15 were successes (i.e. 75 per cent response rate). A chi-square test that this difference is significant (with Yates' correction) gives a value of 1.71 which, with one degree of freedom, signifies a probability between 10 per cent and 20 per cent that such a difference could arise by mere chance when in fact there is no treatment difference. This is not sufficiently low to allow us to confidently conclude that such a result is so improbable that we should reject the null hypothesis that the difference is zero. However, the data did show a 25 per cent difference between the treatments. If the groups in the trial had comprised 40 patients, this 25 per cent difference would have given a probability of less than 5 per cent as judged by chi-square. Is it therefore safe to conclude the treatments do not differ?

By far the most useful way to view the results of a clinical trial, or indeed the results of any other experiment, is to attempt to guess the truth. In the trial, the question of interest is how large is the difference, if any, between the two treatments? Our intuition tells us that a guess based on, say, five patients per treatment would not be as accurate as a guess based on 500 patients per treatment. Such guesses are, in logic, inductive inferences, and as such can never be logically valid. As Popper (1959) remarked, 10, 1000, or 1 000 000 white swans do not prove that all swans are white. What is possible, using the estimated standard error for the difference between the two percentages or means, as the case may be, is to estimate an interval or range within which it is likely the true answer lies. Such intervals are termed *Confidence intervals*, and the degree of confidence most often employed is 95 per cent.

An approximate estimated 95 per cent confidence interval for the difference between two percentages of success, or two means, is given by the observed difference $\pm$ 1.96 standard errors of the difference. Usually two is used instead of 1.96. The 1.96 is, of course, the appropriate deviation about the mean of the standard normal distribution to give a 95 per cent interval. This is to say that we can expect that 95 per cent of the time the difference between two success rates or means will fall within two standard errors of the observed difference.

In the small non-significant trial described above, it can be easily computed that the estimated standard error of the difference is 15.3 per cent. The estimated approximate 95 per cent confidence interval is therefore given by 25 per cent $\pm$ 2 $\times$ 15.3 per cent, which is 25 per cent $\pm$ 30.6 per cent, or $-$ 5.6 to 55.6 per cent. There are three principal comments to make about such an interval. First, the most likely 'true' answer, known as the 'point estimate' is the difference actually seen in the data, namely 25 per cent. Thus, although the result was not significant in the significance test, our best guess of the true difference is 25 per cent. Second, the 95 per cent confidence interval does happen to include the possibility that the true difference is indeed zero. This is indeed another way of expressing the conclusion that the result obtained, a difference of 25 per cent between the treatments, is not all that unlikely even if the difference is indeed zero—i.e. is not statistically significant. Third, and most important of all perhaps is to note the tremendous width of the interval—from $-$ 5.6 to 55.6 per cent, over 61 per cent wide. Even after this clinical trial we have still only a vague notion as to the likely size of any treatment difference. It can be added at this point that the situation would not be very different even if the difference between the two treatments had been significant. Suppose the response rates in the two groups of 20 patients were 85 and 40 per cent. This gives a chi-square of 6.83, and therefore a probability of occurrence of less than 1 per cent. The 95 per cent confidence interval for the difference now becomes 45 $\pm$ 30.6 per cent, or 14.6–75.6 per cent. It is possible that one of the treatments is a relatively modest improvement over the other, or alternatively is a vastly superior treatment. Freiman *et al.* (1978) illustrated the vagueness and imprecision resulting from the use of small samples in clinical research and concluded that of 71 trials with non-significant differences, 67 (94 per cent) had a greater than 10 per cent chance of missing a therapeutic difference of 25 per cent. Examination of so-called 'significant' differences would doubtless have revealed a similar degree of imprecision. Clinical trials with more than 100 patients per treatment are rare. With a qualitative binary response, the standard error of the treatment difference with 100 patients per group is in the region of 5–7 per cent, which gives confidence intervals 20 to 28 per cent wide. Thus, the answer from a significant trial could be that the difference is likely to be between 5 and 25 per cent. With a non-significant trial, the answer would be, perhaps, that the difference is probably between $-$ 5 and 15 per cent.

Usually, quantitative measurements will give more precise answers on smaller numbers of patients, depending, of course, on the variability of the measurement concerned. The problem, of course, is that the really important assessments in any trial are usually the qualitative ones. It may be possible to say that the difference between the two treatments is 3 $\pm$ 6 points on Price and McVitie's scale of despondency, but 10 $\pm$ 35 per cent in terms of the number of patients judged clinically cured in six weeks. Once more, a careful consideration of the answer required from the trial should be undertaken beforehand, so that enough patients will be treated in order to achieve a suitably precise result.

Interim analyses—when can we stop a trial?

It is clearly both ethical and economical for a clinical trial to be as small as possible, particularly if a marked treatment difference is indeed present. Sequential analysis of the accumulating data is an approach to this problem (e.g. Armitage 1975), but there are often practical difficulties making continuous monitoring of the data as they accumulate unrealistic. Instead, one or more interim analyses may be a more feasible alternative, so that a trial may, under appropriate circumstances, be terminated early. Several authors have addressed themselves to this problem (McPherson 1974, 1982; O'Brien and Fleming 1979; Pocock 1977, 1982), and the problems are now well understood.

The basic scenario of the interim analysis approach is to look at the data a pre-determined number of times as they accrue, and to stop the study if a difference statistically significant at a pre-assigned level of statistical significance is found. If the difference is not significant at the pre-assigned level, the study continues. So, the number of looks at the data has to be decided on, and the statistical significance criterion at each look has to be specified.

In general (e.g. McPherson 1982; Pocock 1982), there is little advantage in having many more than five looks at the data, depending of course on whether the difference actually present in the study is very large. For example, for a given real treatment effect, Pocock (1982) showed that even one interim analysis (at the half-way point) reduces the expected size of the trial to 72 per cent of the fixed sample size n. Using up to 5 analyses (i.e. every 20 per cent of the data) reduces the expected trial size to 60 per cent of the fixed n, but increasing the number of looks to 10 in all gives an expected size of 57 per cent of the fixed n.

The foregoing expected trial sizes apply if each of the analyses, interim or final, is made at a constant level of significance. For a total of five looks (four interim and one final) the significance level of the trial is 0.05 if each of the looks at the data uses a nominal significance level of 0.016. O'Brien and Fleming (1979) and Richard Peto (personal communication) suggested alternative approaches, which permit the trial to be stopped early only if a very large effect is seen at the earlier analyses, thus allowing the final analysis to be carried out using a nominal significance level close to the usual 0.05. O'Brien and Fleming suggested using 0.00001, 0.0013, 0.0084, 0.025, and 0.041 for five analyses. Peto's suggestion is 0.001 for the four earlier looks, and 0.049 for the final analysis. While the expected sample size is somewhat larger than the constant 0.016, these two designs do not require the maximum sample size for the trial to be increased much (if at all) over that used for a fixed n study having just one analysis at the end. The constant 0.016 for all five analyses should, on the other hand, aim to recruit about 20 per cent more patients in total—i.e. at worst the trial may be 20 per cent larger than the fixed n trial, even although the expectation (if there is a difference to find) is to need just 60 per cent of the fixed n.

Finally, sometimes the aim of the interim analysis is to see if the trial is worth continuing. This problem has not been formalized in the same way as interim analyses that are intended to stop the study if a difference *is* present. However, the problem is an important and real one at times, so some advice on this point seems appropriate. As a negative conclusion is the matter at issue, it seems prudent to look at the data only when a substantial proportion (at least half) of the intended final *n* have been assessed. As with a negative conclusion based on the full trial *n*, a confidence interval approach would seem to be the most appropriate way to place the observed treatment difference in perspective. Usually, factors such as finance, availability of patients, and interest in other possible treatments to study will be as important as purely statistical considerations if a trial is to be terminated for negative reasons.

Conclusion

The clinical trial, however ideal in theory as a means of evaluating treatment, presents formidable difficulties. The medical profession can be helped only to a degree by statisticians in dealing with these problems, for recognition of potential sources of allocation and assessment bias will rely heavily on a full understanding of the clinical realities of the disease being studied and its treatment. Also, the acquisition of large numbers is an insoluble problem for the majority of individual clinicians. The attempt to overcome the 'numbers problem' through the use of multicentre trials has often resulted in poor control over the quality of the data. The answer to these problems must lie in increasing professionalism of clinical research and in the end of the tendency to view trials as a means of acquiring quick answers and as a source of plentiful publications.

THE EFFECT OF EPIDEMIOLOGICAL FACTORS AND SELECTION OF CASES ON THE APPARENT EFFECTIVENESS OF TREATMENT

The evidence reviewed in Chapter 7 shows that social experience makes a major contribution to treatment response which is independent of the influence of medication, and the medication and social factors each can modify the effect of the other. We will now consider how these and other factors associated with the measurement of clinical response can greatly enhance or diminish the apparent effect of a treatment, in the sense that the treatment will appear to be more or less effective depending on the selection of cases. This chapter argues that epidemiological factors relating to case selection can have as great or greater an effect in determining the outcome of a research study than the treatment itself and must therefore be seriously considered when planning and interpreting a clinical trial.

This point becomes clearer with a few examples. In 1971 Leff and Wing published a Medical Research Council trial of maintenance treatment for schizophrenia in which the experimental group received chlorpromazine or

TABLE 8.3. *Relapse rates in two maintenance treatment trials for schizophrenia*

Trial	Placebo (per cent)	Drug (per cent)	Design
Leff & Wing 1971 (*n* = 37)	80	35	Began on leaving hospital
Hirsch *et al.* 1973 (*n* = 81)	66	8	Withdrawal study patients well-established on treatment

stelazine as maintenance medication for one year from the time they left hospital, while controls received placebo. In 1973, Hirsch *et al.* published the results of a Medical Research Council withdrawal study of depot long-acting maintenance medication for out-patients who had been well-established on treatment, mostly more than one year; all patients had had two or more relapses, and half of the sample had placebo injections substituted for active medication and were observed for nine months. Both studies were double-blind, with random allocation to treatments. The results, shown in Table 8.3, show higher relapse rates for both active drug and placebo in Leff's study of patients treated from the time they left hospital than in Hirsch's withdrawal study.

Two trials of lithium maintenance treatment, analogous to the maintenance neuroleptic trials, were reported about the same time for patients with recurrent bi-polar affective illness. Coppen *et al.* (1971) carried out a multi centre trial of patients studied for two years from the time they left hospital. Patients were randomly allocated to lithium or placebo. Baastaup *et al.* (1970), in Sweden, reported a withdrawal study of lithium in patients who had been well-maintained in treatment for several years; half the patients had placebo substituted for lithium. A comparison of their results is given in Table 8.4.

For both treatments (Tables 8.3 and 8.4) the relapse rates were higher in the trials of patients treated from the time they left hospital, whether treated with active drug or placebo, than the respective relapse rates observed in the withdrawal studies of patients entering the study after being well-established on treatment. Moreover, the relapse rates for patients on medication in the withdrawal studies were lower than in the trials of patients studied from the time of discharge from hospital. The differences between the two lithium

TABLE 8.4. *Relapse rates in two lithium maintenance trials for bi-polar affective illness*

Trial	Placebo (per cent)	Drug (per cent)	Design
Coppen *et al.* 1971 (*n* = 65)	95	50	Began on leaving hospital
Baastaup *et al.* 1970 (*n* = 84)	55	0	Withdrawal study

trials were especially remarkable. Here, the relapse rates of placebo patients who were studied when they left hospital was over twice that for placebo patients withdrawn from treatment later on. This can be only partly accounted for by the fact that Coppen's study lasted two years, while Baastaup's study was stopped after five months, when sequential analysis revealed a significant difference between groups. Note that both the maintenance studies of patients well-established on treatment had very low relapse rates on active medication, 8 and 0 per cent, respectively, which is lower than one might expect from clinical experience.

These examples serve to demonstrate that the success or failure rate of treatment can be affected by the criteria for selection of patients—in this case patients newly-administered maintenance medication on the one hand, and patients well-maintained on the medication, but withdrawn from it, on the other.

The remainder of this chapter is intended to demonstrate the influence of various aspects of patient selection which can markedly enhance or diminish the apparent treatment effect. The term 'apparent' is used advisedly because it is intended to demonstrate that the result of any single clinical trial cannot be taken as the true therapeutic potency of a treatment as this will vary, depending on the conditions under which it is measured.

Five aspects of case selection which influence the outcome of clinical trials will be discussed:

1. When the trial is begun in the course of treatment—acute or chronic stage, after remission has occurred etc;
2. In- or out-patient exposure to social influences;
3. Previous treatment;
4. Diagnostic criteria used in selection;
5. Length of follow-up.

Trials of newly initiated treatment versus withdrawal studies

The influence of factors affecting case selection can explain the higher relapse rates reported by Leff and Wing (1971) and Coppen *et al.* (1971) (see discussion above) in comparison to those reported by Hirsch *et al.* (1973) and Baastaup and colleagues (1970). The first two trials began when maintenance medication was introduced; the second two after the treatment had been well established. This is summarized in Table 8.5.

Trials, such as Leff and Wing's, which begin when the patients are put on maintenance treatment at the time they leave hospital, are more likely to include patients who have not yet fully remitted from the acute episode as well as patients who may not respond to the treatment—both of which situations may contribute to a higher relapse rate. Moreover, a study of treatment from the time it is initiated is likely to include patients who will drop out because they developed side-effects, or show poor compliance. Both factors will contribute to a higher drop-out rate and a higher rate of treatment failures, thereby diminishing the success of the treatment.

TABLE 8.5. *Effects on case selection: trials of newly initiated treatment versus withdrawal studies*

Trial	Treatment effect	
	Enhanced by	Diminished by
Trial of newly initiated treatments	Inclusion of spontaneous remissions	1. Inclusion of non-responders 2. Side-effects from withdrawal 3. Compliance worse
Withdrawal studies of patients well established on treatment	Early treatment non-responders eliminated before Bias to patients who respond well and tend to relapse if treatment stopped Low drop-out rate	

Withdrawal studies of patients well-established in treatment such as those of Hirsch and Baastaup will have excluded non-responders from the sample, as well as patients who do not benefit because they fail to take the treatment, and patients who will have failed the treatment and dropped out. Because the trials are directed at chronic patients, both trials will have included mostly patients who have had previous attacks. As the subjects are selected from patients who are currently well maintained on the treatment, the sample will be biased toward including patients who apparently respond well to treatment. Thus, the sample will have been biased to include only those who are potentially most in need of maintenance treatment, and the response rate will not be representative of the effect of this treatment for *all* patients suffering with the disorder. This explains the unusually good response to treatment in the depot medication and lithium withdrawal studies.

In a trial of patients where a high spontaneous improvement rate can be expected, the number of patients responding to the medication will be enhanced by the group who respond spontaneously due to unidentifiable or non-specific factors, such as the change of milieu which patients experience when they escape from the pressures of their home and work environment by entering hospital.

Withdrawal studies are more likely to exaggerate a treatment effect, if it is present, because the patients chronically maintained on treatment are those with the strongest propensity to relapse, or those who never achieve more than a partial remission of symptoms. If the therapeutic potency of the treatment is slight or non-existent, such patients will respond poorly and show a higher than expected relapse rate. If the therapeutic effect is strong, the difference between no treatment (placebo) and treatment will be greater, but the test of therapeutic efficacy in such a sample will be more rigorous than in more heterogeneous samples which include milder cases.

As Table 8.5 shows, a number of factors favour an enhanced success rate with withdrawal studies. Earlier treatment failures are eliminated, patients likely to drop out or relapse because of non-compliance will have been previously eliminated, and the sample will have been biased to include patients who are likely to relapse if the treatment is stopped. A further theoretically important factor is the possibility of rebound effects when medication is withdrawn in the placebo group—this too could account for high relapse rates in withdrawal studies.

In- or out-patient studies

The influence of social factors will obviously be different for in-patients and out-patients. In contrast to the high relapse rates reported by Hirsch *et al.* (1973) and others when placebo was substituted for active medication, Letemandia and Harris (1967) found no difference between drug and placebo in a sample of chronic in-patient schizophrenics, half of whom were randomly withdrawn from medication. If the arousal engendered by high Expressed Emotion, Life Events, or a change in the demands from occupational therapy are necessary to provoke a florid relapse in most patients, then chronic well-stabilized in-patients are less likely to be pushed into relapse if they are treated in their accustomed social milieu, even though the previous history of chronic severe illness would otherwise increase their risk of relapse and diminish the apparent treatment effect.

The evidence referred to in Table 8.6 and summarized above would indicate that patients deprived of treatment in an out-patient study would have a lower success rate if they are exposed to high Expressed Emotion and Life Events. Remember that a variable as simple as more or less than 35 hours contact per week in the same room with the key relative predicted a 53 per cent versus 15 per cent lapse rate in the combined sample of 128 patients reported by Vaughn and Leff (1976) (also see Chapter 7). Out-patients as a group are not as ill as in-patients, so a higher proportion could be expected to improve. An out-patient sample should, by nature, be more stable and less liable to relapse.

TABLE 8.6.   *In- versus out-patient trials*

Trials	Treatment effect	
	Enhanced by	Diminished by
Out-patient	Illness less severe	Exposure to greater social stress (a) Family (b) Life Events (c) Other stresses
In-patient	Less social stress	Illness more severe

Previous treatment

Trials of patients selected because they failed to respond to previous treatment may yield important results which are different from the effect achieved

TABLE 8.7.   *Selection of cases based on previous treatment*

Trials	Treatment effect	
	Enhanced by	Diminished by
Trials of patients who failed to respond to conventional treatment	A special subgroup (which responds better to the trial medication than previous treatment) may do better than unselected cases	Cases selected because they are resistant to previous treatment

in more heterogeneous samples (see Table 8.7). For example, cloxacillin, a special penicillin, is effective in patients who have a penicillin-resistant strain of staphylococcus—a small subgroup of patients with staphylococcal infection. However, cloxacillin is less potent than crystalline penicillin in ordinary staphylococcal infections. Studies of high-dose chlorpromazine for schizophrenia, 1–2 g daily, failed to show any advantage for the total sample over standard doses, up to 800 mg daily, but there was an advantage to high doses for younger and less chronic patients within the sample (Prien and Cole 1968). High-dose trials of patients selected because they were refractory to standard doses of neuroleptics showed a significant beneficial effect favouring high dosage (Gardos and Cole 1973). Generally, if patients were selected because of their failure to respond to a previous treatment one would expect a poorer result because the patient comes from a refractory group. It follows that a positive response to a treatment in a specially selected group should be treated cautiously and not generalized to all patients with the same diagnostic label.

Diagnostic criteria

Diagnostic criteria have an effect on the treatment response similar to that of a selection by previous treatment. Diagnostic criteria vary according to local practice. In parts of the USA the criteria for schizophrenia have been very broad (Cooper *et al.* 1972). Sargent and Slater (1948) broadened the criteria for schizophrenia to include 'early cases' for insulin therapy. A sample chosen on the basis of broad criteria may tend to give better results because milder cases are included, or give worse results because the negative result on the more broadly diagnosed groups may swamp the positive effect present in a small target subgroup (Table 8.8).

But we must equally be aware of trials based on *narrowly* defined criteria, lest the results be falsely generalized to the larger group. With narrow criteria we may falsely miss a subgroup who would respond or mistakenly generalize the effect when the drug is only effective on a narrowly diagnosed subgroup.

The Medical Research Council trial (1965) on antidepressants illustrates this point. It was found that phenelzine, a monoamine oxidase inhibitor (MAOI), was no better than placebo. This result has often been incorrectly interpreted (by those who overlook the diagnostic criteria used on the trial) as demonstrating that MAOIs are ineffective in the treatment of depression. In

TABLE 8.8.   *Effect of diagnostic criteria on case selection*

| Diagnostic criteria | Treatment effect | |
	Enhanced by	Diminished by
Broadly defined	Less severe cases may be included with higher spontaneous rate of recovery	May include disorders which would not respond
		May miss a small subgroup of responders
Narrowly defined	May pick out the most responsive group	May miss a positive effect in those excluded

fact, only endogenous, severe depressives were included in the trial. On the other hand, the therapeutic potency of the tricyclic imipramine, which was shown to be effective in the Medical Research Council trial could be over-rated as a treatment for all depression if one overlooked the fact that this trial had *not* included neurotic depressives. Whatever the size or selection criteria of the sample, beneficial effects on specific subgroups may be missed because they were not included in sufficient numbers, or because the effect was swamped by being averaged in with that of a larger, dissimilar group. The truth of the matter is that the Medical Research Council trial did not test the effects of antidepressants on neurotic depression, for which MAOIs have since been proved to be effective.

A large sample of patients with less severe illness will tend to show higher rates of recovery. Small samples of narrowly diagnosed patients may pick out a specific response not generally applicable to the larger reference group, thereby enhancing the apparent efficacy of the treatment if the trial is mis-interpreted to have implications for the larger reference group. Equally, they may miss a subsample of patients who would respond and falsely conclude that the treatment has no effect.

Length of follow-up

When introducing new treatments it is fashionable to carry out brief studies to see if there is *any* pharmacological response (e.g. Smith *et al.* 1978). These studies have the added advantage of overcoming ethical objections to placebo-controlled comparisons. However, brief studies can be misleading because so many variables can be confounded (Table 8.9). For example, the

TABLE 8.9.   *Length of follow-up*

| Length of follow-up | Treatment effect | |
	Enhanced by	Diminished by
Short	Rapid-acting medication, even if effect not sustained e.g. ECT in acute schizo-phrenia	Slowly developing treatment effect, e.g. antituberculous therapy for tuberculosis
Long	Maintenance but not acute therapy	Acute but not maintenance therapy

investigator must decide whether the aim of the trial is to establish the speed of action in the initial phase, or how long the effect is sustained if the treatment is continued, or how long it lasts if the treatment is discontinued?

ECT has been shown to speed the treatment response in schizophrenia (Taylor and Fleminger 1980) and depression (Johnston *et al*. 1980) but both these studies failed to find a significant advantage over placebo after two months. The general belief is that neuroleptic maintenance treatment is required in schizophrenia and lithium or tricyclic maintenance is required for depression. In one study of oral maintenance treatment for schizophrenia, neuroleptics were significantly better than placebo up to two years, by which time as many patients had had at least one relapse on medication as placebo (Engelhardt *et al*. 1967). Often the effect of continuing treatment is to reduce the frequency, length of time, and severity of relapses without eliminating them altogether. In general, every treatment has a point of elapsed time which reflects the maximum differences between the treated and untreated groups, or between two treatments if they really differ as time goes on. After that point, other factors tend to diminish the overall drug effect (the difference between drug and placebo) unless the treatment has been totally curative.

General discussion

Leff and Wing's analysis of their study of oral maintenance treatment inspired this chapter and usefully illustrates many points made in it (Leff and Wing 1971; Leff 1973). In their study, a continuous sample of 116 documented schizophrenics was identified using the Present State Examination, a standardized method of assessment and the Catego computerized criteria for diagnosis (Wing *et al*. 1974). Only 35 patients entered the trial; most of the remainder were excluded for a variety of reasons, depending on actions of the patient or the views of their consultant. Of the 35 cases 83 per cent relapsed on placebo during nine months, compared to 33 per cent on drugs. This was a decisive advantage for the experimental group, but can the results on this subsample be generalized to apply to the remaining 81 cases? To answer this Leff analysed the reasons why the responsible clinicians excluded 70 per cent of their schizophrenic patients from study (Leff and Wing 1971). He noted that the response to treatment depended on the reason they were excluded, as shown in Table 8.10.

In contrast to the randomized sample who entered the trial and showed a significant advantage to the medicated group, patients excluded from the trial in order to be sure they received drugs did worse than those who did not receive drugs. Of the excluded but drug-treated group 69 per cent relapsed within a year, compared to 51 per cent of the unmedicated group. If relapse rate on drugs is computed for the entire cohort of 116 schizophrenics including the 35 patients in the trial and 81 excluded patients, 64 per cent those given drugs relapsed compared to 47 per cent of the untreated group. This result is the reverse of the trial group of randomized patients who

TABLE 8.10.   *Outcome for patients excluded from the trial of oral maintenance treatment. (From Leff and Wing 1971.)*

Reason for exclusion	*n*	Subgroup relapse rate (per cent)	Overall relapse rate (per cent)
Given drugs other than trial medication			
Consultant's choice: too precarious, different drug	27	67	
Poor response to drugs	7	100	} 69
Moved	2	0	
Not on drugs			
Patient's choice — default	24	67	
Consultant's choice — too well	11	27	} 51
Miscellaneous	6	33	

showed a significant advantage for the maintence medication. But this analysis does not invalidate the results for the randomized subsample of trial patients. Leff suggested that patients included in this trial were an appropriate middle prognosis group for whom maintenance treatment is effective. Indeed, the analysis by Davis (1975) of 24 other well-conducted randomized trials of maintenance treatment involving a total of over 300 patients yielded essentially the same result as Leff and Wing. But it is also clear that in their study, selection factors were more powerful than the therapeutic potency of maintenance neuroleptics. Patients who were excluded because they needed maintenance treatment had a high relapse rate, and those excluded because they did not need maintenance treatment had a low relapse rate.

Conclusion—epidemiological influence on clinical trials

The importance of placebo controls

Scientific method involves the testing of hypotheses and a systematic approach to observation in order to obtain a reliable and valid result. The discussion of statistics indicates how the randomized controlled trial is intended to eliminate allocation bias by ensuring that unknown or unspecified factors will have an equal chance of occurring in all groups. Assessment bias is avoided by the double-blind technique. Under these conditions when all variables except the experimental variable are the same in each group, any difference in outcome between groups can be attributed to the experimental variable. Clinicians are interested in the size of the treatment response as measured by the percentage of patients who recover or improve, or the amount of change in patients over time. The controlled trial, comparing different treatments, helps to determine whether the treatment response can be attributed to the specific qualities of the experimental treatment. A placebo-controlled drug trial indicates whether improvement can be accounted for by the pharmacological effect because the placebo controls for concomitant environmental and unspecified influences, including the possibility that patients will improve without treatment. In practice, it is difficult to measure the 'treatment effect', if this is defined as the difference between treatment and no treatment, because any treatment involves not only the medication but the person and situation in which it is applied. To help the reader to appreciate this, a chapter on social and environmental influences on treatment outcome has been included (Chapter 7). The most effective means of measuring these non-specific effects is to include a placebo control. The response to placebo is a measure of the influence of unspecified factors including spontaneous improvement, nursing care, hospital milieu, and other social factors. The drug effect is the difference between improvement on medication and improvement on placebo. Unless a placebo control is employed it is not possible to determine the extent to which spontaneous improvement or non-specific factors account for improvement.

Epidemiological influences on treatment response

These techniques control the influence of bias within a trial and provide a measure of the treatment effect. However, they fail to deal with the problem that the selection of patients tends to enhance or diminish the treatment response and will influence the magnitude of the difference between active medication and placebo. Chapter 7 on the influence of epidemiological and selective factors was meant to highlight this.

Every trial will have a tendency to increase or diminish the magnitude of difference between a treatment and placebo—no trial could encompass all the factors which determine the use of a treatment—for acute illness, for maintenance therapy, for mild cases, or refractory ones. A clinical trial provides a 'window' for making observations under defined conditions at a particular point in the course of the illness. Only a series of studies looking at the value of a treatment in different social and clinical settings can give a *general* picture of the 'effectiveness' of a treatment over and above those which were present in a single trial.

References

Armitage, P. (1975). *Sequential medical trials*, 2nd edn. Blackwell, Oxford.

Baastaup, P. C., Poulsen, J. C., Schou, M., Thomsen, K., and Amdisen, A. (1970). Prophylactic lithium: double blind discontinuation in manic depressive and recurrent depressive disorders. *Lancet* ii, 1970, pp. 326–30.

Barnes, B. A. (1977). In *Costs, risks and benefits of surgery* (ed. J. P. Bunker, B. A. Barnes, and F. Mosteler), p. 109. Oxford University Press, New York.

Bloom, H, J. G. (1968). In *Prognostic factors in breast cancer* (ed. A. P. M. Forrest and P. B. Kunkler), p. 3. Livingstone, Edinburgh.

Cooper, J. E., Kendell, R. E., Garland, B. J., Sharpe, L., Copeland, J. R., and Simon, R. (1972). *Psychiatric diagnosis in New York and London*. Oxford

232   *The psychopharmacology and treatment of schizophrenia*

Univeristy Press, London.

Coppen, A., Noguera, R., Bailey, J., Burns, B. H., Swani, M. S., Hare, E. H., Gardner, R., and Mahgs, R. (1971). Prophylactic lithium in affective disorder. *Lancet* **ii**, 275–9.

Davis, J. M. (1975). Overview: maintenance therapy in psychiatry: 1. Schizophrenia. *Am. J. Psychiat.* **132**, 1237–45.

Engelhardt, D., Rosen, B., Freedman, N., Mann, D., and Margolis, R. (1967). Phenothiazines in prevention of psychiatric hospitalization. IV. Delay or prevention or rehospitalization—a re-evaluation. *Arch. gen. Psychiat.* **16**, 98–101.

Freiman, J. A., Chalmers, T. C., Smith, H., and Kuebler, R. (1978). The importance of beta, the type II error and sample size in the design and interpretation of the randomized controlled trial. *New Engl. J. Med.* **299**, 690–4.

Gardos, C. and Cole, J. (1973). The importance of dosage in antipsychotic drug administration: a review of dose response studies. *Psychopharmacology* **29**, 221–30.

Hempel, C. G. (1966). *Philosophy of natural science*. Prentice-Hall, Englewood Cliffs, New Jersey.

Hirsch. S., Gaind, R., Rohde, P., Stevens, B., and Wing, J. K. (1973). Outpatient maintenance treatment of chronic schizophrenics with fluphenazine decanoate injections: a double-blind placebo trial. *Br. med. J.* **1**, 633–7.

Johnston, E., Lawler, P., Stevens, M., Deakin, J., Frith, C., Mc Pherson, K., and Crow, T. (1980). The Northwick Park electro-convulsive trial. *Lancet* **ii**, 1317–20.

Kastenbaum, M. A., Hoel, D. G., and Bowman, K. O. (1970). Sample size requirements: one-way analysis of variance. *Biometrika* **57**, 421–30.

Leff, J. (1973). The influence of selection of patients on results of clinical trials. *Br. med. J.* **4**, 156–8.

—— and Wing, J. K. (1971). Trial of maintenance therapy in schizophrenia. *Br. med. J.* **3**, 599–604.

Letemandia, F. J. J. and Harris, A. D. (1967). Chlorpromazine and the untreated chronic schizophrenic: a long-term trial. *Br. J. Psychiat.* **123**, 950–8.

Medical Research Council (1965). Clinical trial of the treatment of depressive illness. *Br. med. J.* **1**, 881–6.

McPherson, K. (1974). Statistics: the problems of examining accumulating data more than once. *New Engl. J. Med.* **290**, 501–2.

—— (1982). On choosing the number of interim analyses in clinical trials. *Stat. Med.* **1**, 25–36.

O'Brien, P. C. and Fleming, T. R. (1979). A multiple testing procedure for clinical trials. *Biometrics* **35**, 549–56.

Paulson, E. and Wallis, W. A. (1947). In *Selected techniques of statistical analysis* (ed. C. Eisenhart, M. W. Hastay, and G. A. Wallis), p. 247. McGraw-Hill, New York.

Pocock, S. J. (1977). Group sequential methods in the design and analysis of clinical trials. *Biometrika* **64**, 191–9.

—— (1982). Interim analyses for randomised clinical trials: the group sequential approach. *Biometric* **38**, 153–62.

Popper, K. R. (1959). *The logic of scientific discovery*. Hutchinson, London.

Prien, R. F. and Cole, J. (1968). High dose chlorpromazine therapy in chronic schizophrenia. *Arch. gen. Psychiat.* **18**, 482–95.

Sargent, W. and Slater, E. (1948). *Introduction to physical methods of treatment in psychiatry*, 2nd edn. Churchill Livingstone, Edinburgh.

Silverman, G. (1980). Placebo effect of changes in response set with re-testing: a further source of bias. *Neuropharmarcology* **18**, 1019–21.

Smith, A. H. W., Naylor, G. S., and Moody, J. P. (1978). Placebo controlled double-blind trial of mianserin hydrochloride. *Br. J. clin. Pharmacol.* **5**, 675–705.

Taylor, P. and Fleminger, J. J. (1980). ECT for schizophrenia. *Lancet* **i**, 1380–2.

Vaughn, C. and Leff, J. P. (1976). The influence of family and social factors on the course of psychiatric illness: a comparison of schizophrenic and depressed neurotic patients. *Br. J. Psychiat.* **129**, 125–37.

Wing, J. K., Cooper, J. E., and Sartorius, N. (1974). *Description and classifications of psychiatric symptoms.* Cambridge University Press, Cambridge.

Woggan, B., Stassen, H., and Angst, J. (1973). Differences between hospitals versus differences between drugs in multicentre trials. A paper given at the CINP meeting, Vienna 1973.

9

Rating scales for clinical studies on schizophrenia

RAHUL MANCHANDA AND STEVEN R. HIRSCH

The measurement of psychopathology and the quantification of therapeutic results are a crucial problem in psychiatric research. The development of psychopharmacology has, since the 1950s rapidly influenced the elaboration of instruments intended to evaluate and analyse changes in the symptomatology of the mentally ill. Information concerning psychiatric patients can be obtained in several ways. The patient can report about himself, observations and inferences about his behaviour and emotional functioning can be made by other professionals or those close to the patient, and information can be obtained from biochemical or psychological tests. The commonest method of evaluating patients in clinical psychopharmacology remains the global judgement, usually based on a scale of worse, unimproved, slightly improved, and moderately or markedly improved. Such ratings are often criticized, but when made by competent clinicians they can be quite accurate in appraising the efficacy of a drug, and have the advantage that they can encompass many aspects of verbal and non-verbal communications which are otherwise difficult to take into account. However, clinical studies which require measurement of change need rating scales which, although perhaps limited in their content and range of applicability, are capable of being easily quantified, are available in a standard form, and are particularly relevant for measuring change in psychopathology.

This chapter reviews the main rating scales used to assess symptom change in schizophrenia in response to treatment, outlining their descriptive characteristics, reliability, validity, and their application and limitations in order to help researchers choose the scale most applicable for their needs. An introductory discussion of reliability, validity, and common sources of error in the use of rating scales is also provided.

RELIABILITY

The reliability of a test or rating is its consistency when measured under different conditions or different occasions, or under the same conditions by different raters, assuming that the data being measured is unchanged. It is used as a means of measuring the error inherent in the instrument which could arise even if the basic data remained unchanged. Despite optimum testing conditions, no test is perfectly reliable. Since all types of reliability are concerned with the degree of consistency or agreement between two or more independently derived sets of scores, they can all be expressed in terms of a correlation coefficient, a perfect positive correlation being 1.00 and no correlation being zero. The coefficients found in actual practice generally fall between these extremes, having some value higher than zero but lower than 1.00.

According to Andersen *et al.* (1974) the degree of agreement between raters is usually dependent upon a number of factors such as:

1. The degree of psychopathology—an extreme degree of psychopathology being easier to rate than a moderate degree.
2. Whether the raters interview the patient on the same occasion or separately, which would then involve retest reliability. In the latter case it is possible that changes in ratings are due to changes in psychopathology between ratings arising from a number of factors, or it may be a practice effect. If the test is unreliable because it does not adequately measure what it is supposed to measure, it is invalid for the purpose for which it is being employed, but, if the data base remains unchanged while the ratings vary, it is the reliability which is at fault.
3. The extent and type of training of the raters, both as regards a common psychopathological frame of reference and with respect to specific training with the rating scale in question. This factor is of special importance when the steps in the scale are subject to different interpretations which require some kind of agreement; this can occur even when definitions seem exact, because in practice they never are. For scales originally constructed in other languages, translation into exactly corresponding terminology can sometimes be insuperable. Another important point made by Hamilton (1961) is that during repeated measurements of clinical status, the rater should not have access to prior ratings because such access results in inflated correlations between observation periods and reduced within-group variance, as shown by Jacobsen (1965).

There are different types of reliability, each of which identifies a source of error variance; These are described below.

1. *Test–retest reliability*: the correlation between the scores obtained by the same person on two administrations of the test. The error variance corresponds to the random fluctuations of performance from one test session to the other. These variations may result in part from uncontrolled testing conditions and to some extent from changes in the condition of the subject himself. The higher the test–retest reliability, the less susceptible the scores are to the random daily changes in the condition of the subject or of the testing environment.
2. *Alternate-form reliability*: the same person can be tested with one form on the first occasion and with another, comparable form on the second. The correlation between the scores obtained on the two forms represents the reliability coefficient of the test and is a measure of both temporal stability and consistency of response to different item

samples. However, the procedure has certain limitations. If the behaviour under consideration has a large practice effect, the use of alternate forms will reduce such an effect. If the practice effect is small, reduction will be negligible.

3. *Split-half reliability*: two scores are obtained for each test by dividing the test into comparable halves. If all items are of equal importance, the two halves should have equal scores. This type of reliability coefficient is sometimes called a coefficient of internal consistency, since only a single administration of a single form is required.

4. *Kuder–Richardson reliability*: based on the consistency of responses between items in a test. This interim consistency is influenced by two sources of error variance: (a) content sampling; (b) heterogeneity of the behaviour domain samples—the more homogeneous the domain, the higher the inter-item consistency.

5. *Scorer reliability*: with clinical instruments employed in intensive individual examinations, there is evidence of considerable 'examiner variance'. Through special experimental designs, it is possible to separate the examiner variance from that attributable to temporal fluctuations in the subject's condition.

VALIDITY

The validity of a test concerns what the test measures and how well it does so. In a very general sense, a rating scale is valid if it does what it is intended to do. A scale may be highly reliable and yet not be a valid measure of anything. Fundamentally, all procedures determining test validity are concerned with the relationships between performance on the test and other independently observable facts about the behavioural characteristics under consideration. The specific methods employed for investigating these relationships are as follows:

1. *Content validity* involves the systematic examination of test content to determine whether it covers a representative sample of the behaviour to be measured. Inevitably, content validity rests mainly on appeals to reason regarding the adequacy with which important content has been sampled and on the adequacy with which the content has been cast in the form of test items. Another type of circumstantial evidence for content validity is obtained by comparing scores before and after treatment. If the test is intended to measure change, the improvement in scores on individual items can be considered evidence for the validity of those items. Another type of evidence for content validity is obtained from correlating scores on different scales purporting to measure much the same thing. Though it is comforting to find high correlations, it does not guarantee content validity—both scales might be inadequate measures.

2. *Construct validity* is the extent to which the test may be said to measure a theoretical construct or trait. It requires the gradual accumulation of information from a variety of sources. A construct represents a hypothesis

that one variety of behaviour will correlate with another in studies of individual differences and/or will be similarly affected by experimental treatments.

3. *Criterion-related validity* indicates the effectiveness of a test in predicting an individual's behaviour in specified situations. For this purpose, performance on the test is checked against a criterion, i.e. a direct and independent measure of that which the test is designed to predict. The APA test standards (1974) differentiate between *concurrent* and *predictive* validity on the basis of these time relations between criterion and test. Concurrent validity is relevant to tests employed for diagnosis of existing status, whereas predictive validity is related to the prediction of outcome.

4. *Sensitivity and specificity* are perimeters which have not been sufficiently appreciated when evaluating rating scales in psychiatry. Sensitivity and specificity are two components of *concurrent validity*. In rating the presence of schizophrenic symptoms the *sensitivity* of a scale is its ability to detect the presence of symptoms when they are present, and the *specificity* is the ability of the scale to avoid rating symptoms as present when they are not. Consider a situation where a series of patients have been given a scale which classifies them into symptoms present (+) and symptoms absent (−),

		Symptoms		
		+	−	
Scale	+	a	b	$a + b$
	−	c	d	$c + d$
		$a + c$	$b + d$	

In this example $a + c$ actually have symptoms. Of these the scale has identified a and missed c. The sensitivity (a measure of how good the scale is in identifying those with symptoms) is

$$\frac{a}{a + c} \times 100 \text{ per cent}$$

or, in other words,

$$\text{Sensitivity} = \frac{\text{No. of patients correctly rated as symptom present}}{\text{No. of patients with symptoms actually present}} \times 100 \text{ per cent.}$$

Further, $b + d$ are actually well. Therefore, specificity (a measure of how good the scale is in identifying those without symptoms) is

$$\frac{d}{b + d} \times 100 \text{ per cent}$$

or, in other words,

$$\text{Specificity} = \frac{\text{No. of patients correctly rated as symptom absent}}{\text{No. of patients with symptom actually absent}} \times 100 \text{ per cent}$$

It can be seen that a scale can be very sensitive if the criteria for rating symptoms are broad or the threshold for rating them as present is low. This could, however, result in poor specificity if symptoms tend to be rated as positive when, in fact, they are not present. When sensitivity is 100 per cent all patients with a symptom are rated as having the symptom. Specificity of 100 per cent means that no one is rated as having the symptom who does not have it. Thus, making a test more sensitive runs the risk of making it unspecific; making a test highly selective to avoid false positives runs the risk of making it less sensitive.

It should, however, be pointed out that 'sensitivity' and 'specificity' are in fact terms which have generally been used in the context of diagnostic decisions and not for testing the ability of scales to detect a symptom rating. Hence, it is not surprising that the sensitivity and specificity of the scales used for measuring change in schizophrenia have not been determined, but can be inferred from an inspection of the scales in Table 9.2, p. 258.

From the example above, the validity, i.e. the percentage of patients correctly classified by the test (rating instrument), is

$$\frac{a + d}{a + b + c + d} \times 100 \text{ per cent,}$$

or, in other words,

$$\text{Validity} = \frac{\text{No. of patients correctly rated as symptoms present} + \text{number of patients correctly rated as symptom absent}}{\text{No. of patients with symptom actually present} + \text{number of patients with symptom actually absent}} \times 100 \text{ per cent}$$

SOURCES OF ERROR

Hamilton (1974) emphasized three fundamental issues in rating any scale: (1) the scoring of items independently; (2) avoiding constant errors; (3) avoiding bias. Scoring of items independently means that any aspect of behaviour which is included in one item should not be included in another. Constant errors are traps for the unwary and there are four important ones. *The error of leniency* describes a reluctance of the rater to use extreme or severe scores. Although not a very satisfactory way of solving the problem, Hamilton suggests the inclusion of an extra grade of severity, not because it will be used, but to ensure that raters will have a sufficient number of grades even if they ignore the last. *The halo effect* describes the tendency for a rater, having given a high score on one variable, to give high scores on others and vice versa. *The error of proximity* describes a tendency to give similar scores to adjacent items. *The logical error* is based on a tendency to give high or low scores where these are sensible or implied by the nature of the material. The most important of biases is known as '*response set*' (Cronbach 1946; Innes 1977). There are two kinds, a central (or neutral) tendency and an extreme tendency. The former describes the inclination of some raters always to give middle scores and to be reluctant to shift to either end of the scale. The latter describes the opposite tendency where the rater tends to give either excessively high or excessively low scores. Another bias may consist of high pre-treatment scores and low post-treatment scores, irrespective of treatment.

Silverman (1979) investigated the changes in response set with retesting. Using the same set of photographs with the same raters he observed that retesting reduced a decline in severity although the raters were fully aware that the same photographs were presented to them. His experiments provided sufficient support for the view that there is a consistent effect whereby scores tend toward a midpoint on retesting and, according to him, this might well contribute much to the so-called placebo response. He considered this a major source of bias in the use of rating scales.

IMPLICIT RATIONALE IN THE STRUCTURE OF RATING SCALES

In order to understand the difference between rating scales it is useful to examine the assumptions on which they have been based and certain general differences in their approach. All scales are constructed so that a higher score corresponds to a greater severity (except Global Assessment Scale (GAS)) (Endicott *et al.* 1976). However, severity implies the degree of disturbance or deviation from normal and is not closely correlated with long-term prognosis. It is of course well known that some of the most severely disturbed psychotic patients respond most rapidly to neuroleptics and ECT with good recovery and good prognosis, while other patients with a less florid array of symptoms and signs do not respond so readily to treatment, and are most likely to have persistent or chronic morbidity. In rating severity in clinical trials, therefore, one is not concerned with the long-term implications of the clinical picture but with the degree of overall disturbances in terms of quantitative and qualitative deviation from the norm.

Adherence to clinical concepts

The first important conceptual difference between rating scales is whether the individual items are defined in non-clinical terms as abnormalities of behaviour and experience or whether the ratings are based on clinical phenomena on the basis of symptoms and signs, defined by operational criteria. There are, of course, an indefinite number of ways that a particular symptom or sign can be described or rated as an abnormality of behaviour. Thus, a Schneiderian First Rank symptom which might be rated as such on a scale such as the Present State Examination (PSE) (Wing *et al.* 1974), could be variously rated on behaviourally based scales as odd or unusual behaviour, paranoid thinking, etc. It could be argued that a scale which rates well-defined clinical symptoms has a sounder conceptual basis, particularly in rating psychoses which are believed to have their roots in abnormalities of biological function. The scales which simply rate the behavioural expressions of these abnormalities are not as likely to yield useful clinical observations when one is looking at the profile of ratings. On the other hand they may be more sensitive to picking up vague and less easily defined changes in behaviour, and therefore might be more suitable for certain kinds of studies, particularly studies of personality disorder and less well-defined neuroses.

Qualitative versus quantitative approach

Closely related to the first difference between scales is the second—that which uses a wide band of ratings, e.g. rating 1–7 for each item, versus that which uses a narrow band of 'not present', 'present', and 'severely present'. The hard-minded approach is that a clearly defined symptom like a delusion or a hallucination is either present or not present. In the area of neurotic symptoms, however, one can argue more cogently that there should be a wide rating band because it is the nature of such symptoms to vary from normal to severely abnormal, as would be the case with anxiety, depression, tension, etc. The problem here is that psychiatric observations are partially based on qualitative changes most notable in the psychoses, and partially based on quantitative variations from the normal, which characterize the neuroses.

Narrow versus broad ratings

The third fundamental difference between scales is whether individual items rate discrete observations of behaviour or symptoms or whether the rating encompasses a whole range of different behaviours broadly grouped under a general heading. An example of the first is ratings for such specific items as 'rapid speech', or 'third person hallucinations'. An example of the second is a rating for 'suspiciousness' in the Brief Psychiatric Rating Scale (BPRS) (Overall and Gorham 1962). In this rating scale 'suspiciousness' covers vague suspiciousness, overvalued ideas, ideas of reference, and delusions of reference. The weakness of such a rating is that it does not make any distinction between definitively psychotic symptoms and symptoms which can occur in neurotic conditions. The advantage of this type of rating is that the observer is required only to make a few ratings to cover the whole range of psychopathology; the scale is therefore quicker to use. A compromise to this approach is, for example, the Schizophrenia (Montgomery *et al.* 1978) or Depression subscale (Montgomery and Asberg 1979) of the Comprehensive Psychopathological Rating Scale (CPRS) (Asberg *et al.* 1978) each of which includes a few items specially selected because they reflect the changes in that disorder which we see with present-day treatments. Such scales are short and easy to use but they may miss non-specific changes, and changes which may be effected with new treatments.

It should be noted that the scales such as the PSE are based on the assumption that the psychiatric syndromes have a hierarchical relationship with each other. For example, a patient with depressive psychosis has depression plus neurotic symptoms while a patient with schizophrenic psychosis may have depressive symptoms and will certainly have neurotic symptoms. As patients improve they give up symptoms from the top of the hierarchy, retaining symptoms from the lower order. There is considerable evidence to support this view which is most cogently argued by Foulds and Bedford (1975) with more recent support from Surtees and Kendall (1979) and Sturt (1981).

Rating symptoms versus rating diagnosis

Whilst some scales can be used both for rating the presence and intensity of symptoms, and for making a diagnoses, these are not the same activity. Many systems such as the DSM III, ICD-9, Research Diagnostic Criteria, etc. discussed in Chapter 6, are not useful for quantitatively rating change. Many of the scales discussed here can be used as diagnostic tools by combining symptom ratings, but changes in the attitude of psychiatrists about the criteria they wish to use to diagnose schizophrenia vary widely and change rapidly. This chapter confines itself to a discussion of the characteristics of the main scales used for providing quantitative estimates of the number and intensity of symptoms and its variation over time in schizophrenia research. In addition we describe a scale for global assessment which is a useful adjunct to a symptom-related rating scale. We are not reviewing Nurses' rating scales as this requires separate consideration.

PRESENT STATE EXAMINATION (PSE)

The Present State Examination schedule is a guide to structuring a clinical interview with the object of obtaining a valid and reliable description of the present mental state of patients suffering from one of the functional psychoses or neuroses. The schedule was first developed in the late 1960s for US–UK diagnostic comparisons (Cooper *et al.* 1972) and the International Pilot Study of Schizophrenia (IPSS) (WHO 1973) but since then it has gone through a number of changes until its present ninth edition (Wing *et al.* 1974). A tenth edition is currently being tested both as a diagnostic instrument and an instrument for measuring change. One of the main differences from the ninth edition is the inclusion of a broader quantitative scale for each item allowing the rater to rate mild severity. However, the tenth edition is still in an early stage of development.

The ninth edition consists of 140 items that systematically cover the phenomena likely to be considered during the examination of a patient's present mental state. For most symptoms a form of questioning is given. An important feature is that, although initial questions are suggested by the questionnaire, the onus is on the interviewer to carry out clinical cross-examination in order to assure himself of the presence or absence of a symptom, according to the criteria listed in the glossary for each symptom. They must be mentioned by the patient or observed during the interview. Normally, only symptoms occurring during the previous month are rated. There is a system of 'cut-off points' following obligatory probes so that the interviewer can move on to another symptom if initial probes suggest that there are no symptoms in a particular area. When symptoms are suggested by the probes, further ratings are required. The items are grouped into sections to facilitate the conduct of the interview. Some items are rated on the basis of frequency of occurrence and some on severity. Most items are rated on a combination of the two (e.g. 1 = occasional or not severe: 2 = continuous or severe). All the items are defined in the glossary and raters have to undergo special training in the use of the schedule. The routine statistical output (using the CATEGO program) provides symptoms and syndrome profiles, subscores and a total score, and a classification into categories which, under certain circumstances, are equivalent to a syndrome diagnosis of functional psychoses and neuroses.

Throughout the development of the PSE the authors have considered the reliability of rating of items, section scores, CATEGO syndromes, and sub-classes. The inter-observer reliabilities of ratings have been studied extensively during the US–UK Diagnostic Project (Cooper *et al.* 1972) and the International Pilot Study of Schizophrenia (WHO 1973). Also, these studies have helped the authors to improve the reliability of items during the progression through earlier editions. The details and points of comparative reliability can be found in Wing *et al.* (1974). During the realiability exercises, the PSE has been used mainly with patients already referred for psychiatric opinion. It was, therefore, difficult to be certain whether the same degree of reliability could be demonstrated in the general population. In such a reliability study (Wing *et al.* 1977) a random sample of 237 women in London were seen by non-medical interviewers trained to use the PSE. Of these woman, 95 were interviewed a second time by psychiatrists who also rated audiotape recordings ($n = 28$). The overall agreement on the frequency of various syndrome profiles in the interviews and tapes was very good ($r = 0.98$). However, it must be mentioned that of the 36 syndromes derived from the rating of PSE symptoms, 17 were not present in the population tested. These 17 syndromes included the psychotic syndromes. The product moment correlation coefficient for the sets of total PSE scores was 0.73 ($n = 123$), for repeated interviews $r = 0.67$ ($n = 95$), and for tape-recorded interviews $r = 0.96$ ($n = 28$). The equivalent correlations for 'all non-psychotic symptoms' reported by Wing *et al.* (1967) were 0.80 (two interviews) and 0.97 (interview–audiotape comparison). However, many of the second interviews took place several weeks after the first, so that the results are not comparable with studies that reported higher reliability with interviews being repeated within a few days.

In a study by Newson-Smith and Hirsch (1979) hospitalized self-poisoning patients with psychiatric symptoms were evaluated at week 0 and week 1 and again at three months with the General Health Questionnaire (GHQ) (Goldberg 1972) and the PSE. The PSE and GHQ scores were compared using the Pearson product moment correlation coefficient. Highly significant correlations were obtained for all interviews at 0.78, 0.81, and 0.77, respectively (significance of all $p < 0.0001$). It is to be noted that the patient sample principally consisted of a non-psychotic group.

Primarily intended as a tool for the classification of psychiatric symptoms, its usefulness as a measure of change was also reported (Hirsch *et al.* 1973;

Newson-Smith and Hirsch 1979; Knights *et al.* 1980). Hirsch *et al.* (1973) carried out a double-blind, placebo-controlled trial of fluphenazine deca-noate in maintenance therapy of chronic schizophrenic out-patients by a single criterion for relapse, namely a decision by the hospital's clinical team that the patient had so deteriorated that he or she must be taken out of the trial to ensure that active medication was prescribed. At the same time, deterioration on PSE was defined as the appearance of new psychotic symptoms or a change in two or more symptoms from partial to full delusions. The investigators observed 85 per cent agreement between the clinical and PSE criteria for relapse. One of the shortcomings in using these criteria is that patients who are non-communicative may not show a rateable change because the PSE relies heavily on reported symptoms, though there is a section for rating observed behaviour during the interview (motor behaviour, affect, speech disorder, etc.).

Knights *et al.* (1980) showed how the PSE could be used to measure change in clinical state for a heterogeneous group of psychiatric patients, the majority of whom were schizophrenics. The measures used in the study are given below.

1. Total score: the sum of all symptoms recorded as present during an interview.

2. Syndromes and subscores: symptoms are combined, in the first stage of CATEGO programme, to form 38 syndromes. There are three degrees of certainty that a syndrome is present ?, + , and + + . Syndrome profiles are plotted showing the proportion of patients in any given group for whom each syndrome is + or + + . Four subscores are derived from summing up the ratings on appropriate symptoms (Wing *et al.* 1977) as follows: DAH, delu-sional and hallucinatory syndromes; BSO, behavioural, speech, and other syndromes; SNR, specific neurotic syndromes; NSN, non-specific neurotic syndromes.

Knights *et al.* (1980) combined DAH and BSO to derive a Psychotic subscore and SNR and NSN to derive a Neurotic subscore.

In an uncontrolled trial of des-tyr-γ-endorphin in the treatment of schizophrenia. Manchanda and Hirsch (1981) used the PSE, Brief Psy-chiatric Rating Scale (BPRS), and the Manchester Scale (MS) for assessing patients. The BPRS and MS are described below. Clinically only two out of 11 patients showed an improvement. Utilizing these scales as a measure of pre- and post-treatment change of the whole group, it was found that a significant change ($p < 0.05$) was observed only in the non-specific score of MS (anxiety, depression and motor retardation) and the Neurotic Score (SNR + NSN) of PSE. Interestingly, although the change in Psychotic Score was not significant (12.9 ± 6.1 before and 11.0 ± 6.0 after) the total score was ($p < 0.05$). Clearly the improvement as seen in total score was influenced by the change in Neurotic Score. It is therefore important to evaluate a change in the more specific psychotic subgroup whenever the antipsychotic effect is being assessed. It can be recommended that when PSE is used in measuring change, investigators should report the change in each of the four syndromes (DAH, BSO, SNR, and NSN) rather than merely use change in total scores.

The PSE should be used by a trained rater only. Training sessions of one week's duration are frequently organized in Britain and somewhere on the continent and in the USA. The time taken for each PSE, though variable, is usually over an hour, but considering its applicability for rating change, besides a syndrome and subclasses categorization, the time spent is worthwhile. Further, its widespread use in different countries helps bring uniformity and clarity into diagnosis and descriptive psychopathology.

Certain limitations need to be mentioned. Organic symptoms are not dealt with in any detail in the PSE and it is expected that these be ruled out in routine clinical evaluation. The PSE is less useful for describing characteristics which are manifested in observed behaviour. It does not help in rating a patient who is uncooperative and at the same time not manifesting behavioural abnormalities in a fairly severe degree. Scales such as In-patient Multidimensional Psychiatric Scale (IMPS) and the Comprehensive Psychopathological Rating Scale (CPRS) have several items for rating mild forms of psychopathology in observed behaviour. However, one should be aware that ratings of observed behaviour are less reliable than subjectively described symptoms. The reliability of PSE is improved by ensuring that these symptoms must be present in fairly severe degree in order to be regarded as present. The majority of the ratings in the PSE are based on the premise that these are moderately severe and present for at least 50 per cent of the time. Thus, some psychopathology at the initial assessment and residual symptoms at the end may be missed. One might, therefore, consider using half scores or a separate score for recording milder forms of psychopathology, or utilize a different scoring procedure as done by Myers *et al.* (1981).

THE AMDP SYSTEM

Beginning in 1961 (Bente *et al.* 1961), this schedule was developed from the tradition of German language descriptive psychopathology in a collaboration of more than 15 years among German, Swiss, and Austrian psychiatrists. This collaboration is called Association for Methodology and Documentation in Psychiatry, and was originally named the 'AMP System'. This system was developed for documentation of information useful in both clinical practice and psychopharmacological research. By 1971, the Association had developed a manual for the initial version of the system (AMP-I) in which its structure and content were described (Scharfetter 1971). The system is now in its revised third edition and the Association as well as the present edition of the manual (English translation, Guy and Ban 1982) have been called AMDP to avoid any confusion with cyclic-AMP.

AMDP-III consists of five integrated parts: (1) demographic data; (2) Life Events; (3) psychiatric history; (4) psychopathological symptoms; (5) somatic signs.

The 'demographic data' consist of 21 items based on the social indicators of Zapf (1974). The items are concerned with patient's socio-demographic and personal data. The information is obtained from the patient, or from a near relative or close friend, or even from the medical records. The 'Life Events' which are related to the present illness and/or influence the present admission are documented. The list of Life Events has been adapted from Dohrenwend and Dohrenwend (1974) and Rahe (1975). Item 22 (precipitating factors) assesses the type and duration of stress as perceived by the patient and by the assessor. Life Events (Item 23) and the age at which they occurred are recorded. Several entries of precipitating factors and Life Events can be made. The 'psychiatric history' consists of 15 items pertaining to the patient's present or past psychiatric illness, previous treatment, and family history of psychiatric illness. One hundred 'psychopathological symptoms' are logically organized under 13 major categories to provide a comprehensive evaluation of psychopathology. These headings consist of: intellectual deficit; disorders of consciousness; disturbances of orientation; disturbances of attention and memory; formal disorders of thought; phobias and compulsions; delusions; disorders of perception; disorders of ego; disturbances of affect; disorders of drive and psychomotility; circadian disturbances; and other disturbances. Each item in this section has been defined to improve the reliability of a rating. The English adaptation includes nine additional psychopathological symptoms for routine assessment while leaving six positions blank for any other symptoms. In rating an item the assessor is required to make a detailed enquiry into it; hence considerable psychiatric experience is expected. A symptom is considered 'inaccessible' if the information necessary for evaluation is not available and the rating is considered 'uncertain' if the presence of an item is questionable. Both 'inaccessibility' and 'uncertainty' are rated as NA (not ascertained). The degree of severity is rated on a 5-point (0–4) scale, namely, mild, moderate, severe, or extremely severe. The judgement of severity is based on the intensity and frequency of the item. In addition to the definitions, the glossary also provides examples for rating 'mild' and 'extremely severe' ratings. The presence and severity of 47 physical symptoms and signs constitute 'somatic symptoms' and are documented whether these symptoms are a part of patient's psychopathology or secondary effects of treatment. Also, five spaces are provided for additional symptoms. The 'somatic symptoms' cover the whole spectrum of physical disorders.

In Europe, the computer programs for the processing of the AMDP system have been developed and installed in Berlin, Munich, Zurich, and Belgium. They are all independent of each other. For the analysis of the present English version only BLIPS (Biometric Laboratory Information Processing System) can be used and that too only in North America. The AMDP system has, for years, been widely used in German-speaking countries for the selection and assessment of patients in therapeutic studies and the routine documentation of hospital admissions. There is evidence that the AMDP system in combination with DiaSika, a computer program, provides psychiatric diagnosis which exhibits higher agreement with clinicians than there is between clinicians and the CATEGO program of the PSE (Schmid *et al.* 1982). For more detailed information about the AMDP system, in English, the reader is referred to the manual (Guy and Ban 1982).

Although much time and effort has been put into the construction and validation of the scale, its routine use in clinical research in schizophrenia is limited for several reasons. Besides the special training required for the raters, the assessments are computerized and programs are not freely available or economical. Thus, there is no easy access to data analysis which involves extensive and sophisticated statistical work. Also, the schedule is too extensive to be routinely used. Furthermore, the items are not specific to schizophrenia. Although stricter operational criteria have been employed in defining the psychopathological symptoms in the latest revision, more than about one-third of symptoms have failed to achieve satisfactory reliability (Guy and Ban 1982). The PSE is comparable in its applicability to the AMDP system. Also, the reliability of the PSE is probably greater than that of the AMDP system because of its structured interview and stronger operational definitions (Helmchen 1974). A large number of items in AMDP are rated on observation and lack a structured enquiry. Moreover, there are no uniformly agreed rules or guidelines in the glossary as to how the information should be elicited—by observation alone or by enquiry, or both. Ratings made on observed behaviour and absence of rating criteria are known to lower the reliability of the information collected. For research workers in the UK, experience in the use of the AMDP system is non-existent. It does appear though that it may have a more useful place in multicentre recording of symptoms for drug trials or for epidemiological, cross-cultural studies if workers have a common training in order to assure uniformity in data collection. In contrast to the PSE, which tends to be used to ascertain the presence of symptoms over a block of time—one week to one month—the AMDP system was originally designed to measure change based on the presence of symptoms around the time of rating, and to record short-term fluctuations in ratings.

INPATIENT MULTIDIMENSIONAL PSYCHIATRIC SCALE (IMPS)

The IMPS was devised by Lorr *et al.* in 1962 for the recording of severe neurotic and psychotic behaviour. The scale has undergone revision (Lorr and Klett 1967) and it consists of 89 item scales stated in terms of a short behavioural description. In addition, most of the items are accompanied by a brief illustration. The information is recorded by means of a clinical interview and the ratings are based on the patient's reported feelings and beliefs. Of the 89 items, 51 are recorded on a nine-point scale, 21 are recorded on a five-point scale of severity and the remainder are two-valued (yes–no) items. Factor analysis of these items has resulted in 12 syndromes as follows: excitement; hostile belligerence; paranoid projection; grandiose expansiveness; perceptual distortions; obsessional-phobic; anxious-depression; impaired functioning; retardation and apathy; disorientation; motor disturbances; and conceptual disorganization. Each syndrome is preceded and followed by the syndrome with which it is most highly correlated. These syndromes are not entirely independent and when the syndrome score correlations are factored, four broader and more general dimensions known as 'major psychotic disorders' are identified. It is claimed (Lorr *et al.* 1967; Overall *et al.* 1967; Lorr and Klett 1968) that these four major disorders, namely, schizophrenic disorganization, paranoid process, psychotic depression, and disorganized hyperactivity, correspond to the ICD-8 major classes of schizophrenia, paranoid states, depression, and mania, respectively.

Schizophrenic disorganization in the IMPS is characterized by psycho-motor retardation, functional disorientation, and motor disturbances. Clinically one might also expect such changes in depressed and hysterical patients. Conceptual disorganization is also associated with schizophrenia, but less frequently than the other three syndromes mentioned above. Paranoid process is characterized by paranoid projection, perceptual distortion, grandiosity, and obsessive thinking. According to Zerssen and Cording (1978), factor analysis of IMPS ratings on 127 psychiatric patients resulted in five syndromes. Factors II and III relate to positive and factor VI to negative symptoms of schizophrenia; factors IV and V, however, reflect depressive symptomatology.

Individual item reliability was computed in the early stages of development of the IMPS. The correlation coefficients of scale items from various samples range from 0.81 to 0.95 and, except for motor disturbance, all items are 0.90 or higher (Klett and McNair 1966). Mariotto and Farrell (1979) assessed interrater reliability in a sample of 10 patients using 11 raters. They found very good reliabilities for ranked scores as did Klett and McNair but also found that the difference in levels of rating did exist among the raters over the whole instrument as well as between the syndrome scales. Cairns *et al.* (1982) questioned the reliability of the scale and explained that such high values are obtained due to their chosen reliability measure of intraclass correlation coefficient for average ratings with between-rater variance excluded. Even higher values tend to be produced by calculating product moment correlation coefficients (Bender 1976).

The particular advantage of the IMPS is its relative simplicity as compared to the PSE or AMDP. The scale is rather comprehensive, at least with respect to the symptomatology of functional psychoses. Organic and neurotic symptoms are not so well covered, but the scale was not intended to measure these. However, the same is true for other instruments used in schizophrenia research. The formulation of psychiatric symptoms in everyday language facilitates the understanding and use of the scale. A great advantage of the scale is the operational definition of the items, and the clear and clinically meaningful factorial structure. Moreover, the scale values are rather sensitive to changes and can be used successfully in longitudinal investigation in schizophrenia (Moller *et al.* 1982; Emrich *et al.* 1977).

The scoring procedure is, however, rather awkward. It has already been mentioned that the items have different scores and any one syndrome may consist of items with different scores. For example, grandiosity is made up of five items: of these three items are scored on two points (0 or 8); one item is scored on nine points (0–8); and another item is scored on five points (0, 2, 4, 6, or 8). Thus the multiple of eight on the scale are frequent. A similar analogy can be drawn from the Paranoid Projection Scale. All items for disorientation can score either zero or eight. A score of eight is thus seen to be particularly common in these syndromes because of the mere presence of a yes–no item. On the other hand, a change from eight to zero (although the change is a forced change of items) would be seen as a major change and is in no way consistent with a change from eight to zero on a nine-item scale. This procedure leads to an undesirable syndrome scale distribution that could distort the results in further analysis as shown by Cairns *et al.* (1982) who recommend that the same rating should be used for all items and also the scoring should be reduced to a four-point scale so that the distortions in change of scores is minimal.

Mariotto and Paul (1974) found that '. . . although the IMPS possessed excellent concurrent validity with clearly independent modes of assessment at different time points, it did not demonstrate the same degree of utility as a measure of change', and that 'extreme caution should be exercised in any use of IMPS where absolute level differences are required (e.g. comparisons across patient groups, assessing change in functioning etc.)'. In order to avoid this, the same rating score should be used for all items including the yes–no items.

For many purposes the biggest limitation of IMPS is that it does not rate the presence or absence of symptoms but only their behavioural manifestations. Thus various behaviours may actually result from one symptom and an improvement or deterioration in these symptoms could affect the rating on several IMPS items, resulting in artificially large effects. For example, there is very little difference between the following ratings: item no. 5 'Verbally express feelings of hostility, ill will, or dislike of others'; item no. 11 'Express a feeling or attitude of contempt, disdain, or scorn towards other people as unworthy or beneath him'; item no. 18 'Manifest a hostile, sullen, or morose attitude towards others, by tone of voice, demeanour, or facial expressions'; and items 28, 32, and 38 could similarly be affected by the same paranoid symptoms.

COMPREHENSIVE PSYCHOPATHOLOGICAL RATING SCALE (CPRS)

In 1971 an interdisciplinary group of psychiatrists, psychologists, and clinical pharmacologists was formed to construct a new scale consisting of items sensitive to change with treatment. The construction of a Swedish and English version of the scale went hand in hand with actual rating of patients, and the scale was published in 1978 (Asberg *et al.* 1978).

The scale consists of 67 items: reported (1–40) and observed (41–65) psychopathology; global rating of illness (66); and assumed reliability of the rating (67). Each item has been described in simple non-technical terms. For each variable the scale steps, 0, 1, 2, and 3 have been operationally defined and the use of half steps is recommended thus making it a scale with seven points of severity. The following general rules have been used in their construction : 0 = absent; 1 = pathological, although it may even be a normal variation; 2 = clearly pathological; and 3 = extreme degree of psychopathology. The dimensions used for defining and ranging the individual items are intensity, frequency, and duration of the symptoms. In the rating of items such as sexual interest or sleep, the rater is asked to judge the severity against the subject's habitual pattern. The essential requirements for a rater are training and experience in interviewing psychiatric patients, and it is recommended that the scale can be used by all trained mental-health workers. An interview technique that is as close to the clinical psychiatric interview as possible is recommended, and the ratings are made on the basis of information elicited and item definition.

Jacobsson *et al.* (1978) conducted an interrater reliability study of the CPRS for 39 items relevant to patients with schizophrenia or paranoid syndromes. Five doctors rated 14 schizophrenics; all except one were using the scale for the first time. The interrater reliability of reported symptoms (n = 16) was over 0.90 for all items except inability to feel (r = 0.78) and reduced sleep (r = 0.84). Sixteen out of 23 observed symptoms had high interrater reliability (r = 0.78–0.97). Low values were obtained for mood disturbance (incontinence of affect 0.20, incongruence affect 0.31, labile emotional responses 0.48, hostility 0.52), distractability (0.30), and speech defects (0.62). Reliability studies have been conducted under different settings (Asberg *et al.* 1978; Kasa and Hitomi 1985). Montgomery *et al.* (1978) utilized conjoint rater pairs consisting of a psychiatrist and a rater from psychology, nursing, or general practice to blindly rater 49 depressed patients undergoing treatment in Sweden and England. Seventeen items were chosen for analysis on the basis of their frequency of occurrence in depressive illness (Montgomery and Asberg 1979). High correlation coefficient values were obtained for all items except agitation (r = 0.33) and fatiguability (r = 0.68) for the psychiatrist–nurse pair, and observed muscular tension (r = 0.58) for the psychiatrist–general practitioner pair.

The CPRS with 67 items falls between a longer scale like the PSE or IMPS and shorter scales like the BPRS and the Manchester Scale (MS). The advantages claimed by the authors of excluding items pertaining to pronounced character traits, of a particular psychiatric syndrome, or those influenced by socio-cultural differences, are shared by other scales like the PSE, BPRS, and MS. The description of each item and rating instructions are indeed a favourable point. Also, the rater is frequently asked to distinguish between items that may appear to convey the same meaning, e.g. inner tension must be distinguished from sadness, worrying, and muscular tension; worrying must be distinguished from pessimistic thoughts, hypochondriasis, compulsive thoughts, phobias, and indecision. Since this caution is mentioned under the respective item, there is no generalization and only specific symptoms are rated. However, similar instructions and guidelines are available for the PSE. Overall, the scale covers a wide spectrum of psychiatric symptoms. Whereas this may be an advantage in the recording of pattern and severity of clinical presentation for different psychiatric disorders, having so many items is no advantage in measuring change during treatment in schizophrenics. Thus the PSE has greater specificity than the CPRS. With so many items and recommendations for using half-scores, a change in the total score may be related to non-specific factors or to the rating bias described by Silverman (1979). Indeed, it is seen that of the total scale, only a small number of items are reliable and valid measures for change in depression and schizophrenia. Ratings based on observations are universally known to have lower reliability and in the CPRS as many as 25 out of 65 items are based on observation.

The schizophrenia subscale

Montgomery *et al.* (1978) constructed a schizophrenia subscale from the CPRS. This is called the 'Montgomery Schizophrenia Scale' (MSS). The complete scale was administered to 50 schizophrenics before treatment and to 36 after they were on a standard dose of neuroleptics for four weeks. Change in scores on individual items were examined to see which were the most sensitive to treatment change. The clinicians' global judgement of responders and non-responders at the end of the treatment allowed testing of the discriminatory power of the change score of the individual items, using the point biserial correlation. The 12 items which discriminated best were presented as the schizophrenia scale. The items in order of greater sensitivity to change during treatment were as follows: feeling controlled; lack of appropriate emotion; disrupted thoughts; commenting voices; depersonalization; perplexity; inability to feel; sadness; pessimistic thoughts; other delusions; ideas of persecution; and delusional mood. According to the authors, the change in scores on the new scale discriminated more significantly than the BPRS. This claim remains to be substantiated. The criteria for selecting items that constitute the schizophrenia subscale is the ability of an item to change over a period. This does not imply a specific treatment effect. For example, delusional mood is characteristically seen in acute schizophrenic episode and is in many cases replaced in time by fully formed delusions. In other words, the items represented in the schizophrenia subscale reflect a change in acute symptomatology. Negative symptoms of schizophrenia, considered unresponsive to currently available nueroleptic medication, are not adequately represented in this subscale. It is important to rate negative symptoms in every treatment trial of schizophrenic patients because a change in acute symptomatology does not mean a specific drug effect on the schizophrenic process. A crucial aspect of schizophrenic symptomatology is thus excluded from assessment. The full CPRS consists of several negative symptoms, namely: indecision; lassitude; withdrawal; and reduced speech; and these should have been included. Further, the 12 items in the subscale are not mutually exclusive. For example, depersonalization and perplexity represent two facets of acute anxiety and in an acute schizophrenic episode these phenomena may be not uncommonly associated with a delusional mood. Hallucinations other than 'commenting voices' are not included in the sub-scale and they are rated under 'other delusions' or not rated at all. Also when the patient is uncooperative or unresponsive the rater uses his judgement to arrive at a score. This obviously introduces a bias. However, the merits of the scale are the clear description of items and of the anchor points. Also, the items are commonly used in current psychiatric practice in English-speaking countries. In our view it has definite advantages over the BPRS but not over the MS. The 12 items of the MSS can be summarized under anxiety, depression, abnormal ideas and beliefs, hallucinations, and blunting or incongruity of affect. The content of this scale is thus even more limited than the MS which shares the merits of being a schizophrenia subscale. The MS has another advantage because it includes rating for incoherence and poverty of thought.

The scales described so far (except the MSS) are multidimensional in that one can rate the presence and/or severity of different symptoms. Alternatively, one can assess change using a scale with fewer items measuring the severity of schizophrenic symptomatology. The BPRS and the MS are examples of rating scales in this group.

BRIEF PSYCHIATRIC RATING SCALE (BPRS)

The BPRS was the first rapid evaluation procedure for use in assessing treatment change in psychiatric patients while at the same time yielding a rather comprehensive description of major symptom characteristics. Even today, it is the most extensively used rating scale in drug trials on schizophrenic patients (Manchanda *et al*. 1986). The original scale consisted of 16 symptom constructs (Overall and Gorham 1962) derived from factor analyses of several larger sets of items, principally Lorr's Multidimensional Scale for Rating Psychiatric Patients (Lorr *et al*. 1953) and the IMPS. The ratings are made on the basis of verbal report and observation of the patient during a brief semi-structured interview lasting between 15 and 30 minutes. Items rated on observation consist of tension; emotional withdrawal; mannerisms and posturing; motor retardation; blunted affect; and unco-operativeness. Items completed on the basis of information obtained during interviews consist of conceptual disorganization; unusual thought content; anxiety; guilt feelings; grandiosity; depressive mood; hostility; somatic concern; hallucinatory behaviour; suspiciousness. Two more items, namely excitement and disorganization, were subsequently added to render the instrument more useful for classification research since these items represent hypomania. Each of these symptoms is identified with a construct, and the definition of each item is provided in the rating form with wider discussion for each construct in the original article (Overall and Gorham 1962). Although each item has its own definition, the severity is rated by virtue of its being:

(1) absent; (2) very mild; (3) mild; (4) moderate; (5) moderately severe; (6) severe; or (7) extremely severe.

Initial studies with the BPRS were concerned with providing objective rating scale descriptions of psychiatric diagnostic stereotypes (Overall and Gorham 1963). Four major diagnostic categories could be discriminated: schizophrenic; paranoid; depressive; and manic. The schizophrenic, paranoid, and depressive profile patterns were used as a basis for classifying patients in drug studies (Hollister *et al.* 1971). However, actual patient profiles were not always well represented by diagnostic subtypes. In the American psychiatric population, six phenomenological types have been repeatedly identified by cluster analyses of BPRS profiles (Overall 1974). They have been given descriptive names as follows: florid thinking disorder; withdrawn – disorganized thinking disturbance; paranoid hostile – suspiciousness; anxious depression; hostile depression; and retarded depression. A seventh, agitation – excitement type has been verified in analyses of ratings of patients with clinical diagnosis of mania and schizoaffective psychosis. These categories were closely replicated in a large sample of French psychiatric patients, with the possible exception that the so-called 'hostile depression' appeared as a more traditional 'agitated' type which was added to complete eight phenomenological patterns. The mean BPRS rating profiles for 2000 French and American psychotic patients were well represented by one of the classification prototypes (Overall 1974). Although one might find some correspondence, the symptom profiles are not to be confused with diagnostic categories. Further, BPRS contains four clusters of symptoms that tend to go together (Overall *et al.* 1967; Pichot *et al.* 1969). Each of these higher order factors can be scored by combining ratings on the relevant scales, as follows:

1. *Thinking disturbance*: conceptual disorganization, hallucinatory behaviour, unusual thought content.
2. *Withdrawal—retardation*: emotional withdrawal, motor retardation, blunted affect.
3. *Anxious depression*: anxiety, guilt feelings, depressive mood.
4. *Hostile suspiciousness*: hostility, suspiciousness, unco-operativeness.

In studies designed to measure change, a global index of improvement can be arrived at by adding all the ratings to obtain a 'total score'. On the basis of overall clinical impression, one could also make a qualitative evaluation on the global scale. Hanssen *et al.* (1974) recommended that in drug trials the scoring should be reduced to fewer items. Yorkston *et al.* (1974) modified the scale by changing the scoring from 1–7 to 0–6 so that the absence of a symptom is designated by zero rather than one. The items were classed into three groups: the 'thought disorder' subscale which corresponds to the thinking disturbance scale mentioned above; the 'other schizophrenic' or 'non-thought disorder' subscale consists of blunted affect; grandiosity; suspiciousness; emotional withdrawal; motor retardation; and mannerisms and posturing. The 'remaining' or 'non-schizophrenic' subscale consists of the items not covered.

The BPRS has obvious advantages as a brief scale. It covers both florid and deficit symptoms of schizophrenia. The symptom clusters can be used for describing the patient population. Furthermore, since it has been extensively used, it is possible to compare studies using the scale. However, there are certain flaws in the use of this scale. The scale was not designed specifically for schizophrenia. Only six items (conceptual disorganization, hallucinatory behaviour, unusual thought content, emotional withdrawal, motor retardation, and blunted affect) or at the most nine items (including suspiciousness, grandiosity, and mannerisms and posturing) are specific to schizophrenia. Even then most of the investigators use change in the total score as the criterion for change (Manchanda *et al.* 1986), though it may merely reflect a change in non-specific symptoms. Furthermore, there is a likely halo effect between groups of symptoms, for example a suspicious and uncommunicative patient may score on suspiciousness; uncooperativeness; motor retardation; emotional withdrawal; and on hostility when the cause may arise solely from a paranoid delusion. Delusions, unless unusual, do not get a rating except under suspiciousness. 'Unusual' paranoid delusions may be rated on both suspiciousness and unusual thought content. Howsoever one might define it, some degree of overlap is seen between emotional withdrawal and blunted affect. It should be noted that the key word for emotional withdrawal is lack of *rapport*, whereas for blunted affect it is reduced *emotional expression*. Somatic concern is rated whether or not there is a physical basis for concern. Conceptual disorganization includes all forms of thought disorder. The fact that a wide range of different phenomena are rated under each heading means that theoretically a symptom would be present and disappears while another symptom in the cluster remains and the rating will remain the same.

Although Overall and Gorham (1962) defined each item, there are no guidelines for rating severity. The rater is asked to compare the degree of severity of symptoms in the patient to the population of patients who do have the symptom in question. This makes the rating very subjective. Manuals for rating have subsequently been prepared. Turner (1963) provided guidelines for moderate and extremely severe ratings and Kolakowska (in Wiles *et al.* 1976) prepared instructions for rating each level of severity. The two sets of instructions for rating the same levels of severity do not correspond. Thus, although two raters at one centre may have high interrater reliability, this does not mean that the constructs used by one investigator in one centre correspond with those used by another investigator in a different centre. Blunted affect, as defined by Overall and Gorham, does not include incongruity of affect but is included by both Turner and Kolakowska. According to Turner, vague, evasive, or shift under slight pressure is rated as 'moderate' conceptual disorganization, but not so by Kolakowska. Thus the BPRS may prove particularly confusing when a beginner is looking for hard, well-specified criteria for rating each item. The absence of set criteria for ratings and the possibility that different centres and different raters will have different reference points for high and low rating limit the reliability of comparing data from one centre to another, except to draw conclusions about its direction of change. Little or nothing can be concluded from trials using such a scale which do not include a blindly rated control group because the inherent bias to rate improvement over time and the high rate of spontaneous improvement shown by untreated psychiatric patients would tend to lead to reduced rating with the passage of time in almost all patient groups.

MANCHESTER SCALE (MS)

This scale, also referred to as the Krawiecka scale is primarily intended for rating psychotic patients fairly quickly by doctors who know them (Krawiecka *et al.* 1977). The ratings are relevant to deficits seen in chronic psychoses and sensitive to changes with treatment. It consists of eight items based on reported (four) and observed (four) psychopathology. The ratings based on replies to questions are: depressed; anxious; delusions; and hallucinations, and the ratings based on observations are: incoherence and irrelevance of speech; poverty of speech, mute; flattened, incongruous affect; and psychomotor retardation. A new rater can train himself in its use from videotaped training tapes from the Department of Psychiatry, Manchester University and then establish his reliability by using additional videotapes especially prepared for this purpose. A manual offers probe questions and guidelines for rating. Manchanda and Hirsch (1979 unpublished) modified the manual by introducing a series of questions derived from the PSE in order to facilitate interviewing and provide adequate coverage of symptoms seen in acute patients. The ratings are made on a five-point (0–4) scale of severity, detailed as follows: zero represents the absence of an item; a rating of one is given when although there is some evidence for the item in question, it is not considered pathological; a rating of two refers to a degree just sufficient to be regarded as pathological; ratings of three and four refer to marked and severe psychopathology but guidelines for each rating vary according to the item being rated. The ratings are made for presence and absence of symptoms during the preceding week. For anxiety and depression, the degree of distress to the patient is an important factor for rating.

In the reliability exercises for the scale there was no difference between five psychiatrists in the mean severity of their ratings (over videotapes) except for 'flattened/incongruous affect'. The correlation coefficients for all five psychiatrists showed that not only do the tape-trained raters tend to agree amongst themselves, but that their ratings were consonant with psychiatrists who had much more extensive experience of using the scale (Krawiecka *et al.* 1977).

The usefulness of the scale has been shown in practical settings. It has been used not only in the assessment of chronic psychotics (Owens and Johnstone 1980) but more commonly, as a measure of change in several acute treatment

TABLE 9.1. *Coefficient correlations (r > 0.80) in the number of items out of a total number of items based on reported or observed symptoms in each of the two scales (BPRS and MS)*

	Inter-rater reliability			
	Single interview		Separate interview	
	Reported	Observed	Reported	Observed
BPRS	8/9	4/9	2/9	0/9
MS	4/4	1/4	3/4	1/4

trials (Johnstone *et al.* 1978; Manchanda and Hirsch 1981; Manchanda and Hirsch 1986). The investigators found it brief, simple to use, and sensitive in recording change. Johnstone *et al.* (1978) subdivided the scale into positive, negative, and non-specific subscales of schizophrenia and, based on the therapeutic response in this trial, together with other relevant findings (Crow 1980), hypothesized the Type I and Type II syndromes of schizophrenia. In our study (Manchanda and Hirsch 1981), improvement in the non-specific symptoms of this scale correlated well with an improvement in neurotic sub-score of the PSE but not with the non-schizophrenia score of the BPRS. In another unpublished study (Manchanda), the BPRS and the MS were used by two raters from different cultural (Indian and German) and different educational backgrounds (psychiatrist and psychologist cum medical student, respectively) without any experience in the use of the two scales. The correlation coefficient of the majority of the items on the MS were higher than those for the BPRS, which in general were low. The higher inter-rater reliability for items on the MS was seen whether the scale was used to rate the patient at one or two points in time (Table 9.1).

The MS, therefore, has the advantage of being a brief scale, valid for rating acute and chronic schizophrenics, and has been shown to be sensitive to change. The instructions for rating are clear cut, making it easy to use, and it can be a reliable substitute for brief scales like the BPRS, providing that one does not need to rate neurotic symptoms or a wide range of pathology.

GLOBAL ASSESSMENT SCALE (GAS)

The GAS (Endicott *et al.* 1976) is a single rating scale for evaluating the overall functioning of a subject on a continuum from psychological sickness to health (score 1–100, respectively). The scale is divided into 10 equal parts (1–10; 11–20; and so on up to 91–100). The severity of the scale is operationally defined for each of 10 grades. It is recommended that the two highest intervals, 81–90 and 91–100 should be used for those individuals who are not only without significant psychopathology but also exhibit traits of a positive mental health e.g. superior functioning, wide range of interests, social effectiveness, warmth, and integrity). The interval from 71 to 80 is for individuals with no or only minimal psychopathology but without the traits referred to above. The authors regard that a vast majority of patients in treatment will be rated between 1 and 70. In making a rating, one selects the lowest interval that describes the overall functioning. The final rating within the scale interval (e.g. 21–30) is done on the basis of the proximity of overall psychopathology to the higher (31–40) or lower (11–20) rating. The time period assessed is generally the week prior to an evaluation. It is recommended that the rating should be based on overall functioning and symptoms and not be influenced by the nature of the disorder.

GAS is by no means specific for use in measuring change in schizophrenia, and can be affectively used in affective and neurotic disorders. Used by itself it does not indicate the patient's symptom profile or symptom-specific response to a treatment, but it provides a rating of the subject's overall functioning which is also relevant in any treatment evaluation. The commonly used global assessments are simple 5- or 7-point (or less) scales, usually self structured with no, or minimal, criteria for rating the anchor points. The GAS, too, is simple, easy to use, takes little time, and, furthermore, provides objective criteria. According to Endicott *et al.* (1976) the intra-class correlation or reliability varies from 0.69 to 0.91 and there was 95 per cent confidence from the ratings to be within 10–11 points from each other. The authors claim it has good validity in measuring overall severity, that it is sensitive to change, and that the scores are a good index of likely rehospitalization. The GAS has been used as a measure of change in several studies recently; it can be recommended as a useful summary statement complimentary to a multidimensional rating scale and should not be used entirely on its own.

CONCLUSIONS

It is difficult to consider one scale as being superior or inferior to another without adequate justification. Arguments for or against a particular scale would vary considerably, depending on the aims of the research and what one wishes to measure. The specific behaviour being rated for measuring change therefore assumes crucial importance. In the PSE the major section refers to psychotic symptomatology. Some initial questions relate to neurotic features. The AMDP system is a detailed documentation system mainly used in German-speaking countries for diagnosis and assessment of psychiatric patients. The MS emphasizes psychotic symptomatology and includes both negative and positive features of schizophrenia. The IMPS, CPRS, and BPRS cover a number of non-specific items and provide a wider measure of symptomatology. BPRS has relatively fewer items but covers some aspects of schizophrenic, depressive, manic, and anxiety symptomatology. Since the present review is restricted to the discussion of schizophrenia, it is perhaps appropriate to compare how these scales fare in recording schizophrenic psychopathology.

In order to use various schedules adequately it is necessary to have the guidelines to convey what each item means as well as how the severity is graded. All schedules define the items but the PSE and MS have the added advantage of detailed description of each item and a standardized set of guidelines for eliciting the phenomena. The gradations on these scales vary. Ratings on the PSE are conservative and every symptom or sign must have moderate or severe intensity to be rated as present. Thus, even when a symptom is present in mild degree, it would get a rating of zero. However, this approach has the advantage of discriminating only moderate or severe symptoms as present. Also, when schizophrenics improve, symptoms diminish in the conviction with which they are held, the degree to which they disturb the patient (reflected in neurotic symptoms), and the number of psychotic symptoms present. Therefore, the problem of evaluating change or severity of symptoms is overcome in the PSE (and to an extent in the AMDP, IMPS, and CPRS) by having ratings for more symptoms e.g. different kinds of delusions and hallucinations. Shorter scales (MS, MSS, and BPRS) group symptoms like delusions and hallucinations under one rating but allow for the observer to subjectively assess severity in terms of either disturbance to the patient or to others but this could be expected to be less reliable because the basis of the ratings is less specific.

Examination of different rating scales would suggest that the PSE should be more specific for schizophrenia and not falsely rate symptoms as present while the IMPS, CPRS, AMDP, BRPS, MSS, MS, and GAS should be more sensitive because they either allow for a low threshold (i.e. 'probably present') or use broad, poorly-defined criteria (including several symptoms under one rating (BPRS), which will increase the likelihood of a rater making a positive rating even when the symptom isn't there. Differences are less marked between scales for rating neurotic symptoms which in any case are more dimensional in character and less specifically defined. Some researchers may feel there is an advantage in less specific scales with vague broad criteria because this allows the rater to rate some of the unspecified aspects of behaviour which more specific scales avoid. The choice of scale should, in the end, be decided on the basis of the aims of the study. Table 9.2 summarizes our comparison of long and short scales for use in clinical studies on schizophrenia.

Much schizophrenia research today involves the need to assess specific effects on core symptoms. If the PSE is used for this purpose, it also provides detailed information on the symptom characteristics of a patient population which can in turn be analysed in a variety of ways. 'Before' and 'after' ratings provide a sensitive measure of change. When the main aim of research is to measure the clinical response of schizophrenic symptoms, the Manchester Scale has advantages over the BPRS and MSS as outlined above. Use of total scores as the only measure of change should always be avoided because this may exclusively reflect changes in neurotic symptoms when the core schizophrenia syndrome persists. Also, one should be on the look-out for any effect of potential antipsychotic agents on both positive and negative symptoms of schizophrenia. There is no additional benefit in using more than one short scale. We recommend rating patients before and after on a long scale, with point interval rating, say weekly, with a short scale, and the possible addition

TABLE 9.2.   *A comparison of scales used for rating schizophrenic symptomatology. The strength of each scale is rated + to + + + +*

	Long scales				Short scales			
	PSE	AMDP	IMPS	CPRS	BPRS	MSS	MS	GAS
Diagnosis	+ + +		+	—	+	—	—	—
Sensitivity	+ +	+ + +	+ + + +	+ + + +	+ + +	+ + +	+ +	+ + + +
Specificity	+ + + +	+ + +	+ + +	+ + +	+ + +	+ + +	+ + +	—
Positive symptoms	+ + +	+ + + +	+ + +	+ + +	+ +	+ + +	+ +	overall functioning
Negative symptoms	+ +	+ + +	+ + +	+ + +	+	+ +	+ +	overall functioning
Neurotic symptoms	+ +	+ + +	+ +	+ + +	+ +	+	+	overall functioning
Glossary and guidelines	+ + + +	+ + +	+ +	+ + +	+	+ + +	+ + + +	+ +
Standardized interview	yes	no	no	no	no	no	yes	no
Scoring	0–2	0–4	0–8*	0–3	0–6 (1–7)	0–3†	0–4	0–100 (units of 10)
Approx. time taken (min)	45–90	45–90	30–45	30–45	15–30	10–15	10–15	<5

* 9 points, 5 points, and 2 points of severity.
† Use of half scores recommended.

of the GAS to get a comprehensive global impression by the clinician most involved in the treatment.

References

APA Test Standards (1974). Standards for educational and psychological tests. American Psychological Association, Washington, DC.

Andersen, K., Malm, U., Perris, C., Rapp, W., and Roman, G. (1974). The inter-rater reliability of scales for rating symptoms and side-effects in schizophrenic patients during a drug trial. *Acta psychiat. scand. Suppl.* **249**, 38–42.

Asberg, M., Montgomery, S. A., Perris, C., Schalling, D., and Sedvall, G. (1978). The comprehensive psychopathological rating scale. *Acta psychiat. scand. Suppl* **271**, 5–27.

Bender, W. (1976). Studie zuer reliabilititaet und differentiellen validitaet der Lorr-scale (IMPS). Unpublished dissertation. Hamburg.

Bente, D., Engelmeirer, N. P., Heinrich, K., Hippius, H., and Schmitt, W. (1961). Zur Documentation medikamentoser Wirkungen bei der psychiatrischen Pharma-kotherapie. *Arzneim. Forsch.* **11**, 886–90.

Cairns, V., Faltermaier, T., Wittchen, H. U., Dilling, H., Mombour, W., and Zerssen, D. V. (1982). Some problems concerning the reliability and structure of the scales in the inpatient multidimensional psychiatric scale (IMPS). *Arch. Psychiat. Nervenkr.* **232**, 395–406.

Cooper, J. E., Kendell, R. E., Gurland, B. J., Sharpe, L., Copeland, J. R. M., and Simon, R. (1972). *Psychiatric diagnosis in New York and London*. Oxford University Press, London.

Cronbach, L. J. (1946). Response set and test validity. *Educ. psychol. Meas.* **6**, 475–94.

Crow, T.J. (1980). Molecular pathology of schizophrenia: more than one disease process? *Br. med. J.* **280**, 66–8.

Dohrenwend, B. S. and Dohrenwend, B. P. (1974). *Stressful life events: their nature and effects*. John Wiley, New York.

Emrich, H. M., Cording, C., Piree, S., Kolling, A., Zerssen, D. V., and Herz, A. (1977). Indication of an antipsychotic action of the opiate antagonist Naloxone. *Pharmakopsychiat.* **10**, 265–70.

Endicott, J., Spitzer, R. L., Fleiss, J. L., and Cohen, J. (1976). The global assessment scale, a procedure for measuring overall severity of psychiatric disturbance. *Arch. gen. Psychiat.* **33**, 766–71.

Foulds, G. A. and Bedford, A. (1975). The hierarchy of classes of personal illness. *Psychol. Med.* **5**, 181–92.

Goldberg, D. P. (1972). *The detection of psychiatric illness by questionnaire*. Oxford University Press, Oxford.

Guy, W. and Ban, T. A. (1982). *The AMDP-system. Manual for the assessment and documentation of psychopathology*. Springer-Verlag, Berlin.

Hamilton, M. (1961). *Lectures on methodology of clinical research*. Churchill Livingstone, Edinburgh.

——(1974). General problems of psychiatric rating scales. In *Psychological measurements in psychopharmacology* (ed. P. Pichot), Vol. 7, 125–8. Karger, Basel.

Hanssen, V., Hagen, A. S., Lehmann, E. H., and Astrup, C. (1974). Simplified symptom registration in psychiatric trials; a statistical approach. *Acta psychiat. scand.* **50**, 492–5.

Helmchen, H. (1974), The AMP system as a method in clinical pharmacopsychiatry.

In *Assessment of pharmacodynamic effects in human pharmacology.* Schattauer Verlag, Stuttgart.

Hirsch, S. R., Gaind, R., Rhode, P. D., Stevens, B. C., and Wing, J. K. (1973). Outpatient maintenance of chronic schizophrenic patients with long acting phenothiazine: double blind placebo trial. *Br. med. J.* **1**, 633–7.

Hollister, L. E., Overall, J. E., Katz, G., Higginbotham, W. E., and Kimbell, I. (1971). Oxypertine and Thioxathene in newly admitted schizophrenic patients. *Clin. Pharmacol. Ther.* **12**, 531–8.

Innes, J. M. (1977). Extremity and 'don't know' sets in questionnaire response. *Br. J. Soc. clin. Psychol.* **16**, 9–12.

Jacobsen, M. (1965). The use of rating scales in clinical research. *Br. J. Psychiat.* **111**, 545–6.

Jacobsson, L., von Knorring, L., Mattsson, B., Perris, C., Edenius, B., Kettner, B., Magnusson, K. E., and Villemoes, P. (1978). The comprehensive psychopathological rating scale—CPRS—in patients with schizophrenic syndromes. Inter-rater reliability and in relation to martens' S-scale. *Acta psychiat. scand. Suppl.* **271**, 39–44.

Johnstone, E. C., Crow, T. J., Frith, C. D., Carney, M. W. P., and Price, J. S. (1978). Mechanism of the antipsychotic effect in the treatment of acute schizophrenia. *Lancet.* **i**, 848–51.

Kasa, M. and Hitomi, K. (1985). Inter-rater reliability of the Comprehensive Psychopathological Rating Scale in Japan. *Acta psychiat. scand.* **71**, 388–91.

Klett, C. J. and McNair, D. M. (1966). Reliability of the acute psychotic types. In *Exploration in typing psychotics* (ed. M. Lorr). Pergamon Press, New York.

Knights, A., Hirsch, S. R., and Platt, S. D. (1980). Measurement of clinical change as a function of brief admission to hospital: a controlled study. *Br. J. Psychiat.* **137**, 170–80.

Krawiecka, M., Goldberg, D., and Vaughan, M. (1977). A standardised psychiatric assessment scale for rating chronic psychotic patients. *Acta psychiat. scand.* **55**, 299–308.

Lorr, M. and Klett, C. J. (1967). *Inpatient Multidimensional Psychiatric Scale (IMPS) revised manual.* Consulting Psychologists Press, Palo Alto, California.

——, ——, (1968). Major psychotic disorders. A cross cultural study. *Arch. gen. psychiat.* **19**, 652–8.

——, ——, Cave, R. (1967). Higher level psychotic syndromes *J. abnorm. Psychol.* **72**, 74–7.

——Jenkins, R. L., and Holsopple, J. Q. (1953). Multi-dimensional scale for rating psychiatric patients. *V. A. Tech. Bull.* **10**, 507.

Manchanda, R. and Hirsch, S. R. (1981). (Des Tyr¹)-γ-endorphin in the treatment of schizophrenia. *Psychol. Med.* **11**, 401–4.

Manchanda, R. and Hirsch, S. R. (1986). Does propranolol have an antipsychotic effect? A placebo controlled study in acute schizophrenia. *Br. J. Psychiat.* **148**, 701–7 (June).

——, ——, Barnes, T. R. E. (1986). Psychopharmacological research in schizophrenia: I. Review of rating scales. (In press).

Mariotto, M. J. and Farrell, A. D. (1979). Comparability of the absolute level of ratings on the Inpatient Multidimensional Psychiatric Scale with a homogenous group of raters. *J. Cons. Clin. Psychol.* **47**, 59–64.

——and Paul, G. L. (1974). A multimethod validation of the inpatient multidimensional rating scale with chronically institutionalised patients. *J. Cons. Clin. Psychol.* **42**, 497–508.

Moller, H., Zerssen, D. V., Werner, Ellert, K., and Wuschner-Stockheim, M. (1982). Outcome in schizophrenic and similar paranoid pyschoses. *Schiz. Bull.* **8 (1)**, 99–108.

Montgomery, S. A. and Asberg, M. (1979). A new depression scale designed to be sensitive to change. *Br. J. Psychiat.* **134**, 382–9.

——Taylor, P., and Montgomery, D. (1978). Development of a schizophrenia scale sensitive to change. *Neuropharmacology* **17**, 1061–3.

Myers, D. H., Campbell, P. L., Cocks, N. M., Flowerdew, J. A., and Muir, A. (1981). A trial of propranolol in chronic schizophrenia. *Br. J. Psychiat.* **139**, 118–21.

Newson-Smith, J. G. B. and Hirsch, S. R. (1979). Psychiatric symptoms in self poisoning patients. *Psychol. Med.* **9**, 493–500.

Overall, J. E. (1974). The brief psychiatric rating scale in psychopharmacology research. In *Psychological measurements in psychopharmacology. Modern problems. Pharmacopsychiat.* (ed. P. Pichot), Vol. 7, pp. 67–78.

——and Gorham, D. R. (1962). The brief psychiatric rating scale. *Psychol. Rep.* **10**, 799–812.

——, ——, (1963). A pattern probability model for classification of psychiatric patients. *Behav. Sci.* **8**, 108–16.

——Hollister, L. E., and Pichot, P. (1967). Major psychiatric disorders. A four dimensional model. *Arch. gen. Psychiat.* **16**, 146–51.

Owens, D. G. C. and Johnstone, E. C. (1980). The disabilities of chronic schizophrenia—their nature and the factors contributing to their development. *Br. J. Psychiat.* **136**, 384–95.

Pichot, P., Overall, J. E., Samuel-Lajeunesse, B., and Dreyfus, J. F. (1969). Structure factorielle de l'échelle abrégée d'appréciation psychiatrique (BPRS). *Rev. Psychol. Appl.* **19**, 217–32.

Rahe, R. H. (1975). Epidemiological studies of life change and illness. *Int. J. Psychiat. Med.* **6**, 133.

Scharfetter, C. (ed.) (1971). *Das AMP system. Manuel zur Documentation psychiatrischer Befunde.* Springer-Verlag, Berlin.

Schmid, W., Bronisch, T., and Zerssen, D. V. (1982). A comparative study of PSE/CATEGO and DiaSika: Two psychiatric computer diagnostic systems. *Br. J. Psychiat.* **141**, 292–5.

Silverman, G. (1979). Placebo effect and changes in response set with retesting; a further source of bias. *Neuropharmacology* **18**, 1019–21.

Sturt, E. (1981). Hierarchical patterns in the distributions of psychiatric symptoms. *Psychol. Med.* **11**, 783–94.

Surtees, P. G. and Kendell, R. E. (1979). The hierarchy model of psychiatric symptomatology: an investigation based on the present state examination ratings. *Br. J. Psychiat.* **135**, 438–43.

Turner, W. J. (1963). *Glossaries for use with the Overall and Gorham Brief Psychiatric Rating Scale and for a Modified Malamud–Sands Rating Scale.* Research Division. Central Islip State Hospital, Central Islip, N.Y.

Wiles, D. H., Kolakowska, T., McNeilly, A. S., Mandelbrote, B. M., and Gelder, M. G. (1976). Clinical significance of plasma chlorpromazine levels, I. Plasma levels of the drug, some of its metabolites and prolactin during treatment. *Psychol. Med.* **6**, 407–15.

Wing, J. K., Birley, J. L. T., Cooper, J. E., Graham, P., and Isaacs, A. (1967). Reliability of a procedure for measuring and classifying 'present psychiatric state'. *Br. J. Psychiat.* **113**, 499–575.

——Cooper, J. E., and Sartorius, N. (1974). *The measurement and classification of psychiatric symptoms.* Cambridge University Press, Cambridge.

——Nixon, J. M., Mann, S. A., and Leff, J. P (1977). Reliability of the PSE (ninth edition) used in a population study. *Psychol. Med.* **7**, 505–16.

WHO (1973). *The international pilot study of schizophrenia.* WHO, Geneva.

Yorkston, N. J., Zaki, S. A., Malik, M. K. U., Morrison, R. C., and Havard, C. W. H. (1974). Propranolol in the control of schizophrenic symptoms. *Br. med. J.* **4**, 633–5.

Zapf, W. (Ed.) (1974). *Working conference on 'social indicators'* Part 2, *Report and Discussions*. Campus, Mannheim.

Zerssen, D. V. and Cording, C. (1978). The measurement of change in endogenous affective disorders. *Arch. Psychiat. Nervenkr.* **266**, 95–112.

10

Evaluating social functioning. A critical review of scales and their underlying concepts

STEPHEN PLATT

INTRODUCTION

One consequence of the major shift from custodial care to community care over the last quarter century has been a growing awareness that new methods are required to evaluate the treatments that are provided for schizophrenia and other psychiatric illness. Prior to the 1960s, the impact of a new drug regime was assessed almost exclusively in terms of its ability to relieve or remove specific symptoms; length of hospital stay and incidence of rehospitalization were also used as measures of treatment effectiveness, especially in North America. However, the advent of new therapeutic methods which sought to maintain the patient's links with the 'real world' outside the hospital necessitated an examination of factors which might influence community tenure and therefore treatment success. As a result, social psychiatrists have extended their interest in the patient by focusing upon functioning or performance in social and instrumental roles in addition to a manifestation of psychiatric symptoms, and they have gone beyond the patient to consider the indirect impact (or burden) of treatment upon the patient's family, household, and significant others. This chapter will review a number of major scales that have been or are currently being used to measure social functioning in psychiatric patients. It also presents a set of criteria which have proved useful in evaluating the potential of these various research instruments.

WHY MEASURE SOCIAL FUNCTIONING?

The distinction between behavioural correlates of psychiatric symptomatology (e.g. 'over-activity', 'slowness', 'depression'), on the one hand, and disturbances in the performance of social roles, on the other, is now widely accepted. Few researchers would disagree with Remington and Tyrer's (1979; p. 151) statement that 'psychological disturbance is multidimensional and inadequately characterized by sole reference to symptoms'. Consequently, independent assessments of both symptoms and social functioning are increasingly found in evaluations of treatment effectiveness. This tendency is likely to become more widespread as the debate about the relationship between symptoms, social functioning, and treatment outcome in different psychiatric populations becomes more heated. (For recent differing views see, e.g. Weissman and Paykel 1974; Tanner *et al.* 1975; Paykel *et al.* 1978; Platt *et al.* 1981; Dohrenwend *et al.* 1981; Hurry and Sturt 1981; Dohrenwend and Dohrenwend 1974; Brown *et al.* 1975; Casey *et al.* 1985; Winoker *et al.* 1969; Dohrenwend *et al.* 1983).

WHAT IS MEANT BY SOCIAL FUNCTIONING?

Social functioning here refers to the performance of social roles that would normally be expected of an individual in his or her habitual social environment. Each member of society is an incumbent of numerous positions or statuses (e.g. mother, worker, female, white, Protestant) and each position involves an array of associated roles. 'Role describes the rights and obligations which are inherent in the occupancy of a social position, the norms or moral rules which define the behaviour you are entitled to receive from your role-partners and that you should engage in with them.' (Bradbury *et al.* 1972; p. 42). Role performance, i.e. how a person actually conducts himself in a role, may not be identical with the standards applied to someone in his position. A man may fail to act towards his family (marital role, parental role) and towards 'society' (economic role) in accordance with generally held norms and expectations: he may desert his children or batter his wife or refuse to pay his taxes to the state. Unfortunately, the evaluation of role performance is rarely straightforward, since role expectations have been shown to be highly variable. Gross and colleagues (1958) showed that the expectations of different audiences or reference groups concerning the school superintendent's role are heterogeneous and often conflicting. Their conclusion, that the degree of consensus about a given role is itself a variable, is echoed in a number of other studies (e.g. Biddle and Thomas 1966; Bott 1957). It is therefore unhelpful to assume the existence of a uniform set of cultural expectations associated with a position. (This crucial point will be considered later because this assumption underpins a number of 'social adjustment' rating scales.)

Most psychiatric rating scales are not so much interested in social functioning or social performance *per se*, i.e. behaviour which is congruent with norms and expectations, as in its converse, i.e. the extent of disturbance in social functioning, or the gap between expectations and performance. However, there is little consensus in the literature on nomenclature. Weissman *et al.* (1981) viewed social role performance as only one aspect of social functioning, the other aspects being social supports, social attachments, social competence, and social status. The general rubric they used to classify scales which measure non-symptomatological aspects of the patient's behaviour is 'social adjustment'. Thus, in their reviews of social adjustment schedules, we can find reference to adjustment, adaptation, and social behaviour, and, conversely, to maladjustment, disability, ineffectiveness, and impairment. The concept of social functioning advocated here is narrower than Weissman's concept of social adjustment. A preliminary classification of criteria for evaluating scales of social functioning, i.e. scales which attempt to measure (disturbance in) social role performance, is developed in the next section. Following this, we will review a number of social functioning scales which are in common use at the present time and especially relevant in the evaluation of treatment for schizophrenia.

CRITERIA FOR EVALUATING SOCIAL FUNCTIONING SCALES

Table 10.1 sets out the major criteria which should be taken into account when attempting to decide which scale (if any) is most appropriate to the investigator's current requirements. The following comments are designed to enlarge upon the more important issues covered in the table.

Informant

In most scales, information about the patient's social functioning is derived almost exclusively from the patient or from the patient's significant others. However, some scales, for example the Psychiatric Evaluation Form (Endicott and Spitzer 1972) and the WHO Disability Assessment Schedule (Jablensky *et al.* 1980), allow or recommend the use of multiple sources of information to complete the ratings. Weissman (1975) argued that this procedure is not to be encouraged: comparisons between patients are difficult to make when non-uniform sources of information are used. Whether the researcher prefers to choose the patient or significant others to obtain information will depend upon a number of factors, including the nature of the patient population under study, the aims of the investigation, and the importance of the generalizability of the findings. While the patient is the most direct and available source of information in out-patient studies, psychotic and delusional in-patients may be unsatisfactory informants since they tend to underreport their disabilities (Prusoff *et al.* 1972; Stevens 1972); they are also liable to fail to complete the interview and show limited grasp of the purpose of the questioning (Spitzer and Endicott 1973). The use of a significant other as informant has considerable advantages when the schizophrenic patient is in hospital or living in the community, but considerably disturbed. Relatives' reports have been found to be both reliable and valid in a number of studies (e.g. Ellsworth *et al.* 1968; Katz and Lyerly 1963; Remington and Tyrer 1979). However, there are also disadvantages with this method. The patient must be able and willing to provide the name of a person who in turn is able and willing to give the relevant information. To the extent that these conditions are not fulfilled, a major research problem ensues: information will only be collected about a very special subgroup of patients which may differ in unknown ways from the total population of such patients (Clausen 1972). Furthermore, a number of aspects of the patient–informant relationship must be evaluated and held reasonably constant in view of their possible association with all the major dependent variables measures in these

TABLE 10.1.   *Criteria for evaluating social functioning scales*

1. *Recognition of scale to which these criteria may apply*
    1.1.   These criteria apply to any scale which measures (disturbances in) the performance of social roles that are expected of an individual in his usual interpersonal environment.
    1.2.   These criteria do not apply to scales whose exclusive or major concern is a clinical assessment of mental state.
    1.3.   Scales to which these criteria are applicable may employ a variety of different terms in place of 'functioning'. These include 'adjustment', 'competence', 'performance', 'attainment', and 'adaptation', and, conversely, 'maladjustment', 'impairment', 'disability', and 'ineffectiveness'.
    1.4   Not all scales which are reviewed by Weissman and colleagues (Weissman 1975; Weissman *et al*. 1981; Weissman and Sholomskas, in press) under the rubric 'social adjustment' are considered to measure 'social functioning' as defined here. In particular, scales measuring 'social supports' are excluded.

2. *Informant*
    2.1.   Patient.
    2.2.   Significant other(s).
        2.2.1.   More than one informant?
        2.2.2.   Relationship to patient (kin, friend, etc.).
        2.2.3.   Frequency of contact with patient.
        2.2.4.   In same household as patient?
        2.2.5.   Quality of interpersonal relationship with patient.
        2.2.6.   Permission to interview granted by patient?
    2.3.   Records.
    2.4.   Mixed sources possible/recommended.

3. *Method*
    3.1.   Self-report.
    3.2.   Mail questionnaire.
    3.3.   Telephone interview.
    3.4.   In-person interview.
        3.4.1.   Non-standardized.
        3.4.2.   Standardized.
            3.4.2.1.   Structured (schedule);
            3.4.2.2.   Semi-structured;
            3.4.2.3.   Unstructured (non-schedule).

4. *Content*
    4.1.   Role areas.
        4.1.1.   Comprehensiveness of coverage.
            4.1.1.1.   Employment;
            4.1.1.2.   Economic;
            4.1.1.3.   Study (education);
            4.1.1.4.   Marital;
            4.1.1.5.   Parental;
            4.1.1.6.   Extended family;
            4.1.1.7.   Community;
            4.1.1.8.   Household;

TABLE 10.1.   *Continued*

                  4.1.1.9.   Social;
                  4.1.1.10. Leisure/recreation;
                  4.1.1.11. Sexual;
                  4.1.1.12. Decision-making;
                  4.1.1.13. Therapeutic;
                  4.1.1.14. Behaviour in emergency/crisis;
                  4.1.1.15. (Other).
          4.1.2.   Derivation of content of roles.
                  4.1.2.1.   Based on other schedules;
                  4.1.2.2.   Based on 'commonsense';
                  4.1.2.3.   Based on piloting in appropriate community.
          4.1.3.   Applicability of roles.
                  4.1.3.1.   By age;
                  4.1.3.2.   By sex;
                  4.1.3.3.   By marital status;
                  4.1.3.4.   By social class;
                  4.1.3.5.   By race;
                  4.1.3.6.   (By other structural variable).

4.2.   Type of norms used to assess (disturbance in) social functioning.
         4.2.1.   Norms based on concept of 'adjustment'.
                  4.2.1.1.   Extent to which behaviour conforms to (deviates from) unattainable ideal;
                  4.2.1.2.   Extent to which behaviour conforms to (deviates from) attainable ideal;
                  4.2.1.3.   Extent to which behaviour conforms to (deviates from) statistical average.
         4.2.2.   Norms based on concept of 'performance'.
                  4.2.2.1.   Extent to which behaviour conforms to (deviates from) cultural expectations of average/normal functioning of a person of same age, sex, background, etc.;
                  4.2.2.2.   Extent to which the patient's current behaviour conforms to (deviates from) own previous/best-ever/pre-illness performance;
                  4.2.2.3.   Extent to which the patient has difficulty in fulfilling the major average components of the role.

4.3.   Dimensions of functioning.
         4.3.1.   Performance;
         4.3.2.   Affect/distress/feeling;
         4.3.3.   Interpersonal friction;
         4.3.4.   Environmental stress;
         4.3.5.   Subjective burden (others);
         4.3.6.   Objective burden (others);
         4.3.7.   Onset of change and/or appearance of 4.3.1–4.3.6.

4.4.   Items.
         4.4.1.   Number of items;
         4.4.2.   Equivalence of items;
         4.4.3.   Standardization/definition of items.

4.5.   Ratings.
         4.5.1.   Number of rating steps;

268   *The psychopharmacology and treatment of schizophrenia*

TABLE 10.1.   *Continued*

        4.5.2.   Definition of ratings;
        4.5.3.   Equivalence of ratings across items.
   4.6   Time period assessed.

5. *Psychometric properties*
   5.1   Validity.
        5.1.1.   Construct;
        5.1.2.   Concurrent;
        5.1.3.   Discriminative.
   5.2.   Reliability.
        5.2.1.   Test–retest;
        5.2.2.   Interrater;
        5.2.3.   Internal consistency.
   5.3.   Sensitivity (to change).
   5.4.   Scoring system.

6. *Analysis*
   6.1.   Rating guide.
   6.2.   Scoring sheets (precoded forms).
   6.3.   Computer program available.
   6.4.   Rules for derivation of summary scores.
        6.4.1.   Overall score for social functioning;
        6.4.2.   Score(s) per role area(s);
        6.4.3.   Score(s) per dimension(s).

7. *Use of scale*
   7.1.   Time taken for completion.
   7.2.   Availability of training manual.
   7.3.   Need for training.
        7.3.1.   Level of training required.
   7.4.   Acceptance of scale by scientific peers.
   7.5.   Successful use of scale in previous empirical studies.
   7.6.   Restrictions on applicability of scale in social psychiatric research.
   7.7.   Flexibility/adaptability of scale to subgroups other than those to whom
       it has been administered.

---

scales (see Table 10.1, Sections 2.2.1–2.2.6). Thus, informants who live in the same household as the patient and meet the patient every day have a greater potential for reporting lower social functioning in the patient than do informants who do not live with the patient and meet him/her regularly. Randomized controlled trials which rely on a significant other as informant should ensure that all factors of the patient–informant relationship are in fact comparably distributed in the groups under investigation.

Method

Mail questionnaires and telephone interviews are not to be recommended as preferred methods of obtaining information; they tend to produce a poor response rate, and data of dubious reliability and validity. The self-report inventory is an economic method of data collection with no threat to validity from interviewer bias. However, it is not appropriate for illiterate informants, nor for psychotic patients who are likely to be too disturbed to understand the questions or to report accurately on their social functioning. Although a costly method, the standardized personal interview usually obtains the most complete and valid information, since the interviewer can probe for more details and check on inconsistencies in responses. The standardized interview can be highly structured with a predetermined wording and sequence of questions, and highly defined, individual rating scales; or unstructured, with global items and/or only general guides to the wording and sequence of questions; or semi-structured, with defined items, fixed leading questions, and precoded ratings, but allowing the interviewer freedom to make additional probes in order to make the final rating. Unless precluded by financial considerations, the semi-structured in-person interview is the most highly recommended method for gathering data on the patient's social functioning.

Content (see Platt 1981)

Dohrenwend *et al.* (1981) and Gurland *et al.* (1972*b*), among others, have provided evidence to show that social functioning should not be viewed as a unidimensional concept: from their research on both community and patient populations they conclude that individual levels of social functioning are not consistent between different areas of life, such as work and family. Thus, an instrument with a comprehensive coverage of role areas is generally to be preferred to one which narrowly focuses upon only a few roles. However, the number, type, and content of roles to be found in any particular institution cannot be decided *a priori*. If we confine our discussion to the institution of the family, we need to know which roles are considered to be appropriate and relevant to family members. Most research instruments which measure 'social functioning' are in agreement that occupational, community, marital, and parental roles are expected of the subject (see Weissman 1975). However, no evidence is presented to support the emphasis on these, rather than other, aspects of family life; Clare and Cairns (1978; p. 570) note that these role areas were established by Barrabee *et al.* (1955) over 20 years ago and have been closely followed ever since. Nye (1974), on the other hand, puts forward the thesis that the family is an institution which has developed new roles and assumed new sets of responsibilities in three areas: sexual relationship, recreation, and therapeutic services. Correspondingly, housekeeping and kinship roles are declining or disappearing. Thus it becomes vital to establish by empirical research which roles are relevant to the institution and sub-culture under investigation, carefully avoiding *a priori* assumptions about which roles do or do not exist.

Even where the general outlines of the role are known, there are still difficulties concerning its more detailed content. For instance there is little doubt that at the start of a typical Western marriage both spouses assume the existence of a sexual component to the relationship. However, the nature of that (sub-) role is nowhere clearly specified. Aspects that have been studied include frequency of sexual intercourse, feelings toward the sexual partner, consideration for the partner's needs, and strength of interest in sex. Again, the content of the role may vary systematically in accordance with local conditions and subcultural settings; empirical research is therefore necessary so that the role can be defined appropriately.

The applicability of roles to position incumbents also requires consideration. Just as each position includes a number of roles, so the same role may be found in more than one position (Bates 1956). The 'breadwinner' role has long been considered the duty of the husband/father alone, but increasingly the role is becoming available to the wife/mother in the family unit. At least partial fulfilment of the child care and child socialization roles, once the exclusive responsibility of the mother, can now be expected of the father. It is therefore unsafe to assume that incumbency of a particular position (e.g. husband) automatically entails the performance of certain roles and the non-performance of others. Instead, information should be gathered concerning the allocation of roles to position incumbents.

The norms explicitly or implicitly used to assess the extent of disturbance in social functioning can be divided into two types. By far the most common are those based on the concept of adjustment, operationally defined as the extent to which performance matches an attainable or unattainable ideal, or (more rarely) a statistical average. The reliance on ideal norms is problematic for two main reasons. First, contrary to the impression given by adjustment theorists, there is little consensual agreement about the characteristics of 'ideal social functioning'. Dependent upon actual circumstances, virtually any subjective personal reaction might be deemed adjusted or appropriate (or, conversely, maladjusted or inappropriate) by some professional expert. Second, by invoking this type of norm, researchers are abandoning any attempt to apply a sociological approach to the measurement of social functioning. This is, in fact, particularly surprising, since the *formal* definition of (mal)adjustment is usually couched in the language of role analysis. Thus, Weissman and Paykel (1974) defined social adjustment as 'the individual's ability to function in roles', while for Gurland *et al.* (1972*a*) maladjustment is 'ineffective performance in the roles and task [*sic*] for which an individual has been socialized'. However, empirical investigation into the actual expectations of the subject's reference groups or the content of the role is conspicuously absent. One final major drawback with scales using a norm of adjustment is that they confound a description of what the individual does (role performance) with an evaluation of such behaviour in terms of its approximation to an ideal. This mixture of evaluation and description is most unhelpful, given the variability in subjective value-judgements concerning what is, or is not, ideal.

Recognizing the difficulties associated with the use of the norm of adjustment, a number of researchers in the field have moved in recent years towards the adoption of a more value-free approach to the measurement of social functioning. Their major concern is to describe what the person does or does not do when performing a certain role. The norm of full or complete performance is not based on a conception of ideal or average behaviour, but upon empirically derived expectations and prescriptions of role-appropriate behaviour. That is to say, the principal components of the role are identified through empirical research with appropriate reference groups, and an assessment is made of the extent to which the individual's actual performance deviates from the prescribed or expected performance. A major difficulty with this procedure is that cultural expectations of average/normal functioning in a role can vary according to the social characteristics of the individual. Thus, criteria of 'full performance' in the household role might well differ between a woman who occupies the positions 'married', 'middle-class', 'parent of young children' and a man who occupies the positions 'married', 'working class', 'parent of older children'. (The *applicability* of the household role to the man is a separate issue. While not in doubt today, this has been a hotly contested issue in the past, and, of course, a non-issue in, say, Victorian Britain.)

Two solutions have been proposed to avoid the necessity of defining criteria of 'full performance' to suit every possible configuration of positions that an individual might occupy. The first consists in avoiding closely defined items and adopting instead a system of global ratings based on the extent to which the individual's performance falls short of what is expected of him/her in his/her sociocultural context. Thus the WHO's Disability Assessment Schedule (Jablensky *et al*. 1980) rates social role performance on a five-point scale, ranging from no dysfunction, (e.g. 'patient participates in household activities about as much as is expected for his/her age, sex, position in household and sociocultural context') to maximum dysfunction (for example, 'patient totally excludes himself/herself . . . from participation in any common household activities'). This kind of global rating is useful for cross-cultural comparisons but almost certainly presents formidable interrater reliability problems. The other drawback is that the rater may tend to assume more homogeneity within his own culture concerning role prescriptions and role expectations than does in fact exist.

The second solution has been to itemize the major average expectations of the role and assess the extent to which the subject's performance has conformed to or deviated from those expectations. One variant of this solution (Remington and Tyrer 1979) adopted the use of the global analogue line for rating 'problems' in performing roles; the line is marked 'no difficulties' at one extreme and 'severe difficulties' at the other. Another variant (Platt *et al*. 1980) uses a conventional three-point categorical scale, with each point clearly defined and corresponding to 'no performance', 'partial performance', and 'full performance'. Either of these methods ensures more reliable ratings, but again can be used mistakenly if the subjects under investigation are culturally heterogeneous or belong to the same subculture which is, however, markedly deviant in its role prescriptions from the 'average' for the parental culture. A further problem is that assessments of social functioning are often undertaken in societies characterized by rapid social change and unstable role norms and prescriptions. Consequently, these scales run a considerable risk of becoming obsolescent. Scales embodying both solutions to the problem of defining what is 'full performance' have included an attempt to compare the subject's present functioning with his/her level of functioning at some determined point of time in the past (WHO Disability Assessment Schedule and the Social Behaviour Assessment Schedule). A purely idiographic approach is not recommended, since comparisons across individuals or groups are thereby made extremely difficult. However, the incorporation of historical information about the subject enables an assessment of current functioning on two axes: deviation from the average/normal/expected performance in the sociocultural context, and deviation from own former self.

In addition to possible variation in performance between role *areas*, there may also be variation between role *dimensions* (Table 10.1, Sections 4.3.1–4.3.7). There is little consensus among researchers about which dimensions should be assessed, with the exception of the patient's performance (instrumental role) and, in self-report instruments, the patient's feelings and satisfactions (affective role). Thus, the Social Behaviour Assessment Schedule (Platt *et al.* 1980) includes scales on burden and change, but not on interpersonal friction. The Structured and Scale Interview to Assess Maladjustment (Gurland *et al.* 1972a, b) measures friction and environmental stress, while the Social Adjustment Scale (Weissman and Paykel 1974) omits consideration of environmental stress. An instrument which measures many of these distinct components (dimensions) is likely to be more precise or of more practical use in assessing different treatment effects than an unidimensional scale (Weissman 1975).

Table 10.1 lists three other aspects of scale contents which merit consideration: the number, equivalence, and definition of items; the number of rating steps, the definition of ratings, and the equivalence of ratings across items; and the time period assessed. When information is sought about the patient's functioning, the period of time under assessment should be explicitly (and, if necessary, repeatedly) stated. If precise information is required, the previous month is probably the longest period that can readily be recalled by the informant (whether subject or significant other). Less than one month may be too short a time to provide adequate examples of the subject's behaviour.

Psychometric properties

It is widely recognized that a new scale or instrument should possess demonstrated reliability, validity, sensitivity to change, and a well-developed, quantitative scoring system (Weissman 1975). However, it is less commonly acknowledged that validity and, especially, reliability are not instrinsic once-and-for-all attributes of any particular scale; they are highly context-dependent, and should always be reestablished when the characteristics of the population under investigation differ from those of the population originally used to test the scale's psychometric properties. In addition, adequate interrater reliability must be confirmed in each new study as a matter of course; this is a particularly important procedure where global rating scales are employed. The validation of a scale by comparing ratings obtained from interviews with a patient and a significant other (e.g. Gurland *et al.* 1972*b*; Spitzer *et al.* 1970) is not highly recommended because their reports may not be truly independent (Platt 1980).

Analysis

A rating scale should be structured in such a way that it facilitates the analysis of data as well as its collection. To that end, it is advisable to provide a detailed rating guide (giving precise instructions about the classification of data) and precoded scoring sheets (which simplify the transfer of data via punched cards or directly to the computer). The availability of a computer program in a universal language, such as for example, FORTRAN, which specifies basic analyses (e.g. frequencies, cross-tabulations) adds to the scale's attractiveness and practical usefulness. Since most users require some overall indication of level of social functioning by role areas, rules about the construction of summary scores are highly desirable. However, the use of factor scores to summarize data on social functioning is problematic, since factors derived from one study may not be obtained/replicated in a different population; the amount of variance left unexplained may be unacceptably large (e.g. the factor analysis of the SSIAM only accounts for 40 per cent of the total variance) (Gurland *et al.* 1972*b*); and too many items may be omitted altogether (24 out of 45 items are not included in the modified factors of the Structured and Scaled Interview to Assess Maladjustment (SSIAM).

Use of scale

Table 10.1 lists a number of criteria related to a scale's use, including features which contribute towards ease of administration (e.g. availability of training manual, reasonable time for completion, a developed training programme, and instructional material) and evidence that it has acquired some degree of acceptance in the field (because of its proven 'track record' and/or its generalizability, flexibility, and adaptability).

SOME CURRENT SCALES FOR RATING SOCIAL FUNCTIONING

A brief description and critique of seven rating scales is presented below. These scales, which are currently available and either used or of potential use in psychiatric research, can be divided into two types: those based on the concept of 'adjustment' (the Katz Adjustment Scale (KAS), the Structured and Scaled Interview to Assess Maladjustment (SSIAM), the Social Adjustment Scale (SAS), and the Standardized Interview to Assess Social Maladjustment (SIASM)); and those based on the concept of 'performance' (the Social Performance Schedule (SPS), the Social Functioning Schedule (SFS), and the Social Behaviour Assessment Schedule (SBAS)). For a more extended review of the SSIAM and the SAS, the interested reader should consult Platt (1981).

Katz Adjustment Scale

The Katz Adjustment Scale (Katz and Lyerly 1963) is a self-report inventory which exists in two forms: one is used by the patient (S scales), the other by a close relative (R scales). The R scales consist of 205 items in five sections: 127 items rating symptoms and social behaviour on a four-point global scale; 16 items rating the performance of 'socially-expected activities' on a three-point global scale; 23 items rating level of free-time activities on a three-point global scale; and the same items rated from the point of view of the relative's satisfaction with performance. The S scales are identical to the R scales (although adapted for patient self-ratings) with the exception of the replacement of the inventory of symptoms and social behaviour by a modified version of the Johns Hopkins Symptom Distress Checklist (55 items rated on a four-point global scale). The instrument has been widely used in a variety of settings, with heterogeneous diagnostic and non-patient populations (see the bibliography in Weissman and Sholomkas, 1982). Data are available on reliability, validity (Katz and Lyerly 1963), and norms (Hogarty and Katz 1971).

Katz's scale is unique in its attempts to measure the informant's level of expectations for socially expected activities carried out by the patient. As such, it is recommended for use by Weissman *et al*. (1978) in conjunction with the SAS (q.v.). However, on reading the advice given to informants in the instruction booklet, it would appear that what Katz is seeking to measure is the informant's expectations of the patient *in the role of sick* (i.e. recently hospitalized) *person* (see Katz and Lyerly 1963). How the instructions are actually interpreted by the informant is another matter. Undoubtedly, the measure is highly ambiguous. A negative rating on an item (e.g. relative did not expect the patient to help with household chores) can have two meanings. On the one hand, it can be used by the informant to signify that he did not consider the activity to be appropriate to the patient's position (his illness being irrelevant in the context). On the other hand, it could mean that the informant grants the patient temporary exemption from the obligation to carry out the activity because he is regarded as ill (whereas normally he would be expected to carry out the activity). Given that the list of 'socially expected activities' includes those which are likely to be expected of the 'healthy' patient and those which are not, this ambiguity renders invalid the conceptualization of the differences between the Performance and Expectation scales as a measure of 'level of satisfaction with performance' (Katz and

Lyerly 1963). The non-performance of an activity which is expected of the patient in both 'health' and 'sickness' is likely to generate higher levels of dissatisfaction than the non-performance of an activity which is expected in 'health' but not in 'sickness'. The non-performance of an activity which is *not* expected of the patient, even when healthy, is likely to generate no dissatisfaction at all. In order to clear up the outstanding ambiguities of these scales, Katz needs to undertake empirical research in order to establish: which activities are expected of the position incumbent in his habitual social milieu; how these expectations vary according to the change in the patient's status (from 'healthy' to 'sick'); and in what way the informant's satisfaction with the patient's level of performance is linked to these different sets of expectations.

Structured and scaled interview to assess maladjustment

This scale (Gurland *et al.* 1974) consists of 60 items, of which 45 assess deviant behaviour, subjective distress, and friction with others in five roles: work, social, family, marital, and sex. The remaining 15 items include an interviewer assessment of the environmental conditions facing the patient, general prognostic measures, and aspects of positive mental health. Information is obtained from the patient by means of a structured interview and the items are rated on an 11-point scale with anchoring definitions on five of the 11 points. Reliability, validity, scoring, and results of factor analysis are discussed in Gurland *et al.* (1972*a*, *b*). The scale was devised as an outcome measure for psychotherapy, and has been used in a number of studies with psychoneurotic and personality disordered out-patients (Candy *et al.* 1972; Hoehn-Saric *et al.* 1972; Sloane *et al.* 1975).

The author has made a fairly detailed critique of the SSIAM elsewhere (Platt 1981). Briefly, it was noted that there is no correspondence between the theoretical and operational definitions of maladjustment put forward by the authors; that the actual evaluation of role performance fails to take account of the expectations of the subject's role set and relies instead upon highly subjective and value-laden judgements about what constitutes 'reasonable adjustment'; and that scanty attention is paid to the social and cultural context in which the subject functions.

Social adjustment schedule

This instrument exists in two versions, one a semi-structured interview with the patient taking 45 to 60 minutes and conducted by a trained interviewer (Weissman and Paykel 1974; Paykel *et al.* 1971), the other (called SAS–SR) a self-report version (Weissman and Bothwell 1976; Weissman *et al.* 1978) which is completed in 15–20 minutes. (The SAS–SR can also be used where the family and significant other are available as informants.) The SAS, which is based largely on the SSIAM, covers five major areas of functioning: (1) work (as worker, housewife, or student); (2) social and leisure activities; (3)

relationships with extended family; (4) marital role; and (5) parental role. In addition, there are global evaluations of each of the areas and a rating of economic inadequacies. Questions in each of the role areas fall into four major categories: (1) the patient's performance at expected tasks; (2) the amount of friction the patient has with others; (3) finer aspects of inter-personal relations; and (4) the patient's feelings and satisfactions. Each item is rated on a five-point scale (except globals, which are rated on a seven-point scale). The SAS-SR is comparable to the SAS interview schedule, although it contains fewer items. Data on reliability, validity, sensitivity, scoring, and results of factor analysis are available for both instruments (see bibliography in Weissman and Sholomskas, 1982). The SAS was designed for a main-tenance trial of antidepressants and psychotherapy in out-patient women. It has been used with non-psychiatric community populations and with para-suicides, alcoholics, methadone-maintained patients, and schizophrenics. The SAS–SR has also been administered to general and psychiatric popula-tions (Weissman and Sholomskas, 1982).

For a critique of this instrument, readers are referred to Platt (1981), where the following problems are highlighted. First, Weissman and Paykel's theoretical and operational definitions of adjustment are not equivalent, so that in the actual ratings the subject's behaviour is not related to the expecta-tions of relevant audiences. Having introduced three different usages of the term 'norm' (an ideal, a statistical average, a community expectation), the authors proceed to ignore the most sociologically relevant definition (i.e. norm as expectation). Second, the derivation of the ideal norm (to which each scale is anchored) is nowhere discussed. However, the assumptions which underpin these norms are reasonably clear. For Weissman and Paykel the ideal world is characterized by harmony, happiness, and consensus, and inhabited by men and women who are consistently interested, active, friendly, adequate, guilt-free, non-distressed, and so on. What is conspicu-ous by its absence in this instrument is the investigation of behaviour and affect in relation to the patient's immediate environment. Instead, the instru-ment measures the fit between certain behaviours and an idealized concep-tion of adjustment or normality which is not explicitly related to the norms or expectations of the patient's milieu.

Standardized interview to assess social maladjustment

This is a semi-structured interview schedule whose aim is 'to provide the material for an evaluation or measurement of the social adjustment of the person interviewed' (Clare and Cairns 1976). The schedule examines the subject's life along three independent dimensions: 'material conditions' (what the subject *has*), 'social management' (what the subject *does* with his life), and 'satisfaction' (what the subject *feels* about his situation). Aspects of social adjustment covered by the instrument are housing, occupation, and 'social role' (i.e. as housewife, retired person, etc.), finance, leisure activities, social interaction, and domestic and family life. Ratings of all but one of the

41 items are made using a four-point scale, ranging from 0, which indicates satisfactory adjustment, to 3, which indicates poor adjustment including severe social difficulties. The terminology used to describe each point on the scale varies according to whether the rating is one of material conditions, management, or satisfaction. The authors are aware that, while it is possible to establish reasonably objective criteria for measuring material conditions, the assessment of the individual's functioning is more problematic, due to the absence of universal, objective norms of what constitutes 'adequate' or 'satisfactory' functioning. (The satisfaction category is oriented entirely towards a faithful reproduction of the patient's subjective perception of his circumstances and functioning.) They note the difficulty of defining adequate functioning in such a way that every individual has the chance of attaining it, regardless of social class, age, sex, etc. 'Indeed particular efforts were made to avoid writing middle-class norms into the rating definitions. To this end, ratings were defined with specific alternatives relating to different social class, occupational or age groups' (Clare and Cairns 1978). In addition, the authors claimed to have set a low threshold for a rating of adjustment, which 'encompasses the merely adequate' and 'does not imply the attainment of an impossibly elevated quality of life beyond the reach of any particular group'. Data on reliability and scoring, in addition to some evidence of validity, were given in Clare and Cairns (1978). The scale has been used in a number of studies of psychosocial morbidity in the community and in general practice (e.g. Cooper *et al.* 1970, 1975; Sylph *et al.* 1969; Kedward and Sylph 1974; Huxley and Goldberg 1975). A self-report version, the Social Problem Questionnaire, is also available (Corney *et al.* 1982).

A major criticism of the scale is that, in spite of their attempt to avoid moralistic judgements, Clare and Cairns are apparently no less concerned with the absence of change and conflict than the authors of the SSIAM and the SAS. Thus, even if the subject is unable to perform any aspect of the housekeeping role, she is still given a rating of '0' (satisfactory) if 'satisfactory and alternative arrangements have been made that are not *disruptive*, for example 'au pair', home help, husband taking over shopping for phobic housewife' (Clare and Cairns 1976, p 14; emphasis added). Again, any involuntary loss of job is given a rating of maladjustment, even where the event is clearly 'independent' of the subject's own behaviour. However, it is necessary to ask whether stability, harmony, and consensus are necessarily 'satisfactory' states and, if so, to whom. Change and conflict may sometimes be necessary for the survival of both the individual and his/her society.

Social performance schedule

The SPS (see Hurry and Sturt 1981 for a description of the most recent, third edition) is a semi-structured interview schedule covering eight areas of social role functioning: household management, employment, management of money, child care, intimate relationship with spouse or close friend, other relationship, social presentation of self, and coping with emergencies. Each section has two cut-off points: one if no significant contribution would be ordinarily be expected and the other if preliminary questioning reveals that no serious problem occurred during the time-period covered (a month before the interview). Examples of 'serious problems' are given for all sections. Each area of performance can be rated, if applicable, on a four-point global scale ('fair-to-good performance', occasional serious problem, serious problem most of the time, virtually no contribution). Questions are also asked systematically about the onset and course of difficulties in performing the role, and the informant's feelings about, and postulated cause of, the problem. Although the scale is designed for use in an interview with the subject, it could be adapted to obtain ratings from an informant. The reliability of the third edition is reported to be 'satisfactory' (Hurry and Sturt 1981), but the scale's sensitivity and validity are not formally discussed. However, partial validity has been established by findings of markedly different problem prevalence in all categories of performance between a community and an out-patient series. In addition, a substantial correlation between the SPS score and a quantitative measure of symptomatology (PSE score) for both community and patient populations was found (Hurry and Sturt 1981).

The SPS was one of the first schedules to abandon both the concept of adjustment and the use of ideal norms of behaviour to anchor rating scales. Instead, it measures the extent of performance in a role, with the norm of 'fair-to-good performance' defined in terms of the absence of 'serious problems.' The underlying assumption here is that there is a reasonable level of societal consensus concerning what constitutes a serious problem in the performance of a role. Even if this is a reasonable assumption, which it may not be, the actual behaviours which are identified as examples of 'serious problems' may differ between cultures and over time. It is therefore necessary to ensure that the definition of serious problems given in the schedule reflects the actual normative beliefs of the target population. It is incumbent upon future users of the SPS to ensure that the cut-off point between problems and non-problems has some empirical foundation in the population under study. Likewise, the first cut-off point (no significant contribution expected) will have to be set differently depending on the social context. This sensitivity to the fact that the appropriateness of a role is an empirical issue which cannot be decided *a priori*, is another major asset of the SPS. Moreover, it is made quite clear that the expected contribution relates to the individual in his 'normal' roles and not in the role of 'sick person' (compare with the KAS). A major reservation about the instrument is centred on the doubtful equivalence of the item 'coping with an emergency' with the other items. In the first place, this is not a recognized structural role in the same way that household, employment, and child care roles are so recognized. Second, elsewhere in the schedule, ratings are obtained from reports of what the informant actually does, whereas the rating of coping is based on reports about likely behaviour in a hypothetical crisis. The validation of this item requires quite a different approach compared to the other items.

Social functioning schedule

The SFS (Remington and Tyrer 1979) is a brief semi-structured interview schedule for assessing social functioning, particularly of non-psychotic patients. It exists in two versions: one for use with the patient, the other for use with the informant. The patient version consists of 12 sections: employment, household chores, money, self-care, marital relationship, child care, patient–child relationships, patient–parent relationships, household relationships, extra-marital relationships (not included in informant version), social contacts, hobbies and spare-time activities. Sections on employment, household chores, money, and spare-time activities are divided into two parts: a 'behaviour' subsection, in which the patient's reports of his own performance are rated, and a 'stress' subsection, in which the patient describes feelings such as strain or worry. Within each of the sections and subsections evidence is sought of any problems in the performance of the role during the past month. On the basis of the patient's (or informant's) report, the interviewer makes a rating on a 10 cm analogue line which is labelled 'severe difficulties' at one extreme and 'none' at the other. 'In each section a number of possible problems are explored based on the results of preliminary interviews with patients. A report of frequent or intense problems in any or all areas warrants a high rating' (Remington and Tyrer 1979). Administration of the full schedule takes no more than twenty minutes. Inter-rater agreement was assessed using audio-tape and independent interviews: the overall intraclass correlation coefficient for both methods was 0.62, with only one scale having a non-significant value. The relationship between the two versions of the SFS was investigated on 73 pairs of patients and informants. All the correlations over 14 sections were significant, ranging from 0.45 to 0.80. Validity was assessed by examining the scale's ability to discriminate between groups of individuals with different diagnoses (personality disorder, neurosis/psychosis, and 'normal'). The prediction of greatest problems in the personality-disordered group was substantially corroborated. Use of the SFS is a study of day- and out-patient care demonstrated the sensitivity of the instrument's scales to changes over time (Tyrer and Remington 1979).

The SFS was constructed partly out of the authors' dissatisfaction with existing social adjustment schedules which assumed the existence of an agreed criterion against which an individual's functioning can be measured. In practice, they note, the anchor points of adjustment scales are usually tied to notions of optimal or ideal functioning, or to arbitrary norms of 'adequate' performance. In contrast, they have 'abandoned norm-referenced criteria altogether and eschewed concepts of social adjustment or attainment which appear to incorporate them' (Remington and Tyrer 1979). They seek instead to establish an inventory of disturbing or distressing events which are scaled in terms of frequency in intensity, 'this being accomplished without reference to normative criteria'. The authors are to be commended on the success of their endeavour. One must be particularly impressed by the fact that the specific items (questions) taped in each role area are based on pilot interviews with the appropriate (patient) population; and the schedule is structured in such a way that these items can be altered to suit the socio-cultural context in which it is applied. Although it is a brief interview, coverage of roles is fairly extensive. Reported validity, reliability, and sensitivity are satisfactory. It is hoped that the suitability of using the SFS with other (e.g. psychotic) populations will be assessed in future.

Social behaviour assessment schedule

The SBAS (Platt *et al.* 1978, 1980, 1983) was specifically designed in order to evaluate behaviour and social performance in relation to some independent variable causing change, such as severity of illness or treatment, and to assess the impact of different treatment regimes on the patient and his/her significant others. It takes the form of a standardized, semi-structured interview with the patient's most closely involved relative or friend. Guidelines for choosing the appropriate informant (e.g. face-to-face contact, lives in the same household, a hierarchy of relatives) have been delineated by the authors. To quantify the impact of the illness, the patient's disturbed behaviour, his/her limited social performance, and the subjective and objective burden on the household are included. The interview takes from 45 to 75 minutes to administer and requires interviewer practice and training. A combined training manual and rating guide is included.

The patient's social performance is assessed in Section C. Twelve items of behaviour are included: household role (two ratings: tasks and management), parental role (three ratings: child care, interest in child, discipline of child), spare-time activities, informant–patient relationship (three ratings: everyday conversation, support, affection/friendliness), sexual relationship, work/study, decision-making. The patient's performance on each (sub-)role is assessed on a three-point scale; each point is fully defined in terms of observable behaviour and corresponds to 'non-performance', 'partial performance', and 'full performance'. Decisions about what constitutes non-performance or incomplete performance are not arbitrary, but are based on objective criteria. An interviewer assessment is made according to the extent to which the patient falls short of certain main items of the role. No distinction is made between patients according to age, sex, class, or any other attribute. All patients are treated alike and have the same standards applied indiscriminately to them. While the presence of any severe physical disability which might prevent the fulfilment of any particular role is taken into account, cultural factors which might affect the role performance are ignored. Thus, for example, a middle-aged woman, a young working man, and an old-age pensioner who are all physically fit would be rated as 'non-participants' (rating 2) if they did nothing at all in the house. The authors believe that those who interpret the results must make decisions about whether non-participation in a certain role constitutes an 'impairment'. 'Our guiding principle has been to keep "facts" and "evaluation" as separate as possible' (Platt *et al.* 1980). For each item there is also a rating of change which compares the patient's present performance in a particular role with his best ever performance; it is a global scale with five points (same, somewhat less, much less, somewhat more, much more). The onset of any change in performance is rated on a further five-point scale. Finally, the informant's distress is measured on a four-point scale in relation to each item of disturbed behaviour: 'no distress', 'moderate distress', 'severe distress', and 'resignation'.

Interrater reliability was originally assessed by comparing the raw scores of four rater on nine interviews carried out by two sociologist research workers. The intraclass correlation coefficient of reliability for the summary social performance score (calculated by aggregating ratings on individual items of behaviour) was 0.98; a comparably high degree of reliability at the item level was also found (Platt *et al.* 1980). In a later study, 30 tape-recorded interviews were rated independently by two interviewers. The weighted kappa for the social performance scale was 0.85 (Gibbons *et al.* 1984). Partial validity of the scale was established by evidence of a non-significant correlation between the social performance score on the SBAS and PSE score for 127 acute psychiatric in-patients taking part in a randomized controlled trial of brief hospitalization (see Hirsch *et al.* 1979). This result confirmed the authors' assumption that the social performance section of the SBAS is tapping a behavioural domain which is separate from mere symptomatology. Evidence of the sensitivity of the social performance section was also demonstrated in the brief hospitalization study. Both brief and standard hospitalization groups were performing their roles to a significantly greater degree two weeks after admission. This improvement was sustained three months later, although no further change was noted. Behavioural (symptomatological) disturbance in the patient (as measured by Section B of the SBAS) improved substantially among the same 127 patients over the three-month follow-up period, whereas social performance improved to a far lesser extent (Platt and Hirsch 1981). In addition to its use in this study, the SBAS has been used in a follow-up study of chronic schizophrenics (Curson *et al.* 1985*a, b, c*), a randomized controlled trial of maintenance anti-psychotic therapy for schizophrenic out-patients (Barnes *et al.* 1983), with families of alcoholic women in Germany (Lutz *et al.* 1980), and in a survey of schizophrenic patients and their families in Southampton, England (Gibbons *et al.* 1984). A full discussion of the rationale, development, and structure of the instrument can be found in Platt *et al.* (1980).

CONCLUSION

For descriptive purposes, scales based on the concept of 'performance' (i.e. the extent to which behaviour conforms to, or deviates from, cultural expectations of average/normal functioning) are to be preferred to scales based on the concept of 'adjustment' (i.e. the extent to which behaviour conforms to, or deviates from, an attainable or unattainable ideal). However, each of the instruments reviewed above undoubtedly has particular advantages in certain research situations. These can be highlighted by reference to the criteria set out in Table 10.1.

Informant

The KAS, SAS, SIASM, and SFS exist in versions for use with both patients and significant others as informants. The SSIAM and SPS have thus far only been used with patients, and the SBAS only with significant others.

Method

While the KAS is a self-report instrument, the remaining scales are based on a structured or semi-structured in-person interview. The SAS and SIASM exist in both self-report and interview versions.

Content

None of the instruments covers all the role areas or dimensions listed in Table 10.1. Choice of a suitable scale will therefore depend upon the interests of the investigator and the purposes of the research project. The KAS is the least comprehensive, while the SBAS is the only scale which evaluates decision-making. Special attention to the economic role is paid by the SIASM, SAS, SPS, and SFS.

Psychometric properties

In general, all seven scales possess demonstrated reliability and validity, although relevant data relating to the SPS are scanty. Further work on the validity of the SSIAM and SIASM is also required. Sensitivity to change has not been shown by the SSIAM and SPS. Each scale is based on a well-developed quantitative scoring system.

References

Barnes, T. R. E., Milavic, G., Curson, D. A., and Platt, S. D. (1983). Use of the Social Behaviour Assessment Schedule (SBAS) in a trial of maintenance antipsychotic therapy in schizophrenic outpatients: pimozide versus fluphenazine. *Soc. Psychiat.* **18**, 193–9.

Barrabee, P., Barrabee, E. L., and Finesinger, J. E. (1955). A normative social adjustment scale. *Am. J. Psychiat.* **112**, 252–9.

Bates, F. L. (1956). Position, role and status: a reformulation of concepts. *Social Forces* **34**, 313–21.

Biddle, B. J. and Thomas, E. J. (eds.) (1966). *Role theory: concepts and research*. Wiley, New York.

Bott, E. (1957). *Family and social network*. Tavistock, London.

Bradbury, M., Heading, B., and Hollis, M. (1972). The man and the mask: a discussion of role theory. In *Role* (ed. J. A. Jackson), p. 42. Cambridge University Press, Cambridge.

Brown, G. W., Bhrolchain, N. W., and Harris, T. O. (1975). Social class and psychiatric disturbance of women in an urban community. *Sociology* **9**, 225–54.

Candy, J., Balfour, F. H., Cawley, R. H., Hildebrand, H. P., Malan, D. H., Marks, I. M., and Wilson, J. (1972). A feasibility study for a controlled trial for formal psychotherapy. *Psychol. Med.* **2**, 345–62.

Casey, P. R., Tyrer, P. J., and Platt, S. (1985). The relationship between social functioning and psychiatric symptomatology in primary care. *Soc. Psychiat.* **20**, 5–9.

Clare, A. W. and Cairns, V. E. (1978). Design, development and use of a standardised interview to assess social adjustment and dysfunction in community studies. *Psychol. Med.* **8**, 589–4.

—— ——(1976). *A Manual for use in conjunction with the general practice unit's standardised social interview schedule*. Institute of Psychiatry, London.

Clausen, G. T. (1972). Some problems of design and inference in studies of community tenure. *J. nerv. ment. Dis.* **155**, 22–35.

Cooper, B., Eastwood, M. R., and Sylph, J. A. (1970). Psychiatric morbidity and social adjustment in a general practice population. In *Psychiatric epidemiology* (ed. E. H. Hare and J. K. Wing), pp. 299–309. Oxford University Press, Oxford.

——Harwin, B. G., Depla, C., and Shepherd, M. (1975). Mental health in the community: an evaluative study. *Psychol. Med.*, **5**, 372–80.

Corney, R. H., Clare, A. W., and Fry, J. (1982). The development of a self-report questionnaire to identify social problems—a pilot study. *Psychol. Med.* **12**, 903–9.

Curson, D. A., Barnes, T. R. E., Bamber, R. W., Platt, S. D., Hirsch, S. R., and Duffy, J. C. (1985a). Long-term maintenance of chronic schizophrenic out-patients: the seven year follow-up of the MRC fluphenazine/placebo trial. I. Course of illness, stability of diagnosis, and the role of a special maintenance clinic. *Br. J. Psychiat.* **146**, 464–9.

—— —— —— —— ——(1985b). Long-term maintenance of chronic schizo-phrenic out-patients: the seven year follow-up of the MRC fluphenazine/placebo trial. II. The incidence of compliance problems, side-effects, neurotic symptoms, and depression. *Br. J. Psychiat.* **146**, 469–74.

—— —— —— —— —— ——(1985c). Long-term maintenance of chronic schizophrenic out-patients: the seven year follow-up of the MRC fluphena-zine/placebo trial. III. Relapse postponement or relapse prevention? The implica-tions for long-term outcome. *Br. J. Psychiat.* **146**, 474–80.

Dohrenwend, B. P. and Dohrenwend, B. S. (1974). Social and cultural influences on psychopathology. *Ann. Rev. Psychol.* **25**, 417–52.

Dohrenwend, B. S., Cook, D., and Dohrenwend, B. P. (1981). Measurement of social functioning in community populations. In *What is a case?* (ed. J. K. Wing, P. Bebbington, and L. N. Robbins), pp. 183–201. Grant McIntyre, London.

——Dohrenwend, B. P., Link, B., and Levav, I. (1983). Social functioning of psy-chiatric patients in contrast with community cases in the general population. *Arch. Gen. Psychiat.* **40**, 1174–82.

Ellsworth, R. B., Foster, L., Childers, B., Arthur, G., and Kroeker, D. (1968). Hospital and community adjustment as perceived by psychiatric patients, their families and staff. *J. consult. clin. Psychol.* **32**, (No. 5, Pt. 2), 1–41.

Endicott, J., and Spitzer, R. L. (1972). What! Another rating scale? The psychiatric evaluation form. *J. nerv. ment. Dis*, **154**, 88–104.

Gibbons, J. S., Horn, S. H., Powell, J. M., and Gibbons, J. L. (1984). Schizophrenic patients and their families: a survey in a psychiatric service based on a DGH unit. *Br. J. Psychiat.* **144**, 70–7.

Gross, N. A., Mason, W. S., and McEachern, W. (1958). *Explorations in role analysis*. Wiley, New York.

Gurland, B. J., Yorkston, N. J., Stone, A. R., Frank, J. D., and Fleiss, J. L. (1972a). The Structured and Scaled Interview to Assess Maladjustment (SSIAM).

I. Description, rationale and development. *Arch. gen. Psychiat.* **27**, 259–64.

—— ——Goldberg, K., Fleiss, J. L., Sloane, R. B., and Cristol, A. H. (1972*b*). The Structured and Scaled Interview to Assess Maladjustment (SSIAM). II. Factor analysis, reliability and validity. *Arch. gen. Psychiat.* **27**, 264–7.

—— ——Stone, A. R., and Frank, J. D. (1974). *Structured and Scaled Interview to Assess Maladjustment (SSIAM)*. Singer, New York.

Hirsch, S. R., Platt, S. D., Knights, A., and Weyman, A. (1979). Shortening hospital stay for psychiatric care: effect on patients and their families. *Br. Med. J.* **1**, 442–6.

Hoehn-Saric, R., Liberman, B., Imber, S., Stone, A. R., Pande, S. K., and Frank, J. D. (1972). Arousal and attitude change in neurotic patients. *Arch. gen. Psychiat.* **26**, 51–6.

Hogarty, G. E., and Katz, M. M. (1971). Norms of adjustment and social behaviour. *Arch. gen. Psychiat.* **25**, 470–80.

Hurry, J., and Sturt, E. (1981). Social performance in a population sample: relation to psychiatric symptoms. In *What is a case?* (ed. J. K. Wing, P. Bebbington, and L. N. Robbins), pp. 202–13. Grant McIntyre, London.

Huxley, P., and Goldberg, D. P. (1975). Social versus clinical predictions in minor psychiatric disorders. *Psychol. Med.*, **5**, 96–100.

Jablensky, A., Schwarz, R., and Tomov, T. (1980). WHO collaborative study on impairments and disabilities associated with schizophrenic disorders. *Acta psychiat. scand.* **62** (Suppl. 285), 152–9.

Katz, M. M., and Lyerly, S. B. (1963). Methods for measuring adjustment and social behaviour in the community. I. Rationale, description, discriminative validity and scale development. *Psychol. Rep.* **13**, 503–35. (Monograph Supplement 4–V13).

Kedward, H. B., and Sylph, J. A. (1974). Social correlates of chronic neurotic disorder. *Soc. Psychiat.* **9**, 91–8.

Lutz, M., Appelt, H., and Cohen, R. (1980). Belastungsfaktoren in den Familien alkoholkranker und depresiver Frauen aus der sicht der Ehemänner. *Soc. Psychiat.* **15**, 137–44.

Nye, F. I. (1974). Emerging and declining roles. *J. Marriage Family* **36**, 238–45.

Paykel, E. S., Weissman, M. M., and Prusoff, B. A. (1978). Social maladjustment and severity of depression. *Comprehens. Psychiat.* **19**, 121–8.

—— —— ——and Tonks, C. M. (1971). Dimensions of social adjustment in depressed women. *J. nerv. ment. Dis.* **152**, 158–72.

Platt, S. (1980). On establishing the validity of 'objective' data: can we rely on cross-interview agreement? *Psychol. Med.*, **10**, 573–81.

——(1981). Social adjustment as a criterion of treatment success: just what are we measuring? *Psychiatry* **44**, 95–112.

——and Hirsch, S. (1981). The effects of brief hospitalisation upon the psychiatric patient's household. *Acta psychiat. scand.* **64**, 199–216.

—— ——and Knights, A. C. (1981). Effects of brief hospitalisation on psychiatric patients' behaviour and social functioning. *Acta psychiat. scand.* **63**, 117–28.

——Weyman, A., and Hirsch, S. (1978). *Social behaviour assessment schedule (SBAS)*, 2nd ed., revised. Department of Psychiatry, Charing Cross Hospital, London.

—— —— ——(1983). *Social behaviour assessment schedule (SBAS)*, 3rd edn. NFER-Nelson, Windsor, Berks.

—— —— ——and Hewett, S. (1980). The social behaviour assessment schedule (SBAS): rationale, contents, scoring and reliability of a new interview schedule. *Soc. Psychiat.* **15**, 43–55.

Prusoff, B. A., Klerman, G. L., and Paykel, E. S. (1972). Pitfalls in the self-report assessment of depression. *Can. Psychiat. Ass. J.* **17**, 101–7.

Remington, M., and Tyrer, P. (1979). The social functioning schedule—A brief semi-structured interview. *Soc. Psychiat.* **14**, 151-7.

Sloane, R. B., Staples, F. R., Cristol, A. H., Yorkston, N. J., and Whipple, K. (1975). Short-term analytically oriented psychotherapy versus behaviour therapy. *Am. J. Psychiat.* **132**, 373-7.

Spitzer, R. L., and Endicott, J. E. (1973). The value of the interview for the evaluation of psychopathology. In *Psychopathology: contributions in the biological, behavioural and social sciences* (ed. J. Hammer, K. Salzinger, and S. Sutton), pp. 397-408. Wiley, New York.

—— ——Fleiss, J. L., and Cohen, J. (1970). The psychiatric status schedule: a technique for evaluating psychopathology and impairment in role functioning. *Arch. gen. Psychiat.* **23**, 41-55.

Stevens, B. (1972). Dependence of schizophrenic patients on elderly relatives. *Psychol. Med.* **2**, 17-32.

Sylph, J. A., Kedward, H. B., and Eastwood, M. R. (1969). Chronic neurotic patients in general practice. *J. R. Coll. gen. Pract.* **17**, 162-70.

Tanner, J., Weissman, M. M., and Prusoff, B. A. (1975). Social adjustment and clinical relapse in depressed outpatients. *Comprehens. Psychiat.* **16**, 547-56.

Tyrer, P. and Remington, M. (1979). A controlled comparison of day hospital and out-patient care for neurotic disorders. *Lancet* **1**, 1014-16.

Weissman, M. M. (1975). The assessment of social adjustment. A review of techniques. *Arch. gen. Psychiat.* **32**, 357-65.

——and Bothwell, S. (1976). Assessment of social adjustment by patient self-report. *Arch. gen. Psychiat.* **33**, 1111-15.

——and Paykel, E. S. (1974). *The depressed woman: a study of social relationships.* University of Chicago Press, Chicago.

——Prusoff, B. A., Thompson, W. D., Harding, P. S., and Myers, J. K. (1978). Social adjustment by self-report in a community sample and in psychiatric out-patients. *J. nerv. ment. Dis.* **166**, 317-26.

——and Sholomskas, D. (1982). The assessment of social adjustment by the clinician, the patient and the family. In *The behavior of psychiatric patients: quantitative techniques for evaluation* (ed. E. I. Burdock, A. Sudilovsky, and S. Gershon). Marcel Dekker, New York.

—— ——and, John, K. (1981). The assessment of social adjustment. An up-date. *Arch. gen. Psychiat.* **38**, 1250-8.

Winoker, G., Clayton, P. J., and Reich, T. (1969). *Manic depressive illness.* C. V. Mosby, St. Louis.

11

Clinical treatment of schizophrenia

STEVEN R. HIRSCH

No-one would deny the revolutionizing effect on psychiatric treatment which followed the discovery that chlorpromazine (Delay and Bernitzer 1952) and reserpine (Kline 1954) had tranquillizing properties especially effective in patients with schizophrenia. Besides the direct effect on symptoms, excitement could be rapidly brought under control and behaviour became more predictable—important changes in the social management of patients within and outside hospital followed and eventually the focus of treatment shifted from the hospital to the community. Despite such dramatic improvements in patient care and their prospects for a speedy return to society, evidence from 12 follow-up studies, each extending over 10 years, suggests that the number of patients who fully recover from schizophrenia has not changed since 1908 when Eugene Bleuler first proposed the term 'schizophrenia' (Stephens 1970; Tsuang 1982). Manfred Bleuler's observation of over 1000 cases, 208 of whom he personally followed for more than 20 years, substantiates this view (Bleuler 1974). Thus, we are discussing treatments which are not curative, but lead to a more speedy remission of the illness in some cases and a considerable decrease in symptoms in most.

EFFECTS OF MEDICATION

Effectiveness

The efficacy of neuroleptic medication for schizophrenia is proven beyond doubt. Neuroleptics are drugs with pharmacological features similar to chlorpromazine, having relatively strong antipsychotic tranquillizing effects relative to their hypnotic effect but also causing extrapyramidal side-effects which were originally thought to be relevant to their antipsychotic action. Davis and Garver (1978) summarized the results of 207 double-blind comparisons between antipsychotics and placebo (Table 11.1). The former were found to be superior to placebo in 86 per cent of trials; barbiturates which had no antipsychotic effect and promazine and mepazine which showed weak antipsychotic activity accounted for the rest. Of 66 trials comparing *chlorpromazine* to placebo, 11 studies did not show a significant treatment effect because the numbers were small or the dosage inadequate. Chlorpromazine proved superior to placebo in all studies using daily doses of 500 mg

TABLE 11.1. *Antipsychotic effect of chlorpromazine in comparison to placebo at different doses*

Mean dose (mg/day)	Number of studies showing chlorpromazine to be (in comparison with placebo)	
	Definitely more effective	The same or only slightly more effective
< 300	11	15
301–400	4	4
401–500	4	1
501–800	14	0
> 800	12	0
Total	45	20

Based on Davis and Garver (1978).

or more. The magnitude of the treatment effect was reflected in a large-scale trial of acutely ill patients (Cole *et al.* 1964). Seventy-five per cent of patients receiving active medication showed considerable improvement compared to 26 per cent receiving placebo. Nearly 90 per cent of patients treated with phenothiazines improved but more than half the patients treated with placebo showed no change or became worse. Similar rates of improvement for acutely admitted schizophrenics were observed in a sample of all admissions during one year to a psychiatric unit from a catchment area population of 90 000 (Knights *et al.* 1980).

Specific antipsychotic effects of neuroleptics

As classically described, neuroleptics have three main effects on psychosis:

1. A specific effect on psychotic features including delusions and paranoid thinking, hallucinations, thought disorder, retardation, mannerisms, and catatonia—these abnormalities may be understood to give rise to other secondary effects such as withdrawal, anorexia, and self-neglect which also respond.

2. A specific sedative effect on psychotic agitation, restlessness, and excitement. These effects can be obtained without clouding consciousness or clinical impairment of intellectual functioning and, unlike barbiturates, large doses do not normally cause ataxia or anaesthesia. The combined effects of (1) and (2) lead to improvement in other features of schizophrenia including negativism, uncooperativeness, hostility, belligerence, bizarre behaviour, and insomnia.

3. A third specific action of neuroleptics is their ability to arrest the development of new symptoms in recently treated acute patients whose florid symptoms have not yet remitted (Goldberg *et al.* 1965) and prevent the re-emergence of symptoms in successfully treated patients who no longer have

psychotic symptoms or whose symptoms are stabilized and relatively quiescent (Davis 1975). In short, neuroleptics reduce symptom intensity, shorten florid psychotic episodes, and lessen the recurrence of psychotic symptoms. They have a much stronger sedative effect in non-psychotic individuals who are more dose-sensititive to the hypnotic effect of these drugs. For this reason they can be used to quell any form of excitement.

Note that these effects are not specific for schizophrenic psychosis but apply equally well to the florid psychotic symptoms of mania, depression, and organic psychosis, though the preventive effects in these conditions has not been established.

During the initial phase of treatment in an acute illness the whole range of schizophrenic, neurotic, and depressive symptoms improve in most patients (Knights *et al.* 1979; Knights and Hirsch 1981). However, Johnstone *et al.* (1978) showed that positive, florid symptoms of hallucinations, delusions, and bizarre behaviour respond differentially better than the negative symptoms of affective flatness and poverty of speech, which in their hands did not respond at all. The failure of negative symptoms to respond to medication in chronic patients is well known, but some improvement occurs in the initial period following an acute exacerbation if change in behaviour is taken as the basis of judgement (Knights *et al.* 1980). The sensitivity of these symptoms to environmental factors is discussed in Chapter 7.

Comparative effectiveness of various neuroleptics

Davis and Garver (1978) evaluated the results from 134 double-blind comparisons between 21 different neuroleptics and chlorpromazine. No drug was superior to chlorpromazine in any trial. Mepazine, promazine, and phenobarbitone were consistently inferior except when chlorpromazine was used in insufficient dosage, usually below 400 mg per day. There was no consistent trend from one study to the next to suggest that any drug was better than another, even in respect to individual symptoms. Thus, taken with their earlier comprehensive review of double-blind studies of antipsychotic medication (Klein and Davis 1969) and Hollister's review of 16 reports each involving more than 250 patients (Hollister 1974), one must conclude that it is impossible to establish a consistent difference between antipsychotic drugs in their effectiveness on specific symptoms, syndromes, or types of schizophrenia subgroup.

The frequent reports in the literature of effects of different drugs on individual symptoms can usually be explained as a chance result occurring when comparisons are made in the data analysis—in no case have such findings been consistently revalidated in subsequent studies. Nor has it been possible to indentify a pattern of symptoms, signs, or demographic variables which can be used to predict the response of an individual patient to any given drug. However, there are differences in the properties of various neuroleptics which depend on their side-effects and are relevant to clinical practice, as we shall see later on.

TABLE 11.2. *Antipsychotic potency and sedation and neuroleptic quotients at average effective antipsychotic dosage*

Group	Name	Antipsychotic Potency	Sedation quotient	Neuroleptic quotient
Phenothiazine				
Aliphatic	Chlorpromazine	+	+ + + +	+ +
Piperidine	Thioridazine	+	+ + +	+
Piperazine	Trifluoperazine	+ + +	+ +	+ + + +
Piperazine	Fluphenazine	+ + + +	+ +	+ + + +
Butyrophenone	Haloperidol	+ + + +	+ +	+ + + +
Diphenylbutylperidine	Pimozide	+ + + +	+	+ + +

Relative strengths: low + ; high + + + + .
From Hirsch (1982*a*).

Time-course of action

Sedative action

There are important differences in the time-course of the specific anti-psychotic effects (Table 11.2). The sedative action is immediate as soon as adequate blood levels are reached, within 10 minutes using intravenous haloperidol. Agitation and excitement which have been controlled by treatment can re-emerge quickly when medication is omitted. Less potent barbiturates and benzodiazepines in high doses as well as paraldehyde can also be used to quell excitement, and it is said that morphine is still the last resort if all else fails. However, barbiturates and opiates are rapidly hypnotic and suppress brainstem functions making medical examination more difficult, and carrying all the other dangers of deep unconsciousness and respiratory failure that can usually be avoided by neuroleptics, if given judiciously but in sufficient dosage.

Antipsychotic action

Comparisons of neuroleptics to placebo in newly-admitted patients shows that the antipsychotic effect develops slowly over two to three weeks, by which time a significant advantage of neuroleptics over placebo is evident (Davis and Garver 1978). Most patients will improve to some extent following admission to hospital, even if treated with placebo, but the response is usually only partial and temporary. The sedative action of neuroleptics is useful in itself in the early stages while the slower antipsychotic action has a chance to develop.

There is some suggestion that the use of anticholinergics in combination with neuroleptics delays the emergence of the antipsychotic effects. In an earlier study (Johnstone *et al.* 1978) of α-flupenthixol in acute schizophrenics, dopamine receptor blockade, as indicated by increased serum prolactin, occurred more rapidly than symptom improvement, but all their patients had received anticholinergics. In a subsequent study (Crow *et al.* 1981, Johnstone *et al.* 1983) with a similar doses, patients who had been randomly assigned not to receive anticholinergics improved more rapidly and the time course of the antipsychotic effect paralleled the rise in prolactin. The comparison group had a similar course of recovery until the tenth day when they received an anticholinergic, procyclidine, and subsequently showed a slower rate of improvement. The authors believe they have demonstrated that anticholinergics delay the antipsychotic effect of neuroleptics, a phenomenon which had been previously reported for benzotropine by Singh and Kay (1975, 1979*b*). Further studies are required to confirm these findings including a comparison of patients randomly allocated to have anticholinergics or not from the onset of treatment.

Generally the most rapid effect on psychotic symptoms is achieved between two and six weeks, after which further improvement takes place slowly over months. Some patients run an erratic course, slowly improving over six months or more, and gradual improvements may be seen to occur over the ensuing five years. For such patients it is difficult to be sure that medication is a definite factor leading to further recovery, although it certainly prevents deterioration. It is of interest to note that there is no evidence to suggest that tolerance to the antipsychotic effects of neuroleptics develops.

Prophylactic action

This probably develops gradually at first, consistent with the antipsychotic effect. New symptoms may be uncovered in the early stages of treatment if the initial features are characterized by inhibition, paranoid guarding, or withdrawal on the one hand, or gross excitement with intolerance on the other. Whether these are new symptoms or only the emergence of the covert psychosis as the patient becomes less guarded and more articulate is perhaps a philosophical point. Generally, psychotic symptoms do not continue to develop once treatment has begun.

Numerous well-controlled trials (Davis 1975) have confirmed the observation of Leff and Wing (1971) that relapse can occur any time after discontinuing prophylaxis but about 50 per cent of patients will relapse between three and ten months; the mode occurs at three to five months. This will be discussed further in the section on maintenance treatment.

RELATIVE EFFECTS OF DIFFERENT DRUGS AND THEIR PHARMACOLOGY

Beliefs about differences between drugs, for example that chlorpromazine is better for excited, disoriented, or hostile patients and fluphenazine better for paranoid or thought-disordered ones, can be explained in terms of differences in their side-effects when drugs are compared at doses necessary to achieve equal antipsychotic effects.

TABLE 11.3. *Relative potencies of neuroleptics compared to chlorpromazine equal to 100*

	Relative potency	Mean daily dose used in clinical trials (mg)	Range of clinical daily dose (mg)
Chlorpromazine (Cpz)	100	734	75–2000
Thioridazine	97	712	75–800*
Perphenazine	9	66	
Molindone	6	44	
Thiothixane	4.4	32	6–120
Trifluoperazine	2.8	21	5–60
Haloperidol	1.6	12	1.5–100
Fluphenazine	1.2	9	1.5–1200†

* Upper limit set to avoid retinal pigmentation.
† One study used 1200 mg/day (Quitkin *et al.* 1975).
After Davis 1976*a*

Potency

Some of the reported differences between treatments may be due to a failure to ensure that drugs are used in equivalent dosage. If the effectiveness of neuroleptics is defined as their ability to achieve the desired antipsychotic effect, *potency* can be defined in terms of the minimum amount of drug in milligrams required to achieve this. In terms of milligram dosage chlorpromazine and thioridazine are low in potency, that is they require high dosage as compared to fluphenazine, haloperidol, or pimozide.

The relative potency of some commercially used neuroleptics is shown in Table 11.3 (after Davis 1976*a*). Davis estimated each drug's mean clinical daily dose by averaging the doses compiled from all the double-blind comparisons of drugs to chlorpromazine which allowed for flexible adjustment of dosage to obtain an optimal clinical response. In some cases the relative potency was calculated indirectly from studies which compared a drug of unknown potency to one whose potency relative to chlorpromazine had been established. The mean dose of chlorpromazine determined by this method may be biased on the high side because prescribing was blind, and studies of chronic patients were not separated from those of acute. However, the method is so far the best approximation available using clinical data to establish the *relative* clinical potencies of different neuroleptics even if absolute dose levels are high. Other methods yield marginally different results, particularly in regard to the relative potencies of the low-dose neuroleptics which may vary slightly in their rank order and be a half or a third as potent in comparison to chlorpromazine as Table 11.3 suggests.

Response to individual drugs and serum levels

It does not follow that because there are no consistent differences in the responses of a group of patients to different drugs, that patients individually will not respond better to one than to another. Neuroleptics differ considerably in clinical structure and 100-fold differences in plasma concentrations have been observed between individuals taking equivalent doses of oral chlorpromazine, though variations in plasma concentrations are said to account for less than 10 per cent of the variation in clinical response (Lader 1979). Variation of plasma concentration in response to dose could be due to differences in absorption, carrier state, metabolism, or excretion (Davis 1976b). For example, Kulhanek and colleagues reported that neuroleptics rapidly form insoluble complexes with coffee and tea which alters their pharmacokinetics (Kulhanek *et al.* 1979; Kulhanek and Linde 1981). This may be one source of the wide variation in blood levels with oral medication and the fact that there is much less variation in blood levels when medication is given by the parenteral route. Though there are reports of correlations between plasma levels and clinical response, including the possibility of a 'therapeutic window' for specific drugs, results are inconsistent and as yet not ready for clinical application. On the basis that the effectiveness of neuroleptics depends on their action as dopamine antagonists, all drugs should be equally effective. If for an individual, drugs differ as to their clinical effectiveness, this must be due to differences in the biological handling of the particular molecule involved. Thus, when excitement and agitation do not respond to increased dose in the acute phase, or psychotic thought content does not respond to high dosage after two or more weeks, a change to a drug in a different chemical class, or to parenteral administration should be considered. These matters are discussed in greater detail in Chapter 4.

Differences in clinical action based on pharmacology

As explained in Chapter 2, the main effects of neuroleptics are due to competitive inhibition of the drug with neurotransmitters, which block the action of the neurotransmitter substances on postsynaptic neurones. Each neuroleptic has its own profile of activity on various neurotransmitter systems, and this explains the drug's sedative, antipsychotic, and extrapyramidal effects. Inhibition of α-noradrenergic transmission centrally is thought to account for the antipsychotic action, and in the nigro-striatal system to account for extrapyramidal side-effects. However, the effect on nigro-striatal dopaminergic systems, and therefore parkinsonian side-effects, tends to be modified by the drug's activity, blocking acetycholine transmission centrally (i.e. their anticholinergic effect) because dopaminergic and cholinergic systems have opposing effects on this system (Snyder *et al.* 1974 and Chapter 12, this volume). Tardive dyskinesia is thought to be due to a different sort of mechanism discussed in Chapter 12.

Sedation and neuroleptic quotients

The clinical psychiatrist can usefully understand the differences between drugs in terms of their effects on different transmitter systems when given in doses necessary to control florid symptoms of schizophrenia. Their effect on α-noradrenergic transmissions may be weak or strong relative to their effect on the dopamine transmission. A *sedation quotient* can be defined as a drug's sedative effect when prescribed at doses necessary to control psychoses. As Table 11.2 shows, chlorpromazine (Cpz) has a high sedation quotient when given at average antischizophrenic doses. Haloperidol has a low sedation quotient. Pharmacologically, at the clinically effective doses, say 500 mg, chlorpromazine has a strong anti-α-noradrenergic effect, but haloperidol, at comparable effective antipsychotic doses of 8 to 12 mg, is weakly sedative in an excited patient (see Peroutka *et al*. 1977). Thus it has a low sedation quotient. Similarly a *neuroleptic quotient* can be defined as the drug's tendency to cause extrapyramidal side-effects when given at clinically effective doses. This is a function of the anticholinergic potency of the drug. Haloperidol is weakly anticholinergic in the 8–15 mg (antipsychotic) dose range when it nevertheless has as strong an antidopamine activity as chlorpromazine. As would be expected it has an equally strong antidopamine action in the nigro-striatal system and because it is a weak anticholinergic at this dose it has a strong tendency to cause drug-induced parkinsonism. Thus, it has a high *neuroleptic quotient*.

The antipsychotic potency, sedation quotient, and neuroleptic quotient of different drugs given in Table 11.2 are based on research reports and clinical impression. The differences between the effects of drugs are only relative to their antipsychotic effective dose. When given in very high doses, say 10 times the usual clinical range, we would expect receptor sites to be saturated, and the dose to exceed a ceiling of any possible effects on the dopamine system.

It must be said in passing that, while the concept of a neuroleptic and sedation quotient expressing the tendency of a drug to produce extrapyramidal side-effects and have strong sedative effects in the early stage of treatment may be useful clinically, the explanation of such differences is controversial. Newer drugs with different pharmacological profiles in respect to animal behaviour, site of absorption, and affinity for specific receptor sites are emerging, and the activities of even well-established drugs give different results in different pharmacological systems (e.g. Loduron and Leysen 1978 versus Yamamura 1976). The clinician must beware of claims by manufacturers and researchers about the specificity of activity of any drug in respect to lack of side-effects. Such claims are often based on inadequate numbers of studies or failure to appreciate that reported differences between drugs may be due to differences in dosage of drugs compared in the studies rather than their inherent activity on different receptor sites. Often, reports are based on studies which use techniques which may not have been validated against other approaches or in other centres. A fair generalization is that when it comes to new products, specific advantages will be overestimated and side-effects, even dangerous ones, underestimated. Only numerous trials by independent investigators and widespread clinical use over time provide a sound basis for an accurate appraisal of benefits and side-effects. This will be punctuated by the rare breakthrough which will alter our basis for treatment.

Paradoxical effects on the extrapyramidal system in high dosage

A popular clinical conundrum is that parkinsonian side-effects are less pre-valent when very high rather than normal doses are prescribed. In some controlled trials using megadoses of neuroleptics, increased frequencies of extrapyramidal symptoms are reported, compared with the control group, but symptoms are less severe or prevalent than would be expected, especially in the initial phase. Other studies do not show any increase of extrapyramidal symptoms with very high dosage (McClelland *et al.* 1976). In the absence of graded dose–response studies one can predict a plateau effect or even a comparative decrease in extrapyramidal effects with very high dosage. Thioridazine has the lowest neuroleptic quotient of any of the established antipsychotics, and the strongest anticholinergic activity of conventional drugs so antiparkinsonian medication is less commonly required. With very high doses of a potent neuroleptic such as haloperidol, the dose required for maximal dopamine blockade will be exceeded, but the relatively weak anti-cholinergic activity will be increased to the point that the anticholinergic and antidopaminergic effects may be balanced and, paradoxically, extra-pyramidal side-effects may if anything decrease rather than increase (Hollister 1978).

Sedation is thought to be due to α-noradrenergic blockade centrally, and hypotension is thought to be due to α-adrenergic blockade peripherally so these actions tend to vary together from one drug to another (Peroutka *et al.* 1977). Sedation has also been attributed to the antihistamine effects of neuro-leptics (Quach *et al.* 1979). Sedation and neuroleptic quotients should influence the choice of drugs provided that the clinician also has a knowledge of other side-effects and takes these into account, together with any general medical problems the patient may present (see Chapters 12 and 13).

CLINICAL USE

Application in psychiatric emergencies

The high-potency neuroleptics offer advantages in psychiatric emergencies when rapid and massive sedation is wanted. At very high doses their sedative action can be equal to large doses of chlorpromazine, but there are fewer problems with hypotension, excessive anticholinergic action, or excessive hypnotic effect, with hardly more extrapyramidal side-effects than would be observed on lower dosage (Ayd 1978). Sedation begins about 30 minutes after oral haloperidol or fluphenazine administration and in 10 to 20 minutes after an intravenous injection. After the initial 10–20 mg intravenous or intra-muscular dose, 10 mg can be given every half hour until the desired calming effect is achieved. Patients chronically exposed to large doses of alcohol, sedative, or neuroleptics will require much higher doses because of tolerance. Large doses of haloperidol have been used safely in post-heart-surgery patients with no effect on arterial pressure, pulse pressure, pulmonary atrial pressure, cardiac rhythm, respiratory rate or ECG (Ayd 1978). Haloperidol, and other butyrophenones, have no untoward effects on cardiac, hepatic, or ectodermal tissue; haloperidol is therefore an excellent drug when treating patients with other forms of physical illness. This is partly accounted for by its relatively weak effect on cholinergic and noradrenergic neuroreceptors.

Dose–response relationships

Our knowledge about dosage largely depends on clinical observation, and further detailed studies are required. Toxicity limits the dose range for most drugs in medicine but conventional neuroleptics are remarkably safe over a wide therapeutic range—up to 1000 times the minimal therapuetic dose. Attention has already been drawn to the wide variation of plasma levels and of clinical response between patients to a given dose of neuroleptic drug. In the same patient, initial plasma levels tend to fall over time due to enzyme induction which speeds up metabolism. The recent development of a simple radioreceptor assay based on inhibition of the dopamine receptor by [³H]haloperidol may simplify plasma monitoring but has proved unreliable and has so far not shown a close link of plasma levels with clinical effects (see Chapters 2, 3, and 4).

The comprehensive reviews of controlled therapeutic trials by Klein, Davis, and Garver have contributed to our understanding of dose–response relationships (Klein and Davis 1969; Davis and Garver 1978). Table 11.1, which is based on 65 double-blind studies, summarizes their findings. While chlorpromazine was significantly more effective than placebo in doses less than 300 mg in some studies, in the majority it was not. On the other hand, every study using a mean dose of chlorpromazine above 500 mg per day showed the drug to be superior to placebo. The fact that some, but not all, studies using doses below 300 mg show an advantage to chlorpromazine suggests that under some conditions patients will respond to lower dosage. There is an increasing likelihood of a good response as the dose rises from 300 to 600 mg per day. We thus conclude that there is considerable variation in patient response at different doses with an increasing likelihood of good response in the 300–600 mg per day range.

Gardos *et al.* (1973) reviewed 12 carefully controlled studies of high-dose regimes, seven dealing with unspecified groups of chronic schizophrenics and five limited to treatment of refractory cases. Prien and Cole (1968) randomized 838 chronic schizophrenics to 2000 mg of chlorpromazine, 300 mg of chlorpromazine, continuation on their 'current treatment', and placebo. The high-dose group did not do better than the other active treatment groups except for a subgroup consisting of 25 per cent of the sample who were under 40 and had less than 10 years' treatment. The younger group responded significantly better to high-dose treatment, but the normal dose of chlorpromazine, 300 mg per day, was probably too low. However, two other studies also found higher doses were better for some groups of younger patients. The remaining five studies did not show an advantage for doses above 600 mg in groups of unspecified chronic patients. However, of the studies limited to the treatment of refractory patients, in four out of five the high-dose regime was significantly more effective, although the treatment was associated with more side-effects. A small but notable minority did better off medication. These findings give support for Davis's suggestion that the dose–response curve is roughly sigmoidal in shape with an increasing response between doses of 300 and 600 mg/day of chlorpromazine or the equivalent reaching a gradual plateau between 600 and 2000 mg, but doses above 600 mg should generally be limited to refractory cases. Hollister (1978) pointed out that, because of variable absorption from the gastrointestinal tract and metabolism during passage through the liver (first-pass effect), parenteral administration can increase potency almost fourfold. A consequence of this would be a much steeper dose–response gradient by the parenteral route achieving a maximal antipsychotic response at a lower dose.

Megadose studies

Quitkin *et al.* (1975) compared 1200 mg of oral fluphenazine daily, equivalent to 100 000 mg of chlorpromazine (Table 11.3), with 30 mg of fluphenazine (equivalent to 2500 mg of chlorpromazine) in the treatment of refractory patients. McClelland and colleagues (1976) compared 250 mg of depot fluphenazine to 12.5 mg intramuscularly per week over six months and others have compared 600 mg trifluoperazine (equivalent to 21 400 mg chlorpromazine) to 60 mg (Wijsenbeck *et al.* 1974). None of these studies showed an advantage for the megadose regime. Doses above 600 mg of chlorpromazine gave better response rates than lower doses, but there was a diminishing return for doses much higher than this. More data are needed on this problem, especially in respect to speed of response in acute studies. However, since medication is relatively safe in high doses for brief periods and trials have only considered average effects between groups, it is advisable to try a treatment-refractory patient on very high dosage maintaining careful observations and not prolonging treatment more than a few weeks in the first instance. Doses generally in use for this purpose are limited by the toxicity of individual drugs—chlorpromazine up to 2000 mg per day, or haloperidol up to 200 mg per day are examples.

Who to treat

Kane *et al.* (1982) carried out a randomized control trial on 28 first-illness schizophrenics with a duration of illness less than three months—for this reason they are classified as schizophreniform psychosis under DSM III. Forty-one per cent of 28 patients relapsed within a year on placebo compared to no relapses on active fluphenazine decanoate. This suggests that within this group of first-illness patients, who on the whole have a better prognosis, there is a group of patients who will relapse if not given maintenance medication. At the same time it is worth nothing that, of the 14 patients given active medication, three dropped out and three developed toxic reactions.

There are many reasons to offer patients a period off treatment at all stages of schizophrenia. Contrary to traditional views schizophrenics rarely show progressive deterioration after five years (Bleuler 1974) unless it is due to harmful treatment or environmental influences such as poverty of stimulation or excessive arousal (see Chapter 7). There is no evidence that early treatment prevents or minimizes deterioration. Up to 25 per cent of unselected schizophrenic admissions to hospital show a remission, even without medication, hence the value of hospitalization before modern somatic treatment (Cole *et al.* 1964).

While spontaneous remission is more likely to occur among the group traditionally recognized to have a good prognosis—first illness, acute florid onset, good previous personality, etc.—it is not possible to identify patients who will spontaneously recover unless they are first tried without medication. Moreover, significant differences between neuroleptics and placebo are not demonstrable during the first two weeks of treatment, after that period those on drugs do better. Once treatment has begun, the patient is likely to remain on it for months, even after discharge. Therefore, there is much to support the practice of having a period of unhurried observation before starting medication in order to make an accurate diagnosis and identify patients who will remit spontaneously; this will spare a number of patients the disadvantage of side-effects and unnecessary medication. Unfortunately, the advantages of such an approach are often counterbalanced by practical considerations in the treatment setting and the pressures for rapid management and discharge.

This rule applies equally to chronic patients stabilized in an unstressful environment. While some chronic patients require neuroleptics for sedation, and others need them to control or prevent the emergence of florid symptoms, a sizeable proportion of chronic patients—30 to 70 per cent—are unchanged in the short run when medication is withdrawn (Prien and Klett 1972). Given the risk of developing tardive dyskinesia and the fact that treatment can be rapidly restarted in patients under observation, consideration should be given to a period off treatment in most chronic cases. A proportion, even of the very disturbed, will improve—probably due to the disappearance of side-effects such as akinesia. However, the quality of the social and psychological environment should be carefully considered before deciding on drug withdrawal (see Chapter 7).

MAINTENANCE TREATMENT

The prophylactic action of neuroleptics preventing the recurrence or recrudescence of schizophrenic symptoms has now been well established in 33 double-blind trials dealing with 3609 chronic in- and out-patients (Davis 1982). Relapse on placebo ranged from 30 to 100 per cent with a mean of 53 per cent but on active medication the range was 0 to 49 per cent with a mean of 20 per cent. Differences between studies mostly depend on the length of study and selection of cases (see Chapter 8). It is interesting to note that when medication was withdrawn, symptoms tended to return in the same order as in previous episodes (Wistedt 1981) and were schizophrenic in nature (Hirsch *et al*. 1973). The powerful prophylactic effect which had been demonstrated by Hirsch *et al*. (1973) for chronic out-patients maintained on long-acting fluphenazine *depot injections* has been replicated in several countries with the same and other forms of depot medication, none of which has proved superior in efficacy to another (Davis 1975).

Oral versus depot injections

Though the value of oral medication had been confirmed earlier (Leff and Wing 1971) a strongly held view has developed among clinicians, especially in Britain, that depot injections are more successful in preventing relapse. The development of special clinics and district psychiatric nurses for administering injections has improved patient care and follow-up, but the route of administration does not prove to be a critical factor when treatments are compared under similar conditions. Large controlled studies comparing oral neuroleptics such as penfluridol (Quitkin *et al*. 1978) and oral fluphenazine (Rifkin *et al*. 1977; Schooler *et al*. 1980) against depot fluphenazine decanoate injections found relapse rates below 30 per cent over one year for both oral and depot medication. About 65 per cent of patients relapsed when switched to placebo, depending on the length of treatment (Davis 1975). In another study of selected patients, clinical differences between those treated with pimozide tablets and fluphenazine injections were not significant (Falloon *et al*. 1978*a*), but differences in social functioning ascribed to extra-pyramidal side-effects and possibly to differences between doses were significant (Falloon *et al*. 1978*b*). In practice, one is likely to achieve better results with long-acting depot injections because schizophrenics are unreliable when left to administer their own medication, and the close nursing supervision associated with depot injection clinics assures reliable supervision.

The problem associated with poor compliance and follow-up may not be reflected in clinical trials such as those quoted in which patients are highly selected and closely observed. Johnson's study (1978) of 287 schizophrenics from a catchment area followed up after discharge supported this. He found that only 23 per cent of the depot-treated patients ($n = 187$) relapsed in a year, compared to 37 per cent on oral medication ($n = 73$) and 63 per cent of dropouts ($n = 27$). However, as the patients were self-selected or prescribed oral or depot medication by clinical choice, bias in selection may account for the different relapse rates of different groups. In a 7–8-year follow-up of patients on depot phenothiazine, there were significant correlations of the number of illness episodes with not turning up to the clinic for injections but having them at home, or failing attendance (Curson *et al*. 1985). Again, it is difficult to unravel whether poor compliance is a cause or effect of clinical deterioration, or a mixture.

Extrapyramidal side-effects: drug differences and treatment during maintenance

Like oral medication, the claim that depot neuroleptics differ in their specific actions does not stand up to scrutiny. Knights and colleagues (1979) were unable to find any meaningful differences in the course or outcome of 57 schizophrenic patients randomly assigned to fluphenazine and flupenthixol, and followed for six months after leaving hospital. However, frequent assessment reveals a high incidence of extrapyramidal side-effects. After six months on maintenance medication a large proportion (89 per cent) experienced at least mild extrapyramidal side-effects (EPSEs) at some time but fewer were affected at any one time. The more recently introduced long-acting neuroleptics, including *cis*-clopenthixol, haloperidol decanoate, penfluridol (oral weekly), and pipothiazine palmitate, have not shown any consistent pattern of superiority to fluphenazine, flupenthixol, or one another, though they may differ in their half-life. The study of Knights and colleagues emphasizes the high frequency of EPSEs during the initial stage of treatment with depot neuroleptics. Assessment by community psychiatric nurses can be useful to achieve frequent observation. For example, a nurse realized that one patient who worked with hot molten iron needed to take a few days off work after each injection because of shaking in his hands which lasted a few days.

When they occur, extrapyramidal symptoms can be abated by reducing the dose in two-thirds of cases or increasing the frequency of injections using smaller doses. Anticholinergic medication is rapidly effective but the necessity for long-term administration after control of the acute symptoms is doubtful and has been called into question (Mindham 1976; Johnson 1978, and see Chapter 12, this volume). At any point in time about 20 per cent of patients on depot maintenance neuroleptic treatment will have parkinsonian symptoms, but there is a constant interchange between those affected and those not. In their seven year follow-up study Curson and colleagues (1985) found no patients with severe extrapyramidal symptoms at follow-up, only 2.6 per cent had moderate ones and 28 per cent had mild symptoms. Only three cases (5.4 per cent) had tardive dyskinesia, but almost all patients were on medication.

Despite the prevalence of extrapyramidal symptoms, McClelland (1976) found that only 4 per cent of patients showed an increase of parkinsonian symptoms when anticholinergic medication was discontinued. Thus, patients may not require antiparkinsonian medication on a prolonged basis. At the same time prolonged use may increase the dose requirement of antipsychotic treatment as a result of enzyme induction and more rapid metabolism of neuroleptics (Lader 1979). They may cause discomforting and, rarely, life-threatening anticholinergic side-effects such as paralytic ileus and in high doses, cerebral toxicity and delirium; they may increase the risk of tardive dyskinesia. The general conclusion can be drawn that parkinsonian side-effects tend to be over treated; gradually increasing the dose of neuroleptics when first administered, and reducing it when parkinsonism appears could avoid symptoms in two-thirds of cases. Anticholinergics have a definite value when quick relief of symptoms is necessary but prolonged use after 6–12 weeks is generally not warranted.

Effects of discontinuing maintenance treatment

Maintenance treatment can be withdrawn from many in- or out-patients for many months without adverse effects. The mean time before relapse is about 4½ months (Letemendia *et al*. 1967; Hirsch *et al*. 1973; Hogarty and Ulrich 1977). After withdrawal, the number who relapse accumulates with time at a rate which decreases exponentially. Hogarty and Ulrich, using life table methods, calculated survival rates for 374 patients treated with oral chlorpromazine or placebo. The longer patients survived without relapse the more the risk declined. In the first months the risk of relapsing on placebo or drug was 13 and 4 per cent, respectively, and by month 24 the probability declined to 3 and 1.5 per cent. However, Davis *et al*. (1980) analysed results from several studies and noted that there was a constant exponential decline in the number of patients who survive without relapse of about 10 per cent per month following withdrawal from drugs. The exponential relationship is accounted for by the decreasing number of patients who are at risk to relapse. Of 100 patients, 90 remain the first month, 81 the second, 73 the third, etc. Medication lowered the risk of relapse by a factor of three.

Extrapolating their results beyond three years, Hogarty and Ulrich estimated that eventually 65 per cent of patients on medication and 87 per cent on placebo would relapse. Thus 13 per cent of patients did not need treatment, and medication should indefinitely prevent relapse for 22 per cent, while in the remaining 65 per cent relapse was only postponed. These predictions have support from Curson and colleagues' 7–8-year follow-up study of 81 patients who had been well maintained in a depot phenothiazine clinic (Curson *et al*. 1985). Discounting 12 who died and five with incomplete data, 83 per cent of the 63 patients followed up had at least one relapse but, as predicted by Hogarty and Ulrich (1977), 68 per cent had a relapse within seven years while taking medication. This compares with a relapse rate of 63 per cent within 13 months for 39 patients during the period they were temporarily off medication. This study again emphasizes that the main effect of maintenance medication is to considerably reduce the rate of relapse and prolong the interval between illness episodes, but only in a minority of cases to eliminate them altogether. Depot medication is likely to give better results because of close follow-up and better compliance. Eventual relapse rate is in any case a crude indicator which does not reflect the large reduction in the frequency and severity of relapse observed in patients following the introduction of depot maintenance treatment (Denham and Adamson 1971).

Relationship of serum drug level to relapse
The period when most relapses peak following discontinuation of depot

phenothiazines is about 4½ months. This coincides with the period when fluphenazine ceases to be detectable in most patients. However, Wiles was able to detect fluphenazine deconoate with a radioimmune assay in the serum of some patients up to six months, but flupenthixol decanoate was not detectable after nine weeks. This corresponded to the trend for patients to relapse on flupenthixol medication at a higher frequency than on fluphenazine depot injections when they were discontinued. It was also noticed that patients who relapsed in the first three months after withdrawal had higher initial serum levels and a significantly greater fall in the serum level during the first three weeks. Drug persisted in the blood longer in elderly patients and relapse occurred more slowly (Wistedt 1981; Wiles and Wistedt 1981).

When can medication be stopped?

These figures demonstrate the continuing benefit to patients of drug maintenance as compared to placebo, but they do not tell the clinicians the answer to the more practical question of what is the likelihood of relapsing if medication is withdrawn after several years treatment. During the first year after discharge if medication is withdrawn the relapse rate is particularly high (Hirsch *et al.* 1973). Three groups report one-year relapse rates on the order of 65 per cent for patients withdrawn from treatment after surviving two or three years on medication (Hogarty *et al.* 1976; Johnson 1976; Cheung 1981). This is a similar rate to that reported by Curson's follow-up study when 63 per cent of patients relapsed who had up to 13 months off medication at some time during the seven-year follow-up (Curson *et al.* 1985).

Recent studies have focused on chronic patients successfully maintained for years and especially selected to come off maintenance medication because they wished to stop, had no symptoms, and had good social control. Dencker *et al.* (1980) selected 32 patients from 200 in their clinic; 82 per cent relapsed in the first year, 92 per cent relapsed in the second. Wistedt (1981) found that 94 per cent of 16 patients relapsed in two years. Thus, there is no indication of recovery taking place in patients even if they have remained well controlled for several years. Rather, it seems possible that we may have created neuroleptic dependence, consistent with the idea of inducing postsynaptic receptor sensitivity by blocking dopamine receptors chronically. This would fit with the concept of Chouinard and Jones (1980) of a supersensitivity psychosis which describes a syndrome of increasing tolerance to neuroleptics and the rapid emergence of psychosis and tardive dyskinesia when drugs are withdrawn. However, there is no evidence of tolerance developing to maintenance neuroleptics—in fact the maintenance dose is usually much lower than the acute treatment dose. Nor can we say that tardive dyskinesia has been a common problem in withdrawal studies.

Low-dose maintenance and drug holidays

Given the disadvantages of long-term treatment including parkinsonian side-effects, tardive dyskinesia, and subtle extrapyramidal symptoms, akathisia and bradykinesia, which alter the patient's social presentation and cause symptoms which look like distress and depression (Rifkin *et al.* 1975), there is much to commend stopping long-term neuroleptics if possible.

Two alternatives to discontinuing medication were examined involving a reduction of the amount and frequency of medication. Caffey and colleagues (1964) randomized patients to three groups; daily treatment; treatment Monday, Wednesday, and Friday (43 per cent of original dose); and placebo. Within four months the relapse rates were 5, 16, and 45 per cent respectively. Prien and colleagues (1973) compared daily treatment to treatment three, four, and five times a week. After four months the relapse rate was 1 per cent and 6–8 per cent, respectively, the dose reductions being 19–43 per cent, respectively. It is clear that dose reduction in this manner carries less risk of relapse than completely discontinuing treatment, but more risk than full treatment. The risks and benefits of treatment must be assessed for each individual patient, but particular attention should be paid to patients in older age groups who are more at risk of developing tardive dyskinesia.

Capstick (1980) attempted gradual withdrawal from medication by increasing the period between injections over six months by one week at each visit and slowly decreasing the dose. When patients were on 3 mg fluphenazine decanoate every eight weeks, medication was stopped. Forty-seven out-patient schizophrenics were studied and by the end of two years 80 per cent of patients had relapsed while medication was being reduced. No variables predicted who would relapse or when, but reactive factors occurred in seven patients during the withdrawal phase compared to one in 22 after medication stopped. Symptoms quickly remitted when medication was reintroduced, even in patients who relapsed with predominantly depressive symptoms. Kane *et al.* (1979) employed a strategy of openly reducing each of 57 patients' medication to one-tenth the usual dose or 1.25–5 mg every 2–4 weeks. Twenty-six per cent relapsed within six months. Sixteen survivors were carefully matched into eight pairs, one of which was given placebo on a random and double-blind basis. Seven of eight on placebo (87 per cent) compared to one of eight continuing on low-dose relapsed. Relapse responded easily to reintroduction of normal dosage, and often did not require admission to hospital.

In a subsequent double-blind controlled study, 126 stable schizophrenics were randomly allocated to the same low- and standard-dose regimes. Fifty-six per cent relapsed within a year on the low-dose regime but only seven patients were hospitalized. Only three patients (7 per cent) relapsed on standard dose, and social sequelae were minimal in both groups (Kane *et al.* 1983).

These findings suggest that a proportion of well-stabilized patients, perhaps half or more, could be maintained on very low dosage, though not for the first year after a major episode. Moreover, the social cost of relapse under conditions of low dose or gradual withdrawal under close supervision does not seem high so the venture may be worthwhile.

Long-term effects of relapse and consequences of placebo-controlled trials

Good clinical practice involves deciding when treatment should be initiated, and when it should be stopped or continued, taking into account a reasoned response to a patient's desire to come off treatment.

This requires an assessment of the benefits of treatment, balanced against its risks. The same clinical judgement is involved when deciding if a patient should enter a controlled clinical trial, especially a placebo-controlled trial. Yet the United States Federal Drug Administration demands such evidence to sanction new products and proof of pharmacological efficacy for clinic use is never complete without a placebo-controlled study (see Chapter 8). Do placebo-controlled trials have long-term disadvantageous consequences for schizophrenics? The follow-up by Curson and his colleagues (1985) of patients who entered a randomized placebo-controlled trial after being well-established and stable on depot fluphenazine decanoate, provides useful evidence. In the original placebo-controlled trial 66 per cent of placebo group and 8 per cent of those on active medication relapsed over nine months (Hirsch *et al.* 1973). Sixty-four patients were subsequently followed up with a repeat assessment of clinical, social, and neurological functioning as well as detailed examination of their clinical experience during the intervening seven to eight years. There were no differences between the original drug and placebo trials groups in subsequent deaths, number of relapses, companionship, marital status, employment status, number of admissions, number of episodes of illness, total time spent on depot medication, status of follow-up, and mean time to relapse if medication was subsequently discontinued. Similarly, comparing those 20 patients who received neuroleptics continuously during the follow-up with 22 who relapsed within 13 months of discontinuing treatment, at follow-up there were no significant differences on the same variables. There was a positive correlation between the number of relapses an individual had and social ($r = 0.49$) outcome which was significant ($p < 0.001$), but this is only to say that the worst patients have the worst outcome. The clear implication from this study is that in general a relapse by itself does not have long-term clinical implications, and that relapse in a placebo-controlled study does not in itself contribute to deterioration, provided that the immediate untoward consequences are dealt with.

THE TREATMENT OF AFFECTIVE SYMPTOMS IN SCHIZOPHRENIA

The relationship between depression and schizophrenia

Depressive symptoms are exceedingly common at all stages of schizophrenia, but usually go unnoticed until the florid psychotic symptoms have settled. They are most prevalent during an acute exacerbation, before medication has been instituted (Shanfield *et al.* 1970; Knights and Hirsch 1981). Using a modern criterion for severity such as a Hamilton score over 15, several authors have reported depression in more than half of first-illness or drug-free schizophrenics (Johnson 1981), acutely hospitalized patients (Moller and von Zerssen 1981, 1982) and patients on maintenance therapy during six months follow-up (Knights *et al*. 1979). Fifty-six per cent of Moller and von Zerssen's series of 237 acute admissions showed prolonged depressive symptoms during their hospital stay but only 14 per cent of admissions developed depression after hospital treatment had been instituted.

We have shown that depressive symptoms diminish significantly during acute hospitalization and their prevalence during the six months immediately following discharge is about 25 per cent. About 50 to 70 per cent of all patients are affected at some point during their six-month period (Knights *et al*. 1979). Johnson (1981) followed 30 chronic schizophrenics for two years from the time of an acute on chronic relapse while on neuroleptics and found that 70 per cent experienced depression at some time. He defined depression as a lowered mood state with subjective changes of sadness, misery, tear-fulness, and hopelessness lasting more than one week and likely to provoke a treatment adjustment or intervention, with a Hamilton or Beck depression score above 15. Patients were rated monthly and 16 of the 30 patients had a depression lasting more than one week. Of the 524 weeks of recorded morbidity, 70 per cent were accounted for by depressive symptoms alone—an average of two months of depressive symptoms per affected patient per year. Moreover, follow-up studies have shown that depression is the main indication for some 40 per cent or more admissions (Falloon *et al*. 1978*a*; Curson *et al*. 1985).

Herz (1980) questioned 145 schizophrenics and their relatives about the symptoms which were present leading up to relapse. Depressed mood, agitation, anger, and social withdrawal were common in the three-week prodomal period. Dencker *et al*. (1980) reported that, in addition, reduced sleep and restlessness were common and Wistedt (1981) noted that retardation, increased sleep, loss of initiative, and withdrawal preceded relapse. Similar findings were reported by Capstick (1980) who found that the symptoms were reversed with increased neuroleptic medication.

The facts that depressive symptoms are part of the developing phase of an acute exacerbation, are most prevalent just after admission, but decrease in frequency during treatment with neuroleptics, and come and go spontaneously with lower prevalence during the recovery phase independent of anti-depressant treatment (Knights *et al*. 1979) are strong evidence against the concept of a pharmacogenic depression due to neuroleptics. On the contrary, the evidence suggests that depressive symptoms are an integral part of the schizophrenic syndrome sharing common pathophysiology (Hirsch 1982*b*) and that depressive symptoms increase rather than decrease when neuroleptics are withdrawn (Wistedt and Palinstlernag 1983). If this is so, then a possible first strategy when depressive symptoms emerge should be to increase the dose of neuroleptics, but this strategy has not been systematically tested.

It is interesting to note that only about half of the schizophrenics in each sample are affected by dysphoria and depression. Singh and Kay (1979*a*) found that those patients (30 per cent) who showed dysphoric symptoms (anxiety, depression, accusativeness, hostility, guilt, and suicidal ideation) had a poorer rate of recovery and a higher relapse rate. Eugene Bleuler made the opposite observation as he thought that patients with affective symptoms had a better prognosis. It remains for future studies to determine how schizophrenics who develop depression are otherwise different from those who do not.

Akinetic depression

Rifkin *et al.* (1975) produced evidence to suggest that depression may be a falsely read extrapyramidal symptom due to akinesia; and Van Putten and May (1978) called this 'akinetic depression' because they thought it was a new symptom of extrapyramidal disorder, not part of the parkinsonian syndrome. To test the theory that the depression is an extrapyramidal disorder, a double-blind controlled comparison of the anticholinergic, orphenadrine, was compared to placebo under double-blind conditions on Feighner-positive chronic schizophrenics who developed depression on depot neuroleptics. They were all thought to be free from drug-induced parkinsonism. Anticholinergics were discontinued for one week, and then either orphenadrine 50 mg bd or placebo were given for four weeks (Johnson 1981). A subjective feeling of muscular weakness and stiffness was the only symptom to significantly favour the antiparkinsonian drug, and 45 per cent of the placebo group improved. However, the trend favoured orphenadrine with 75 per cent improving; half the eight orphenadrine responders who showed a good improvement regressed when the drug was stopped. The response to an intravenous injection of an anticholinergic should help to identify patients with akinesia which presents as depression, but the negative results with anticholinergics by other authors (e.g. Singh and Kay 1979*b*) suggest that this group will be small.

The role of antidepressant medication

Chronic symptoms of schizophrenia

Antidepressants have been tried in different ways and for different aspects of schizophrenia but most studies have not selectively tested their use in schizophrenia with well documented depression. In a comprehensive review Siris *et al.* (1978) reported eight double-blind studies of tricyclics and six of monoamine oxidase inhibitors, all of which failed to find any benefit for symptoms in acute on chronic schizophrenics. Of a further 16 studies combining tricyclics with a neuroleptic, usually perphenazine, only Collins and Dundas (1967) found the combination significantly better for chronic anergic schizophrenics (58 per cent of 58 responded) than perphenazine or placebo alone (29 per cent responded) (*n* = 108). Flatness of affect was the symptom most improved by the addition of amitriptyline to perphenazine.

The remaining studies either found no effect, or did not sufficiently distinguish between schizophrenic and non-schizophrenic patients to determine which group benefited. Many studies focused on chronic inactive, apathetic, and withdrawn patients but did not distinguish patients affected by depression. Twelve studies combining monoamine oxadase inhibitors and phenothiazines showed no benefit for acute on chronic schizophrenics. Thus the value of antidepressants for the withdrawn chronic schizophrenic as such is slight or non-existent.

Depression in schizophrenia

There are remarkably few studies limited to depressed schizophrenics. In chronic patients it is difficult to differentiate between flatness of affect, apathy, and withdrawal on the one hand and symptoms of depression on the other. Moreover, institutionalized patients with these symptoms respond well to activation and social management (Wing and Brown 1970) so increased attention and care, which might occur in a research project, could itself have a beneficial effect, improving the patient's sociability and level of activity which is unrelated to the effect of medication. Such an effect can account for the improvement noted in all patients in a placebo-controlled trial of anticholinergic withdrawal in chronic schizophrenics (McClelland *et al*. 1974, and Chapter 7, this volume).

Siris *et al*. (1978) reported two studies of tricyclics alone in acute on chronic schizophrenics identified as being depressed. The first (Leuthold *et al*. 1961) showed only a trend toward improved mobility on imipramine, and improved affect on nialamide, while the second (Pishkin 1972) showed improved information processing. The clinical relevance of these studies is marginal as depression itself was not shown to improve. The small number of more substantial studies should be mentioned. Prusoff *et al*. (1978) reported results in 35 ambulatory schizophrenics who developed depressive symptoms. Depression scores significantly decreased at four months in the group receiving amitriptyline 100–200 mg, compared to the seven patients on placebo, but there were no significant differences at the end of the trial. Seventy-five per cent of those receiving combined treatment suffered an increase in blood pressure and body weight. Brockington *et al*.'s study (1978) suggested that chlorpromazine alone was as good as or better than combined treatment with amitriptyline for schizodepressives. The best trial of antidepressants for depression in schizophrenia is a comparison of nortriptyline, 50 mg three times daily, to placebo in 50 chronic non-florid schizophrenics who developed an episode of lowered mode state, with subjective sadness, misery, tearfulness, and hopelessness, of at least one week's duration, with a Hamilton Rating Scale score over 15 (Johnson 1981). All patients had Schneiderian First Rank symptoms or were Feighner-positive schizophrenics, and free of extrapyramidal side-effects. All were being maintained on fluphenazine or flupenthixol decanoate depot injections. There was no significant difference between placebo and nortriptyline or recovery rate, but 40 per cent of both groups showed some improvement.

A final complicating factor is that tricyclic antidepressants have an anticholinergic effect. Butterworth (1972) showed that the extrapyramidal symptoms of 80 per cent of 30 institutionalized patients significantly improved when imipramine was added. Thus the minimal benefit of imipramine to mobility, activity, etc. may be interpreted as an antidepressant action when it could be due to an effect on akinesia, an extrapyramidal side-effect difficult to distinguish from depression. Such results stress the importance of distinguishing akinesia from true depression and show the risks of attempting diagnosis on the basis of a specific response to treatment.

One must conclude that, though this important area is underresearched, there are no studies that suggest a strong therapeutic advantage in using antidepressants to treat the negative or positive symptoms of schizophrenia, or the symptoms of depression when they occur in conjunction with schizophrenia. Further studies need to address themselves to the serious methodological difficulties in distinguishing between depression, akinesia, and the effects of institutionalism in chronic patients which confound the issues in most of the previous work. There is only one study (Johnson 1981) which adequately separates these features in order to distinguish between specific and non-specific effects, and this had a negative outcome. A rational approach to treatment would be to identify the symptoms to be treated, and first test the effect of increasing the dose of neuroleptics. If this is unsuccessful, give a test dose of intravenous or intramuscular anticholinergics on the basis that the patient may have an akinetic drug-induced parkinsonian syndrome, for which anticholinergics should be prescribed. Tricyclics would be considered as a last resort, though a propitious delay before this intervention, which is unlikely to produce any benefit, may well reveal a spontaneous remission of depressive features within a month.

Lithium for schizophrenic and schizoaffective disorders

The methodological difficulties concerning the value of lithium for schizophrenia or for schizoaffective disorders are analogous to the problem in evaluating antidepressants and render any conclusion about their value premature. The effectiveness of lithium in schizophrenia has not been tested with adequate controls or sufficiently large samples, and any beneficial effect raises the question whether the sample included misdiagnosed atypical manic-depressives (Prien 1979). The study of Brockington and colleagues (1978) suggested that chlorpromazine has the edge when treating depressed-type schizoaffectives, but lithium is as good as chloropromazine for schizomanics if they are not grossly excited. However, the number of patients studied is small. Van Kammen and colleagues (1980) tried lithium for schizoaffective patients who had largely recovered from their psychoses but developed depression. Large doses, 1800–2100 mg per day, were used to obtain blood levels of 0.7 to 1.3 meq/l. The group effect was unimpressive but six of the 11 patients showed a marked decrease of their depressive scores while on lithium, with a return of symptoms when it was stopped after three weeks—this suggested the possibility of a lithium-responsive subgroup.

Delva and Letemendia (1982) suggested that there is a lithium-responsive schizophrenia subgroup after noticing that delusions, hallucinations, and thought-disorder recurred in one patient each of the four times that lithium was discontinued. The review of the literature by Delva *et al*. (1982) suggested that just under half of schizophrenics and more than 75 per cent of schizoaffectives respond to lithium; they considered that a number of patients in 15 mostly uncontrolled trials of lithium in schizophrenia and in 29 trials in schizoaffectives, respectively, improved on lithium, though the controlled studies gave conflicting results about the benefits in schizophrenia. An interesting strategy was adopted by Edelstein and colleagues (1981) who noted that cholinergic drugs had produced a positive response in catatonic and refractory schizophrenics in three papers, though two other studies had found negative results. Other studies had looked at the effect of increasing cholinergic function by giving physostigmine in manic depressives, which had a beneficial effect. This approach was based on the theory that the rate disturbance in mania is due to a relative high noradrenergic to low cholinergic ratio (Janowsky *et al*. 1972*a, b*; Davis and Berger 1978). They infused 11 Research Diagnostic Criteria schizophrenics and schizoaffectives with physostigmine for 1½ hours after a two-week wash-out. Peripheral cholinergic effects were blocked with probanthine. Those patients who showed a significant reduction of BPRS-rated Thinking Disturbance without increased retardation during the infusion responded to a two-week course of lithium carbonate when they had a 25 per cent reduction of schizophrenic symptoms, as rated on the New Haven Schizophrenic Index. Patients who did not improve during physostigmine infusion did not respond to lithium. Thus, the physostigmine test may differentiate a lithium-responsive group of schizophrenics or schizomanics.

Zemlan and colleagues (1984) suggested a clinical test for identifying lithium responders among schizophrenics and schizoaffectives. A criterion of 20 per cent improvement, or more, in hallucinations, delusions, or formal thought disorder at seven days identified over 88 per cent of responders, and less than 20 per cent improvement indicated more than 90 per cent of non-responders. If replicated, the test could have 90 per cent diagnostic efficiency.

More convincing evidence of the potential for lithium in schizophrenic-related disorders comes from Perris's report (1978) of 30 patients diagnosed and treated as cycloid psychoses (see Chapter 6). Using a mirror image design, the 21 patients who took this medication regularly, as confirmed by blood levels, showed a significant reduction of morbidity time in hospital.

Miller and Libman (1979) reviewed the use of lithium in schizophrenia and schizoaffective disorders. Ten papers are quoted as reporting case reports claiming lithium is of value in both affective symptoms and schizophrenic ones, but two others—both controlled studies—found no effect. Another eight papers reported a selective effect for lithium in the affective symptoms of schizoaffective patients. The authors suggested that the diagnostic complexities can be avoided by using the presence of psychomotor acceleration and periodicity as the criteria for its use. Psychomotor acceleration is a symptomatic complex consisting of restlessness and hyperactivity associated with pressure of speech and rapid thoughts. Periodicity refers to an intermittent course in which successive episodes are similar in content, onset, and duration and there is a return to pre-psychotic levels of functioning. Such an approach will nicely avoid the diagnostic problems, if indeed these syndromes can be confirmed to improve selectively to lithium carbonate, supporting the view that lithium is effective for both the affective and the schizophrenic symptoms of schizomanic states. Biederman and colleagues (1979) carried out a five-week study of haloperidol with and without lithium, randomly allocated to 36 psychiatric patients admitted with elevated mood or hyperactivity. Haloperidol with lithium conferred significant advantages for both affective-schizoaffectives and schizophrenics with affective changes. On a broad range of items on the manic and BPRS scales, 34 of 42 items showed greater change in the group receiving lithium with haloperidol than haloperidol alone; six of these changes were significant and included depression, suspiciousness, and guilt feelings. However, affective-schizoaffectives improved significantly more than schizophrenic schizoaffectives regardless of treatment. The point to be noticed is that all of the patients had a rate-related disorder in addition to psychotic thought content.

A novel treatment for schizoaffective states is the use of carbamazepine with haloperidol in refractory schizoaffective states; this has been tested in one small controlled trial (n = 43) in which placebo or carbamazepine were added to haloperidol, with good results (Klein *et al.* 1984). This is considered with a growing number of reports that suggest carbamazepine is a useful adjunct to lithium in manic-depressive states.

Schizoaffective disorders present problems for treatment evaluation because the relationship between schizophrenia and affective symptoms is not understood, and different diagnostic systems are used to define the condition (see Chapter 6). The best working hypothesis is that lithium is effective against excitement and abnormal affective states associated with schizophrenia, and may be effective against core psychotic symptoms in up to half of affected patients.

Treatment with lithium should be tried on a symptomatic basis and continued if there is a good response for a period longer than that of the patient's previous episode of affective swings or excitement.

OTHER PHYSICAL TREATMENTS

Electroconvulsive therapy

The popularity of electroconvulsive treatment (ECT) has waxed and waned since its introduction in 1938 by Cerletti and Bini. For the past decade or more it has had only a limited place in the treatment of schizophrenia in Britain and the United States; a few practitioners use it widely, but most restrict ECT to the occasional patient with catatonic stupor or excitement, or patients with hypomanic excitement in schizoaffective states. This is in marked contrast to practice in the late 1950s when ECT was the commonest form of treatment for schizophrenia (Baker *et al.* 1958), and is different from prevailing practice in many developing countries where a premium is placed on short rapid but effective treatment to minimize hospital stay. Despite problems in the quality and quantity of research to date, almost all reports point in the same direction—that ECT is broadly effective in acute schizophrenia, but less so or not at all in long-standing stable chronic states, that it speeds recovery in the early stages, and that some patients respond to ECT who have not responded to neuroleptics. Given the fact that the safety record of modern ECT is probably better than medication because it has no long-term side-effects and the only contraindications are the risks of anaesthesia in the presence of brain tumour (Maltbie *et al.* 1980), ECT may deserve a more central place in the first-line treatment of schizophrenia. Here we will consider the evidence.

The effect of ECT with and without drugs: an acceleration of the treatment response

Systematic research into the value of ECT for schizophrenia is limited, and earlier studies suffer from the absence of adequate rating scales and tend to rely on clinical impression and length of hospitalization as a crude intention of outcome. Studies with mostly acutely ill patients suggest that, in combination with neuroleptics, ECT speeds the course of recovery in the early stages of treatment and lowers the patient's requirement for medication. Controlled studies support this. Turek (1973) reviewed 14 studies, albeit most are uncontrolled and methodologically dubious, but together they cover a large number of patients. In a preliminary retrospective study of 109 schizophrenics, Childers (1964) noted an improvement of 47 per cent on drugs alone, which increased to 63 per cent following ECT. In a subsequent cross-over study, 80 patients were randomly allocated to have 12 ECT alone: ECT plus chlorpromazine 1 g daily; chlorpromazine alone; or fluphenazine alone—80 per cent of the combined ECT–CPZ group and ECT-alone group each had a 55 per cent diminution of symptoms or better, compared to 45 per cent in the two drug groups. Half the 22 patients who did not respond to drugs alone responded when subsequently given ECT—giving about the same improvement as giving ECT in combination with drugs from the start.

Smith and colleagues (1967) randomly allocated 54 acutely admitted schizophrenics to receive ECT plus chlorpromazine (mean dose 400 mg), or chlorpromazine only (mean dose 655 mg). Although there was no important difference between treatments at the six-week and six-month follow-up on the IMPS and ward behaviour rating scales, the group having combined treatment improved more rapidly in a number of symptom areas and significantly more patients were discharged at two and six months. Wells (1973) followed up 276 schizophrenics given ECT, of whom over 80 per cent of those with depression and catatonia had a good or moderate improvement compared with 55 per cent of catatonics and 40 per cent of other schizophrenics who had made the same level of improvement previously.

Two studies compared ECT with simulated ECT in which all aspects of ECT administration were given to both groups except the passage of current—thereby controlling for all non-specific aspects of the treatment. Taylor and Fleminger (1980) randomly assigned 20 acutely admitted schizophrenics with symptoms of less than six months' duration to real or simulated ECT. All patients were on neuroleptics for two weeks and required further treatment. The diagnosis was based on CATEGO criteria of schizophrenia using the Present State Examination, and 25 joules of bilateral or unilateral undirectional ECT was given thrice weekly to the experimental groups; simulated ECT, including the anaesthetic but no electricity, was given to controls. Experimental conditions were double-blind, thus the study controlled for all variables and measured the effect of ECT itself. A significant advantage to the real ECT group was noted by two weeks. By the end of four weeks, only one of 10 patients receiving ECT had signs of schizophrenia, compared to nine of 10 of controls ($p < 0.004$). After an additional four weeks there was still a nearly significant advantage to the ECT group ($p < 0.07$) but by three months three of the ECT group had relapsed while some controls had improved (four had ECT during the uncontrolled treatment period from four weeks to 16 weeks) and the difference between the experimental and control group was not significant.

This showed a significant advantage to neuroleptics plus ECT as compared to neuroleptics alone for the first two months, an impressive result considering that little importance can be given to the placebo group after the first four weeks when restrictions on treatment were lifted. Depressive symptoms were better relieved by ECT than placebo at two, four, and eight weeks, and none of the ECT group were depressed by the end of treatment, although the difference between groups in Beck's score was not quite significant ($p = 0.068$ at 4 weeks).

These findings were further confirmed by the Leicester ECT trial of 19 patients (Brandon *et al.* 1984) who fulfilled the Present State Examination criteria for schizophrenia. Patients were randomized to eight bilateral chopped sinusoidal wave ECT treatments or no electricity two times per week under double-blind conditions. Patients receiving real ECT improved significantly more than simulated controls at two and four weeks. Five of nine of the real ECT group will not require the full course of eight treatments, but all the simulated group did, and five of eight simulated ECT were given ECT in the post-trial treatment period, after four weeks. Thus the fact that there were no significant differences in outcome at 12 and 28 weeks can be accounted for by differences in additional treatment. The effect on depressive symptoms, though evident, was not as great as on the schizophrenic symptoms as measured by the Montgomery Schizophrenic Scale (Montgomery *et al.* 1978).

Neither of these studies gave information on the effect of neuroleptic dosage in relation to the efficacy of ECT. Janakiramaiah and colleagues

(1982) tested the response of ECT and no ECT at two levels of chlorpromazine on 60 acutely schizophrenic patients hospitalized for six weeks. ECT enhanced the therapeutic response at the 300-mg level of chlorpromazine but was not better than no ECT when combined with chlorpromazine at 500 mg or more per day.

Thus, there is strong evidence that ECT confers a beneficial physiological effect in combination with neuroleptics, offering a more rapid recovery than neuroleptics without ECT in several studies, but one study, controlling for dose level, found no advantage to ECT when used in combination with higher doses of neuroleptics. Patients who had not responded initially to medication alone improved considerably when ECT was added. Whether this latter group are slow responders who would have improved with time in the absence of ECT has not been adequately tested.

Longer-term effects of ECT and regressive ECT

The longer-term effects of ECT are hard to gauge from these studies because it is generally not feasible to control treatment beyond a few months, particularly additional treatments after a course of ECT is completed, because of a well-established clinical view that ECT should be combined with maintenance treatment. Kalinowsky *et al.* (1969) stated that relapse rapidly follows if ECT is given alone unless followed by 10 or 20 further shocks at decreasing intervals. Others who have reviewed the subject state that ECT has been undervalued in schizophrenia because it is incapable by itself of leading to sustained improvement (Weinstein and Fisher 1971). The implication is that the effect of ECT is not unlike the effect of medication in its ability to bring about temporary recovery, but the patient remains vulnerable without continued treatment.

There is some evidence of longer-term effects of ECT. In the study by Smith and colleagues (1967) a greater proportion of drug-plus-ECT patients were discharged at two and six months.

May and colleagues (1965, 1976) compared ECT alone to drugs and controls with and without psychotherapy in 100 middle prognosis acute schizophrenics. The worst and best prognosis patients were excluded. The outcome over three years for patients treated with ECT alone occupied an intermediate position between patients treated with drugs and those given no physical treatment, though ECT by itself was not significantly better than controls. The main treatment effect was due to medication alone but the effect of drugs combined with ECT was not tested. More patients initially allocated to receive ECT were discharged at two and five years than patients who received psychotherapy or milieu therapy, even though all groups were eligible to receive any treatment after the first year.

The studies of Exner and Murillo (1973) claimed long-term effects on the social and clinical functioning of acute schizophrenics with moderate and poor prognosis. They employed so-called 'regressive' ECT, given twice daily until the patient becomes confused, mute, helpless, ataxic, or has positive Babinski signs. They reported that recovery from this state usually takes 7–10 days and improvement is marked (Murillo and Exner 1973). The authors produced evidence that 32 patients so treated had significantly more clinical and social improvement after two months than 21 patients who refused ECT but were treated with adequate doses of neuroleptics. At one year post-discharge 22 of 24 patients treated with 'regressive' ECT, compared to eight of 13 who received neuroleptics in adequate doses were working (Exner and Murillo 1973). Only two of the ECT-treated group were on medication compared to 11 of 13 who originally had neuroleptics. A battery of psycho-metric tests including WAIS, MMPI, Bender Gestalt, and others failed to show any difference between the two groups at 24–30 months post-discharge, but both groups were inferior to 'normal controls'; however, the mean IQ of the control group was above normal, 118 on the WAIS (Exner and Murillo 1977). This result needs to be confirmed by a randomized controlled trial before general consideration can be given to applying the method which many psychiatrists would find harsh and extreme. However, given the efficacy of psychotropic medication in maintaining patients, and the evidence that ECT effects are not sustained without maintenance treatment, there is little to support the use of ECT alone or in this extreme form.

The importance of affective and other symptoms

There are particular problems in assessing the role of ECT in schizophrenia. First, in several studies the patients who responded best had affective symptoms. Given the previous prevailing practice in the United States of diagnosing schizophrenia on the basis of broad, ill-defined diagnostic criteria (this has now been corrected by DSM III which has an ultra-narrow defini-tion), many patients with affective symptoms in earlier studies may have been suffering from an affective illness misdiagnosed as schizophrenia. For example, Wells (1973) found that, of 276 schizophrenics given ECT, those who responded best had moderate or severe depression and these made up 76 per cent of his sample, of whom 85 per cent did well. Second, patients who responded best are said to be those who have an acute onset and are being treated in the first year of illness (Abrams and Taylor 1977). This is a self-fulfilling prophecy since these characteristics describe patients who are most likely to have a spontaneous recovery and have the most favourable long-term prognosis regardless of treatment. Neither trials of simulated versus real ECT discussed above (Taylor and Fleminger 1980; Brandon *et al.* 1984) examined the effect of length of previous illness on response, and about half the patients in both studies had strong affective symptoms which responded to treatment. Whether there was a better response in those with affective symptoms was not considered. Koehler and Sauer's (1983) retrospective study of 142 schizophrenics who had ECT found that patients with affective symptoms did better as did schizophrenics who did not have Schneiderian symptoms of the First Rank. No particular type of First Rank symptom was predictive of a better or worse response. Data from other studies re-analysed and quoted supported their findings. Generally in the UK about half of patients diagnosed as having schizophrenia have a depressive syndrome as well (Hirsch 1982*b*), so the question whether patients who respond best to ECT are those with affective symptoms is of interest. Notwithstanding, First Rank symptoms of schizophrenia responded to ECT in several studies (e.g. Taylor and Fleminger 1980; Brandon *et al.* 1984) and it should be remembered that affective symptoms in schizophrenia respond to neuroleptics, so improvement with ECT need not imply a change of diagnosis.

Catatonia

Because acute catatonic stupor or excitement is a medical emergency and cases are rare, there are no controlled trials, but few would doubt the effectiveness of ECT treatment in aborting the acute state or bringing hypomanic excitement under control. Treatment can be given daily or even twice daily in extreme cases, where control of excitement presents an urgent problem; otherwise three times a week will normally suffice. Amelioration of symptoms is usually seen after three or four treatments, if not sooner. Neuroleptic treatment should be given with ECT and continued to maintain the improvement.

The nosological status of catatonia and its relation to affective psychoses and schizophrenia remains an unresolved question. Abrams and Taylor (1977) studied 55 catatonic patients treated with ECT, 70 per cent of whom had three or more catatonic symptoms. Patients who responded had a lower mean age of onset and a positive history of affective disorder or co-existing affective symptoms. On the other hand all the poor responders satisfied Feighner's narrow criteria for schizophrenia and had a poorer long-term outcome. They suggest that catatonia occurs in affective states and should not always be equated with schizophrenic states. In Morrison's follow-up study (1973) 28 per cent of 67 excited-typed catatonics were rediagnosed as affective disorder. In practice, diagnostic distinctions often follow the treatment of catatonic states, and the combination of neuroleptics, plus ECT if required, is the surest initial approach.

Chronic schizophrenia

A different question is whether ECT is of therapeutic value in the absence of affective and catatonic symptoms, particularly in chronic patients. The limited evidence available for chronic non-depressed schizophrenics shows that ECT is no better than anaesthesia without ECT (Brill *et al.* 1959; Heath *et al.* 1964; Miller *et al.* 1953). In chronic patients there is difficulty distinguishing between depression and the inert, withdrawn social poverty syndrome. Any attempt to do so would need to control for changes in social environment, ward milieu, and level of activity—all of which are highly correlated with social withdrawal and the presence or absence of the negative symptoms of schizophrenia. The improvements seen in control as well as treated chronic patients are probably due to changes in these unspecific factors associated with being in a trial. This is illustrated by McClelland and colleagues (1974) who reported a study of the effects after three months of withdrawing antiparkinsonian medication in 99 chronic hospitalized schizophrenics. There was a general trend for more patients to improve, rather than deteriorate, in both treatment groups. Frank psychotic behaviour, laughter and talking to oneself, and pronounced mannerisms all improved, irrespective of treatment—evidently as a result of being included in a research study. Thus, frequent reports of improvement in chronic patients based on uncontrolled observations are probably based on improvement in response to the unspecific aspects of the treatment and not to ECT itself.

This review fails to deal with a host of technical questions regarding the form, frequency, and length of ECT because of the dearth of systemic studies. Adequate research is not available to know which patients need more, which require less. For example, Robin and de Tissera (1982) reported a significant correlation between the energy of each ECT and clinical effect irrespective of whether a convulsion occurred, but their work was done with depressives.

There is every indication that ECT has a place in the treatment of schizophrenia to bring about a more rapid resolution of symptoms, to control catatonia and states of excitement, and to treat patients whose symptoms have not fully responded to neuroleptics. There is little evidence to support the value of ECT for chronic states but research is sparse. Technical aspects of ECT in schizophrenia are virtually unresearched, though if this 'lost treatment' is to be brought into more general use, the time for a resurgence of studies to deepen and refine our knowledge will have to be recognized.

Chemically-induced convulsive treatment

Von Meduna introduced convulsive treatment in schizophrenic patients in 1934. He used camphor oil injected intramuscularly but soon changed to a soluble synthetic camphor preparation, pentamethylentetrazol or metrazole. Since 1957, the most popular chemical convulsive agent has been hexafluorediethyl called fluethyl or indoklon. It can be given intravenously but causes sclerosis of veins—inhalation is therefore the usual route of administration. The details of technique were summarized by Kalinowsky and colleagues (1982) and the research on its clinical value was well reviewed by Small and Small (1972). Ulett *et al.* (1956) found convulsive shock by ECT or by hexazol, plus photostimulation, led to a significant higher rate of recovery (46 per cent versus 21 per cent) than subconvulsive shock or controls in 84 patients, but only 20 of these were diagnosed as schizophrenic. Many studies, including a double-blind evaluation in 100 patients, suggest it is clinically as effective as ECT but no more. The evidence suggests that the essential therapeutic factor is whether seizures have been induced—a fact which is relevant to the issue of whether electricity or seizures is the key factor in ECT. Disadvantages of fluethyl include difficulty of administration, occasional multiple seizures, plus other side-effects equivalent to ECT. It may produce fewer amnestic effects. Its main advantage is as an alternative to ECT when there is a need to avoid electrical induction of seizures. Against occasional use of this sort is the fact that most psychiatrists today are unfamiliar with the technical aspects of its use.

Insulin coma treatment

This treatment which has a reported mortality of 0.5 per cent is mentioned for historical interest as it was the first biological treatment of importance to be used in schizophrenia. Experimenting with insulin subcoma in various psychiatric patients, Manfred Sakel noticed that some schizophrenics who developed coma, although as an unintended complication, came out of it remarkably improved. He reported it as a treatment for schizophrenia in 1933 and it rapidly became established, later to be joined by ECT as the main treatment for schizophrenia until the advent of phenothiazines. The method was well reviewed by Kalinowsky and colleagues (1982). Although a respectable number of series have reported positive results, there are few controlled trials. Fink *et al*. (1958) randomly allocated patients to 50 insulin coma treatments or to chlorpromazine, 300–2000 mg per day, and found no difference in outcome on weekly observation over four months following completion of treatment.

About the same time, Ackner and colleagues' (1957) classic double-blind trial failed to show a difference between insulin coma and barbiturate coma followed by amphetamines. Their study of 50 patients aged 18 to 40 included only first episode cases, and the largest number were paranoid. Eventually 66 patients were included, and a three-year follow-up showed a significantly greater re-admission rate for the insulin-treated group, who then spent more time in hospital (Ackner *et al*. 1957; Ackner and Oldham 1972). In themselves, these studies are limited in scope and cannot be regarded as decisive. Because the treatment is difficult, dangerous, uneconomic, and has nothing to offer over standard chemotherapy, it rapidly gave way to neuroleptics and has largely disappeared from use even in centres where it had the greatest support.

Psychosurgery

The problems of conducting controlled trials are most evident in relation to surgical techniques. There are no adequately controlled or randomized studies of note where psychosurgery has been used in schizophrenia. Stengel (1950) reported that hallucinations were unchanged in 75 per cent of 154 cases and delusions undiminished in 72 per cent of 160 cases following leucotomy, but when psychosurgery is considered today, selection is much more stringent. The use of psychosurgery fell dramatically following the introduction of phenothiazines. The general dictum is that anxiety, tension, agitation, and depression form the main indication, regardless of the underlying condition. Centres which specialize in psychosurgery do not regard schizophrenia as an indication *per se*, but an occasional patient whose symptoms are both very distressing and unresponsive to all reversible means of treatment can be considered. While the symptoms may not abate, their distressing quality can be expected to.

EXPERIMENTAL TREATMENTS

Propranolol

The interest in this treatment emanates from the original observation by Atsmon and Blum (1970) that propranolol ameliorated florid psychotic symptoms in patients with acute porphyria variegata and that it had ameliorative effects in functional psychosis (Atsmon *et al.* 1971, 1972). This was supported by an open study of Yorkston and colleagues (1974) who reported remission of schizophrenia in 17 of 55 patients, acute and chronic, and improvement amongst an additional 11 using high doses, 160–3000 mg/day. Subsequent studies have not reported such impressive results and many have been negative. Summing the results of 13 studies published up to 1981, about a third of acute, mixed, or chronic schizophrenics showed at least a moderate response to propranolol. However, this obscures the lack of consistent results from one study to another. Can this be resolved by focusing on double-blind randomized controlled trials?

There are three questions that need to be answered. The first is whether propranolol is a useful adjunct to neuroleptic medication in refractory or mixed psychosis. The second is whether it has a therapeutic effect as a first-line agent in acute treatment. The third is an important scientific question, whether a substance which has no effect on dopamine binding and does not cause hyperprolactaemia or extrapyramidal side-effects has an antipsychotic action.

There are several controlled trials comparing propranolol to placebo as an adjunct to neuroleptics in chronically hospitalized refractory schizophrenics. Yorkston and colleagues (1977) found that seven chronic schizophrenics did significantly better with propranolol than placebo, as an adjunct to neuroleptics, while Lindström and Persson (1980) found that 6 of 12 patients improved on propranolol using a two-week cross-over design. In contrast, Myers and colleagues (1981) reported an unequivocal negative result. They allocated 20 chronically hospitalized schizophrenics with one or more First Rank symptoms to receive propranolol or placebo in addition to fortnightly fluphenazine (25 mg) or flupenthixol decanoate (400 mg). The dose of propranolol was increased from 160 mg to 1920 mg/day over the first month and then maintained for three months. Patients were rated on a modified Present State Examination (Wing *et al.* 1974). No significant differences were noted at any point in time between propranolol and placebo. Pugh and colleagues (1983) had a more equivocal result with refractory schizophrenics ill for at least one year. They added propranolol or placebo to existing neuroleptics obtaining a dose of 640 mg/day in 13 of 26 patients treated for three months, but of three scales employed, BPRS, CPRS, and NOISE, only the

NOISE showed an advantage for propranolol at the end of 12 weeks. These unimpressive results of propranolol adjunct therapy were substantiated by Peet and colleagues (1981) who failed to obtain a better than placebo response over four months in 40 chronically hospitalized schizophrenics randomly allocated to propranolol 640 mg, placebo, or chlorpromazine 400 mg, though tremor and drowsiness were more evident with chlorpromazine.

The history of therapeutic reports not uncommonly starts with excellent results and proceeds to less enthusiastic ones. An overview of some 20 reports in the light of controlled studies suggests to the author that propranolol offers no major therapeutic benefit in chronic refractory schizophrenics who still show evidence of delusions and/or hallucinations.

A different question is whether propranolol has a measurable pharmacological effect on schizophrenic symptoms which may be evident on rating scales, but does not reflect itself in the number of patients who make a moderate or better improvement. Eccleston and colleagues (1985) randomly treated 45 chronic schizophrenics who had not responded satisfactorily to neuroleptics. RAC-positive chronic schizophrenics were given propranolol or thioridazine about two weeks after discontinuing previous treatment, reaching a dose of 640 mg and 400 mg respectively, over seven days. By the end of four weeks there was a significantly greater improvement with propranolol than with thioridazine on the BPRS total scores, and in both positive and negative symptoms. Taken separately, the number of patients who lost early symptoms did not differ, and only 9 of 22 patients on propranolol and 5 of 23 on thioridazine showed a moderate or better improvement on global ratings. While this could not be considered impressive evidence of an important clinical effect, it does suggest that pharmacological effect can be detected on the rating scales. Peet and colleagues (1981) suggested that many of the positive responses in previous studies could be related to their finding that the level of neuroleptics in the body is higher when propranolol is used as an adjunct. However, the evidence for the interaction is confined to chlorpromazine sulphoxide in patients treated for seven weeks with chlorpromazine with or without propranolol. Whether this effect could be important in patients such as those in Eccleston's trial, who have been treated with propranolol two weeks after conventional neuroleptics have been withdrawn, is not yet known.

Observations by those of us who have used propranolol suggest that, if it has an effect on acute schizophrenia, it is not a powerful one and lacks the benefit of sedation during the initial phase of treatment. The remaining question is whether it has a specific antipsychotic effect. This can best be tested in acute patients. We randomly treated 46 acutely admitted florid schizophrenics with an average dose of propranolol of about 500 mg/day, and of chlorpromazine, about 300 mg/day and did not find a significant overall difference between treatments; there was a wide variation of outcome within each group, and there were significant differences favouring chlorpromazine over propranolol on a number of items of the BPRS (Yorkston *et al.* 1981).

Subsequently, we have carried out a double-blind comparison of *d*-propranolol and placebo over four weeks in 36 acutely admitted schizophrenics, all of whom received haloperidol for the first week. The *d*-isomer of propranolol has very little β-adrenergic blocking effect. An initial improvement was seen in both groups over the first two weeks, then deterioration toward the baseline, which was significantly greater in the placebo group (Manchanda and Hirsch 1986). The subjects participating in the trial were a treatment-responsive group, as they improved further with haloperidol after the end of the trial. This study, somewhat like that of Eccleston and colleagues, showed significant pharmacological, but not clinical, effect of propranolol on ratings of both positive and negative schizophrenic features on the BPRS and Manchester (MS) scales. When compared to placebo, propranolol had a small but discernible effect sustaining the improvement obtained from one week's treatment with haloperidol, but three weeks' treatment did not lead to further improvement in the propranolol-treated group, which occurred subsequently when haloperidol was re-introduced.

The conclusion seems to be that propranolol and its *d*-isomer which is not a beta-adrenergic blocker, have a smaller pharmacological effect on schizophrenic symptomatology, but the effect does not compare favourably with conventional neuroleptics as a clinical agent. These findings should, however, be of interest to neuropharmacologists because they do point to the possibility that a non-neuroleptic agent with no known effect on the dopaminergic system is pharmacologically active in ameliorating psychoses. Could the action of similar substances be modified to produce an effective treatment?

High-dose diazepam

Because benzodiazepine anxiolytics are often used to sedate patients in clinical trials the possible effect of high-dose benzodiazepam on schizophrenic symptoms could be an important factor affecting the interpretation of results. Beckman and Haas (1980) gave 15 consecutively admitted acute schizophrenics and schizoaffective patients 200 mg of benzodiazepam per day; four patients had 260 mg/day up to day 10 and two patients had 400 mg/day. A significant reduction of psychotic symptoms was noted in 10 patients and 7 of 9 paranoid schizophrenics had a complete remission. Five patients, all schizoaffective, needed to be withdrawn because of excitement, loss of sexual inhibition, and sleep loss with drive enhancement. While all patients were sedated at 50 mg, sedation disappeared with higher dosage. Because of the risk of dependence with withdrawal symptoms on prolonged benzodiazepines and the fact that all patients became ataxic, especially older patients, high-dose diazepam does not seem to have a role in ordinary treatment. There are implications of these findings for our understanding of neuropharmacological interaction mechanism.

Narcotic antagonists—naloxone and naltrexone

Since the discovery of endogenous opiate peptides and receptor sites in the mid-1970s, the possibility of using endorphins and opiate antagonists to treat schizophrenia has intrigued many researchers. In over 30 studies of the opiate antagonists, naloxone or naltrexone hydrochloride have been given to symptomatic schizophrenics with conflicting results. Details were discussed by Mueser and Dysken (1983) who suggested that all the double-blind studies which found positive effects used between 4 and 40 mg of naloxone, intravenously. Relief followed in three to six hours in most cases, and only persisted transiently for hours or a day. Hallucinations are the symptom most commonly affected but several studies report improvement in the psychotic symptoms.

Mueser and Dysken reviewed the results of six studies of catatonic patients; four reported a beneficial effect, but the total number of patients was only 14. Schenk and colleagues (1978) reported an initial response to naloxone 1.6 to 19.2 mg/day intravenously, in eight of nine movement-inhibited schizophrenics and five of seven patients clinically benefited from three to twenty-one days. Less success was noted with naltrexone in that only one of eight investigations reported positive results. Of 42 schizophrenics investigated who received 50 to 800 mg of oral naltrexone per day for intervals ranging from two to six weeks, only seven patients responded favourably, and 10 had a negative outcome.

Because clinical response is so short and medication must be administered intravenously, narcotic antagonists to date must be regarded as having more theoretical than clinical interest.

Even in this regard there are various explanations for their antipsychotic effect including an endorphin rebound effect because symptom relief takes two to four hours, a direct effect on non-opioid neurotransmitters, and an effect through dopaminergic modulation though not directly on dopamine receptors. The fact that naltrexone, a powerful opioid antagonist does not seem to have effects on schizophrenic symptoms creates problems in explaining the effects of naloxone with the opiate model.

Haemodialysis

Considerable interest in the feasibility of removing possible toxic substances from the plasma of schizophrenics followed the report by Wagemaker and Cade (1977; Wagemaker 1978) that 10 out of 15 schizophrenics improved with haemodialysis, although Feer and colleagues had reported that four of five patients improved in 1960. A review of an uncontrolled study comprising 92 patients (Fogelson *et al*. 1980) reported that 47 per cent of patients made a marked or partial improvement. The influence of non-specific factors on the patients' response must be powerful under such a dramatic procedure; its effect can only be judged under double-blind controlled conditions. Three such trials comparing real dialysis with sham dialysis have all yielded unequivocally negative results (Diaz-Buxo *et al.* 1980; Schultz *et al.* 1981; Vanherweghan *et al.* 1983). Given the expense and life-threatening hazards of the procedure, there is little justification for further research.

Megavitamin therapy

Originally based on the use of vitamin B_3 (nicotinamide, nicotinic acid) as advocated by Hoffer *et al.* (1957), the concept of megavitamin therapy has been broadened to include the use of vitamin C, and to some extent vitamin B_6 (pyridoxine), vitamin B_{12}, folic acid, vitamin E, and a variety of minerals. It includes a school of nutritional thought which encompasses conventional somatic treatments such as neuroleptics and ECT but advocates supplementation with large doses of vitamins. The main focus is on the amelioration of chronic and recurrent states, allowing for conventional treatment in the acute initial stages of schizophrenia. Unfortunately, the evidence is non-existent or very weak (American Psychiatric Association 1973) but we will review it here.

Vitamin B_3, nicotinic acid, niacin, nicotinamide

Three controlled trials (Hoffer and Osmond 1964; Osmond and Hoffer 1962; Denson 1962) and one open study (Hoffer *et al.* 1957) reported significantly lower relapse rates, or a shorter period in hospital, over a two- to three-year period following a brief controlled trial on vitamin B_3, but in these studies authors either failed to report measures of schizophrenic symptoms or improvements were not noted. They all suffered from poor controls, inadequate statistical analysis, and loose undefined criteria for diagnosis and outcome. The majority of double-blind controlled studies failed to find any greater improvement than placebo during a six-month to two-year follow-up using nicotinamide and nicotinic acid (Greenbaum 1970), niacin (Wittenborn *et al.* 1973), or broad megavitamin therapy (Ban *et al.* 1977), and several studies reported untoward side-effects in the absence of beneficial effects such as increased time in hospital due to vitamin B_3 treatment (Ananth 1973), increased irritability and hostility (Kline *et al.* 1967; Meltzer *et al.* 1969), and increased need for phenothiazines.

Vitamin C (ascorbic acid)

Milner (1963) treated 34 schizophrenics with ascorbic acid or placebo and noted improvement in the vitamin-C-treated group on the affective and paranoid measures of the Wittenborn scale, but not on other subscales associated with schizophrenia. The possibility of subclinical scurvy in these patients as an explanation of the treatment response was not ruled out. Pitt and Pollitt (1971), on the other hand, matched for diet and length of hospitalization and did not find any benefit of vitamin C over placebo, and Ban and colleagues (1977), already mentioned, failed to find a better response to chlorpromazine plus megavitamins than to chlorpromazine plus placebo—in fact the trend favoured placebo. The vitamin therapy, given to

20 chronically hospitalized schizophrenics included ascorbic acid (vitamin C) 1–3 g daily, nicotinic acid 1–9 g daily, thiamine 300 mg daily, pyridoxine 150 mg daily, and hydroxycobalamine 5 mg daily, given over a 24-week period.

After 30 years advocacy for megavitamin therapy, which is not infrequently instituted as a last hope measure by families of schizophrenics, one would have expected to find more credible clinical reports as well as adequate controlled research if the treatment has any substantial value.

Endorphins

The discovery that endorphins played a role in brain metabolism and reports of abnormal quantities of endorphin fragments in the cerebral spinal fluid raised the possibility that an abnormality of endorphin production or metabolism could be important in the aetiology of schizophrenia. Attention was brought to the possible therapeutic role of endorphins in schizophrenia when de Wied and colleagues (1978) reported that des-tyr-γ-endorphin, a β-lipotropin fragment, facilitated extinction of active avoidance behaviour in rats in a similar way to the neuroleptic drug, haloperidol, but lacked other properties of neuroleptics in animal models including sedation and reduced locomotion. They also reported that γ-endorphin fragments do not compete for neuroleptic binding sites in brain homogenates. Subsequently, de Wied and his group published various reports of open and controlled studies on a small sample of patients which suggested that des-try-γ-endorphin had anti-schizophrenic activity (Verhoeven *et al*. 1979). Unfortunately, attempts to replicate these results have largely been negative (Tamminga *et al*. 1981; Casey, *et al*. 1981; Manchanda and Hirsch 1981). More recently, the same authors have had more encouraging results with des-enkephalin-γ-endorphin (Verhoeven *et al*. 1982) and studies are now under way to replicate these findings. As yet it is far too early to draw conclusions about the possible therapeutic role of endorphins in schizophrenia.

Gluten-free diets

The possibility that dietary measures could have an influence on the course of schizophrenia has been suggested by Dohan who observed that severe restrictions of gluten, normally found in cereal grain, led to more rapid improvement of schizophrenics (Dohan 1966, 1976). Moreover, he found a 0.96 correlation between changes in the rate of mental hospital admissions for female schizophrenics and wheat consumption in the United States, Canada, Finland, and Norway during World War II. In subsequent studies he showed that a cereal-free, milk-free diet, combined with neuroleptics, decreased the number of days hospitalization on a locked ward, but that the trend did not continue when gluten was blindly added to the diet (Dohan *et al*. 1969) and that schizophrenics on such a diet spent half the number of days in hospital (Dohan and Grasberger 1973).

As yet, there are not enough studies to corroborate or disconfirm Dohan's hypothesis, but a reduction in the wartime admission rate for mental disorder is a general finding, not specific for schizophrenia, which has many possible alternative explanations. Singh and Kay (1976) reported an interruption of recovery when gluten was given double-blind to schizophrenics improving on such a diet. More seriously ill patients had a worse outcome. Rice and colleagues (1978) obtained a good response over four weeks in only two of 16 patients on a gluten- and milk-free diet, though one patient had been hospitalized over 23 years. Potkin *et al.* (1981) had a completely negative result—eight young chronic schizophrenics on the diet were challenged with gluten or placebo in a double-blind manner, daily for at least five weeks, producing no deterioration in any patient studied.

Ashkenazi and colleagues (1979) demonstrated that both schizophrenics and non-schizophrenics showed an antigenic response to gluten on peripheral lymphocytes to gluten, not unlike that of coeliac patients—implying a defect in absorption in both conditions though there were no signs of malabsorption. Although the evidence is weak, gluten intolerence could be a factor in a subgroup of schizophrenics and further investigation is warranted.*

Future developments in medication

The future promises the marketing of a new generation of neuroleptics with few extrapyramidal side-effects, and possibly less risk of developing tardive dyskinesia. Several compounds with interesting pharmacological properties are in the experimental stage, not yet available for large-scale clinical testing. Possible early forerunners which have been in clinical use are sulpiride and the substituted benzamides which differ from most available neuroleptics in either their pharmacological mode of action, or their neuropharmacological and behavioural effects, particularly as demonstrated in animal behavioural models. Clozapine, possibly the most promising of this group, had to be withdrawn from the market because of idiosyncratic severe toxic reactions. However, as not uncommonly occurs, drugs which have distinctive pharmacological profiles suggesting selective actions of one sort or another do not always prove to be selective or different in clinical practice, and such is the case with oxypertine and sulpiride. The distinctive quality of the latter is its specificity for the dopamine receptor in the absence of anticholinergic or sedative effects. Several companies have tested other chemicals which share some of the pharmacological actions of neuroleptics such as inhibiting aggressivity without causing marked sedation and inhibiting learned avoidance behaviour but without animal behavioural effects which suggest striatal activity, such as the induction of catalepsy in mice and rats. The implication is that these drugs will prove to have selective actions on the mesolimbic system and forebrain in the absence of extrapyramidal side-

* The author is indebted to Dr Brian Robinson for his assistance in reviewing the literature on dietary treatments of schizophrenia.

effects. Early clinical studies suggest that some of these compounds (e.g. clozapine) may have antipsychotic activity in man, promising a new era of antipsychotic treatments in man in the not-too-distant future. If an anti-psychotic activity can be confirmed in man which is not associated with extra-pyramidal side-effects, the mode of action will bear explanation. Various possibilities have been suggested, but the evidence is conflicting. It has been suggested that the action of 'selective' neuroleptics of this sort could be due to differential absorption in various areas of the brain, or that these drugs may have selective actions on dopamine receptors, which is the case for sulpiride. Alternatively, the failure to demonstrate extrapyramidal side-effects with clozapine may be due to its action on dopamine receptors in the striatum. One can but hope that work in progress to develop neuroleptics which have both a powerful antipsychotic effect and minimal or no effects on the striatal system will be realized, especially as these drugs offer a faint hope of also giving benefit to the patient who has predominantly negative symptoms of schizophrenia.

PSYCHOLOGICAL AND SOCIAL TREATMENTS

Chapter 7 deals with the influence of social factors on the course and prognosis of schizophrenia, and Chapter 8 discusses how they and other variables can influence the outcome of clinical trials. Here we will review the evidence for the effectiveness of psychological and social therapies in the treatment of schizophrenia.

Relative contributions of experiential factors and drug treatment

The importance of antipsychotic medication in terms of it's effect on the recurrence of acute and chronic symptoms and relapse rates is less than psychiatrists generally appreciate. Davis (1976a) calculated a strong correlation of r_P = 0.60 between medication–no medication and improve-ment–deterioration from a large series of placebo-controlled studies where r_P is the Pearson correlation coefficient. However, this means that drugs explain only 36 per cent of the varience between improvement and no improvement in acute patients randomly given medication or not. The results of Vaughn and Leff's (1976) follow-up, discussed in Chapter 7, replicated previous research on patients returning to live with relatives who had been rated high on Expressed Emotion (high EE). The correlation between continuation on maintenance medication and relapse was only r_P = 0.39, explaining 15 per cent of the variance. Returning to live with a relative who was rated high on Expressed Emotion had a similar correlation with relapse (r_P = 0.45), but continuation of medication was not related to the type of relative (r_P = 0.01), so taking medication is independent of Expressed Emotion in the social environment. Even the amount of time spent in contact with a high-EE relative has a significant effect on the relapse rate independent of medication; 69 per cent of those spending more than 35 hours a week with a high-EE relative relapsed compared to 35 per cent of those spending less. Patients who returned to live with relatives rated low on Expressed Emotion had a low relapse rate whether they were on medication or not; this was about 13 per cent in the first year, but an advantage emerged even in low-EE patients on medication when they were followed for two years (Leff and Vaughn 1981). In contrast, patients living in the high-risk, high-EE environments experienced a significant protective effect from medication which was strongly evident, even in the first years decreasing their relapse rate by a third to a half. Thus, contact with a high-EE relative played as strong a role in determining whether a patient relapsed as whether or not the patient was on medication, and the two acted independently. A protective effect of prophylactic medication, against everyday life experience was also suggested in three Life Events studies (Leff *et al.* 1973; Leff and Vaughn 1980; Leff 1982). These studies are discussed in greater detail in Chapter 7. They suggest that social experience is a strong factor in provoking relapse, but drugs can modify the influences remedially in the acutely ill, and prophylactically after patients have recovered. The comparative effectiveness of psychosocial versus pharmacological treatments is discussed below.

The effectiveness of psychosocial treatments

A different aspects of the question is whether psychological and social treatments have a remedial effect on the illness process itself, beyond reducing the relapse rate. The question is complex and the evidence has been reviewed in detail elsewhere (Mosher and Keith 1980; Wallace *et al.* 1980; Davis and Chang 1978). There are three basic issues: Do psychological and social treatment interventions have effects on the underlying illness process? Do they have an effect on social functioning and well-being by improving coping skills and interpersonal relationships which is independent of any effect on the schizophrenic process? Do they have a prophylactic effect improving prognosis and reducing the relapse rate?

Specific effects of psychotherapy on the schizophrenic process—individual and group therapy

Because we know so little about the underlying pathology of schizophrenia this question can only be answered indirectly. However, it would appear axiomatic that if psychosocial treatments are able to abate the illness process, it should be possible to demonstrate a main effect in controlling acute or florid symptoms including delusions, hallucinations, thought disorder, and the symptoms of schizophrenia such as incoherent thought, social withdrawal, catatonia, and defects of drive, warmth, mannerisms, etc. General environmental changes such as withdrawal from life pressures by admission to hospital without medication can lead to remission of symptoms in 10 to 25 per cent of schizophrenics and improvement has been noted under placebo conditions in acutely admitted schizophrenics (Johnstone *et al.* 1978). Similarly changes in milieu can have a considerable effect on some of the negative features of schizophrenia which develop under conditions of social understimulation (see Chapter 7). Consequently studies of psychotherapy must control for these and unspecified influences, especially the effect of medication.

There are four studies bearing on the problem which employ a controlled research design. Greenblatt and colleagues (1965) studied the effect of social therapies on chronic schizophrenics in hospital more than five years. Grinspoon and colleagues (1968) studied the effect of approximately 200 hours of intensive treatment by experienced psychoanalysts on 10 chronic schizophrenics and 10 controls; Rogers and colleagues (1967) studied the effect of twice-weekly psychotherapy on 16 acute and chronic patients and controls, and May and colleagues (May and Tuma 1965; May *et al*. 1976) studied the effect on psychotherapy given by training psychiatrists to acutely admitted 'middle prognosis' schizophrenics. All of these studies controlled for the effects of medication, except Rogers who found little or no effect of psychotherapy on schizophrenic symptoms also controlled for the effects of medication. The general finding was a clear-cut beneficial effect of drugs on schizophrenic symptoms with an equal or slightly better effect if drugs are combined with psychotherapy or social therapy. (Greenblatt and colleagues (1965) found them to be 10 per cent better). Patients who did not receive drugs did significantly worse, and psychosocial therapies had no effect without drugs. When patients were followed up for one to five years there were no significant differences on any measures in Grinspoon and colleagues' study, but there was a slight tendency for patients having psychotherapy in May and colleagues' study to do better than patients who only had medication. This was pioneering work to try to test clinical impressions of the efficacy of psychotherapeutic measures on severe chronic and moderately severe acute patients. It may not be the negative results of these earlier studies as much as the obvious beneficial effects of medication and the benefits of straightforward social and rehabilitative treatments which explain the dearth of research into the specific effects of psychotherapy.

A different approach attempted to see if differences in the amount of individual, group, or milieu therapy which patients received was associated with differences in outcome. This failed to show positive results. Brief to medium-term hospitalization in a therapeutic environment was compared with longer-term hospital care, but there were no significant or noteworthy differences in outcome when treatment groups were compared at equivalent times after onset of the episode (Glick *et al*. 1975, 1976; Herz *et al*. 1971, 1974; Caffey *et al*. 1971).

Effects on social functioning and coping skills

An indication of more promising results emerged from the studies of maintenance medication (Goldberg *et al*. 1977; Hogarty *et al*. 1974; Hogarty and Goldberg 1973). They compared the effects of social work and support plus vocational rehabilitation which they called Major Role Therapy (MRT) with the effect of maintenance medication. Patients were randomly assigned to be maintained on placebo or drug treatment with or without MRT. Although the placebo-treated group had a much higher relapse rate in the first six months, whether they received MRT or not, patients who survived six months without relapse and had MRT had a significantly lower relapse rate at two years (44 per cent) than the subgroup of patients who did not have MRT (58 per cent relapsed). This suggests that MRT can have beneficial effects in patients who remain well or are stabilized by drugs or natural remission. However, Hogarty's group were unable to confirm the advantage of MRT in a subsequent study (Hogarty *et al.* 1979). Nevertheless, the fact that psychological treatments were unlikely to be effective in the absence of medication or some other method of controlling the underlying biological disturbance is now well established (see section on maintenance treatment) and the possible effect of social treatments like MRT would have to be regarded as adjuncts to biological treatment.

Mosher and Keith (1980) reviewed the efficacy of group therapy and other approaches. They found general problems of poor design, poor expertise of therapists, inadequate intensity of treatment, and imprecise measures of outcome among these studies. Results are inconsistent but group therapy more often emerges as better than individual psychotherapy, but no study could pretend to claim an effect on the illness process reflected in significant effects on the core symptoms of schizophrenia. Several studies suggested possible non-specific but important effects such as improved motivation and social functioning. It can be concluded that, notwithstanding the design problems and many limitations of the evidence to date, there is still no convincing data to suggest an effect of psychotherapeutic treatments on the schizophrenic process. There is evidence to suggest that psychotherapeutic interventions can improve the patient's general functioning, but as we shall see below, a number of other treatment approaches may be equally or more effective and possibly less costly. Whether psychotherapy given by experts in sufficient amounts under ideal conditions can alter the long-term outcome or have a prophylactic effect in reducing relapse remains an unanswered question.

Behavioural therapies

The important research in this area has been directed at assessing improvements in social skills and coping abilities of patients with chronic disabilities, and their ways of relating to others. They have not been directed at the illness as such, except indirectly in terms of its manifestations and consequences. They have not been concerned with internal states—the patient's feeling, attitudes, and perception of what is going on; but on aspects of behaviour such as the rate of eye contact, hand gestures, body postures, voice volume etc., and the effect on others, as well as the patient's ability to achieve his own goals. Wallace and colleagues (1980) made an extensive review of the literature with regard to social skills training and allied approaches.

They found, unfortunately, that little attention has been given to diagnostic criteria and almost all the studies reviewed failed to control for medication. A considerable body of evidence showed that, while self-reports of anxiety and certain aspects of behaviour could be modified, other aspects of behaviour considered critical in the process of producing improved social skills did not generalize from the treatment situation. Eye contact, leaning forward postures, and voice quality could be improved, but more complex behaviour changes would not carry over to new situations if they were not typical of the training venue, and substantial changes in the patient's quality of life usually did not occur.

Family therapy

In contrast to the disappointing results reported with individual treatments, a therapeutic effect of therapy with the families of schizophrenics has been established. Treatment of the families of schizophrenics with or without the patient implies a concern for the social context in which the patient functions. Intervention is not aimed at the illness process but at the factors in the patient's environment to which he or she is vulnerable. Consideration of the research reviewed in Chapter 7 would lead to the hypothesis that a change in the patient's environment which lowered arousal and stress would decrease the recurrence rate of florid symptoms, and improving an understimulated socially impoverished environment would improve the functions of chronic regressed patients with only negative symptoms (Wing and Brown 1970; Leff *et al.* 1982).

Earlier studies gave promising evidence but failed to be a control for medication: for example, Langsley and colleagues (1968, 1969) studied 300 patients with diverse diagnoses requesting emergency treatment with drugs and psychotherapy. There was no difference at 6, 12, and 18 months in the patient's ability to deal with stressful events, though the family-treated group as a whole had fewer admissions. We do not know if this is true for the schizophrenia subgroup.

Goldstein and colleagues (1978) controlled for medication using low- (0.25 mg) and medium-dose (25 mg) depot fluphenazine from discharge, with and without six two-hourly family sessions. The sessions were aimed at accepting the occurrence of psychosis and dealing with stress. General beneficial effects on adjustment and the Brief Psychiatric Rating Scale were present at six weeks but not six months in the family therapy group. The main therapeutic effect occurred with higher-dose medications, except for patients with good premorbid personality ratings in the higher-dose treatment group who did better at six months if they had family therapy. The studies of Leff and colleagues (1982) and Falloon and colleagues (1982) have been discussed in detail in Chapter 7. These were both well controlled trials which showed that intervention in families with a schizophrenic, whether the relative is a parent or spouse, can significantly reduce the relapse rate of schizophrenics after leaving hospital from a predicted 50 per cent to about 15 per cent over nine months. The therapy was first of all aimed at educating the relatives who had been identified as having a hostile, critical, or overinvolved attitude towards the patient about the nature of schizophrenia, viewed as an illness. Relatives were also helped to learn to cope with intrafamilial tension created by the patient, using dynamic and supportive means (Leff's D group) or behavioural ones (Falloon's group). Both studies were limited to patients who were in close contact with relatives who had been rated high on the Expressed Emotion variable. Thus the patients were known to have a high risk for relapse, despite maintenance treatment with depot phenothiazines (see Chapter 7). Other centres are repeating these studies which suggest that for vulnerable patients with a high risk of relapse, a powerful therapeutic effect can be obtained by psychological and social treatments. For this special group living with high EE families, family intervention is as potent as medication in preventing relapse, and acts independently but complementarily to the effects of medication. These effects are consistent with the hypothesis that neuroleptics alter basic biological processes which effect the patient's response to social over-arousal and are part of the schizophrenic's tendency to relapse in the face of overstimulation. The evidence for this model is discussed in Chapter 7. It can be concluded that medication is still the mainstay for acute and maintenance treatment of schizophrenia, and that psychosocial treatments have a complementary role in the recovery phase, which has only just begun to be effectively exploited.

References

Abrams, R. and Taylor, A. (1977). Catatonia: prediction of response to somatic treatments. *Am. J. Psychiat.* **134**, 78–80.

Ackner, B., Harns, A., and Oldham, A. J. (1957). Insulin treatment of schizophrenia. *Lancet* ii, 607–11.

——and Oldham, A. J. (1972). Insulin treatment of schizophrenia—A three-year follow-up of a controlled study. *Lancet* ii, 504–6.

American Pyschiatric Association. (1973). *A report of the A.P.A. task force on vitamin therapy in psychiatry. megavitamin and orthomolecular therapy in psychiatry.* A.P.A. Washington DC.

Ananth, J. V., Ban, T. A., and Lehmann, H. E. (1973). Potentiation of therapeutic effects of nicotinic acid by pyridoxine in chronic schizophrenia. *Can. Psychiat. Ass. J.* **18**, 409–14.

Ashkenazi, A., Krasilowsky, D., Levin, S., Idap, D., Kalianky O. R. A. Gonat, Y., and Halperin, B. (1979). Immunological reaction of psychotic patients to fractions of gluten. *Am. J. Psychiat.* **136**, 1306–9.

Atsmon, A. and Blum, I. (1970). Treatment of acute porphyria variegata with propranol. *Lancet* i, 196–7.

—— ——Steiner, M., Laty, A., and Wigsenbeck, H. (1972). Further studies with propranolol in psychotic patients. *Psychopharmacologia* **27**, 249–54.

—— ——Wigsenbeck, H., Maoz, R., Steiner, K., and Zielgelman, G. (1971). The short term effect of adrenergic blocking agents in a small group of psychotic patients. *Psychiat. Neurol. Neurochir.* **74**, 251–8.

Ayd, F. J. (1978). *Intravenous haloperidol therapy.* International Drug Therapy Newsletter, Hezd Publications, Baltimore, Maryland.

330   *The psychopharmacology and treatment of schizophrenia*

Baker, A. A., Game, J. A., and Thorpe, J. G. (1958). ECT—the commonest form of treatment for schizophrenia in the UK. *J. ment. Sci.* **104**, 860–4.

—— —— ——(1960). Some research into the treatment of schizophrenia in the mental hospital. *J. ment. Sci.* **106**, 203–13.

Ban, T. A., Lehman, H. E., and Deutsch, M. (1977). Negative findings with megavitamins in schizophrenic patients: preliminary report. *Commun. Psychopharmacol.* **I**, 119–22.

Beckman, H. and Haas, S. (1980). High dose diazepam in schizophrenia. *Psychopharmacology* **1980**, 71–82.

Biederman, J., Lerner, Y., and Belsmaker, R. H. (1979). Combination of lithium carbonate and haloperidol in schizoaffective disorder. *Arch. gen. Psychiat.* **36**, 327–33.

Bleuler, M. (1974). The long-term course of the schizophrenic psychoses. *Psychol. Med.* **4**, 244–54.

Bowers, M. and Astrachan, B. (1967). Depression in acute schizophrenic patients. *Am. J. Psychiat.* **123**, 976–9.

Brandon, S., Cowley, P., McDonald, C., Neville, P., Palmer, R., and Wellstood-Eason, S. (1984). Electroconvulsive therapy results in depressive illness from Leicestershire trial. *Br. med. J.* **288**, 22–5.

Brill, N. Q., Crumpton, E., Erduson, S., Grayson, H. M., Hellman, L. I., and Richards, R. A. (1959). Relative effectiveness of various components of electroconvulsive therapy. *Arch. Neurol. Psychiat.* **81**, 627–35.

Brockington, I. F., Kendell, R. E., Kellett, J. M., Curry, S. H., and Wainwright, S. (1978). Trials of lithium, chlorpromazine and amitriptyline in schizoaffective patients. *Br. J. Psychiat.* **133**, 162–8.

Butterworth, A. T. (1972). Inhibitions of extrapyramidal side-effects of haloperidol through the joint use of imipramine-type drugs. *Psychosomatics* **13**, 328–32.

Caffey, E. M., Diamond, L. S., Frank, T. V., Grasberger, J. C., Herman, L., Klett, C. J., and Rothstein, R. (1964). Discontinuation or reduction of chemotherapy in chronic schizophrenics. *J. chron. Dis.* **17**, 347–59.

——Galbrecht, C., and Klett, C. J. (1971). Brief hospitalisations and aftercare in the treatment of schizophrenia. *Arch. gen. Psychiat.* **24**, 81–6.

Capstick, N. (1980). Long-term fluphenazine decanoate. Maintenance dosage requirements of chronic schizophrenic patients. *Acta psychiat. scand.* **61**, 256–62.

Casey, D., Korsgaard, S., Gerlach, J., Jorgensen, W., and Summelsgaard, H. (1981). Effect of des-tyrosene-gamma-endorphin in tardive dyskinesia. *Arch. gen. Psychiat.* **38**, 158–60.

Cerletti, U., and Bini, L. (1938). L'electroshock. *Arch. gen. Neurol. Psychiat. Psychoanal.* **19**, 2666–8.

Cheung, H. K. (1981). Schizophrenics fully remitted on neuroleptics for 3–5 years—to stop or continue drugs. *Br. J. Psychiat.* **138**, 490–4.

Childers, R. T. (1964). Comparison of four regimes in newly-admitted female schizophrenics. *Am. J. Psychiat.* **120**, 1010–11.

Chouinard, G. and Jones, B. (1980). Neuroleptic-induced supersensitivity psychosis with clinical and pharmacological characteristics. *Am. J. Psychiat.* **137**, 16–21.

Cole, J., Kleberman, G. L., and Goldberg, S. C. (1964). Phenothiazine treatment of acute schizophrenia. *Arch. gen. Psychiat.* **10**, 246–61.

Collins, A. D. and Dundas, J. (1967). A double-blind trial of amitriptyline? Perphenazine, perphenazine and placebo in chronic withdrawn inert schizophrenics. *Br. J. Psychiat.* **113**, 1425–9.

Crow, T. J., Frith, C. D., Johnson, E. C., and Owens, D. G. (1981). The influence of anti-cholinergic medication on the extrapyramidal and anti-psychotic effects of neuroleptic drugs in the treatment of acute schizophrenia. *Biol. Psychiat.* 790–2.

Curson, D. A., Barnes, T. R., Bamber, R. W., Platt, S. D., Hirsch, S. R., and Duffy, J. A. (1985). 7-year follow-up study of MRC. 'Modecate' trial. *Br. J. Psychiat.* **146**, 464–80.

Davis, J. M. (1975). Overviews: maintenance therapy in psychiatry in schizophrenia. *Am. J. Psychiat.* **132**, 1237–45.

——(1976a). Comparative doses and costs of anti-psychotic medication. *Arch. gen. Psychiat.* **33**, 858–61.

——(1976b). Recent developments in the drug treatment of schizophrenia. *Am. J. Psychiat.* **133**, 208–14.

——and Chang, S. (1978). In *A look at the data. Controversy in psychiatry* (ed. J. P. Brady and H. K. Brodie). W. R. Saunders, Philadelphia.

——Dysken, M., Haberman, S., Javaid, I., Chang, S., and Killian, G. (1980). Use of survival curves in analysis of anti-psychotic relapse studies with long-term effects of neuroleptics. In *Advances in biochemistry and psychopharmacology*, Vol. 24 (ed. F. Cattabens *et al.*). Raven Press, New York.

——and Garver, D. L. (1978). Neuroleptics: clinical use in psychiatry. Chapter 10 in Iverson, Iverson and Snyder; *Handbook of psychopharmacology*. Plenum Press, New York and London.

——Janicah, P., Chang, S., and Klerman, K. (1982). *Recent advances in the treatment of schizophrenia*. Unpublished (manuscript from authors).

Davis, K. L. and Berger, P. A. (1978). Pharmacological investigations of cholinergic imbalance hypothesis of movement disorder and psychosis. *Biolog. Psychiat.* **12**, 23–49.

Delay, J. and Bernitzer, P. (1952). *Le traitement des psychoses par une méthode neurolytique dérivée de l'hibernothérapie*. Congrès de Médecins Alienistes et Neurologistes de France (ed. P. C. Ossa), pp. 497–502. Masson Editeurs Libraires de l'Academie de Médecine, Paris and Luxembourg.

Delva, N. J. and Letemendia, F. J. J. (1982). Lithium treatment in schizophrenia and schizo-affective disorders. *Br. J. Psychiat.* **141**, 387–400.

—— ——and Prowse, A. W. (1982). Lithium withdrawal trial in chronic schizophrenia. *Br. J. Psychiat.* **141**, 401–6.

Dencker, S. J., Lepp, M., and Malm, U. (1980). Do schizophrenics well adapted in the community need neuroleptics? A depot withdrawal study. *Acta psychiat. scand. Suppl.* **279**, 64–6.

Denham, J. and Adamson, L. (1971). The contribution of fluphenazine enanthate and decanoate in the prevention of readmission of schizophrenic patients. *Acta psychiat. scand.* **47**, 420–30.

Denson, R. (1962). Nicotinomide in the treatment of schizophrenia. *Dis. nerv. Syst.* **23**, 167–72.

deWied, D., Bohus, J. M., van Ree, J. M., and Urban, F. (1978). *J. Pharmacol. exp. Ther.* **204**, 570–80.

Diaz-Buxo, J., Caudle, J., Chandler, J. T., Farmer, C. D., and Holbrook, N. D. (1980). Dialysis of schizophrenic patients: a double-blind study. *Am. J. Psychiat.* **137**, 1220–2.

Dohan, F. C., (1966). Cereals and schizophrenia: Data and hypothesis. *Acta psychiat. scand.* **42**, 125–52.

——(1976). The possible pathogenic effect of cereal grains in schizophrenia—celiac disease as a model. *Acta neurol.* **31**, 195–205.

——and Grasberger, J. C. (1973). Relapsed schizophrenia: early discharge from hospital after a cereal-free diet. *Am. J. Psychiat.* **130**, 686–8.

—— ——Lowell, F. M., Johnston, H. T. and Abegast, Ann W. (1969). Relapsed schizophrenics: more rapid improvement on a milk and cereal-free diet. *Br. J. Psychiat.* **115**, 595–6.

Eccleston, D., Fairbairns, F., Hassanyeh, F., McClelland, H., and Stephens, D. (1986). The effect of propranolol and thioridazine on positive and negative symptoms of schizophrenia. *Br. J. Psychiat.* (in press).

Edelstein, P., Schultz, J., Hirschowitz, J., Kanter, D., and Garver, D., (1981). Physostiginine and lithium response in schizophrenics. *Am. J. Psychiat.* **138**, 1078–81.

Exner, J. and Murillo, L. (1973). Effectiveness of regressive ECT with process schizophrenia. *Dis. nerv. Syst.* **34**, 44–8.

—— ——(1977). A long-term follow-up of schizophrenics treated with regressive ECT. *Dis. nerv. Syst.* **38**, 162–8.

Falloon, I., Boyd, J., McGill, C., Razani, J., Moss, H., and Gilderman, A. (1982). Family management in the prevention of exacerbation of schizophrenia; a controlled study. *New Engl. J. Med.* **306**, 1437–40.

——Watt, D. C., and Shepherd, M. (1978a). A comparative controlled trial of pimozide and fluphenazine decanoate in continuation therapy of schizophrenia. *Psychol. Med.* **8**, 59–70.

—— —— ——(1978b). The social outcome of patients in a trial of long-term continuation therapy in schizophrenia and pimozide vs. fluphenazine I. M. *Psychol. Med.* **8**, 265–74.

——Feer, H., Thoelen, H., Massini, M. A., and Staub, H. (1960). Haemodialysis in schizophrenia. *Comprehens. Psychiat.* **1**, 338.

Fink, M., Shaw, R., Cross, C. E., and Coleman, F. S. (1958). Study of chlorpromazine and insulin used in therapy of psychosis. *J. Am. med. Ass.* **166**, 1846–50.

Fogelson, D. L., Marder, S. R., and van Putten, T. (1980). Dialysis for schizophrenia. A review of clinical trials and implications for further research. *Am. J. Psychiat.* **137**, 605.

Gardos, I., Cole, J., and Urzack, M. (1973). The importance of dosage in antipsychotic drug administration—a review of dose response studies. *Psychopharmacology* **29**, 221–30.

Glick, I. D., Hargreaves, W., Drues, J., and Showstack, J. (1976). Short vs. long hospitalization. A prospective controlled study. IV. One-year follow-up results for schizophrenic patients. *Am. J. Psychiat.* **133**, 509–14.

—— ——Raskin, M., and Kutner, S. (1975). Short vs long hospitalization. A prospective controlled study II. Results for schizophrenic in-patients. *Am. J. Psychiat.* **132**, 385–90.

Goldberg, S. C., Klerman, G. L., and Cole, J. O. (1965). Changes in schizophrenic psychopathology and ward behaviour as a function of phenothiazine treatment. *Br. J. Psychiat.* **111**, 120–33.

——Schooler, N., Hogarty, G., and Roper, M. (1977). Prediction of relapse in schizophrenic outpatients treated by drug and sociotherapy. *Arch. gen. Psychiat.* **34**, 171–84.

Goldstein, M., Rodnich, E., Evans, J., May, P., and Steinberg, M. (1978). Drug and family therapy in the aftercare of acute schizophrenics. *Arch. gen. Psychiat.* **35**, 1169–77.

Greenbaum, G. H. E. (1970). An evaluation of niacinamide in the treatment of childhood schizophrenia. *Am. J. Psychiat.* **127**, 89–93.

Greenblatt, M., Solomon, M., Evans, A. S., and Brooks, G. W. (1965). *Drugs and social therapy in chronic schizophrenia* Charles C. Thomas, Springfield, Illinois.

Grinspoon, L., Ewalt, J., and Shardu, R. (1968). Psychotherapy and pharmacotherapy in chronic schizophrenics. *Am. J. Psychother.* **124**, 62–74.

—— —— ——(1977). *Schizophrenia: pharmacotherapy and psychotherapy*. William and Wilkins, Baltimore, Maryland.

Heath, E. S., Adams, A., and Wakeling, P. G. (1964). Short. courses of ECT and simulated ECT in chronic schizophrenics. *Br. J. Psychiat.* **110**, 800.

Herz, M., Endicott, J., Spitzer, R., and Mesnihoff, T. A. (1971). Day versus inpatient hospitalization: a controlled study. *Am. J. Psychiat.* **127**, (10), 107–8.

—— and Melville, C.(1980). Relapse in schizophrenia. *Am. J. Psychiat.* **137**, 801–5.

——Spitzer, R., Gibbon, M., Greenspan, K., and Reibel, S. (1974). Individual versus group aftercare treatment. *Am. J. Psychiat.* **131**, 808–12.

Hirsch S. R. (1982a). Medical and physical treatment of schizophrenia. In *Handbook of psychiatry*, Vol. 3 (ed. J. K. Wing). Cambridge University Press, Cambridge.

——(1982b). Depression 'revealed' in schizophrenia. *Br. J. Psychiat.* **140**, 421–524.

——Gaind, R., Rohde P. D., Stevens, B. C., and Wing, J. C. (1973). Outpatient maintenance of chronic schizophrenic patients with long-acting fluphenazine: double-blind placebo trial. *Br. med. J.* **1**, 633–7.

——Manchanda, R., Weller, M. and Malcolm P. I. (1981). Dextro-propranolol in schizophrenia. *Programme of Neuro-Psychopharmacology* **4**, 633–7.

Hoffer, A., and Osmond, H. (1964). A treatment of schizophrenia with nicotinic acid—a 10-year follow-up. *Acta psychiat. scand.* **40**, 171–89.

—— ——and Callbeck, M. J. (1957). Treatment of schizophrenia with nicotinic acid and nicotinamide. *J. clin. exp. Psychopathol.* **18**, 131–58.

Hogarty, G. E. and Goldberg, S. C. (1973). Drug and sociotherapy in the after care of schizophrenic patients. *Arch. gen. Psychiat.* **28**, 54–64.

—— ——Schooley, N., and Ulrich, R. (1974). Drugs and sociotherapy in the aftercare of schizophrenia Patients. II. 2-year relapse rates. *Arch. gen. Psychiat.* **31**, 603–8.

——Schooler, N., Ulrich R., Mussare F., Ferro, P., and Herron, E. (1979). Fluphenazine and social therapy in the aftercare of schizophrenic patients. *Arch. gen. Psychiat.* **36**, 1283–4.

——and Ulrich, R. (1977). Temporal effects of drug and placebo in delaying relapse in schizophrenic outpatients. *Arch. gen. Psychiat.* **34**, 297–301.

—— ——Mussare, F., and Aristigueta, N. (1976). Drug discontinuation among long-term, successfully-maintained schizophrenic outpatients. *Dis. nerv. Syst.* **37**, 494–500.

Hollister, L. E. (1974). Clinical differences among phenothiazines in schizophrenics. In *Advances in biomedical psychopharmacology*, Vol. 9, pp. 667–73. WHO, Geneva.

——(1978). *Antipsychotics: clinical pharmacology of psychotherapeutic drugs*, ch. 5. Churchill Livingstone, Edinburgh.

Janakiramaiah, N. Channabasavanna, S. M., and Narasimha Morthy, N. S. (1982). *Acta psychiat. scand.* **66(6)** 464–70.

Janowsky, D., El-Yousef, M. K., Davis, J. M., Hubbard, B., and Sekerke, H. J. (1972a). Cholinergic reversal of manic symptoms. *Lancet* i, 1236–7.

—— —— ——and Sekerke, H. J. (1972b). A cholinergic—adrenergic hypothesis of mania and depression. *Lancet* ii, 632–5.

Johnson, D. A. W. (1976). The duration of maintenance therapy in chronic schizophrenia. *Acta psychiat. scand.* **53**, 298–301.

——(1978). The prevalence and treatment of drug-induced extrapyramidal symptoms. *Br. J. Psychiat.* **132**, 27–30.

——(1981). Studies of depression in schizophrenia. *Br. J. Psychiat.* **139**, 89–101.

Johnstone, E., Crow, T., Ferrier, N., Frith, C., Owens, D., Bourne, R., and Gamble, S. (1983). Adverse effects of anticholinergic medication on positive schizophrenic symptoms. *Psychol. Med.* **13**, 513–27.

—— ——Frith, C., Carney, M., and Price, J. (1978). The mechanism of the anti-psychotic effect in the treatment of acute schizophrenia. *Lancet* i, 848–51.

Kalinowsky, M. D., Lothan, B., and Hippius, H. (1969). *Pharmacological, convulsive and other somatic treatments in psychiatry*. Grune and Stratton, New York.

Kalinowsky, L. B., Hippius, H., and Klein, H. E. (1982). *Biological treatments in psychiatry*. Grune and Stratton, New York.

Kane, J., Rifkin, A., Quitkin, F., Nayah, D., Saraf, K., Ramos Lorenzi, J., Klein, D., and Secha, E. J. (1979). How does fluphenazine decanoate aid in maintenance treatment of schizophrenia. *Psychiat. Res.* 1, 341–8.

—— —— ——and Klein, D. F. (1982). Fluphenazine vs. placebo in patients who remitted, acute first-episode schizophrenia. *Arch. gen. Psychiat.* 39, 70–3.

—— ——Woerner, M., Reardon, G., Sarrantakos, S., Schiebel, D., and Ramos Lorensi, J. (1983). Low dose neuroleptic treatment of out-patient schizophrenics. *Arch. gen. Psychiat.* 40, 893–6.

Klein, D. F., and Davis, J. M. (1969). Review of anti-psychotic drug literature. In *Diagnosis and treatment of psychiatric disorders* Chapter 5, pp. 51–137 (ed. D. F. Klein and J. M. Davis). Williams and Wilkins, Baltimore.

Klein, E., Bewlat, E., Leven, B., and Belmaher, R. (1984). Carbamazepine and haloperidol v. placebo and haloperidol in excited psychoses. *Arch. gen. Psychiat.* 41, 165–70.

Kline, N. S. (1954). Use of *Rauwolfia serpentinia bentyl* in neuropsychiatric conditions. *Ann. NY Acad. Sci.* 59, 107–32.

——Barclay, G. L., Cole, J. O., Esser, A. H., Lehmann, H., and Wottenborn, J. R. (1967). Controlled evaluation of nicotinamide adenine dinucleotide in the treatment of chronic schizophrenic patients. *Br. J. Psychiat.* 113, 731–42.

Knights, A. and Hirsch, S. R. (1981). Revealed depression and drug treatment for schizophrenia. *Arch. gen. Psychiat.* 38, 806–11.

—— ——and Platt, S. (1980). Clinical change as a function of brief admission to hospital in a controlled study using the P.S.E. *Br. J. Psychiat.* 137, 170–80.

——Okasha, M. S., Salih, M. and Hirsch, S. R. (1979). Depressive and extrapyramidal symptoms and clinical effects: a trial of fluphenazine versus flupenthixol in maintenance of schizophrenic outpatients. *Br. J. Psychiat.* 135, 515–24.

——Koehler, K. and Sauer, H. (1983). First Rank symptoms as predictors of E.C.T. response in schizophrenia. *Br. J. Psychiat.* 142, 280–3.

Kulhanek, F. and Linde, O. K. (1981). Coffee and tea influence pharmacokinetics of anti-psychotics. *Lancet* ii, 359–60.

—— ——and Meisenberg, G. (1979). Precipitations of antipsychotic drugs in interaction with coffee and tea. *Lancet* ii, 1130.

Lader, M. (1979). Monitoring plasma concentrations of neuroleptics. *Pharmacopsychology* 9, 170–7.

Langsley, D., Mchotka, and Flomenhaft, K. (1968). Family crisis therapy—results and implications. *Family Process* 7, 145–58.

——Pittman, F., and Swank, G. (1969). Family crisis in schizophrenics and other mental patients. *J. nerv. ment. Dis.* 149 (3), 270–6.

Leff, J. P. (1982). *Family and social influences in schizophrenia*, Vol. 1, No. 6. S.K. and F. Publications.

——Hirsch, S., Gainde, R., Rohde, P., Steven, B. (1973). Life Events and maintenance therapy in schizophrenic relapse. *Br. J. Psychiat.* 123, 659–80.

——Kuipers, L., Berkowitz, R., Ebstein-Vries, R., and Sturgeon, D. (1982). A controlled trial of social intervention in the families of schizophrenic patients. *Br. J. Psychiat.* 141, 121–34.

——and Vaughan, C. (1980). The inte . . of life events and relatives'—expressed emotion in schizophrenia and depressive neurosis. *Br. J. Psychiat.* 136, 146–53.

—— ——(1981). The role of maintenance therapy and relatives'—expressed emotion in relapse of schizophrenia: a two-year follow-up. *Br. J. Psychiat.* 139, 102–4.

——and Wing, J. K. (1971). Trial of maintenance therapy in schizophrenia. *Br. med. J.* **3**, 599–604.

Letemendia, F. J. J., Harris, A. D., and Williams, P. J. A. (1967). The clinical effects on a population of chronic schizophrenic patients of administrative changes in hospital. *Br. J. Psychiat.* **113**, 959–71.

Leuthold, C. A., Bradshaw, F., Arndt, G., *et al.* (1961). Behaviour evaluation of imipramine and nialamide in regressed schizophrenic patients with depressive features. *Am. J. Psychiat.* **118**, 354–5.

Lindström, L. H. and Persson, E. (1980). Propanolol in chronic schizophrenia: A controlled study in neuroleptic-treated patients. *Br. J. Psychiat.* **137**, 126–30.

Loduron, P. and Leysen, J. (1978). Is the incidence of extrapyramidal side-effects of antipsychotics associated with anti-muscarinic properties? *J. Pharm. Pharmacol.* **30**, 120–1.

Maltbie, A. A., Wingfield, M. S., Volon, M. R., Werner, R. D., Sullivan, J. L., and Cavernar, J. O. (1980). Electroconvulsive therapy in the presence of brain tumour. *J. nerv. ment. Dis.* **168**, 400–5.

Manchanda, R. and Hirsch, S. R. (1981). (Des-tyr)-γ-endorphin in the treatment of schizophrenia. *Psychol. Med.* **2**, 401–4.

—— ——(1982) (Des-tyr)-γ-endorphin for schizophrenia. *Int. Pharmacopsychiat.* **17**, 147–52.

—— ——(1986). Does propranolol have an anti-psychotic effect—a placebo-controlled trial in acute patients. *Br. J. Psychiat.* (in press).

May, P. R. A. and Tuma, A. H. (1965). Treatment of schizophrenia—an experimental study of five treatment methods. *Br. J. Psychiat.* **111**, 503–10.

—— ——Yale, C., Dotepan, P., and Nixon, W. (1976). Schizophrenia—a follow-up study of the results of treatment. *Arch. gen. Psychiat.* **33**, 481–6.

McClelland, H. A. (1976). Discussion on assessment of drug-induced extrapyramidal reactions. *Br. J. clin. Pharmacol. Suppl.* **2**, 401–3.

——Blessed, G., Bhate, S., Ali, N., and Clarke, P. (1974). The abrupt withdrawal of anti-parkinsonian drugs in schizophrenic patients. *Br. J. Psychiat.* **124**, 151–9.

——Farquharson, R. G., Leyburn, P., Furness, J. A., and Schiff, A. A. (1976). Very high dose fluphenazine decanoate. *Arch. gen. Psychiat.* **33**, 1435–42.

Meltzer, H., Shader, R., and Grinspoon, L. (1969). The behavioural effects of nicotinamide adenine dinucleotide in chronic schizophrenia. *Psychopharmacologia, Berlin* **15**, 144–52.

IOD. H., Clancy, J., and Cumming, E. (1953). A comparison between unidirectional current non-convulsive electrical stimulation given with Reiter's machine, standard alternating current electroshock (Cerletti method) and pentothal in chronic schizophrenia. *Am. J. Psychiat.* **109**, 617–20.

Miller, F., and Libman, H. (1979). Lithium carbonate in the treatment of schizophrenia and schizo-affective disorder: Review and hypothesis. *Biol. Psychiat.* **14**, 705–10.

Milner, G. (1963). Ascorbic acid in chronic psychiatric patients: a controlled trial. *Br. J. Psychiat.* **109**, 294–9.

Mindham, R. H. S. (1976). Assessment of drug-induced extrapyramidal reactions and of drugs given for their control. *Br. J. clin. Pharmacol. Suppl.* **2**, 395–400.

Moller, H. J., and Von Zerssen, D. (1981). Depressive Symptomatik und stationären Behandlungsverlauf von 280 Schizophrenen Patienten. *Pharmacopsychiatria* **14**, 172–9.

—— ——(1982). Frequency and course pattern of depressive states during the neuroleptic treatment of 81 patients with acute schizophrenia or similar psychoses. *Schiz. Bull.* **8**, 109–17.

Montgomery, S. A., Taylor, P., and Montgomery D. (1978). Development of a schizophrenia scale sensitive to change. *Neuropharmacology* **1710**, 61–3.

Morrison, J. R. (1973). Catatonia. *Arch. gen. Psychiat.* **28**, 39–41.

Mosher, L. and Keith, S. (1980). Psychosocial treatment: individual group, family and community support approaches. *Schiz. Bull.* **6** (1), 10–41.

Mueser, K. and Dysken, M. (1983). Narcotic antagonists in schizophrenia: a methodological review. *Schiz. Bull.* **9** (2), 213–25.

Murillo, L. and Exner, J. (1973). The effects of regressive E.C.T. with process schizophrenics. *Am. J. Psychiat.* **130**, 267–73.

Myers, D. H., Campbell, P. L., Cocks, N. M., Flowerdew, J. A., and Muir, A. (1981). A trial of propranolol in chronic schizophrenia. *Br. J. Psychiat.* **139**, 118–21.

Osmond, H. and Hoffer, A. (1962). Massive niacin treatment in schizophrenia. *Lancet* **i**, 316–19.

Peet, M., Bethell, M. S., Coates, A., Khamnee, A. K., Hall, P., Cooper, D. J., King, D. J., and Yates, R. A. (1981). Propranolol in schizophrenia: I. Comparison of propranolol, chlorpromazine and placebo. II. Clinical and biochemical aspects of combining propranolol with chlorpromazine. *Br. J. Psychiat.* **139**, 105–17.

Peroutka, S. J., Prichared, D. C., Greenberg, D. A., and Snyder, S. H. (1977). Neuroleptic drug interactions with noreprinephrine alpha receptor binding sites in rat brains. *Neuropharmacology* **16**, 549–56.

Perris, C. (1974). A study of cycloid psychosis. *Acta psychiat. scand.* **50**, Suppl. 253.

——(1978). Morbidity suppressive effect of lithium carbonate in cycloid psychosis. *Arch. gen. Psychiat.* **35**, 328–31.

Pishkin, V. (1972). Concept identification and psychophysiological parameters in depressed schizophrenics as functions of imipramine and malamide. *J. clin. Psychol.* **28**, 335–95.

Pitt, B. and Pollitt, N. (1971). Ascorbic acid and chronic schizophrenia. *Br. J. Psychiat.* **118**, 227–8.

Potkin, S. G., Weinberger, D., and Kleinman, J. (1981). Wheat gluten challenge in schizophrenic patients. *Am. J. Psychiat.* **138**, 1208–21.

Prien, R. F. (1979). Lithium in the treatment of schizophrenia and schizoaffective disorders. *Arch. gen. Psychiat.* **36**, 852–3.

——and Cole, J. O. (1968). High dose chloropromazine therapy in chronic schizophrenics. *Arch. gen. Psychiat.* **18**, 482–95.

——Gillis, R. D., and Caffey, E. M. (1973). Intermittent pharmacotherapy in chronic schizophrenia. *Hosp. Community Psychiat.* **24**, 317–22.

——and Klett, C. C. (1972). An appraisal of the long-term use of tranquilizing medication with hospitalized chronic schizophrenics. *Schiz. Bull.* **5**, 64–73.

Prusoff, B., Williams, D. H., Wensmann, M., and Astrachan, B. (1978). Treatment of secondary depression in schizophrenia. *Psychopharmacol. Bull.* **15**, (2) 80–1.

Pugh, C. R., Steinert, J., and Priest, R. G. (1983). Propranolol in schizophrenia: a double-blind placebo-controlled trial of propranolol as an adjunct to neuroleptic medication. *Br. J. Psychiat.* **143**, 151–5.

Quach, T., Duchemin, A., Rose, C., and Schwartz, J. (1979). *In vivo* occupation of cerebral histamine H_{13}—receptors evaluated with H-megapyramine may predict sedative properties of psychotropic drugs. *Eur. J. Pharmacol.* **60**, 391–2.

Quitkin, F., Rifkin, A., and Klein, D. E. (1975). Very high dosage vs. standard dosage fluphenazine in schizophrenia. *Arch. gen. Psychiat.* **32**, 1276, 1281.

—— ——Kane, J., Ramos-Lorenzi, J., and Klein, D. (1978). Long-action oral vs injectable antipsychotic drugs in schizophrenics. *Arch. gen. Psychiat.* **35**, 889–92.

Rice, J., Ham, C. H., and Gore W. E. (1978). Another look at gluten in schizophrenia. *Am. J. Psychiat.* **135**, 1417–18.

Rifkin, A., Quitkin, F., and Klein, D. F. (1975). Akinesia: A poorly-recognised drug-induced extrapyramidal disorder. *Arch. gen. Psychiat.* **32**, 672–4.

—— ——Rabiner, C., and Klein, D. (1977). Fluphenazine decanoate, fluphenazine hydrochloride given orally, and placebo in remitted schizophrenics. *Arch. gen. Psychiat.* **34**, 43–7.

Robin, A. and de Tissera, S. (1982). A double-blind controlled comparison of the therapeutic effects of low energy and high energy electroconvulsive therapy. *Br. J. Psychiat.* **241**, 357–66.

Rogers, C. R., Gondlin, E., Kiesler, D., and Truax, C. (1967). *Relationship and its impact.* University of Wisconsin Press, Madison.

Schenk, G. K., Enders, P., Engelmeier, M., Ewert, T., Herdemerten, S., Kohler, K., Lodeman, E., Matz, D., and Pacrh, J. (1978). Application of the morphine antagonist haloxone in psychic disorders. *Arzneim. Forsch.* **28**, 1274–7.

Schooler, N. R., Lerme, J., Severo, J. B., Brauzen, B., DiMascio, A., Klerman, G. L., and Tuason, V. B. (1980). Prevention of relapse in schizophrenia. *Arch. gen. Psychiat.* **37**, 16–26.

Schultz, C. S., van Kammen, D. P., Balow, J. E., Flye, M. W. and Bunney, W. (1981). Dialysis in schizophrenia: a double-blind evaluation. *Science* **211**, 1066–8.

Shanfield, S., Tucker, G., Harrow, M., and Detre, T. (1970). The schizophrenic patient and depressive symptomatology. *J. nerv. ment. Dis.* **151**, 203–10.

Singh, M. M. and Kay, S. R. (1975). A comparative study of haloperidol and chlorpromazine in terms of clinical effects and therapeutic reversal with benzotropine in schizophrenia. *Psychopharmacologia* **43**, 103–13.

—— ——(1976). Wheat gluten as a pathogenic factor in schizophrenia. *Science* **191**, (4225), 401–2.

—— ——(1979*a*). Dysphoric response to neuroleptic treatment in schizophrenia: its relationship to autonomic arousal and prognosis. *Biol. Psychiat,* **14**, 277–94.

—— ——(1979*b*). Therapeutic antagonism between anticholinergic antiparkinsonian agents and neuroleptics in schizophrenia. *Neuropsychobiology* **5**, 74–86.

Siris, S., von Kaummer, D., and Docharty, J. (1978). Use of anti-depressant drugs in schizophrenia. *Arch. gen. Psychiat.* **35**, 1368–77.

Small, J. and Small, I. (1972). Clinical results: indoklan versus E.C.T. *Seminars Psychiat.* **4**, 13–26.

Smith, K., Surphlis, W., Gynther, M., and Shimkunas, A. (1967). E.C.T.—chlorpromazine and chloropromazine compared in the treatment of schizophrenia. *J. nerv. ment. Dis.* **144**, 284–90.

Snyder, S., Greenberg, D., and Yamamura, H. I. (1974). Anti-cholinergic drugs and brain cholinergic receptors. *Arch. gen. Psychiat.* **31**, 58–61.

Stengel, E. C. (1950). A follow-up investigation of 330 cases treated by prefrontal leucotomy. *J. ment. Sci.* **96**, 633–62.

Stephens, J. H. (1970). Long-term course and prognosis in schizophrenia. *Seminars Psychiat.* **2**, 464–85.

Tamminga, C., Tighe, P., Chase, T., Fraites, G., and Schaffer, M. (1981). Des-tyrosine-gamma-endorphin administration in chronic schizophrenics. *Arch. gen. Psychiat.* **38**, 167–8.

Taylor, P. and Fleminger, J. J. (1980). E.C.T. for schizophernia. *Lancet* **i**, 1380–2.

Tsuang, M. T. (1982). Long-term outcome in schizophrenia. *Trends Neurosci.* June, 203–7.

Turek, I. S. (1973). Combined use of E.C.T. and psychotropic drugs—antidepressive and antipsychotic. *Comprehens. Psychiat.* **14**, 495–504.

Ulett, G. A., Smith, K., and Glesser, G. (1956). Evaluation of convulsive and sub-convulsive shock therapies utilizing a control group. *Am. J. Psychiat.* **12**, 795–802.

Vanherweghan, J. L., Linkowski, P., and Mendlewicz, T. (1983). Haemodialysis in

338   *The psychopharmacology and treatment of schizophrenia*

schizophrenics. *Arch. gen. Psychiat.* **40**, 211–14.

Van Kammen, D., Alexander, P., and Bunney, Jr., W. (1980). Lithium treatment in post-psychotic depression. *Br. J. Psychiat.* **136**, 479–85.

Van Putten, T. and May, P. R. A. (1978). 'Akinetic depression' in schizophrenia. *Arch. gen. Psychiat.* **35**, 1101–7.

Vaughn, C. and Leff, J. (1976). The influence of family and social factors on the course of psychiatric illness. *Br. J. Psychiat.* **129**, 125–37.

Verhoeven, M. M. A., Van Praag, H. M., van Ree, J. M., and de Wied, D. (1979). Improvement of schizophrenic patients by treatment with des-tyr-endorphin. *Arch. gen. Psychiat.* **36**, 294–302.

——Westenberg, H. G. M., Gerritsen, A. W., van Praag, H. M., Thijssen, J. H. H., Schwarz, F., van Ree, J. M., and de Weid, D. (1981). (Des-tyrosine I) gamma-endorphins in schizophrenia: clinical, biochemical and hormonal aspects. *Psychiat. Res.* **5**, 293–309.

——van Ree, J. M., van Bentum, A. H., de Wied, D., and van Praagg, H. M. (1982). Antipsychotic properties of des-enkephalin-endorphin in treatment of schizophrenic patients. *Arch. gen. Psychiat.* **39**, 648–54.

Wagemaker, H. (1978). The effect of haemodialysis on fifteen chronic process schizophrenics. *Artificial Organs* **2** (2), 205–6.

——and Cade, R., (1977). The use of haemodialysis on chronic schizophrenics. *Am. J. Psychiat.* **134**, 684–5.

Wallace, C., Nelson, C., Liberman, R., Aitchison, R., Lukoff, D., Elder, J., and Ferris, C. (1980). A review and critique of social skills. Training with schizophrenic patients. *Sociol. Bull.* **6**(1) 42–63.

Weinstein, M. R. and Fisher, A. (1971). Combined treatment with E.C.T. and antipsychotic drugs in schizophrenia. *Dis. nerv. Syst.* **32**, 801–8.

Wells, D. A. (1973). Electroconvulsive treatment for schizophrenia, a ten-year survey. *Comprehens. Psychiat.* **14**, 291–8.

Wijsenbeck, H., Steiner, M., and Goldberg, S. C. (1974). Trifluoperazine; a comparison between regular and high doses. *Psychopharmacologia* **36**, 147–50.

Wiles, D. and Wistedt, B. (1981). The relationship of serum fluphenazine decanoate levels to relapse following withdrawal of medicayion. Poster F522, Third World Congress of Biology and Psychiatry, Stockholm.

Wing, J. K. and Brown, G. W. (1970). *Institutionalism and schizophrenia*. Cambridge University Press, Cambridge.

——Cooper, J. F., and Sartorius, N. (1974). *The description of psychiatric symptoms*. Cambridge University Press, Cambridge.

Wistedt, B. (1981). A depot neuroleptic withdrawal study. *Acta psychiat. scand.* **64**, 65–84.

——and Palinstlernag, T. (1983). Depressive symptoms in chronic schizophrenic patients after withdrawal of long-acting neuroleptics. *J. clin. Psychiat.* **14**, 369–71.

Wittenborn, J. R., Weber, E. S., and Brown, M. (1973). Niacin in the long-term treatment of schizophrenia. *Arch. gen. Psychiat.* **28**, 308–15.

Yamamura, H. (1976). Muscarinic cholinergic receptor binding: influence of pimozide and chlorpromazine metabolites. *Life Sci.* **18**, 685–92.

——Manian, A., and Snyder, S., (1976). Cholinergic receptor bindings: influence of pimozide and chlorpromazine metabolites. *Life Sci.* **18**, 685–92.

Yorkston, J. J., Gruzelier, J. H., Zaki, S. A., Hollander, D., Pitcher, D. R., and Sargent, H. G. (1977). Propranolol in chronic schizophrenia. *Lancet* **ii**, 1082–3.

——Zakin, S. A., Malifk, M. K. U., Morrison, R. C., and Harvard, C. H. (1974). propranolol in the control of schizophrenic symptoms. *Br. med. J.* **4**, 633–5.

—— ——Weller, M. D., Gruzelier, J. H., and Hirsch, S. R. (1981). Dh-propranolol and chloropromazine following admission for schizophrenia. *Acta psychiat. scand.* **63**, 13–27.

Zemlan, F., Hirschowitz, J., Sautter, F., and Garver, D. (1984). Impact of lithium, therapy on core psychotic symptoms of schizophrenics. *Br. J. Psychiat.* **144**, 64–9.

12

Extrapyramidal movement disorders produced by antipsychotic drugs

C.D. MARSDEN, R.H.S. MINDHAM, AND A.V.P. MACKAY

INTRODUCTION

Very soon after their introduction into clinical practice, it was found that antipsychotic drugs could produce a range of extrapyramidal side-effects. The commonest was drug-induced parkinsonism, which mirrored idiopathic Parkinson's disease in practically all of its clinical aspects (Steck 1954). A peculiar state of mental and motor restlessness, termed akathisia, was seen often in conjunction with drug-induced parkinsonism (Steck 1954), but also occurred in isolation. A small proportion of patients developed explosive and bizarre acute dystonic reactions in the first days or weeks of treatment (Delay and Deniker 1957). Finally, a more sinister abnormal movement disorder, chronic tardive dyskinesia, became recognized after months or years of therapy (Sigwald *et al.* 1959; Uhrbrand and Faurbye 1960).

These various extrapyramidal movement disorders are of considerable interest to both psychiatrists and neurologists. To psychiatrists they represent one of the major problems of neuroleptic therapy. Acute dystonic reactions may prevent the successful introduction of treatment, while parkinsonism and akathisia may limit dosage and efficacy. Finally, the emergence of chronic tardive dyskinesia is a worrying long-term development because in a proportion of patients it appears that this complication can be permanent, despite stopping the offending drug. To neurologists, these conditions are of great interest because they mimic, in many respects, a range of spontaneously occurring extrapyramidal motor disorders, many of which are of completely unknown origin. Thus, drug-induced dyskinesias provide a clue to the pathophysiology of spontaneous dystonia, oro-facial dyskinesias, chorea, and other such abnormal movement disorders.

In this chapter we will discuss the clinical features of each of these major extrapyramidal syndromes in turn, and then consider their likely pathophysiology.

DRUG-INDUCED PARKINSONISM

Clinical features

In its fully developed form drug-induced parkinsonism has all the features of

Parkinson's disease itself. These include the cardinal signs of rigidity, tremor, and akinesia, with a variety of subsidiary clinical features such as changes in gait and posture, excessive salivation, difficulty in speaking and swallowing, a characteristic facies, and greasy skin. In most patients, however, the syndrome is seen in a less severe form.

Akinesia is especially common, occurring soon after the initiation of treatment with neuroleptic drugs, and frequently is the only sign of parkinsonism to occur (Ayd 1961). Akinesia is shown in many ways. The face, characteristically, is blank and expressionless. Associated movements are lost, so that the arms fail to swing on walking, and gesture on talking disappears. The patient sits still without the usual flow of postural adjustments that occur in normal subjects; seldom does he cross his legs or fold his arms. All voluntary movement becomes laboured, being slow in initiation and execution, and reduced in amplitude; the voice becomes soft and the handwriting small. All these signs of akinesia may occur in individuals taking neuroleptic drugs, without the rigidity, tremor, or other signs of parkinsonism.

Minor degrees of akinesia pose an important problem in management because of the resemblance the condition has to some of the features of schizophrenia. The characteristic facies, the slowness and economy of movements, and the lack of spontaneity may be confused with emotional changes which may occur in schizophrenia, namely blunting and depression of affect. The management of drug-induced akinesia, depression of mood, or blunting of affect in schizophrenia may be quite different; for this reason it is important that the distinction is correctly made and appropriate treatment instituted. The incidence of mild akinesia is difficult to estimate accurately as it is often ignored, even in studies of drug-induced syndromes (Ayd 1961).

Tremor is seen less frequently; it may appear as the characteristic 'pill-rolling' tremor of Parkinson's disease, as a finer tremor of the limbs occurring both at rest and in action, or alternatively as a fine peri-oral tremor referred to as 'the rabbit syndrome' (Villeneuve 1972). This syndrome develops late in the course of treatment and improves with anticholinergics (Jus *et al*. 1974).

Although all effective neuroleptic drugs are capable of producing parkinsonism, they vary greatly in potency, and this particular unwanted effect may not be proportional to the therapeutic action of the drugs in psychiatric disorders.

Epidemiology

There have been a number of surveys of drug-induced parkinsonism and related syndromes. Some of these will be reviewed briefly.

Ayd (1961) examined 3775 patients who were receiving phenothiazine drugs; of these 1472 (or 38.9 per cent) developed some kind of extrapyramidal reaction to the drugs; 21.2 per cent showed akathisia; 15.4 per cent parkinsonism; and 2.3 per cent acute dystonic reactions. The most common change was akinesia but this was regarded as a mild reaction, not amounting

TABLE 12.1.   *Relative frequency of extrapyramidal syndromes in patients receiving neuroleptic drugs*

Drug	Number of patients taking the drug	Patients with extrapyramidal syndromes	
		Number	Per cent
Chlorpromazine	1500	525	35
Trifluopromazine	325	117	36
Thiopropazate	300	132	44
Prochlorperazine	350	115	43
Perphenazine	900	324	36
Trifluoperazine	200	120	60
Fluphenazine	200	104	52

Data reported by Ayd (1961).

to an extrapyramidal syndrome, and was not recorded. In fact, as indicated above, pure akinesia is very much an indication of extrapyramidal deficit, so the incidence of parkinsonism in this series was much greater than reported. Where akinesia was a part of a more fully developed parkinsonian syndrome it was recorded as such. Most of the patients showed only one neurological syndrome as a complication of medication; where parkinsonism eventually appeared it was recorded as drug-induced parkinsonism and not under other categories.

The frequency of drug-induced syndromes varied with the different phenothiazine drugs (Table 12.1) and bore some relationship to the potency of the

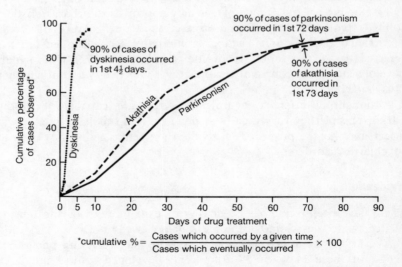

FIG. 12.1.   Time of onset of extrapyramidal reactions to neuroleptic drugs. Dyskinesia refers to acute dystonic reactions; data for tardive dyskinesias, which appear after about six months of treatment, is not shown. (Redrawn from Ayd (1961), with permission.)

drug when used in the treatment of psychiatric disorders (see Chapter 11). The potency of phenothiazines is increased by the piperazine side-chain and by the attachment of halogen atoms to the nucleus; these drugs are especially likely to cause acute dystonic reactions and akathisia (but see below).

Women were more likely to have unwanted extrapyramidal effects of phenothiazines than men of the same age. Akathisia and parkinsonism were twice as common in women as in men, but acute dystonic reactions, a much less frequent complication generally, were twice as common in men.

Ninety per cent of the cases of acute dystonic reactions occurred in the first four-and-half days of administration of the drugs; akathisia and parkinsonism were later in onset but 90 per cent occurred within the first 10 weeks of drug administration (Fig 12.1). The more potent drugs led to the appearance of extrapyramidal syndromes more rapidly. Younger patients tended to show acute dystonic reactions and akathisia, and older patients parkinsonism. The age distribution of patients showing parkinsonism resembled that of Parkinson's disease itself; drug-induced parkinsonism being uncommon in early adult life and most common in late middle age and early old age (Fig 12.2). In cases who showed parkinsonism (ignoring those with pure akinesia), 65 per cent presented with rigidity, and 35 per cent presented with tremor as the first sign.

Kennedy *et al.* (1971) reported a detailed survey of extrapyramidal disorders in 63 chronic hospitalized schizophrenics who had received trifluoperazine for between three and 13 years. Tremor was present in 88 per cent, muscular rigidity in 68 per cent, choreiform dyskinesia in 56 per cent, and motor restlessness in 38 per cent. Factor analysis of the data showed that a syndrome resembling Parkinson's disease accounted for 19.1 per cent of the

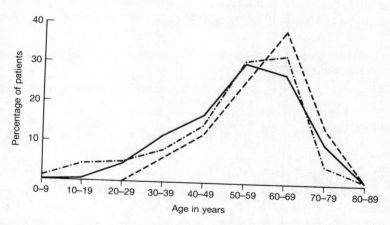

FIG. 12.2.   Age distribution of drug-induced parkinsonism and Parkinson's disease (paralysis agitans). Data for patients with Parkinson's disease obtained from Ayd (1961), Schwab *et al.* (1956), and Mjönes (1949). — Drug-induced parkinsonism (Ayd); --- Naturally-occurring parkinsonism (Schwab *et al.*); –·–·– Paralysis agitans (Mjönes). (Redrawn from Ayd (1961), with permission.)

patients studied, compared with 32 per cent showing a syndrome resembling akathisia, and 13 per cent showing a syndrome which resembled chorea.

The study of drugs in the treatment of schizophrenia reported by the National Institute of Mental Health Psychopharmacology Service Centre (1964) is of particular interest because it enables comparisons to be made between the three main types of phenothiazines, namely: chlorpromazine, a dimethylamino phenothiazine; thioridazine, a piperidine derivative; and fluphenazine, a piperazine derivative. The frequency of some of the reported unwanted effects is shown in Table 12.2.

The different drugs were given according to flexible dosage schedules and administration was continued for at least six weeks. Both chlorpromazine and thioridazine were given in an average dose of approximately 700 mg daily, and fluphenazine in a dosage approximately one-hundredth of this. These dosages produced similar clinical effects, but differing effects on the extrapyramidal nervous system. Of the active treatments, fluphenazine produced most unwanted effects and thioridazine least. Some unwanted effects were recorded among patients receiving the placebo. The study showed that the phenothiazine drugs vary in their potency in causing neurological unwanted effects and that this is not closely related to therapeutic potency.

A detailed study of phenothiazine-induced extrapyramidal effects by Simpson *et al.* (1964) showed that some evidence of disturbance in the extrapyramidal system was present in all of 20 patients receiving perphenazine 24 mg daily. In the majority of patients the signs were maximal between the fifth and tenth weeks of treatment, but declined in severity after 10 to 12 weeks. In some of the patients these signs appeared as soon as two weeks after the administration of drugs began and others showed a maximum severity of symptoms after only three weeks. Five patients still showed signs of extrapyramidal disturbance 105 days after the provocative drug was withdrawn.

TABLE 12.2.   *Unwanted effects of three phenothiazine drugs and placebo on the extrapyramidal nervous systems*

Unwanted effects	Thioridazine $n = 91$	Chlorpromazine $n = 88$	Fluphenazine $n = 91$	Placebo $n = 74$
Muscle rigidity	4.4	12.5	24.2	8.1
Facial rigidity	8.8	12.5	14.3	5.4
Tremor of hands, arms and face	13.2	5.7	12.1	5.4
Loss of associated movements	0	3.4	19.8	2.7
Akathisia	3.3	5.7	12.1	4.1
Increased salivation	3.3	5.7	8.8	0
Dystonia	1.1	4.5	6.6	0
Oculogyric causes	0	1.1	0	0

Percentage of patients exhibiting the particular effect is shown. (From National Institute of Mental Health 1964.)

A study of 57 patients who were treated for schizophrenia with injections of a depot preparation of fluphenazine, either the enanthate or the decanoate, showed that 88 per cent experienced extrapyramidal unwanted effects at some time during six months observation (Knights *et al.* 1979). Seventy-four per cent developed the unwanted effects after the test dose; 74 per cent showed extrapyramidal effects during the trial (not always those who showed the effects with the test dose); and 54 per cent showed the unwanted effects after six months treatment. This study confirms a high incidence of extrapyramidal effects with some types of phenothiazine and shows that in a proportion of patients these effects may be persistent.

A study by Myrianthopoulos *et al.* (1962) examined the relationship between the occurrence of drug-induced parkinsonism and a family history of Parkinson's disease. A survey was made of 728 relatives of 59 patients who developed drug-induced parkinsonism; the incidence of Parkinson's disease among them was compared with its incidence among 777 relatives of 67 patients who failed to develop parkinsonism while receiving phenothiazines. Among the relatives of the index group there were 13 cases of Parkinson's disease compared with three cases among the relatives of the controls. A very similar study was carried out a few years later by the same group of workers. Among 1079 relatives of sufferers from drug-induced parkinsonism, 14 cases of Parkinson's disease were found as compared with five cases among 1208 patients who received neuroleptic drugs but did not develop parkinsonism. The authors regard these findings as confirming those of their earlier study. Interestingly, the findings were restricted to white patients, negroes showing no difference between the groups (Myrianthopoulos *et al.* 1967). The findings may be due to a hereditary predisposition to parkinsonism, but are not conclusive proof of such a tendency. Indeed, there is now some doubt that Parkinson's disease itself has any hereditary origin, for few cases of similarly affected identical twins have been reported.

Although a great part of the literature on drug-induced parkinsonism concerns the phenothiazine drugs, the neuroleptics of other classes, such as the butyrophenones and the thioxanthenes also are capable of producing extrapyramidal syndromes. Of considerable theoretical importance is the observation that drugs such as reserpine and tetrabenazine, which also antagonize the effects of dopamine (but by a different mechanism) also cause drug-induced parkinsonism.

The liability to drug-induced parkinsonism has occasionally been shown to be linked with other physical features. A study of acutely ill female schizophrenic patients showed the appearance of parkinsonism in response to a low dosage of trifluoperazine to occur in patients with a higher taste sensibility to quinine. Conversely, parkinsonism which appeared on higher dosage levels of trifluoperazine occurred in patients with low taste sensibility (Knopp *et al.* 1966). In another study an excess of blue-eyed men was found amongst patients developing facial dyskinesia (Brandon *et al.* 1971). The relevance of these observations is, as yet, unclear.

Relationship between parkinsonism and therapeutic effects

The effect of chlorpromazine on the extrapyramidal system has been known almost from the discovery of its therapeutic action. Delay and Deniker (1952) suggested that the effect of chlorpromazine in controlling agitation and violence might be due to the induction of parkinsonism. As new phenothiazines and their analogues have come into use in the treatment of schizophrenia and of other conditions, they have all been found to share the property of inducing parkinsonism, although their potency in this respect is not necessarily proportional to their therapeutic actions (Herman and Pleasure 1963).

Psychiatrists have varied in their view of the importance of the relationship of drug-induced parkinsonism and of other extrapyramidal syndromes to the therapeutic effect; some have argued that extrapyramidal complications must be produced for a therapeutic effect to be seen; others have regarded extrapyramidal complications as unfortunate unwanted effects, not essential for satisfactory treatment. Haase (1961) for example, believed the induction of impairment of fine movements to be essential for a therapeutic action; he described this as a 'conditio sine qua non' for therapeutic effectiveness. Other workers have reached similar conclusions (Brune *et al.* 1962), and some have even deliberately sought the development of severe extrapyramidal signs in regulating phenothiazine dosage in psychiatric patients (Delay and Deniker 1961).

The view that extrapyramidal signs are not essential for a good therapeutic effect has been argued by many (Bishop *et al.* 1965). In a review of 4030 patients, comparing the discharge rates among those who had developed drug-induced parkinsonism with those who had not, it was concluded that a good therapeutic effect can be produced in most patients without the development of parkinsonism (Goldman 1961). A similar study showed no differences in therapeutic effects of phenothiazines between patients who developed extrapyramidal signs and those who did not (Hollister *et al.* 1960). A survey of published reports contrasts the low incidence of extrapyramidal signs in patients treated with thioridazine with the high incidence of these complications in patients treated with fluphenazine but with both drugs showing similar therapeutic efficiency in the treatment of chronic schizophrenia (Cole and Clyde 1961). An experimental study of the relationship in 20 chronic schizophrenic patients treated with perphenazine showed a negative correlation between the severity of parkinsonism and therapeutic effect (Simpson *et al.* 1964).

The National Institute of Mental Health (1964) collaborative study of the effects of chlorpromazine, thioridazine, fluphenazine, and placebo in the treatment of schizophrenia showed the drugs to have similar therapeutic properties but to differ in the number of unwanted effects produced. The authors believe that this observation suggests that the therapeutic properties of the drugs are independent of their action on the extrapyramidal system.

In a review of this controversy, Chien and Dimascio (1967) attributed the early view, that extrapyramidal signs were essential to therapeutic effect, to a series of methodological problems in early studies. First, there was confusion in the recognition and terminology of drug-induced extrapyramidal syndromes; second, many earlier investigators approached the topic with a bias arising from certain theoretical assumptions; third, most of the early studies were methodologically unsound and rarely included satisfactory control groups or reliable methods of measuring symptomatology; fourth, most studies were retrospective and open to different methods of interpretation; and finally, many opinions were based on insufficient data.

It is now generally agreed that overt extrapyramidal side-effects are not required for therapeutic effect. Indeed, some of the newer novel antipsychotic drugs, such as clozapine, rarely produce drug-induced parkinsonism despite effective therapeutic action (Gerlach *et al.* 1974; Ekblom and Haggstrom 1974; Simpson and Varga 1974). (Unfortunately, agranulocytosis led to the withdrawal of clozapine in most countries.)

The relation between therapeutic action and extrapyramidal side-effects is complicated, however, by the differences in inherent anticholinergic activity of the various neuroleptic drugs. Miller and Hiley (1974) pointed out that many neuroleptics possess powerful inherent anticholinergic action, and that this would protect against drug-induced acute dystonic reactions and parkinsonism. Strongly anticholinergic drugs such as thioridazine and clozapine produce much less extrapyramidal dysfunction than drugs such as trifluoperazine or fluphenazine which possess little inherent anticholinergic action.

Drug treatment of drug-induced parkinsonism

Not unnaturally, remedies used in the treatment of Parkinson's disease have been employed in the management of drug-induced parkinsonism; these include a large number of anticholinergic drugs, and a few other substances. These drugs have been used in two ways: to control the symptoms once they have appeared, or they are given before symptoms appear with the intention of preventing them. For either purpose the anticholinergic drugs are given in the same dosage as is used in Parkinson's disease (Table 12.3).

Following the introduction of L-DOPA as a treatment for Parkinson's

TABLE 12.3. *Anticholinergic drugs in common use for the treatment of drug-induced parkinsonism*

Drug	Daily dosage (mg)
Benzhexol	6–10
Benztropine methane sulphanate	1–2
Biperiden	2–6
Methixene	15–60
Orphenadrine	150–300
Procyclidine	20–30

disease, it was tried in drug-induced parkinsonism (Yaryura-Tobias *et al.* 1970*a, b*). Two effects were observed: the parkinsonism either remained the same or the symptoms increased, and there was a behavioural change for the worse. The effect on psychiatric states was such that only four of 20 patients completed the study as planned. There is further evidence that the administration of amine precursors to schizophrenic patients may cause a deterioration in the mental state which suggests that such treatment is inappropriate for drug-induced parkinsonism (Angrist *et al.* 1973; Lauer *et al.* 1958).

More recently the administration of relatively small amounts of L-DOPA to schizophrenic patients has been reported to lead to improvements in some patients without provoking a serious deterioration in others (Inanga *et al.* 1972; Ogura *et al.* 1976; Garfinkel and Stancer 1976). The main effect appears to be one of activation, with improvement in social behaviour and spontaneity. The advantageous effect was most seen in withdrawn, solitary schizophrenic patients and was absent in those with predominantly paranoid illnesses. A small number of patients showed irritability, anxiety, and akathisia with a worsening of hallucinations and delusions.

Other dopaminergic drugs which might be expected to lead to an improvement in symptoms of drug-induced parkinsonism include nomifensine; this drug has been clinically evaluated in both Parkinson's disease and in depressive states. The evidence that it is effective in Parkinson's disease is, so far, limited (Bedard *et al.* 1977*b*; Park *et al.* 1981). As yet, no reports of the evaluation of the drug in the treatment of drug-induced parkinsonism have been reported. Piribedil, a drug claimed to be a dopamine agonist, has been shown to be ineffective in the treatment of drug-induced parkinsonism (Mindham *et al.* 1977).

Evidence on the effectiveness of amantadine in drug-induced parkinsonism is conflicting. An uncontrolled study which employed amantadine in a dosage of 200 mg daily reported to show effective control of drug-induced parkinsonism and, furthermore, that the degree of control was related to the plasma levels of amantadine achieved (Pacifici *et al.* 1976). In this study the patients investigated were receiving a variety of neuroleptic drugs together with anticholinergic drugs which had produced an unsatisfactory degree of control of parkinsonism. Another study compared the effects of amantadine (600 mg daily) in controlling fluphenazine-induced parkinsonism with that of placebo and orphenadrine; no differences were found between the treatments (Mindham *et al.* 1972).

The limited effectiveness of dopaminergic substances in the treatment of drug-induced parkinsonism is difficult to understand in pharmacological terms. Conventionally, where the effect of a drug is blocked by another substance, an increased concentration of the drug in use would be expected to overcome the effect of the blocking agent.

Anticholinergic drugs in treatment

Although the anticholinergic drugs are so widely used in the management of drug-induced parkinsonism, the evidence for their effectiveness is less convincing than might be expected (Mindham 1976). Many of the substances used have never been fully assessed in the treatment of Parkinson's disease itself. Anticholinergic drugs were introduced many years ago, before the advent of controlled clinical trials, and were replaced by newer preparations largely on the basis of clinical impressions. These substances have rarely been compared with placebo; more often with one another. Procyclidine is one of the few drugs which have been compared with placebo in the treatment of Parkinson's disease and was shown to be more effective (Strang 1965).

Studies of the use of anticholinergic drugs in the management of drug-induced parkinsonism fall into three main categories: those which compared the effects of a drug or drugs with placebo; those which compared the efficacy of different drugs; and those which studied the effects of withdrawal of anticholinergic drugs. Examples of these studies will be described.

Anticholinergic drugs vs. placebo

A small series of studies of the treatment of drug-induced parkinsonism was reported by Simpson (1970*a*). In the first, a rising dosage of benztropine mesylate and biperiden was given by intravenous injection on alternate days to patients suffering from drug-induced parkinsonism. The patients were rated 'blind' prior to the injections, after 30 and 60 minutes, and then at 60-minute intervals for seven hours. The experiment was then repeated 10 days later using different raters. On both occasions the greatest therapeutic effect followed the first injection of the series. In the second experiment intravenous injections of 2 mg of benztropine mesylate or of a placebo were given randomly over six successive days. Ratings of parkinsonism were performed as before. There was no difference between the effects of the injections. In the third experiment six patients received nine injections, three each of biperiden, benztropine mesylate, and placebo. No differences were found between the treatments. The same patients then received biperiden 3 mg daily for three weeks, 4 mg daily for one week, and 6 mg daily for five weeks. In five patients no changes were found in parkinsonism, but in one there was a diminution in the severity of symptoms.

The effects of amantadine, orphenadrine, and placebo on parkinsonism induced by depot injections of fluphenazine decanoate were compared in a double-blind cross-over trial (Mindham *et al.* 1972). The severity of symptoms and signs of parkinsonism were assessed using standard methods. No differences were found between the effects of the three treatments. A rather similar study showed procyclidine to be superior to placebo; piribedil was similar to placebo in the control of parkinsonism but produced more unwanted effects (Mindham *et al.* 1977).

Comparisons between anticholinergic drugs

A study reported a comparison of the effects of orphenadrine, procyclidine and methixene in drug-induced parkinsonism (Ekdawi and Fowke 1966). Little difference was found between the remedies; the impression was gained that all improved the symptoms but without controlling them fully.

The effects of orphenadrine and its demethylated derivative tofenacin on parkinsonism induced by fluphenazine decanoate were reported (Capstick and Pudney 1976). Both substances appeared to reduce the symptomatology to a similar degree but without abolishing parkinsonism.

A rather different approach was employed in a study of the effects of exchanging three anticholinergic drugs and placebo in patients who had developed parkinsonism on major tranquillizers (St. Jean *et al.* 1961). All the patients began the study of benzhexol for one month, and then were randomly allocated to promethazine, ethopropazine, and placebo in turn, for one month each. The active drugs showed similar degrees of effectiveness in controlling parkinsonism and all were superior to placebo (Table 12.4).

Withdrawal of anticholinergic drugs

Quite a number of studies have been made of the effects of withdrawal of anticholinergic drugs from patients receiving major tranquillizers.

In two early studies benzhexol was withdrawn from patients showing parkinsonism caused by a variety of phenothiazines. In the first, in which chlorpromazine, fluphenazine, perphenazine, prochlorperazine, and trifluoperazine were used, withdrawal of benzhexol resulted in the reappearance of parkinsonism in 41 per cent of subjects; in the second, in which the phenothiazine drug was thioperazine, 80 per cent of patients developed parkinsonism (Mandel and Oliver 1961; Mandel *et al.* 1961).

In another early study 88 female patients, who were receiving phenothiazine drugs and anticholinergic antiparkinson drugs, had their anticholinergic medication withdrawn for a nine-week period (Stratas *et al.* 1963). Of the 88 patients, 64 showed no extrapyramidal signs following drug withdrawal. Of those showing parkinsonism, 16 were given a lower dosage of phenothiazine and 13 of these were free of parkinsonism after two weeks; the remaining three had their phenothiazines substituted for thioridazine. Eight patients who had changed directly to thioridazine lost their signs of parkinsonism. The authors conclude that most patients do not require antiparkinson medication and that many of those who do show drug-induced parkinsonism respond to reduction in dosage or substitution of the phenothiazine they are receiving by thioridazine. Eighty patients receiving a variety of phenothiazines who had shown drug-induced parkinsonism, which had led to the administration of an anticholinergic drug, were randomly allocated to groups to continue anticholinergic medication or to stop it abruptly (Ananth *et al.* 1970). Six patients in the control group and thirteen patients in the withdrawal group showed an increased severity of extrapyramidal signs, one control and three withdrawal patients improved and the remainder were unchanged. Only four patients in the withdrawal group returned to anticholinergic drugs on account of the severity of parkinsonism. Withdrawal of anticholinergic drugs did not cause any serious changes in the psychiatric states of the subjects.

Another study clearly showed how important the length of the period of administration of major tranquillizers is to the need for anticholinergic

TABLE 12.4. *Trials of drugs in the control of drug-induced parkinsonism*

Authors	Design	Neuroleptics	Anticholinergic drugs	Other drugs	Placebo control	Result
St. Jean *et al.* (1961)	Random multiple substitution	Unspecified	Promethazine 10 mg daily Ethopropazine 25 mg daily Benzhexol 2 mg daily Oral	None	Oral	Active drugs similar and all superior to placebo in control of parkinsonism
Ekdawai and Fowke (1966)	Cross-over	Various	Methixene 5 mg, 3 or 4 daily Procyclidine 5 mg, 3 or 4 daily Orphenadrine 50 mg, 3 or 4 daily Oral	None	None	Parkinsonism equally improved by each drug
Simpson (1970)	Random intravenous injections	Unspecified	Benztropine mesylate 2 mg Biperiden 2.5–7.5 mg	None	Placebo given intravenous injection	Little difference between treatments
Mindham *et al.* (1972)	Cross-over	Fluphenazine decanoate depot injection 25–50 mg every 4 weeks	Orphenadrine 50 mg tds oral	Amantadine 200 mg tds oral	Oral tds	No difference between treatments
Capstick and Pudney (1976)	Cross-over	Fluphenazine decanoate depot injection every 4 weeks	Orphenadrine 50 mg tablets Tofenacin 40 mg tablets Constant dosage in each subject	None	None	Remedies equally effective in controlling parkinsonism
Mindham *et al.* (1977)	Cross-over	Fluphenazine decanoate depot injection 25–50 mg every 4 weeks	Procyclidine 5 mg qds oral	Piribedil 20 mg qds oral	Oral qds	Procyclidine superior to placebo. Piribedil similar to placebo.

medication (Orlov *et al.* 1971). A group of 78 patients who had received anti-parkinson drugs for over three months had their anticholinergic drugs withdrawn on a particular date. Some patients were unhappy about the withdrawal of the drugs, but of the total only seven (9%) showed symptoms of sufficient severity for drugs to be prescribed again. In these there was recurrence of parkinsonism, and a variety of other symptoms apparently caused by drug withdrawal. In all these patients the symptoms reappeared within seven days of drug withdrawal. The authors draw attention to their earlier observation that when anticholinergic drugs have been given for over three months less than 10% of patients show a severe return of symptoms on withdrawal; whereas in those patients who have received anticholinergic drugs for only one month, withdrawal leads to the appearance of severe unwanted effects in two-thirds. The authors conclude that few patients require chronic administration of anticholinergic drugs, and that withdrawal is only likely to lead to a serious recurrence of parkinsonism where medication has only been given for a relatively short time.

A study of patients receiving depot fluphenazine enanthate injections gave rather different results (Grove and Crammer 1972). Sixteen patients who had received phenothiazine injections and benzhexol orally for some months were divided into two groups: one group continued with benzhexol and the other group had placebo tablets blindly substituted for benzhexol. Four of the patients in the withdrawal group showed severe parkinsonism, but the other four were unaffected by the change. The authors believe that many patients require continued administration of anticholinergic drugs for control of drug-induced parkinsonism and that abrupt withdrawal is unwise. They suggest that a pharmacological dependency may have been induced.

A large-scale collaborative withdrawal study is reported from the United States of America (Klett and Caffey 1972). Five hundred and eighteen patients who were receiving treatment with a variety of phenothiazines or haloperidol, and one of a variety of anticholinergic antiparkinson drugs, were allocated to groups for abrupt withdrawal of anticholinergic drugs by substitution with placebo, or for substitution of existing anticholinergic medication by benztropine mesylate. Eighty per cent of patients were allocated to the placebo group and 20 per cent to the active drug group. The new treatments were given for six weeks unless the patients were withdrawn prematurely. Of the 403 patients who received placebo 7 per cent were withdrawn on account of a recurrent parkinsonism requiring medication; 11 per cent were judged to be worse but did not necessitate further medication; the remaining 82 per cent of patients were either free from parkinsonism or showed signs of minimal severity. Of the patients on the active drug, 1 per cent were withdrawn on account of worsening of parkinsonism; 9 per cent were worse but were not withdrawn; and 90 per cent were little changed or showed only temporary worsening. Following the withdrawal of anticholinergic drugs symptoms of parkinsonism reappeared between five and 38 days afterwards; 50 per cent appearing within two weeks and about 25 per cent in the second two weeks. The authors concluded that many of the patients receiving anticholinergic drugs for parkinsonism do not require them.

A study is reported from the United Kingdom of the effects of withdrawing anticholinergic drugs from patients on phenothiazines or butyrophenones (McClelland *et al.* 1974). In the study, patients were divided into two groups receiving one or more oral preparations, depot injections alone, or with oral drugs. These groups were then further subdivided into those from whom anticholinergic drugs were withdrawn, and those who continued to take them. Two of the patients withdrawn showed marked parkinsonism, and a further two were somewhat worse, making a total relapse rate of only 8 per cent. Some other patients who were withdrawn showed an increase in rigidity but this did not cause the patients to complain of discomfort. Most of the patients studied had received anticholinergic drugs continuously for longer than three months, and the majority for more than one year. The authors concluded that the majority of patients receiving phenothiazine drugs and their analogues do not require antiparkinson medication.

A more recent study was reported by Manos *et al.* (1981) in which the effects of withdrawal of anticholinergic drugs from chronic schizophrenic patients who were receiving treatment with a variety of neuroleptic drugs, alone and in combination were observed. Seventy-five per cent of the patients were withdrawn to receive placebo and the remainder to receive trihexyphenidyl. The patients were then assessed weekly for severity of drug-induced parkinsonism and other changes over a period of six weeks. The results of this study were that the patients withdrawn from antiparkinson drugs more frequently showed evidence of distress from drug-induced parkinsonism than those given an alternative antiparkinson drug.

Methodological problems in trials of treatment

Accounts of studies of drug treatments of drug-induced parkinsonism make it clear that satisfactory trials are difficult to carry out; the results of trials are often inconsistent and their results conflicting. Several factors are important in the design of such trials and these will be discussed briefly.

A failure to take the drug which causes the parkinsonism can result in an improvement in the unwanted effect on the extrapyramidal nervous system. Thus it is important that the provocative drug is taken in the dosage known to cause drug-induced parkinsonism in particular subjects, and that the drug is taken in the same dosage throughout the study. This problem can be partly overcome by using depot injections of drugs, but even this can cause difficulty as the drug may be unevenly released from the injection site (Lamb *et al.* 1976).

Drugs vary in their potency in provoking drug-induced parkinsonism. This means that the effects of antidotes cannot be compared unless groups of subjects take the same drug throughout the study.

The severity of parkinsonism probably declines with the passage of time, and this must be allowed for in the design of a study. This is normally done by using prospective comparison with a control group, both groups being subject to the effects to a similar degree.

Control treatments are required for comparison with the remedy under investigation. This may be a placebo treatment or a 'standard treatment'. The results of a number of trials show that few treatments of known and reliable efficacy are available and that the use of placebo controls may radically alter the interpretation of findings. Thus, the choice of a satisfactory control group is an important aspect of trial design.

Satisfactory methods of assessing symptoms and signs must be used. A number of methods of rating extrapyramidal signs have been developed (Simpson and Angus 1970; Godwin-Austen *et al*. 1969; Klett and Caffey 1972; Chouinard *et al*. 1979*a*). These methods work fairly well, but suffer from the disadvantage of being more suitable for severely affected rather than mildly affected patients, having been developed for the most part for patients suffering from Parkinson's disease. The scale described by Chouinard *et al*. is possibly the most sensitive in detecting minor signs of parkinsonism and hence the most generally suitable for studying drug-induced parkinsonism. The scale developed by Webster and his colleagues is also very satisfactory (Webster 1968).

Performance tests have been used in the assessment of symptoms and signs of drug-induced parkinsonism and Parkinson's disease. These included:

1. Timing a walk of 25 yards with a turn.

2. Squeezing a sphygmomanometer cuff blown up to 60 mm of mercury—each hand being tested in turn and the results averaged (Onuaguluchi 1964).

3. The groove pegboard test in which the patient places grooved pegs in holes in a board while the procedure is timed (Meier and Martin 1970).

4. Bead tests in which the subject transfers beads from one container to another using tweezers while the procedure is timed (Horne 1973). There are several variations on this test using coloured beads and interrupting the procedure with other tasks.

5. The tapping test in which a metal stylus is used to tap one or two metal plates and the number of taps in a short period, say ten seconds, is timed (Simpson *et al*. 1964).

6. Various tests of writing. Some involve timed writing of a familiar address, others measure size and style of writing, and others the area of paper covered (Angus and Simpson 1970). Performance tests clearly reflect various functions and are influenced by tremor, rigidity, difficulty in initiating movements, and other clinical changes. Unfortunately, they have been shown to correlate poorly with clinical signs and to be generally less sensitive to change (Simpson *et al*. 1964; Mindham *et al*. 1977).

There may be fluctuations in the severity of symptoms and signs which make the evaluation of a remedy difficult (Ekdawi and Fowke 1966). This can be partly overcome by the use of large numbers of patients and studying them over an extended period of time.

The co-operation of the subject in assessment should be satisfactory and consistent; this may be difficult to achieve, especially amongst the patients who are mentally ill. Symptomatic enquiries made of chronically hospitalized patients have been shown to give inconsistent results (Mindham *et al.* 1972).

Ideally, an objective assessment should be made of co-operation in taking antiparkinson treatment. This can be attempted by tablet counts, urine tests, or possibly plasma estimations of drug concentrations. Unfortunately, plasma estimations are not always possible in the presence of other substances and rarely show whether or not the full prescribed dose has been taken (Mindham *et al.* 1977).

In view of all these problems it is perhaps not surprising that so few methodologically sound trials have been conducted of antidotes to drug-induced parkinsonism; it is more surprising that many of these points have not even been considered in the design of many trials.

Dangers of anticholinergic drugs

The anticholinergic antiparkinson drugs show a variety of unwanted effects, some of them of particular importance where the drugs are used in the management of drug-induced parkinsonism.

The acute toxic state which may follow an excessive dose of anticholinergic drugs is well documented and well known to clinicians (Schwab *et al.* 1951; Porteous and Ross 1956; Stephens 1967). The clinical features of these episodes, which are typical of acute toxic confusional states, include excitement, agitation, violence, disorientation in time and place, delusions, and both visual and auditory hallucinations. Patients affected usually respond rapidly to the withdrawal of the anticholinergic medication.

With the recognition of tardive dyskinesia it has been suggested that the concurrent administration of a major tranquilliser and an anticholinergic antiparkinson drug may increase the risk of tardive dyskinesia appearing (Klawans 1973*b*; Kiloh *et al.* 1973; Klawans and Rubovitz 1974). Two experimental studies showed that some patients with tardive dyskinesia were clinically worse when receiving anticholinergic drugs (Turek *et al.* 1972; Chouinard *et al.* 1979*b*). This effect is clearly of great clinical importance. The administration of anticholinergic drugs to subjects on long-term neuroleptic medication has been suggested as an aid to the early detection of tardive dyskinesia (Chouinard *et al.* 1979*c*).

More recently, it has been suggested that anticholinergic drugs may contribute to the development of hyperthermic episodes, some of which are fatal. One report is of two cases of hyperpyrexia in male schizophrenics receiving phenothiazine and anticholinergic drugs in combination. Both presented with deep coma, rectal temperatures in excess of 108°F, tachycardia, tachypnoea, and dry skin and mucous membranes. One patient recovered without ill effect and reported that he had experienced no warning symptoms before losing consciousness. The other patient died from respiratory and cardiovascular failure with pneumonia. Both patients were receiving chlorpromazine 1 g daily and benztropine methane sulphonate 6 mg daily (Sarnquist and Larson 1973).

Another report is of three cases of hyperpyrexia in patients taking major tranquillizers with anticholinergic drugs. The clinical features were as described above, and in all three cases heat stroke was suspected initially. All three patients responded to cooling and rehydration and recovered without apparent ill effect. The authors attributed the hyperpyrexial episodes to the peripheral inhibition of sweating by anticholinergic drugs, together with a central effect on thermoregulatory centres from the phenothiazines (Westlake and Rastegar 1973). These effects are particularly important in heat waves, in hot countries, and in conditions of prolonged exposure to cold.

For some years occasional papers have suggested that the administration of anticholinergic drugs for the control of extrapyramidal unwanted effects reduces the therapeutic effectiveness of the drug causing the unwanted effects (Haase 1965; Singh and Smith 1973). Two studies are reported which appear to support these observations with experimental evidence (Singh and Kay 1975*a, b*). In both studies a small number of chronic schizophrenic patients were treated with chlorpromazine or haloperidol. In the first study the drugs were given in a cross-over design, with patients acting as their own controls, and benztropine was administered for a part of the period on each drug. In the second study, matched pairs of patients were given either chlorpromazine or haloperidol, and benzhexol was given for part of the period of administration of each drug. In both trials a flexible dosage schedule was used and the relative potencies of the drugs were found to be of the order of 50 mg of chlorpromazine to 1 mg of haloperidol. In both studies it was found that during the period of administration of the anticholinergic antiparkinson drugs there was a worsening of the schizophrenic symptomatology. This effect was found to be more marked in the case of chlorpromazine-treated schizophrenics; it is suggested that the anticholinergic activity of chlorpromazine counters its antischizophrenic effects in some degree, and that this effect is potentiated by the administration of an additional anticholinergic substance. The authors argue that a disturbance of cholinergic transmission in the nervous system may occur in schizophrenia. This is discussed further in Chapter 11.

The effects described may be attributable to changes in the plasma concentration of phenothiazine. Both phenobarbitone and orphenadrine have been shown to reduce the plasma levels of chlorpromazine when the drugs are given over a period of weeks (Loga *et al.* 1975). Twelve patients were studied intensively over a period of 15 weeks; it was noted that the plasma levels of chlorpromazine reached their maximum values in the first week of treatment and then gradually fell; this phenomenon was held to suggest an induction of enzymes metabolizing the drug. When phenobarbitone or orphenadrine was added, the same general pattern was found but the plasma levels of chlorpromazine were lower.

Another study, primarily concerned with the therapeutic effects of chlorpromazine, reported a fall in plasma levels of chlorpromazine following the addition of benzhexol; the chlorpromazine levels rose when the anticholinergic drug was withdrawn (Rivera-Calimlim *et al.* 1976). A subsequent study of chlorpromazine levels in rats suggested that the effect on plasma levels might be due to impaired absorption from the intestine (Rivera-Calimlim 1976).

Management of drug-induced parkinsonism

The possible complications of the use of anticholinergic antiparkinson drugs have made clinicians more sparing of their use. General guidelines for the management of drug-induced parkinsonism can be drawn from research on the subject (Stratas *et al.* 1963; Dimascio and Demirgian 1970; Klett and Caffey 1972; Johnson 1978).

1. The routine prescription of anticholinergic drugs with neuroleptics should be avoided; this practice results in many patients who do not require drugs receiving them.

2. Where drug-induced parkinsonism gives rise to distressing symptoms, consideration should first be given to reducing the dosage of the offending drug. In many cases this will be possible without prejudicing the main aims of treatment.

3. Where reduction of dosage of the provocative drugs is inappropriate, another drug with less potency in producing parkinsonism but giving adequate therapeutic effect might be substituted.

4. When antiparkinson medication is deemed necessary the drugs should be given only for as long as symptoms are unpleasant to the patient.

5. Antiparkinson drugs should not be given for more than three or four months, as there is good evidence that a longer period of administration is neither necessary nor effective.

6. If parkinsonism re-appears after withdrawal of antiparkinsonism medication the drugs should be re-introduced for a limited period only.

If these principles are followed a relatively small proportion of patients who require neuroleptic medication will be given antiparkinson drugs in addition and the others will, as a consequence, be spared their various unwanted effects in both the short and long term.

AKATHISIA

Akathisia, a state of motor restlessness, is often seen following the administration of a wide range of neuroleptic drugs. The major manifestation of the syndrome is the *subjective* feeling of motor unease. The unfortunate patient feels that he cannot sit still, but must move to gain relief from his discomfort. The subject constantly shifts his legs and taps his feet, and this behaviour is accompanied by tension, a feeling of being driven to move, and an inability to tolerate inactivity. In more severely affected subjects there is constant rocking of the body, shifting from foot to foot, and walking or running movements. Such florid movement may be misinterpreted as due to a recurrence of schizophrenic behaviour, leading to an inappropriate increase in drug dosage (Marsden *et al.* 1975).

Following the administration of neuroleptic drugs, akathisia appears more slowly than acute dyskinesia but more quickly than parkinsonism (Ayd 1961; Marsden *et al.* 1975). Ninety per cent of those patients who develop akathisia do so within 10 weeks of starting treatment. Akathisia commonly co-exists with drug-induced parkinsonism, and occurs often in idiopathic Parkinson's disease. In both conditions, the subjective mental urge to move contrasts with the physical akinesia of the condition. Women are almost twice as frequently affected as men.

Drugs vary in their tendency to produce akathisia; for example, chlorpromazine produced the syndrome in 20 per cent of Ayd's sample as compared with 30 per cent among those receiving trifluoperazine. The syndrome is difficult to control as response to anticholinergic drugs is very limited. Reduction in dosage is the most effective method of management. Occasionally, the syndrome subsides only slowly following withdrawal of the provocative drug, or may even become worse (Hershon *et al.* 1972).

ACUTE DYSTONIC REACTIONS (ACUTE DYSKINESIAS)

Perhaps the most dramatic of the neuroleptic-induced disorders of striopallidal function are the acute dystonic reactions. The term dystonia has been reserved by some for the signs of sustained tonic contraction of a muscle or muscle group (Denny-Brown 1968), yet it is commonly used to describe certain involuntary hyperkinetic movements of facial and limb musculature. Acute dyskinesia perhaps is more accurate, but in view of the general usage of the term dystonia, acute dystonic reaction will be used here.

Clinical features

The array of clinical phenomena constituting this syndrome is the richest of all the extrapyramidal reactions. The syndrome consists primarily of intermittent or sustained muscular spasms and abnormal postures (Ayd 1961; Marsden *et al.* 1975).

Involvement of the cephalic musculature may be expressed as protrusion or twisting of the tongue, trismus, blepharospasm, oculogyric crises, grimacing, forceful opening of the jaw, and glossopharyngeal contractions. Dysarthria, dysphagia, jaw dislocation, and respiratory stridor with cyanosis may ensue.

Oculogyric crisis is characterized by a brief prodromal fixed stare, followed by upward and lateral rotation of the eyes. If the eyelids are forced open against blepharospasm, the irises are typically found to be hidden beneath the upper canthus of the eye, leaving only the sclera visible. Associated with these quite alarming ocular signs, the head is usually tilted backwards and laterally, the mouth is open and the tongue protruded.

Involvement of neck muscles can produce spasmodic torticollis and retrocollis. Trunk involvement may be expressed as opisthotonos, scoliosis, lordosis, trunk flexion, writhing movements, or tortipelvis accompanied by dystonic gait. The limbs may show slow writhing movements, with exaggerated postures of hyperpronation and adduction. Rigidity usually is evident and tendon reflexes are increased.

Acute reactions unaccompanied by severe muscle spasm can also occur. They include protrusion of the tongue, lip-smacking, blinking, athetosis of the fingers and toes, shoulder-shrugging, and a variety of myoclonic muscle contractions of the face, neck, and extremities. Subtle forms of these disturbances such as muscular cramps or tightness of the jaw and tongue, with dysphagia and dysarthria, may occur by themselves or may precede the more obvious manifestations (Marsden *et al.* 1975).

In a study of 1152 neuroleptic-treated patients Swett (1975) found the following five phenomena to be the commonest manifestations of acute dystonia: torticollis (30 per cent); contraction of the tongue (17 per cent); trismus (15 per cent); oculogyric crises (6 per cent); and opisthotonos (3 per cent).

The character of the reaction varies according to the age of the patient. In children under the age of 15 years the syndrome appears to affect predominantly the axial and limb musculature, with increasing cephalic and upper limb involvement occurring towards early and middle adulthood (Ayd 1961; Gupta and Lovejoy 1967; Marsden *et al.* 1975). However, the face is by no means spared in children. In a report of dystonic reactions to metoclopramide in children between the ages of 5 and 11 years, Casteels-Van Daele *et al.* (1970) found frequent oculogyric crises and facial grimacing.

The urgency of the clinical situation often created by the acute dystonic reactions comes not only from their striking appearance but also from the pain and severe distress experienced by the patient. The pain is a result of sustained muscle spasm, and the bizarre involuntary contortions occurring in clear consciousness understandably evoke considerable anxiety. The clinical picture is exacerbated by any additional emotional stress and can be influenced by suggestion.

Dystonic reactions are often episodic and recurrent, even after only a single intake of neuroleptic. Attacks may last seconds, minutes, or hours.

The dystonia caused by neuroleptics closely resembles the dystonic reactions produced by a variety of other toxic, metabolic, infectious, traumatic, or degenerative disorders of the basal ganglia. Dystonia musculorum deformans (idiopathic torsion dystonia) closely resembles the neuroleptic-induced syndrome, not only in phenomenology but also in its age-specific character and its reactivity to stress and suggestion (Marsden *et al.* 1975; Marsden 1976).

Differential diagnosis

The practising psychiatrist who regularly prescribes neuroleptic drugs should have little difficulty in making the diagnosis. In other situations, however, the diagnosis may not spring so easily to mind. Outside psychiatric practice, neuroleptics (such as metoclopramide) may be exhibited to alleviate nausea, vomiting, and dizziness. In children or young adults, the possibility of neuroleptics, unless specifically enquired about, is often overlooked—particularly in the emergency surrounding an accidental or intended overdose. Erroneous diagnoses such as tetanus, status epilepticus, meningitis, or encephalitis have all been documented, resulting in antibiotic therapy, lumbar puncture, and even tracheotomy before the situation was properly assessed (Ayd 1960). On the basis of clinical presentation in the absence of a drug history, the diagnosis of dystonia musculorum deformans might be made, but the commonest error is to dismiss the events as hysterical. The curious, bizarre pattern of rapid remission and fluctuation in response to stress or suggestion, and the accompanying distress and anxiety, can often lead the unwary casualty officer to diagnose a hysterical reaction.

The simple precaution of a careful drug history should avoid these pitfalls. Delay in diagnosis is inexcusable; the condition is painful, profoundly distressing, and can be rapidly ameliorated by appropriate treatment (see below).

Time of onset

Acute dystonic reactions are the earliest extrapyramidal disorders to appear after instituting neuroleptic therapy. In adults, some 90 per cent of cases appear within the first 4½ days of treatment and with a variety of neuroleptics, many presenting within the first few hours (Ayd 1961; Swett 1975). The more potent dopamine receptor-blocking agents (such as piperazinyl phenothiazines) tend to provoke the earliest reactions (Ayd 1961), presumably because effective receptor-blocking concentrations are low and achieved quickly.

Ayd (1975) reported that dystonic reactions to the depot intramuscular neuroleptics occur, on average, significantly sooner than with oral neuroleptics. He found that 90 per cent of cases present within 12 to 24 hours of injection. The pharmacokinetic explanation for this is not immediately obvious, given that the active drug is dispensed in esterified form in any oily vehicle so as to provide slow and sustained release. It may be that a small fraction of the total dose is in a non-esterified form which is rapidly absorbed from the oily depot, giving an early and fleeting peak in plasma drug concentration (Wiles and Gelder 1980).

Incidence

Frequency

In days before the advent of the butyrophenones and the depot neuroleptics, acute dystonic reactions were recorded in approximately 2 per cent of patients, making this the least frequent of the drug-induced extrapyramidal disorders (Ayd 1961). There has been a growing suspicion that the frequency has increased significantly with the use of the intramuscular depots. Ayd (1975) contended that this is a false impression generated by the unusually rapid occurrence of dystonias after intramuscular administration rather than by any real increase in overall incidence. However, the careful study by Swett (1975), in which over 1000 patients were monitored following the administration of a range of neuroleptics (including 142 patients receiving depot phenothiazines), recorded an overall incidence of dystonia of 10.1 per cent. Even higher incidence rates of up to 30 per cent were reported by Simpson (1970*b*).

Although it is clear that the incidence of acute dystonia is lower than that of akathisia, pseudo-parkinsonism, or tardive dyskinesia, it does seem that reported rates have recently shown an upward trend. The reasons for this probably lie both with the introduction of more potent and selective dopamine receptor antagonists (such as the butyrophenones which possess little anticholinergic activity) and the more widespread use of depot intramuscular preparations (Groves and Mandel 1975; Swett 1975).

Influence of age and sex

It has long been known that acute dystonic reactions are particularly common in young males. Ayd (1961) reported that such reactions were unusual over the age of 30 years, and in those patients showing acute dystonic reactions the male-to-female ratio was 2:1. A more recent study has confirmed both the particular susceptibility of the young and also the male preponderance, but only in cases under the age of 50 years (Swett 1975). Thus acute dystonia was found to be approximately three times more common under the age of 30, when the male:female ratio was 1.6:1.0, whereas in patients over the age of 50 there was a sex ratio of one (Table 12.5).

TABLE 12.5. *Frequency of dystonia by age and sex*

Age (years)*	Men		Women	
	Number of patients	Per cent with dystonia	Number of patients	Per cent with dystonia
Less than 30	259	20.5	206	12.6
30–49	174	8.1	241	4.6
50 and older	87	4.6	184	4.4

* The age of one patient was unknown.
Data reported by Swett (1975).

TABLE 12.6.   *Frequency of dystonia attributed to various neuroleptics*

Drug	Number of patients taking the drug	Patients with dystonia*	
		Number	Per cent
Butyrophenone			
Haloperidol	200	32	16.0
Phenothiazines			
Piperazine side-chain			
Fluphenazine enanthate	137	16	11.7
Fluphenazine decanoate	4	1	25.0
Fluphenazine hydrochloride	80	2	2.5
Trifluoperazine	219	18	8.2
Perphenazine	89	5	5.6
Aliphatic side-chain			
Chlorpromazine	679	24	3.5
Piperidine side-chain			
Thioridazine	313	2	0.6
Mesoridazine	20	1	5.0
Thioxanthenes			
Thiothixene	24	2	8.3
Chlorprothixene	2	0	0.0

* Thirteen patients developed dystonia that was attributed to combinations of two or more drugs.
Data reported by Swett (1975).

Type of neuroleptic

Acute dystonic reactions appear to occur more commonly with the potent and pharmacologically selective neuroleptics, such as the phenothiazines with a nuclear halogen substitution and a piperazine side-chain (Ayd 1961) and the butyrophenones (Swett 1975). Drugs such as fluphenazine, trifluoperazine, and haloperidol are not only potent dopamine receptor antagonists but they lack the atropinic activity of drugs such as thioridazine which attenuate the net acute disturbance of striatal function.

It seems likely that the depot neuroleptics in general are more guilty of acute dystonia than their oral counterparts (Table 12.6), for reasons suggested above. While few figures are available for flupenthixol decanoate, it appears that fluphenazine enanthate is more likely to provoke dystonia than fluphenazine decanoate (Groves and Mandel 1975).

The recently developed substituted benzamides, such as metoclopramide, which have selectivity for D_2 over D_1 dopamine receptors, have a propensity to induce acute dystonia (Casteels-Van Daele *et al.* 1970; Pinder *et al.* 1978). While all dopamine receptor antagonists seem to share this ability, it may be significant that presynaptic amine depletors such as reserpine have not been reported as causing acute dystonia (Marsden *et al.* 1975).

Dose of neuroleptic

While there does appear to be an individual predisposition required for acute dystonia, within any individual the probability of occurrence seems clearly dose-dependent (Marsden *et al.* 1975).

In patients receiving oral chlorpromazine, Swett (1975) found that daily doses of 300 mg or more were three times more likely to induce dystonia than were daily doses of 100 mg or less. In an elegant study of the pharmaco-kinetics of butaperazine, and their relationship to acute dystonia, Garver and associates (1976*b*) demonstrated that the concentration of drug found within patients' erythrocytes correlated closely with the occurrence of dystonic reactions.

Individual predisposition

In addition to youth and male sex, there may exist a genetically inherited predisposition to neuroleptic-induced dystonia. It has been suggested that the incidence of drug-induced dystonia is higher than expected in relatives of patients with dystonia musculorum deformans (Edridge 1970) and a familial tendency to drug-induced dystonia has been described (Ayd 1960). The clinical picture of the neuroleptic syndrome can certainly mimic torsion dystonia but, as Marsden and Jenner (1980) pointed out, the frequency of carriers of the recessive gene for the naturally-occurring disorder is most unlikely to be as high as the incidence of dystonia in a neuroleptic-treated population.

The presence of hypoparathyroidism with hypocalcaemia appears to confer particular susceptibility to neuroleptic-induced dystonia. Schaaf and Payne (1966) described five hypoparathyroid patients who developed dystonia shortly after small doses of prochlorperazine. Correction of the hypocalcaemia reversed this susceptibility. Although likely to be a rare situation, the development of sudden and severe dystonia with very low doses of neuroleptic should prompt an investigation of serum calcium concentrations and parathyroid status.

Management

The signs of dystonia will subside as the offending drug is cleared from the body; thus simple drug withdrawal will allow resolution.

The urgency of the clinical situation, however, often demands more defini-tive therapeutic action. The vast majority of acute dystonic reactions will rapidly subside after an intramuscular injection of an antiparkinson anti-cholinergic drug such as procyclidine or benztropine. The therapeutic effect is usually evident within 10 minutes, with maximal effect after 30 minutes. If recovery is not complete after 30 minutes, the injection may be repeated. Thereafter, three or four oral doses of a similar drug at four-hourly intervals should protect against recurrence (Ayd 1961).

If continued neuroleptic medication is required, further dystonic reactions should be avoided by lowering the dose of neuroleptic. If no reduction in dose is possible, then regular concurrent anticholinergic medication can be prescribed, but the prime therapeutic aim should be to find a dose of neuroleptic which is just high enough to control the psychosis and low enough to avoid dystonia.

The distress of an acute dystonic reaction may be a patient's introduction to neuroleptic medication. There is evidence that early experience of extrapyramidal side-effects is a significant determinant of subsequent default in patients chosen for chronic neuroleptic medication (Johnson 1977). It is thus very important that such reactions are avoided if at all possible. While there is usually no easy way of predicting individual susceptibility, the likelihood of acute dystonia is crudely dose-dependent. Thus care should be taken over the choice of initial dose, taking into account the age, sex, and weight of the patient. This is particularly important when instituting depot intramuscular therapy where blind adherence to manufacturers' recommended test doses appears to be prevalent. Patients' relatives and nursing staff should all be adequately prepared for this potentially alarming but rapidly reversible side-effect.

TARDIVE DYSKINESIA

Nosology

Most observers agree that oro-facial dyskinesia occurs in a high proportion of psychiatric patients. The status of 'tardive dyskinesia' as a nosological entity, however, depending for its justification upon an aetiological link with chronic neuroleptic medication, has been and is, the subject of dispute. Within five years of the introduction of phenothiazine drugs for the treatment of psychosis, Schonecker (1957) drew attention to an involuntary hyperkinesia, apparently associated with neuroleptic medication, which was distinguished from the acute dystonias and from pseudo-parkinsonism on the basis of both phenomenology and time-course. Sigwald *et al.* (1959) identified involuntary movements of the branchiomeric musculature as the crucial element of this syndrome, and applied the descriptive term 'facio-bucco-linguo-masticatory dyskinesia'—later abbreviated to the 'bucco-linguo-masticatory triad' or BLM syndrome. It is to Uhrbrand and Faurbye (1960) that we owe the significant term tardive dyskinesia, a nosological term which embodies both a phenomenological element (dyskinesia) and an aetiological assumption—that the dyskinesia is necessarily a late outcome of neuroleptic treatment. This causal relationship has been widely questioned, partly it would seem, as a reflection of reluctance on the part of psychiatric practitioners to incriminate such useful psychotherapeutic drugs, but more compellingly because the BLM syndrome could be observed in patients who had never been exposed to neuroleptic medication (Brandon *et al.* 1971). Why then have some observers recorded an appreciable prevalence of the BLM syndrome in non-neuroleptic treated individuals? Involuntary hyperkinesis can of course occur in the setting of several discrete clinical syndromes such as Huntington's chorea, thyrotoxicosis, hypoparathyroidism, disseminated lupus erythematosus, Henoch–Schönlein purpura, Syden-ham's chorea, and cranial trauma, but the total clinical picture usually renders the clinical diagnosis obvious.

Senile chorea

There is an undoubted association between facial dyskinesia and ageing. A typical dyskinetic syndrome can arise spontaneously in people over the age of 60 (Weiner and Klawans 1973; Kidger *et al.* 1980) and it is against this back-ground that all of the evidence given in support of the diagnosis of tardive dyskinesia must be considered (Table 12.7). In a study of 365 people over the age of 65, Varga *et al.* (1982) observed oral dyskinesia in 10 per cent of those who had never received antipsychotic, antidepressant, or anticonvulsant drugs. Kane and Smith (1982) found published estimates of the prevalence of abnormal involuntary movements in elderly non-neuroleptic-treated samples to be as high as 38 per cent. There appears to be an association between involuntary movements and dementia, and with associated neurological signs such as the snout and grasp reflexes in the elderly. When only elderly patients are considered who do not exhibit significant neurological findings apart from bucco-linguo-facial dyskinesia, the prevalence of cephalic dyskinesia is around 3 per cent (Kane and Smith 1982). Weiner and Klawans (1973) considered lingual-facial-buccal movements in the elderly to be a precursor of full-blown senile chorea.

Drug effect or illness

The question which continues to provoke doubt about the very existence of tardive dyskinesia as a nosological entity is not whether the movements might be an early sign of senile chorea or Huntington's chorea or disseminated lupus, but whether the movements might be an expression of the neuro-pathology of schizophrenic illness. While it now seems clear that the BLM syndrome occurring in neuroleptic-treated patients is not specifically associated with any particular medical diagnosis (Klawans *et al.* 1974; Gerlach 1979), there is no doubt that the syndrome is seen predominantly in patients with a diagnosis of schizophrenia.

TABLE 12.7. *Prevalence of tardive dyskinesia according to age and neuroleptic exposure*

Age (years)	Exposed to neuroleptics*	Never exposed to neuroleptics
Under 50	7 (202)	11 (26)
51–70	31 (256)	18 (124)
Over 70	37 (167)	23 (135)

Figures shown are percentages, with sample sizes in parentheses. Data calculated from the report by Brandon *et al.* (1971) of a study of facial dyskinesia (BLM syndrome) in 910 in-patients of both sexes.
* Includes patients on drugs and withdrawn from drugs at time of assessment; mini-mum period of neuroleptic exposure = 3 months.

The frequent occurrence of dyskinesia in neuroleptic-treated outpatients (Smith *et al.* 1979) makes it unlikely that the syndrome is merely a behavioural product of institutionalization. Manneristic and stereotyped behaviour of the facial musculature was well documented in certain forms of schizophrenia in the pre-phenothiazine era (Kraepelin 1913) but such repetitive behaviours are usually clearly distinguishable from the fragmented involuntary movements of the BLM syndrome. Manschreck *et al.* (1982) recently identified abnormalities of volitional motor activity in schizophrenic patients which appear to be similar to those highlighted in the original descriptions of schizophrenia (Marsden 1982) but such abnormalities are not to be confused with the involuntary dyskinesias coming within the term tardive dyskinesia. Bleuler (1911) was in no doubt that true chorea, facial or otherwise, was rarely seen in association with schizophrenic illness. However, a recent report by Owens and his colleagues (1982) on schizophrenic patients in a British hospital suggested that involuntary dyskinesia occurs in a high percentage of those patients with a diagnosis of schizophrenia who have never received neuroleptic drugs. Psychiatric diagnosis was well defined and the prevalence of dyskinesia in 47 drug-free patients was 36 per cent, whereas in 364 drug-treated patients it was 56 per cent. Involuntary movements were rated on the AIMS (Abnormal Involuntary Movement Scale) and Rockland scales, but while these scales are reliable instruments for the recording of severity and distribution of abnormal movements, their validity as diagnostic instruments is not established. While this report is intriguing and provocative, it is possible that the abnormal movements of the drug-free sample were of an essentially different nature to those of the neuroleptic-treated sample. Replication of these important findings will be difficult in view of the scarcity of drug-naïve subjects, but the blind evaluation of the videotapes of these subjects by independent experienced observers would tend to increase the validity of the conclusions.

After carefully considering all of the evidence available in 1973, the American College of Neuropsychopharmacology in co-operation with the US Food and Drug Administration (1973*a, b*) made an authoritative statement to the effect that they considered the balance of evidence strongly in favour of an aetiological relationship between neuroleptic exposure and the BLM syndrome. Ten years later there seems to be no compelling reason to alter that view. In a recent exhaustive review of the literature comparing non-neuroleptic- and neuroleptic-treated subjects, Kane and Smith (1982) formulated overwhelming statistical support for this opinion. In pooled data from nearly 35 000 neuroleptic-treated patients the prevalence of abnormal involuntary movements was 20 per cent, in data from 11 000 untreated subjects the prevalence was 5 per cent. The statistical significance of this difference was $p < 10^{-5}$.

The consensus view throughout the world today is that the dyskinesia is a neurological reaction pattern which can occur spontaneously, with or without psychosis, particularly with advancing age, and that the probability of its appearance is significantly increased by chronic exposure to neuroleptic agents (Baldessarini 1974; Crane 1975; Marsden *et al.* 1975; Gerlach 1979; Kane and Smith 1982). In the absence of any independent diagnostic criterion, the aetiological inference is merely by association, but a syndrome of involuntary dyskinesia occurring in someone exposed to chronic neuro-leptic medication can reasonably be labelled tardive dyskinesia.

Clinical features

The most widely described phenomena comprise the BLM syndrome; this consists of pursing and smacking movements of the lips, lateral jaw movements, inflation of the cheeks against pursed lips, rolling or thrusting ('fly-catching') of the tongue, and 'chewing-the-cud' type of movements. The frequency of such involuntary facial movements is usually 1–2 (Jus *et al.* 1973). More rarely, other cephalic movements are evident such as grimacing and contraction of the peri-orbital muscles. Not uncommonly, cephalic dyskinesia is associated with choreic movements of the limbs and rhythmic dystonic contraction of axila muscles, giving rise to torticollis and pelvic thrusting. Rarely the muscles of deglutition and respiration may be implicated, in which case the dyskinesia can be life-threatening. In children and adolescents the hyperkinesia can affect preferentially trunk musculature and peripheral sites such as arms and hands and in these cases the character of the movements often is more dystonic than choreic (McAndrew *et al.* 1972; Polizos *et al.* 1973; Marsden *et al.* 1975; McLean and Casey 1978). On the other hand, Kidger and his colleagues (1980) found that axial and limb movements (their component II) were as clearly associated with old age as were cephalic movements (their component I). It may be that the axial and limb movements seen in the elderly, usually coexisting with the BLM syndrome, are of a typical choreic type and that, when these sites are affected in the very young, the movements tend to be dystonic and to occur without the BLM syndrome. In any event, it seems clear that the particular combination of elements which makes up the pattern in any individual patient is quite idiosyncratic.

Muscle tone usually is reduced but the BLM syndrome can co-exist with features of drug-induced parkinsonism such as cog-wheel rigidity of limb muscles and, in young people, axial and limb dyskinesias may be associated with hypertonus.

It is the exception rather than the rule for patients to report distress from their dyskinesia, more commonly a complaint will come from relatives or nursing staff.

Arousal plays a key role in determining the severity and perhaps even the distribution of hyperkinetic movements. Tardive dyskinesia disappears during sleep and is often intensified during periods of anxiety. Although essentially involuntary and repetitive, the movements can be consciously suppressed for limited periods. Thus, if a patient is waiting to be examined but not being observed, anxiety will exacerbate the syndrome whereas under direct examination embarrassment may provoke conscious suppression.

Rebound exacerbation then follows such temporary suppression. Conscious use of musculature in one area of the body will usually allow the expression of the full-blown dyskinesia in another area—for example, performance of a simple manual task will often disinhibit a facial dyskinesia.

Diagnosis

There is at present no generally agreed diagnostic check list for tardive dyskinesia. As with schizophrenic illness, in the absence of any independent objective diagnostic criterion, the diagnosis must be operational and must depend upon the presence of a specified cluster of phenomena.

Time on neuroleptic

In the diagnosis of tardive dyskinesia the only absolutely necessary criterion is previous exposure to neuroleptic medication, but the length of such exposure required to qualify for the term 'tardive' is not clear. The peak emergence of tardive dyskinesia is after approximately two years of regular neuroleptic medication, but cases have been recorded after exposure for only a few months (Evans 1965) and attempts to correlate duration of neuroleptic treatment with prevalence of tardive dyskinesia have had variable results (see below). However, the majority of patients develop tardive dyskinesia after years rather than days or weeks of neuroleptic treatment and this sort of time-course clearly distinguishes the disorder from other commonly encountered extrapyramidal side-effects.

Symptom clusters

In severe cases of facial dyskinesia the diagnosis is easy. However, whilst most observers agree that the BLM syndrome is of cardinal importance for the diagnosis of tardive dyskinesia, it need not always be present; certainly the BLM syndrome is often not seen in young patients with axial and peripheral movements characteristic of tardive dystonia.

Attempts to resolve this issue have been made by performing multivariate analyses of all abnormal involuntary movements in patients receiving chronic neuroleptic medication in the hope that discrete phenomenological clusters would emerge (Kennedy *et al*. 1971; Crane *et al*. 1971; Kidger *et al*. 1980). Kidger and his colleagues examined 182 medicated psychiatric patients and 85 non-medicated, non-psychiatric controls. Principal-component analysis of abnormal movements at eight anatomical sites revealed three major components: a cephalic dyskinesia (component I); an axial and limb dyskinesia (component II); and a third component incorporating high-frequency tremor of the lips and hands. The latter component undoubtedly corresponds to parkinsonian tremor and it was concluded that the other two (cephalic and axial/peripheral dyskinesia) represent central and peripheral subsyndromes of tardive dyskinesias. This is largely in agreement with previous work, but Kidger *et al*. took care to make the important distinction between peripheral dyskinesia and akathisia, an essentially subjective phenomenon. By making systematic enquiry about feelings of inner restlessness they could conclude that there was no special relationship between akathisia and peripheral dyskinesias (component II). The relationship of akathisia to extrapyramidal disorder in general seems to require systematic investigation.

It is clear that even with the cephalic hyperkinesias, the BLM triad must be distinguished from the 'rabbit syndrome', a high-frequency (5/s) lip movement associated with increased muscle tone and behaving pharmacologically like Parkinson's disease (Jus *et al*. 1973).

At the present time it seems that obvious repetitive involuntary movements of appropriate character and frequency occurring anywhere in the body provide phenomenological support for a diagnosis of tardive dyskinesia, bearing in mind that the overall picture may be dictated by the age of the patient.

Diagnostic threshold

It has been the fashion to use published scales of severity of dyskinesia (such as the AIMS and Rockland scales) as diagnostic instruments for tardive dyskinesia. This implies a misunderstanding of these scales, which were developed to quantify severity but not necessarily to provide a diagnostic check-list.

There are two main problems in stating diagnostic criteria. First, how obvious and therefore how severe must a movement be to be judged abnormal? This question would present no problem if the components of the dyskinetic syndrome were all clearly and qualitatively distinguishable from normal—they are not. Aspects of the BLM syndrome, for instance licking of the lips, can be seen in normal subjects as simple paroxysmal habits. Severity might incorporate amplitude of muscular contraction, frequency of muscular contraction within bursts of activity, and frequency of bursts interspersed with periods of quiescence. Second, given that abnormal movement of appropriate character has been detected, is it sufficient for the diagnosis of tardive dyskinesia to identify dyskinesia in only one, perhaps narrowly restricted, anatomical area? These questions have not yet been resolved and the continued use of severity scales for diagnosis will do little to help. Only by basic investigations of phenomenological clustering and correlation with independent clinical judgements of 'abnormality' will an operationally useful and valid set of diagnostic criteria be established. The only tolerably justifiable use of severity scales in diagnosis is when a 'criterion level of symptomatology' is clearly stated. Thus, Smith *et al*. (1979), using the AIMS, decided on the basis of clinical face validity that an average rating of 2.5 or more by at least two observers on any one of seven body areas was sufficient to justify a diagnosis of tardive dyskinesia. Their approach is to be commended since it allows other observers to know exactly how they arrived at their diagnostic threshold.

The approaches of Kidger *et al*. (1980) and of Smith *et al*. (1979) are procedurally most important if we are to arrive at clinically valid diagnostic rules for tardive dyskinesia. Until such rules are generally agreed it is essential that observers state, in the clearest possible terms, what thresholds of severity and anatomical involvement they used for diagnosis.

Prevalence

Prevalence rate

For a neurological syndrome such as tardive dyskinesia the discrepancy in published prevalence rates is disappointingly wide. In a review of 12 published reports, Jus *et al.* (1976) found prevalence rates to vary between 0.5 and 41.3 per cent. This is perhaps understandable in view of the lack of generally accepted diagnostic rules and standardized observation conditions. Differing diagnostic thresholds probably account for most of the disagreement over point prevalence rates (Table 12.8). In the American study of Smith *et al.* (1979) in which an apparently valid criterion level of symptomatology was identified, the overall prevalence of tardive dyskinesia in in-patients was 45.9 per cent and in out-patients 40.9 per cent. Such strikingly high figures, however, have been reported by several other groups using different diagnostic procedures in different countries. The Canadian workers Jus *et al.* (1976) reported an overall prevalence of 56 per cent and the British workers Barnes and Kidger (1979) reported an overall in-patient prevalence of 55 per cent. Despite disquiet over different diagnostic habits it seems that tardive dyskinesia is a common disorder in neuroleptic-treated patients whether they be out-patients or in-patients (Smith *et al.* 1979; Asnis *et al.* 1977).

TABLE 12.8.   *Prevalence (per cent) of tardive dyskinesia as a function of criterion level of symptomatology*

Criterion level* (derived from the AIMS scale)	In-patient prevalence (n = 293) (per cent)	Out-patient prevalence (n = 213) (per cent)
2.0	62.2	72.3
2.5	45.9	40.9
3.0	30.2	33.7
3.5	13.8	8.6
4.0	6.9	2.4

Data taken from Smith *et al.* (1979).
Values are the average prevalence rates (per cent) for male and female patients.
* Level of symptomatology defined as mean scores required in at least one of seven body areas examined.

One other factor, in addition to diagnostic definition, bears heavily on observed prevalence and that is the age of the population sample. It has been repeatedly shown that prevalence increases sharply after middle age (Fig. 12.3). For example, Smith *et al.* (1979) recorded a prevalence in female in-patients of 14.8 per cent between the ages of 20 and 49 years, 59.1 per cent

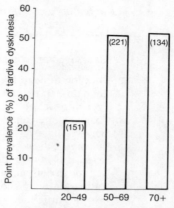

FIG. 12.3.   Prevalence of tardive dyskinesia according to age in neuroleptic-treated patients. Figures calculated from the report by Smith *et al.* (1979) of studies involving 506 neuroleptic-treated patients. Average prevalence values for male and female in- and out-patients satisfying a criterion level of symptomatology (mean AIMS rating of at least 2.5 on at least one of seven body area items).

between 50 and 69 years and 64 per cent in patients aged 70 years and over. Any age bias between patient samples used for prevalence studies could clearly have a potent influence on observed rates and thus published prevalence figures should be scrutinized closely for age specificity as well as diagnostic specificity.

Factors influencing prevalence

This leads us to a broader aetiopathological consideration of the factors which appear to influence the occurrence of tardive dyskinesia. Of the many variables investigated for an association with point prevalence, age is the only one upon which the published literature agrees (Crane 1973; Jus *et al.* 1976; Chouinard *et al.* 1979c; Smith *et al.* 1979; Smith and Baldessarini 1980; Perris *et al.* 1979; Kidger *et al.* 1980) (Table 12.9). As for other variables, the vast majority of reports come from retrospective correlative exercises which inevitably leave room for soft data but the weight of evidence implicating age as a predisposing factor is impressive. The influence of age is not merely a reflection of the duration of neuroleptic treatment, but appears to denote a particular vulnerability of the ageing brain. While it is almost impossible to isolate duration of treatment as a variable uncontaminated by age, it is possible to investigate the relationship between age at first exposure to neuroleptic (quite independent of duration of treatment) and the prevalence of tardive dyskinesia. Thus Jus *et al.* (1976) found that the age at which a patient is first prescribed a neuroleptic is positively associated with the likelihood of tardive dyskinesia (Fig. 12.4).

Contrary to expectation, there is no general agreement over any quantitative relationship between either the duration or the dose of neuroleptic

TABLE 12.9.   *Variables investigated for an association with the occurrence of tardive dyskinesia*

General agreement over positive association	No association/controversial
Age	Duration of neuroleptic exposure
	Total dose of neuroleptic
	Type of neuroleptic
	Constant/interrupted treatment
	Sex
	Psychiatric diagnosis (including organic states)
	Severity of psychiatric illness
	In-patient/out-patient status
	Antiparkinson medication
	Previous drug-induced parkinsonism
	ECT
	Leucotomy

For references see text.

medication and prevalence of tardive dyskinesia. Some have found a positive association between the duration of neuroleptic exposure and tardive dyskinesia (Crane 1974; Gardos *et al.* 1977; Allen and Stimmel 1977; Smith *et al.* 1979), whereas other have failed to do so (Perris *et al.* 1979; Jus *et al.* 1976; Smith *et al.* 1978). Since duration of treatment is usually contaminated by age, there is clearly a danger of false positive correlation.

Although Jus *et al.* (1976) reported that intermittent neuroleptic exposure appeared to be associated with a lower prevalence than continuous exposure,

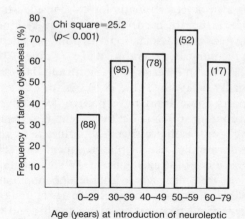

FIG. 12.4.   Frequency of tardive dyskinesia according to age at first exposure to neuroleptics. Taken from the report by Jus *et al.* (1976) in which 330 chronic schizophrenics (both sexes) were examined for tardive dyskinesia and grouped according to age at the first month of treatment with any kind of neuroleptic. Results expressed as percentages, with numbers of patients given in parentheses.

the beneficial effect of 'drug holidays' is still very much an open question (see below) and this important issue may only be resolved through prospective study.

Crane (1974) and Gibson (1978) reported an association between the dose of neuroleptic and the occurrence of tardive dyskinesia, but others (Perris *et al.* 1979; Smith *et al.* 1978) failed to confirm this and as Simpson (1973) and Thornton and Thornton (1973) observed, tardive dyskinesia may occur in sensitive individuals even after modest doses of neuroleptic. The dose variable is difficult to quantify since patients have rarely been maintained chronically on any one particular dose.

Even more problematic is the investigation of which types of neuroleptic might be more likely to cause tardive dyskinesia than others—not only do patients tend to be switched from one drug to another over the years but at any one time they are often receiving a neuroleptic cocktail. Most observers have failed to identity any particular types of neuroleptic as worse culprits than others for tardive dyskinesia (Jus *et al.* 1976; Perris *et al.* 1979; Brandon *et al.* 1971; Crane 1973; Smith *et al.* 1978). As each new addition to the neuroleptic family appears, hopes are raised that it will be innocent of tardive dyskinesia. So far, there is little cause for optimism; as evidenced by pimozide (Freeman 1979) and by the substituted benzamides such as metoclopramide (Kataria *et al.* 1978). It seems that any agent exerting chronic postsynaptic inhibitory effects on central dopamine transmission incurs the risk of producing tardive dyskinesia.

There is no clear association between the prevalence of tardive dyskinesia and sex (Jus *et al.* 1976; Bell and Smith 1978; Perris *et al.* 1979). Early studies claiming an increased prevalence in females mostly failed to control for age. Organic factors such as brain damage (Smith *et al.* 1978; Jus *et al.* 1976; Perris *et al.* 1979; Gerlach 1979), leucotomy (Hunter *et al.* 1964; Faurbye *et al.* 1964; Brandon *et al.* 1971), and previous exposure to ECT (Uhrbrand and Faurbye 1960; Faurbye *et al.* 1964; Degkwitz and Wenzel 1967; Brandon *et al.* 1971) were implicated in early studies but later refuted by others.

If tardive dyskinesia is a maladaptive response to chronic DA receptor blockade in the basal ganglia, then it might be expected that patients showing tardive dyskinesia would also show a particularly high rate of previous drug-induced parkinsonism. Crane (1972) reported this to be the case, but in a careful retrospective study Jus *et al.* (1976) failed to find such an association. Although anticholinergic antiparkinsonian drugs may accentuate existing tardive dyskinesia, or even uncover latent tardive dyskinesia, it is not clear whether chronic antiparkinson medication (or the atropinic tricyclic antidepressants) exhibited in parallel with neuroleptics increases the risk of development of tardive dyskinesia (Gerlach 1979).

Reversibility

Reversibility rate

From a review of over 20 studies in which patients were withdrawn from

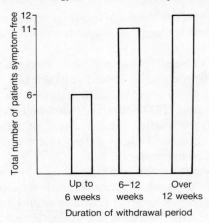

FIG. 12.5. Cumulative figures for recovery from tardive dyskinesia according to length of time after neuroleptic withdrawal. Data from the report of Jeste *et al.* (1979) in which 21 hospitalized patients were observed for an average period of 13 months following neuroleptic withdrawal.

continuous neuroleptic treatment, the average rate of reversibility was only approximately 30 per cent (Jeste and Wyatt 1979). In a recent prospective study of in-patients Jeste *et al.* (1979) reported that whereas after six weeks following neuroleptic withdrawal only 29 per cent of patients had recovered, after an average withdrawal period of 13 months the recovery rate had risen to 57 per cent (Fig. 12.5). In evaluating published reports of reversibility it is thus important to bear in mind that tardive dyskinesia may continue to improve for several months or even years after withdrawal, and that a minimum observation period of six months is required before reversibility can even start to be assessed. For a proper assessment of reversibility, a neuroleptic-free period of three years is probably necessary. Given the short-comings of some studies in this respect it seems reasonable to predict that, overall, at least approximately one-half of patients will eventually recover if the neuroleptic is discontinued.

Factors determining irreversibility

Of the factors shown to bear on the likelihood of persistence of tardive dyskinesia, the following seem the most important; age (Crane 1974; Gerlach 1979; Smith and Baldessarini 1980), duration of neuroleptic exposure (Jeste *et al.* 1979), and duration of dyskinesia (Quitkin *et al.* 1977). A literature survey by Smith and Baldessarini (1980) revealed a strong inverse relationship between recovery from dyskinesia and age. There is evidence to suggest that the anatomical site of the dyskinesia may be related to reversibility. Movements of the trunk and limbs (more commonly occurring in young people) seem more readily reversible as compared to the typical BLM which seems more likely to prove persistent (Polizos *et al.* 1973; Tarsy *et al.* 1977;

Chouinard and Bradwejn 1982). There is also some consensus in the literature that coincident organic brain disorder militates against reversibility (Jeste and Wyatt 1979). Thus there is a good chance that the young patient who develops a non-cephalic dyskinesia after a relatively short exposure to neuroleptic will recover if the drug can be withdrawn promptly after tardive dyskinesia is diagnosed.

In their comparison of 12 cases of reversible tardive dyskinesia with nine cases of irreversible tardive dyskinesia Jeste *et al*. (1979) found that the one factor which discriminated best between these groups was the number of drug-free intervals (assessed retrospectively) of at least three months duration.

In this study it was those patients who had experienced a greater number of prolonged 'drug holidays' who were liable to have irreversible tardive dyskinesia, a finding which supported the earlier observation of Degkwitz (1969). This is a most significant and disturbing finding in view of the increasingly popular strategy of drug holidays. The findings of Jeste and Wyatt (1979) require urgent confirmation, preferably through prospective study.

Severity

Arousal is probably the most potent variable which can cause fluctuation in the severity of existing tardive dyskinesia (Gerlach 1979). Factors which have been claimed to be positively associated with an enduring degree of severity of tardive dyskinesia are age, 'organicity', and male sex (Chouinard *et al*. 1979c). The use of anticholinergic antiparkinsonian medication is generally seen to worsen existing tardive dyskinesia (Perris *et al*. 1979; Gerlach 1979). It is reasonable to expect any atropinic agent to aggravate the dyskinesia. Apart from the antiparkinsonian drugs, the likeliest anticholinergic drugs to be exhibited concurrently with a neuroleptic are the tricyclic antidepressants. Although there is no clear evidence that any one type of neuroleptic is more likely than another to actually cause tardive dyskinesia, it might be expected that highly atropinic neuroleptics (such as thioridazine) will exacerbate existing dyskinesia.

It has been reported that mood changes along the manic-depressive axis can influence severity, depression being associated with a reduction and mania with an exacerbation of dyskinesia (Gerlach 1979).

Therapeutic trials in tardive dyskinesia

A recent exhaustive review of the therapeutic literature on tardive dyskinesia included over 130 published reports from pharmacological trials (Jeste and Wyatt 1979). Such a profusion of reports attests to the uncertain and generally unsatisfactory situation pertaining to the treatment of tardive dyskinesia.

TABLE 12.10.　*Summary of published results of the chemotherapy of tardive dyskinesia*

Treatment	Number of studies		Double-blind studies only	
	Total	Double-blind	No. of patients	Per cent improved
Inhibitors of dopamine transmission	55	15	153	67.3
Acetylcholine potentiators	40	10	109	32.1
γ-Aminobutyric acid potentiators	10	3	42	54.8
Dopamine potentiators	12	2	29	10.3
Acetylcholine antagonists	6	1	16	0

Data calculated from Tables 1–5 and 10 of Jeste and Wyatt (1979).

Therapeutic strategies

Most therapeutic trials have been conceived within the context of the currently popular neurochemical models for dyskinesia which focus on the functional interactions of neurotransmitters in the basal ganglia. Dopamine, acetylcholine, and γ-aminobutyric acid have received most attention and the therapeutic strategies have been aimed at decreasing the functional ratio of dopamine to acetylcholine and γ-aminobutyric acid. Thus postsynaptic dopamine receptor antagonists, monoamine depletors, anticholinesterases, cholinergic precursors, γ-aminobutyric acid transaminase inhibitors, and directly-acting γ-aminobutyric acid agonists have all been evaluated. Results are summarized in Table 12.10 and for details the reader is directed to the reviews of Jeste and Wyatt (1979) and of Mackay and Sheppard (1979).

Methodological problems

The overall picture is one of wide variability in both the nature and extent of any response to medication. As with other aspects of tardive dyskinesia, the interpretation of published trials is often clouded by inadequate methodology. Insufficient attention is often given to obvious requirements such as double-blind design and the use of rating instruments which are both reliable and valid (Mackay and Sheppard 1979). Less obvious requirements may have potent effects upon the reliability of severity ratings in a therapeutic trial. For example, the environmental conditions under which the patient is rated can influence arousal and therefore need to be strictly standardized. The reversibility of tardive dyskinesia in the face of neuroleptic withdrawal may be an important variable determining the feasibility of pharmacological intervention in individual subjects. In therapeutic trials which are not preceded by a lengthy withdrawal period this characteristic will remain obscure, so that the experimental sample may comprise a mixture of 'good risk' and 'poor risk' subjects.

Pharmacological subtypes

Methodological problems such as these undoubtedly contribute to the variable picture which has emerged from published trials. However, it may be that a more heuristic interpretation of this variability is possible. On the basis of results from a small number of patients with tardive dyskinesia, each of whom was given a single dose of a battery of four pharmacological agents (affecting both dopamine and acetylcholine systems), Casey and Denney (1977) concluded that discrete pharmacological subtypes of tardive dyskinesia may exist. One subtype responded typically in that the dyskinesia improved with a dopamine antagonist or a cholinomimetic. The other subtype showed an improvement in dyskinesia when treated with a dopamine potentiator or an anticholinergic. If such pharmacologically disparate subtypes exist, then therapeutic experiments which failed to distinguish between them might produce results which were equivocal and variable as a result of dilution. It will be of interest to discover if Casey and Denney's pharmacological subtypes correspond to the phenomenological subtypes of Kidger *et al.* (1980).

At the present time, then, there is no generally satisfactory pharmacological treatment for established tardive dyskinesia and the practising clinician must therefore seek to minimize the incidence and severity of the disorder according to the few facts which are available from public experience.

Clinical implications

From what has been said, it should be clear that neuroleptic drugs are not trivial therapeutic agents. Of course, many psychotic patients will continue to require chronic neuroleptic medication and for these patients certain guidelines seem evident. Neuroleptics should be prescribed with forethought and for clear indications. A useful analogy might be the prescription of opiates, where their use has traditionally been confined to cases of clear morbidity in which the dangers of chronic use are outweighed by the clinical need. In the absence of an effective treatment for tardive dyskinesia, prevention must be the prime consideration.

Prophylaxis

The first step is to develop a high level of suspicion. Regular neurological examination for all forms of extrapyramidal dysfunction is mandatory for all patients on chronic neuroleptic regimes. This is easy to establish at discrete contact points such as depot injection clinics, and here a useful routine to establish is for the patient to be examined by a doctor at every second visit. Patients in long-stay hospital wards tend to be relatively neglected in this respect but every effort must be made to achieve regular neurological assessment. Signs of dystonia or pseudo-parkinsonism denote substantial disturbance of dopamine transmission in the basal ganglia and should prompt early reduction in the dose of neuroleptic rather than the prescription of anticholinergic agents. Routine indiscriminate use of antiparkinson drugs as adjuncts to neuroleptic therapy is to be avoided. It robs the clinician of an important sign in determining the dosage ceiling, analogous to the prescription of an anti-emetic during digitalization.

Chronic neuroleptic medication should be taken particularly seriously in the elderly and close watch should be kept for early signs of tardive dyskinesia. Such signs may emerge first as dyskinesia of the tongue (observed with the tongue retracted in the open mouth), as apparently innocuous facial tics, or as restlessness of the limbs.

Treatment

Although the value or dangers of 'drug holidays' remain to be firmly established, it would seem that periodic limited drug withdrawal (for a period of, say, one month) might unmask a latent tardive dyskinesia and therefore give the clinician the chance of a useful early warning. At the first signs of tardive dyskinesia, early withdrawal of the neuroleptic at that stage, if compatible with the psychiatric state, should offer a good chance of complete recovery. In the case of established tardive dyskinesia where complete drug withdrawal is not feasible it seems prudent to minimize the dose of neuroleptic.

The most difficult group of patients are those in whom the severity of active psychosis makes any reduction in neuroleptic medication virtually impossible. One fairly sure way of ameliorating the dyskinesia is to increase the dose of neuroleptic but, just as avoidance of withdrawal signs from opiates requires ever-increasing doses, so with the neuroleptics any advantage is likely to be short-lived and counter-productive. The presynaptic dopamine-depleting agent tetrabenazine is interesting in this regard. As a neuroleptic, it can be expected to ameliorate tardive dyskinesia if added to existing medication, but the danger of a 'breakthrough' dyskinesia may be less than with the conventional postsynaptic dopamine antagonists. The published incidence of tardive dyskinesia associated with the long-term use of tetrabenazine (or reserpine) is very low (Degkwitz 1969; Duvoisin 1972; Marsden *et al.* 1975) and its introduction might at least allow a reduction in the dose of existing neuroleptic medication. Both tetrabenazine and reserpine, however, may provoke depression. In patients requiring continued neuroleptic medication or in patients with irreversible tardive dyskinesia, the so-called cholinomimetic agents deanol, choline, and lecithin would also seem to merit a therapeutic trial. They are relatively safe and have been said by some to be of value in a few cases of tardive dyskinesia. The benzodiazepines might be expected to exert some beneficial effect through their anxiolytic action, let alone any specific potentiating action on γ-aminobutyric acid transmission in the basal ganglia. Their place in the treatment of tardive dyskinesia remains to be established in double-blind trial, but in view of the fact that they are both safe and innocuous, a trial in individual cases would seem to be a reasonable clinical option.

Given the state of the field, a useful guiding principle in any therapeutic endeavour with tardive dyskinesia is summed up in the traditional saying of the Scottish apothecary: 'If it does ye nae guid, it should dae ye nae herm'.

Antiparkinson medication tends, in general, to make existing tardive dyskinesia worse, and thus avoidance of this or any other group of drugs with potent anticholinergic properties is to be recommended. For example, while a neuroleptic such as thioridazine may diminish the intensity of drug-induced parkinsonism because of its inherent anticholinergic properties, it may have the opposite effect on tardive dyskinesia.

Management summary

Some simple clinical guidelines for the prevention and management of tardive dyskinesia are summarized in Table 12.11. In view of the high degree of uncertainty and ignorance which currently surrounds the pathophysiology of tardive dyskinesia the reader is urged to treat most of these recommendations as tentative. They are meant as no more than pragmatic suggestions which may, in the light of increasing knowledge, require considerable revision.

THE PATHOPHYSIOLOGY OF DRUG-INDUCED EXTRAPYRAMIDAL SYNDROMES

Each of the four major categories of drug-induced extrapyramidal disorders—parkinsonism, akathisia, acute dystonic reactions, and chronic tardive dyskinesia—has a different pathogenesis. Each is currently attributed, however, to a disorder of dopamine function in the brain.

Dopamine receptors exist at a number of sites in the brain (Fig. 12.6). Dopamine receptors in the region of the area postrema are exposed to chemicals in the bloodstream since this area of the medulla oblongata has a poor blood–brain barrier. As a result, circulating substances with dopaminergic agonist action stimulate the area postrema to cause vomiting. Dopaminergic fibres within the hypothalamus are concerned with the control of the release of certain hormones, particularly prolactin and growth hormone. Dopaminergic fibres originating in the pars compacta of the substantia nigra innervate the striatum (caudate nucleus and putamen). Dopaminergic fibres arising in the ventral tegmental area of the midbrain innervate certain mesolimbic structures, including the nucleus accumbens, olfactory tubercle, and septal area, and project to restricted areas of the cerebral cortex including parts of the medial frontal cortex, the cingulate gyrus, and the entorhinal cortex. It is believed that the nigro-striatal dopaminergic pathway is concerned with the control of movement, as to some extent is the mesolimbic dopaminergic system. The roles of the mesocortical and mesolimbic dopamine pathways are not clear, but it is believed that both may be concerned in some way with mental events.

The complex sequence of transmitter synthesis, release, receptor activation, and termination of action occurring at dopamine synapses has been

TABLE 12.11.   *Guidelines for the prevention and management of tardive dyskinesia*

Prophylaxis	Treatment
1. Neuroleptic exhibited for serious indication only	1. Withdrawal of any anticholinergic medication
2. Use of minimum effective dose for shortest time	2. Gradual withdrawal of neuroleptic. Worsening before improvement is to be expected. Reversibility can only be ascertained after drug-free periods of at least 6 months.
3. Particular care in patients over 50	3. If neuroleptic withdrawal is clinically unjustifiable, then dose reduction is the next best strategy
4. Regular (monthly) neurological examination	4. In cases where tardive dyskinesia is irreversible in the face of neuroleptic withdrawal or reduction:
5. Occasional brief 'drug holidays' to expose covert tardive dyskinesia and identify 'at risk' population in whom early withdrawal is given priority	a. Trial of benzodiazepine (such as clonazepam). Innocuous and may evoke some improvement
6. Early detection maximizes the chances of recovery. Early signs often detected in the tongue; observed retracted in the open mouth	b. Trial of cholinomimetic such as deanol or lecithin. Fairly innocuous, published data suggests efficacy, but double-blind trials awaited
	c. Trial of tetrabenazene. May allow reduction in dose of other neuroleptics, without loss of antipsychotic effect, while ameliorating dyskinesia. Danger of subsequent breakthrough, and risk of depression

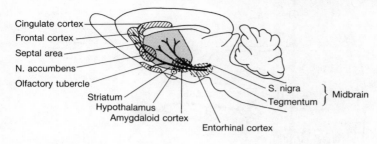

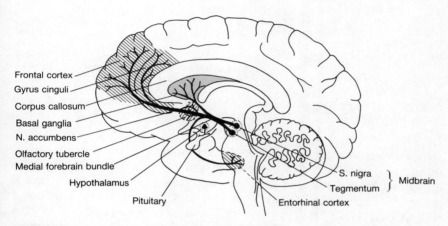

FIG. 12.6. Dopamine neurones in rat and human brain. The major systems are the nigro-striatal pathway from the zona compacta of the substantia nigra to the neo-striatum (caudate nucleus and putamen); mesolimbic pathway from the midbrain tegmentum to mesolimbic structures including septal nuclei (i.e. nucleus accumbens septi) and olfactory tubercle; a closely related *mesocortical* pathway arising with the mesolimbic system and projecting to prefrontal, cingulate, and temporal areas of cortex; and a *tuberoinfundibular* pathway within the hypothalamus. (From Baldessarini and Tarsy (1979), with permission.)

studied extensively (Fig. 12.7). The rate-limiting step in dopamine synthesis is the conversion of the precursor amino acid L-tryrosine to L-DOPA by the enzyme tyrosine hydroxylase. The subsequent conversion of L-DOPA to dopamine requires the enzyme DOPA decarboxylase, which is a non-specific aromatic amino acid decarboxylase present in many sites other than dopamine neurones. Dopamine synthesized intraneuronally is stored in synaptic vesicles, from which release occurs into the synaptic cleft consequent upon neuronal depolarization and the influx of calcium. The released amine acts directly on the post-synaptic membrane at a surface recognition site or receptor molecule. Activation of one type of dopamine recognition site (D_1) initiates adenylate cyclase activity to convert adenosine triphosphate (ATP) to adenosine-3'-5'-(cyclic) monophosphate (cylic AMP). The neurotransmitter is inactivated largely by high affinity reuptake from the

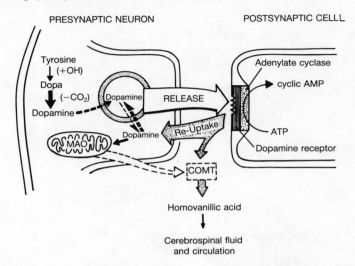

FIG. 12.7.   Dopamine synapse. See text for details. (From Baldessarini and Tarsy (1979), with permission.)

synaptic cleft into the presynaptic nerve terminals. Excess intra-neuronal dopamine is metabolized by monoamine oxidase (MAO) in mitochondria to dihydroxyphenylacetic acid (DOPAC) and subsequently by extraneuronal methylation by catechol-*O*-methyltransferase (COMT) to homovanillic acid (HVA). DOPAC and HVA are removed from the cerebrospinal fluid into the venous circulation by a probenecid-sensitive uptake mechanism, operating largely at the choroid plexus.

Dopamine release and the activity of dopaminergic neurones is controlled by a variety of synaptic and neuronal feedback mechanisms. Activation of the postsynaptic dopamine receptor in the striatum is believed to initiate impulse traffic in a descending strio-nigral loop which inhibits nigral firing. Strio-nigral pathways utilizing γ-aminobutyric acid, substance P, and enkephalins have been identified. The strio-nigral pathway, however, is not essential for many of the compensatory changes in nigrostriatal dopaminergic activity; it also is a powerful output pathway from the striatum via synapses on to non-dopaminergic cells in the pars reticulata of the substantia nigra. Dopamine released into the synaptic cleft is believed to act upon presynaptic dopamine terminals to inhibit further dopamine release. Autoreceptors for dopamine also exist on nigral cell bodies, and perhaps on dendrites of dopaminergic neurones, which themselves release dopamine in the substantia nigra. Dopamine released at striatal synapses may affect activity of recurrent collaterals of striatal interneurones synapsing presynaptically on dopamine nerve terminals, while dendritically-released dopamine may affect the activity of presynaptic nerve terminals synapsing within the substantia nigra itself. All these various mechanisms, and others, act in concert to control the activity of dopaminergic neurones in such a way as to prevent neuronal firing and dopamine release. Similar feedback control mechanisms are believed to exist within the other dopaminergic projection systems to mesolimbic areas and to cortex, but these have been studied less.

Against this brief background of the topography, biochemistry, and neuronal organization of dopaminergic pathways we will now turn to examine the pathophysiology of each of the drug-induced extrapyramidal syndromes.

Drug-induced pseudo-parkinsonism

Parkinson's disease (and post-encephalitic parkinsonism) are both due to degeneration primarily of pigmented brainstem neurones, particularly those of the substantia nigra and locus coeruleus in the brainstem. Such cell loss is associated with a profound depletion of cerebral catecholamines, particularly dopamine in the caudate nucleus and putamen (the corpus striatum) as a result of degeneration of the nigro-striatal dopaminergic pathway. There is also probably a loss of dopamine in mesolimbic areas such as the nucleus accumbens, and mesocortical areas such as the parolfactory gyrus, which are innervated by mesolimbic and mesocortical dopamine pathways originating in the ventral tegmental area of the brainstem. The main clinical features of Parkinson's disease are due to this profound dopamine depletion in the brain.

Drug-induced parkinsonism also is due to dopamine deficiency. Drugs producing pseudo-parkinsonism do so either by (1) acting presynaptically to prevent dopamine release, by disrupting intraneuronal granular storage of dopamine (reserpine and tetrabenazine) or by preventing dopamine synthesis (for example, α-methyl-p-tyrosine which inhibits tyrosine hydroxylase), or (2) by blocking postsynaptic dopamine receptors in the brain. All neuroleptics (apart from drugs such as reserpine) are dopamine receptor antagonists, at least on acute administration (Carlsson and Lindqvist 1963; Janssen *et al.* 1965; van Rossum 1966). The evidence that drugs such as phenothiazines, butyrophenones, thioxanthenes, and substituted benzamides are cerebral dopamine receptor antagonists comes from many sources (see Chapter 2), but it must be pointed out that nearly all this data has been obtained in experiments in which such drugs were administered acutely.

Blockade of postsynaptic dopamine receptors in the brain, particularly those in the striatum and mesolimbic areas, is taken to be the cause of pseudo-parkinsonism produced by neuroleptic drugs but there are certain clinical observations which deserve comment.

In general, drug-induced parkinsonism is dose-dependent. Everyone probably would develop obvious clinical features of parkinsonism if given a large enough dose of a neuroleptic drug. In routine clinical practice, however, only a proportion of patients taking neuroleptic drugs develop obvious clinical signs of parkinsonism. Clearly, there is individual susceptibility to development of this unwanted effect in response to a given dose of neuroleptic. The fact that the age incidence of drug-induced parkinsonism parallels that of the idiopathic disease (Ayd 1961) (Fig. 12.2) strongly hints that a propensity to the latter may determine the incidence of the former. This is not surprising, for it is known that an extensive loss of brain dopamine (80 per cent or more) is required before the signs of idiopathic Parkinson's disease are evident. This suggests that there is a pre-symptomatic phase of the illness during which brain dopamine declines, until it reaches the critical level necessary for producing clinical symptoms and signs. Indeed, there is evidence from a number of studies to suggest that brain dopamine synthesis progressively declines with age in apparently normal subjects (McGeer and McGeer 1976; McGeer *et al.* 1977). It seems reasonable to suggest those who develop drug-induced parkinsonism on relatively low doses of neuroleptics do so because they already have some degree of cerebral dopamine deficiency. Some recent biochemical evidence supports this conclusion, for three patients who developed drug-induced parkinsonism during life were found, after death, to have abnormally low concentrations of dopamine in the striatum (Rajput *et al.* 1979). Such an analysis suggests that the few cases of apparent permanent drug-induced parkinsonism may represent patients with idiopathic Parkinson's disease, whose illness was unmasked by the administration of a neuroleptic. Pre-existing, but asymptomatic, Parkinson's disease in some patients who develop drug-induced parkinsonism might also explain the not uncommon asymmetry of signs. It is difficult to conceive how a purely pharmacological effect on an otherwise intact central nervous system should produce an unwanted effect obviously worse in one arm and leg than in the other.

Although florid drug-induced parkinsonism occurs only in a proportion of patients on usual neuroleptic treatment, there is a question as to whether more subtle signs of the condition are present in a much greater percentage of patients. The earliest signs of drug-induced parkinsonism, in particular mild akinesia, are often hard to detect. A slight loss of facial expression and arm-swing on walking, a slowing of movement and diminution in the many associated movements that occur in the normal subject, a deterioration in hand-writing, as well as an emotional and volitional poverty, often are attributed to a degree of psychomotor retardation due to the psychotic disease for which the drugs are administered. Such signs are, however, typical of early parkinsonism.

There is often delay in the appearance of drug-induced parkinsonism after starting treatment with conventional doses of neuroleptics. The incidence of this unwanted effect increases in the first few weeks and months of therapy. This may be due to accumulation of drugs, because the pharmacokinetics of most neuroleptic agents are characterized by long half-life, and accumulation in tissue stores (Salzman and Brodie 1956 and see Chapter 4, this volume), but whether this is the sole reason is not certain. Significance has been attached to the observation that the antipsychotic effect of administration of neuroleptic drugs may take some weeks to develop (see, for example, Crow *et al.* 1979), but since the same is true for drug-induced parkinsonism it may be that it takes this length of time for full dopamine receptor blockade to be achieved.

Another clinical observation is that drug-induced parkinsonism once apparent may gradually disappear despite continuing the offending neuroleptic. Likewise, anticholinergic drugs given to counteract drug-induced parkinsonism may be withdrawn with no recurrence of the syndrome some months later. Although there is some evidence of increased neuroleptic metabolism with chronic administration (Sakalis *et al.* 1972; Loga *et al.* 1975; see Chapter 4, this volume), this seems unlikely to be the sole explanation if only because the therapeutic action of the drugs appears to continue. An alternative explanation is provided by the discovery that the pharmacological action of neuroleptics changes during long-term administration, such that initial dopamine receptor blockade gradually disappears during chronic therapy to be replaced, finally, by dopamine receptor supersensitivity in some circumstances (see below). The disappearance of dopamine receptor blockade during chronic treatment certainly would explain why drug-induced parkinsonism may remit during continued therapy.

Drug-induced akathisia

The cause of akathisia is unknown, but a reasonable hypothesis can now be proposed. Two observations suggest that, like drug-induced parkinsonism, it is due to deficient dopamine action in the brain. First, akathisia identical to that seen in patients treated with neuroleptic drugs occurs in idiopathic Parkinson's disease. Second, presynaptically acting drugs such as reserpine and tetrabenazine also may produce intense akathisia. The fact that akathisia commonly coexists with drug-induced parkinsonism also supports the notion that it is due to antagonism of dopamine actions in the brain.

The essential ingredient of akathisia is the intense subjective feeling of restlessness. This conscious mental element of akathisia suggests that it may be due to some effect of the drugs upon the cerebral cortex, and it is reasonable to propose that it is due to neuroleptic blockade of mesocortical dopamine receptors.

There is experimental evidence in animals indicating that the mesocortical dopamine system influences movement in such a way as normally to inhibit it (Iversen 1971; Tassin *et al.* 1978; Carter and Pycock 1978). Blockade of mesocortical dopamine receptors might be expected to increase some aspects of motor activity, and to have an impact upon conscious experience of such behaviour.

Acute dystonic reactions

Animal experiments have suggested possible mechanisms responsible for acute dystonic reactions to neuroleptic drugs. Several species of primate exposed to the acute administration of a variety of neuroleptic drugs have developed a clinical syndrome indistinguishable from that seen in human patients with acute dystonic reactions (Gunne and Barany 1976; Bedard *et al.* 1977*a*; Meldrum *et al.* 1977; Weiss *et al.* 1977). The clinical character of such acute dystonic reactions in primates, dystonic spasms of mouth, neck, jaw, back, and limbs, resembles in some respects the behavioural effects of administration of the dopamine agonist apomorphine, although the latter also provokes marked chewing and gnawing (Meldrum *et al.* 1977). Likewise, abnormal movements provoked by levodopa in patients with Parkinson's disease occasionally may have a frankly dystonic form. That acute dystonic reactions may be due to over-activity of certain dopaminergic mechanisms in the brain is supported by the observation that they are prevented by pre-treatment with drugs disrupting presynaptic dopaminergic activity. Thus, pretreatment of baboons with a combination of reserpine (to prevent granular storage of dopamine) and α-methyl-*p*-tyrosine (to prevent dopa-mine synthesis) antagonized the induction of acute dystonic reactions by a subsequent dose of haloperidol in sensitive animals (Meldrum *et al.* 1977). This result indicates that acute dystonic reactions are dependent on some pre-synaptic dopaminergic (or perhaps noradrenergic) event mediated by both storage and synthesis of catecholamines. The fact that dopamine receptor antagonists with little noradrenaline receptor blocking action, such as haloperidol and pimozide, are just as capable of producing acute dystonic reactions as neuroleptics with a greater capacity to block noradrenaline as well as dopamine receptors, such as chlorpromazine, suggests that the important catecholamine is dopamine.

What action of neuroleptics on presynaptic dopamine mechanisms could be responsible for acute dystonic reactions? The obvious candidate is the well-known compensatory increased dopamine synthesis and release that is provoked by acute administration of neuroleptic drugs. Neuroleptics do not greatly affect brain dopamine concentration, but they do cause a consider-able increase in dopamine synthesis and release, at least initially (Carlsson and Lindqvist 1963; Laverty and Sharman 1965; Anden 1972; Gey and Pletscher 1968; Nybäck and Sedvall 1970). This biochemical effect is inter-preted as an attempt to compensate for the blockade of postsynaptic dopamine receptors produced by neuroleptic drugs. Such a compensatory increase in dopamine turnover, like acute dystonic reactions themselves, is apparent only on acute administration. Repeated administration is asso-ciated with a decline and eventual disappearance of such evidence of increased dopamine turnover (Asper *et al.* 1973; Scatton 1977). Anti-cholinergic drugs which diminish the dopamine release provoked by neuro-leptics, also prevent or reverse acute dystonic reactions in man (O'Keefe *et al.* 1970; Anden 1972; Corrodi *et al.* 1972).

All this evidence suggests that acute dystonic reactions in man and animals may be due to increased dopamine release resulting from the acute administration of a neuroleptic drug. But a paradox immediately is apparent. How can the dopamine released by this compensatory mechanism stimulate postsynaptic dopamine receptors, which themselves are blocked by the neuroleptic? A number of mechanisms may be invoked to explain this, such as the presence of more than one type of dopamine receptor in the brain (see Kebabian and Calne 1979). It is possible that dopamine released as a result of neuroleptic administration may act on a population of dopamine receptors not antagonized by that neuroleptic. There is another phenomenon, however, which seems more likely to be responsible.

An important clinical observation concerning acute dystonic reactions is that they usually occur hours or days after the administration of a single dose of a drug, presumably at a time of falling brain concentrations of the active agent. It is now known that even a single dose of a neuroleptic may produce long-lasting changes in the sensitivity of the postsynaptic dopamine receptor. Thus, 24 hours or so after the acute administration of a neuroleptic, animals showed enhanced behavioural responses to dopamine agonists indicating the development of supersensitivity, which lasts for a matter of a few days to a week (Christensen 1973; Christensen and Møller-Nielsen 1974; Christensen *et al.* 1976; Martres *et al.* 1977). The implication of this observation is that, as the neuroleptic concentration decreases after acute administration, it will leave exposed a supersensitive, postsynaptic dopamine receptor, a receptor exposed to a residual enhanced release of dopamine.

This sequence of events is illustrated by the studies of Kolbe *et al.* (1980) who investigated the biochemical and behavioural effects of single dose of butaperazine. This phenothiazine was chosen for study because it had been investigated clinically by Garver *et al.* (1976*a, b*), who, in the course of administering a single dose to a group of 13 schizophrenics, had provoked acute dystonic reactions in no less than eight. These unwanted effects occurred usually 20–28 hours after the administration of butaperazine, at a time when measured blood levels of the drug were rapidly falling. Administration of a similar dose of butaperazine to rats initially abolished apomorphine-induced stereotypy, due to postsynaptic dopamine receptor blockade, and increased the concentration of dopamine metabolites, due to increased dopamine release. But by 12 hours after drug administration post-synaptic dopamine receptor blockade began to wear off, and increased dopamine release began to decline. By 24 hours after butaperazine, apormorphine induced a normal or exaggerated stereotyped behavioural response and, although concentrations of dopamine metabolites in striatum were falling, they were still increased. In other words, at this critical time when acute dystonic reactions occurred in man, striatal dopamine receptors responded normally or in an exaggerated manner to apomorphine, while striatal dopamine turnover and release was still increased. The net sum of these two events would be an increased striatal dopaminergic activity, at this critical time after drug administration when the majority of acute dystonic reactions occurred in the human studies with this drug.

While acute dystonic reactions may be due to a combination of these two events in postsynaptic and presynaptic dopamine mechanisms occurring on acute neuroleptic administration, it remains to be explained why they occur only in such a small proportion of individuals. No definite answer can be given at this time, but the work of Garver *et al.* (1976*a, b*) suggests that a pharmacokinetic explanation may be responsible, at least in part. Thus, those who developed acute dystonic reactions to butaperazine in these studies had elevated red cell concentrations of the drug in comparison to those who did not. The difference was, however, not dramatic and perhaps other factors such as an idiosyncratic reaction or hereditary predisposition may also be involved.

Finally, it is necessary to speculate on why acute dystonic reactions frequently occur in the young. The mechanism proposed involves compensatory presynaptic dopamine release in response to acute neuroleptic administration, and presumably the extent of this will depend on the capacity of presynaptic dopamine mechanisms. Evidence has already been quoted to show that there is a progressive decline in cerebral dopamine with ageing in the normal population, so perhaps acute dystonic reactions become less frequent with age because of a progressive decline in the extent of the compensatory presynaptic response to these drugs.

Chronic tardive dyskinesia

Of all the extrapyramidal complications of neuroleptic treatment, tardive dyskinesia is potentially the most serious. The fact that, in a proportion of cases, the abnormal movements that comprise the chronic tardive dyskinesia syndrome may persist despite stopping the drugs that caused them, suggests that neuroleptics may induce some long-term change in the brain that outlasts their administration. Indeed, in a proportion of patients tardive dyskinesia appears permanent, suggesting that such a change itself may be life-long.

The clinical pharmacology of tardive dyskinesias indicates that they are due to overstimulation of dopamine mechanisms in the brain (Klawans 1973*a, b*). The evidence in support of this conclusion is summarized in Table 12.12.

A paradox immediately is apparent. How can a condition whose patho-

TABLE 12.12.   *Dopamine hypothesis of tardive dyskinesias*

1. The oro-bucco-lingual syndrome of tardive dyskinesias is identical to the commonest movement provoked by levodopa in patients with Parkinson's disease.
2. The whole clinical syndrome of tardive dyskinesia may be mimicked by levodopa administration to patients with Parkinson's disease.
3. Tardive dyskinesia can be suppressed, at least partially and temporarily, by drugs that interfere with dopaminergic neuro-transmission:

   (a) Presynaptic agents such as tetrabenazine, reserpine, α-methyl-p-tyrosine inhibit tardive dyskinesias;
   (b) Dopamine receptor antagonists such as neuroleptics inhibit tardive dyskinesias.

4. Tardive dyskinesias often are enhanced by administration of high doses of dopamine agonists.

For original references see Klawans (1973*a*), Marsden (1975), Marsden and Jenner (1980), Mackay and Sheppard (1979).

physiology is that of dopaminergic over-activity be produced by drugs whose prime mode of action is to block dopamine receptors? Carlsson (1970) and Klawans (1973*a, b*) overcame this problem by invoking the concept of drug-induced supersensitivity.

It has long been known that denervation or pharmacological inactivation of neurones produces a state of postsynaptic receptor supersensitivity to applied transmitter in the peripheral somatic and autonomic nervous systems (see Axelsson and Thesleff 1959; Trendelenburg 1963*a, b*; Langer and Trendelenburg 1966; Langer *et al.* 1967). Carlsson and Klawans argued that blockade of postsynaptic cerebral dopamine receptors might have a similar effect by depriving receptor sites of their normal stimulation by the natural transmitter, dopamine. Experimental support for this hypothesis was soon obtained by Tarsy and Baldessarini (1973, 1974) who demonstrated that administration of a neuroleptic drug for a few weeks, followed by withdrawal of the drug, led to a supersensitive behavioural response to administration of dopamine agonists during the withdrawal phase. Many subsequent studies have confirmed this observation, which applies to a wide range of neuroleptics including phenothiazine, butyrophenones, and clozapine. Other investigations have established that, during the phase of supersensitivity after drug withdrawal, the number of dopamine receptors in the striatum labelled by specific binding of [^{3}H]haloperidol is increased (Burt *et al.* 1977; Muller and Seeman 1977). In addition, some authors (Gnegy *et al.* 1977; Heal *et al.* 1976), but not others (von Voigtlander *et al.* 1975; Rotrosen *et al.* 1975; Seeber and Kuchinsky 1976), have demonstrated an enhanced response of striatal adenylate cyclase to added dopamine during this withdrawal phase.

All these studies indicate that striatal dopamine mechanisms become supersensitive after a few weeks administration of neuroleptics and their subsequent withdrawal, but a paradox remains. Many tardive dyskinesias appear while patients are continuing to take their antipsychotic drugs which, at least for the first few weeks, appear effectively to block dopaminergic neurotransmission in the central nervous system.

Recent work, however, has shown that administration of neuroleptic drugs for months, rather than weeks, leads to a gradual disappearance of behavioural and biochemical evidence of dopamine receptor blockade in the striatum (Clow *et al.* 1978, 1979*a, b*, 1980*a*). In the first month or so of drug treatment of rats with phenothiazines, behavioural evidence of dopamine receptor stimulation by apomorphine is abolished. *In vitro* tests of dopamine receptor function indicate blockade at this time; for example, there is inhibition of stimulation of striatal adenylate cyclase by dopamine, and a marked increase in the dissociation constant (K_D) for [^{3}H]-spiperone binding with no change or a slight reduction in receptor numbers (B_{max}). Between one and six months of drug treatment a change occurs. The stereotyped behavioural response to apomorphine begins to re-appear, dopamine stimulation of striatal adenylate cyclase begins to return, receptor affinity begins to increase (K_D falls) and receptor numbers begin to rise. All this points to a disappearance of dopamine receptor blockade by neuroleptic drugs, despite their continuation and regular intake during this time. Between six months and a year of drug administration, this gradual disappearance of dopamine receptor antagonism in the striatum progressively changes into a state of dopamine receptor over-activity. Apomorphine begins to provoke excessive stereotypy, dopamine overstimulates striatal adenylate cyclase, and the number of dopamine receptors identified by [^{3}H]-spiperone binding increases above control levels. These behavioural and biochemical changes indicate that the animals are developing dopamine receptor supersensitivity in the striatum, despite continuation of drug intake. These changes are summarized in Fig. 12.8.

Similar changes occur in the mesolimbic areas of the brain during chronic phenothiazine administration to rats (Clow *et al*. 1980*b*). Initial blockade of dopamine function in mesolimbic areas is indicated by inhibition of dopamine stimulation of mesolimbic adenylate cyclase. But during a six-month period of drug administration, dopamine stimulation of striatal adenylate cyclase returns to normal and there is a tendency towards an increase in binding of [^{3}H]-spiperone to mesolimbic homogenates.

Whether such changes occur during neuroleptic administration in cortical dopamine-containing areas is not known, because it is difficult to measure either cortical dopamine-sensitive adenylate cyclase or cortical dopamine-specific receptor binding.

Other studies indicate that similar changes occurred during chronic administration of haloperidol (Owen *et al*. 1980) and flupenthixol (Jenner *et al*., unpublished observations; Waddington *et al*. unpublished observations).

All this evidence indicates that, for a wide range of neuroleptics, their chronic administration leads to loss of dopamine receptor blockade in the striatum and mesolimbic areas of the rat brain, and the appearance of a supersensitive dopaminergic system at least within the striatum. The latter may reasonably be considered to be responsible for the generation of tardive dyskinesias.

The question then arises as to whether the changes found in animals during chronic neuroleptic administration persist on drug withdrawal, in the light of the observation that tardive dyskinesias may sometimes be permanent. In the studies of Clow *et al*. (1980*c*), animals treated with trifluoperazine for a year were subsequently studied for a further six months after the drug was withdrawn. Behavioural supersensitivity to apomorphine gradually disappeared by about three months, and dopamine receptor numbers in the striatum had returned to normal by six months after drug withdrawal. Excessive stimulation of striatal adenylate cyclase by dopamine, however, was still evident at the end of the six-month period, when the study was terminated (Fig. 12.8). The fact that some of the evidence of dopamine receptor supersensitivity persisted for at least six months after withdrawal of drugs in these animal studies adds weight to the clinical concern that these agents may provoke long-lasting, perhaps even permanent, changes in the brain. It should be emphasized that administration of a drug for a year to a rat represents exposure of approximately a third of its life, while persistence

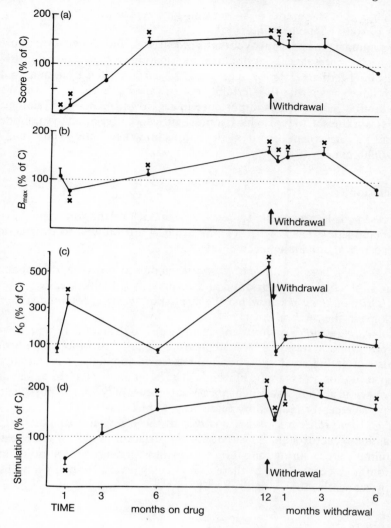

FIG. 12.8. Effects of chronic (12 months) trifluoperazine administration to rats, followed by drug withdrawal (6 months) on striatal dopamine function. Trifluoperazine dihydrochloride (2.5–3.5 mg/kg/day p.o.) was given in drinking water to half of a colony of rats. Age-matched control animals were maintained in identical conditions, and all results are shown in relation to findings obtained at the same time in these control animals as a percentage of control (% of C). (a) Intensity of stereotypy induced by the dopamine agonist apomorphine (0.5 mg/kg s.c.); (b) The number of specific (dopamine 10^{-4}) binding sites for [^{3}H]spiperone (0.125–4.0 nM) to striatal homogenates (B_{max}); (c) The dissociation constant (K_D) for such specific [^{3}H]spiperone striatal binding; (d) The stimulation of striatal adenylate cyclase by dopamine (50 μM). x denotes $p < 0.05$ or less. (From Marsden and Jenner (1980), with permission.)

of a change in the brain for six months may represent a change lasting 10 years or so in a human being.

In summary, the original hypothesis of Carlsson and Klawans that tardive dyskinesias represent the development of dopamine receptor supersensitivity during long-term neuroleptic treatment has been vindicated by animal studies which have shown that this certainly occurs, at least in the striatum. While such studies have obvious importance in regard to the pathophysiology of tardive dyskinesia, they also have some significance in relation to the mode of action of neuroleptic drugs in controlling psychotic behaviour in schizophrenia.

Conclusion

At present, it is reasonable to consider that each of the four major extra-pyramidal side-effects of neuroleptic drugs is attributable to their actions upon cerebral dopamine mechanisms.

1. *Drug-induced pseudo-parkinsonism* is due to postsynaptic dopamine receptor blockade in the striatum and perhaps mesolimbic areas.

2. *Drug-induced akathisia* may be due to postsynaptic dopamine receptor blockade in the cerebral cortex.

3. *Acute dystonic reactions* appear to be due to the interaction of the pre- and postsynaptic response to acute neuroleptic administration. The former consists of an increased synthesis and release of dopamine in an attempt to compensate for postsynaptic blockade. The latter consists of the appearance of behavioural (but not biochemical) supersensitivity of the postsynaptic dopamine receptor induced by acute drug administration.

4. *Chronic tardive dyskinesia* is due to the emergence of postsynaptic dopamine receptor super-sensitivity in the striatum, and to a lesser extent mesolimbic area, during long-term treatment with neuroleptics for a matter of months or years. Some of these changes may persist for many months, if not permanently, following drug withdrawal.

References

Allen, R. E. and Stimmel, G. L. (1977), Neuroleptic dosage, duration and tardive dyskinesia, *Dis. nerv. Syst.* **38**, 385–7.

American College of Neuropsychopharmacology, Food and Drug Administration Task Force. (1973*a*). Neurological syndromes associated with antipsychotic drug use. *Arch. gen. Psychiat.* **28**, 463–7.

——(1973*b*). Neurological syndromes associated with antipsychotic drug use. *New Engl. J. Med.* **289**, 20–3.

Ananth, J. V., Horodesky, J., Lechman, H. E., and Bon, T. A. (1970). Effect of withdrawal on chronically hospitalised schizophrenics. *Laval Med.* **41**, 934–8.

Anden, N. E. (1972). Dopamine turnover in the corpus striatum and the limbic system after treatment with neuroleptic and anti-acetylcholine drugs. *J. Pharm. Pharmacol.* **24**, 905–6.

Angrist, B., Sathananthan, G., Gershon, S. (1973). Behavioural effects of L-dopa in schizophrenic patients. *Psychopharmacologia, Berlin* **31**, 1–12.

Angus, J.W.S., Simpson, G.M. (1970). Handwriting changes and response to drugs. *Acta psychiat. scand. Suppl.* **212**, 28–37.

Asnis, G. M., Leopold, M. A., Duvoisin, R. C., and Schwartz, A. H. (1977). A survey of tardive dyskinesia in psychiatric outpatients. *Am. J. Psychiat.* **134**, 1367–70.

Asper, H., Baggiolini, M., Burki, H. R., Lauener, H., Ruch, W., and Stille, G. (1973). Tolerance phenomena with neuroleptics: catalepsy, apomorphine stereotypies and striatal dopamine metabolism in the rat after single and repeated administration of loxapine and haloperidol. *Eur. J. Pharmacol.* **22**, 287–94.

Axelsson, J. and Thesleff, S. (1959). A study of supersensitivity in denervated mammalian skeletal muscle. *J. Physiol., London* **147**, 178–93.

Ayd, F. J. Jr. (1960). Drug-induced extrapyramidal reactions: their clinical manifestations and treatment with Akineton. *Psychosomatics* **1**, 143–50.

——(1961). A survey of drug-induced extrapyramidal reactions. *J. Am. med. Ass.* **175**, 1054–60.

——(1975). The depot fluxphenazines: a reappraisal after 10 years' clinical experience. *Am. J. Psychiat.* **132**, 491–500.

Baldessarini, R. (1974). Tardive dyskinesia: an evaluation of the etiologic association with neuroleptic therapy. *Can. psychiat. Ass. J.* **19**, 551–4.

——and Tarsy, D. (1979). Relationship of the actions of neuroleptic drugs to the pathophysiology of tardive dyskinesia. *Int. Rev. Neurobiol.* **21**, 1–45.

Barnes, T. R. E. and Kidger, T. (1979). Tardive dyskinesia and problems of assessment. In *Current themes in psychiatry*, Vol. II (ed. R. Gaind and B. L. Hudson), pp. 145–62. Macmillan, London.

Bedard, P., Delean, J., Lafleur, J., and Larochelle, L. (1977*a*). Haloperidol-induced dyskinesias in the monkey. *J. Can. Sci. Neurol.* **4**, 197–201.

——Parkes, J. D. and Marsden, C. D. (1977*b*). Nomifensine in Parkinson's disease. *Br. J. clin. Pharmacol.* **4**, 187–90.

Bell, R. C. H. and Smith, R. C. (1978). Tardive dyskinesia; characterization and prevalence in a statewide system. *J. clin. Psychiat.* **39**, 39–47.

Bishop, M. P., Gallant, D. M., and Sykes, T. F. (1965). Extrapyramidal side-effects and therapeutic response. *Arch. gen. Psychiat.* **13**, 155–62.

Bleuler, E. (1911). *Dementia praecox or the group of schizophrenias*. Translated by H. Zinkin (1950). International Universities Press, New York.

Brandon, S., McClelland, H. A., and Protheroe, C. (1971). A study of facial dyskinesia in a mental hospital population. *Br. J. Psychiat.* **118**, 171–84.

Brune, G. C., Morpurgo, C., Bielkus, A., Kobayashi, T., Tourlentes, T., and Himwich, H. (1962). Relevance of drug-induced extrapyramidal reaction to behavioural changes during neuroleptic treatment: I. Treatment with trifluoperazine singly and in combination with trihexyphenidyl. *Comp. Psychiat.* **3**, 227–34.

Burt, D. R., Creese, I., and Snyder, S. H. (1977). Antischizophrenic drugs: chronic treatment elevates dopamine receptor binding in brain. *Science* **196**, 326–8.

Capstick, N. and Pudney, H. (1976). A comparative trial of orphenadrine and tofenacin in the control of depression and extrapyramidal side effects associated with fluphenazine decanoate therapy. *J. int. med. Res.* **4**, 435–40.

Carlsson, A. (1970). Biochemical implications of dopa-induced actions on the central nervous system with particular reference to abnormal movements. In *L-Dopa and parkinsonism* (ed. A. Barbeau and F. H. McDowell), pp. 205–13. Davis, Philadelphia.

——and Lindqvist, M. (1963). Effect of chlorpromazine or haloperidol on formation of 3-methoxytyramine and normetanephrine in mouse brain. *Acta pharmacol. toxicol.* **20**, 140–4.

Carter, C. J. and Pycock, C. J. (1978). Studies on the role of catecholamines in the frontal cortex. *Br. J. Pharmacol.* **42**, 402P.

Casey, D. E. and Denney, D. (1977). Pharmacological characterization of tardive dyskinesia. *Psychopharmacology* **54**, 1–8.

Casteels-Van Daele, M., Jaeken, J., Van der Schueren, P., Zimmerman, A., and Van den Bon, P. (1970). Dystonic reactions in children caused by metoclopramide. *Arch. Dis. Child.* **45**, 130–3.

Chien, C. P. and Dimascio, A. (1967). Drug-induced extrapyramidal symptoms and their relation to clinical efficacy. *Am. J. Psychiat.* **123**, 1491–8.

Chouinard, G., Annable, L., Ross-Chouinard, A., and Kropsky, M. L. (1979*a*). Ethopropazine and benztropine in neuroleptic-induced Parkinsonism. *J. clin. Psychiat.* **40**, 147–52.

—— —— ——and Nestoros, J. N. (1979*c*). Factors related to tardive dyskinesia. *Am. J. Psychiat.* **136**, 79–83.

——and Bradwejn, J. (1982). Reversible and irreversible tardive dyskinesia: A case report. *Am. J. Psychiat.* **139**, 360–2.

——de Montigny, C. and Annable, L. (1979*b*). Tardive dyskinesia and anti-Parkinson medication. *Am. J. Psychiat.* **136**, 228–29.

Christensen, A. V. (1973). Acute and delayed effects of a single dose of neuroleptic drug. *Acta physiol. scand. Suppl.* **396**, 78.

——Fjalland, B., and Møller-Nielsen, I. (1976). On the supersensitivity of dopamine receptors induced by neuroleptics. *Psychopharmacology* **48**, 1–6.

——and Møller-Nielsen, I. (1974). Influence of flupenthixol and flupenthixol-decanoate on methylphenidate and apomorphine induced compulsive gnawing in mice. *Psychopharmacologia, Berlin* **34**, 119–26.

Clow, A., Jenner, P., and Marsden, C. D. (1978). An experimental model of tardive dyskinesias. *Life Sci.* **23**, 421–24.

—— —— ——(1979*b*). Changes in dopamine mediated behaviour during one year's neuroleptic administration. *Eur. J. Pharmacol.* **57**, 365–75.

—— ——Theodorou, A., and Marsden, C. D. (1979*a*). Striatal dopamine receptors become supersensitive while rats are given trifluoperazine for six months. *Nature, Lond.* **278**, 59–61.

——Theodorou, A., Jenner, P., and Marsden, C. D. (1980*a*). Changes in rat striatal dopamine turnover and receptor activity during one year's neuroleptic treatment. *Eur. J. Pharmacol.* **63**, 135–44.

—— —— —— ——(1980*b*). A comparison of striatal and mesolimbic dopamine function in the rat during six months trifluoperazine administration. *Psychopharmacology* **69**, 135–44.

—— —— —— ——(1980*c*). Cerebral dopamine function in rats following withdrawal from 1 years continuous neuroleptic administration. *Eur. J. Pharmacol.* **63**, 145–57.

Cole, J. O. and Clyde, D. J. (1961). Extrapyramidal side-effects and clinical response to phenothiazines. *Rev. Can. Biol.* **20**, 565–74.

Corrodi, H., Fuxe, K., and Lidbrink, P. (1972). Interaction between cholinergic and catecholaminergic neurones in rat brain. *Brain Res.* **43**, 397–416.

Crane, G. E. (1968). Dyskinesia and neuroleptics. *Arch. gen. Psychiat.* **19**, 700–3.

——(1972). Pseudoparkinsonism and tardive dyskinesia. *Arch. Neur.* **27**, 426–30.

——(1973). Persistent dyskinesia. *Br. J. Psychiat.* **122**, 395–405.

——(1974). Factors predisposing to drug-induced neurological effects. In *The phenothiazines and structurally related drugs* (ed. I. S. Forrest, C. J. Carr, and E. Usdin), pp. 269–79. Raven Press, New York.

——(1975). Tardive dyskinesia. A review. In *Neuropsychopharmacology* (ed. J. R. Boissier, H. Hippius, and P. Pichot), pp. 346–54. Excerpta Medica, America, Elsevier, New York.

——Naranjo, E. R., and Chase, C. (1971). Motor disorders induced by neuroleptics—a proposed new classification. *Arch. gen. Psychiat.* **24**, 179–84.

Crowe, T. J., Johnstone, E. C., and Owen, F. (1979). Research on schizophrenia. In *Recent advances in clinical psychiatry* (ed. K. Granville-Grossman), Vol. 3, pp. 1–36. Churchill Livingstone, London.

Degkwitz, R. (1969). Extrapyramidal motor disorders following long-term treatment with neuroleptic drugs. In *Psychotropic drugs and dysfunctions of the basal ganglia* (ed. G. E. Crane, and R. Gardner), Public Health Service Publication 1938. US Government Printing Office, Washington DC.

——and Wenzel, W. (1967). Persistent extrapyramidal side effects after long-term application of neuroleptics. In *Neuropsychopharmacology* (ed. H. Brill, J. O. Cole, H. Hippius, and P. B. Bradley) pp. 608–18. Excerpta Medica, Elsevier, Amsterdam.

Delay, J. and Deniker, P. (1952). Le traitement des psychoses par une méthode neurolytique dérivée de l'hibernothérapie (le 4560 RP utilisé—seul en curé prolongée et continue). In *Le congrès de Psychiatrie et de Neurologie de langue française*, p. 503. Masson et Cie, Luxembourg.

—— ——(1957). Caractéristiques neuro-physiologiques des médicaments neuroleptiques. In *Psychotropic drugs* (ed. S. Garratini and V. Ghetti), pp. 485–501. Elsevier, Amsterdam.

—— ——(1961). Rapport de la clinique a la connaisance de l'action des neuroleptiques. In *Extrapyramidal system and neuroleptics* (ed. J. Bourdelean). Editions Psychiatriques, Montreal.

Denny-Brown, D. (1968). Clinical symptomatology of diseases of the basal ganglia. In *Handbook of clinical neurology* Vol. 6. *Diseases of the basal ganglia* (ed. P. J. Vinken and G. W. Bruyn), pp. 133–72. North-Holland, Amsterdam.

Dimascio, A. and Demirgian, E. (1970). Antiparkinson drug over-use. *Psychosomatics* **11**, 596–601.

Duvoisin, R. (1972). Reserpine for tardive dyskinesia. *New Engl. J. Med.* **286**, 611.

Ekblom, B. and Haggstrom, J. E. (1974). Clozapine (Leponex) compared with chlorpromazine: a double-blind evaluation of pharmacological and clinical properties. *Curr. ther. Res.* **16**, 945–57.

Ekdawi, M. Y. and Fowke, R. (1966). A controlled trial of antiparkinson drugs in drug-induced Parkinsonism. *Br. J. Psychiat.* **112**, 633–6.

Eldridge, R. (1970). The torsion dystonias: literature review and genetic and clinical studies. *Neurology, Minneapolis* **20**, Part 2.

Evans, J. H. (1965). Persistent oral dyskinesia in treatment with phenothiazine derivatives. *Lancet* **i**, 458–60.

Faurbye, A., Rasch, P. J., Peterson, P. B., Brandborg, G., and Pakkenberg, H. (1964). Neurological symptoms in pharmacotherapy of psychosis. *Acta psychiat. scand.* **40**, 10–27.

Freeman, H. (1979). Pimozide as a neuroleptic. *Br. J. Psychiat.* **135**, 82–3.

Gardos, G., Cole, J. O., and La Brie, R. A. (1977). Drug variables in the etiology of tardive dyskinesia. Application of discriminant function analysis. *Prog. Neurol. Pharmacol.* **1**, 147–54.

Garfinkel, P. E. and Stancer, H. C. (1976). L-dopa and schizophrenia. *Can. Psychiat. Assoc. J.* **21**, 27–9.

Garver, D. L., Davis, J. M., Dekirmenjian, H., Ericksen, S., Gosenfield, L., and Haraszti, J. (1976*a*). Dystonic reactions following neuroleptics; time course and proposed mechanisms. *Psychopharmacology* 47, 199–201.
—— —— ——Jones, F. D., Casper, B., and Haraszti, J. (1976*b*). Pharmacokinetics of red blood cell phenothiazine and clinical effects; acute dystonic reactions. *Arch. gen. Psychiat.* 33, 862–6.
Gerlach, J. (1979). Tardive dyskinesia. *Dan. med. Bull.* 46, 209–45.
——Koppelius, P., Helweg, E., and Monrad, A. (1974). Clozapine and haloperidol in a single-blind cross-over trial: therapeutic and biochemical aspects in the treatment of schizophrenia. *Acta psychiat. scand.* 55, 410–24.
Gibson, A. C. (1978). Depot injections and tardive dyskinesia. *Br. J. Psychiat.* 132, 361–5.
Gey, K. F. and Pletscher, A. (1968). Acceleration of turnover of [^{14}C]-catecholamines in rat brain by chlorpromazine. *Experientia* 24, 335–6.
Gnegy, M., Uzunov, P., and Costa, E. (1977). Participation of an endogenous Ca^{++}-binding protein activator in the development of drug-induced supersensitivity of striatal dopamine receptors. *J. Pharmacol. exp. Ther.* 202, 558–64.
Godwin-Austen, R. B., Tomlinson, E. B., Frears, C. C., and Kok, H. W. L. (1969). Effects of l-dopa in Parkinson's disease. *Lancet* ii, 165–8.
Goldman, D. (1961). Parkinsonism and related phenomena from administration of drugs; their production and control under clinical conditions and possible relation to therapeutic effect. *Rev. Can. Biol.* 20, 549–60.
Grove, L. and Crammer, J. L. (1972). Benzhexol and side effects with long-acting fluphenazine therapy. *Br. med. J.* 1, 276–9.
Groves, J. E. and Mandel, M. R. (1975). The long-acting phenothiazines. *Arch. gen. Psychiat.* 32, 893–900.
Gunne, L. M. and Barany, S. (1976). Haloperidol-induced tardive dyskinesia in monkeys. *Psychopharmacology* 50, 237–40.
Gupta, J. M. and Lovejoy, F. H. (1967). Acute phenothiazine toxicity in childhood. A five-year survey. *Paediatrics* 39, 771–4.
Haase, H. J. (1961). Extrapyramidal modification of fine movements: a 'conditio sine qua non' of the fundamental therapeutic action of neuroleptic drugs. *Rev. Can. Biol.* 20, 425–49.
——(1965). Clinical observations on the actions of neuroleptics. In *The action of neuroleptic drugs. A psychiatric, neurological and pharmacological investigation* (ed. H. J. Haase and P. Janssen), pp. 1–118. North Holland, Amsterdam.
Heal, D. J., Green, A. R., Boullin, D. J., and Grahame-Smith, D. G. (1976). Single and repeated administration of neuroleptic drugs to rats: effect on striatal dopamine-sensitive adenylate cyclase and locomotor activity produced by tranylcypromine and L-tryptophan or L-dopa. *Psychopharmacology* 49, 287–300.
Herman, E. and Pleasure, H. (1963). Clinical evaluation of thioridazine and chlorpromazine in chronic schizophrenics. *Dis. nerv. Syst.* 24, 54–9.
Hershon, H. I., Kennedy, P. F., and McGuire, R. J. (1972). Persistence of extrapyramidal disorders and psychiatric relapse after withdrawal of long-term phenothiazine therapy. *Br. J. Psychiat.* 120, 41–50.
Hollister, L. E., Chaffey, E. M. Jr, and Klette, C. J. (1960). Abnormal symptoms, signs and laboratory tests during treatment with phenothiazine derivatives. *Clin. Pharmacol. Ther.* 1, 284–93.
Horne, D. J. de L. (1973). Sensorimotor control in Parkinsonism. *J. Neur. Neurosurg. Psychiat.* 36, 742–6.
Hunter, R., Earl, C. J., and Thornicroft, S. (1964). An apparently irreversible syndrome of abnormal movements following phenothiazine medication. *Proc. R. Soc. Med.* 57, 758–62.

Inanga, K., Inoue, K., Tachibana, H., Oshima, M., and Kotorii, T. (1972). Effects of l-dopa in schizophrenia. *Fol. Psychiat. Neurol.* **26**, 145–57.

Iversen, S. D. (1971). The effect of surgical lesions to frontal cortex and substantia nigra on amphetamine responses in rats. *Brain Res.* **31**, 295–311.

Janssen, P. A. J., Niemegeers, C. J. E., and Schellekens, K. H. L. (1965). Is it possible to predict the clinical effects of neuroleptic drugs (Major tranquillizers from animal data) 1. Neuroleptic activity spectra for rats. *Arzneim. Forsch.* **15**, 104–12.

Jeste, D. V., Potkin, S. G., Sinha, S., Feder, S., and Wyatt, R. J. (1979). Tardive dyskinesia—reversible and persistent. *Arch. gen. Psychiat.* **36**, 585–90.

——and Wyatt, R. J. (1979). In search of treatment of tardive dyskinesia: review of the literature. *Schiz. Bull.* **5**, 251–93.

Johnson, D. A. W. (1977). Practical considerations in the use of depot neuroleptics for the treatment of schizophrenia. *Br. J. hosp. Med.* **17**, 546–58.

——(1978). The prevalence and treatment of drug-induced extrapyramidal symptoms. *Br J. Psychiat.* **132**, 27–30.

Jus, K., Jus, A., Gautier, J., Villeneuve, A., Pires, P., Pineau, R., and Villeneuve, R. (1974). Studies on the action of certain pharmacological agents on tardive dyskinesia and on the rabbit syndrome. *Int. J. clin. Pharmacol.* **9**, 138–45.

—— ——and Villeneuve, A. (1973). Polygraphic profile of oral tardive dyskinesia and of the rabbit syndrome. *Dis. nerv. Syst.* **34**, 27–32.

——Pineau, R., Lachance, R., Perchat, G., Jus, K., Pires, P., and Villeneuve, R. (1976). Epidemiology of tardive dyskinesia, Parts I and II. *Dis. nerv. Syst.* **37**, 210–14, 257–61.

Kane, J. M. and Smith, J. M. (1982). Tardive dyskinesia. *Arch. gen. Psychiat.* **39**, 473–81.

Kataria, M., Traub, M., and Marsen, C. D. (1978). Extrapyramidal side-effects of metoclopramide. *Lancet* **ii**, 1254–5.

Kebabian, J. W. and Calne, D. B. (1979). Multiple receptors for dopamine. *Nature, Lond.* **277**, 93–6.

Kennedy, P. F., Hershon, H. I., and McGuire, R. J. (1971). Extrapyramidal disorders after prolonged phenothiazine therapy. *Br. J. Psychiat.* **118**, 509–18.

Kidger, T., Barnes, T.R.E., Trauer, T., and Taylor, P.J. (1980).Subsyndromes of tardive dyskinesia. *Psychol. Med.* **10**, 513–20.

Kiloh, L. G., Smith, S. J., and Williams, S. E. (1973). Anti-parkinson drugs as causal agents in tardive dyskinesias. *Med. J. Austral.* **2**, 591–3.

Klawans, H. L. (1973*a*). The pharmacology of extrapyramidal movement disorders. In *Monograph in neural science* (ed. M. M. Cohen). S. Karger, Basel.

——(1973*b*). The pharmacology of tardive dyskinesias. *Am. J. Psychiat.* **130**, 82–6.

——Bergen, D., Bruyn, G. W., and Paulson, G. W. (1974). Neuroleptic-induced tardive dysinesias in non-psychotic patients. *Arch. Neurol.* **30**, 338–9.

——and Rubivits R. (1974). Effect of cholinergic and anticholinergic agents on tardive dyskinesias. *J. Neurol. Neurosurg. Psychiat.* **27**, 941–7.

Klett, C. J. and Caffey, E. (1972). Evaluating the long-term need for anti-parkinson drugs by chronic schizophrenics. *Arch. gen. Psychiat.* **26**, 374–9.

Knights, A., Okasha, M. S., Salih, M. A., and Hirsch, S. R. (1979). Depressive and extrapyramidal symptoms and clinical effects: a trial of fluphenazine versus flupenthixol in maintenance of schizophrenic out-patients. *Br. J. Psychiat.* **135**, 515–23.

Knopp, W., Fischer, R., Beck, J., and Teitelbaum, A. (1966). Clinical implications of the relation between taste sensitivity and the appearance of extrapyramidal side effects. *Dis. nerv. Syst.* **26**, 729–35.

398   *The psychopharmacology and treatment of schizophrenia*

Kolbe, H., Clow, A., Jenner, P., and Marsden, C. D. (1981). Neuroleptic-induced acute dystonic reactions may be due to enhanced dopamine release onto supersensitive post-synaptic receptors. *Neurology, Minneapolis* **31**, 434–9.

Kraepelin, E. (1913). *Dementia praecox and paraphrenia.* Translated by R. M. Barclay and G. M. Robertson, (1919). E. & S. Livingstone, Edinburgh.

Lamb, P., Mindham, R. H. S., and Ezzat, M. A. (1976). Parkinsonism induced by fluphenazine decanoate. *Lancet* **i**, 484.

Langer, S. Z., Draskoczy, P. R., and Trendelenburg, U. (1967). Time course of the development of supersensitivity to various amines in the nictitating membranes of the pithed cat after denervation and decentralization. *J. Pharmacol. exp. Ther.* **157**, 255–73.

——and Trendelenburg, U. (1966). The onset of denervation supersensitivity. *J. Pharmacol. exp. Ther.* **151**, 73–86.

Lauer, J. W., Inskip, W. M., Bernsohn, J., and Zeller, E. A. (1958). Observations on schizophrenic patients after iproniazid and tryptophan. *Arch. Neur. Psychiat,* **80**, 122–30.

Laverty, R. and Sharman, D. F. (1965). Modification by drugs of the metabolism of 3, 4-dihydroxyphenylethylamine, noradrenaline and 5-hydroxytryptamine in the brain. *Br. J. Pharmacol.* **24**, 759–72.

Loga, S., Curry, S., and Lader, M. (1975). Interactions of orphenadrine and phenobarbitone with chlorpromazine; plasma concentrations and effects in man. *Br. J. clin. Pharmacol.* **2**, 197–208.

Mackay, A. V. P. and Sheppard, G. P. (1979). Pharmacotherapeutic trials in tardive dyskinesia. *Br. J. Psychiat.* **135**, 489–99.

Mandel, W. and Oliver, W. A. (1961). Withdrawal of maintenance antiparkinson drug in the phenothiazine-induced extrapyramidal reaction. *Am. J. Psychiat.* **118**, 350–1.

——Claffey, B., and Margolis, L. H. (1961). Recurrent thioperazine-induced extrapyramidal reaction following placebo substitution for maintenance antiparkinson drug. *Am. J. Psychiat.* **118**, 351–2.

Manos, N., Gkiouzepas, J., and Logthetis, J. (1981). The need for continuous use of anti-Parkinson medication with chronic schizophrenic patients receiving long-term neuroleptic therapy. *Am. J. Psychiat.* **138**, 184–8.

Manschreck, T. C., Maher, B. A., Rucklos, M. E., and Vereen, D. R. (1982). Disturbed voluntary motor activity in schizophrenic disorder. *Psychol. Med.* **12**, 73–84.

Marsden, C. D. (1975). The neuropharmacology of abnormal involuntary movement disorders (the dyskinesias). In *Modern trends in neurology*, Vol. 6 (ed. D. Williams). Butterworth, London.

——(1976). Dystonia: the spectrum of the disease. In *The basal ganglia* (ed. M. D. Yahr), pp. 351–67. Raven Press, New York.

——(1982). Motor disorders in schizophrenia. *Psychol. Med.* **12**, 13–15.

——and Jenner, P. (1980). The patholophysiology of extrapyramidal side-effects of neuroleptic drugs. *Psychol. Med.* **10**, 55–72.

——Tarsy, D., and Baldessarini, R. J. (1975). Spontaneous and drug induced movement disorders in psychotic patients. In *Psychiatric aspects of neurologic disease* (ed. D. F. Benson and D. Blumer), pp. 219–66. Grune & Stratton, New York.

Martres, M. P., Costentin, J., Baudry, M., Marcais, H., Protais, P., and Schwartz, J. C. (1977). Long-term changes in the sensitivity of pre- and post-synaptic dopamine receptors in mouse striatum evidence by behavioural and biochemical studies. *Brain Res.* **136**, 319–37.

McAndrew, J. B., Case, W., and Treffert, D. A. (1972). Effects of prolonged phenothiazine intake on psychotic and other hospitalised children. *J. Autism chld Schiz.* **2**, 75-9.

McClelland, H. A., Blessed, G., Bhate, S., Ali, N., and Clarke, P. A. (1974). The abrupt withdrawal of antiparkinson drugs in schizophrenic patients. *Br. J. Psychiat.* **124**, 151-9.

McGeer, P. L. and McGeer, E. G. (1976). Enzymes associated with the metabolism of catecholamines, acetylcholine and GABA in human controls and patients with Parkinson's disease and Huntington's chorea. *Neurochemistry* **26**, 65-76.

——— ———Suzuki, J. S. (1977). Ageing and extrapyramidal function. *Arch. Neurol.* **34**, 33-5.

McLean, P. and Casey, D. E. (1978). Tardive dyskinesia in an adolescent. *Am. J. Psychiat.* **135**, 969-71.

Meier, M. J. and Martin, W. E. (1970). Measurement of behavioural changes in patients on L-dopa. *Lancet* **i**, 352-3.

Meldrum, B. S., Anlezark, G. M., and Marsden, C. D. (1977). Acute dystonia as an idiosyncratic response to neuroleptic drugs in baboons. *Brain* **100**, 313-26.

Mindham, R. H. S. (1976). Assessment of drug-induced extrapyramidal reactions and of drugs given for their control. *Br. J. clin. Pharmacol.* **3**, 395-400.

———Gaind, R, Anstee, B. H., and Rimmer, L. (1972). Comparison of amantadine, orphenadrine and placebo in the control of phenothiazine-induced parkinsonism. *Psychol. Med.* **2**, 406-13.

———Lamb, P., and Bradley, R. (1977). A comparison of piribedil, procyclidine and placebo in the control of phenothiazine-induced parkinsonism. *Br. J. Psychiat.* **130**, 581-5.

Mjönes, H. (1949). Paralysis agitans: a clinical and genetic study. *Acta psychiat. neurol. Suppl.* **54**, 1-195.

Miller, R. and Hiley, R. (1974). Antimuscarinic properties of neuroleptics and drug-induced parkinsonism. *Nature, Lond.* **248**, 596-7.

Muller, P. and Seeman, P. (1977). Brain neurotransmitters after long-term haloperidol: dopamine, acetylcholine, serotonin, α-noradrenergic and naloxene receptors. *Life Sci.* **21**, 1751-8.

Myrianthopoulos, N. C., Kurland, A. A., and Kurland, I. T. (1962). Hereditary predisposition in drug-induced parkinsonism. *Arch. Neurol.* **6**, 5-9.

———Waldrop, F. N., and Vincent, B. L. (1967). A repeat study of hereditary predisposition to drug-induced Parkinsonism. *Prog. Neurogene.* **175**, 486-91.

National Institute of Mental Health (1964). Psychopharmacology Service Center Collaborative Study Group. Phenothiazine treatment in acute schizophrenia. *Arch. gen. Psychiat.* **10**, 246-61.

Nybäck, H. and Sedvall, G. (1970). Further studies on the accumulation and disappearance of catecholamines formed from tyrosine-14C in the mouse brain. *Eur. J. Pharmacol.* **10**, 193-205.

Ogura, C., Kishimoto, A., and Nakao, T. (1976). Clinical effect of L-dopa on schizophrenia. *Curr. ther. Res.* **20**, 308-18.

O'Keefe, R., Sharman, D. F., and Vogt, M. (1970). Effect of drugs used in psychoses on cerebral dopamine metabolism. *Br. J. Pharmacol.* **38**, 287-304.

Onuaguluchi, G. (1964). *Parkinsonism*, p. 125. Butterworths, London.

Orlov, P., Kasporian, G., Dimascio, A., and Cole, N. O. (1971). Withdrawal of anti-Parkinson drugs. *Arch. gen. Psychiat.* **25**, 410-12.

Owen, F., Cross, A. J., Waddington, J. L., Poulter, M., Gamble, S. J., and Crow, J. J. (1980). Dopamine-mediated behaviour and ³H-spiperone binding to striatal membranes in rats after nine months haloperidol administration. *Life Sci.* **26**, 55-9.

Owens, D. G. C., Johnston, E. C., and Frith, C. D. (1982). Spontaneous involuntary disorders of movement. *Arch. gen. Psychiat.* **39**, 452–61.

Pacifici, G. M., Nardini, M., Ferrari, P., Latini, R., Fieschi, C., and Morselli, P. L. (1976). Effect of amantadine on drug-induced Parkinsonism: relationship between plasma levels and effect. *Br. J. clin. Pharmacol.* **3**, 883–9.

Park, D. M., Findley, L. J., Hanks, G., and Sandler, M. (1981). Nomifensine: effect in Parkinsonian patients not receiving levodopa. *J. Neurol. Neurosurg. Psychiat.* **44**, 352–4.

Perris, C., Dimitrijevic, P., Jacobsson, L., Paulson, P., Rapp, W., and Froberg, H. (1979). Tardive dyskinesia in psychiatric patients treated with neuroleptics. *Br. J. Psychiat.* **135**, 509–14.

Pinder, R. M., Brogden, R. N., Sawyer, P. R., Speight, T. M., and Avery, G. S. (1978). Metoclopramide: a review of its pharmacological properties and clinical use. *Drugs* **12**, 81–131.

Polizos, P., Engelhardt, D. M., and Hoffman, S. P. (1973). Neurological consequences of psychotropic drug withdrawal in schizophrenic children. *J. Autism and Childhood Schizophrenia* **3**, 247–53.

Porteous, H. B., and Ross, D. N. (1956). Mental symptoms in Parkinsonism following benzhexol hydrochloride therapy. *Br. med. J.* **2**, 138–40.

Quitkin, F., Rifkin, A., Gochfield, L., and Klein, D. F. (1977). Tardive dyskinesia: are first signs reversible? *Am. J. Psychiat.* **134**, 84–7.

Rajput, A. H., Rozdilsky, B., Hornykiewicz, O., Shannak, K., Lee, T., and Seeman, P. (1979). Susceptibility to drug-induced Parkinsonism. *Neurology, Minneapolis* **29**, 567.

Rivera-Calimlim, L. (1976). Impaired absorption of chlorpromazine in rats given trihexyphenidyl. *Br. J. Pharmacol.* **56**, 301–5.

——Narallah, H., Strauss, J., and Lasagna, L. (1976). Clinical response and plasma levels: effect of dose, dosage schedules, and drug interactions on plasma chlorpromazine levels. *Am. J. Psychiat.* **133**, 646–52.

Rotrosen, J., Friedman, E., and Gershon, S. (1975). Striatal adenylate cyclase activity following reserpine chronic chlorpromazine administration in rats. *Life Sci.* **17**, 563–8.

Sakalis, G., Curry, S. H., Mould, G. P., and Lader, M. H. (1972). Physiologic and clinical effects of chlorpromazine and their relationship to plasma level. *Clin. Pharmacol. Ther.* **13**, 931–46.

Salzman, N. P. and Brodie, B. B. (1956). Physiological disposition and fate of chlorpromazine and a method for its estimation in biological materials. *J. Pharmacol. exp. Ther.* **118**, 46–54.

Sarnquist, F. and Larson, C. P. (1973). Drug-induced heatstroke. *Anesthesiology* **39**, 348– .

Scatton, B. (1977). Differential regional development of tolerance to increase in dopamine turnover upon repeated neuroleptic administration. *Eur. J. Pharmacol.* **46**, 363–9.

Schaaf, M. and Payne, C. A. (1966). Dystonic reactions to prochlorperazine in hypoparathyroidism. *New Engl. J. Med.* **275**, 991–5.

Schonecker, M. (1957). Ein eigentümliches Syndrome in oralen Bereich bei Megaphenapplikation. *Nerventartz* **28**, 35.

Schwab, R. S., Doshay, L. J., Garland, H., Bradshaw, P., Garvey, E., and Crawford, B. (1956). Shift to older age distribution in parkinsonism. A report on 1 000 patients covering the past decade from three centres. *Neurology* **6**, 783–90.

——Fabing, H. D., and Prichard, J. S. (1951). Psychiatric symptoms and syndromes in Parkinson's disease. *Psychiat. Neurol.* **150**, 345–57.

Seeber, U. and Kuchinsky, K. (1976). Dopamine-sensitive adenylate cyclase in homogenates of rat striata during ethanol and barbiturate withdrawal. *Arch. Toxicol. Berlin* **35**, 247–53.

Sigwald, J., Bouttier, D., Raymondeaud, C., and Piot, C. (1959). Quatre cas de dyskinesie facio-bucco-linguo-masticatrice à evolution prolongée secondaire à un traitement par les neuroleptiques. *Rev. Neurol.* **100**, 751–5.

Simpson, G. M. (1970a). Controlled studies of antiparkinson agents in the treatment of drug-induced extrapyramidal symptoms. *Acta psychiat. scand. Suppl.* **212**, 44–51.

——(1970b). Long-acting antipsychotic agents and extrapyramidal side-effects. *Dis. nerv. Syst.* **31**, (Suppl. 9), 12–14.

——(1973). Tardive dyskinesia. *Br. J. Psychiat.* **122**, 618.

——Amuso, D., Blair, J. H., and Farkas, T. (1964). Phenothiazine-produced extrapyramidal system disturbance. *Arch. gen. Psychiat.* **10**, 127–36.

——and Angus, J. W. S. (1970). A rating scale for extrapyramidal side-effects. *Acta psychiat. scand. Suppl.* **212**, 11–19.

——Varga, E. (1974). Clozapine—a new antipsychotic agent. *Curr. ther. Res.* **16**, 679–86.

Singh, M. M. and Kay, S. R. (1975a). A comparative study of haloperidol and chlorpromazine in terms of clinical effect and therapeutic reversal with benztropine in schizophrenia. Theoretical implications for potency differences among neuroleptics. *Psychopharmacologia, Berlin* **43**, 103–13.

—— ——(1975b). A longitudinal therapeutic comparison between two prototypic neuroleptics (haloperidol and chlorpromazine) in matched groups of schizophrenics. Non-therapeutic interactions with trihexyphenidyl. Theoretical implications for potency differences. *Psychopharmacologia, Berlin* **43**, 115–23.

——and Smith, J. M. (1973). Reversal of some therapeutic effects of an antipsychotic agent by an antiparkinsonism agent. *J. nerv. ment. Dis.* **157**, 50–8.

Smith, J. M., Kucharski, L. T., Eblen, C., Knutsen, E., and Linn, C. (1979). An assessment of tardive dyskinesia in schizophrenic outpatients. *Psychopharmacologia, Berlin* **64**, 99–104.

——and Baldessarini, R. J. (1980). Changes in prevalence, severity and recovery in tardive dyskinesia with age. *Arch. gen. Psychiat.* **37**, 1368–73.

Smith, R., Strizich, M., and Klass, D. (1978). Drug history and tardive dyskinesia. *Am. J. Psychiat.* **135**, 1402–3.

St. Jean, A., Donald, M., and Bann, T. A. (1961). A survey of drug-induced extrapyramidal reactions. *J. Am. med. Assoc.* **175**, 102–8.

—— —— ——(1964). Interchangeability of antiparkinson medication. *Am. J. Psychiat.* **120**, 1189–90.

Steck, H. (1954). Le syndrome extrapyramidal et diencephalique au cours des traitements au Largactil et au Serpasil. *Ann. Medico-psychol.* **112**, 737–43.

Stephens, S. A. (1967). Psychotoxic effects of benzhexol hydrochloride (Artone). *Br. J. Psychiat.* **113**, 213–18.

Strang, R. R. (1965). Kemadrin in the treatment of Parkinsonism: a double-blind and one-year follow-up study. *Curr. Med. Drugs* **5** (8), 27–32.

Stratas, N. E., Philips, R. D., Walker, P. A., and Sandifer, M. G. (1963). A study of drug-induced parkinsonism. *Dis. nerv. Syst.* **24**, 180.

Swett, C. Jr (1975). Drug-induced dystonia. *Am. J. Psychiat.* **132**, 532–4.

Tarsy, D., and Baldessarini, R. J. (1973). Pharmacologically-induced behavioural supersensitivity to apormorphine. *Nature, Lond.* **245**, 262–3.

—— ——(1974). Behavioural supersensitivity to apomorphine following chronic treatment with drugs which interfere with the synaptic function of catecholamines.

Neuropharmacology **13**, 927–40.

—— ——Granacher, R., and Bralower, M. (1977). Tardive dyskinesia in young adults. *Am. J. Psychiat.* **134**, 1032–4.

Tassin, J. P., Stinus, L., Simon, M., Blanc, G., Thierry, A. M., le Moal, M., Cardo, B., and Glowinski, J. (1978). Relationship between the locomotor hyperactivity induced by AlO lesions and the destruction of the fronto-cortical dopaminergic innervation in the rat. *Brain Res.* **141**, 267–81.

Thornton, W. and Thornton, B. (1973) Tardive dyskinesia. *J. Am. med. Assoc.* **226**, 274.

Trendelenburg, U. (1963*a*). Supersensitivity and subsensitivity to sympathomimetic amines. *Pharmacol. Rev.* **15**, 225–76.

——(1963*b*). Time course of changes in sensitivity after denervation of the nictitating membrane of the spinal cat. *J. Pharmacol.* **142**, 335–42.

Turek, I., Kurland, A., Hanlon, T., and Bohm, M. (1972). Tardive dyskinesia: its relation to neuroleptic and antiparkinson drugs. *Br. J. Psychiat.* **121**, 605–12.

Uhrbrand, L. and Faurbye, A. (1960). Reversible and irreversible dyskinesia after treatment with perphenazine, chlorpromazine, reserpine and electroconvulsive therapy. *Psychopharmacologia, Berlin* **1**, 408–19.

Van Rossum, J. M. (1966). Significance of dopamine-receptor blockage for mechanism of action of neuroleptic drugs. *Arch. Int. pharmacodynamic Ther.* **160**, 492–4.

Varga, E., Sugerman, A., Varga, V., Zomorodi, A., Zomorodi, W., and Menken, M. (1982). Prevalence of spontaneous oral dyskinesia in the elderly. *Am. J. Psychiat.* **139**, 329–31.

Villeneuve, A. (1972). The rabbit syndrome, a peculiar extrapyramidal reaction. *Can. Psychiat. Ass. J.* **17**, 69.

Von Voigtlander, P. F., Losey, E. G., and Triezenberg, H. J. (1975). Increased sensitivity to dopaminergic agents after chronic neuroleptic treatment. *J. Pharmacol. exp. Ther.* **193**, 88–94.

Webster, D. (1968). Critical analysis of the disability in Parkinson's disease *Mod. Treat.* **5**, 257–82.

Weiner, W. and Klawans, H. (1973). Lingual-facial buccal movements in the elderly. II. Pathogenesis and relationship to senile chorea. *J. Am. geriat. Soc.* **21**, 318–20.

Weiss, B., Santelli, S., and Lusink, G. (1977). Movement disorders induced in monkeys by chronic haloperidol treatment. *Psychopharmacology* **53**, 289–93.

Westlake, R. J. and Rastegar, A. (1973). Hyperpyrexia from drug combinations. *J. Am. med. Assoc.* **225**, 1250.

Wiles, D. H. and Gelder, M. G. (1980). Plasma fluphenazine levels by radio-immuno-assay in schizophrenic patients treated with depot injections of fluphenazine decanoate. In *Long-term effects of neuroleptics (Advances in biochemistry and psychopharmacology*, Vol. 24) (ed. F. Cattabeni, G. Racagni, P. F. Spano, and E. Costa), pp. 599–602. Raven Press, New York.

Yaryura-Tobias, J. A., Diamond, B., and Meris, S. (1970*b*). The action of L-dopa on schizophrenic patients. *Curr. ther. Res.* **12**, 528–31.

——Wolpert, A., Dana, L., and Merlis, J. (1970*a*). Action of L-dopa in drug-induced extrapyramidalism. *Dis. nerv. Syst.* **31**, 60–3.

13

The untoward effects of antipsychotic drugs: pathogenesis and management

J. GUY EDWARDS

The ideal antipsychotic drug would be one that has a beneficial effect on the psychosis being treated but no untoward effects on other physiological systems. Unfortunately, no such drug exists and the price we have to pay for progress in pharmacotherapy is a wide range of effects on other systems. Those relevant to clinical practice will be reviewed in this chapter. Attention will be paid to the most widely used antipsychotic drugs—phenothiazines, thioxanthene derivatives, and butyrophenones. Reference will be made more to the effects of categories of drugs than individual compounds. Details concerning individual drugs, including less frequently used antipsychotic agents, have been provided by Shepherd *et al.* (1968*a*, 1972), Shader and Dimascio (1970), Mindham (1975, 1977, 1978), Davies (1977), Caldwell (1977), Lipton *et al.* (1978), Rudenko and Lepakhin (1979), Baldessarini (1980), Dukes (1980), Korczyn (1980), and others. In this chapter the mechanisms and management of some of the more serious and common effects will also be discussed.

SOME GENERAL CONSIDERATIONS

Drug effects result from interactions between the drug, the patient, and the patient's pathophysiological state, but are also influenced by psychological and social factors. Untoward effects may be categorized as type A (augmented) reactions and type B (bizarre) reactions (Rawlins and Thompson 1977). Type A reactions form part of the normal pharmacological spectrum of the drug, and are qualitatively normal though quantitatively abnormal. They include oversedation and anticholinergic effects. Such augmented reactions are predictable and largely dose-dependent. In contrast, type B reactions are unusual, bizarre, qualitatively abnormal, and unrelated to the normal pharmacology of the drug. They include allergic or hypersensitivity reactions, mediated through antigen–antibody mechanisms (for example an exanthematous rash) and idiosyncratic reactions appearing in those genetically or constitutionally predisposed (such as drug-induced convulsions). The causes of both types of reactions can be pharmaceutical, pharmacokinetic, or pharmacodynamic. Untoward effects may also result from drug interactions, overdoses, and faulty administration.

In attempting to establish a cause-and-effect relationship between drug and effect problems arise because: (1) symptoms identical to side-effects may be reported in healthy untreated subjects (Reidenberg and Lowenthal 1967) or as placebo side-effects (Pogge 1963); (2) an apparent effect may be due to psychological factors, such as anxiety concerning treatment or resentment at being given a drug to control disturbed behaviour (Appleton 1968), or due to more florid psychopathology, such as a delusion of being poisoned; (3) an effect may be a symptom of the illness for which the drug was originally given or of a concomitant disorder; (4) an effect may be due to other drugs being given concurrently or recently withdrawn: and (5) a clinician who has an intense interest in a particular effect may overdiagnose it (Edwards 1977). The best we can hope for therefore is an assessment of the probability of a causal connection. An effect is more likely due to a drug if: (1) it differs from the symptoms and signs of the disorder being treated; (2) no others drugs are being given or withdrawn when the effect occurs; (3) there is a close temporal relationship between the effect and taking the drug or the occurrence of toxic levels of drug or metabolites in blood or other body fluids; (4) it disappears on stopping treatment, and especially if it recurs if the drug is re-introduced.

There are many deficiencies in existing systems of reporting and monitoring drug effects. Voluntary reporting of single cases varies with the awareness, initiative, and knowledge of the clinician. Cases may be missed or not reported and even when reported it is often difficult to relate them to the drug. Reactions are more likely to be reported if they occur during a clinical trial, but even in trials the methodology of eliciting unwanted effects often leaves much to be desired. Furthermore, most trials are of short duration and therefore do not allow for the recognition of adverse effects that occur after prolonged treatment. For these reasons, and because many effects are rare, larger-scale methods have been used. Some investigators compare retrospectively the frequency of exposure to a drug in patients who have experienced a particular reaction with those who have not had such a reaction. Others compare prospectively the frequency of occurrence of reactions in patients exposed to a drug with the occurrence of those effects in a control group that has not received the drug. Yet others assess prospectively the frequency of occurrence of all unwanted effects in populations exposed to a wide variety of drugs. An example of this is the British Committee on Safety of Medicines which relies on voluntary reporting but this varies considerably with the clinician, the drug, and the reaction. Because of its limitations systems of 'recorded release', 'registered release', and 'monitored release' have been recommended for new drugs (*British Medical Journal* 1977; Gross and Inman 1977; Inman 1980).

Because of the difficulties in proving a causal relationship between drug and effect and deficiencies in the systems of reporting and monitoring unwanted effects the size of the problem is not known. Some think it is small and a trivial price to pay for the benefits that antipsychotic drugs provide; others believe we are seeing merely the tip of an iceberg.

CENTRAL NERVOUS SYSTEM

Antipsychotic drugs can affect cognition, perception, and affect although the reactions that result are also dependent on psychological and social factors. At high doses and in susceptible individuals neuroleptics can impair concentration, attention, memory, and intellectual functioning. They can affect components of complex skills, such as reaction time and visuomotor co-ordination, and performance in driving simulation tests. This suggests that they can be a threat to safety, for example by contributing to road traffic accidents, and can lead to impaired precision and decreased productivity in industry. It is thought that traffic accidents are more likely to occur when antipsychothic drugs are first introduced or when used in combination with alcohol or other drugs (Milner and Landauer 1971; Milner 1972; Willette 1977).

Antipsychotic drugs, particularly chlorpromazine and thioridazine, can cause oversedation that in turn may lead to toxic confusional states, falls, injuries, and hypostatic pneumonia. Oversedation occurs particularly when the drugs are given in large doses or in combination with other drugs such as antiparkinson agents. It also occurs when they are administered to susceptible individuals, particularly the elderly. In general schizophrenic patients are less susceptible to the sedative effects of drugs than are normal subjects (Okuma *et al.* 1976). The reasons for this are not known; differences in rates of absorption and differences in levels of arousal have been considered as possible explanations. Non-smokers are more prone to chlorpromazine-induced drowsiness than are smokers, possibly due to the stimulation in smokers of enzymes involved in the metabolism of chlorpromazine (Swett 1974). In general, sedation is dose-dependent and time-limited. The tendency for individual neuroleptics to cause sedation correlates with their capacity to block alpha-adrenoceptor sites (Creese *et al.* 1978; also see Chapter 2, this volume, for discussion of pharmacological effects in relation to activity in different neuroreceptor systems).

Neuroleptics have been said to cause 'paradoxical' reactions which are opposite to the expected effect and 'pendular' reactions in which the patient swings too far in the direction of the desired effect (Shader and Dimascio 1970). For example, they have been alleged to increase anxiety or cause excitement instead of calming the patient, and to subdue excessively patients who were pathologically excited. They may cause exacerbations of the illness being treated; some of these respond to decreasing the dose of neuroleptics, others to antiparkinson agents (Van Putten *et al.* 1974; Simpson *et al.* 1976). It was suggested by Chouinard and Jones (1980) that, just as dopaminergic receptor hypersensitivity occurs in the neostriatal system and is thought to be the cause of tardive dyskinesia, neuroleptic-induced supersensitivity of dopamine receptors occurs in the mesolimbic system, as a result of which there is an increased tendency to relapse and a need to increase the dose of antipsychotic drug to maintain its therapeutic effect. The phenomenon is associated with high plasma prolactin levels, due to the dopamine blockage required to control the psychosis, and sexual dysfunction.

Neuroleptics have also been alleged to cause 'depression' and such catatonic phenomena as mutism, negativism, posturing, and waxy flexibility (Behrman 1972; Gelenberg and Mandel 1977; Weinberger and Kelly 1977). It is uncertain whether these occurrences are predominantly due to intrinsic properties of the drug or to predisposing factors in the patient. Alternatively, they may be features of the schizophrenic illness for which the drug was given. In the case of excitement, restlessness, and aggression induced by high doses of fluphenazine and flupenthixol, there is disagreement as to whether these effects are due to enhancement of the presynaptic release of dopamine (Barnes and Bridges 1980) or due to akathisia (Guirguis and Bawden 1980). A psychoanalytic view of adverse behavioural effects of neuroleptics was put forward by Nevins (1977).

Tolerance to some of the effects of antipsychotic drugs, for example autonomic effects, occurs and cross-tolerance between antipsychotic drugs has been reported. Withdrawal of neuroleptics may be followed by a variety of symptoms including those due to autonomic dysfunction and an exacerbation of extrapyramidal effects including dyskinesia (Gardos *et al.* 1978). In one instance multiple tics and spontaneous vocalizations as seen in Gilles de la Tourette syndrome were encountered (Klawans *et al.* 1978). Withdrawal phenomena are often mistaken for a worsening of the psychosis for which the drug was originally given. Antipsychotic agents do not have pleasurable effects and are only very rarely abused on the 'drug scene'. They are not drugs of addiction.

Antipsychotic drugs may cause a slowing of the electroencephalogram with a decrease in alpha and beta activity and an increase in theta and to a lesser extent delta waves (Fink 1981). They may also induce spikes or sharp waves and paroxysmal features (Fink 1969; Itil 1978). Some antipsychotic drugs can precipitate convulsive seizures (Logothetis 1967; Toone and Fenton 1977). There is usually no preceding aura, focal disturbance, or residual neurological deficit. Convulsions are more likely to occur at high doses and when there is a rapid change in dose. They occur more often in those with pre-existing brain damage or epilepsy and when the antipsychotic agent is given in combination with other potentially epileptogenic drugs. The differential effects of neuroleptics on dopaminergic and cholinergic transmission have been said to be important in determining the relative epileptogenic potential of antipsychotic drugs, as is the case with extrapyramidal effects (Cools *et al.* 1975; Remick and Fine 1979). It is thought that in therapeutic doses low-potency neuroleptics are more likely to cause seizures, possibly due to their higher anticholinergic activity.

During an epileptic attack the patient should be prevented from injury and an anticonvulsant, such as phenytoin sodium or diazepam, should be administered parenterally. Possible predisposing causes of the attack should be investigated. The antipsychotic drug should be reduced in dose or a high-potency neuroleptic substituted. If it is thought necessary to continue the original drug while the risk of fits remain high, an anticonvulsant, such as phenytoin, should be added to the treatment regime and its blood levels monitored. In general, however, unnecessary drug combination should be avoided.

Neuroleptics can cause non-specific neuropsychiatric symptoms, such as headache, but these often occur in normal subjects and as placebo side-effects. They are also seen in such a wide variety of disorders that it is usually difficult to relate them to the drug. In large doses antipsychotic drugs cause cerebellar signs, including nystagmus, dysarthria, and ataxia of the extremities. Muscle pain, spasms, twitches, and weakness may also be encountered. Chlorpromazine may aggravate myasthenia gravis presumably because of its neuromuscular blocking action (McQuillen *et al.* 1963).

The central nervous effects discussed above are reversible. Lyon *et al.* (1981) carried out brain density measurements using computerized tomography print-out matrices of chronic schizophrenic patients who had received prolonged treatment with various neuroleptics. Although there were acknowledged limitations to the study, the investigators found a significant correlation between density measurements in the posterior quadrants of both hemispheres and life-long drug consumption, suggesting that permanent drug-induced effects may occur.

A serious complication that is sometimes encountered is the 'neuroleptic malignant syndrome'. In this there is muscular rigidity, akinesia, hyperthermia, fluctuating levels of consciousness, dyskinesia, sialorrhoea, dysphagia, tachycardia, labile blood pressure, profuse sweating, and incontinence. Complications such as pneumonia or pulmonary embolism may occur. Laboratory investigations reveal leucocytosis and high creatinine phosphokinase. Generalized electroencephalographic abnormalities similar to those found in metabolic encephalopathies can be demonstrated. The mortality in reported cases is about 20 per cent, death being due to cardiovascular, respiratory, and renal causes.

The aetiology of the syndrome is unknown. Most reported cases have occurred during treatment with high-potency neuroleptics, especially fluphenazine decanoate given by depot injections. Young adult males and patients who are physically exhausted or dehydrated appear to be most susceptible (Caroff 1980).

There is no satisfactory treatment so the emphasis should be on prevention. The antipsychotic drug should be discontinued and intensive medical and nursing care instituted as soon as the syndrome is suspected. Fluid and electrolyte imbalance should be corrected, hyperthermia controlled, and the patient's cardiovascular and respiratory state carefully monitored. Antiparkinson drugs have been tried and, as the clinical picture resembles malignant hyperthermia associated with anaesthesia, attempts have been made at treatment with dantrolene sodium.

AUTONOMIC NERVOUS SYSTEM

The most widely known autonomic effects of antipsychotic drugs are due to their cholinergic and α-adrenergic blocking actions, but they also have adrenergic activity (due to the blocking of neuronal re-uptake of noradrenaline) and antihistaminic and antiserotonergic properties as part of their pharmacological spectrum. Because of the complexity of their actions on neurotransmission, clinical effects on the autonomic nervous system are difficult to predict. However, autonomic effects occur more often during treatment with aliphatic and piperazine phenothiazines, although they are mostly mild and decrease in severity as tolerance develops.

Anti-α-adrenergic effects include nasal congestion, inhibition of ejaculation (especially with thioridazine), and postural hypotension. Hypotension may be caused by depression of medullary vasopressor reflexes with decreased peripheral vascular resistance and α-adrenoceptor blockade (Alexander and Nino 1969). Hypotensive episodes may result from previous sensitization and occur more often than is generally realized (Mann and Chen 1973). Patients with phaeochromocytomas given phenothiazines parenterally may have a particularly sudden and severe drop of blood pressure with generalized circulatory failure (Brody 1959; Lund-Johansen 1962). Chlorpromazine-induced hypotension, like drowsiness, occurs more often in non-smokers, possibly due to the stimulation in smokers of enzymes concerned with the metabolism of chlorpromazine (Swett *et al.* 1977). The tendency for individual neuroleptics to cause hypotension (again like drowsiness) is related to their capacity to block α-adrenoceptor sites (Creese *et al.* 1978). It is therefore greater in the case of low-potency neuroleptics such as chlorpromazine and thioridazine. In most instances tolerance to the hypotensive effects of antipsychotic drugs occurs but in some patients orthostatic hypotension persists for as long as the drug is continued. Hypotension is a particular hazard to the elderly. It can result in falls, fractures, cerebrovascular ischaemia (with toxic confusional states, strokes, or unconsciousness), and myocardial ischaemia with or without infarction.

Anticholinergic effects include decreased salivation (which can cause polydipsia), decreased sweating, blurred vision due to decreased accommodation, tachycardia with or without palpitations, constipation, and, more seriously though occurring less frequently, angle-closure glaucoma, urinary retention, and paralytic ileus (which may be fatal). (See sections on 'The eye', 'Urinary tract', and 'Alimentary tract', respectively).

Phenothiazines have central (hypothalamic) and peripheral (anti-α-adrenergic) effects on temperature regulatory mechanisms. Interference with temperature regulation may cause hypothermia, less frequently hyperthermia. The effects are influenced by the ambient temperature and the rate of heat production which is affected by physical activity and the subject's pathophysiological state. Hypothermia may be accompanied by vasodilation, an increase in superficial temperature of the extremities, and suppression of shivering. Chlorpromazine can precipitate hypothermic coma in myxoedematous patients (Jones and Meade 1964). In contrast, hyperpyrexia with profuse perspiration may occur (Garmany *et al.*, 1954) and the combination of heat, physical exertion, and neuroleptics can be life-threatening or even lethal (Mann and Boger 1978; Cooper 1979). Heat stroke can be aggravated by antiparkinson agents as these drugs decrease sweating. A slight increase in temperature early in treatment is probably due to drug fever.

Antipsychotic drugs can cause difficulty in obtaining or maintaining an erection and inability to achieve an orgasm. Thioridazine is one of the worst offenders and in one study there was a 60 per cent incidence of sexual difficulty. Ejaculatory problems were most common, with a third of the patients having retrograde ejaculation probably due to a specific α-adrenoceptor blocking effect (Kotin *et al.* 1976). Persistent priapism, possibly due to peripheral adrenergic blockade, has been reported on rare occasions (Meirez and Fishelovitch 1969; Doorman and Schmidt 1976).

Patients who are troubled by dryness of the mouth should be advised to rinse their mouths with water frequently. They should not suck sweets or chew gum because sugar increases the chance of fungal infections, especially candidiasis (moniliasis), and in the longer term promotes caries formation. Asymptomatic hypotension does not usually call for treatment. Troublesome hypotensive attacks can mostly be treated successfully by laying the patient supine and elevating the foot of the bed. If they continue, the dose of the offending drug should be reduced or a drug with less anti-adrenergic activity substituted. Severe and persistent hypotension is serious but rare. It calls for emergency medical treatment with intravenous fluids and sometimes infusions of a vasopressor agent such as noradrenaline. Adrenaline should not be used because its hypertensive effects are antagonized by phenothiazines. Hypothermia and hyperpyrexia should be treated symptomatically by external or core-re-warming or cooling, respectively. In the case of hyperpyrexia possible causes of the raised temperature other than drugs, such as infections, should be investigated and appropriately treated. Antipyretic drugs may be indicated.

ENDOCRINE AND METABOLIC SYSTEM

There is a particularly intimate relationship between the nervous and endocrine systems. Psychiatric disorders frequently occur during the course of endocrine diseases and endocrine dysfunction occurs in psychiatric illnesses. Antipsychotic drugs have direct effects on the endocrine system and metabolic processes and also secondary effects mediated by changes in arousal or behaviour.

Antipsychotic drugs may influence hypothalamic–pituitary function through their effects on neurotransmission, as a non-specific action mediated haemodynamically or via their influence on thermoregulation (de Wied 1967). Neuroleptics stimulate the release of some hormones and suppress others. Phenothiazines, for instance, stimulate the release of prolactin, melanocyte stimulating hormone (MSH), and antidiuretic hormone (ADH) and suppress corticotrophin (ACTH), growth hormone (GH), thyrotrophin (TSH), follicle-stimulating hormone (FSH), and luteinizing hormone (LH). The effects may be determined by actions on hypothalamic releasing and inhibiting hormones and factors. The release of prolactin, for example, is kept under tonic inhibition by dopamine as well as by other quantitatively less important neurotransmitters and small peptides of unknown chemical sequence, collectively known as prolactin inhibitory factor (PIF). Prolactin, by enhancing the release of PIF, controls its own release. In addition to this negative feedback, prolactin is also influenced by releasing factors. Antipsychotic drugs decrease the availability of dopamine at its receptors by receptor blockade, which in turn leads to increased plasma prolactin levels (Beumont *et al.* 1974*a, b*; Meltzer and Fang 1976; Gruen *et al.* 1978; Rubin and Hays 1980; Beumont 1981).

Only some of the known hormonal changes are associated with clinical effects. Neuroleptic-induced hyperprolactinaemia, for instance, may contribute to the production of galactorrhoea, increased MSH to ocular and cutaneous hyperpigmentation (see section on 'The skin'). High prolactin levels are also related to extrapyramidal symptoms (Wiles, *et al.* 1976; Kolakowska *et al.* 1979).

Amenorrhoea may result from specific inhibitory effects associated with changes in FSH and LH, while its occurrence with drug-induced galactorrhoea suggests that it is mediated via the hypothalamus (Shader *et al.* 1970). However, amenorrhoea is particularly difficult to relate to antipsychotic drugs because it often occurs as a symptom of the psychoses being treated. In general, the tendency for drugs to produce hormonal effects may be related to dose, duration of treatment, and predisposing factors; in the case of galactorrhoea, for example, predisposing factors in the hypothalamic–pituitary–mammary gland axis (Shader *et al.* 1970).

Inappropriate lactation has been reported with a frequency ranging from 10–80 per cent, depending on the degree of awareness of the effect, whether or not the breasts are examined, and the concomitant use of other drugs such as oral contraceptives. Those who have galactorrhoea are more likely to come to the attention of the investigator while interpretation of frequency rates is also complicated by the occurrence of lactation in normal women who have borne children, menopausal women, and those with menstrual disorders. Gynaecomastia in men is unrelated to neuroleptic-induced lactation and is dependent on the ratio of androgen to oestrogens (Beumont 1981).

Elevated serum prolactin levels increase the incidence of spontaneously occurring mammary tumours in mice and increase the growth of established carcinogenic-induced breast tumours in rats. Concern has therefore been expressed about the possibility of antipsychotic drugs increasing the risk of carcinoma of the breast in humans. To date, however, epidemiological studies have failed to show an increased risk of cancer (Brugmans *et al.* 1973; Ettigi *et al.* 1973; Overall 1978; Schyve *et al.* 1978; Wagner and Mantel 1978).

Other endocrine effects include decreased libido in men, increased libido in women, and infertility allegedly due to phenothiazines. These may be related to changes in urinary gonadotrophin, oestrogen, progesterone, and other hormones (Baldessarini 1980). Impotence in men also occurs and may in part be explained by a decrease in plasma testosterone. Little is known about the effects of antipsychotic drugs on spermatogenesis but aspermia without impairment of sexual excitation or the ability to obtain an erection and orgasm has been reported in patients receiving thioridazine (Shader *et al.* 1970). Phenothiazines may produce a false-positive pregnancy test (Marks and Shackeloth 1966; Paoletti *et al.* 1966). Reference has already been made to the effects of antipsychotic drugs on erection and ejaculation (see section on 'Autonomic nervous system').

The syndrome of inappropriate secretion of ADH has been described in patients receiving fluphenazine, thioridazine, and haloperidol (Matuk and Kalyanaraman 1977; Vincent and Emory 1978; Smith and Clark 1980), but also in schizophrenic patients not taking neuroleptics.

Antipsychotic drugs can cause changes in appetite and weight, especially increased weight which can be quite troublesome. Weight gain may also be caused by increased appetite (which may be related to an improvement in mental state), decreased activity, and, rarely, water retention (which may be accompanied by oedema). Phenothiazines, especially chlorpromazine given in high doses, can inhibit insulin secretion and cause hyperglycaemia and glycosuria (Thonnard-Neumann 1966; Erle *et al.* 1977). Drug-induced changes in glucose tolerance may precipitate overt diabetes in potential diabetics and cause instability in the control of patients receiving antidiabetic treatment. In some studies, however, the effects of antipsychotic drugs on glucose metabolism are difficult to interpret, because of a possibly higher prevalence of diabetes mellitus in the patients studied or in their families and because the research has been carried out in older and more obese subjects who may have been intolerant to glucose.

IMMUNOLOGICAL SYSTEM

The terms allergic and hypersensitivity reactions are often used inaccurately to describe effects that are not mediated through immunological mechanisms. True allergic reactions are not dose-related and occur in only a small minority of those who receive the offending drug. Their manifestations are typically those of protein allergy. They require an induction period following primary exposure but not if the drug is readministered. They disappear when the drug is withdrawn but reappear if it is reintroduced or a chemically-related substance given. Drugs with small molecules cannot on their own stimulate an immunological response. To act as an allergen they or one of their metabolites must act as a hapten; that is they must combine with endogenous macromolecules, usually proteins, to produce a covalently-bonded complex known as an antigen or immunogen. To elicit an allergic response the antigen must form a bridge between antibody molecules. They then react with complement to release cytoactive peptides (Assem 1977; McQueen 1980).

Allergic reactions fall into one or other of four main categories (Coombs and Gell 1975). Their clinical manifestations may be generalized or confined to specific tissues. There may be a generalized anaphylactic reaction with urticaria or angioneurotic oedema, asthma, and/or gastrointestinal symptoms or serum sickness, with fever, rash, lymphadenopathy, arthritis, periarteritis, oedema, and/or haematological abnormalities. Alternatively, the patient may have localized urticaria or angioneurotic oedema or reactions against specific organs, for example cholestatic jaundice. Identical reactions can be produced by different drugs or the same drug may produce different reactions in different individuals or in the same individual at different times. Specific reactions are described under the appropriate system headings.

THE SKIN

Antipsychotic drugs, particularly phenothiazines, have been alleged to cause many different types of dermatological reactions although the causal link is often difficult to prove (Baker 1972; Beerman and Kirshbaum 1975; Cluff *et al.* 1975; Wintroub *et al.* 1979). Unrelated lesions such as acne vulgaris, neurodermatitis, and allergic reactions to other drugs and chemicals have mistakenly been attributed to neuroleptics. There are few dermatological symptoms and signs that cannot be caused by drugs, but most fall into a number of familiar patterns. Each drug tends to cause a limited range of reactions but is capable of producing any type. In the case of allergic skin reactions a chemically-related drug sometimes produces cross-sensitivity. Occasionally, an offending drug may be reintroduced without an exacerbation of the eruption.

One of the most frequently reported dermatological effects is an erythematous reaction (red rash), most cases allegedly being caused by phenothiazines. The rash may resemble that seen in measles (morbilliform rash) or it may be unlike that which accompanies any of the infectious diseases. Eczematous reactions may also occur and rarely progress to life-threatening exfoliative dermatitis. Urticaria, with histamine release from the antigen–antibody reaction, may occur as a complication of phenothiazine treatment and may be associated with other features of anaphylaxis or serum sickness. Vesicular-bullous eruptions are also rarely encountered. Phenothiazines have been said to cause lichenoid eruptions and erythema multiforme which may be of the Stevens–Johnson variety with oro-anal, genital, ophthalmic, and respiratory involvement. They have also been alleged to precipitate systemic lupus erythematosus-like illnesses (see section on 'The respiratory system') and purpura due to a direct toxic effect on capillaries (rather than due to an allergic reaction or thrombocytopenia). Haloperidol has been reported as causing an acneiform eruption and loss of hair colour.

Some rashes are photosensitive, being either phototoxic or photo-allergic, with the involvement of immunological mechanisms. One of the most widely recognized drug-effects is in fact a chlorpromazine-induced photosensitive sunburn reaction (Epstein 1968). Phototoxic reactions depend on the ability of the subject to absorb light energy of wavelengths above 4100 A and those in the ultraviolet range (Satonova and McIntosh 1967). They can be induced by fluorescent lighting.

Prolonged treatment with high doses of chlorpromazine can lead to blue-grey or purple-brown pigmentation of the skin (Greiner and Berry 1964; Satonova 1965; Bond and Yee 1980). This is not associated with blistering or changes in the texture of the skin. It occurs more often in women than in men and is most conspicuous in parts of the skin exposed to sunlight. It is usually associated with corneal and lenticular opacities (see section on 'The eye'). Pigmentary deposits also occur throughout the reticuloendothelial system and in the parenchymal cells of internal organs—the heart, lungs, gastro-intestinal tract, liver, kidneys, endocrine glands, and brain (Greiner and Nicolson 1964).

Melanin is formed in the cytoplasm of melanocytes by oxidation of the amino-acid tyrosine in the presence of the enzyme tyrosinase. Production is under hormonal and neural control. The most important darkening factors are α-and β-melanocyte-stimulating hormones (MSH), androgen, oestrogen, and thyroid hormones. Lightening factors, include adrenaline, noradrena-line, 5-hydroxytryptamine (5-HT, serotonin), and, most importantly, melatonin present in the pineal gland and peripheral nerves. It is thought that phenothiazines disturb the balance between darkening and lightening factors by decreasing the release of adrenaline and noradrenaline as a result of which there is a relative excess of MSH and overproduction of melanin (Greiner and Nicholson 1964).

Different views have been expressed on the cause of the purple hue. It has been suggested for instance that 7-hydroxy-chlorpromazine, or a further metabolite, accumulates in the skin and other tissues and becomes converted to a purple toxic compound on exposure to ultraviolet light; the violaceous hue is believed to be due to this purple metabolite or a pseudo-melanin with a colour distinct from normal melanin (Perry 1964). However, measurements of skin melanin by reflectance spectrophotometry has shown that the pigmentation is due solely to melanin (Robins 1972, 1975).

Allergic contact dermatitis may occur in industrial employees who handle chlorpromazine. This drug is absorbed through the skin and may be stored in the stratum corneum for up to two weeks. Fluspirilene, administered by long-acting depot injections, may cause toxic necrosis of subcutaneous tissue, possibly due to the rapid absorption of the aqueous vehicle and the sub-sequent precipitation of crystals which have a toxic effect (McCreadie *et al.* 1979).

Phenothiazines should be used with caution in patients with a predisposition to allergic reactions. When rashes occur, the suspect drug should be discontinued because of the risk of serious, though rare, effects. Patients prone to phototoxic reactions should avoid exposure to excessive sunlight and a topical preparation containing para-aminobenzoic acid which acts as a sunscreen may be helpful. The chances of abnormal drug-induced pigmentation occurring can be minimized by avoiding high doses and the judicious use of drug holidays. If it does occur, a low-dose high-potency pheno-thiazine or a different type of neuroleptic should be substituted. The copper-chelating agent D-penicillamine has been successfully employed in decreasing pigmentation (Greiner *et al.* 1964) but is not generally recommended because toxic effects are common. These include such serious reactions as thrombocytopenia and renal tubular damage. Attempts have also been made to decrease pigmentation by keeping patients in darkened rooms. This is thought to increase the production of melatonin but is not a practical form of treatment.

THE EYE

Most ophthalmic effects of antipsychotic drugs occur as part of a more generalized reaction. The eyelids and conjunctiva, for example, may be involved in a widespread allergic skin reaction while cycloplegia and mydriasis may result from the drug's antimuscarinic effects and oculogyric crises may occur alongside other manifestations of extrapyramidal dysfunction.

Acute glaucoma may result from mydriasis, itself due to autonomic paralysis. Mydriasis allows the peripheral part of the iris to occlude access of aqueous humour to the drainage canals. The outflow of humour is thereby impeded causing increased intraocular pressure. Various mechanisms have been described: angle-closure caused by bunching or bowing forward of the iris in the case of those with narrow irido-corneal angles and over-relaxation of the pupillary muscle which can occur in any eye (Reid *et al.* 1976).

Whatever the mechanism, glaucoma is a rare and exaggerated complication of neuroleptic treatment, though one may need to be cautious in giving antipsychotic drugs to patients with widely dilated pupils and to those with a previous or family history of acute glaucoma or of such suggestive symptoms as blurred vision, pain in the eye, and seeing coloured rings around lights. In cases of doubt, there is a simple test which can be carried out by any psychiatrist; it is the oblique illumination test which is highly sensitive in separating patients with and without known attacks of angle-closure glaucoma (Vargas and Drance 1973). In dimmed light the beam of a flashlight is directed from the temporal side tangentially towards the pupil. In eyes with narrow anterior chambers the nasal part of the iris is in shadow whereas in normal eyes the nasal and temporal portions of the iris are equally well illuminated.

Phenothiazines, notably chlorpromazine and thioridazine, cause pigmentary changes in the eye as well as in the skin (see section on 'The skin') (Greiner and Berry 1964; Siddall 1965, 1966, 1968; Mathalone 1966; Cameron 1967; Edler *et al.* 1971; Bond and Yee 1980). Patients with skin pigmentation invariably have ophthalmic lesions but most of those with eye changes do not have excessive cutaneous pigmentation. Reported frequencies of occurrence of pigmentation in the eye vary widely and depend on such variables as the criteria for diagnosis, dose of drug, duration of treatment, sex of patient, amount of exposure to light, and climate. The effects are seen more often in women and in those with dark complexions, and may be intensified by sunlight.

Brown pigmentation occurs in exposed parts of the bulbar conjunctiva and cornea. Isolated brownish dust-like specks are seen in the lens which become aggregated and eventually form anterior capsular and subcapsular star-shaped (stellate) opacities. Although there have been reports of impaired visual acuity due to corneolenticular pigmentary deposits, in most instances there is no interference with vision. It is only on rare occasions that white pearl-like polar cataracts occur. Chlorpromazine may also cause epithelial keratopathy (Johnson and Buffaloe 1966). This also does not impair visual acuity and is at least partially reversible. The keratopathy is thought to be related to high rather than total dose of drug.

Drug-induced pigmentation also occurs in the fundus. Doses of thiorida-zine in excess of 800 mg per day and chlorpromazine greater than 300 mg per day can result in pigmentary retinopathy, with loss of retinal pigment epithelium and choriocapillaries (Connell *et al.* 1964; Davidorf 1973; Meredith *et al.* 1978). In the past, the clinical picture was likened to retinitis pigmentosa. Night blindness, transient central and ring scotomata confined to the central part of the visual field, and decreased visual acuity may occur. Most reports of pigmentary retinopathy have suggested that there is no per-manent visual loss and that vision improves on stopping treatment, though progressive deterioration occurs in severe cases.

The blood–eye barrier in many ways resembles the blood–brain barrier. The ability of a drug to penetrate the eye depends on many factors including its chemical structure, water and lipid solubility, polarity, and ionic charge (Leopold 1968). Phenothiazines enter the eye and in experimental animals (but not albino rabbits) reach concentrations in the uveal tissue 50 times the mean distribution value (Potts 1962). It has been shown that chlorpromazine enters the eye and decreases the metabolism of lens epithelium. Guinea pigs fed with large doses of chlorpromazine develop opacities similar to those seen in humans. It is thought that the drug or one of its metabolites, acting as a photosensitizing agent, interacts with lens protein to cause denaturation and flocculation. The resulting opacities are said to have no apparent relation to melanin because they occur in albino as well as pigmented animals (Howard *et al.* 1969).

Other reported ophthalmic effects include depression of tear function, meiosis, mydriasis, iridoplegia, and cycloplegia induced by phenothiazines and toxic amblyopia caused by perphenazine (Crews 1962, 1974; Walsh and Hoyt 1969; Garner *et al.* 1974; Grant 1974).

Antipsychotic drugs should be prescribed with caution and aliphatic and piperazine phenothiazines avoided altogether if there are any suggestions of raised intraocular pressure, while symptoms suggestive of glaucoma should be assessed by an ophthalmologist. The risk of pigmentary changes in the eye like that of cutaneous pigmentation can be minimized by avoiding unnecessarily large doses of neuroleptics and by allowing patients drug holidays. If corneo-lenticular opacities occur, high-dose low-potency pheno-thiazines should be discontinued and other antipsychotic drugs substituted. This applies even more so if pigmentary retinopathy is encountered. Drug-induced ocular pigmentation has been treated by D-penicillamine and by keeping patients in a darkened room, but the disadvantages of these treatments have been discussed in the section on 'The skin'.

THE BLOOD

Antipsychotic drugs can cause various haematological abnormalities, but the most serious is agranulocytosis. This presents with fever, fatigue, and prostration and is followed by ulceration at sites where bacteria are normally present in greatest numbers—commonly the mouth and throat but also the nose, rectum, and vagina. It has a mortality rate of about 30 per cent, death being caused by bacteraemia. The majority of cases have been attributed to phenothiazines (Pisciotta 1968, 1974; Ayd 1969; Swett 1975). Reported prevalence rates range from 1 in 700 to 1 in 200 000 (Shepherd *et al.* 1968*b*), a more recent estimation being 1 in 1250 (Pisciotta 1974). The incidence seems to have declined since the late-1960s, possibly because of the increased use of high-potency neuroleptics (Ducomb and Baldessarini 1977). Agranulocytosis occurs more often during treatment with high doses. Although it is usually encountered during the first three months of treatment and often within the first 10 days (Pisciotta 1971), cases have been reported after more prolonged phenothiazine administration. Susceptibility increases with age and agranulocytosis has been reported more often in women than men, possibly because phenothiazines have been prescribed more often for women.

Allergic mechanisms have been suspected because of the time relationship between the introduction of the drug and onset of the dyscrasia and the association in some cases of other hypersensitivity manifestations such as a rash. It is now thought, however, that agranulocytosis is more likely to result from a toxic effect on white blood cells which have limited proliferative potential and reduced deoxyribonucleic acid (DNA) synthesis (Pisciotta 1968, 1974) and it has been suggested that in those with such a predisposition bone marrow suppression occurs anew each time an antipsychotic agent is introduced (Ducomb and Baldessarini 1977).

Other haematological reactions that have allegedly been caused by antipsychotic agents, particularly chlorpromazine, are leucopenia, thrombocytopenia, pancytopenia, leucocytosis, eosinophilia, iron deficiency, haemolytic and aplastic anaemia (de Gruchy 1975; Girdwood 1976; Wintrobe *et al.* 1977). In many reported cases, however, the evidence is no more than circumstantial and although toxic and allergic mechanisms have been incriminated, the mechanisms of production of the reactions are not fully understood. It has also been shown that chlorpromazine prolongs the bleeding time in healthy individuals, a finding that the investigators suggested could lead to a new approach to the prevention of arterial thrombosis (Zahavi and Schwartz 1978).

When haematological abnormalities occur it is essential to investigate the possibility of causes other than drug reactions and a haematologist's opinion should be sought. In the case of agranulocytosis or neutropenia, the offending drug should be discontinued and not reintroduced. Appropriate material, such as smears and blood, should be taken for culture and sensitivity tests whenever there is fever, and antibiotics should be prescribed to prevent overwhelming sepsis. When the results of the culture and sensitivity tests are available, appropriate changes in bactericidal drugs should be made if necessary. Oral hygiene should receive particular attention to prevent the development of painful ulceration. Drugs to stimulate bone marrow activity, and therefore granulocyte formation, are sometimes given but their value has not been proven. Neutrophil transfusions are recommended by some haematologists when there is life-endangering infection. Drug-induced thrombocytopenia does not usually call for specific treatment because withdrawal of the offending drug is usually followed by spontaneous recovery though platelet transfusions may be helpful in tiding patients over life-threatening episodes. The evidence for the value of steroids is not convincing (Wintrobe *et al.* 1975).

It was once hoped that leucopenia could be detected early and agranulocytosis prevented by carrying out regular white blood cell counts. The reaction develops so rapidly, however, that this practice has now been abandoned. Leucocyte counts need only be carried out in patients who develop fever or other manifestations of sepsis. A low white blood cell count noted before starting treatment with an antipsychotic drug could indicate a low proliferative potential within the marrow and is therefore an indication for choosing a neuroleptic, such as fluphenazine or haloperidol, that is not known to cause agranulocytosis. Although cross-sensitivity reactions to other antipsychotic drugs can occur, these drugs may also be used as alternative treatments on recovery from agranulocytosis.

THE HEART

Some antipsychotic drugs, especially thioridazine which has a quinidine-like action on the heart, can cause ECG abnormalities, cardiac conduction defects, and arrhythmias (Alexander and Nino 1969; Lapierre *et al.* 1969; Ayd 1970; Crane 1970; *British Medical Journal* 1971; Raj and Benson 1975; Fowler *et al.* 1976; Deglin *et al.* 1977; Wheatley 1981).

The ECG abnormalities are non-specific. Prolonged PR (PQ) and QT intervals, widening of QRS complexes, depression of ST segments and most commonly blunting, flattening, or notching of T-waves, and the appearance of U-waves may occur. These changes are seen more often in those with pre-existing heart disease (Swett and Shader 1977). In those without cardiac disease they are harmless and reversible. The abnormalities resemble those seen in hypokalaemia and may disappear after administering potassium. It is thought, in fact, that phenothiazines affect the T-waves and U-waves by shifting potassium into the intracellular compartment (Alvarez-Mena and Frank 1973). Some effects—RST segment and T-wave changes—can be caused by excessive anxiety.

Antipsychotic drugs, especially high-dose low-potency phenothiazines given in large doses, may also cause atrio-ventricular block, bundle branch block, atrial and ventricular extrasystoles, atrial flutter, ventricular tachycardia, and fibrillation. They may precipitate congestive cardiac failure in those predisposed. The elderly, particularly those with pre-existing atherosclerotic and hypertensive heart disease, are especially vulnerable to cardiac effects. The exact mechanism of production of these effects is not known but anticholinergic, adrenolytic, and other actions have been incriminated and the high levels of circulating catecholamines that are sometimes found may be relevant.

Lesions in intramyocardial arterioles and the arteriolar-capillary bed, deposition of acid mucopolysaccharide in and near these altered arterioles, and degeneration of myocardial muscle have been demonstrated histologically in patients dying after many years' treatment with phenothiazines (Richardson *et al*. 1966). It has been suggested that these sub-endothelial lesions are responsible for the ECG changes and conduction defects. It has been speculated that the temporary increase in plasma aminotransferase activity observed in some patients could possibly be due to microinfarcts resulting from these vascular changes (Crane 1970).

Patients receiving phenothiazines may die suddenly for no apparent reason (Kelly *et al*. 1963; Hollister and Kosek 1965; Leestma and Koenig 1968; Crane 1970; Moore and Book 1970; Peele and von Loetzen 1973; Wendkos 1979). Sudden death has also been reported in a patient receiving haloperidol (Ketal *et al*. 1979). To date 16 cases of cardiac arrest occurring during treatment with antipsychotic drugs have been reported to the British Committee on Safety of Medicines. Thirteen of these were fatal; the suspect drugs were chlorpromazine, clopenthixol, droperidol, fluphenazine, haloperidol, prochlorperazine, thioridazine, and trifluoperazine. Sudden death is more likely to occur when the drugs are given in large doses and in those with pre-existing heart disease or general physical disability. Hyperpyrexia, aspiration and asphyxia, vasodilation and hypotension, and inhibition of regulatory centres in the brain have all been incriminated as mechanisms leading to death although cardiotoxicity is now the most widely accepted explanation. It is thought that a toxic cardiomyopathy leads to death by ventricular fibrillation or cardiac arrest. Ultrastructural damage to the heart associated with circulating auto-antibodies, especially those to skeletal muscle, heart, DNA, mitochondria, and smooth muscle has been found in patients who have died from such fatal arrhythmias (Guillan *et al*. 1977).

The occurrence of cardiac complications during treatment with antipsychotic drugs, especially serious conduction defects and arrhythmias, calls for a cardiological assessment. The possibility of previously unrecognized heart disease should be investigated and treatment of arrhythmias may need to be initiated. Fainting episodes or 'blackouts' occurring for the first time during treatment call for monitoring of the cardiac rhythm. Those with pre-existing heart disease, especially if associated with serious arrhythmias or delayed intraventricular conduction, are more prone to cardiac reactions, but in general it is impossible to predict for prophylactic reasons which individuals will be the victims of the more serious untoward effects.

RESPIRATORY SYSTEM

Antipsychotic drugs given in therapeutic doses have few clinically relevant effects on the respiratory system although respiratory depression may occur if they are taken in overdose or in combination with other drugs that depress respiration. This is of clinical relevance only in patients with obstructive airways disease. Neuroleptic-induced dystonia and dyskinesia can affect respiratory muscles as well as muscles elsewhere. Flaherty and Lahmeyer (1978), for example, reported two cases of patients who were found cyanotic and gasping for breath after receiving haloperidol. It was thought that they might have had laryngeo–pharyngeal dystonia. Asthma may result from an anaphylactic reaction to phenothiazines and chlorpromazine has been alleged to cause pulmonary infiltration associated with eosinophilia and other clinical manifestations of a hypersensitivity reaction (Shear 1978). There have also been isolated case reports of systemic lupus erythematosus-like illnesses with pulmonary involvement and pleural effusions (Dubois *et al.* 1972; Goldman *et al.* 1980). In general, special care need only be taken when prescribing antipsychotic drugs for patients with severe asthma or respiratory depression, especially when these compounds are given with other drugs that depress respiration.

THE ALIMENTARY TRACT

Symptoms referable to the alimentary tract, such as dry mouth, nausea, abdominal discomfort, and bowel dysfunction, are difficult to relate to drug treatment because they occur in normal subjects and as manifestations of psychiatric disorders. They also occur as placebo side-effects. Antipsychotic drugs can, however, cause oral and gastrointestinal symptoms occurring either in isolation or as manifestations of a generalized disturbance. Dryness of the mouth, for example, may be the only symptom or a manifestation of generalized autonomic dysfunction. It may be a contributing factor to the development of dental caries, oral candidiasis (moniliasis), and bacterial parotitis. Dislocation of the jaw (although not strictly part of the alimentary tract) can result from neuroleptic-induced dystonia (Abelson 1968; Ryan and LaDow 1968; Smith 1973) or angioneurotic oedema caused by pheno-thiazines (Lutz and Rotov 1964). When drug-related, oral and gastro-intestinal symptoms may be mediated through central or peripheral mechanisms. Anticholinergic and anti-adrenergic mechanisms may be involved in their production. Gastrointestinal effects tend to be dose-related and dependent on individual susceptibility. Pre-existing disorders, such as gastric atrophy, peptic ulceration, coeliac disease, and ulcerative colitis, predispose to their occurrence. Vomiting occurring during treatment with phenothiazines seems paradoxical because of the anti-emetic properties of these drugs.

The occurrence of paralytic ileus has already been noted (see section on

'Autonomic nervous system'). Of 27 cases induced by phenothiazines, 10 resulted in death, underlining the seriousness of the condition. Seven of the patients who died had also been receiving antiparkinson drugs (Evans *et al.* 1979) which is perhaps a further reason why they should not be prescribed routinely as often as they are (see section on 'Interactions with antipsychotic drugs'). Death results from the retention of gas and fluids, causing mucosal damage and ischaemia which in turn leads to septicaemia and peritonitis due to invasion by enteric organisms.

Constipation and faecal impaction with or without colonic dilation induced by antipsychotic drugs occurs much more often than adynamic ileus (Goulston 1976; Sriram *et al.* 1979). Gut motility is controlled by the autonomic nervous system and various neurotransmitters are involved. These include acetylcholine, noradrenaline, dopamine, and 5-HT. Circulating neuropeptides also play a part. Motilin, a polypeptide produced in the duodenal and jejunal mucosa, influences myoelectrical activity in the colon (Christofides and Bloom, 1981; Itoh 1981). Antipsychotic drugs affect gut motility by their effects on neurotransmitters, especially dopamine and acetylcholine (Lechin and Van der Dijs 1979), but motilin may also be involved as it is found in the serum in increased amounts in patients receiving neuroleptics (Allen *et al.* 1982). It is not known, however, if this is due to a direct drug effect or if it is a secondary phenomenon that comes into play in an attempt to restore normal gut motility.

When anticholinergic mechanisms are thought to be involved in the production of gastrointestinal side-effects, the dose of the offending agent should be reduced or an antipsychotic drug with less anticholinergic action substituted. Paralytic ileus calls for urgent medical treatment. It may require decompression of the small bowel via a nasogastric tube or of the colon by intubation, depending on the site of maximum distention, and sometimes digital evacuation of faeces. A surgical opinion should be obtained as soon as possible.

THE LIVER

The liver is particularly prone to adverse drug effects because it is the principal organ involved in detoxification. However, it is often difficult to relate hepatic reactions to the administration of drugs, especially in patients with nutritional deficiencies or infectious diseases, in those with a previous history of alcoholism or other disorders that affect liver function, and in those who have received other potentially hepatotoxic drugs. Adverse effects are mostly mild, clinically unrecognizable, and only identifiable by liver function tests (LFTs) because of the liver's large functional reserve. Their severity depends on hepatic blood flow, oxygenation, and enzyme activity. These may be adversely affected by liver disease and the concomitant use of other drugs metabolized in the liver.

Hepatic reactions may be predictable or unpredictable, occurring in susceptible individuals with an immunological defect or an inherent abnormality of hepatic enzymes. The resulting damage may be hepatocellular, cholestatic, or mixed. Antipsychotic drugs tend to produce cholestatic jaundice, but variations can occur.

Cholestatic jaundice may be caused by phenothiazines and rarely other neuroleptics (e.g. Fuller *et al.* 1977). The clinical picture is similar to that seen in other cases of obstructive jaundice with malaise, weakness, fatigue, anorexia, nausea, abdominal discomfort, fever, pale stools, and dark urine. There may be hepatosplenomegaly and, if jaundice is prolonged, widespread xanthelomata. Laboratory investigations reveal hyperbilirubinaemia and bile in the urine. There are increased levels of serum alkaline phosphatase, aspartate aminotransferase (AST, previously known as serum glutamic oxalacetic transaminase), and alanine aminotransferase (ALT, previously called serum glutamic pyruvic transaminase). Liver biopsy shows centrilobular cholestasis with little or no parenchymal damage and only a mild inflammatory response. Inspissated bile in the hepatic canaliculi may be caused by the intrahepatic precipitation of protein and glycoprotein (Clarke *et al.* 1972).

Reports of chlorpromazine-induced jaundice, once relatively common, are now rare. It was therefore suggested that there might have been impurities in earlier products. Subclinical reactions with abnormalities of liver function tests only (Dickes *et al.* 1957) or abnormalities found on liver biopsy (Hollister and Hall 1966) occur more often than those with jaundice. Spontaneous recovery usually occurs and jaundice has been known to regress despite continued treatment (Skromak *et al.* 1957). Rarely, cholestatic jaundice leads to cirrhosis (Kohn and Myerson 1961; Read *et al.* 1961).

Hypersensitivity mechanisms have been incriminated in the production of cholestatic jaundice because it is not dose-related and it sometimes occurs after a single dose of drug. It occurs after a latent period of two to four weeks and may be accompanied by other allergic manifestations such as eosinophilia. Jaundice may recur if the offending drug is re-introduced and cross-sensitivity between phenothiazines has been said to occur. Antimitochondrial antibodies have been reported in some patients (Rodriguez *et al.* 1969).

Diffuse hepatocellular jaundice occurs during treatment with neuroleptics very much less frequently than cholestatic jaundice, but hypersensitivity mechanisms have been suspected with this reaction also. It has been suggested that liver cell damage occurs as a result of covalent-bonding to hepatocyte fractions or an immunological attack directed towards a metabolite-liver cell complex (Read 1979). The hepatitis, however, is mostly indistinguishable from viral hepatitis and could be due to a coincidental viral infection. It is possible that the drug facilitates the emergence of viral hepatitis or aggravates a pre-existing infection. Despite these considerations, spread from one person to another does not occur and the mortality from drug-induced hepatitis is greater than that from viral hepatitis.

When a patient being treated with an antipsychotic drug becomes jaundiced it should not be assumed that the drug is necessarily responsible;

other causes should be excluded. But at the same time the suspect drug should be discontinued and another agent less prone to cause hepatic reactions, such as haloperidol, substituted. Recovery usually occurs spontaneously within a few weeks.

URINARY TRACT

Reference has already been made to difficulty in micturition as an anticholinergic effect of antipsychotic drugs (see section on 'Autonomic nervous system'). This may lead to retention of urine particularly in the elderly if autonomic effects are superimposed on genito-urinary disease such as prostatic hypertrophy. Retention is associated with vesical atonicity allegedly due to competitive antagonism of acetylcholine at the neuromuscular junctions within the detrusor. Incomplete emptying of the bladder, distention with overflow, and eventually permanent loss of bladder tone due to damage to smooth muscle, elastic and collagenous tissue may occur (Merrill and Markland 1972). On rare occasions, urinary obstruction may be complicated by water intoxication provoked by an excessive intake of fluids due to decreased salivary secretion (Glomaud *et al.* 1976). Urinary incontinence not due to overflow has been reported (Nurnberg and Ambrosini 1979) and this may be seen in patients with neuroleptic-induced catatonia (see section on 'Central nervous system') (Behrman 1972; Gelenberg and Mandel 1977). Acute renal failure can result from massive destruction of muscle with myoglobinuria in subjects who have phenothiazine-induced hyperpyrexia (Mann and Boger 1978).

If anticholinergic mechanisms are thought to be contributing to urinary difficulty, as in the case of gastrointestinal side-effects the dose of the offending drug should be decreased or a neuroleptic with less anticholinergic properties substituted. If underlying organic pathology is suspected, the opinion of a urologist should be sought.

EMBRYO AND FETUS

Antipsychotic drugs are prescribed during pregnancy not only for the treatment of psychoses but also in the management of complications of pregnancy such as hyperemesis gravidarum. Most antipsychotic drugs cross the placenta and may therefore affect the fetus. The rates of transfer of drugs from mother to fetus depend on the concentration gradient, surface area and thickness of the placental membrane, rate of blood flow in the intervillous space, placental enzyme activity and molecular weight, configuration, polarity, protein-binding capacity, and lipid solubility of the drug (Moya and Thorndike 1962; Barnes 1974). The effects of a drug on the embryo and fetus are not the same as those on the mother because of immaturity of detoxification mechanisms and metabolic degradation processes in the fetus. The effects vary according to the drug, its concentration, and the genetic constitution and stage of development of the embryo and fetus. Some drugs have a predilection for specific organs. Prolonged exposure at a low dose is generally less harmful than transient high concentrations at vulnerable stages of development.

Dysmorphogenesis may occur as a direct or indirect action of the drug. Alternatively, the drug may act as a co-factor or may sensitize the embryo to the harmful effects of some other agent. Potentially harmful drugs given before the blastocyst is embedded may lead to its destruction and resorption. The embryo is most susceptible during the period of rapid growth between implantation and complete organogenesis, that is from the first to the ninth week. Individual organs are most vulnerable at the time of maximum differentiation. Drugs given after the fourth month do not cause dysmorphogenesis; they enter the fetal circulation in concentrations similar to that of the mother but produce exaggerated effects because of immaturity of the fetus's metabolic and enzyme systems.

There is little specific knowledge about the effects of antipsychotic drugs *in utero*. Few conclusions can be drawn from animal experiments because of species differences. Large-scale epidemiological studies have either not been carried out or their methodological limitations do not allow definite conclusions to be reached. Because significant numbers of apparently normal human pregnancies end in spontaneous abortion or in the birth of babies with congenital abnormalities, vast numbers of mothers would have to be investigated to decide if a small increase in the frequency of occurrence of a common congenital abnormality could be attributable to a particular drug. Added to these difficulties are the facts that mothers forget what drugs they have taken during pregnancy, medical record-keeping is often deficient, and there is usually no record at all of over-the-counter medication taken or other chemicals to which the mother may have been exposed such as preservatives and pesticide residues in food.

There have been isolated reports of congenital abnormalities in the offspring of mothers who have taken antipsychotic drugs during pregnancy, for example a case of ectromelia in an infant whose mother was given chlorpromazine and meclazine (O'Leary and O'Leary 1964), complete transformation of the great vessels with a patent foramen ovale in a baby whose mother had received thioridazine and trifluoperazine (Vince 1969), and multiple congenital limb malformations in the stillborn infant of a mother who had taken haloperidol (Kopelman *et al.* 1975). These could well have been coincidental, and there is evidence to suggest that antipsychotic drugs are not teratogenic (Ananth 1975) and do not increase the incidence of death *in utero* (Rieder *et al.* 1975). On the other hand, large-scale surveys have suggested that exposure to phenothiazines may result in a greater than expected incidence of congenital abnormalities (Rumeau-Rouquette *et al.* 1977), for example cardiovascular malformations attributed to prochlorperazine (Heinonen *et al.* 1977).

Attention has been paid not only to dysmorphogenesis but also to behavioural teratogenicity. Animal experiments have suggested that drugs that are teratogens of the CNS are also behavioural teratogens, even when given in doses lower than those that cause congenital malformations. The behavioural effects depend on the stage of development at which the drug is administered and the dose administered. The period of susceptibility is longer than that in which malformations occur, although maximum susceptibility is similar to that for dysmorphogenesis. Some agents that are behavioural teratogens are specific in the effects they produce (Vorhees *et al*. 1979). The implications for humans of these observations in animals is not understood. Until it can be established beyond all reasonable doubt that antipsychotic drugs do not have permanent harmful effects on the embryo and fetus they should be given during pregnancy only when absolutely essential. Rarely if ever is the patient more in need of a prolonged drug holiday than during the first nine weeks of pregnancy.

THE NEWBORN

Newborn infants may be affected by antipsychotic drugs received through the placenta. The newborn, especially if premature, is particularly vulnerable to drug effects because of deficiencies in the immature liver and kidney of drug-metabolizing enzymes, limited renal clearance, low protein-binding capacity, and greater permeability of the blood–brain barrier. Immaturity of the glucuronyl transferase system is one of the most important of these.

Phenothiazines given to pregnant women may lead to neurological disturbances such as hypertonia, tremor, restlessness, and athetoid movements (presumed to be due to extrapyramidal dysfunction), respiratory depression, hypothermia, and hypotension in their newborn babies (Hill *et al*. 1966; Levy and Wisniewski 1974). It has been suggested that high doses of phenothiazines given for long periods during pregnancy may cause retinal damage in the newborn (Stirrat and Beard 1973). It has also been suspected that they increase the incidence of jaundice in premature infants but not in those born at full-term (Scokel and Jones 1962), although this is disputed by other clinicians. Phenothiazines can potentiate analgesics and anaesthetics given during labour to produce neonatal depression with respiratory difficulties (Hodges and Bennett 1959; Cohen and Olson 1970).

Most drugs are excreted in breast milk. The concentration reached depends on the dose, duration of treatment, pharmacokinetics of the drug in the mother, her hepatic and renal function, the drug's lipid solubility, protein-binding properties and degree of ionization, the volume and constituents of the milk, and other factors (Knowles 1965; Ayd 1973; *British Medical Journal* 1979). Relatively little research into the effects of antipsychotic drugs on the newborn due to excretion in breast milk has been carried out, but in general they do not appear to produce serious adverse reactions.

Whether or not antipsychotic drugs given during the late stages of pregnancy or delivery are known to have effects on the newborn, they should be avoided whenever possible. When it is essential that they should be given for the health of the mother they should be prescribed in the lowest dose possible. When reactions occur, other possible causes should be investigated, and the appropriate perinatal and neonatal paediatric care given.

EFFECTS OF OVERDOSES

If antipsychotic drugs are taken in overdoses the patient may develop a toxic confusional or delirious state with clouding of consciousness, disorientation, agitation, and perceptual disturbances. Drowsiness may progress to stupor or coma. Twitching of muscles, dystonic reactions, and convulsions may occur. The pupils become meiotic and the tendon reflexes diminished. Hypothermia frequently occurs but it may later be superseded by pyrexia and hyperthermia. The patient also develops tachycardia and hypotension. Cardiotoxicity may occur, especially after overdoses of piperazine phenothiazines (Donlan and Tupin 1977). The electroencephalogram is of low voltage with diffuse slowing. Death may result from respiratory failure, prolonged shock, or cardiac arrest; it occurs only rarely and mostly in children. Adult patients have survived overdoses of 9.75 g of chlorpromazine and 8 g of chlorprothixene, while no deaths have been reported as a result of overdoses of haloperidol (Hollister 1983). The most lethal neuroleptic taken in overdose is thioridazine, death sometimes occurring within a few hours of ingestion (Donlon and Tupin 1974).

After a patient takes an overdose, gastric lavage should be carried out and the general principles of caring for the unconscious patient attended to. Convulsions should be treated with parenteral diazepam or phenytoin unless there is a high risk of respiratory failure. Hypotension should be treated with an α-adrenoceptor stimulant, such as noradrenaline, and hypothermia countered by the use of warm blankets and a heat cradle.

INTERACTIONS WITH ANTIPSYCHOTIC DRUGS

Antipsychotic drugs may interact with a wide variety of other drugs. Some interactions occur consistently, but most are idiosyncratic occurring in only a small proportion of those exposed to the risk. They cannot always be predicted from animal pharmacology, but are more likely to be when the pharmacokinetics and mechanisms of action of the drugs are known. Many interactions are of theoretical rather than practical interest. Those of clinical importance form a relatively small proportion of the total but their seriousness should be appreciated.

Interactions with antipsychotic drugs are mediated through different mechanisms including; (1) interference with absorption; (2) potentiation or antagonism at the same site or affecting the same process; (3) interference with intracellular transport (amine uptake by sympathetic neurones); and (4) stimulation or inhibition of metabolism (Prescott 1973). Examples of these are shown in Table 13.1. Further details concerning these and other examples of interactions with neuroleptics were summarized by Stockley (1972), Prestcott (1973), Hansten (1976), Griffin and D'Arcy (1979), and Avery and

TABLE 13.1.   *Interactions with antipsychotic drugs*

Drugs with which antipsychotic drugs interact	Effect	Mechanism
Adrenaline	Chlorpromazine blocks action of adrenaline	α-Adrenergic blockade
Alcohol	Enhanced CNS and respiratory depression	Summation
Anaesthetics (halogenated)	Profound hypotension	Summation
Antacids	Decreased absorption of chlorpromazine	Formation of adsorption complexes
Anti-anxiety agents	Enhanced CNS and respiratory depression	Summation
	Phenobarbitone decreases plasma levels of neuroleptics	Hepatic enzyme induction $\rightarrow$ increased metabolism
Anticoagulants	Increased anticoagulant effect $\rightarrow$ prolonged bleeding time	Inhibition of hepatic metabolism
Anticonvulsants	Phenothiazines decrease plasma phenytoin levels (opposite effect may occur)	Hepatic enzyme induction $\rightarrow$ increased metabolism (inhibition of metabolism)
Antidepressants		
Monoamine oxidase inhibitors (MAOIs)	Hypotension	Summation
	Increased extrapyramidal reactions	?MAOIs inhibit metabolism of phenothiazines
Tricyclics	Enhanced CNS depression	Summation
	Enhanced anticholinergic effects	Summation
	Chlorpromazine, perphenazine and haloperidol increase plasma levels of tricyclic antidepressants, decrease plasma levels of metabolites	Inhibition of hepatic metabolism
Antidiabetic agents	Phenothiazines interfere with diabetic control	Phenothiazine-induced hyperglycaemia
Antihistamines	Promethazine may antagonize effects of antipsychotic drugs	Not known
Antihypertensive drugs	Phenothiazines decrease antihypertensive effect of guanethidine, bethanidine, and debrisoquine	Decreased neuronal uptake of antihypertensive drugs by adrenergic neurones
Methyldopa	Severe hypotension	Summation
Antiparkinson agents	Enhanced CNS depression	Summation
	Increased anticholinergic effects	Summation

TABLE 13.1. *Continued*

Drugs with which antipsychotic drugs interact	Effect	Mechanism
	Antiparkinson agents may decrease plasma levels of neuroleptic	Enzyme induction increased metabolism
	Possible increased chance of tardive dyskinesia	Not known
	Hypothermia	Interference with thermoregulatory system, exact mechanism not known
Corticosteroids	Phenothiazines increase absorption of corticosteriods	Decreased gastrointestinal motility due to anticholinergic effects of phenothiazine
	Increased risk of thioridazine-induced cardiotoxicity	Hypokalaemia
Digoxin	Phenothiazines increase lithium toxicity	Decreased gastrointestinal motility due to anticholinergic effects of phenothiazine
Diuretics	Increase risk of thioridazine-induced cardiotoxicity	Hypokalaemia
Lithium	Antipsychotic drugs increase lithium toxicity	Decreased lithium excretion (opposite effect has been reported)
	'Neuroleptic malignant syndrome'	Not known
Metaclopramide	Increased extrapyramidal effects	Summation of antidopaminergic action
Narcotic analgesics	Enhanced CNS and respiratory depression	Summation
Oral contraceptives	Oestrogen-containing oral contraceptives increase neuroleptic-induced galactorrhoea	Enhanced prolactin secretion (may also occur with other drugs that stimulate prolactin secretion, e.g. reserpine, methyldopa)
Quinidine	Thioridazine-induced cardiotoxicity	Summation of quinidine-like effects
Succinylcholine	Prolonged neuromuscular blockade	Decreased anticholinesterase

Heel (1980). Psychotropic drugs may interact not only with other drugs, but also with other chemicals and foodstuff. It has been shown for instance that antipsychotic drugs form insoluble precipitates with coffee and especially tea (Kulhanek *et al.* 1979).

Some of the most frequently occurring drug effects are due to summation. Oversedation, a particularly troublesome problem in the elderly, may result from the additive effects of anti-anxiety (including hypnotic), antidepressant, and antihistaminic agents (including over-the-counter preparations) taken with antipsychotic drugs. Excessive sedation may also occur when patients on neuroleptics drink alcohol. The anticholinergic effects of antipsychotic drugs summate with those of antiparkinson agents and tricyclic antidepressants while their α-adrenoceptor-blocking effects may be added to those of a variety of drugs, including antidepressants and antihypertensive agents, to produce hypotensive episodes. The antidopaminergic actions of metaclopramide summate with those of neuroleptics with an increased risk of extrapyramidal effects.

A drug combination that has caused concern is that of haloperidol and lithium. Cohen and Cohen (1974) reported severe encephalopathic symptoms, including weakness, lethargy, fever, tremulousness, increasing confusion, extrapyramidal and cerebellar dysfunction, associated with leucocytosis and increased blood urea nitrogen, fasting blood sugar, and serum enzymes, in four patients receiving large doses of these drugs (the patients were also receiving benztropine mesylate). Two of the patients had widespread irreversible brain damage. Other investigators have also reported untoward effects of neuroleptics combined with lithium (e.g. Spring 1979; Spring and Frankel 1981; Singh 1982) though most of these were not as severe as those described by the Cohens. Baastrup *et al.* (1976) found no evidence of severe untoward effects in a retrospective study of 425 patients who had been treated simultaneously with haloperidol and lithium, albeit only occasionally at high doses. They concluded that clinicians should not be discouraged from using the combination so long as there is adequate monitoring of drug effects. Ayd (1975) also supported the carefully monitored use of the combination and, while accepting that there were puzzling aspects of the cases reported by the Cohens, concluded that at least some effects were due to lithium rather than its combination with haloperidol. Ayd also suggested that the patients might have had an underlying organic brain syndrome and highlighted violations of the rules of safe and proper prescribing that had been carried out—the injudicious use of the combination (especially in high doses) when the patient was already improving, failure to decrease the dose when signs of toxicity were noted, and failure to stop treatment when the patient's condition was worsening.

Many interactions can be prevented if unnecessary drug combinations are avoided. One of the combinations most frequently used in the treatment of psychoses is that of antiparkinson agents and antipsychotic drugs which are often given together as a 'routine' treatment of schizophrenia. Such a routine should be abandoned because only a relatively small proportion of patients need antiparkinson drugs for long periods and discontinuing them does not necessarily lead to a return of extrapyramidal effects (Edwards 1979*b*). Furthermore, some antiparkinson agents decrease plasma chlorpromazine levels (Rivera-Calimlim *et al.* 1973; Loga *et al.* 1975) and may thereby decrease its antipsychotic effect (Singh and Kay 1975). The combination increases the risk of toxic confusional states or anticholinergic crises (Hollister 1967; Dynes 1968), tardive dyskinesia (Hunter *et al.* 1964; Crane 1968; Kiloh *et al.* 1973; Klawans 1973), hyperthermia (Westlake and Rastegar 1973), and death from paralytic ileus (Evans *et al.* 1979) (see section on 'The alimentary tract'). This is discussed further in Chapter 12.

COMPARATIVE DRUG EFFECTS

There is no entirely convincing evidence that one antipyschotic drug is therapeutically superior to another (see Chapter 11). The effect of individual drugs on other physiological systems has therefore become of increasing importance in determining drug choices. Reference to differential effects have been made throughout this chapter, but many of the statements made should be interpreted with caution for the following reasons.

Many claims concerning relative unwanted effects have been based on clinical impressions or comparisons in which drugs have not been given under identical conditions. It is generally accepted that double-blind randomized controlled trials are essential for comparing the therapeutic effectiveness of drugs. It is also well known that the course of such trials, from their inception to the presentation of the final results, is littered with potential sources of bias. But it seems to be less well appreciated that the methodology of studies comparing the effects of drugs on other systems should be equally sophisticated. One often finds that the more meticulous the methodology the fewer the differences shown. Some reactions have been reported as a result of the offending agent being given in enormous doses. It is possible that similar effects would have occurred if other drugs, regarded as being free from these effects, had been given in equally large quantities. The more intensively a drug is investigated the more likely it is that adverse effects will be found. As a result a more thoroughly tested drug is sometimes erroneously regarded as being more toxic than a less intensively investigated compound.

Despite these considerations, there are widely held beliefs, sometimes supported by experimental evidence, that different antipsychotic drugs have quantitatively different effects on the same system. It is thought, for instance, that low-potency neuroleptics such as chlorpromazine and thioridazine have a greater tendency to produce sedation, hypotension, and ECG changes than have high-potency drugs like fluphenazine and trifluoperazine. These differential effects are believed to be dependent on the drugs' anticholinergic and anti-adrenergic potency relative to their antidopaminergic properties (see Chapter 11). Table 11.2, p. 289, gives some clues as to the relative tendency of a small range of widely-used antipsychotic drugs to produce some common effects, although this is in no way intended to be comprehensive or accurately quantified for the reasons discussed above.

It will be noted from Table 11.2 that chlorpromazine and thioridazine appear to have more severe unwanted effects than other antipsychotic drugs. Yet in a questionnaire study of the prescribing habits of British teachers of psychiatry it was shown that these two drugs ranked first and sixth, respectively, amongst all other antipsychotic drugs (Edwards 1982). In fact chlorpromazine comfortably outranked all other drugs. This suggests either that university teachers of psychiatry and psychiatric tutors are so conservative in their prescribing that they are uninfluenced by drug reactions or that concern by psychopharmacologists over the comparative effects of antipsychotic drugs on other systems is less important that it seems. Whichever the case, it is unfortunate that there is not a more objective basis for choosing antipsychotic drugs and that one drug may be compared unfavourably with others on the flimsiest of evidence.

TREATMENT AND PREVENTION OF ADVERSE EFFECTS

Many of the less severe effects of antipsychotic drugs on other systems improve or disappear spontaneously while treatment continues. Others respond to reassurance or disappear when the dose is decreased or treatment discontinued. Sometimes reintroducing the drug or substituting a related compound does not lead to a recurrence, which is not surprising when one considers all the variables involved. Minor unwanted effects may also respond to symptomatic treatment or placebos. While most reactions should be managed by the psychiatrist who prescribed the offending drug some, for example paralytic ileus or urinary retention, call for urgent specialist treatment (see sections on 'The alimentary tract' and 'Urinary system').

Many untoward effects can be prevented if drugs are used with caution or avoided altogether in conditions where pathological disturbances of tissue sensitivity or pharmacokinetics lead to exaggerated reactions. Depending on the drug, such reactions may occur in patients with organic brain disease, cardiac, hepatic, and renal pathology, angle-closure glaucoma, prostatic hypertrophy, blood dyscrasias, and a predisposition to allergy. When treating patients with these conditions and particularly when 'rapid neuroleptization' is called for care should be taken in the choice of antipsychotic drug. In the case of a patient with severe heart disease, for instance, a drug regarded as being free from significant cardiovascular effects such as haloperidol should be administered (Ayd 1978). Particular care should also be taken when prescribing antipsychotic drugs for children and the elderly, especially those who are debilitated. Drugs that are not essential for the treatment of severely disabling mental illnesses should be avoided during pregnancy whether or not they are known to affect the fetus. Unless they are really necessary they should also be avoided during breast feeding. They should be used with great care in patients who drive or work in dangerous situations.

The greater the number of patients exposed to drugs the greater the prevalence of unwanted effects. Avoiding unnecessary drugs and adhering to sound principles of prescribing are therefore important preventive measures (Edwards 1979a, b). Drug combinations that are not essential should be avoided. Such combinations provide particularly serious problems for the elderly and it is well known how mentally disturbed elderly patients often improve dramatically simply by discontinuing the large numbers of drugs that have been prescribed for them. Ironically, these often include antipsychotic drugs given for the disturbed behaviour itself.

CONCLUSIONS

In a review which highlights the unwanted effects of neuroleptics it is difficult to avoid giving an apparently biased impression of antipsychotic drug treatment. It should therefore be reiterated that many of the serious effects reported are very rare and many others occur mainly in patients with pre-existing physical illnesses. The more commonly occurring reactions are a relatively small price to pay for the immense relief from suffering that neuroleptics have produced.

It is essential to study unwanted effects of drugs, not only to balance the risks and benefits of treatment, but also because knowledge of the mechanism of production of effects on other physiological systems may one day provide inroads into the understanding of the mode of therapeutic action of drugs. This in turn may throw light on the aetiology of mental illnesses. But before the causes of these illnesses are found a long journey lies ahead and millions of mentally ill people will be treated with antipsychotic drugs. The untoward effects of these can be kept to a minimum by adhering to sound principles of prescribing.

References

Abelson, C. B. (1968). Phenothiazine induced neck-face syndrome: report of case. *J. oral Surg.* **26**, 649–50.

Alexander, C. S. and Nino, A. (1969). Cardiovascular complications in young patients taking psychotropic drugs. *Am. Heart J.* **78**, 757–69.

Allen, J. M., Christofides, N. D., Cramer, P. A., Steiner, J., and Bloom, S. R. (1982). Elevated motilin levels in patients treated with antidepressant and neuroleptic drugs. *Br. J. Psychiat.* **141**, 27–9.

Alvarez-Mena, S. C. and Frank, M. J. (1973). Phenothiazine-induced T-wave abnormalities. *J. Am. med. Assoc.* **224**, 1730–3.

Ananth, J. (1975). Congenital malformations with psychopharmacologic agents. *Comprehens. Psychiat.* **16**, 437–45.

Appleton, W. S. (1968). The false drug side-effect: which patients complain. *Br. J. Psychiat.* **114**, 197–201.

Assem, E-S, K. (1977). Drug allergy. In *Textbook of adverse drug reactions* (ed. D. M. Davies), pp. 380–96. Oxford University Press, Oxford.

Avery, G. S. and Heel, R. C. (1980). Guide to the clinically more important drug interactions. In *Drug treatment: principles and practice of clinical pharmacology* (ed. G. S. Avery), pp. 1252–72. ADIS Press, Sydney.

Ayd, F. J. (1969). Phenothiazine-induced agranulocytosis: the 'at risk' patient. *Int. Drug. Ther. Newslett.* **4**, 13–20.

—— ——(1970). Cardiovascular effects of phenothiazines. *Int. Drug. Ther. Newslett.* **5**, 1–8.

——(1973). Excretion of psychotropic drugs in human breast milk. *Int. Drug. Ther. Newslett.* **8**, 33–40.

——(1975). Lithium–haloperidol for mania: is it safe or hazardous? *Int. Drug Ther. Newslett.* **10**, 29–36.

——(1978). Intravenous haloperidol therapy. *Int. Drug Ther. Newslett.* **13**, 20–3.

Baastrup, P. C., Hollnagel, P., Sorensen, R., and Schou, M. (1976). Adverse reactions in treatment with lithium carbonate and haloperidol. *J. Am. med. Assoc.* **236**, 2645–6.

Baker, H. (1972). Drug reactions. In *Textbook of dermatology*, 3rd ed, Vol. 1 (ed. A. Rook, D. S. Wilkinson, and F. J. J. Ebling), pp. 1111–49. Blackwell, London.

Baldessarini, R. J. (1980). Drugs and the treatment of psychiatric disorders. In *The pharmacological basis of therapeutics*, 6th ed. (ed. A. G. Gilman, L. S. Goodman, and A. Gilman), pp. 391–447. Macmillan, New York.

Barnes, C. G. (1974). *Medical disorders in obstetric practice*. Blackwell, London.

Barnes, T. R. E. and Bridges, P. K. (1980). Disturbed behaviour produced by high-dose antipsychotropic drugs. *Br. med. J.* **2**, 274–5.

Beerman, H. and Kirshbaum, B. A. (1975). Drug eruptions (dermatitis medicamentosa). In *Dermatology* Vol. 1 (ed. S. L. Mioschella, D. M. Pillsbury, and H. J. Hurley, pp. 350–84. W. B. Saunders, Philadelphia.

Behrman, S. (1972). Mutism induced by phenothiazines. *Br. J. Psychiat.* **121**, 599–604.

Beumont, P. (1981). Endocrine effects of psychotropic drugs: a historical perspective. In *Handbook of biological psychiatry*. Part VI. *Practical applications of psychotropic drugs and other biological treatments* (ed. H. M. Van Praag, M. H. Lader, O. J. Raphaelson, and E. J. Sachar), pp. 39–56. Marcel Dekker, New York.

——Gelder, M. G., Friesen, H. G., Harris, G. W., MacKinnon, P. C. B., Mandelbrote, B. M., and Wiles, D. H. (1974*a*). The effects of phenothiazines on endocrine function: I. Patients with inappropriate lactation and amenorrhea. *Br. J. Psychiat.* **124**, 413–19.

——Corker, C. S., Friesen, H. G., Kolakowska, T., Mandelbrote, B. M., Marshall, J., Murray, M. A. F., and Wiles D. H. (1974*b*). The effects of phenothiazines on endocrine function: II. Effects in men and post-menopausal women. *Br. J. Psychiat.* **124**, 420–30.

Bond, W. S. and Yee, G. C. (1980). Ocular and cutaneous effects of chronic phenothiazine therapy. *Am. J. hosp. Pharm.* **37**, 74–8.

British Medical Journal (1971). Cardiovascular complications from psychotropic drugs. *Br. med. J.* **1**, 3.

——(1977). New strategies for drug monitoring. *Br. med. J.* **1**, 861–2.

——(1979). Drugs and breast-feeding. *Br. med. J.* **1**, 642.

Brody, I. A. (1959). Shock after administration of prochlorperazine in patient with phaeochromocytoma. Report of a case with spontaneous tumor destruction. *J. Am. med. Assoc.* **169**, 1749–51.

Brugmans, J., Verbruggen, F., Dom, J., and Schuermans, V. (1973). Prolactin, phenothiazines, admission to mental hospital, and carcinoma of the breast. *Lancet* **ii**, 502–3.

Caldwell, J. (1977). Toxic effects of psychotherapeutic agents. In *Psychotherapeutic drugs* (ed. E. Usdin and I. S. Forrest), pp. 437–81. Marcel Dekker, New York.

Cameron, M. E. (1967). Ocular melanosis with special reference to chlorpromazine. *Br. J. Ophthalmol.* **51**, 295–305.

Caroff, S. N. (1980). The neuroleptic malignant syndrome. *J. clin. Psychiat.* **41**, 79–83.

Chouinard, G. and Jones, B. D. (1980). Neuroleptic-induced supersensitivity psychosis; clinical and pharmacological characteristics. *Am. J. Psychiat.* **137**, 16–21.

Christofides, N. D. and Bloom, S. R. (1981). Motilin. In *Gut hormones* (ed. S. R. Bloom and J. M. Polak), pp. 273–9. Churchill Livingstone, Edinburgh.

Clarke, A. E., Maritz, V. M., and Denborough, M. A. (1972). Phenothiazines and jaundice. *Aust. NZ. J. Med.* **4**, 376–82.

Cluff, L. E., Caranosos, G. J., and Stewart, R. B. (1975). *Clinical problems with drugs.* W. B. Saunders Co., London.

Cohen, S. N. and Olson, W. A. (1970). Drugs that depress the newborn infant. *Pediat. Clin. N. Am.* **17**, 835–50.

Cohen, W. J. and Cohen, N. H, (1974). Lithium carbonate, haloperidol, and irreversible brain damage. *J. Am. med. Assoc.* **230**, 1282–7.

Connell, M. M., Poley, B. J., and McFarlane, J. R. (1964). Chorioretinopathy associated with thioridazine administration. *Arch. Ophthalmol.* **71**, 816–21.

Cools, A. R., Hendriks, G., and Korten, J. (1975). The acetylcholine–dopamine balance in the basal ganglia of rhesus monkeys and its role in dynamic, dystonic, dyskinetic and epileptoid motor activities. *J. neur. Transmission* **36**, 91–105.

Coombs, R. R. A. and Gell, P. G. H. (1975). Classification of allergic reactions responsible for clinical hypersensitivity and disease. In *Clinical aspects of immunology*, 3rd ed. (ed. P. G. H. Gell and R. R. A. Coombs), pp. 761–81. Blackwell, London.

Cooper, R. A. (1979). Heat and neuroleptics: a deadly combination. *Am. J. Psychiat.* **136**, 466–7.

Crane, G. E. (1968). Tardive dyskinesia in patients treated with major neuroleptics: review of the literature. *Am. J. Psychiat.* **124**, (suppl.), 40–8.

——(1970). Cardiac toxicity and psychotropic drugs. *Dis. nerv. Syst.* **31**, 534–9.

Creese, I., Burt, D. R., and Synder, S. A. (1978). Biochemical action of neuroleptic drugs. Focus on the dopamine receptor. In *Handbook of psychopharmacology*, Vol. 10, *Neuroleptics and schizophrenia* (ed. L. L. Iversen, S. D. Iversen, and S. H. Snyder). Plenum Press, New York.

Crews, S. J. (1962). Toxic effects on the eye and visual apparatus resulting from the systemic absorption of recently introduced agents. *Trans. Ophthal. Soc. UK.* **82**, 387–404.

——(1974). Adverse drug reactions in neuro-ophthalmology. In *Aspects of neuro-ophthalmology* (ed. S. I. Davidson), pp. 148–63. Butterworths, London.

Davidorf, F. H. (1973). Thioridazine pigmentary retinopathy. *Arch. Ophthalmol.* **90**, 251–5.

Davies, D. M. (Ed.) (1977). *Textbook of adverse drug reactions.* Oxford University Press, Oxford.

Deglin, S. M., Deglin, J. M., and Chung, E. K. (1977). Drug-induced cardiovascular diseases. *Drugs* **14**, 29–40.

de Gruchy, G. C. (1975). *Drug-induced blood disorders.* Blackwell, London.

de Wied, D. (1967). Chlorpromazine and endocrine function. *Pharmacol. Rev.* **19**, 251–88.

Dickes, R., Schenker, V., and Deutsch, L. (1957). Serial liver function and blood studies in patients receiving chlorpromazine. *New Engl. J. Med.* **256**, 1–7.

Donlon, P. T. and Tupin, J. P. (1977). Successful suicides with thioridazine and mesoridazine. A result of probable cardiotoxicity. *Arch. gen. Psychiat.* **34**, 955–7.

Doorman, B. W. and Schmidt, J. D. (1976). Association of priapism in pheno-thiazine therapy. *J. Urol.* **116**, 51–3.

Dubois, E. L., Tallman, E., and Wonka, R. A. (1972). Chlorpromazine-induced systemic lupus erythematosus. *J. Am. med. Assoc.* **221**, 595–6.

Ducomb, L. and Baldessarini, R. J. (1977). Timing and risk of bone marrow depression by psychotropic drugs. *Am. J. Psychiat.* **134**, 1294–5.

Dukes, M, N. G. (Ed.) (1980). The major tranquillizers. In *Side effects of drugs annual 4; a worldwide yearly survey of new data and trends* (ed. M. N. G. Dukes), pp. 38–41. Excerpta Medica, Amsterdam.

Dynes, J. B. (1968). Drug-induced parkinson-like syndrome. *Virginia med. Monthly* **95**, 746–50.

Edler, K., Gottfies, C. G., Haslund, J., and Ravn, J. (1971). Eye changes in connection with neuroleptic treatment especially concerning phenothiazines and thioxanthenes. *Acta psychiat. scand.* **47**, 377–85.

Edwards, J. G. (1977). Unwanted effects of psychotropic drugs. I.—some general considerations. *Practitioner* **218**, 556–62.

——(1979a). Overprescribing of psychotropic drugs. In *Current themes in psychiatry* (ed. R. Gaind and B. Hudson), pp. 97–115. Macmillan, London.

——(1979b). Principles of prescribing of psychotropic drugs. In *Current themes in schizophrenia* (ed. Guy Edwards), pp. 61–74. University of Southampton, Southampton.

——(1982). Psychotropic drug choices of teachers of psychiatry. *Br. J. clin. soc. Psychiat.* **1**, 88–9.

Epstein, S. (1968). Chlorpromazine photosensitivity. Phototoxic and photoallergic reactions. *Arch. Dermatol.* **98**, 354–63.

Erle, G., Basso, M., Federspil, G., Sicolo, N., and Scandellari, C. (1977). Effect of chlorpromazine on blood glucose and plasma insulin in man. *Eur. J. clin. Pharmacol.* **II**, 15–18.

Ettigi, P., Lal, S., and Friesen, H. G. (1973). Prolactin, phenothiazines, admission to mental hospital, and carcinoma of the breast. *Lancet* **ii**, 266–7.

Evans, D. L., Rogers, J. F., and Peiper, S. C. (1979). Intestinal dilation associated with phenothiazine therapy: a case report and literature review. *Am. J. Psychiat.* **136**, 970–2.

Fink, M. (1969). EEG and human psychopharmacology. *Ann. Rev. Pharmacol.* **9**, 241–58.

——(1981). Classification of psychoactive drug: quantitative EEG analysis in man. In *Handbook of biological psychiatry. VI. Practical application of psychotropic drugs and other biological treatments* (ed. M. H. van Praag, M. H. Lader, O. J. Rafaelsen, and E. J. Sacher), pp. 309–26. Marcel Dekker, New York.

Flaherty, J. A. and Lahmeyer, H. W. (1978). Laryngeal and pharyngeal dystonia as a possible cause of asphyxia with haloperidol treatment. *Am. J. Psychiat.* **135**, 1414–15.

Fowler, N. O., McCall, D., Chou, T. C., Holmes, J. C., and Hanenson, I. B. (1976). Electrocardiographic changes and cardiac arrhythmias in patients receiving psychotropic drugs. *Am. J. Cardiol.* **37**, 223–30.

Fuller, C. M., Yassinger, S., Donlon, P., Imperato, T. J., and Ruebner, B. (1977). Haloperidol-induced liver disease. *West. J. Med.* **127**, 515–18.

Gardos, G., Cole, J. O., and Tarsy, D. (1978). Withdrawal syndromes associated with antipsychotic drugs. *Am. J. Psychiat.* **135**, 1321–4.

Garmany, G., May, A. R., and Folkson, A. (1954). The use and action of chlorpromazine in psychoneuroses. *Br. med. J.* **2**, 439–41.

Garner, L. L., Wang, R. I. H., and Hieb, E. (1974). Ocular effects of phenothiazines. *Drug Ther.* **4**, 30–7.

Gelenberg, A. J., and Mandel, M. R. (1977). Catatonic reactions to high-potency neuroleptic drugs. *Arch. gen. Psychiat.* **34**, 947–50.

Girdwood, R. H. (1976). Drug-induced haematological abnormalities. In *Haema-*

tological aspects of systemic disease (ed. M. C. G. Israels and I. W. Delaware), pp. 495–528. W. B. Saunders, London.

Glomaud, D., Chodkiewicz, J. P., Merienne, L., and Salamagne, J. C. (1976). Intoxication par l'eau et syndrome de levee d'obstacle urinaire en cours de traitement neuroleptique prolonge. A propos de trois observations. *Anesth. Analg. Reanim.* **33**, 833–44.

Goldman, L. S., Hudson, J. I., and Weddington, W. W. (1980). Lupus-like illness associated with chlorpromazine. *Am. J. Psychiat.* **137**, 1613–14.

Goulston, E. (1976). Diverticular disease of the colon and megacolon. Incidence in a psychiatric centre compared with a teaching hospital. *Med. J. Aust.* **2**, 863–4.

Grant, W. M. (1974). *Toxicology of the eye.* Charles C. Thomas, Springfield, Illinois.

Greiner, A. C. and Berry, K. (1964). Skin pigmentation and corneal and lens opacities with prolonged chlorpromazine therapy. *Can. med. Ass. J.* **90**, 663–5.

——and Nicolson, G. A. (1964). Pigment deposition in viscera associated with prolonged chlorpromazine therapy. *Can. med. Assoc. J.* **91**, 627–35.

—— ——and Baker, R. A. (1964). Therapy of chlorpromazine melanosis: a preliminary report. *Can. med. Assoc. J.* **91**, 636–8.

Griffin, J. P. and D'Arcy, P. F. (1979). *A manual of adverse drug interactions.* John Wright, Bristol.

Gross, F. H. and Inman, T. H. W. (Eds.) (1977). *Drug monitoring.* Academic Press, London.

Gruen, P. H., Sachar, E. J., Langer, G., Altman, N., Leifer, M., Frantz, A., and Halpern, F. S. (1978). Prolactin responses to neuroleptics in normal and schizophrenic subjects. *Arch. gen. Psychiat.* **35**, 108–16.

Guillan, R. A., Yang, C—P., and Hocker, E. V. (1977). Antibody phenothiazines. Multiple antibody screening of patients under high doses. *J. Kansas med. Soc.* **78**, 221–7.

Guirguis, W. R. and Bawden, S. E. (1980). Disturbed behaviour induced by high-dose antipsychotic drugs. *Br. med. J.* **2**, 617–18.

Hansten, P. D. (1976). *Drug interactions.* Lea and Febiger, Philadelphia.

Heinonen, O. P., Slone, D., and Shapiro, S. (1977). *Birth defects and drugs in pregnancy.* Publishing Sciences Group, Littleton, Massachusetts.

Hill, R. M., Desmond, M. M., and Kay, J. L., (1966). Extrapyramidal dysfunction in an infant of schizophrenic mother. *J. Pediat.* **69**, 589–95.

Hodges, R. J. H. and Bennett, J. R. (1959). Some contra-indications to the use of chlorpromazine (with particular reference to obstetric analgesia and anaesthesia). *J. Obst. Gynaecol. Br. Emp.* **66**, 91–8.

Hollister, L. E. (1967). Newer complications of psychotherapeutic drugs. *Int. J. Neuropsychiat.* **3**, 141–8.

—— ——(1983). *Clinical pharmacology of psychotherapeutic drugs,* 2nd edn. Churchill Livingstone, New York.

——and Hall, R. A. (1966). Phenothiazine derivatives and morphological changes in the liver. *Am. J. Psychiat.* **123**, 211–12.

——and Kosek, J. C. (1965). Sudden death during treatment with phenothiazine derivatives. *J. Am. med. Assoc.* **192**, 1035–8.

Howard, R. O., McDonald, C. J., Dunn, B., and Creasey, W. A. (1969). Experimental chlorpromazine cataracts. *Invest. Ophthalmol.* **8**, 413–21.

Hunter, R., Earl, C. J., and Thornicroft, S. (1964). An apparently irreversible syndrome of abnormal movements following phenothiazine medication. *Proc. R. Soc. Med.* **57**, 758–62.

Inman, W. H. W. (Ed.) (1980). *Monitoring for drug safety.* Medical and Technical Publishing Co., Lancaster.

Itil, T. M. (1978). Effects of psychotropic drugs on qualitatively and quantitatively analysed human EEG. In *Principles of psychopharmacology*, 2nd edn (ed. W. G. Clark and J. de Guidice), pp. 261–77. Academic Press, New York.

Itoh, Z. (1981). Effect of motilin on gastrointestinal tract motility. In *Gut hormones* (ed. S. R. Bloom and J. M. Dolak), pp. 280–9. Churchill Livingstone, Edinburgh.

Johnson, A. W. and Buffaloe, W. J. (1966). Chlorpromazine epithelial keratopathy. *Arch. Ophthalmol.* **76**, 664–7.

Jones, I. H. and Meade, T. W. (1964). Hypothermia following chlorpromazine therapy in myxoedematous patients. *Geront. Clin.* **6**, 252–6.

Kelly, H. G., Fay, J. E., and Laverty, S. G. (1963). Thioridazine hydrochloride (Mellaril): its effect on the electrocardiogram and a report of two fatalities with electrocardiographic abnormalities. *Can. med. Assoc. J.* **89**, 546–54.

Ketal, R., Mathews, J., and Mozdzen, J. J. (1979). Sudden death in a patient taking haloperidol. *Am. J. Psychiat.* **136**, 112–13.

Kiloh, L. G., Smith, J. S., and Williams, S. E. (1973). Antiparkinson drugs as causal agents in tardive dyskinesia. *Med. J. Aust.* **2**, 591–3.

Klawans, H. L. (1973). The pharmacology of tardive dyskinesia. *Am. J. Psychiat.* **130**, 82–6.

——Falk, D. K., Nausieda, P. A., and Weiner, W. L. (1978). Gilles de la Tourette Syndrome after long-term chlorpromazine therapy. *Neurology* **28**, 1064–8.

Knowles, J. A. (1965). Excretion of drugs in milk—a review. *Pediat. Pharmacol. Ther.* **66**, 1068–82.

Kohn, N. N. and Myerson, R. M. (1961). Xanthomatous biliary cirrhosis following chlorpromazine. *Am. J. Med.* **31**, 665–70.

Kolakowska, T., Orr, M., Gelder, M., Heggie, M., Wiles, D., and Franklin, M. (1979). Clinical significance of plasma drug and prolactin levels during acute chlorpromazine treatment: a replication study. *Br. J. Psychiat.* **135**, 352–9.

Kopelman, A. E., McCullar, F. W., and Heggeness, L. (1975). Limb malformations following maternal use of haloperidol. *J. Am. med. Assoc.* **231**, 62–4.

Korczyn, A. D. (1980). The major tranquillisers. In *Meyler's side effects of drugs. An Encyclopedia of adverse reactions and interactions* 9th edn. (ed. M. N. G. Dukes), pp. 76–89. Excerpta Medica, Amsterdam.

Kotin, J., Wilbert, D. E., Verburg, D., and Soldinger, S. M. (1976). Thioridazine and sexual dysfunction. *Am. J. Psychiat.* **133**, 82–5.

Kulhanek, F., Linde, O. K., and Meisenberg, G. (1979). Precipitation of antipsychotic drugs in interaction with coffee or tea. *Lancet* **ii**, 1130.

Lapierre, Y. D., Lapointe, L., Bordeleau, J. M., and Tetreault, L. (1969). Phenothiazine treatment and electrocardiographic abnormalities. *Can. Psychiat. Assoc. J.* **14**, 517–23.

Lechin, F. and Van der Dijs, D. D. (1979). Effects of dopaminergic blocking agents on distal colon motility. *J. clin. Pharmacol.* **19**, 617–26.

Leestma, J. E. and Koenig, K. L. (1968). Sudden death and phenothiazines. A current controversy. *Arch. gen. Psychiat.* **18**, 137–48.

Leopold, I. V. (1968). Ocular complications of drugs. Visual changes. *J. Am. med. Assoc.* **205**, 631–3.

Levy, W. and Wisniewski, K. (1974). Chlorpromazine causing extrapyramidal dysfunction in newborn infant of psychotic mother. *NY St. J. Med.* **74**, 684–5.

Lipton, M. A., Dimascio, A., and Killman, K. F. (1978). *Psychopharmacology: a generation of progress*. Raven Press, New York.

Loga, S., Curry, S., and Lader, M. (1975). Interactions of orphenadrine and phenobarbitone with chlorpromazine: plasma concentrations and effects in man. *Br. J. Pharmacol.* **2**, 197–208.

Logothetis, J. (1967). Spontaneous epileptic seizures and electroencephalographic changes in the course of phenothiazine therapy. *Neurology* **17**, 869–77.

Lund-Johansen, P. (1962). Shock after administration of phenothiazines in patients with phaeochromocytoma. *Acta med. scand.* **172**, 525–9.

Lutz, E. G. and Rotov, M. D. (1964). Angioneurotic edema of the tongue with phenothiazine administration. Report of two cases. *Dis. nerv. Syst.* **25**, 419–22.

Lyon, K., Wilson, J., Golden, C. J., Graber, B., Coffman, J. A., and Bloch, S. (1981). Effects of long-term neuroleptic use on brain density. *Psychiat. Res.* **5**, 33–7.

Mann, P. L. and Chen, C. H. (1973). Severe shock caused by chlorpromazine hypersensitivity. *Br. J. Psychiat.* **122**, 185–7.

Mann. S. C. and Boger, W. P. (1978). Psychotropic drugs, summer heat and humidity, and hyperpyrexia: a danger restated. *Am. J. Psychiat.* **135**, 1097–100.

Marks, V. and Shackeloth, P. (1966). Diagnostic pregnancy tests in patients treated with tranquillisers. *Br. med. J.* **1**, 617–19.

Mathalone, M. B. R. (1966). Ocular complications of phenothiazines. *Trans. Ophthal. Soc. UK* **86**, 77–88.

Matuk, F. and Kalyanaraman, K. (1977). Syndrome of inappropriate secretion of anti-diuretic hormone in patients treated with psychotherapeutic drugs. *Arch. Neurol.* **34**, 374–5.

McCreadie, R. G., Kiernan, W. E. S., Venner, R. M., and Denholm, R. B. (1979). Probable toxic necrosis after prolonged fluspiriline administration. *Br. med. J.* **1**, 522–3.

McQueen, E. G. (1980). Pharmacological basis of adverse drug reactions. In *Drug treatment: Principles and practice of clinical pharmacology* (ed. G. S. Avery), pp. 202–35. Churchill Livingstone, Edinburgh.

McQuillen, M. P., Gross, M., and Jones, R. J. (1963). Chlorpromazine-induced weakness in myasthenia gravis. *Arch. Neurol.* **8**, 286–90.

Meirez, D. and Fishelovitch, J. (1969). Priapism and Largactil medication. *Isr. J. med. Sci.* **5**, 1254–6.

Meltzer, H. Y. and Fang, U. S. (1976). Serum prolactin levels in schizophrenia—effect of antipsychotic drugs: a preliminary report. In *Hormones, behaviour and psychopathology* (ed. E. J. Sachar). Raven Press, New York.

Meredith, T. A., Aaberg, T. M., and Willerson, D. (1978). Progressive chorioretinopathy after receiving thioridazine. *Arch. Ophthalmol.* **96**, 1172–6.

Merrill, D. C. and Markland, C. (1972). Vesical dysfunction induced by the major tranquillizers. *J. Urol.* **107**, 769–71.

Milner, G. (1972). *Drugs and driving.* Karger, Basle.

——and Landauer, A. A. (1971). Alcohol, thioridazine and chlorpromazine effects on skills related to driving behaviour. *Br. J. Psychiat.* **118**, 351–2.

Mindham, R. H. S. (1975). Major tranquillisers. In Meyler's *Side effects of drugs*. Vol. VIII, *A survey of unwanted effects of drugs reported in 1972–1975* (ed. M. N. G. Dukes), pp. 84–98. Excerpta Medica, Amsterdam.

——(1977). The major tranquillisers. In *Side effects of drugs annual 1; a worldwide survey of new data and trends* (ed. M. N. G. Dukes), pp. 30–48. Excerpta Medica, Amsterdam.

——(1978). The major tranquillizers. In *Side effects of drugs annual 2; a worldwide survey of new data and trends* (ed. M. N. G. Dukes), pp. 45–60. Excerpta Medica, Amsterdam.

Moore, M. T. and Book, M. H. (1970). Sudden death in phenothiazine therapy. *Psychiat. Quart.* **44**, 389–402.

Moya, F. and Thorndike, V. (1962). Passage of drugs across the placenta. *Am. J. Obstet. Gynecol.* **84**, 1778–98.

Nevins, D. B. (1977). Adverse response to neuroleptics in schizophrenia. *Int. J. Psychoanal. Psychother.* **6**, 227–41.

Nurnberg, H. G. and Ambrosini, P. L. (1979). Urinary incontinence in patients receiving neuroleptics. *J. clin. Psychiat.* **40**, 271–4.

Okuma, T., Koga, I., and Uchida, Y. (1976). Sensitivity to chlorpromazine effects on brain function of schizophrenics and normals. *Psychopharmacology* **5**, 101–5.

O'Leary, J. L. and O'Leary, J. A. (1964). Nonthalidomide ectromelia. Report of a case. *Obstet. Gyn.* **23**, 17–20.

Overall, J. E. (1978). Prior psychiatric treatment and the development of breast cancer. *Arch. gen. Psychiat.* **35**, 898–9.

Paoletti, F., Juan, A., Vazquez, J., and Wolf, P. L. (1966). Positive pregnancy test in an 82-year old woman. *Am. J. med. Sci.* **252**, 570–2.

Peele, R. and von Loetzen, I. S. (1973). Phenothiazine deaths: a critical review. *Am. J. Psychiat.* **130**, 306–9.

Perry, T. L., Culling, C. F. A., Berry, K., and Hansen, S. (1964). 7-hydryoxy-chlorpromazine: potential toxic drug metabolite in psychiatric patients. *Science* **146**, 81–3.

Pisciotta, A. V. (1968). Mechanisms of phenothiazine induced agranulocytosis. In *Psychopharmacology: a review of progress 1957–1967* (ed. D. F. Efron). US Government Printing Office, Washington, DC.

——(1971). Drug-induced leukopenia and aplastic anaemia. *Clin. Pharmacol. Ther.* **12**, 13–43.

——(1974). The effect of chlorpromazine on peripheral leukocytes. In *Drugs and hematologic reactions*, The Twenty-Ninth Hahnemann Symposium (ed. N. V. Dimitrov and J. H. Nodine), pp. 233–47. Grune and Stratton, New York.

Pogge, R. C. (1963). The toxic placebo. *Medical times* **91**, 773–8.

Potts, A. M. (1962). The concentration of phenothiazines in the eye of experimental animals. *Invest. Ophthalmol.* **1**, 522–30.

Prescott, L. F. (1973). Clinically important drug interactions. *Drugs* **5**, 161–86.

Raj, M. V. J. and Benson, R. (1975). Phenothiazines and the electrocardiogram. *Postgrad. med. J.* **51**, 65–8.

Rawlins, M. D. and Thompson, J. W. (1977). Pathogenesis of adverse drug reactions. In *Textbook of adverse drug reactions* (ed. D. M. Davies), pp. 10–31. Oxford University Press, Oxford.

Read, A. E. (1979). The liver and drugs. In *Liver and biliary disease. Pathophysiology, diagnosis, management*. (ed. R. Wright, K. G. M. M. Alberti, S. Karran, and G. H. Milward-Sadler), pp. 822–47. W. B. Saunders, Co., London.

——Harrison, C. V., and Sherlock, S. (1961). Chronic chlorpromazine jaundice with particular reference to its relationship to primary biliary cirrhosis. *Am. J. Med.* **31**, 249–57.

Reid, W. W., Blouin, P., and Schermer, M. (1976). A review of psychotropic medications and the glaucomas. *Int. Pharmacopsychiat.* **11**, 163–74.

Reidenberg, M. M. and Lowenthal, D. T. (1967). Adverse nondrug reactions. *New Engl. J. Med.* **279**, 678–9.

Rieder, R. O., Rosenthal, D., Wender, P., and Blumenthal, H. (1975). The offspring of schizophrenics. Fetal and neonatal deaths. *Arch. gen. Psychiat.* **32**, 200–11.

Remick, R. A. and Fine, S. H. (1979). Antipsychotic drugs and seizures. *J. clin. Psychiat.* **40**, 78–80.

Richardson, H. L., Graupner, K. I., and Richardson, M. E. (1966). Intramyocardial lesions in patients dying suddenly and unexpectedly. *J. Am. med. Assoc.* **195**, 114–20.

Rivera-Calimlim, L., Castaneda, L., and Lasagna, L. (1973). Effects of mode of management on plasma chlorpromazine in psychiatric patients. *Clin. Pharmacol. Ther.* **14**, 978–86.

Robins, A. H. (1972). Skin malanin concentrations in schizophrenia. II. Patients treated by phenothiazines. *Br. J. Psychiat.* **121**, 615–17.
——(1975). Melanosis after prolonged chorpromazine therapy. *S. Afr. med. J.* **49**, 1521–4.
Rodriguez, M., Paronetto, F., Schaffner, F., and Popper, H. (1969). Antimitrochondrial antibodies in jaundice following drug administration. *J. Am. med. Assoc.* **208**, 148–50.
Rubin, R. T. and Hays, S. E. (1980). The prolactin secretory response to neuroleptic drugs: mechanisms, applications and limitations. *Psychoneuroendocrinology* **5**, 121–37.
Rudenko, G. M. and Lepakhin, V. K. (1979). The major tranquillizers. In *Side effects of drugs annual 3; a worldwide survey of new data and trends* (ed. M. N. G. Dukes), pp. 39–58. Excerpta Medica, Amsterdam.
Rumeau-Rouquette, C., Goujard, J., and Huel, G. (1977). Possible teratogenic effects of phenothiazines in human beings. *Teratology* **15**, 57–64.
Ryan, M. and LaDow, C. (1968). Subluxation of the temperomandibular joint after administration of prochlorperazine. *J. oral Surg.* **26**, 646–8.
Satonova, A. and McIntosh, J. (1967). Phototoxic reactions induced by high doses of chlorpromazine and thioridazine. *J. Am. med. Assoc.* **200**, 121–4.
Schyve, P. M., Smithline, F., and Meltzer, H. Y. (1978). Neuroleptic-induced prolactin level elevation and breast cancer. *Arch. gen. Psychiat.* **35**, 1291–301.
Scokel, P. W. and Jones, W. N. (1962). Infant jaundice after phenothiazine drugs for labour: an enigma. *Obstet. Gynaecol.* **20**, 124–7.
Shader, R. I., Dimascio, A., and associates (1970). *Psychotropic drug side effects: Clinical and theoretical perspectives.* Williams and Wilkins, Baltimore.
Shear, M. K. (1978). Chlorpromazine-induced PIE syndrome. *Am. J. Psychiat.* **135**, 492–3.
Shepherd, M., Lader, M. H., and Lader, S. R. (1968a). Central nervous system depressant drugs. In *Side effects of drugs. Volume VI. A survey of unwanted effects of drugs reported in 1965–1967* (ed. L. Meyler and A. Herxheimer), pp. 51–93. Excerpta Medica, Amsterdam.
—— —— ——(1972). Major tranquillizers. In *Side effects of drugs.* Vol. VII. *A survey of unwanted effects of drugs reported in 1968–1971* (eds. L. Meyler and A. Herxheimer), pp. 69–97. Excerpta Medica, Amsterdam.
—— ——and Rodnight, R. (1968b). *Clinical psychopharmacology.* English University Press, London.
Siddall, J. R. (1965). The ocular toxic findings with prolonged and high dosage chlorpromazine intake. *Arch. Ophthalmol.* **74**, 460–4.
——(1966). Ocular toxic changes associated with chlorpromazine and thioridazine. *Can. J. Ophthalmol.* **1**, 190–8.
—— ——(1968). Ocular complications related to phenothiazines. *Dis. nerv. Syst.* **29** (suppl.), 10–13.
Simpson, G. M., Varga, E., and Haher, J. (1976). Psychotic exacerbations produced by neuroleptics. *Dis. nerv. Syst.* **37**, 367–9.
Singh, M. M. and Kay, S. R. (1975). A comparative study of haloperidol and chlorpromazine in terms of clinical effects and therapeutic reversal with benztropine in schizophrenia. Theoretical implications for potency differences among neuroleptics. *Psychopharmacologia* **43**, 103–13.
Singh, S. V. (1982). Lithium carbonate/fluphenazine decanoate producing irreversible brain damage. *Lancet* **ii**, 278.
Skromak, S. J., Schreader, C. J., O'Neil, J. F., and Ciccone, E. F. (1957). Observations of chlorpromazine induced jaundice with continued use of the drug. *Am. J. med Sci.* **234**, 85–90.

Smith, A. J. (1973). Perphanazine side effects presenting in oral surgical practice. *Br. J. oral Surg.* **10**, 349–51.

Smith, W. O. and Clark, M. L. (1980). Self-induced water intoxification in schizophrenic patients. *Am. J. Psychiat.* **137**, 1055–9.

Spring, G. and Frankel, M. (1981). New data on lithium and haloperidol incompatibility. *Am. J. Psychiat.* **138**, 818–21.

Spring, G. K. (1979). Neurotoxicity with combined use of lithium and thioridazine. *J. clin. Psychiat.* **40**, 135–8.

Sriram, K., Schumer, W., Ehrenpreis, S., Comaty, J. E., and Scheller, J. (1979). Phenothiazine effect on gastrointestinal tract function. *Am. J. Surg.* **137**, 87–91.

Stirrat, G. M. and Beard, R. W. (1973). Drugs to be avoided or given with caution in the second and third trimesters of pregnancy. *Prescribers J.* **13**, 135–40.

Stockley, I. H. (1972). *Drug interactions and their mechanisms.* Pharmaceutical Press, London.

Swett, C. (1974). Drowsiness due to chlorpromazine in relation to cigarette smoking. *Arch. gen. Psychiat.* **31**, 211–13.

——(1975). Outpatient phenothiazine use and bone marrow depression. A report from the Drug Epidemiology Unit and the Boston Collaborative Drug Surveillance Program. *Arch. gen. Psychiat.* **32**, 1416–18.

——Cole, J. O., Hartz, S. C., Shapiro, S., and Slone, D. (1977). Hypotension due to chlorpromazine. Relation to cigarette smoking, blood pressure, and dosage. *Arch. gen. Psychiat.* **34**, 661–3.

Swett, C. P. and Shader, R. I. (1977). Cardiac side effects and sudden death in hospitalized psychiatric patients. *Dis. nerv. Syst.* **38**, 69–72.

Thonnard-Neumann, E. (1968). Phenothiazines and diabetes in hospitalised women. *Am. J. Psychiat.* **124**, 978–82.

Toone, B. K. and Fenton, G. W. (1977). Epileptic seizures induced by psychotropic drugs. *Psychol. Med.* **7**, 265–70.

van Putten, T., Mutalipassi, L. R., and Malkin, M. D. (1974). Phenothiazine-induced decompensation. *Arch. gen. Psychiat.* **30**, 102–5.

Vargas, E. and Drance, S. M. (1973). Anterior chamber depth in angle-closure glaucoma, *Arch. Ophthalmol.* **90**, 438–9.

Vince, D. J. (1969). Congenital malformations following phenothiazine administration during pregnancy. *Can. med. Assoc. J.* **100**, 223.

Vincent, F. M. and Emory, S. (1978). Antidiuretic hormone syndrome and thioridazine. *Ann. intern. Med.* **89**, 147–8.

Vorhees, C. V., Brunner, R. L., and Butcher, R. E. (1979). Psychotropic drugs as behavioural teratogens. *Science* **205**, 1220–5.

Wagner, S. and Mantel, N. (1978). Breast cancer at a psychiatric hospital before and after the introduction of neuroleptic agents. *Cancer Res.* **38**, 2703–8.

Walsh, F. B. and Hoyt, W. F. (1969). *Clinical neuro-ophthalmology*, Vol. 3. Williams and Wilkins, Baltimore.

Weinberger, D. R. and Kelly, M. J. (1977). Catatonia and malignant syndrome: a possible complication of neuroleptic administration. Report of a case involving haloperidol. *J. nerv. ment. Dis.* **165**, 263–8.

Wendkos, M. H. (1979). *Sudden death and psychiatric illness.* S.P. Medical and Scientific Books, New York.

Westlake, R. J. and Rastegar, A. (1973). Hyperpyrexia from drug combinations. *J. Am. med. Assoc.* **225**, 1250.

Wheatley, D. (Ed.) (1981). *Stress and the heart.* Raven Press, New York.

Wiles, D. H., Kolakowska, T., McNeilly, A. S., Mandelbrote, B. M., and Gelder, M. G. (1976). Clinical significance of plasma chlorpromazine levels. I: Plasma levels of the drug, some of its metabolites and prolactin during acute treatment. *Psychol. Med.* **6**, 407–15.

Willette, R. E. (ed.) (1977). *Drugs and driving*. National Institute on Drug Abuse, Monograph II. Department of Health, Education and Welfare, Washington, DC.

Wintrobe, M. M., Lee, G. R., Boggs, D. R., Bithell, T. C., Athens, J. W., and Foerster, J. (1975). *Clinical hematology*. Lee and Febiger, Philadelphia.

Wintroub, B. V., Shiffman, N. J., and Arndt, K. A. (1979). Adverse cutaneous reactions to drugs. In *Dermatology in general medicine* (ed. T. B. Fitzpatrick, A. Z. Eisen, K. Wolff, I. M. Freedberg, and K. F. Austen), pp. 555–67. McGraw-Hill, New York.

Zahavi, J. and Schwartz, G. (1978). Chlorpromazine and platelet function. *Lancet* **ii**, 164.

Index

444 *Index*